READINGS IN CONTEMPORARY SOCIOLOGICAL THEORY

READINGS IN CONTEMPORARY SOCIOLOGICAL THEORY: FROM MODERNITY TO POST-MODERNITY

Edited by
DONALD MCQUARIE
Bowling Green State University

with contributions by
R. Serge Denisoff

Prentice Hall, Englewood Cliffs, New Jersey 07632

Library of Congress Cataloging-in-Publication Data

Readings in contemporary sociological theory : from modernity to post-
   modernity / edited by Donald McQuarie ; with contributions by R.
   Serge Denisoff.
      p.   cm.
   Includes bibliographical references.
   ISBN 0-13-104266-1
   1. Sociology.   I. McQuarie, Donald.   II. Denisoff, R. Serge.
HM51.R363 1995
301—dc20   94-3991
                                                           CIP

Editorial/production supervision
   and interior design: *Joan E. Foley*
Acquisitions editor: *Nancy Roberts*
Editorial assistant: *Pat Naturale*
Copy editor: *Margo Quinto*
Cover director: *Rich Dombrowski*
Production coordinator: *Mary Ann Gloriande*

 © 1995 by Prentice-Hall, Inc.
A Paramount Communications Company
Englewood Cliffs, New Jersey 07632

Printed in the United States of America
10 9 8 7 6 5 4

ISBN 0-13-104266-1

Prentice-Hall International (UK) Limited, *London*
Prentice-Hall of Australia Pty. Limited, *Sydney*
Prentice-Hall Canada Inc., *Toronto*
Prentice-Hall Hispanoamericana, S.A., *Mexico*
Prentice-Hall of India Private Limited, *New Delhi*
Prentice-Hall of Japan, Inc., *Tokyo*
Simon & Schuster Asia Pte. Ltd., *Singapore*
Editora Prentice-Hall do Brasil, Ltda., *Rio de Janeiro*

CONTENTS

PREFACE

Contemporary sociology presents a dizzying array of theories, schools, and approaches. Some have been around for over a century (e.g., functionalism, Marxism); others have sprouted within the last decade (postmodernism, sociology of the emotions). The one thing that has characterized sociology since the 1970s is the astonishing proliferation of theoretical approaches within the discipline. Only four decades ago, sociology was seemingly unified under the theoretical aegis of Parsonian functionalism. Today there is a cacophony of competing voices, and the trend seems to be toward ever-increasing diversity.

Sociologists themselves are deeply divided in their attitudes toward this dramatically increasing diversity within sociological theory. Some long for the days of a field unified behind a dominant functionalism, and others applaud the new diversity in sociological theory as a positive step forward that reflects the increasing diversity of modern postindustrial society. Yet other sociologists work toward a new hegemony of an as-yet-untried new contender; still others work to refurbish old and abandoned theories that are now promoted under new rubrics suggesting continuity within change—for example, neofunctionalism, neo-Marxism.

This book is meant to serve as a guide to the maze of modern sociological theory. It can be used as a supplement to one of the many excellent textbooks in contemporary sociological theory, or it can be used alone. I have provided for each group of readings a rather extensive preface that introduces both the particular theoretical approach covered in the chapter and the accompanying selections. It has always struck me that, no matter how thorough the interpretation offered by a particular textbook may be, there is something to be said for allowing students to read theorists in their own words and on their own terms. Reading *about* Talcott Parsons' work, for example, can never substitute for the experience of actually *reading* Parsons' work itself—even though, admittedly, doing so might not be an experience that my hypothetical student of sociological theory would want to repeat often!

The terms *modern* and *contemporary sociology*, as they are used in this book, deserve some explanation. Although I have tried to include "classic" statements from each of the theoretical schools covered in this reader, an attentive person will quickly note that there are no selections by the giants of nineteenth-century European theory. This omission reflects two considerations. The first was the need to draw a line somewhere in order to conserve space. The second was my decision to narrow the selection of readings to the last fifty years of sociological work—roughly from the end of World War II to the present. This is the period during which sociology achieved full academic acceptance in the United States, developing a departmental presence in almost every major American university. The period also encompassed the full flowering of the first dominant theoretical perspective in American sociology—structural functionalism—and the subsequent explosion of new contending approaches since the 1960s. Although the works of the classical European and early American theorists remain of enduring value to modern sociology, they are covered only indirectly in this reader through the more contemporary writings of social theorists working in the theoretical traditions that those classic figures founded. It is in that sense that this book is a reader in *contemporary* sociological theory.

In addition to its focus on modern sociological theory, I have also endeavored to give this reader something of an international emphasis. For many years, American sociology remained a largely insular discipline. (Although even during the 1950s and 1960s, when American sociology seemed most isolated from international influences, some of the most influential theorists in American sociology were European émigrés—Peter Berger, Lewis Coser, Herbert Marcuse, and Peter Blau, for example.) Many of the most important contemporary theorists are European scholars, and I have tried to arrange the readings to reflect this renewed internationalism in sociological theory, including essays by such important contemporary European theorists as Niklas Luhmann, Jürgen Habermas, Anthony Giddens, and Pierre Bourdieu. I have also tried to give a special emphasis to feminist theory, which receives coverage in this text as a theoretical perspective in its own right in Chapter 6, but is also drawn on in Chapters 3 and 4 in the form of feminist critiques of other theoretical approaches. Perhaps more than any other contemporary approach in sociology, feminism has profoundly challenged the assumptions and theoretical "blind spots" of the traditional male-centered perspectives with its characteristic question, What about the women?

The structure of this book is as follows: Chapter 1 reviews the development of the functionalist approach from its origins in British social anthropology through its high point in 1950s American sociology in the work of Talcott Parsons and Robert Merton. It concludes with an assessment of functionalism's revival in the 1980s under the rubric of neofunctionalism. Chapter 2 reviews the career of conflict theory, which emerged during the 1960s and 1970s as the main challenger to the dominance of the functionalist paradigm. This chapter begins with some of the major early statements of the conflict approach and concludes with a couple of recent essays by Randall Collins, the leading contemporary proponent of the conflict approach. Chapter 3 examines the last several decades of Marxist and Marxist-influenced approaches in sociology, beginning with an essay by Herbert Marcuse, one of the leading figures of the German Frankfurt School. This essay is followed by a couple of essays on the role of the state— one by a leading contemporary representative of the Frankfurt School's approach, Jürgen Habermas. The chapter concludes with two essays that discuss recent innovations within the Marxist perspective—world-systems theory and analytical Marxism—and a final article that offers a critical feminist reflection on the Marxist approach.

In Chapter 4 we shift focus from the macrolevel world of events and structures to the microlevel scale of interpersonal relations. This chapter surveys the four major "micro-orientations": symbolic interactionism, ethnomethodology, exchange theory, and Erving Goffman's dramaturgical approach. Each approach is represented in essays by its major proponents; in addition, I have included a feminist critique by Nancy Hartsock of the exchange model. Chapter 5 departs somewhat from the structure of the preceding chapters. Rather than presenting a major perspective, this chapter takes up a body of recent literature in sociological theory concerning a central problem—the link between micro and macro levels of analysis. This is an area in which much of the most interesting and innovative work in theory is currently being done. I have included several recent contributions to this body of literature, beginning with a statement by theorists defending an exclusive focus on, respectively, the micro approach (George Homans) and the macro approach (Bruce Mayhew). These essays are followed by several theoretical reflections on the problem of translation and synthesis between these two levels of analysis. Among these essays are contributions by two important European theorists, Pierre Bourdieu and Anthony Giddens, each of whom pioneered a distinctive theoretical approach in the 1980s; in their essays, each theorist introduces the basic elements of his approach to theory.

Chapter 6 presents an array of recent approaches in sociological theory that are important perspectives in their own right but that have not yet achieved the status within the discipline of the approaches set forth in the first four chapters. These new approaches include sociobiology, environmental sociology, feminist theory, sociology of the emotions, historical sociology, and postmodernism. This list is certainly not meant to be exhaustive of recent approaches that have emerged in the discipline, but it is intended to offer the reader a brief introduction to some of the more vital and interesting new theoretical perspectives to have appeared in the last few decades.

Finally, I would like to say a few words about the criteria that guided me in selecting essays for this reader. All the readings have previously appeared, most of them as articles published in leading journals in the field of sociology, some originally as essays in books. The selections were chosen for three qualities: First, I tried to pick seminal works by important theorists in the field. Second, as previously indicated, I tried to provide a representative sampling of the many varieties of contemporary theory. Finally, I emphasized *readability* in the selection of these essays, on the grounds that no matter how important an article might be, it must be suited to the reading abilities of an advanced undergraduate or beginning graduate student audience to be included in this book. This last criterion sometimes made finding appropriate selections difficult. Many important theoretical approaches—perhaps most—rely on an arcane language and set of concepts that can appear bewildering to the uninitiated. I hope I have succeeded in finding articles that present sociology's major theories in language that can be readily comprehended without sacrificing complexity or theoretical rigor.

Finally, I include here a word of thanks to the many persons who aided me in the completion of this project, beginning with the copyright holders and authors of the essays, who have graciously granted permission to reprint their work. I also thank the editors at Prentice Hall for their support, advice, and patience, especially Nancy Roberts, sociology editor at Prentice Hall; her able assistant, Pat

Naturale, who was especially helpful in guiding me through the process of obtaining the necessary reprint permissions; and the production editor for the manuscript, Joan Foley. I thank my former colleague in the sociology department at Bowling Green State University, R. Serge Denisoff, for his work in coauthoring Chapter 1. I especially thank my frequent coauthor, friend, and guide in all things having to do with sociology, Patrick McGuire of the University of Toledo, who spent an inordinate amount of time reading and critiquing early drafts of the chapter introductions. Also, thanks go to the various readers for Prentice Hall, who made useful suggestions at various stages in the preparation of the manuscript. Among these, I especially thank Craig Calhoun of the University of North Carolina for his extremely helpful comments on the last draft. And thanks to the copy editor at Prentice Hall, Margo Quinto, whose meticulous attention to detail was invaluable. Finally, I want to thank my graduate students, Art Jipson, Ian Ritchie, Amy Barlow, and Renxin Yang, for taking the time to go over various parts of the manuscript and give me their comments. To them I say thank you and xie-xie. Lastly, I must aver that any errors remaining in the manuscript, whether of fact or interpretation, remain my responsibility.

CHAPTER 1

FUNCTIONALISM
AND NEOFUNCTIONALISM*

The analysis of societies by analogy with biological organisms and the assessment of social institutions in terms of the role they play in social life are the main premises of functionalist theory. They are among the oldest forms of social theorizing and are easily traceable to the intellectual thought of ancient Greece (see Brumbach 1964). Functionalism is a theory that seeks to answer the question: What holds societies together? The answer functionalism offers stresses the importance of social order and stability, and emphasizes the role of specialized social institutions such as the family, religion, and education in preserving that order.

Functionalism rose to a position of absolute dominance in American sociology for a period after World War II and gained acceptance as *the* theory of modern sociology. Robert Nisbet, one of the most influential figures in American sociology, claimed that "functionalism is, without doubt, the single most significant body of theory in the social sciences in the present century" (quoted in Turner and Maryanski 1979; xi).

Yet by the late 1960s, functionalism had come under mounting criticism—criticism that became so sustained that by 1970 the very survival of functionalism as a coherent perspective in American sociology had been called into question (see Friedrichs 1970). But old traditions die hard, and, like the phoenix that springs reborn from the ashes of its own funeral pyre, functionalism has reemerged in the last decade as an important sociological theory under the updated title of neofunctionalism (see Alexander 1985). Retaining some of the assumptions of traditional functionalist theory while discarding others and incorporating insights from competing theories, the neofunctionalists have sought to reinvigorate functionalism as a tool of contemporary sociological analysis.

*This chapter is coauthored with R. Serge Denisoff.

CLASSICAL FUNCTIONALISM

The classical functionalist analogy between society and the human organism began with Plato (428–348 B.C.). In *The Republic* (Cornford 1945), the Greek philosopher presented man as an organism with three basic needs for survival: food, shelter, and clothing. Early men organized themselves into groups in order to satisfy the needs of self-preservation. From this organization arose occupational groups, such as hunters and food gatherers, called classes. Because each class had an essential skill and a task to perform, the result was the *division of labor*. Inherent in Plato's reasoning was the concept that society is the result of the unification of humans allied with one another in order to meet basic needs, and the achievement of those needs is the natural order of events. Because they have fundamental or basic needs, humans developed social harmony or common values, which constitute the "social mind."

As Alvin Gouldner has argued, Plato is the father of the notion that Emile Durkheim eventually would call *social integration:*

Social integration no less than economic efficiency depends directly upon (what he construes to be) a proper division of labor. Like Durkheim some two thousand years later, Plato is fully aware that a highly specialized division of labor contributes to social cohesion by creating mutual interdependence. (1966, 55)

With the introduction of the concept of historical quest, Plato strayed from the simple organic "what is" into the world of "what ought to be." In time this line of thinking would give birth to the conflict perspective in sociology, to be discussed in Chapter 2. The classical Greek notion of organism pervaded the philosophical writings of the early social philosophers throughout the Enlightenment period and into the nineteenth century. The British sociologist Herbert Spencer (1820–1903), in developing his theory of social evolution equated society with the human body. "In societies," Spencer reasoned, "as in living bodies, increase of mass is habitually accompanied by increases of structure" (Spencer 1967, 10). Influenced by the writings of the famous theorist of biological evolution Charles Darwin, Spencer maintained that social processes are the same as biological processes. The animal world became the model for human organizations; their processes are "analogous to those of growth, structure and function in an animal," according to Spencer. A sociological *function*, for Spencer, was the contribution of the individual unit to the survival and growth of society.

Despite Spencer's adoption of the word *function*, it was the French sociologist Emile Durkheim (1858–1917) to whom most modern functionalists give credit for its popularization. Durkheim, in the sociological classic *The Division of Labor in Society* (1946a), introduced the idea that function is akin to a biological subunit in an organism. He wrote, "Digestion has as its function the incorporation into the organism of liquid or solid substances designed to replenish its losses, ... respiration has for its function the introduction of necessary gases into the tissues of an animal for the sustainment of life" (1964a, 49). A function, therefore, could be found and defined by seeking "the need which it supplies." This "need" was social preservation. He elaborated this notion in an obscure passage in *The Division of Labor* that asserts that functions are "ways of definite action, which are identically repeated in given circumstances, since they cling to general, constant conditions of social life" (1964a, 365–66).

Durkheim asserted that the social system has needs that must be met repeatedly. A function, therefore, is a contribution to the maintenance of social life and society. In *The*

Elementary Forms of Religious Life (1965), for example, Durkheim presented a classic discussion of the social significance of ceremony. Ritual fulfills the structural needs for social cohesion by performing four functions. First, ritual prepares an individual for social life by imposing discipline upon him. Second, the rite has a cohesive function in that it serves to reaffirm common social ties. Third, ceremony revitalizes the individual's commitment to tradition. Finally, Durkheim asserted, a sense of social euphoria or a sensation of comfort is generated by participation in a religious ceremony. In these four ways the ritual makes its contribution to the needs of life and society. Kingsley Davis and Wilbert Moore (1945), in presenting a functionalist approach to social stratification, aptly illustrated how Durkheim's notion of societal needs can be used to explain existing social practices (see Tumin 1953, for a critique of this approach). The implication in Durkheim's work is that each unit in society is inextricably related to society and to all other units within it. Like Plato, Durkheim believed that when this natural state was recognized, social harmony would be achieved.

The anthropologist A.R. Radcliffe-Brown (1881–1955) continued and elaborated Durkheim's organic analogy. "The concept of function," he maintained, "applied to human societies is based on analogy between social life and organic life" (1956, 178). Need, according to Radcliffe-Brown (Reading 1), is explicitly the "necessary condition of existence." Function, again, was seen as a contribution to the continuing existence of the social structure. Institutions and individuals alike work toward this goal:

The continuity of structure is maintained by the process of social life, which consists of the activities and interactions of the individual human beings and of the organized groups into which they are united. The social life of the community is here defined as the *functioning* of the social structure. The *function* of any recurrent activity, such as the punishment of a crime, or a funeral ceremony, is the part it plays in the social life as a whole and therefore the contribution it makes to the maintenance of the structure's continuity. (Radcliffe-Brown 1956, 189)

For Radcliffe-Brown, maintenance involves harmonious relationships between groups, social continuity or the nurturing of tradition, and the existence of those institutions necessary for survival (see Cohen 1968, 34–45). Like Durkheim and others, he characterized society as an organism with "needs" and consequently posited relationships between social facts and the requirements of that organism to maintain itself. In fact, Durkheim, in *The Rules of Sociological Method* (1964b), published in 1895, had already contended that social facts may be classified as either normal or abnormal on the basis of their contributory nature. While most social facts should be interpreted as playing a positive function in terms of meeting the requirements of the social organism, those actions and facts not contributing to the solidarity and maintenance of the society are *dysnormic,* or abnormal, and their presence is a sign of social ill health (see Durkheim 1951).

MODERN FUNCTIONALISM

Some American sociologists, such as Robert K. Merton (Reading 2), have modified Durkheim's thinking to stress the relationship between institutions and units rather than the notion of the necessary condition of existence. Others, the most important of whom is Talcott Parsons (1951), continued this organic analogy, discussing the functional imperatives and prerequisites of society or the social system. Significantly, the foremost imperative is adaptation or boundary maintenance, which can be simply interpreted to signify "the need for survival." This alteration was due in part to the types of questions they were addressing. For example, Merton and those sociologists who applied his modifications to Durkheim's notion of function in the area of crime and delinquency were primarily concerned with deviant events rather than contributory ones (see Hinkle 1964, Pierce 1964). In *Social Theory and Social Structure* (1968), Merton reviewed five definitions of function and called for a "paradigm for functional analysis." In this schema, the concept of *function* applies to "observed consequences which make for the adaptation or adjustment of a given system, and *dysfunction* to those observed consequences which lessen the adaptation or adjustment of the system" (Merton 1968, 105). To illustrate this alteration, Merton (1968) examined a New York political machine and pointed out its manifest and latent functions. In his analysis, function comes to mean consequence rather than the vague classical notion of emergent society: *X* has *Y* consequence.

No twentieth-century functionalist theorist, of course, has been more influential than the Harvard sociologist Talcott Parsons (Reading 3). In 1937, Parsons published *The Structure of Social Action,* a book that proved to be a landmark work in the emergence of modern sociological theory (Parsons 1968). In that work, he attempted to bring together the writings of four major classical theorists: Durkheim, the German sociologist Max Weber, the Italian conservative theorist Vilfredo Pareto, and the English economist Alfred Marshall. As Parsons explained,

The main concern of the study is with the outline of a theoretical system. Its minor variations from writer to writer are not a matter of concern to this analysis. It is necessary to work out this logical structure in the clearest form attainable. . . . Hence the choice has been made of intensive analysis from the relevant point of view of the work of a small number of the most eminent men. (1968, 14)

In this theoretical mix, the work of two of these theorists, Durkheim and Weber, was to prove especially important. At the most basic level, Parsons attempted to wed in grandiose fashion the strengths of Durkheim's functional analysis with the social psychological assumptions of Weber. He saw the weakness of classical functionalism as lying in the functionalists' stress on social structure and institutions rather than on the individuals in them. This weakness, he believed, could be overcome by integrating a "theory of action" into the functionalist model. This new theory of action, however, was constructed by Parsons squarely within the mainstream of the classical functionalist assumptions about the relationship between the individual and society. In Parsons' view, the individual seeks to attain goals *within* society, always taking account of the expectations and generalized needs of social groups and institutions. Thus, social values and norms at every point impinge upon the individual, and his motivations are in keeping with the values and needs of the social system.

In his later work, Parsons went on to develop a complex theory of the various "action systems" and their interrelationships (Parsons 1951, 1970; Parsons and Shils 1951). Increasingly, Parsons saw his goal to be the construction of a complex analytical map of the social system that could be used as the framework of a functionalist "Grand Theory" of society in which the various structures of society are defined and explained in terms of the positive functions they play for one another. Talcott Parsons was clearly the dominant American sociological theorist of his generation, and his work was enormously influential among sociologists schooled between 1940 and 1970. Parsons' *structural functionalism*, as it was developed by him and his associates and graduate students, offered a system that attempted to integrate the basic concepts and findings of sociology into a coherent theoretical whole. Without competition in terms of its comprehensive nature, systematic development, and theoretical abstraction, it achieved novel status as a theoretical orientation within the discipline. Friedrichs (1970, 13) noted that, by the 1950s, an intimate knowledge of Parsons' work was a prerequisite for a doctorate in sociology in the United States.

CRITICS OF FUNCTIONALISM AND THE EMERGENCE OF NEOFUNCTIONALISM

By the late 1960s, numerous critics had taken issue with functional analysis. Percy Cohen (1968, 47) summarized these criticisms in three basic categories. The first, articulated by Harry Bredemeir (1935) and Ronald Dore (1961), was that functionalist explanations are often *tautological.* That is, X is seen as producing Y, while simultaneously Y accounts for the occurrence of X; thus, both statements are true *by definition.* For example, Davis and Moore (1945) suggested that social class exists *because it is functional.* But they then explained that social class is functional *because it exists.* This criticism is closely related to the charge that functionalist explanations are often *teleological,* meaning that they attempt to explain natural phenomena in terms of some final cause or design that cannot be scientifically known or proved to be true. For example, Durkheim's functional explanation of ritual has been criticized for stating that ceremony exists *in order to maintain the fiber of society.* At best, this teleological statement offers a vague sociological generalization, not a causal explanation.

The second area of dissent to functionalism attacked its basic reliance on unity at the expense of differences that may arise in society. The conflict perspective, epitomized by Ralf Dahrendorf (1959; Reading 8) and Lewis Coser (1956; Reading 9), maintained that the relationship of groups in society is marked by differences in goals rather than similarities. Alvin Gouldner (1959) urged that more insight can be gained by examining the different strengths and weaknesses of social ties. Coser (1956), Harold Fallding (1961), Pierre van den Berghe (1963), and others attempted to compensate for these shortcomings in functionalist analysis by stressing the competitive nature of society and by attempting to integrate the insights of functionalism with conflict theory (although this attempt at synthesis itself generated considerable controversy; see Frank 1966).

The final and most bitter criticism of functional analysis was a sociopolitical one. Many sociologists (Gouldner 1970, Horton 1964, Mills 1959, Tumin 1953, and many others) charged the functionalists with being apologists for the status quo. They argued that articles such as the Davis-Moore analysis of social class or Merton's treatment of political bossism confuse the "is" with the "ought." Functionalists accepted many of these charges as having some merit; however, they still insisted that the functionalist variant of order theory was no less useful than other conceptual models.

During the late 1960s and the 1970s, functionalism fell into general disrepute in sociology, disappearing under a barrage of criticism leveled by younger sociological adherents of the many new sociological paradigms that entered the field during this period of social crisis and ferment. Already by the late 1950s, the dominant model within the functionalist paradigm, Talcott Parsons' Grand Theory, had been coming under increasing attack. Although firmly anchored within the prevailing functionalist perspective, Lewis Coser's 1956 essay *The Functions of Social Conflict* drew embarrassing attention to the major weakness within Parsonian theory, its inability to account for and analyze conflict. This essay was closely followed by David Lockwood's

(1956) seminal paper on Parsons' concept of the social system. In this essay, Lockwood focused on what was to become the major complaint among critics of the functionalist model: the inability of the theoretical system to provide an explanation for the process of social change. Lockwood's essay was followed two years later by Ralf Dahrendorf's polemical "Out of Utopia" (1958), which openly declared a break with functionalism, opposing it to a vaguely sketched "conflict model" (see Chapter 2). The 1960s saw a flood of articles and books attacking functionalism written from within the new "conflict" perspective. Already by 1964, a questionnaire distributed to 3,500 sociologists revealed that the conflict paradigm had as many adherents as the functionalist model. By the 1970s, functionalism had become the "straw man" of sociological theory, the subject of ritual denunciations and attacks from almost every other theoretical perspective.

Seemingly dead, functionalism made a significant comeback during the 1980s in the work of several primarily American scholars influenced by the work of Jeffrey Alexander (see Alexander 1978, 1982–1984, 1985; Alexander and Colomy 1985, 1990a). At the same time, a similar revival of interest in Talcott Parsons' work was taking place in Germany (see Luhmann 1982, 1990; Münch 1990). This recent interest in functionalist models in German sociology was part of a more general revival of conservative ideologies among European intellectuals during the 1980s, in the wake of the decline of traditionally influential Marxist ideas. The renewed international interest in functionalism has led to important collaborative efforts between American and European functionalists (see Haferkamp and Smelser 1992, Münch and Smelser 1992).

While working within the general functionalist tradition, these "neofunctionalists" (a term popularized by Jeffrey Alexander)

have attempted to expand the explanatory base of traditional functionalism by borrowing from other theoretical traditions. Neofunctionalists have attempted to respond to the criticisms raised against the traditional functionalist model in several ways. First, neofunctionalists have largely eliminated references in their work to functional needs or requisites in order to defuse the charge of teleology. Second, neofunctionalists have dropped the assumption of functional unity in society. Instead, neofunctionalists look at the varied (and often conflicting) relationships between various systems and subsystems in ways that allow for considerable organizational complexity and "looseness" of fit. Finally, neofunctionalists have attempted to deal with the charge of conservatism and lack of attention to social change by focusing much of their work on developing the traditional functionalist concept of *differentiation* as a master tool for the explanation of social conflict and change (see Luhmann, Reading 4; Colomy, Reading 5; see also the essays collected in Alexander 1985, Alexander and Colomy 1990b).

These revisions have led to a contemporary functionalism that is much more theoretically open and that, in the work of theorists such as Alexander (1987), is much less scientistic and more in tune with contemporary antipostivist currents in the philosophy of science than was the original concept of functionalism. At the same time, Luhmann (Reading 4) and others (the German neofunctionalists, especially) have retained functionalism's traditional focus on macro-level phenomena and the central organizing concept of the social system. In Reading 6, Turner and Maryanski survey these recent developments and raise the question of whether all these revisions of the classical functionalist model have saved it or transformed it beyond recognition—they ask, in other words, has the baby been thrown out with the bath water?

Despite its many difficulties, functionalism was one of the most widely used approaches in the sociological literature before the mid-1960s. Substantial areas of criminology, deviant behavior, social stratification, and the sociology of religion especially have been influenced by the theoretical labors of Durkheim, Parsons, Merton, Davis, and others. Recent works by neofunctionalists have restored this venerable tradition to some of its former glory, and it seems likely that the functionalist tradition will continue to develop as a living theoretical program well into the twenty-first century.

REFERENCES

ALEXANDER, JEFFREY. 1978. "Formal and Substantive Voluntarism in the Work of Talcott Parsons: A Theoretical and Ideological Reinterpretation." *American Sociological Review* 43 (April):177–98.

———. 1982–1984. *Theoretical Logic in Sociology*, 4 vols. Berkeley: University of California Press.

———, ed. 1985. *Neofunctionalism.* Beverly Hills: Sage Publications.

———. 1987. "The Centrality of the Classics," Pp. 11–57 in *Social Theory Today*, ed. Anthony Giddens and Jonathan Turner. Stanford: Stanford University Press.

ALEXANDER, JEFFREY, AND PAUL COLOMY. 1985. "Toward Neofunctionalism." *Sociological Theory* 3 (Fall):11–23.

———. 1990a. "Neofunctionalism Today: Reconstructing a Theoretical Tradition." Pp. 33–67 in *Frontiers of Social Theory*, ed. George Ritzer. New York: Columbia University Press.

———, eds. 1990b. *Differentiation Theory and Social Change: Comparative and Historical Perspectives.* New York: Columbia University Press.

BREDEMEIR, HARRY. 1935. "The Methodology of Functionalism." *American Sociological Review* 20 (April):173–79.

BRUMBACH, ROBERT. 1964. *The Philosophers of Greece.* New York: Thomas Y. Crowell.

COHEN, PERCY. 1968. *Modern Social Theory.* New York: Basic Books.

CORNFORD, FRANCIS. 1945. *The Republic of Plato.* Oxford, Oxford University Press.

COSER, LEWIS. 1956. *The Functions of Social Conflict.* New York: Free Press.

———. 1958. "Out of Utopia: Towards a Reorientation of Sociological Analysis." *American Journal of Sociology* 64 (September):115–27.

DAHRENDORF, RALF. 1959. *Class and Class Conflict in Industrial Society.* Stanford: Stanford University Press.

DAVIS, KINGSLEY, AND WILBERT MOORE. 1945. "Some Principles of Stratification." *American Sociological Review* 10 (April):242–49.

DORE, RONALD. 1961. "Function and Cause." *American Sociological Review* 46 (December):843–53.

DURKHEIM, EMILE. 1951. *Suicide: A Study in Sociology.* 1897. Reprint, New York: Free Press.

———. 1964a. *The Division of Labor in Society.* 1893. Reprint, New York: Free Press.

———. 1964b. *The Rules of Sociological Method.* 1895. Reprint, New York: Free Press.

———. 1965. *The Elementary Forms of Religious Life.* 1912. Reprint, New York: Free Press.

FALLDING, HAROLD. 1961. "Functional Analysis in Sociology." *American Sociological Review* 28 (February):5–13.

FRANK, ANDRE GUNDER. 1966. "Dialectic and Functionalism." *Science and Society* 30 (Spring):62–73.

FRIEDRICHS, ROBERT. 1970. *A Sociology of Sociology.* New York: Free Press.

GOULDNER, ALVIN. 1959. "Reciprocity and Autonomy in Functional Theory." Pp. 241–70 in *Symposium on Sociological Theory*, ed. Llewellyn Gross. New York: Harper and Row.

———. 1966. *Enter Plato: Classical Greece and the Origins of Social Theory.* New York: Harper and Row.

———. 1970. *The Coming Crisis of Western Sociology.* New York: Basic Books.

HAFERKAMP, HANS, AND NEIL J. SMELSER, eds. 1992. *Social Change and Modernity.* Berkeley: University of California Press.

HINKLE, ROSCOE. 1964. "Durkheim in American Sociology." Pp. 267–95 in *Essays on Sociology and Philosophy by Emile Durkheim, et al.*, ed. Kurt Wolff. New York: Harper Torchbooks.

HORTON, JOHN. 1964. "The Dehumanization of Anomie and Alienation—A Problem in the Ideology of Sociology." *British Journal of Sociology* (December):283–300.

LOCKWOOD, DAVID. 1956. "Some Remarks on 'The Social System'." *British Journal of Sociology* 7 (June):134–45.

LUHMANN, NIKLAS. 1982. *The Differentiation of Society.* New York: Columbia University Press.

———. 1990. *Essays on Self-Reference.* New York: Columbia University Press.

MERTON, ROBERT. 1968. *Social Theory and Social Structure.* New York: Free Press.

MILLS, C. WRIGHT. 1959. *The Sociological Imagination.* New York: Oxford University Press.

MÜNCH, RICHARD. 1990. *Theory of Action: Towards a New Synthesis Going beyond Parsons.* London: Routledge and Kegan Paul.

MÜNCH, RICHARD, AND NEIL J. SMELSER, eds. 1992. *Theory of Culture.* Berkeley: University of California Press.

PARSONS, TALCOTT. 1951. *The Social System.* Glencoe: Free Press.

_____. 1968. *The Structure of Social Action.* New York: Free Press.

_____. 1970. *Social Structure and Personality.* New York: Free Press.

PARSONS, TALCOTT, AND EDWARD SHILS, eds. 1951. *Toward a General Theory of Action.* Cambridge: Harvard University Press.

PIERCE, ALBERT. 1964. "Durkheim and Functionalism." Pp. 154–69. *Essays on Sociology and Philosophy by Emile Durkheim, et al.,* ed. Kurt Wolff. New York: Harper Torchbooks.

RADCLIFFE-BROWN, A.R. 1956. *Structure and Function in Primitive Society.* Glencoe, Ill.: Free Press.

SPENCER, HERBERT. 1967. *The Evolution of Society.* Chicago: University of Chicago Press.

TUMIN, MELVIN. 1953. "Some Principles of Stratification—A Critical Analysis." *American Sociological Review* 18 (August):387–93.

TURNER, JONATHAN, AND ALEXANDRA MARYANSKI. 1979. *Functionalism.* Menlo Park: Benjamin/Cummings Publishing.

VAN DEN BERGHE, PIERRE. 1963. "Dialectic and Functionalism." *American Sociological Review* 28 (October):695–705.

ON THE CONCEPT OF FUNCTION
IN SOCIAL SCIENCE*

A. R. RADCLIFFE-BROWN

The concept of function applied to human societies is based on an analogy between social life and organic life. The recognition of the analogy and of some of its important implications is at least as old as Protagoras and Plato. In the nineteenth century the analogy, the concept of function, and the word itself appear frequently in social philosophy and sociology. So far as I know the first systematic formulation of the concept as applying to the strictly scientific study of society was that of Émile Durkheim in 1895.

Durkheim's definition is that the "function" of a social institution is the correspondence between it and the needs of the social organism. This definition requires some elaboration. In the first place, to avoid possible ambiguity and in particular the possibility of a teleological interpretation, I would like to substitute for the term "needs" the term "necessary conditions of existence," or, if the term "need" is used, it is to be understood only in this sense. It may here be noted, as a point to

be returned to, that any attempt to apply this concept of function in social science involves the assumption that there *are* necessary conditions of existence for human societies just as there are for animal organisms, and that they can be discovered by the proper kind of scientific enquiry.

For the further elucidation of the concept it is convenient to use the analogy between social life and organic life. Like all analogies it has to be used with care. An animal organism is an agglomeration of cells and interstitial fluids arranged in relation to one another not as an aggregate but as an integrated whole. For the bio-chemist, it is a complexly integrated system of complex molecules. The system of relations by which these units are related is the organic structure. As the terms are here used the organism *is not* itself the structure; it is a collection of units (cells or molecules) arranged in a structure, i.e., in a set of relations; the organism *has* a structure. Two mature animals of the same species and sex consist of similar units combined in a similar structure. The structure is thus to be defined as a set of relations between the entities. (The structure of a cell is in the same way a set of re-

*Reproduced by permission of the American Anthropological Association from *American Anthropologist* 37:3, July-September 1935. Not for further reproduction.

lations between complex molecules, and the structure of an atom is a set of relations between electrons and protons.) As long as it lives the organism preserves a certain continuity of structure although it does not preserve the complete identity of its constituent parts. It loses some of its constituent molecules by respiration or excretion; it takes in others by respiration and alimentary absorption. Over a period its constituent cells do not remain the same. But the structural arrangement of the constituent units does remain similar. The process by which this structural continuity of the organism is maintained is called life. The life-process consists of the activities and interactions of the constituent units of the organism, the cells, and the organs into which the cells are united.

As the word function is here being used the life of an organism is conceived as the *functioning* of its structure. It is through and by the continuity of the functioning that the continuity of the structure is preserved. If we consider any recurrent part of the life-process, such as respiration, digestion, etc., its *function* is the part it plays in, the contribution it makes to, the life of the organism as a whole. As the terms are here being used a cell or an organ has an *activity* and that activity has a *function*. It is true that we commonly speak of the secretion of gastric fluid as a "function" of the stomach. As the words are here used we should say that this is an "activity" of the stomach, the "function" of which is to change the proteins of food into a form in which these are absorbed and distributed by the blood to the tissues. We may note that the function of a recurrent physiological process is thus a correspondence between it and the needs (i.e., necessary conditions of existence) of the organism.

If we set out upon a systematic investigation of the nature of organisms and organic life there are three sets of problems presented to us. (There are, in addition, certain other sets of problems concerning aspects or characteristics of organic life with which we are not here concerned.) One is that of morphology—what kinds of organic structures are there, what similarities and variations do they show, and how can they be classified? Second are the problems of physiology—how, in general, do organic structures function, what, therefore, is the nature of the life-process? Third are the problems of development—how do new types of organisms come into existence?

To turn from organic life to social life, if we examine such a community as an African or Australian tribe we can recognize the existence of a social structure. Individual human beings, the essential units in this instance, are connected by a definite set of social relations into an integrated whole. The continuity of the social structure, like that of an organic structure, is not destroyed by changes in the units. Individuals may leave the society, by death or otherwise; others may enter it. The continuity of structure is maintained by the process of social life, which consists of the activities and interactions of the individual human beings and of the organized groups into which they are united. The social life of the community is here defined as the *functioning* of the social structure. The *function* of any recurrent activity, such as the punishment of a crime, or a funeral ceremony, is the part it plays in the social life as a whole and therefore the contribution it makes to the maintenance of the structural continuity.

The concept of function as here defined thus involves the notion of a *structure* consisting of a *set of relations* amongst *unit entities*, the *continuity* of the structure being maintained by a *life-process* made up of the *activities* of the constituent units.

If, with these concepts in mind, we set out on a systematic investigation of the nature of human society and of social life, we find presented to us three sets of problems. First, the problems of social morphology—what kinds of social structures are there, what are their similarities and differences, how are they to be classified? Second, the problems of social physiology—how do social structures function? Third, the problems of development—how do new types of social structure come into existence?

Two important points where the analogy between organism and society breaks down must be noted. In an animal organism it is possible to observe the organic structure to a large extent independently of its functioning. It is therefore possible to make a morphology which is independent of physiology. But in human society the social structure as a whole can only be *observed* in its functioning. Some of the features of social structure, such as the geographical distribution of individuals and groups can be directly observed, but most of the social relations which in their totality constitute the structure, such as relations of father and son, buyer and seller, ruler and subject, cannot be observed except in the social activities in which the relations are functioning. It follows that a social morphology cannot be established independently of a social physiology.

The second point is that an animal organism does not, in the course of its life, change its structural type. A pig does not become a hippopotamus. (The development of the animal from germination to maturity is not a change of type since the process in all its stages is typical for the species.) On the other hand a society in the course of its history can and does change its structural type without any breach of continuity.

By the definition here offered "function" is the contribution which a partial activity makes to the total activity of which it is a part. The function of a particular social usage is the contribution it makes to the total social life as the functioning of the total social system. Such a view implies that a social system (the total social structure of a society together with the totality of social usages, in which that structure appears and on which it depends for its continued existence) has a certain kind of unity, which we may speak of as a functional unity. We may define it as a condition in which all parts of the social system work together with a sufficient degree of harmony or internal consistency, i.e., without producing persistent conflicts which can neither be resolved nor regulated.

This idea of the functional unity of a social system is, of course, a hypothesis. But it is one which, to the functionalist, it seems worth while to test by systematic examination of the facts.

There is another aspect of functional theory that should be briefly mentioned. To return to the analogy of social life and organic life, we recognize that an organism may function more or less efficiently and so we set up a special science of pathology to deal with all phenomena of dysfunction. We distinguish in an organism what we call health and disease. The Greeks of the fifth century B.C. thought that one might apply the same notion to society, to the city-state, distinguishing conditions of *eunomia*, good order, social health, from *dysnomia*, disorder, social ill-health. In the nineteenth century Durkheim, in his application of the notion of function, sought to lay the basis for a scientific social pathology, based on a morphology and a physiology. In his works, particularly those on suicide and on the division of labor, he attempted to find objective criteria by which to judge whether a given society at a given time is normal or pathological, eunomic or dysnomic. For example, he tried to show that the increase of the rate of suicide in many countries during part of the nineteenth century is symptomatic of a dysnomic or, in his terminology, anomic, social condition. Probably there is no sociologist who would hold that Durkheim really succeeded in establishing an objective basis for a science of social pathology.

In relation to organic structures we can find strictly objective criteria by which to distinguish disease from health, pathological from normal, for disease is that which either threatens the organism with death (the dissolution of its structure) or interferes with the activities which are characteristic of the organic type. Societies do not die in the same sense that animals die and therefore we cannot define dysnomia as that which leads, if unchecked, to the death of a society. Further a society differs from an organism in that it can change its structural type, or can be absorbed as an integral part of a larger society. Therefore we cannot define dysnomia as a disturbance of the usual activities of a social type (as Durkheim tried to do).

Let us return for a moment to the Greeks. They conceived the health of an organism and the eunomia of a society as being in each instance a condition of the harmonious working together of its parts. Now this, where society is concerned, is the same thing as what was considered above as the functional unity or inner consistency of a social system, and it is suggested that for the degree of functional unity of a particular society it may be possible to establish a purely objective criterion. Admittedly this cannot be done at present; but the science of human society is as yet in its extreme infancy. So that it may be that we should say that while an organism that is attacked by a virulent disease will react thereto, and, if its reaction fails, will die, a society that is thrown into a condition of functional disunity or inconsistency (for this we now provisionally identify with dysnomia) will not die, except in such comparatively rare instances as an Australian tribe overwhelmed by the white man's destructive force, but will continue to struggle toward some sort of eunomia, some kind of social health, and may, in the course of this, change its structural type. This process, it seems, the "functionalist" has ample opportunities of observing at the present day, in native peoples subjected to the domination of the civilized nations, and in those nations themselves.

Space will not allow a discussion here of another aspect of functional theory, viz., the question whether change of social type is or is not dependent on function i.e., on the laws of social physiology. My own view is that there is such a dependence and that its nature can be studied in the development of the legal and political institutions, the economic systems and the religions of Europe through the last twenty-five centuries. For the preliterate societies with which anthropology is concerned it is not possible to study the details of long processes of change of type. The one kind of change which the anthropologist can observe is the disintegration of social structures. Yet even here we can observe and compare spontaneous movements towards reintegration. We have, for instance, in Africa, in Oceania, and in America the appearance of new religions which can be interpreted on a functional hypothesis as attempts to relieve a condition of social dysnomia produced by the rapid modification of the social life through contact with white civilization.

The concept of function as defined above constitutes a "working hypothesis" by which a number of problems are formulated for investigation. No scientific enquiry is possible without some such formulation of working hypotheses. Two remarks are necessary here. One is that the hypothesis does not require the dogmatic assertion that everything in the life of every community has a function. It only requires the assumption that it *may* have one, and that we are justified in seeking to discover it. The second is that what appears to be the same social usage in two societies may have different functions in the two. Thus the practice of celibacy in the Roman Catholic Church of to-day has very different functions from those of celibacy in the early Christian church. In other words, in order to define a social usage, and therefore in order to make valid comparisons between the usages of different peoples or periods it is necessary to consider not merely the form of the usage but also its function. On this basis, for example, belief in a Supreme Being in a simple society is something different from such a belief in a modern civilized community.

The acceptance of the functional hypothesis or point of view outlined above results in the recognition of a vast number of problems for the solution of which there are required wide comparative studies of societies of many diverse types and also intensive studies of as many single societies as possible. In field studies of the simpler peoples it leads, first of all, to a direct study of the social life of the community as the functioning of a social structure, and of this there are several examples in recent literature. Since the function of a social activity is to be found by examining its effects upon individuals, these are studied, either in the average individual or in both average and exceptional individuals. Further, the hypothesis leads to attempts to investigate directly the functional consistency or unity of a social system and to determine as far as possible in each instance the nature of that unity. Such field studies will obviously be different in many ways from studies carried out from other points of view, e.g., the ethnological point of view that lays emphasis on diffusion. We do not have to say that one point of view is better than another, but only that they are different, and any particular piece of work should be judged in reference to what it aims to do. . . .

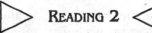

PREVAILING POSTULATES
IN FUNCTIONAL ANALYSIS*

ROBERT K. MERTON

Chiefly but not solely in anthropology, functional analysts have commonly adopted three interconnected postulates which, it will now be suggested, have proved to be debatable and unnecessary to the functional orientation.

Substantially, these postulates hold first, that standardized social activities or cultural items are functional for the *entire* social or cultural system; second, that *all* such social and cultural items fulfill sociological functions; and third, that these items are consequently *indispensable.* Although these three articles of faith are ordinarily seen only in one another's company, they had best be examined separately, since each gives rise to its own distinctive difficulties.

POSTULATE OF THE FUNCTIONAL UNITY OF SOCIETY

It is Radcliffe-Brown who characteristically puts this postulate in explicit terms:

The function of a particular social usage is the contribution it makes to the *total social life* as the functioning of the *total social system.* Such a view implies that a social system (*the total social structure* of a society together with the totality of social usages, in which that structure appears and on which it depends for its continued existence) has a certain kind of unity, which we may speak of as a functional unity. We may define it as a condition in which all parts of the social system work together with a sufficient degree of harmony or internal consistency, i.e., without producing persistent conflicts which can neither be resolved nor regulated.[1]

It is important to note, however, that he goes on to describe this notion of functional unity as a hypothesis which requires further test.

It would at first appear that Malinowski was questioning the empirical acceptability of this postulate when he notes that "the sociological school" (into which he thrusts Radcliffe-Brown) "exaggerated the social solidarity of primitive man" and "neglected the individual."[2] But it is soon apparent that Malinowski does not so much abandon this dubious assumption as he succeeds in adding another to it. He continues to speak of standardized practices and beliefs as functional "for culture as a whole," and goes on to assume that they are *also* functional for every member of the society. Thus, referring to primitive beliefs in the supernatural, he writes:

Here the functional view is put to its acid test. . . . It is bound to show in what way belief and ritual work for social integration, technical and economic efficiency, for *culture as a whole*—indirectly therefore for the biological and mental welfare *of each individual member.*[3]

If the one unqualified assumption is questionable, this twin assumption is doubly so. Whether cultural items do uniformly fulfill functions for the society viewed as a system and for all members of the society is presumably an empirical question of fact, rather than an axiom.

Kluckhohn evidently perceives the problem inasmuch as he extends the alternatives to include the possibility that cultural forms "are adjustive or adaptive . . . for the members of the society *or* for the society considered as a perduring unit."[4] This is a necessary first step in allowing for variation in the *unit* which is subserved by the imputed function. Compelled by the force of empirical observation, we shall have occasion to widen the range of variation in this unit even further.

It seems reasonably clear that the notion of functional unity is *not* a postulate beyond the reach of empirical test; quite the contrary. The degree of integration is an empirical variable,[5] changing for the same society from time to time and differing among various societies. That all human societies must have *some* degree of integration is a matter of definition—and begs the question. But not all societies have that *high* degree of integration in which *every* culturally standardized activity or belief is functional for the society as a whole and uniformly functional for the people living in it. Radcliffe-Brown need in fact have looked no further than to his favored realm of analogy in order to suspect the adequacy of his assumption of functional unity. For we find significant variations in the degree of integration even among individual biological organisms, although the commonsense assumption would tell us that here, surely, all the parts of the organism work toward a "unified" end. Consider only this:

One can readily see that there are *highly integrated organisms* under close control of the nervous system or of hormones, the loss of any major part of which will strongly affect the whole system, and frequently will cause death, but, on the other hand, there are the lower *organisms much more loosely correlated,* where the loss of even a major part of the body causes only temporary inconvenience pending the regeneration of replacement tissues. Many of these more loosely organized animals are *so poorly integrated that different parts may be in active opposition to each other.* Thus, when an ordinary starfish is placed on its back, part of the arms may attempt to turn the animal in one direction, while others work to turn it in the opposite way. . . . On account of its *loose integration,* the sea anemone may move off and leave a portion of its foot clinging tightly to a rock, so that the animal suffers serious rupture.[6]

If this is true of single organisms, it would seem a fortiori the case with complex social systems.

One need not go far afield to show that the assumption of the complete functional unity of human society is repeatedly contrary to fact. Social usages or sentiments may be functional for some groups and dysfunctional for others in the same society. Anthropologists often cite "increased solidarity of the community" and "increased family pride" as instances of functionally adaptive sentiments. Yet, as Bateson[7] among others has indicated, an increase of pride among individual families may often serve to disrupt the solidarity of a small local community. Not only is the postulate of functional unity often contrary to fact, but it has little heuristic value, since it diverts the analyst's attention from possible disparate consequences of a given social or cultural item (usage, belief, behavior pattern, institution) for diverse social groups and for the individual members of these groups.

If the body of observation and fact which negates the assumption of functional unity is as large and easily accessible as we have suggested, it is interesting to ask how it happens that Radcliffe-Brown and others who follow his lead have continued to abide by this assumption. A possible clue is provided by the fact that this conception, in its recent formulations, was developed by social *anthropologists*, that is, by men primarily concerned with the study of non-literate societies. In view of what Radin has described as "the highly integrated nature of the majority of aboriginal civilizations," this assumption may be tolerably suitable for some, if not all, non-literate societies. But one pays an excessive intellectual penalty for moving this possibly useful assumption from the realm of small non-literate societies to the realm of large, complex and highly differentiated literate societies. In no field, perhaps, do the dangers of such a transfer of assumption become more visible than in the functional analysis of religion. This deserves brief review, if only because it exhibits in bold relief the fallacies one falls heir to by sympathetically adopting this assumption without a thorough screening.

The Functional Interpretation of Religion. In examining the price paid for the transfer of this tacit assumption of functional unity from the field of relatively small and relatively tightknit non-literate groups to the field of more highly differentiated and perhaps more loosely integrated societies, it is useful to consider the work of sociologists, particularly of sociologists who are ordinarily sensitized to the assumptions on which they work. This has passing interest for its bearing on the more general question of seeking, without appropriate modification, to apply to the study of literate societies conceptions developed and matured in the study of non-literate societies. (Much the same question holds for the transfer of research procedures and techniques, but this is not at issue here.)

The large, spaceless and timeless generalizations about "the integrative functions of religion" are largely, though not of course wholly, derived from observations in non-literate societies. Not infrequently, the social scientist implicitly adopts the findings regarding such societies and goes on to expatiate upon the integrative functions of religion *generally*. From this, it is a short step to statements such as the following:

The reason why religion is necessary is apparently to be found in the fact that human society *achieves its unity* primarily through the possession by its members of certain ultimate values and ends in common. Although these values and ends are subjective, they influence behavior, and their integration enables this society to operate as a system.[8]

In an extremely advanced society built on scientific technology, the priesthood tends to lose status, because sacred tradition and supernaturalism drop into the background ... [but] *No society* has become so completely secularized as to liquidate *entirely* the belief in transcendental ends and supernatural entities. Even in a secularized society *some system* must exist for the integration of ultimate values, for their ritualistic expression, and for the emotional adjustments required by disappointment, death, and disaster.[9]

Deriving from the Durkheim orientation which was based largely upon the study of non-literate societies, these authors tend to single out *only* the apparently integrative consequences of religion and to neglect its possibly disintegrative consequences *in certain types of social structure.* Yet consider the following very well-known facts and queries. (1) When different religions co-exist in the same society, there often occurs deep conflict between the several religious groups (consider only the enormous literature on inter-religious conflict in European societies). In what sense, then, does religion make for integration of "the" society in the numerous multireligion societies? (2) It is clearly the case that "human society achieves its unity [insofar as it exhibits such unity] primarily through the possession by its members of certain ultimate values and ends in common." But what is the evidence indicating that "non-religious" people, say, in our own society less often subscribe to certain common "values and ends" than those devoted to religious doctrines? (3) In what sense does religion make for integration of the larger society, if the content of its doctrine and values is at odds with the content of other, non-religious values held by many people in the same society? (Consider, for example, the conflict between the opposition of the Catholic Church to child-labor legislation and the secular values of preventing "exploitation of youthful dependents." Or the contrasting evaluations of birth control by diverse religious groups in our society.)

This list of commonplace facts regarding the role of religion in contemporary literate societies could be greatly extended, and they are of course very well known to those functional anthropologists and sociologists who describe religion as integrative, without limiting the range of social structures in which this is indeed the case. It is at least conceivable that a theoretic orientation derived from research on non-literate societies has served to obscure otherwise conspicuous data on the functional role of religion in multi-religion societies. Perhaps it is the transfer of the assumption of functional unity which results in blotting out the entire history of religious wars, of the Inquisition (which drove a wedge into society after society), of internecine conflicts among religious groups. For the fact remains that all this abundantly known material is ignored in favor of illustrations drawn from the study of religion in non-literate society. And it is a further striking fact that the same paper, cited above [notes 8 & 9], that goes on to speak of "religion, which provides integration in terms of sentiments, beliefs and rituals," does not make a single reference to the possibly divisive role of religion.

Such functional analyses may, of course, mean that religion provides integration of those who believe in the *same* religious values, but it is unlikely that this is meant, since it would merely assert that integration is provided by any consensus on any set of values.

Moreover, this again illustrates the danger of taking the assumption of functional unity, which *may* be a reasonable approximation for some non-literate societies, as part of an implicit model for *generalized* functional analysis. Typically, in non-literate societies, there is but one prevailing religious system so that, apart from individual deviants, the membership of the total society and the membership of the religious community are virtually co-extensive. Obviously, in this type of social structure, a common set of religious values may have as *one* of its consequences the reinforcement of common sentiments and of social integration. But this does not easily lend itself to defensible generalization about other types of society.

We shall have occasion to return to other theoretic implications of current functional analyses of religion but, for the moment, this may illustrate the dangers which one inherits in adopting the unqualified postulate of functional unity. This unity of the total society cannot be usefully posited in advance of observation. It is a question of fact, and not a matter of opinion. The theoretic framework of functional analysis must expressly require that there be *specification* of the *units* for which a given social or cultural item is functional. It must expressly allow for a given item having diverse consequences, functional and dysfunctional, for individuals, for subgroups, and for the more inclusive social structure and culture.

POSTULATE OF UNIVERSAL FUNCTIONALISM

Most succinctly, this postulate holds that all standardized social or cultural forms have positive functions. As with other aspects of the functional conception, Malinowski advances this in its most extreme form:

The functional view of culture *insists* therefore upon the principle that in *every type of civilization, every custom, material object, idea and belief fulfills some vital function.* . . .[10]

Although, as we have seen, Kluckhohn allows for variation in the unit subserved by a cultural form, he joins with Malinowski in postulating functional value for all surviving forms of culture. ("My basic postulate . . . is that *no* culture forms survive unless they constitute responses which are adjustive or adaptive, in some sense. . . ."[11]) This universal functionalism may or may not be a heuristic postulate; that remains to be seen. But one should be prepared to find that it too diverts critical attention from a range of non-functional consequences of existing cultural forms.

In fact, when Kluckhohn seeks to illustrate his point by ascribing "functions" to seemingly functionless items, he falls back upon a type of function which would be found, *by definition* rather than by inquiry, served by all persisting items of culture. Thus, he suggests that

The at present mechanically useless buttons on the sleeve of a European man's suit subserve the "function" of preserving the familiar, of maintaining a tradition. People are, in general, more comfortable if they feel a continuity of behavior, if they feel themselves as following out the orthodox and socially approved forms of behavior.[12]

This would appear to represent the marginal case in which the imputation of function adds little or nothing to the direct description of the culture pattern or behavior form. It may well be assumed that all *established* elements of culture (which are loosely describable as "tradition") have the minimum, though not exclusive, function of "preserving the familiar, of maintaining a tradition." This is equivalent to saying that the "function" of conformity to *any* established practice is to enable the conformist to avoid the sanctions otherwise incurred by deviating from the established practice. This is no doubt true but hardly illuminating. It serves, however, to remind us that we shall want to explore the *types of functions* which the sociologist imputes. At the moment, it suggests the provisional assumption that, although any item of culture or social structure *may* have functions, it is premature to hold unequivocally that every such item *must* be functional.

The postulate of universal functionalism is of course the historical product of the fierce, barren and protracted controversy over "survivals" which raged among the anthropologists during the early part of the century. The notion of a social survival, that is, in the words of Rivers, of "a custom . . . [which] cannot be explained by its present utility but only becomes intelligible through its past history,"[13] dates back at least to Thucydides. But when the evolutionary theories of culture became prominent, the concept of survival seemed all the more strategically important for reconstructing "stages of development" of cultures, particularly for non-literate societies which possessed no written record. For the functionalists who wished to turn away from what they regarded as the usually fragmentary and often conjectural "history" of non-literate societies, the attack on the notion of survival took on all the symbolism of an attack on the entire and intellectually repugnant system of evolutionary thought. In consequence, perhaps, they over-reacted against this concept central to evolutionary theory and advanced an equally exaggerated "postulate" to the effect that "every custom [everywhere] . . . fulfills some vital function."

It would seem a pity to allow the polemics of the anthropological forefathers to create splendid exaggerations in the present. Once discovered, ticketed and studied, social survivals cannot be exorcized by a postulate. And if no specimens of these survivals can be produced, then the quarrel dwindles of its own accord. It can be said, furthermore, that even when such survivals are identified in contemporary literate societies, they seem to add little to our understanding of human behavior or the dynamics of social change. Not requiring their dubious role as poor substitutes for recorded history, the sociologist of literate societies may neglect survivals with no apparent loss. But he need not be driven, by an archaic and irrelevant controversy, to adopt the unqualified postulate that all culture items fulfill vital functions. For this, too, is a problem for investigation, not a conclusion in advance of investigation. Far more useful as a directive for research would seem the provisional assumption that persisting cultural forms have a *net balance of functional consequences* either for the society considered as a unit or for subgroups sufficiently powerful to retain these forms intact, by means of direct coercion or indirect persuasion. This formulation at once avoids the tendency of functional analysis to concentrate on positive functions and directs the attention of the research worker to other types of consequences as well.

POSTULATE OF INDISPENSABILITY

The last of this trio of postulates common among functional social scientists is, in some respects, the most ambiguous. The ambiguity becomes evident in the aforementioned manifesto by Malinowski to the effect that

in every type of civilization, every custom, material object, idea and belief fulfills some *vital* function, has some task to accomplish, represents an *indispensable part* within a working whole.[14]

From this passage, it is not at all clear whether he asserts the indispensability of the *function,* or of the *item* (custom, object, idea, belief) fulfilling the function, or *both.*

This ambiguity is quite common in the literature. Thus, the previously cited Davis and Moore account of the role of religion seems at first to maintain that it is the *institution* which is indispensable: "The reason why religion is necessary . . . "; " . . . religion . . . plays a unique and indispensable part in society."[15] But it soon appears that it is not so much the institution of religion which is regarded as indispensable but rather the functions which religion is taken typically to perform. For Davis and Moore regard religion as indispensable only insofar as it functions to make the members of a society adopt "certain ultimate values and ends in common." These values and ends, it is said,

must . . . appear to the members of the society to have some reality, and it is the role of religious belief and ritual to supply and reinforce this appearance of reality. Through ritual and belief the common ends and values are connected with an imaginary world symbolized by concrete sacred objects, which world in turn is related in a meaningful way to the facts and trials of the individual's life. Through the worship of the sacred objects and the beings they symbolize, and the acceptance of *supernatural prescriptions* that are at the same time codes of behavior, a powerful control over human conduct is exercised, guiding it along lines sustaining the institutional structure and conforming to the ultimate ends and values.[16]

The alleged indispensability of religion, then, is based on the assumption of fact that it is through "worship" and "supernatural prescriptions" *alone* that the necessary minimum of "control over human conduct" and "integration in terms of sentiments and beliefs" can be achieved.

In short, the postulate of indispensability as it is ordinarily stated contains two related, but distinguishable, assertions. First, it is assumed that there are certain *functions* which are indispensable in the sense that, unless they are performed, the society (or group or individual) will not persist. This, then, sets forth a concept of *functional prerequisites,* or *preconditions functionally necessary* for a society, and we shall have occasion to examine this concept in some detail. Second, and this is quite another matter, it is assumed that *certain cultural or social forms* are indispensable for fulfilling each of these functions. This involves a concept of specialized and irreplaceable structures, and gives rise to all manner of theoretic difficulties. For not only can this be shown to be manifestly contrary to fact, but it entails several subsidiary assumptions which have plagued functional analysis from the very outset. It diverts attention from the fact that alternative social structures (and cultural forms) have served, under conditions to be examined, the functions necessary for the persistence of groups. Proceeding further, we must set forth a major theorem of functional analysis; *just as the same item may have multiple functions, so may the same function be diversely fulfilled by alternative items.* Functional needs are here taken to be permissive, rather than determinant, of specific social structures. Or, in other words, there is a range of variation in the structures which fulfill the function in question. (The limits upon this range of variation involve the concept of structural constraint, of which more presently.)

In contrast to this implied concept of indispensable cultural forms (institutions, standardized practices, belief-systems, etc.), there is, then, the concept of *functional alternatives,* or *functional equivalents,* or *functional substitutes.* This concept is widely recognized and used, but it should be noted that it cannot rest comfortably in the same theoretical system which entails the postulate of indispensability of particular cultural forms. Thus, after reviewing Malinowski's theory of "the functional necessity for such mechanisms as magic," Parsons is careful to make the following statement:

. . . wherever such uncertainty elements enter into the pursuit of emotionally important goals, if not magic, at least *functionally equivalent* phenomena could be expected to appear.[17]

This is a far cry from Malinowski's own insistence that

Thus magic fulfills *an indispensable function* within culture. It satisfies a definite need *which cannot be satisfied by any other factors of primitive civilization.*[18]

This twin concept of the indispensable function and the irreplaceable belief-and-action pattern flatly excludes the concept of functional alternatives.

In point of fact, the concept of functional alternatives or equivalents has repeatedly emerged in every discipline which has adopted a functional framework of analysis. It is, for example, widely utilized in the psychological sciences, as a paper by English admirably indicates.[19] And in neurology, Lashley has pointed out on the basis of experimental and clinical evidence, the inadequacy of the "assumption that individual neurons are specialized for particular functions," maintaining instead that a particular function may be fulfilled by a range of alternative structures.[20]

Sociology and social anthropology have all the more occasion for avoiding the postulate of indispensability of given structures, and for systematically operating with the concept of functional alternatives and functional substitutes. For just as laymen have long erred in assuming that the "strange" customs and beliefs of other societies were "mere superstitions," so functional social scientists run the risk of erring in the other extreme, first, by being quick to find functional or adaptive value in these practices and beliefs, and second, by failing to see which alternative modes of action are ruled out by cleaving to these ostensibly functional practices. Thus, there is not seldom a readiness among some functionalists to conclude that magic or certain religious rites and beliefs are functional, because of their effect upon the state of mind or self-confidence of the believer. Yet it may well be in some instances, that these magical practices obscure and take the place of accessible secular and more adaptive practices. As F. L. Wells has observed,

To nail a horseshoe over the door in a smallpox epidemic may bolster the morale of the household but it will not keep out the smallpox; such beliefs and practices will not stand the secular tests to which they are susceptible, and the sense of security they give is preserved only while the real tests are evaded.[21]

Those functionalists who are constrained by their theory to attend to the effects of such symbolic practices *only* upon the individual's state of mind and who therefore conclude that the magical practice is functional, neglect the fact that these very practices may on occasion take the place of more effective alternatives. And those theorists who refer to the indispensability of standardized practices or prevailing institutions because of their observed function in reinforcing common sentiments must look first to functional substitutes before arriving at a conclusion, more often premature than confirmed.

Upon review of this trinity of functional postulates, several basic considerations emerge which must be caught up in our effort to codify this mode of analysis. In scrutinizing, first, *the postulate of functional unity*, we found that one cannot assume full integration of all societies, but that this is an empirical question of fact in which we should be prepared to find a range of degrees of integration. And in examining the special case of functional interpretations of religion, we were alerted to the possibility that, though human nature may be of a piece, it does not follow that the structure of non-literate societies is uniformly like that of highly differentiated, "literate" societies. A difference in degree between the two—say, the existence of several disparate religions in the one and not in the other—may make hazardous the passage between them. From critical scrutiny of

this postulate, it developed that a theory of functional analysis must call for *specification* of the social units subserved by given social functions, and that items of culture must be recognized to have multiple consequences, some of them functional and others, perhaps, dysfunctional.

Review of the second *postulate of universal functionalism*, which holds that all persisting forms of culture are inevitably functional, resulted in other considerations which must be met by a codified approach to functional interpretation. It appeared not only that we must be prepared to find dysfunctional as well as functional consequences of these forms but that the theorist will ultimately be confronted with the difficult problem of developing an organon for assessing the net balance of consequences if his research is to have bearing on social technology. Clearly, expert advice based only on the appraisal of a limited, and perhaps arbitrarily selected, range of consequences to be expected as a result of contemplated action, will be subject to frequent error and will be properly judged as having small merit.

The postulate of indispensability, we found, entailed two distinct propositions: the one alleging the indispensability of certain functions, and this gives rise to the concept of *functional necessity* or *functional prerequisites;* the other alleging the indispensability of existing social institutions, culture forms, or the like, and this when suitably questioned, gives rise to the concept of *functional alternatives, equivalents or substitutes.*

Moreover, the currency of these three postulates, singly and in concert, is the source of the common charge that functional analysis inevitably involves certain ideological commitments. Since this is a question which will repeatedly come to mind as one examines the further conceptions of functional analysis, it had best be considered now, if our attention is not to be repeatedly drawn away from the analytical problems in hand by the spectre of a social science tainted with ideology.

NOTES

1. A.R. Radcliffe-Brown, "On the concept of function," *The Andaman Islanders* (Glencoe, Illinois: The Free Press, 1948), 397 [italics supplied].

2. See B. Malinowski, "Anthropology," *Encyclopaedia Britannica*, First Supplementary Volume (London and New York, 1926), 132 and "The group and the individual in functional analysis," *American Journal of Sociology*, 1939, 44, 938–64, at 939.

3. Malinowski, "Anthropology," op. cit., 135.

4. Clyde Kluckhohn, *Navaho Witchcraft*, Papers of the Peabody Museum of American Archaeology and Ethnology, Harvard University (Cambridge: Peabody Museum, 1944), XXII, No. 2, 46b [italics supplied].

5. It is the merit of Sorokin's early review of theories of social integration that he did not lose sight of this important fact. Cf. P.A. Sorokin, "Forms and problems of culture-integration," *Rural Sociology*, 1936, 1, 121–41; 344–74.

6. G.H. Parker, *The Elementary Nervous System*, quoted by W.C. Allee *Animal Aggregation* (University of Chicago Press, 1931), 81–82.

7. Gregory Bateson, *Naven* (Cambridge [England] University Press, 1936), 31–32.

8. Kingsley Davis and Wilbert E. Moore, "Some principles of stratification," *American Sociological Review*, April 1945, 10, 242–49, at 244 [italics supplied].

9. Ibid., 246 [italics supplied].

10. Malinowski, "Anthropology," op. cit., 132. [The italics, though supplied, are perhaps superfluous in view of the forceful language of the original.]

11. Kluckhohn, *Navaho Witchcraft*, 46 [italics supplied].

12. Ibid., 47.

13. W.H.R. Rivers, "Survival in sociology," *The Sociological Review*, 1913, 6, 293–305.

14. Malinowski, "Anthropology," op. cit., 132 [italics supplied].

15. Kingsley Davis and Wilbert E. Moore, op. cit., 244, 246.

16. Ibid., 244–45 [italics supplied].

17. Talcott Parsons, *Essays in Sociological Theory, Pure and Applied* (Glencoe, Illinois: The Free Press, 1949), 58.

18. Malinowski, "Anthropology," op. cit., 136 [italics supplied].

19. Horace B. English, "Symbolic versus functional equivalents in the neuroses of deprivation," *Journal of Abnormal and Social Psychology*, 1937, 32, 392–94.

20. K.S. Lashley, "Basic neural mechanisms in behavior," *Psychological Review*, 1930, 37, 1–24.

21. F.L. Wells, "Social maladjustments: adaptive regression," in Carl A. Murchison, ed., *Handbook of Social Psychology* (Clark University Press, 1935), 880.

THE CONCEPT OF "SOCIAL SYSTEM" AS A THEORETICAL DEVICE*

CHARLES ACKERMAN AND TALCOTT PARSONS

THE ANALYST'S COGNITIVE MAP

Sociology is not a *tabula rasa* upon which things called "facts" inscribe their determinate and essential paths and shapes. No disciplined inquiry is. We approach our data as humans; and, as humans, we approach with differential receptivity and intentionality everything toward which we propose a cognitive orientation. In this respect one need only recall Tolman's famous and provocative concept of "the cognitive map." Data do not simply impose their structure on our inquiring and open minds: we *interact* with "facts." We are not naive, we are not innocent; and, as we shall argue, "no fact is merely itself": a completely open mind is a completely empty one. There is a formative input to analysis, the components of which are not born *ex nihilo* in or of the moment of encounter with "facts"; rather, they are grounded in the orientation and frame of reference of the analyst. Indeed, in major part we create, we do not merely encounter, facticity.

*From Gordon J. DiRenzo, ed., *Concepts, Theory, and Explanation in the Behavioral Sciences* (New York: Random House, 1966), pp. 24–25, 28–35. Reproduced with permission of McGraw-Hill, Inc.

Two grand and ultimate models have traditionally (and, of course, differently) guided sociological conceptualization and research—the *mechanical* and the *organic*. In recent years a third has emerged—the symbolic-interaction or *cybernetic* model—synthesizing to some degree important aspects of the traditional two. The virtues and vices of these models are irrelevant to the point we want to make, which is, simply, that they have been, and are, for many theorists and researchers, generators of ideas, orientational devices guiding conceptualization, research, and explanation.

We are at least as intelligent as Tolman's thoughtful rats, and we take into the analytical situation—a situation, we repeat, of interaction with the data—a cognitive map. There may be more or less "goodness of fit" of our map to the data, and we may be more or less sensitive to this, more or less willing to "learn," to adjust our map; but our learning does not make us inhuman and we always have maps before we encounter the "facts." Our maps tell us what *are* the "facts." We select, and we ascribe importance; and we select and ascribe importance according to criteria that are not simply immanent "in" the data.

Our criteria transcend the array of data under analysis.

We feel it appropriate that an analyst attempt conscious recognition of the general structure of his cognitive map, his "input" to analysis. *Hier stehe ich; ich kann nicht anders* (Here I stand; I cannot do otherwise). The statement frequently attributed to Luther is one of flamboyant self-assertion and the sound of hammering echoes in it still. Although flamboyance, self-assertion, and hammering are not appropriate to a scientific symposium, honesty, introspection, and the attempt to reveal standpoint are. The purpose of this paper is to make as explicit as possible—at least in silhouette—the grounding of our approach, our cognitive map, our orientation, our standpoint, and some of the consequences of all these.

In some respects we are the ragpickers of sociological theory, having derived many of our primary concepts from other disciplines. For example, system, in our usage, implies to an important degree its origin in physiological theory. The nineteenth-century French physiologist Claude Bernard pointed out that systems are less randomly ordered than the environment in which they are embedded. Indeed, one very highly generalized way of conceptualizing a minimal aspect of a system might be to consider it *an area of relative nonrandomness*. It is also the case that system boundaries are permeable: the system and its environment *interpenetrate* each other. A system is an ordered aggregate embedded in, and in interaction with, a fluctuating environment.

Given this conceptualization of system, the analyst immediately finds implications. He may ask such relevant questions as, for example, "How is the degree of order maintained 'against' environmental fluctuation?" and "How are the internal system components ordered vis-à-vis each other?" The analyst will consider *system problems,* for example, problems of boundary maintenance, problems of resource procurement and allocation, and problems of pattern maintenance. If he wants theory rather than empirical generalizations, he will define and identify these problems in generic terms, that is, in terms not specific to any class of action systems, but specifiable to all, in principle, isomorphically. He will be drawn toward attempting: (1) to define problems, and (2) to identify *mechanisms* that, however adequately or inadequately, "resolve" the problems, and (3) to state the conditions and consequences of adequate or inadequate resolution.

Consider, for an example, the "adaptive" problems *implied* by interpenetration and differential randomness. Not only must system boundaries, by some mechanism(s), be maintained in relative integrity, but by some mechanism(s) the system must both draw "sustenance" from the environment and "defend itself" against extreme environmental fluctuation. At the boundary of the system—permeable, open to environmental impingement and intrusion—there must be *filtration* mechanisms, accepting and rejecting possible environmental inputs, and *regulatory* mechanisms, minimizing environmental fluctuation either by direct action into the environment toward control of its relevant aspects or, at least, by neutralizing those effects of such fluctuation as cannot effectively be controlled.

Thus, at the start, by the implication of two of our primary abstractions—system and interpenetration—we are required to consider the "connectedness" of what we study. We are required to do so in a *generic* fashion: by the very nature of the case, our definitions of problems and identification of mechanisms cannot be specific to any given class of action system. We are, in other words, goaded toward general theory. Interpenetration and system are "sticks in the mouth of a croco-

Deductive approach

dile": they force consideration and analysis of connectedness.

Connectedness is not *fusion*, however. Consideration of connectedness does not in any way negate our necessary insistence upon the analytical distinction to be maintained between system and environment. To state, for example, that the two action systems, "personality" and "social system," constitute environments each for the other and that there is an energic input to the social system from the personality system, these systems interpenetrating each other, is not to deny the analytical integrity and "separateness" of the two systems. "Personality" and "social system" are not, from our point of view, fused into *a* system, nor is one epiphenomenal to the other; rather, they constitute two analytically independent *sub-systems of a system* (the general "action" system) in interaction and interpenetration. In the same sense we distinguish between the personality system and the behavioral organism: well and good that through the Id (the adaptive sub-system of the personality) "resources" enter the personality system from the behavioral organism, but the fact that these systems are connected does not mean that they are fused or that such resources "cause" personality.

An analogy may be helpful. (We use it with trepidation, since too often analogies are taken as definitive; we intend this one to *evoke*, not to define.) Imagine that we itemize a vast number of "behavioral" variables, not knowing their labels (such as "physiological," "psychological," and so on), and that we build with these variables an *n*-by-*n* correlation matrix. We submit the matrix for factor analysis. The areas of (relatively) dense intercorrelation suggest factors, and these factors in turn constitute systems. There are, we contend, four such analytically independent factors or systems in the "behavioral" area: those of the "behavioral organism," the "personality," the "social" system, and the "cultural" system. To fuse these would be to ignore the fact of the patterning of the intercorrelations within the matrix: the analytical integrity of a factor is not denied or threatened by the fact that many of its constitutive variables may be correlated with variables external to the factor. Of course, components within each system are intercorrelated with components of another system; this is evidence of connectedness, interpenetration, and function.

Interpenetration is only one of two aspects of the external connectedness of systems. We mentioned previously that there is an energic input to the social system from the personality system, and we mentioned also that resources from the behavioral organism enter the personality through what has been called the Id. In general terms, we are describing a set of "input-receptor" relationships; and consideration of such relationships will, we feel, clarify the second aspect of external systemic connectedness—*function*. Simultaneously, we hope, two further concepts of action theory will be made clear—the energic hierarchy of conditions and the informational hierarchy of controls.

It is convenient to begin with a definition, in summary form, of function. *A function is an energic output of an action system into another system, controlled informationally by the adaptive mechanisms of that receptor system.* As output, what is delivered flows "outward-bound" across the goal-attainment boundary of the delivering system; as input, what is received flows "inward-bound" across the adaptive boundary of the receiving system. *The locus of function is the goal-attainment sector of the relevant delivering system.* (Of course, the analyst may be interested in intrasystemic interchanges; in such case, the term "sub-system" is substituted for the term "system." The categories and dynamics are isomorphic.)

Since there are many ways of using any

term, it would be presumptuous of any analyst to insist that his usage be granted normative status; moreover, there seems to be little general agreement among sociologists about the meaning to be ascribed to the word "function." We can only state what *we* mean and hope that our intended meaning will be understood. From our point of view, function is a term most appropriately used in the context of "output" and "contribution." (Is it necessary to point out that this does not beg the questions of eufunction and dysfunction?) As one example of our usage, we would say: the primary function of the Ego as a sub-system of the personality is the articulation of the personality system with the social system, energizing the latter; this articulation and input of energy are accomplished at the adaptive boundary of the social system, that is, through the *role.* As a second example: the function of the economy is production, not profit-making, the latter being more properly considered analytically as an adaptive aspect of empirical organizations. And for a third example: the function of role is to deliver motivational energy toward, and in a form suitable for, collective action. (Here, of course, we are conceptualizing wholly at the sub-systemic level, that is, within the social system.)

In function there are always directionality and contribution: a function delivers up and contributes to. It is an output of a delivering system. As such, the concept is itself "functional" for theory-building. Along with the concept of interpenetration, function holds open our formulations, is a built-in correction mechanism allowing us—*requiring* us—to avoid the premature closure threatened by the establishment of analytical system boundaries. Function and interpenetration are two conceptual bridges between systems.

We have not yet discussed the two hierarchies mentioned, namely, the energic hierarchy of conditions and the informational hierarchy of controls. We have, however, implied them by pointing out that the concept "system" leads us to the further concept of control mechanisms existing at the adaptive boundary and adjusting possible environmental inputs. These control mechanisms are informational in the cybernetic sense, just as the inputs are energic in the cybernetic sense. It is information which guides, constrains, adjusts; it is energy which activates.

We conceptualize the energic factor as being a flow out of the delivering system into the receptor system. It flows across an output boundary of the delivering system and across an input boundary of the receptor system; these boundaries are connected and they are both external aspects of the two systems concerned. Although in minimal (that is, undifferentiated) systems these output-input boundaries may be empirically the same, they are not analytically the same; and in differentiated systems they are not empirically the same. (Analytical distinctions are not angels either in or on pinheads. Analytical distinctions become empirical ones eventually, as nature rewards us by its isomorphism to thought.) From our point of view these input-output boundaries are most conveniently conceptualized as "adaptation" (input boundary) and "goal-attainment" (output boundary). We say, therefore, that energic inputs flow into the system through the adaptive sector and flow out of the system through the goal-attainment sector, which is linked in turn to the adaptive sector of the next receptor system. Our use of the cybernetic concept "information" rounds out the analytical picture of these aspects of connectedness, as the energic flow into the system is controlled informationally by the adaptive mechanisms of that system and the energic flow out of the system is controlled informationally by the adaptive mechanisms of the next receptor system.

We should like at this point in our exposition to return momentarily to our earlier statement about the purpose of this paper. It is our intention, we said, to make as explicit as possible the grounding of our approach to analysis, our cognitive map. Our purpose, then, is not the technical exposition of general theory; rather, it is to describe most generally what we think we see from where we stand. Thus far *we have attempted, above all, to sketch a picture of vibrant systems in sensitive interpenetration of each other, stimulating and responding to each other, linked and made lively by the flow of energy, controlled and regulated by information.* This is, in barest silhouette, our vision and model; it orients us to the analytical situation. We cannot isolate *a* variable or *a* restricted set of variables, except for analytical emphasis. We can "bracket" (to use Husserl's term) what we do not choose to consider for short-run purposes; but ultimately we are forced to break our brackets. Although we, too, use what Whitehead called "the single fact in isolation," we know that its isolation is artificial, and our whole orientation leads us eventually to correct the artifice, or device, and to consider the connectedness of a network of looser and tighter areas of structure through which energy and messages flow.

In orienting us, our model guides our attention to specific and empirical issues. As we have mentioned, it causes us to search for the specific adaptive mechanisms controlling the energic inputs into the system in question. It also leads us to consider the degree to which they are efficient and the circumstances under which they might fail to control the energy, as well as to consider the circumstances under which the energic outputs of the delivering system might fail. Referring once again to the interpenetration of the personality and social systems, we are guided by our conceptual framework to ask: "Under what circumstances might the Ego withdraw from cathec-

tic commitment to role occupancy—might it, in a word, become *alienated?*" Role occupancy is only one aspect of role in which pathological situations might be found; another is role performance. "Under what circumstances," we ask, "might the informational controls internal to the system itself become inadequate? Under what circumstances, that is, might the Ego find itself in an *anomic* situation?"

On the one hand, the existence of the social system depends upon energic inputs from the personality, that is, cathectic commitment to role occupancy. On the other hand, the existence of the social system depends equally upon role performance; and for role performance, information is essential, information adequate to the specificity of the occasion—situational contingency, in other words. Thus, in a most general way, we would perceive in our conceptual framework the problems referred to by the terms "alienation" and "anomic," the first with a strong cathectic primacy with reference to role occupancy, the second with a strong cognitive primacy with reference to role performance.

Other important inferences can be drawn from our conceptual framework. Certainly it leads us to reject any reductionism whatsoever, while giving us a convenient device for categorizing reductionistic attempts.

Our conceptual framework also implies two hierarchies, already mentioned—one of energy and conditions, one of information and controls. We visualize these as interactive and of opposed directionality. Those aspects of a system that are high in information (tightly structured) exercise control over those that are lower in information but high in energy; reciprocally, those aspects of a system that are high in energy but lower in information constitute the conditions for the activation and realization of informational purpose and maintenance. To use Freud's famous analogy of the horse and the rider, in the interaction system composed of the horse and the rider, the rider—low in energy relative to the horse—controls and guides, by superior information, the path taken by the horse-rider system. He may do so by the merest and most delicate outputs of energy at strategic points. *Of course,* for the system to move at all, the energy of the horse must be utilized; and it constitutes a condition for system action. An analyst interested in explaining either "how" or "why" the system has moved from one village to the next must refer to both the energy and the information, since it is the interchange of energic and informational factors which determines—as, in a sense, a vectored resultant—the sequential path of the system.

THE WORLD SOCIETY
AS A SOCIAL SYSTEM*

NIKLAS LUHMANN

THE CONCEPT OF SOCIETY

Within the European tradition, a very general notion of society survived from the time of Aristotle until about 1800. The concept of society (*koinonoía, societas*) was almost identical with what we would call social system. The *encompassing* system was seen as a *special* case, namely as the political society (*koinonoía politiké, societas civilis*). This conceptualization lost its significance with the emerging development of the modern state and of an industrialized economy. The old tradition cannot be revived. It has, however, never been replaced with an adequate theoretical framework. There are attempts to change the dominant position of politics and to put economy or culture in its place. Such theories use a part of the reality of social life to represent the whole. Without giving sufficient reasons, economic or cultural or again political processes are postulated as the basic phenomenon. But the theory of these basic processes can claim only an historical and relative validity, since

*From Niklas Luhmann, "The World Society as a Social System," *International Journal of General Systems* 8:3 (July 1982), 131–35. Reprinted with permission of Gordon and Breach Science Publishers.

these processes are themselves part of sociocultural evolution.

General systems theory offers a new approach. At first sight, it looks like Aristotelian theory. A general notion of the social system is used to define the *encompassing* system as a *special* case of social systems. The content, however, has changed. Systems theory does not refer to the city or the state in order to characterize the special features of the encompassing system. Our society is too highly differentiated for this kind of design. Instead, systems theory uses systems analysis to disclose the structures and processes that characterize the societal system—"the most important of all social systems which includes all others."

Moreover, to conceive of societies as social systems excludes the traditional understanding that human beings, with body and soul, are "parts" of the society. Social systems are self-referential systems based on meaningful communication. They use communication to constitute and interconnect the events (actions) which build up the systems. In this sense, they are "autopoietic" systems. They exist only by reproducing the events that serve as components of the system. They consist therefore of events, i.e., actions, which they themselves reproduce, and they exist only as long as this is possible. This, of course, presupposes a highly complex environment. The environment of social systems includes other social systems (the environment of a family includes, for example, other families, the political system, the economic system, the medical system, and so on). Therefore, communication between social systems is possible; and this means that social systems have to be observing systems, being able to use, for internal and external communication, a distinction between themselves and their environment, perceiving other systems within their environment.

Society is an exceptional case. It is the encompassing social system that includes all communications, reproduces all communications, and constitutes meaningful horizons for further communications. Society makes communication between other social systems possible. Society itself, however, cannot communicate. Since it includes all communication, it excludes external communication. It has no external referent for communicative acts, and looking for partners would simply enlarge the societal system. This, of course, does not mean that society exists without relations to an environment, or without perceptions of environmental states or events; but input and output are not carried by communicative processes. The system is closed with respect to the meaningful content of communicative acts. This content can be actualized only by circulation within the system. At the same time, but at another level of reality, the system uses the bodies and minds of human beings for interaction with its environment.

The logic of a theory of self-referential communicative systems requires this notion of an encompassing system as a limiting case. The theory of social systems, by its own logic, leads to a theory of society. We do not need

political or economic, "civil" or "capitalistic" referents for a definition of the concept of society. This, of course, does not persuade us to neglect the importance of the modern nation-state or the capitalist economy. On the contrary, it provides us with an independent conceptual framework with which to evaluate these phenomena, their historical conditions, and their far-reaching consequences. In this way, we avoid prejudices toward particular facts; we avoid a *petitio principii.*

TYPES OF SOCIETAL SYSTEMS

One consequence of this general approach is the way in which different historical types of societies can be distinguished. A society cannot be characterized by its most important part, be it a religious commitment, the political state, or a certain mode of economic production. Replacing all this, we define a specific type of societal system by its primary mode of internal differentiation.

Internal differentiation denotes the way in which a system builds subsystems, i.e., repeats the difference between system and (internal) environments within itself. Forms of differentiation determine the degree of complexity a society can attain. Sociocultural evolution began with segmentary systems. Some of these societies developed a higher order of differentiation, above that of families or villages, namely stratification according to rank. All traditional societies that produced enough complexity to develop a high culture were stratified societies and, in this sense, hierarchical systems. Since these societies evolved from different regional sources, and since their aristocracies based themselves on land and/or cities, it was quite natural to conceive of different coexisting societies in spite of a certain degree of reciprocal awareness of each other's existence and of ensuing communication. The idea of society therefore assumed a territorial reference, however unclear its extension and frontiers.

Modern society has realized a quite different pattern of system differentiation, using specific *functions* as the focus for the differentiation of subsystems. Starting from special conditions in medieval Europe, where there existed a relatively high degree of differentiation of religion, politics, and economy, European society has evolved into a functionally differentiated system. This means that function, not rank, is the dominant principle of system building. Modern society is differentiated into the political subsystem and its environment, the economic subsystem and its environment, the scientific subsystem and its environment, the educational subsystem and its environment, and so on. Each of these subsystems accentuates, for its own communicative processes, the primacy of its own function. All of the other subsystems belong to its environment and vice versa.

Basing itself on this form of functional differentiation, modern society has become a completely new type of system, building up an unprecedented degree of complexity. The boundaries of its subsystems can no longer be integrated by common territorial frontiers. Only the political subsystem continues to use such frontiers, because segmentation into "states" appears to be the best way to optimize its own function. But other subsystems like science or economy spread over the globe. It therefore has become impossible to limit society as a whole by territorial boundaries, and consequently it is no longer sensible to speak of "modern societies" in the plural. The only meaningful boundary is the boundary of communicative behavior, i.e., the difference between meaningful communication and other processes. Neither the different ways of reproducing capital nor the degrees of development in different countries provide convincing grounds for distinguishing different societies.

The inclusion of all communicative behavior into one societal system is the unavoidable consequence of functional differentiation. Using this form of differentiation, society becomes a global system. For structural reasons there is no other choice. Taking the concept of the world in its phenomenological sense, all societies have been world societies. All societies necessarily communicate within the horizon of everything about which they can communicate. The total of all the implied meanings constitutes their world. Under modern conditions, however, and as a consequence of functional differentiation, only one societal system can exist. Its communicative network spreads over the globe. It includes all human (i.e., meaningful) communication. Modern society is, therefore, a world society in a double sense. It provides one world for one system; and it integrates all world horizons as horizons of one communicative system. The phenomenological and the structural meanings converge. A plurality of possible worlds has become inconceivable. The worldwide communicative system constitutes one world that includes all possibilities.

In defining my concept of society, I carefully avoided any reference to social integration. The concept does not presuppose any kind of pooled identity or pooled self-esteem (like the nation-state). Modern society in particular is compatible with any degree of inequality of living conditions, as long as this does not interrupt communication. A self-referential system defines itself by the way in which it constitutes its elements and thereby maintains its boundaries. In systems theory, the *distinction* between system and environment replaces the traditional emphasis on the *identity* of guiding principles or values. Differences, not identities, provide the possibility of perceiving and processing information. The sharpness of the difference between system and environment may be more important than the degree of system integration (whatever this means), because morphogenetic processes use differences, not goals, values, or identities, to build up emergent structures.

Given its clear-cut boundaries, differentiating communicative behavior from noncommunicative facts and events, modern society is a social system to a higher degree than any of the traditional societies. It depends more on self-regulative processes than any previous society. And this may be one of the reasons why it cannot afford too high a degree of social integration.

PLANNING AND EVOLUTION

No society so far has been able to organize itself, that is, to choose its own structures and to use them as rules for admitting and dismissing members. Therefore no society can be planned. This is not only to say that planning does not attain its goal, that it has unanticipated consequences, or that its costs will exceed its usefulness. A first obstacle to planning relates to problems of observation and description. The observation of differentiated systems presents serious difficulties. Systems theorists normally presuppose hierarchical structures as a condition of in-depth observation and description. Hierarchy, in this context, does not denote a chain of command, but the transitivity of subsystem building. Subsystems, according to this rule, are allowed to develop only within the boundaries of a subsystem. This expectation may, to some extent, be realistic at the level of organizations. It is highly unrealistic at the level of the whole society and its primary subsystems. No pattern of differentiation, be it according to rank or according to function, can channel all further subsystem building into the primary scheme

of differentiation. The society, therefore, lacks the inherent rationality required for its observation and, so much more, for planned change.

Planning society is also impossible because the elaboration and implementation of plans always have to operate as processes within the societal system. Trying to plan the society would create a state in which planning and other forms of behavior exist side by side and mutually influence each other. Planners have to use a description of the system, and will thus introduce a simplified version of the complexity of the system into the system. But this will only produce a hypercomplex system that contains within itself a description of its own complexity. The system then will stimulate reactions to the fact that it includes its own description and it will thereby falsify the description. Planners, then, will have to renew their plans, extending the description of the system to include hypercomplexity. They may try reflexive planning, taking into account reactions to their own activity. But, in fact, they can only write and rewrite the memories of the system, using simplistic devices which they necessarily invalidate by their own activity.

All of this, of course, does not prevent planners from being active and activities from being planned. By planning we are able to commit resources and activities in advance and to decide, more or less effectively, about the premises of further decisions. This may influence the state of the social system. We know how to handle production plans and electoral campaigns. We plan wars (defensive ones only, of course) and insurance schemes, school curricula, traffic flows, mass media programs, and many other things. Within small systems, and even within large organized social systems, chances are relatively high that activities are carried out as designed. This does not necessarily mean that effects turn out as intended. And it certainly does not mean that the society as a whole develops in a planned direction.

The societal system can change its own structures only by evolution. Evolution presupposes self-referential reproduction and changes the structural conditions of reproduction by differentiating mechanisms for variation, selection, and stabilization. It feeds upon deviations from normal reproduction. Such deviations are in general accidental but in the case of social systems may be *intentionally* produced. Evolution, however, operates without a goal and without foresight. It may bring about systems of higher complexity; it may in the long run transform improbable events into probable ones, and an observer may see this as "progress" (if his own self-referential procedures persuade him to do so). Only the theory of evolution can explain the structural transformations from segmentation to stratification, and from stratification to functional differentiation, which have led to present-day world society. And again: only observers may see this as progress.

Whereas the post-Darwinian decades were fascinated by the alternative of creation (with author) versus evolution (without author), the idea of planned human evolution, in distinction to organic evolution, later replaced the first wave of social Darwinism. Recent research, however, strongly suggests a third version of the relation between planning and evolution. Evolution itself can never be planned; this would be a *contradictio in adiecto*. But a self-referential system that tries to absorb planning may speed up its own evolution, because it becomes hypercomplex and will force itself to react to the ways in which it copes with its own complexity. If this is true, world society will have to face conditions in which more intentional planning will lead to more (and more rapid) unintentional evolution.

PARADOXES OF FUNCTIONAL DIFFERENTIATION

Problems are a consequence of the way in which a distinction between system and environment is made. Therefore, all of the most urgent problems of a societal system are the direct or indirect effects of its way of stimulating internal differentiation of systems and environments. In this sense they are, in our society, consequences of functional differentiation. They are the results of evolutionary developments, not the results of planning, and they are interconnected with all of the advantages of modern life. We cannot seriously want to change this condition of modern life; we cannot imagine an alternative to its mode of primary system differentiation; and in any case, we cannot plan to change the type of differentiation of our society.

We can, however, analyze the special risks we run with this type of society. Evolution is, as I have said, a transformation of improbable into probable states with increasing "costs." Without intending to "change the society," we can become aware of the relations between structures and their trains of consequential problems. Apparently, there are even self-defeating mechanisms at work. For example, functional differentiation both presupposes equality and creates inequality. It *presupposes equality* because it can discriminate only according to special functions (e.g., in schools according to school performance and prospects of further education) and because it operates best if everybody is included on the basis of equal opportunity in each functional subsystem (avoidance of exclusions, of *marginalidad,* and so on). But it *creates inequality,* because most functional subsystems (particularly the economic and the educational subsystem) tend to increase differences. Small differences in the beginning—be it in credit, in educational prospects, but also in scientific, artistic, and political "reputation"—become large differences in the end, because functional subsystems utilize differences and employ differences in pursuing their specific functions, and there no longer exists a superior mechanism such as stratification that controls and limits this process. The entire society, therefore, tends to proceed in the direction of increasing inequality; it accumulates differences between classes and between regions without being able to make use of these differences or provide functions for them, i.e., without being able to regress into the state of meaningful stratificatory differentiation.

Another example of this kind of built-in mechanism that may become self-defeating can be described as the relation between dissolution and recombination. Elements that formerly were regarded as natural units ("individual") have become decomposable, and their components have become available for recombination. We may think of the advances of physics, chemistry, and genetic biology, but also of the breaking up of persons ("individuals") into roles, actions, or motives as a consequence of advances in economic differentiation and organization. These advances, too, are consequences of functional differentiation. Dissolution or decomposition, however, not only provides *chances* for recombination, it also requires new forms of *control of interdependencies*. Singularized particles or motives (or even singularized persons) may associate in unpredictable ways. This problem has been underestimated; it was for a long time hidden behind distinctions of system and environment. To dissolve and to recombine were strategies of systems, and the changes of interdependencies came about in their environments. The famous problem of the "social cost" of economic production may illustrate this situation. Systems, generally, may control selected facts or events in their environment, related to their own inputs and outputs. They

cannot control interdependencies in their environment. The more we rely on systems for improbable performances, the more we shall produce new and surprising problems, which will stimulate the growth of new systems, which will again interrupt interdependencies, create new problems, and require new systems.

It is a comfortable self-deception to attribute all of this to "capitalism." Capitalism in itself is nothing other than the differentiation of the economic system out of societal bonds, and it is by no means the only instance of functional differentiation. The concept of "capitalist society" makes it easy to locate structures in the system whose change would lead us toward a noncapitalist society, presumably a better society. From a systems point of view, however, this is a highly questionable procedure, because it is not possible to define the *unity* of a system by pointing to *specific structures within the system* which can then be changed. The unity of the system is the self-reference of the system, and its change will always require operating within, not against, "the system."

EVOLUTION AT THE LEVEL OF FUNCTIONAL SUBSYSTEMS

My argument can be summarized by two statements: (1) a functionally differentiated world system seems to undermine its own prerequisites; and (2) planning cannot replace evolution—on the contrary, it will make us more dependent on unplanned evolutionary developments. If this is indeed the case, then the prospects of further evolution deserve a second look.

There may be a continuing process of biological evolution on the level of human organisms, given society and culture as their environment. This is not my topic. Social systems are not a *late branch*, they are a *different level* of the evolution of order in general. If all social systems today belong to one single world society, the theory of evolution faces a new kind of problem: the level of sociocultural evolution is represented by one system only. There are no longer many societies from which evolution can select successful ones. A one-system evolution: is this possible? And is this possible without the almost certain prospect of destruction? In this situation, one alternative needs further consideration. Functional differentiation constitutes a kind of self-referential autonomy at the level of functional subsystems. This type of order, once attained, may set off evolutionary processes at the level of these functional subsystems. Within the general framework of the societal system we may have a plurality of evolutionary developments. The economic subsystem will evolve, but also the scientific subsystem, and possibly others too—each taking the others as the environment for its own evolution. The system of world society provides a sufficiently domesticated "internal environment" for its internal evolutions, whereas its own evolution becomes more or less dependent on the outcome of evolutionary processes within this internal environment.

In fact, if we scan the relevant literature, we find several attempts to reconstruct the history and development of functional domains in terms of concepts that are derived from a Darwinian theory of evolution. Each subsystem may realize its own self-referential mode of reproduction—for example reproduction of a sufficient amount of liquid capital in the economy or reproduction of legal "cases" in the legal system—and may therefore find its own ways to deviate from its mode of reproduction, releasing processes of variation, selection, and restabilization. There may be different "accelerators" in different subsystems—for example, credit in the economic system, legislation in the legal system—increasing the chances for, and the speed of, structural transformations. This may "upgrade" the "adaptive capacity" of the whole system, but it by no means guarantees a viable relation between the system of society and its own natural and human environment. Evolution is unpredictable anyway. The separate but interrelated evolutions of the different functional domains within our differentiated society will reinforce this unpredictability. Their independence will bring about a higher degree of uncertainty with respect to the future.

RECENT DEVELOPMENTS IN THE FUNCTIONALIST APPROACH TO CHANGE*

PAUL B. COLOMY

THE FUNCTIONALIST REVIVAL

Functionalism is not dead. To the contrary, there are signs that the functionalist tradition is being revitalized, a development producing the predictable, contradictory reactions in the discipline. This revival is most clearly apparent in Germany where several outstanding theorists, including Niklas Luhmann (1979, 1982) and Richard Munch (1981, 1982, 1986), are re-casting the Parsonian legacy in various ways. (For preliminary reviews of this work see Alexander, 1984a, and Turner, 1986:102–25.) But this renewed interest is not restricted to Germany. Comprehensive and relatively sophisticated interpretations of Parsons' work have appeared throughout Europe and in Canada (Hamilton, 1983; Rocher, 1975; Adriaansens, 1980; Bourricaud, 1981). In the United States, the period of knee-jerk aversion to Parsons' work is apparently now being superseded by more objective scholarly evaluations, appreciative appraisals, and even festschrifts (Bershady, 1973; Savage, 1981; Mayhew, 1982:1–62; Alexander, 1983, 1984a; Loubser et al., 1976). The most recent issue of the *Annual Review of Sociology*, which has quickly become the discipline's measure of intellectual respectability, brazenly features a review article of contemporary theoretical developments and empirical research in action theory (Sciulli and Gerstein, 1985:369–87). Finally, a recently published collection of articles entitled *Neofunctionalism* (Alexander, 1985a), produced not only the expected critical response (Page, 1985) but also a spirited defense calling for a careful reconsideration of the merits of this approach (Alexander, 1986a; Sciulli, 1986).

This resurgence is manifest in a second and, in light of functionalism's recent status as the discipline's favorite straw man, remarkable intellectual development. Scholars identified with purportedly antagonistic intellectual traditions have begun to appropriate significant elements of Parsons' analytic framework. Proponents of critical theory, conflict theory, and various strands of Marxism and Weberian sociology have all employed action theoretic concepts and models in innovative and productive ways (Alexan-

*From Paul B. Colomy, "Recent Developments in the Functionalist Approach to Change," *Sociological Focus* 19:2 (April 1986), 139–45, 150–58. Reprinted with permission of *Sociological Focus*.

der, 1983:3–5, 312–6; 1984a; 1985b; Sciulli and Gerstein, 1985).

This revival, it should be clear, emanates from disparate sources. Even when characterizing the work of those whose contributions fall more or less squarely within the functionalist fold, it is more accurate to speak of an "intellectual tendency" rather than an integrated theory and research program. General adherence to a common core of tenets—e.g., treating society as an intelligible system consisting of relatively autonomous but interdependent parts, a focus on differentiation as a central feature of modernity, the recognition of the "independent" role of theorizing in science, and conceptualizing personality, society, and culture as analytically distinctive features of social structure—enables this intellectual tendency to cohere (Alexander, 1985a:7–18). Within this broad framework there is room for extraordinarily diverse work, ranging from highly sophisticated treatments of "technical" problems indigenous to the original paradigm (e.g., Baum's [1976a, 1976b] analysis of the media of interchange, Lidz and Lidz's [1976] investigation of the behavioral system, and Warner's [1978] discussion of cognitive processes in action theory), to excursions into ostensibly hostile intellectual camps with the aim of extending functionalist theorizing or research and/or remedying perceived weaknesses in its conventional approach to a given problem (e.g., Gould's [1985] attempt to wed elements of functionalist theorizing with the developmental approaches of Marx and Piaget and Sciulli's [1985] effort to bring together aspects of Parsons' and Habermas' work).

My primary concern, however, is not with this broadly-based functionalist revival. Rather, this paper is more narrowly focused on recent developments and revisions in that perspective's approach to social change. After describing the basic tenets of modern functionalism's initial, systematic conception of change, I will indicate how contemporary work is moving the theory in new directions.

THE EMERGENCE
OF DIFFERENTIATION THEORY

Specific sociological theories often grow and develop in response to criticisms formulated by those outside the particular theory group. Frequently, it is a school's competitors who are especially attuned to the theoretical and empirical weaknesses of a given approach. Critics often provide a school with a theoretical and research agenda, and a theory's progress can be measured by its ability to produce satisfactory revisions.

The initial formulation and subsequent revisions of modern differentiation theory can be partially understood as responses to criticisms directed at functional theory. With respect to functionalism's approach to social change, these "external" criticisms appeared in two overlapping waves. In response to each surge, action theory has initiated significant extensions or revisions of its model.

In the mid-1950s functionalism provoked several critical rejoinders, with Lockwood (1956), Mills (1959), Coser (1956), and Dahrendorf (1958, 1959) issuing the sharpest and most polemical rebukes. These critiques claimed that structural-functionalism, premised on value consensus and the internalization of norms, could not account for social change or conflict. They also asserted that action theory was excessively abstract and could not be applied empirically. Although those charges were not entirely correct when issued (Parsons, 1942, 1947, 1951:480–535; Baum and Lechner, 1981; Alexander, 1981a), they nevertheless quickly achieved a virtually unimpeachable status. Indeed, such claims have become cardinal tenets of the discipline's folklore and persist in the face of overwhelmingly contradictory evidence.

Partially in response to such criticisms, scholars aligned with the functionalist approach initiated systematic theorizing and empirical research on the issue of change. Differentiation theory was the product of this collective intellectual effort, and its early formulation rested on three fundamental tenets.

First, this approach identified a "master trend" of social change. The master trend of differentiation asserted that one of the most theoretically and empirically significant aspects of modern social change is the replacement of multi-functional institutions and roles by more specialized units. Parsons (1966, 1971) described the trend for "total societies," arguing that sociocultural evolution has traversed primitive, archaic, intermediate, and modern stages. Several other scholars documented the trend toward greater specialization in distinctive institutional spheres: Bellah (1964) for religious ideas, institutions and action; Smelser (1959) for familial and work roles: Parsons and Smelser (1956:246–94) for economic roles; Keller (1963) for leadership roles; Parsons and Platt (1973) for the modern university; Eisenstadt (1963) for the emergence of historic, bureaucratic empires; Fox (1976) for medical institutions; Mayhew (1984, 1990) for the public sphere; and Alexander (1980, 1981b) for both solidarity relations and the mass media.

Second, when modern differentiation theory was not used primarily as a classificatory device, it typically invoked a societal need explanatory framework to account for the transition from a multi-functional unit to a more specialized structure. Often, that model was tied to the idea of structural strain, the contention being that when functional prerequisites were not being effectively met, strain appeared which, in turn, prompted the creation of more efficient, differentiated arrangements.

Smelser (1959) presented the most sophisticated version of the strain-produces-differentiation argument. Adopting a problem-solving model of society, Smelser maintained that differentiation was precipitated by an inadequately functioning structure which generated widespread dissatisfaction. A given episode of change concluded with the institutionalization of a more differentiated and a more effective unit—indeed, the more effective performance of a given function was presumed to be a motive force behind the impulse to create more differentiated structures. In addition, the model presumed a single dominant value system which served to legitimate the initial dissatisfaction and, subsequently, to sanctify the more efficient innovation. The model also sharply distinguished between those elements of the population who expressed dissatisfaction and a "disinterested" authority structure which handled and channeled "disturbances." Finally, it was assumed that more effective, differentiated arrangements would produce widespread satisfaction.

The third tenet of differentiation theory asserted that the institutionalization of more specialized units increases the effectiveness and efficiency of a social system or sub-system. It was argued that high levels of differentiation throughout a given system were correlated with value generalization and greater inclusion. The latter processes ostensibly contributed to the "reintegration" of a system grown more complex through differentiation.

Formulated, in part, as a response to critics who charged that functionalism could not analyze change, this initial version of differentiation theory instigated, in turn, a second round of criticism that indicted the theory on the following grounds: a lack of historical and empirical specificity (Nisbet, 1969:268–70; 1972:40–5; Smith, 1973:115–24; Stinchcombe, 1978:77–104; Turner and Maryanski, 1979:109–13); a failure to examine the role of concrete groups and social processes involved in change and an undue neglect of power and conflict, both sets of omissions dramatically undermining functionalist explanation of differentiation (Rueschemeyer, 1977; Smith, 1973:42–50; Abrahamson, 1978:40–8); and, finally, an overemphasis on the integrative consequences of structural change (Granovetter, 1979; Rueschemeyer, 1977; Smith, 1973:70–6).

Acknowledging the partial legitimacy of these objections, recent work has pushed differentiation theory in three major directions. First, it has elaborated the empirical scope of the original model, supplementing the description of the master trend of change with the identification of patterned departures from that trend. Second, this revisionist impulse has opened up the explanatory framework of differentiation theory, giving greater attention both to how concrete groups affect the course of change and to the role of power, conflict, and contingency in structural differentiation. Finally, the original characterization of the effects of differentiation has been modified, with greater efficiency and reintegration treated as a subset of a much larger array of possible consequences.

SUPPLEMENTING THE MASTER TREND

The macro-sociological study of social change presupposes an analytic description of the pertinent phenomena. Accordingly, fertile theories of change invariably posit a conceptual master trend which serves as a guide to subsequent theorizing and research. For example, Marx's emphasis on class struggle and the movement toward a classless society, Weber's depiction of rationalization, Tocqueville's description of an irreversible trend toward equality, and Durkheim's discussion of organic solidarity and the "cult of the individual," though differing significantly in their level of generality, all represent ambitious efforts to divine a central direction of modern social change. Further, contemporary students of change share with their classic forebearers the same penchant for organizing their analyses around the description of a master trend—e.g., convergence theory's description of the increasing similarities across industrial societies (Moore, 1979), world systems theory's discussion of the growth of a capitalist world system and the accompanying tensions between core and periphery (Chirot and Hall, 1982), and conflict theory's depiction of a movement toward power as the primary distributive principle in modern societies (Lenski, 1984).

Like these other approaches to change, differentiation theory also postulates an analytic master trend. As noted earlier, differentiation theory's master trend presumes that a significant aspect of social change is the replacement of multi-functional institutions and roles by more specialized units. Nevertheless, despite the central analytic importance of a master trend, the identification of such a trend constitutes only the first step in a fully satisfactory theory of social change. The extension of any theory of change requires the description of departures from its postulated master trend.

Prompted, in part, by the criticism that differentiation theory's preoccupation with abstract depictions of societal and institutional master trends unduly sacrifices historical specificity, recent elaborations aspire to a more theoretically variegated and empirically fruitful conception of change. This revisionist current has begun to yield a more comprehensive description of structural change.

The concern for a more supple conceptualization of structural change is reflected first in work that extends Parsons' earlier analyses of dedifferentiation (Baum and Lechner, 1981; Lechner, 1984, 1985, 1990). Dedifferentiation designates a type of structural change that rejects societal complexity and moves toward less differentiated levels of social organization. It is argued that the emergence of "dedifferentiating" movements in modernizing societies is profitably understood as a response to analytically distinguishable "discontents" engendered by modernity. Several dedifferentiating "syndromes" are identified on the basis of the primary principle or criteria each "reductionist" movement invokes in its effort to restore "meaningful order." Specifically, the "fundamentalist syndrome" promotes dedifferentiation on the basis of an absolute, substantive value principle; "romantic syndromes" move toward dedifferentiation on the basis of integrative or solidary criteria; "expressive-therapeutic syndromes" utilize goal-attainment criteria as the basis for dedifferentiation; and, finally, the "Promethean syndrome" designates dedifferentiation on the basis of adaptive primacy. (For a more empirically oriented discussion of dedifferentiating or backlash movements see Lipset and Raab, [1970].)

In a more general way, Tiryakian (1985) has examined dedifferentiation through Durkeheimian eyes and emphasized what he regards as the heretofore neglected, "positive" features of dedifferentiation. He asserts that such retreats from complexity constitute means by which the societal community is renewed. Through such collective episodes as religious revivals, revolutions, and nationalist movements, the social differences separating individuals are leveled and participants re-establish their commonality through intense interaction. This periodic rejuvenation, Tiryakian hypothesizes, may provide large-scale social systems with renewed energy and commitment to common symbols and values. He also suggests that a general model of modernity may require the coupling of structural differentiation and dedifferentiation as alternating phases of social development.

The growing interest in "unequal develop-ment" represents another important step toward a more variegated conception of structural change. This notion maintains that the rate and degree of differentiation often vary across distinct social spheres and that such variation frequently produces systemic strain. Depending on the specific character of unequal development, the broader structural and cultural constraints of the environing system, and the actions of powerful groups, a variety of responses to that strain is possible, including: political corruption (Smelser, 1971); the breakdown of modernization (Eisenstadt, 1973); anomie (Rueschemeyer, 1976); or, cycles of inflation and deflation (Alexander, 1981b). The examination of unequal development is of great significance both because of its more accurate portrayal of the concrete contours of societal transformations and its sensitivity to the potential sources of conflict and contradiction attendant upon modernization.

Building upon these earlier elaborations, the concept of "uneven differentiation" has been introduced (Colomy, 1985). That idea refers to the varying rate and degree of differentiation of a single institutional sector or role structure within a given social system. Uneven differentiation extends the logic underlying unequal development and suggests that variation in the rate and degree of structural differentiation is evident both within a single institutional complex as well as across distinct social sectors. Thus, a detailed investigation of political party development in the antebellum United States found that differentiated, mass political parties appeared more rapidly and were more fully institutionalized in New York and Pennsylvania than in Massachusetts, South Carolina, and Virginia.

The notion of "incomplete differentiation" has been devised to refer to situations where the initial steps toward differentiation are not consummated and, consequently, two or more structures share or compete for the authority to carry out a given function (Surace, 1982). An examination of Italy's post-war politics indicates that both labor unions and political parties compete for the "function" of organizing and representing the interests of the working class.

Finally, Smelser's (1985b) discussion of English mass education in the first three-quarters of the nineteenth century provides a rich historical-sociological account of what can be called "blunted differentiation." His materials indicate that during this period, the establishment and institutionalization of primary education for working class children were impeded by a concatenation of social forces (particularly the demands of early British capitalism as mediated through the working class "family economy") that pulled mass education in opposing directions.

Each of the preceding patterns of change is oriented to long-run and large-scale transformations. Recently, however, more attention has been devoted to relatively short-term alterations. This research has produced a broader conception of structural change, and has re-cast differentiation, with its diverse modalities, as but a single, albeit very important, type of change among an array of other options.

For example, Smelser's (1974) examination of California public higher education indicates that in response to its increased growth during the 1950s and 1960s, that system could, in principle, have produced several distinct structural responses. In addition to differentiation, a system confronted with substantial growth can adopt any one or any combination of the following alternatives: increases in scale; the creation of similar segmented structures; shifting the relative emphasis of different functional activities (e.g., giving more attention to teaching graduate students); adding functions to existing structures; or adding new structures with different functions without substantially modifying existing arrangements. Smelser's analysis invites students of structural change to investigate the conditions under which differentiation, as opposed to other structural alterations, is adopted in response to the strains induced by rapid growth.

In an analogous way, several potential structural responses available to an institution confronted with declining resources have been identified (Colomy and Tausig, 1986). The possible options include: decreases in scale, winnowing (i.e., the elimination of some units similar in structure to others which persist), reallocation of available resources to specific functional activities, adding or discarding functions, adding new structures to or eliminating existing structural components from an on-going system, differentiation or dedifferentiation, and reconstitution (i.e., re-structuring the entire normative and organizational basis of a given institution). In addition to enumerating various reactions to resource reduction, it is also suggested that a given episode of differentiation may be preceded by a particular sequence of other modes of structural change. In the face of declining support, it is hypothesized, a system may initially opt for relatively less ramifying alterations (e.g., decreases in scale or winnowing). Differentiation or dedifferentiation, if they occur at all, might be usefully regarded as a response to the perceived failure of previous and more moderate structural "solutions."

In sum, recent work has begun to elaborate functionalism's conception of change, moving beyond a preoccupation with the postulated master trend and devising a more variegated approach. These revisions have modified the functionalist approach in two ways. First, several of the distinct types of differentiation—especially unequal, uneven, blunted, and dedifferentiation—suggest that the assumption of a "clean break" with the past implicit in differentiation theory's master trend must be modified (Bendix, 1967). Rather than presuming that there is a perfect inverse relation between advancing differentiation and eroding traditionalism, that more efficient specialized units completely supplant less effective, diffuse structures, these revisionist notions indicate that vestiges or enclaves of traditionalism persist in ostensibly modern systems. At the same time, this more inclusive conception of change also recognizes that those traditionalist patterns and practices, which manage to persist despite encroaching modernity are, nevertheless, likely to experience significant strains.

Secondly, these revisions impart a greater sense of empirical specificity to differentiation theory and provide an impetus to create more historically informed explanations of social transformations (Alexander, 1984c)....

THE CONSEQUENCES OF DIFFERENTIATION: BROADENING THE POSSIBILITIES

In earlier renditions, differentiation theory concentrated on two primary consequences of differentiation: increased efficiency and reintegration. Increased structural specialization, it was argued, fostered greater efficiency and augmented a system's capacity to adapt flexibly to its environment. Moreover, some formulations implied that a systemic imperative for greater efficiency was a primary impetus to structural differentiation. Those early discussions also acknowledged that the master trend toward differentiation made social integration more problematic. The appearance of more general cultural codes and specialized "integrative" institutions purportedly served to integrate relatively complex social orders.

Treating increased efficiency and integration as theoretically and empirically possible, but not invariable outcomes, subsequent analyses provide a broader conception of the consequences of differentiation. Accordingly, the contention that differentiation automatically increases systemic efficiency and effectiveness has been modified. More recent work argues that differentiated institutions establish new bases of interest around which constituencies rally when confronted with perceived threats (e.g., Smelser and Content, 1980; Smelser, 1985a). Structural innovations produce new roles, each of which constitutes the basis for the formation of collectivities that may become "political" constituencies concerned with maintaining or advancing their interests. A preoccupation with protecting vested interests introduces an element of rigidity and inflexibility into a system, and thereby reduces its capacity for efficient and effective adaptation to a changing environment.

In an analogous fashion, the notion of reintegration has also been refined. Recent analytic characterizations of modern social systems, for example, contend that differentiation produces both conflict and integration. Alexander (1983:142–50) maintains that the emergence of functionally differentiated and relatively autonomous subsystems and elites serve to increase the amount of conflict in modern societies. Discordant specifications of general cultural codes, strain inducing changes in a system's or subsystem's environments, advancement of "particularlistic" subsystem interests at the expense of others, and the unresolved tensions with each subsystem are likely to provoke conflict. At the same time, he argues that in a highly differentiated system such contention is more likely to be contained by other specialized subsystems and is less likely to be generalized to the entire system. Therefore, although the amount of conflict is expected to rise with modernity, it is predicted that the scope of that conflict will decline.

In a similar vein, Luhmann (1982) characterizes modern systems as "loosely joined" entities whose endemic "bottlenecks" and imperfect coordination invariably produce deviance and conflict. At the same time, modern society's highly differentiated nature ensures increased tolerance for those tensions.

Munch's (1981, 1982) discussion of the distinctive inter-relationships between relatively autonomous subsystems is assuredly one of the more impressive attempts to assess the consequences of differentiation. Distinguishing between regulative or controlling subsystems and dynamizing subsystems and asserting that there are fundamental tensions between distinct subsystems of action, Munch argues that there are several possible relations that may actually obtain between subsystems. "Interpenetration" denotes that "form of relation through which opposed spheres or subsystems can both expand without thereby creating mutual interference. Interpenetration is the mechanism by which the potential of every system is converted into actuality" (Munch, 1982:772–3). He rejects Parsons' assumption that interpenetration was the modal concrete relation between differentiated subsystems, and claims that many different types of relations may obtain empirically. Therefore, Munch treats interpenetration analytically, as one possible subsystem relation among an array of alternatives which include: the accommodation of the potentially controlling subsystem to the dynamizing subsystem; their mutual isolation; and the one-sided domination of the potentially dynamizing subsystem by the controlling one. Munch's revisions, then, transcend earlier discussions of conflict vs. integration, and provide a powerful analytic lens for examining empirical variation and tensions in the relations between differentiated subsystems.

Sciulli's (1985, 1990) notion of "societal constitutionalism" represents another intriguing reconceptualization of integrative processes in highly differentiated systems. He maintains that the entropic drift toward arbitrary power and bureaucratic authoritarianism, initiated by "purposive rationalization" in the political and socioeconomic orders, can be most effectively controlled by "collegial formations" premised on procedural norms. The standard of societal constitutionalism eschews exclusive reliance on internalized substantive beliefs as the sole basis for reintegration, and maintains that shared recognition of procedural restraints and the institutionalization of collegial formations across differentiated social functions establishes the possibility that actors can determine collectively when power is being exercised arbitrarily. (For a more empirical assessment of the tensions inherent in a setting where the collegial formation complex is highly developed, see Alexander 1986b).

Recent work has also begun to specify some of the particular ways in which differentiation contributes to conflict and integration. Some of the most interesting work in this area focuses on the relation between differentiated cultural and social systems. Eisenstadt (1971), for example, suggests that the charismatic and sacred elements of a given cultural system can serve as a critical standard against which prevailing social institutions and practices can be invidiously compared, and in terms of which reform of or revolt against those institutions and practices is legitimated. In Eisenstadt's view, the quest for direct, unmediated participation in the symbolic order, the desire to realize the sacred, can easily become a focus of dissension, conflict, and change.

In a more empirical fashion, Smelser (1974) demonstrated that when systems are oriented to potentially conflicting values, those inconsistent standards can serve to legitimate competing claims for resources, policies, and innovations. His study of California public higher education indicates how the institutionalization of conflicting value principles, viz., competitive and populist egalitarianism, contributed to the emergence of conflict between different academic estates.

Emphasizing the contingent character of integrative processes, Alexander (1984b, 1988) draws together several intellectual traditions to indicate how actors' "symbolic work" re-forms and revivifies elements of cultural systems during periods of crisis. His detailed analysis of the Senate Watergate hearings indicates how participants' conscious and unconscious employment of symbolic strategies—e.g., bracketing, ritualistic reaffirmation of societal myth, moral degradation ceremonies, and value generalization—simultaneously reaffirmed and altered the American civil religion, while generating the new, redolent symbol of "Watergate." Presuming that periods of rapid social differentiation often produce polarization and societal crisis, Alexander weds a contingent and strategic approach toward symbolization and civic ritual, to a muscular theory of social structure and process. If civic rituals are to resolve societal crises successfully, he asserts, five conditions must be present: (1) sufficient social consensus so that a norm-violating event can be considered deviant or polluting; (2) perception by significant social groups who share in this consensus that the event threatens the "center" of society; (3) the activation of institutional social controls; (4) mobilization and struggle by elites and publics that are differentiated from the structural center of society; (5) effective processes of symbolic interpretation.

Parenthetically, it should be noted that these recent attempts to analyze culture-society relations and, in particular, to identify the potentially tension producing "interchanges" between these systems belie the still widely accepted charge that functionalism invariably treats culture both in an overly determinist way and solely as a source of stability and consensus.

CONCLUSION

Arguing that differentiation theory has developed, in part, as a response to two waves of criticism, this paper has focused on some of the recent developments in the functionalist approach to structural change. In brief, these developments consist of a more variegated conception of change, a more elaborate and empirically grounded explanatory framework, and a more expansive treatment of the possible consequences of differentiation. Some have argued that the modifications reported here are so substantial that they warrant a new appellation, e.g., "neofunctionalism" (Alexander, 1985a), while others prefer that the phrase "action theory" be retained to describe current developments (Munch, 1985). Squabbles over terminology are of secondary interest, however. The more important issue is that a growing segment of the discipline finds considerable intellectual sustenance in a critically appreciative approach to Parsons' work and the tradition he established.

A general review of recent developments in the functionalist approach to change has been presented. These developments constitute a new beginning. It is reasonable, at this juncture, to speculate about the future of this scholarly tradition. In our view, it is likely that this approach will proceed along at least three distinct paths: an increasing emphasis on empirical research; the refinement and modification of the idea of social evolution, and a more critical assessment of its ostensible achievements; a more sympathetic stance toward purportedly antagonistic sociological approaches.

A sophisticated and comprehensive analytic framework for the study of change has always been functionalism's great strength. However, a truly successful theory requires substantial empirical specification of abstract models. In a more general context, Sciulli and Gerstein (1985:384) made the same point, proclaiming that the future acceptance of Parsonsian theorizing depends upon "the quality and quantity of empirical work inspired by it." That empirical work has already begun. Smelser's (1959) classic study of work and family roles and Eisenstadt's (1963) analysis of historic, bureaucratic empires established high standards for historical and comparative research in the functionalist tradition. More recently, Baum's (1981) examination of fascism, Gould's (1986) study of the English revolution, and Prager's (1986) investigation of democracy in Ireland combine far-reaching theoretical elaborations with systematic empirical research. In the immediate future, it is reasonable to expect that the functionalist tradition will produce a large number of similar studies, and by means of such empirical specification elaborate the general model of change.

Second, the existing evolutionary cast of functionalism may require partial modification. There are several elements in this evolutionary framework, and it is important to underscore some fundamental distinctions. First, a pro-Western and American bias permeates several earlier formulations of this approach. More recent work challenges that bias, and has been fairly successful in disengaging the theory's evolutionary elements from its parochial trappings. Second, more contemporary scholarship is critical of the determinist thrust of much evolutionary theory and has introduced an element of contingency into the study of structural change. Accordingly, it is emphasized that the transition from an existing level of differentiation to a more complex stage is not regarded as inevitable or irreversible. Moreover, transitions between stages are increasingly viewed as partially dependent on such contingent factors as group mobilization and leadership, and inter-group conflict. Attention to these contingent processes lends an element of flexibility to functionalism's evolutionary scheme, and renders it more sensitive to empirical variation. Finally, the simple equation of differentiation with progress is now being re-evaluated. In the past, progress denoted both moral and "adaptive" improvement. Today, the assumption that higher levels of differentiation invariably mean moral progress is no longer accepted. The apparent correlation between differentiation and greater adaptiveness, on the other hand, is a more complex issue. Despite the difficulty in operationalizing this concept and despite the realization that the vested interests associated with more differentiated structures can, in principle, reduce effective adaptation, several differentiation theorists argue that differentiation does represent a master trend which has been "hit upon" by many different societies and is increasingly hit upon by all societies. For example, it is maintained that bureaucratization, mass education, and cultural generalization are becoming more prevalent in many societies. Differentiation theory suggests as a working hypothesis that the emergence of a small number of such "evolutionary universals" may have something to do with the greater flexibility required by institutions and societies confronted with a more complex environment. However, it is important to note that a few contemporary renditions of this argument couple tentative statements about evolutionary universals with the acknowledgment that despite the appearance of a delimited number of universals, significant differences between societies still prevail.

Finally, it's likely that the functionalist approach to change will expand its conceptual richness and empirical specificity by borrowing from other intellectual traditions. Such borrowing has a long history in functionalism and contemporary students of change have readily adopted the practice of their predecessors. Accordingly, concepts and research associated with such purportedly hostile traditions as symbolic interaction, exchange theory, some versions of neo-Marxism, Weberian and Durkheimian sociology, symbolic anthropology, hermeunetic and cultural sociology, and world systems theory have been borrowed and adapted by differentiation theorists. This cross-fertilization reflects both a modest decline in the level of discord between sociological traditions and a broadly based effort on the part of some functionalists to revise their approach in a way that remedies perceived weaknesses and extends existing areas of strength.

At the beginning of this paper we asserted that functionalism is experiencing a revitalization. The success of this intellectual rebirth and even its direction cannot be determined exactly at present. However, we regard the increasing scholarly attention now being given to the Parsonsian tradition, this sifting of the intellectual chaff from the wheat, as a positive step toward the judicious appropriation of a powerful and often incisive sociological tradition.

REFERENCES

ABRAHAMSON, MARK. 1978. Functionalism. Englewood Cliffs: Prentice-Hall.

ADRIAANSENS, HANS P.M. 1980. Talcott Parsons and The Conceptual Dilemma. London: Routledge and Kegan Paul.

ALEXANDER, JEFFREY. 1980. "Core solidarity, ethnic outgroups, and social differentiation: A multidimensional model of inclusion modern societies." Pp. 5–28 in Jacques Dofny and Akinsola Akiwowo (eds.), National and Ethnic Movements. Beverly Hills: Sage.

_____. 1981a. "Revolution, reaction and reform: The change theory of Parsons' middle period." Sociological Inquiry 52:267–80.

_____. 1981b. "The mass media in systemic, historical and comparative perspective." Pp. 17–52 in Elihu Katz and Thomas Szeckso (eds.), Mass Media and Social Change. Beverly Hills: Sage.

_____. 1982. Positivism, Presuppositions, and Current Controversies. Berkeley: University of California Press.

_____. 1983. The Modern Reconstruction of Classical Thought: Talcott Parsons. Berkeley: University of California Press.

_____. 1984a. "Notes on the Parsonians revival in Germany." Sociological Theory 2:330–42.

_____. 1984b. "Three models of culture and society relations: Toward an analysis of Watergate." Sociological Theory 2:290–314.

_____. 1984c. "Social structural analysis: Some notes on its history and prospects." Sociological Quarterly 25:5–26.

_____. 1985a. "Introduction." Pp. 7–18 in J. Alexander (ed.), Neofunctionalism. Beverly Hills: Sage.

_____. 1985b. "Review essay: Habermas' new critical theory: Its promise problems." American Journal of Sociology 91:400–24.

_____. 1986a. "Why Neofunctionalism?" Footnotes 14 (1):5.

_____. 1986b. "The university and morality: A revised approach to autonomy and its limits." Journal of Higher Education 57:463–76.

_____. 1988. "Culture and political crisis: Watergate and Durkheimian sociology." In J. Alexander (ed.), Durkheimian Sociology. New York: Cambridge University Press.

BAUM, RAINER C. 1976a. "Communication and media." Pp. 553–56 in J.J. Loubser et al. (eds.), Explorations in General Theory in Social Science. New York: Free Press.

_____. 1976b. "On societal media dynamics." Pp. 579–608 in J.J. Loubset et al. (eds.), Explorations in General Theory in Social Science. New York: Free Press.

_____. 1981. The Holocaust and the German Elite: Genocide and National Suicide in Germany, 1871–1945. Totowa: Rowman and Littlefield.

BAUM, RAINER C., AND FRANK J. LECHNER. 1981. "National Socialism: Toward an actional-theoretical interpretation." Sociological Inquiry 51:281–308.

BELLAH, ROBERT. 1964. "Religious evolution." American Sociological Review 29:358–74.

BERSHADY, HAROLD J. 1973. Ideology and Social Knowledge. New York: John Wiley and Sons.

BOURRICAUD, FRANCOIS. 1981. The Sociology of Talcott Parsons. Chicago: University of Chicago Press. (Originally published in French in 1977.)

CHIROT, DANIEL, AND ROBERT HALL. 1982. "World system theory." Annual Review of Sociology 81:81–106.

COLOMY, PAUL. 1982. Stunted differentiation: A sociological examination of political elites in Virginia, 1720–1850. Unpublished Ph.D. dissertation. U.C.L.A.

_____. 1985. "Uneven structural differentiation: Toward a comparative approach." Pp. 131–56 in Jeffrey Alexander (ed.), Neofunctionalism. Beverly Hills: Sage.

COLOMY, PAUL, AND MARK TAUSIG. 1986. "The rise of applied sociology: A case study of institutional change dynamics." Paper accepted for Presentation at the Annual Meetings of the American Sociological Association, New York City.

COSER, LEWIS A. 1956. The Functions of Social Conflict. New York: Free Press.

DAHRENDORF, RALF. 1958. "Out of Utopia." American Journal of Sociology 64:115–27.

_____. 1959. Class and Class Conflict in Industrial Society. Stanford: Stanford University Press.

EISENSTADT, S.N. 1963. The Political Systems of Empires. New York: Free Press.

_____. 1971. "Introduction." In S.N. Eisenstadt (ed.), Weber on Charisma and Institution Building. Chicago: University of Chicago Press.

_____. 1973. Tradition, Change and Modernity. New York: John Wiley & Sons.

FOX, RENEE. 1976. "Medical evolution." Pp. 773–87 in J.J. Loubser et al., (eds.), Explorations in General Theory in Social Science. New York: Free Press.

GOULD, MARK. 1985. "Prolegomena to any future theory of societal crisis." Pp. 50–73 in J. Alexander (ed.), Neofunctionalism. Beverly Hills: Sage.

_____. 1986. Revolution in the Development of Capitalism. Berkeley: University of California Press.

GRANOVETTER, MARK. 1979. "Notes on evolutionary theory." American Journal of Sociology 85:489–515.

HAMILTON, PETER. 1983. Talcott Parsons. London: Tavistock.

KELLER, SUZANNE. 1963. Beyond the Ruling Class. New York: Random House.

LECHNER, FRANK. 1984. "Ethnicity and revitalization in the modern world system." Sociological Focus 17:243–56.

_____. 1985. "Modernity and its discontents." Pp. 157–76 in J. Alexander (ed.), Neofunctionalism. Beverly Hills: Sage.

_____. 1990. "Fundamentalism and sociocultural revitalization: on the logic of dedifferentiation." Pp. 88–118 in J. Alexander and P. Colomy (eds.), Differentiation Theory and Social Change. New York: Columbia University Press.

LENSKI, GERHARD E. 1984. Power and Privilege. New York: McGraw-Hill.

LIDZ, CHARLES W., AND VICTOR M. LIDZ. 1976. "Piaget's psychology of intelligence and the theory of action." Pp. 195–239 in J. Loubser et al. (eds.), Explorations in General Theory in Social Science. New York: Free Press.

LIPSET, S., AND E. RAAB. 1970. The Politics of Unreason. New York: Harper and Row.

LOCKWOOD, DAVID. 1956. "Some remarks on the social system." British Journal of Sociology 7:134–45.

LOUBSER, J.J., R.C. BAUM, A. EFFRAT, AND V.M. LIDZ (eds.). 1976. Explorations in General Theory in Social Science: Vols. 1 and 2. New York: Free Press.

LUHMANN, NIKLAS. 1979. Trust and Power. New York: John Wiley and Sons.

_____. 1982. The Differentiation of Society. New York: Columbia University Press.

MAYHEW, LEON (ed.). 1982. Talcott Parsons: On Institutions and Social Evolution. Chicago: University of Chicago Press.

_____. 1984. "In defense of modernity: Talcott Parsons and the utilitarian tradition." American Journal of Sociology 89:1273–1305.

_____. 1990. "The differentiation of the solidarity public." Pp. 294–322 in J. Alexander and P. Colomy (eds.), Differentiation Theory and Social Change. New York: Columbia University Press.

MILLS, C. WRIGHT. 1959. The Sociological Imagination. London: Oxford University Press.

MOORE, W. 1979. World Modernization: The Limits of Convergence. New York: Elsevier-North Holland.

MUNCH, RICHARD. 1981. "Talcott Parsons and the theory of action I: The structure of Kantian lore." American Journal of Sociology 86:709–39.

_____. 1982. "Talcott Parsons and the theory of

action II: The continuity of development."
American Journal of Sociology 87:771–826.

_____. 1985. "Commentary: Differentiation, consensus and conflict." Pp. 225–37 in J. Alexander (ed.), Neofunctionalism. Beverly Hills: Sage.

_____. 1986. Theory of Action: Reconstructing the Contributions of Talcott Parsons, Emile Durkheim, and Max Weber. Frankfurt: Suhrkamp.

NISBET, ROBERT A. 1969. Social Change and History. London: Oxford University Press.

_____. 1972. Social Change. New York: Harper and Row.

PAGE, CHARLES H. 1985. "On Neofunctionalism." Footnotes 13(7):10.

PARSONS, TALCOTT. 1942. "Some sociological aspects of the Fascist movements." Social Forces 21:138–47.

_____. 1947. "Certain primary sources and patterns of aggression in the social structure of the western world." Psychiatry 10:167–81.

_____. 1951. The Social System. New York: Free Press.

_____. 1966. Societies: Evolutionary and Comparative Perspectives. New York: Free Press.

_____. 1971. The System of Modern Societies. Englewood Cliffs: Prentice Hall.

PARSONS, TALCOTT, AND GERALD PLATT. 1973. The American University. Cambridge: Harvard University Press.

PARSONS, TALCOTT, AND NEIL SMELSER. 1956. Economy and Society. New York: Free Press.

PRAGER, JEFFREY. 1986. Building Democracy in Ireland. Cambridge: Cambridge University Press.

ROCHER, GUY. 1975. Talcott Parsons and American Sociology. New York: Barnes and Noble.

RUESCHEMEYER, DIETRICH. 1976. "Partial modernization." Pp. 756–72 in J.J. Loubser et al. (eds.), Explorations in General Theory in Social Sciences. New York: Free Press.

_____. 1977. "Structural differentiation, efficiency and power." American Journal of Sociology 83:1–25.

SAVAGE, STEPHEN. 1981. The Theories of Talcott Parsons: The Social Relations of Action. New York: St. Martin's Press.

SCIULLI, DAVID. 1985. "The practical groundwork of critical theory: Bringing Parsons to Habermas (and vice versa)." Pp. 21–50 in J. Alexander (ed.), Neofunctionalism. Beverly Hills: Sage.

_____. 1986. "Why neofunctionalism." Footnotes 14(1):5.

_____. 1990. "Differentiation and collegial formations: Implications of societal constitutionalism." Pp. 367–405 in J. Alexander and P. Colomy (eds.), Differentiation Theory and Social Change. New York: Columbia University Press.

SCIULLI, DAVID, AND DEAN GERSTEIN. 1985. "Sociological theory and Talcott Parsons in the 1980s." Annual Review of Sociology 11:369–87.

SMELSER, NEIL. 1959. Social Change in the Industrial Revolution. Chicago: University of Chicago Press.

_____. 1971. "Stability, instability and the analysis of political corruption." Pp. 7–29 in B. Barber and A. Inkeles (eds.), Stability and Change. Boston: Little, Brown.

_____. 1974. "Growth, structural change and conflict in California higher education, 1950–1970." Pp. 9–141 in N. Smelser and G. Almond (eds.), Public Higher Education in California. Berkeley: University of California Press.

_____. 1985a. "Evaluating the model of structural differentiation in relation to educational change in the nineteenth century." Pp. 113–29 in J. Alexander (ed.), Neofunctionalism. Beverly Hills: Sage.

_____. 1985b. "The contest between family and schooling in nineteenth-century Britain." Paper presented at the Annual Meeting of the American Sociological Association. Washington, D.C.

SMELSER, NEIL, AND ROBIN CONTENT. 1980. The Changing Academic Market. Berkeley: University of California Press.

SMITH, ANTHONY D. 1973. The Concept of Social Change: A Critique of the Functionalist Theory of Social Change. London: Routledge and Kegan Paul.

STINCHCOMBE, ARTHUR L. 1978. Theoretical Methods in Social History. New York: Academic Press.

SURACE, SAMUEL. 1982. "Incomplete Differentiation." Unpublished manuscript. U.C.L.A.

TIRYAKIAN, EDWARD A. 1985. "On the significance of dedifferentiation." Pp. 118–34 in S.N. Eisenstadt and H.J. Helle (eds.), Macro-Sociological Theory: Perspectives on Sociological Theory, Vol. 1. Beverly Hills: Sage.

TURNER, JONATHAN. 1986. The Structure of Sociological Theory. Chicago: Dorsey Press. Fourth Edition.

TURNER, JONATHAN, AND ALEXANDRA MARYANSKI. 1979. Functionalism. Menlo Park: Benjamin/Cummings.

WARNER, R. STEPHEN. 1978. "Toward a redefinition of action theory: Paying the cognitive element its due." American Journal of Sociology 83:1317–49.

Is "Neofunctionalism" Really Functional?*

Jonathan H. Turner and Alexandra R. Maryanski

In his presidential address to the American Sociological Association, Kingsley Davis (1959) proclaimed that there is little which can be considered distinctive about functional analysis. After all, he emphasized, each sociologist is concerned with the "interpretation of phenomena in terms of their interconnections with societies as going concerns" (Davis, 1959:760). Davis' view was in response to the early and mounting criticisms being leveled at functionalism, in general, and its Parsonian variant, in particular. More recently, Jeffrey Alexander (1985:7–8) has made an argument similar to Davis', although the old structural functionalism has been resurrected as "neofunctionalism." For Alexander as for Davis before him, functionalism studies the interrelationships of social phenomena within their systemic and environmental context. Moreover, Alexander echoes Davis in his assertion that the term functionalism "indicates nothing so precise as a set of concepts, a method, a model, or an ideology" (Alexander, 1985:9).

We argue that both Davis and Alexander are incorrect in their respective assertions. While we share both Alexander's and Davis' beliefs that functional analysis and its greatest exponent, Talcott Parsons, have been subject to unfair criticism, there is nonetheless something very distinctive about functional sociology. It *does* dictate a logic, a method, model, and perhaps even an ideology, although this last point has been overemphasized by unreflective and unfair critics. And contrary to Davis' contention, there is nothing "mythical" about functional analysis.

One way to appreciate the distinctiveness of functionalism is to review its emergence, ascendance, decline, and apparent resurrection as neofunctionalism. In this way, we can see what became distinctive about functionalism, what alarmed its critiques, and what its current apologists—from Davis to Alexander—wish to sweep under the rug. Functionalism may indeed have a future in sociological theory, but we had best look into the past to see if this is a good thing.

*From Jonathan H. Turner and Alexandra R. Maryanski, "Is Neofunctionalism Really Functional?" *Sociological Theory* 6:1 (Spring 1988), 110–21. Reprinted with permission of the American Sociological Association and the authors.

THE EMERGENCE
OF FUNCTIONALISM

As with his predecessors, Auguste Comte was a conservative, seeking to restore order in the chaotic aftermath of the French Revolution. In light of this concern, it is little wonder that the emergence of sociology as a self-conscious discipline would ask the question: what can social structures "do for" and "contribute to" the construction and maintenance of social order? This tendency to analyze and assess parts in terms of their consequences for the social whole was furthered by Comte's efforts to legitimize the new science of society. He went to great lengths to separate sociology from the speculative moral philosophy that dominated the social thought of his time. And, as he sought to emancipate sociology from moral philosophy, he began to link the new science to biology. Thus, the science of society was inexorably linked to biology, allowing Comte (1875:234) to invoke the "organismic analogy" in which "a true correspondence between Statical Analysis of the Social Organism in Sociology, and that of the Individual Organism in Biology . . ." could be confidently proclaimed. This form of analogizing marks a critical moment in sociological theorizing. It communicated a vision of the social world as a complex whole with each part contributing to its maintenance and survival. When society is seen as an organism, it is a short analytical step to asking: What does a structure "do for" society? Comte was disposed to ask such questions because of his desire to use sociology as a way of restoring social equilibrium.

It is of enormous significance, we think, that sociology was born as a discipline with this kind of intellectual orientation. For such questions are at the heart of functionalism, and they are what make functionalism distinctive. While Comte never employed the word "function" nor carried his argument very far,

subsequent scholars were to transform his ideas into an explicit form of functionalism—sociology's first theoretical perspective.

Herbert Spencer was the next key figure in the emergence of functionalism. Spencer wore two intellectual hats: (1) As a philosopher, he was a staunch utilitarian who will forever be remembered for the phrase, "survival of the fittest," which was later the rallying cry for Social Darwinists. (2) But Spencer was also an organicist who begrudgingly was to give Comte credit for teaching him that "the principles of organization are common to societies and animals . . . and . . . that the evolution of structures advance from the general to the special." Many contemporaries were to chide Spencer for the inconsistencies in his philosophical and sociological views—that is, society, on the one hand, consists of competitive struggles while, on the other hand, it involves functional integration and cooperation. But the critical point is that Spencer continued Comte's tendency to analogize to organicisms, making both general comparisons between social and animal organisms as well as highly detailed analogies. Spencer thus codified organismic analogizing in the social sciences, making it a highly respectable form of analysis. But his most important contribution resides in the distinction between structure and function (Spencer, 1876:1–2):

There can be no true conception of a structure without a true conception of its function. To understand how an organization originated and developed, it is requisite to understand the *need* subserved at the outset and afterwards.

This quote marks the first time in sociological thought that the concept of "functional needs" is used as an explanatory device for understanding why a structure emerges and why it persists within a systemic whole. Such an emphasis is unique to functionalism, and consequently, Spencer is the explicit founder of functionalism in the social sciences.

Spencer's star was to fade by the latter part

of the 19th century, at just the time when another key figure, Émile Durkheim, was gaining prominence in France. Durkheim was one of Spencer's harshest critics, since the libertarian thrust of Spencer's philosophy conflicted with the long tradition of French collectivism. But Durkheim borrowed extensively from Spencer's sociology and organicism, often without proper citation. In so doing, he was to couple Spencer's insights with Comte's advocacy for a "science of society" and extend the functional approach into the 20th century.

Much like Comte before him, Durkheim viewed the science of society as providing insights into how social integration and order could be created. Yet, Durkheim recognized that functional analysis must be separated from causal analysis, since the reasons for a structure's existence are not typically the social needs that it functions to meet (Durkheim, 1895:90). For Durkheim, therefore, sociological analysis must ask two questions: What are the antecedent causes of a structure? And, what need of the larger social system does it meet? To Durkheim, an answer to *both* questions was essential to scientific *explanation* (Durkheim, 1895:96):

When, then, the explanation of a social phenomenon is undertaken, we must seek separately the efficient cause which produces it and the function it fulfills. We use the word "function" in preference to "end" or "purpose," precisely because social phenomena do not generally exist for the useful results they produce.

Durkheim had difficulty maintaining this distinction, for he often hinted that needs for integration cause such structures as the division of labor and religious ritual to emerge and meet these needs. But far more important than Durkheim's unintended lapses is the fact that those who were to carry the banner of functionalism to the mid-point of this century deliberately obliterated his carefully drawn distinction between cause and func-

tion. The result, as we will examine shortly, was for functional analysis to fall prey to a host of logical problems which even neofunctionalism cannot obviate.

THE PRESERVATION OF FUNCTIONALISM

If we examine the intellectual climate of the early 20th century in America, there was little reason for functionalism to prosper in sociology, especially in America. The first generation of American theorists—Ward, Sumner, and Keller, for example—were heavily influenced by Spencer's evolutionary theory, but remained unresponsive to either Spencer's or Durkheim's functionalism. Indeed, they knew very little about Durkheimian sociology. And, as this early generation of theorists was replaced by the Chicago School and its attendant concern for first-hand research, Spencer was forgotten and Durkheim had still not burst on the theoretical scene in America. Even Talcott Parsons' *The Structure of Social Action* (1937), which finally brought Durkheim to the forefront of the sociological imagination, does not deal with Durkheim's functionalism and, of course, the founder of functionalism is dismissed with the book's opening query: "Who now reads Spencer?"

Thus, in light of the ignorance of Durkheim and the rejection of Spencer, how was functionalism preserved? Here, we believe, is yet another critical moment in the history of functionalism, but a moment that belongs to anthropology and the efforts of two scholars, A.R. Radcliffe-Brown and Bronislaw Malinowski. For these two thinkers, Durkheim's functionalism represented a solution to certain intellectual problems in anthropology and it is their solution to these problems that spawned modern sociological functionalism.

We can best recognize these problems by

visualizing the intellectual milieu of early 20th century anthropology. Travelers, missionaries, explorers, and amateur anthropologists had been accumulating data on traditional peoples, with three competing orientations seeking to order and interpret these accumulating data: (1) diffusionism in which cultural traits are seen as moving out from certain "cultural centers"; (2) evolutionism in which humankind is viewed as progressing on one evolutionary path culminating, coincidently, in Western European civilization and in which "primitive" cultures are conceptualized as existing at different states of evolutionary development; and (3) historical reconstruction in which traits are not viewed as the result of diffusion or evolutionary development, but rather, as the result of unique historical events operating to produce a given culture.

As Malinowski, Radcliffe-Brown, and their students began to grapple with the problems of conducting ethnographies and of interpreting data on traditional peoples, the inadequacies of these dominant approaches became all too clear. Traditional societies do not keep written historical records and their verbal accounts are idealized and sketchy. Traditional peoples, as soon became evident to serious ethnographers, are not at a lower stage on an evolutionary line culminating in Western civilization; and traditional populations are often isolated from hypothesized "cultural centers," a fact which became all too obvious to ethnographers in the far reaches of the globe.

How, then, were ethnographers like Radcliffe-Brown and Malinowski to interpret their data? A critical period appears to have been between 1912 and 1913, when Durkheim (1912), Malinowski (1913), Radcliffe-Brown (1913), and Freud (1913) all published analyses of the Arunta aborigines as described in Spencer and Gillian's (1899) well-known travel log. Indeed, Malinowski (1913) was so impressed with Durkheim's (1912) *Elementary Forms of the Religious Life* that, at the last moment before publication, he incorporated some of its ideas in his *The Family among the Australian Aborigines.* While both Malinowski and Radcliffe-Brown had read Durkheim's (1895) methodological statements on functional explanation, it was only when functional analysis was actually applied by Durkheim to "ethnographic data" of interest to anthropologists that the seeds of their subsequent conversion to functionalism were planted. Curiously, Spencer, who reported and catalogued literally volumes of far superior ethnographic data within a functional framework, was forgotten or ignored by the anthropologists of this era; and thus, as functionalism entered the 20th century, it was Malinowski and Radcliffe-Brown who were to carry it forward, reformulating Durkheim's ideas to their specific projects.

Radcliffe-Brown's conception of function is virtually the same as Durkheim's: a structure is to be assessed in terms of its consequences for meeting the "necessary conditions of existence" in a system, of which there are two (Radcliffe-Brown, 1952): (1) The need for social systems to evidence "consistency" of structure whereby rights and duties over persons and possessions are specified; and (2) the need for social systems to reveal "continuity" in which rights and duties between persons are specified. In a vein similar to Durkheim, Radcliffe-Brown visualized these two conditions as the minimal necessary to avoid conflict and to assure system integration.

Radcliffe-Brown and his followers believed that by understanding how a structure functioned to meet these two "necessary conditions," it would be possible to discover explanatory "laws" about human social systems. In this effort to generate explanatory laws, however, Radcliffe-Brown made an important departure from Durkheim: He abandoned the search for historical causes—thereby disregarding Durkheim's insistence on separate causal and functional analysis. Instead, he suggested that historians are to seek antecedent causes, while sociologists must attempt to find the "sociological origins" of social structures. Through some rather fancy conceptual footwork, the "sociological origins" turn out to be the discovery of the function of a structure (Radcliffe-Brown, 1952:43):

Any social system, to survive, must conform to certain conditions. If we can define adequately one of these universal conditions, i.e., one to which all human societies must conform, we have a sociological law. Thereupon if it can be shown that a particular institution in a particular society conforms to the law, i.e., to the necessary condition, we may speak of this as the "sociological" origin of the institution. Thus an institution may be said to have its general ... sociological origin and its particular ... historical origin. The first is for the sociologist or social anthropologist to discover. ... The second is for the historian ...

For Radcliffe-Brown, then, notions of "needs" or "necessary conditions of existence" now constitute concepts that will be incorporated into theoretical *explanations* of why structures emerge and persist. Twentieth century functionalism was increasingly to view system "needs" as somehow critical for *explanatory* purposes, but without the benefit of Durkheim's carefully drawn (but rarely practiced) distinction between cause and function.

Malinowski was to depart significantly from Radcliffe-Brown's emphasis on the concept of "function" as an explanatory tool and to advocate a functional *method* for collecting and arranging data (Malinowski, 1944). Malinowski began to view the social world as comprised of system levels—the biological, psychological, social, and symbolic—and to advocate inquiry into the properties of each level as they affect the social and symbolic activities of humans. In this emphasis, he was to anticipate by

twenty years Parsons' parallel emphasis on system levels and integration among them. Malinowski was also to advocate the assessment of the functional needs of each system level, arguing that each system level has needs which must be met if it is to remain viable.

Malinowski's scheme has been subject to some misinterpretation, primarily because he was a figure of great controversy. Yet, misinterpretations aside, his orientation can be viewed as stressing several points. First, humans must first satisfy their biological or "basic needs," but to satisfy these they must organize collectively. Secondly, as they organize, new "derived needs" are created and must be met if patterns of collective organization are to remain viable. Malinowski (1944) then provided a list of "basic needs," but his conceptualization of the two types of "derived needs" is far more crucial to subsequent functional analysis. One type of derived need he termed "instrumental," or those conditions necessary for (1) education and socialization, (2) social control, (3) economic adaptation, and (4) political authority. (We should note how this catalogue anticipates Parsons' later conceptualization of his famous four functional requisites.) The other type of "derived need" is what Malinowski termed "integrative," or those conditions necessary for (1) the transmission of knowledge (technology), (2) the creation of a sense of control over destiny (magic and religion), and (3) the maintenance of a sense of communal rhythm (art, rules of games, ceremonial rules).

Malinowski's scheme was designed to facilitate the comparative analysis of ethnographic data. His cataloguing of functional needs at different system levels was only a part of a much more comprehensive methodological strategy. Because social institutions operate to meet basic and derived needs, Malinowski felt that by specifying the common elements of all institutions, the comparisons of diverse cultures in terms of a common analytical yardstick would be possible. By displaying data in comparable categories which are connected to fundamental survival requisites, sociological laws about human organization could be induced (Malinowski, 1941:198). Thus, for Malinowski functional needs were only one element of social institutions, as can be seen by his listing of elements common to all institutions: (a) personnel, (b) charter, (c) norms, (d) material apparatus, (e) division of activities, and (f) function. Thus, by comparing social patterns of different cultures with respect to elements (a) through (f), Malinowski felt that data could be arrayed in ways that would facilitate generalization.

Because Malinowski's scheme is often misrepresented, he has been used as a "straw man" by subsequent sociological functionalists, such as Robert Merton (1949:25–37) who should know better. Yet, Malinowski extended Durkheim's and Radcliffe-Brown's limited functional orientation into directions that were to be adopted by the first sociological functionalists of the 1940s and early 1950s. This fact is rarely acknowledged, but there can be little doubt that Malinowski's work shaped the course of sociological functionalism. Malinowski's ideas thus represent, we feel, the critical link between earlier functionalisms and its more modern variants. His legacy can best be summarized as follows (Turner and Maryanski, 1978): (1) Social reality exists at different levels, minimally at the biological, psychological, social, and cultural (symbolic). (2) The properties of these levels must be analyzed by separate sciences, but the interconnectedness of levels forces sociologists to examine how biological, psychological, and cultural needs impinge upon social structural arrangements. (3) Systems can be analyzed in terms of needs and it is appropriate to investigate the relation of system parts to different needs or requisites. (4) At the social system level, the needs for economic adaptation, political control, legal and moral integration, and socialization are important in understanding the place and operation of institutions in social systems.

THE ASCENDANCE OF FUNCTIONALISM IN SOCIOLOGY

In the late 1930s, Robert K. Merton's arrival at Harvard as a graduate student and part time instructor marks the beginning of modern sociological functionalism. While Talcott Parsons, then a young instructor, had studied briefly for one year with Malinowski in the early 1920s, it was Merton who began to introduce Radcliffe-Brown and Malinowski to a sociological audience. Much of this introduction was critical, as was to become evident with Merton's (1949) classic article, "Manifest and Latent Functions." Yet, the influence was decisive, for it was during the late 1940s and 1950s that functionalism became the dominant theoretical perspective in American sociology.

Functionalism took hold in sociology not only because of the strategic location of Merton and Parsons in the academic world, but also because American sociology lacked the conceptual capacity to examine total social systems. The perspectives of the Chicago School were clearly inadequate for explaining total societies, or even large social systems. And, the evolutionary analysis of Spencer and his early American followers, such as Ward, Sumner, and Keller, had been discredited at the same time that anthropological evolutionary theory was also being discarded. Thus, functionalism held the promise of filling a theoretical vacuum and providing sociology with a way to "explain" both macrostructural and microstructural processes. In a very real sense, this adoption in the 1940s of a perspective that asks what system parts "do for" social wholes is not dissimilar to Comte's use of the organismic analogy a hundred years earlier as a means for legitimatizing the new "science of society."

The emphasis in these early sociological functionalisms was on "functional requisites" as a way to explain social processes. For example, the first clearly functional explanation of the modern era, the famous "Davis-Moore hypothesis" (1945), relied heavily on the concept of "functional importance" as an explanation of stratification processes. Merton's more tempered statement (except for his criticism of Malinowski) in "Manifest and Latent Functions" (1949) also stressed functional requisites, although the emphasis was on empirically established requisites for each particular system. But, a more analytical thrust soon came to dominate. In this analytical approach, universal system requisites were postulated, as is clearly evident in David Aberle's et al. (1950), effort to specify the functional requisites of society, in Kingsley Davis' *Human Society* (1948), and in Marion J. Levy's *The Structure of Society* (1952).

In these works, Malinowski's use of the concept of function as a heuristic device or methodological tool for the comparison of cross-cultural data is replaced by Radcliffe-Brown's emphasis on function as an *explanatory principle*. This shift from descriptive to explanatory logic was, in turn, to encourage the development of abstract theory of social system *in general*. Indeed, except for Merton's (1949) advocacy, the concern for specific empirical systems was soon replaced by an attempt to understand "analytical" systems by reference to the functional requisites met by their various subsystems.

Talcott Parsons' action theory, especially as it developed in the 1950s (Parsons, 1951; Parsons, Bales, and Shils, 1953; Parsons and Smelser, 1956), represents the culmination of this analytical approach. Borrowing from Malinowski, if only subconsciously, the social universe is divided into four system levels in terms of their importance for meeting four universal functional requisites and much like Radcliffe-Brown, Parsons began to visualize these functional categories as offering an explanatory theory.

THE CRITIQUE AND DECLINE OF FUNCTIONALISM IN SOCIOLOGY

In the 1950s and 1960s, as functionalism came to dominate sociological inquiry, a series of logical and substantive criticisms were increasingly leveled at Parsons' action theory. The substantive criticisms concerned the image of the social world connoted by the functional orientation, while the logical criticisms questioned the legitimacy of functional explanations. Until the emergence of neofunctionalism, this two-pronged attack led to the decline of explicitly functional analysis and, for a time, to the virtual disappearance of those who would proclaim themselves to be "functionalists."

These criticisms are well known, but since they represent a crucial turning point in functionalism's (and sociological theory's) history, we should briefly review them. Moreover, since neofunctionalism is often viewed as having avoided and/or incorporated these criticisms, we need to review them in order to assess the claims of neofunctionalists.

Substantive Criticisms

Through all the acrimony of the 1960s, three general lines of substantive criticism were leveled against functionalism (Turner, 1974, 1986; Turner and Maryanski, 1978): (1) Functionalism is ahistorical; (2) functionalism is conservative and supports the status quo; and (3), functionalism cannot adequately account for social change.

(1) *The Question of History.* Durkheim's functionalism was historical in that it sought "antecedent causes" of present events, but as functionalism was adopted by anthropologists, it became decidedly ahistorical. Subsequent sociological functionalisms did not evidence much concern with history. Yet, Parsons' (1966, 1971) later evolutionary events and current neofunctionalists' projects are decidedly historical. The criticism is, therefore, without much merit.

(2) *The Question of Conservatism.* There can be little doubt that since its origins functionalism has been concerned with order, stability, and integration. Comte and Durkheim worked to create a "healthy" and "integrated" society; Radcliffe-Brown consistently assessed structures in terms of their "integrative" functions; and notions of "survival," "equilibrium," "homeostasis," and "adaptive upgrading" were prominent in Parsonian functionalism. Yet, neofunctionalists argue that this criticism can be met by incorporating the analysis of conflict, protest, dissent, and other potentially disintegrative and disequilibrating processes. And we sense that they are correct, since there is no logical barrier to the analysis of disintegrative processes by functionalism.

(3) *The Question of Change.* Critics often argued that functionalists' concern with order and equilibrium precluded the analysis of change, especially revolutionary social change. Comte, Spencer, Durkheim, and Parsons certainly emphasized evolutionary change, and Radcliffe-Brown and Malinowski studied small systems where revolution and conflict are unlikely. Yet, neofunctionalists are correct in their assertion that there is no reason why specific structures cannot be analyzed with respect to their potential (or actual) effects on conflict and change in social systems.

In sum, then, we would agree with the neofunctionalists that there is little merit to the substantive criticisms leveled against functionalism. Critics have assumed that, because early functionalists chose to emphasize some topics and underemphasize others, there is something inherent in the logic of functional analysis that precludes the analysis of history, disorder, and change. Such is clearly not the case, as the works of such contemporary scholars as Smelser, Eisenstadt, Alexander, Prager, Barber, Gould, Colomy, and others clearly document.

Logical Criticism

We can now turn to the logical criticisms leveled against functionalism, of which there were two: (1) Functional explanations are tautologous; and (2), functional explanations are illegitimate teleologies.

The Question of Teleology. An illegitimate teleology can be said to exist when end or goal states are presumed to cause the events leading to their realization, without being able to document the specific causal processes by which this is so. The concept of requisites is the most vulnerable on this score, for many functional explanations appear to argue that the "need for" meeting some requisite brings about the very structures that met this need. Such explanations are likely, though not necessarily, to be illegitimate teleologies.

Durkheim sought to avoid this problem with his distinction between causal and functional explanation, but Radcliffe-Brown plunged back into the problem by abandoning this distinction. Subsequent functionalists have, to varying degrees, often slipped into this logical trap and have appeared to argue that a satisfactory explanation of why a particular structure should exist is rendered by the discovery of its function for the social whole. In order to make such explanations legitimate, it is usually necessary to invoke a "selection" process in which the need or requisites creates selection pressures for a particular structure to emerge. In such an argument, it is not assumed that the relevant structures will inevitably emerge, only that the environment is receptive to their creation, whether by design, planning, chance, trial and error, or luck. For example, it might be argued that a state-government became more centralized and authoritarian to deal with public unrest and protest (translation: the need for integration created selection pressures for social control which, in this case, emerged through centralization of power.) Sociologists frequently make such selection arguments, although they are often implicit and the needs or requisites that create these pressures are unacknowledged.

The problem with these kinds of explanations, however, is that unless one can document the historical processes—usually some combination of chance, intent, design, and luck—by which a particular requisite-failing situation led to the requisite-fulfilling end state, the explanation will be an illegitimate teleology. Durkheim recognized this necessity in his distinction between causal and functional analysis, but Radcliffe-Brown submerged it; and most Parsonian theory is insensitive to the problem, because it assumes that explanation has occurred when the functional requisite of a structure has been determined.

Thus, while this logical problem of illegitimate teleology can be avoided, it surfaces so frequently in functional analysis as to render suspect this perspective as an *explanatory* tool. Perhaps it is for this reason that neofunctionalists avoid the issue of system needs, with a few noticeable exceptions (e.g., Münch, 1982, although Münch obviates the problem of illegitimate teleology by using Parsons' A, G, I, L framework to generate abstract propositions, with the predictive capacity of the propositions, rather than the location of empirical

events in a functional grid, constituting the explanation). But among neofunctionalists, Münch is virtually alone in translating problematic functional explanations into deductive-nomothetic ones. Most neofunctionalists tip-toe around questions of needs; and in so doing, they abandon what is distinctive about functional analysis. Thus, much neofunctionalism is not functional at all, since needs and requisites do not appear as part of the theoretical explanation of events. And, to the extent that they do appear, they generally have not obviated this problem of illegitimate teleology.

The Question of Tautology. Many functional explanations boil down to statements of the following form: A structure is a part of a surviving systemic whole; it therefore must be meeting some crucial need or requisite of this whole; and the structure exists and persists because the system's needs are being met. Again, while the problem of tautology can be avoided, through invocation of a selection argument or translation of functional statements to propositions connecting variables, it occurs so frequently in functional explanations employing the concept of requisites or needs that questions about functionalism as a useful *explanatory* strategy are appropriate. Neofunctionalists avoid the problem to the extent that they expunge notions of needs and requisites which, ironically, no longer makes them functionalists. Or, as is often the case, neofunctionalists slip in and out of functional arguments. For example, Robert Wuthnow's (1987) recent book on cultural analysis makes many statements along the lines that the function of ritual or ideology is to dramatize and stabilize social relations (translation: the need for integration is why human societies have rituals), without offering any clues about the selection processes involved. Alongside these purely functional statements, however, are propositional ones (if *x*, then *y*; or *y* is a function of *x*) which are not functional (except in the mathematical sense). Thus, much neofunctionalism is a mixture of functional and nonfunctional statements. Perhaps quasi-functional is a better term than neofunctional.

These logical difficulties are far more severe than the imputed substantive problems. They raise questions as to whether or not functionalism is capable of consistently generating non-problematic theoretical explanations. Since functionalism has, since its inception, been considered a useful explanatory tool, this is a serious charge which neofunctionalists have tended to ignore and avoid in favor of addressing the substantive criticisms leveled against Parsonian functionalism.

THE RESURRECTION
OF FUNCTIONALISM
BY NEOFUNCTIONALISTS

In Alexander's (1985:7–17) short manifesto for neofunctionalism, he admits that "although not providing a model in an explanatory sense, functionalism does provide a picture of the interrelation of social parts" (p. 9). Here again, we have the Kingsley Davis ploy: deny what made functionalism unique. That is, the defining quality of sociological functionalism is a model of explanation in terms of need states of systemic wholes. Alexander then goes on to list the other general features of neofunctionalism as a concern with action as well as structure; a recognition of the dialectic among control, integration, and deviance; a reformulation of equilibrium in Keynes' sense of systemic strains; a maintenance of the distinctions among, as well as a description of the strains between, personality, culture, and social structure; and an emphasis on differentiation as a major mode of change.

What is distinctly functional about these? In fact, if we can believe them, neofunctionalists have not resurrected functionalism, but killed it off. Only to the extent that the above list of activities is carried out with a view to explaining events in terms of their consequences for meeting need states in system wholes is their analysis functional. Most neofunctionalists, with some notable exceptions, have avoided just this point of emphasis.

What, then, is neofunctionalism? In actual practice, notions of functional needs often slip back into analysis, and so neofunctionalists are much like old-functionalists, except they are more attuned to the substantive criticisms of Parsonian action theory. For example, Niklas Luhmann's (1982) systems theory is, in fact, clearly functional because it analyzes system processes in terms of an implicit functional requisite: systems' need to reduce environmental complexity. That is, Luhmann analyzes structures (law, the state, organizations, etc.) and cultural codes in terms of their function for reducing environmental complexity. This basic need is, in actuality, several related needs to reduce complexity with respect to (1) perceptions of time, (2) organization of space, and (3) use of symbols. At the most general level, three types of systems meet these requisites—interaction systems, organization systems, and societal systems; and while Luhmann never specifies the process, there is an implicit selection argument: requisites to reduce complexity over the infinite reaches of time (both the future and past), over the manifold ways for ordering social relations, and over the infinite number of arbitrary signs as well as their combination and permutation into an unlimited number of symbol systems forces (read: exerts selection pressures on) actors to reduce this complexity. But this selection argument is typically left implicit, making much of Luhmann's scheme an illegitimate teleology, or tautology, at least to the extent that it is assumed to explain anything. Other modern-day neofunctionalists, such as Richard Münch

(1982), are even more in the mainstream of old functionalism, extending and elaborating upon Parsons' four requisite model, but as we mentioned above, Münch often moves out of the functional mode of analysis and into a more nomothetic, deductive mode. For example, in one article (Münch, 1989), he discusses a variety of theories within the Parsonian A, G, I, L framework, but this is not the end-point of his analysis. Instead, he develops specific propositions or laws on economic achievement, political accumulation, associational inertia, and the like. Moreover, he employs the laws, not the A, G, I, L framework, for comparing the structure of the United States, France, Britain, and Germany. Thus, for Münch, functionalism is a preliminary procedure for formulating testable propositions, and it is in this way that he avoids the logical problems associated with functional explanations. In a sense, Münch increasingly becomes a nonfunctionalist by the time he develops explanatory principles. In addition, many prominent scholars identified with functionalism—including Bernard Barber, Neil J. Smelser, and S.N. Eisenstadt, to name but a few—appear less prone in recent years to begin analysis with assumptions of need-states and requisites, and so, they too do not fall into the logical traps evident in much functional analysis.

Thus, in a sense, Alexander is correct in his portrayal of the current scene as one where "nothing so precise as a set of concepts, a method, a model, or an ideology" characterizes these self-proclaimed neofunctionalists. What, then, unifies these scholars? Our answer is close to Alexander's, but it is not functionalism that unites them. Rather, it is concern with theory that conceptualizes social phenomena in terms of: (1) analytical levels (particularly, the cultural, structural, and individual); (2) systems and subsystems as well as their interchanges; (3) normative processes (in an era where many are trying to rid sociology of this central concept); (4) differentiation dynamics (from conflict between groups through social movements to long term historical changes); and (5) differentiated substructures (particularly the interrelations among institutional subsystems).

Hence, much of the substance of the Parsonian action scheme is retained, but the propensity to explain social phenomena in terms of need states and requisites is attenuated, except perhaps in the work of Luhmann and in occasional lapses in others, such as Wuthnow (1987). In fact, a careful review of much neofunctionalist work reveals that it is far more descriptive than explanatory which, given the problems of earlier functionalism, is probably just as well. But is there something lost in abandoning the notion of needs and requisites? Can they be used in some creative manner in sociological analysis?

SHOULD WE ABANDON NOTIONS OF "NEEDS" AND "REQUISITES"?

As tools for explanations, notions of needs should probably be dropped, as the neofunctionalists have quietly done. The reason for this conclusion is that while "selection arguments" can be invoked to "save" many functional statements, such is not always the case and, even when it is, selection arguments will often appear too historical (as opposed to deductive) for many theorists. Our sense is that, if an approach causes so many potential problems in generating explanations, why stick with it?

Yet, though functionalism may not provide adequate theoretical explanations, it can perhaps still be a useful *method* for collecting and organizing data on empirical systems. This conclusion may seem surprising, since the work of such functionalists as Talcott Parsons has been considered obstructive to empirical inquiry. Yet, the fact that Parsons' own examinations of empirical events, from the American school classroom to the American kinship system, are regarded by functionalists and nonfunctionalists alike as insightful should alert us to the potential of functional analysis as a way to describe empirical events. Moreover, Spencer's and Malinowski's effective use of system needs as a device for arraying data should also alert us to potential along these lines. And, to further buttress this conclusion, much of the work by supposed neofunctionalists—i.e., Eisenstadt, Smelser, Alexander, etc.—is insightfully descriptive, making one suspect that hidden notions of requisites are guiding descriptions of historical and current events.

Thus, before "throwing the methodological baby out with the explanatory bathwater," we should pause and consider functionalism as method, not theory. Like Spencer before him, Malinowski recognized that social anthropology must develop a common set of categories if it is to compare diverse cultures. While sociologists have tended to rely on Max Weber's ideal type method or on elaborate correlational analyses to compare different social systems, the anthropologist Walter Goldschmidt (1966) once advocated an alternative approach which is highly compatible with Spencer's advocacy in his *Descriptive Sociology* (1873–1934) and later Murdock's (1936) effort to develop the Human Relation Area Files [HRAF].

Like Spencer, Murdock, and Malinowski (and Weber in his advocacy of "ideal types"), Goldschmidt recognizes that descriptions of diverse social systems require a common yardstick for comparison. He has recommended that functional requisites can best provide this comparative yardstick. For example, a list of basic problems that social systems confront can provide a common frame of reference for comparing diverse systems. Thus, by providing detailed lists of necessary functions, the diversity of ways that systems have become structured with respect to these problems can be recorded. For example, Goldschmidt provides a list of requisites that would allow for comparisons of different societies with respect to certain critical activities. (1) Delineation of rights to sexual access, including the public presentation of those rights and sanctions against breach. (2) Provision for the nurture of infants and care of pregnant and lactating mothers including the definition of rights and obligation. . . . (3) Provision of a defined social status and social identity for the child. (4) Provision of education and indoctrination of the child. . . . (5) Provision of an identification object for both parents through which they may project themselves into the future through sociologically established descendants. By comparing societies with respect to these other lists of requisites, problems over definitions of structures are obviated and a common analytical yardstick for comparison is provided. Much as Spencer (1873–1934) sought to do in his *Descriptive Sociology*, such data will be presented in comparable categories and will thus be more amenable to interpretation by nonfunctional theorizing.

The list of functional requisites will, of course, represent *assumptions* about what is crucial and important for describing social systems. But this has always been the appeal of functionalism: It has addressed the question of what is essential for the survival of the social whole. And it is always an assumption in description: scholars describe what they think is most important, but this is often done idiosyncratically. Would it not be better to have common categories that would allow data to be arrayed for comparative purposes? Categories based upon notions of requisites are not a very good way to begin a theoretical explanation, but we argue that it is a reasonable way to begin a description of a social system. For without such assumptions, it will be difficult to discern important processes and to compare diversely structured systems.

It can be questioned, however, as to whether or not it is feasible to separate a requisite-inspired methodology from theoretical explanations. If one describes empirical processes in terms of requisites, will not explanations, incorporate, at least implicitly, these needs or requisites? Such need not be the case, we believe, because descriptions do not have to be conducted in a functional manner. For example, if one assumes that "adaptation," to take one of Parsons' and Münch's favorite requisites, as our descriptive category, we become alerted to (1) how a given empirical situation secures resources, (2) converts these resources into usable commodities, and (3) distributes them. Description of events with respect to these three processes does not, in our view, force one into a functional mode of explanation. There are many nonfunctional theories that could be used to explain regularities in these data. And, if many different situations were described in terms of how adaptation occurs, a set of reasonably comparable data with respect to securing resources, converting them, and distributing them would be generated.

Another question could be raised here: Of what use would piles of data arrayed in terms of some scheme of functional requisites be to researchers and theorists? Our sense is that too much historical and comparative work is ad hoc. Investigators gather their own data, in their own way, and for their own purposes, with the result that their analyses and conclusions are difficult to assess or compare to those of others working with yet another ad hoc data set. Spencer and Murdock had the right idea in their efforts to catalogue data in ways that would make them comparable and less idiosyncratic; and while we have forgotten this simple methodological insight, it is what a successful science depends upon. To test alternative hypotheses, or to assess one in varying contexts, we need some degree of compatibility in the data. If we collect new data, or

analyze old data, with a brand new methodology each and every time we test a theory, it becomes difficult to cumulate knowledge, since the data are about somewhat different things. Thus, if sociologists could agree (of course, we know how naive this is) upon a limited number of requisites—and A, G, I, L, as these are defined by Parsons would not be a bad set—and if they could consent to array data with respect to these, the test of nonfunctional theories would be greatly facilitated, especially those that require comparative data sets.

In fact, this is just what Spencer (1873–1934) in his *Descriptive Sociology* and Murdock in his HRAF tried to do; and Malinowski's and Goldschmidt's similar efforts represent a further appeal to this kind of methodology. Functionalism can help implement this methodology, but alas, neofunctionalists seem unaware, at least explicitly, of this potential. One consequence, we believe, is that sociology, and anthropology as well, seem more and more relativistic and less interested in theory testing.

CONCLUSION

What, then, can we conclude about neofunctionalism. First, it downplays what is distinctly functional, and instead, emphasizes culture, system levels, and problems of differentiation and integration. Second, it does not seem to recognize explicitly that there is a difference between functional methods and explanations. Explanations in terms of needs and requisites are almost always going to be problematic; and so, the "neofunctionalists," who are really nonfunctionalists, are perhaps wise to downplay notions of requisites. But since so much of neofunctionalism is macro and comparative, it is important, we argue, that a reassessment of functionalist-inspired methodology be undertaken. Sociology desperately needs a way to record, catalogue, and array comparative data; notions of requisites might serve this truly "neo" function in sociology.

REFERENCES

ABERLE, D.F., et al. 1950. "The Functional Requisites of Society." *Ethics* 60:100–111.

ALEXANDER, JEFFREY C., ed. 1985. *Neofunctionalism.* Beverly Hills: Sage.

COMTE, AUGUSTE. 1875. *A System of Positive Polity or Treatise on Sociology.* London: Burt Franklin.

DAVIS, KINGSLEY. 1948. *Human Society.* New York: Macmillan.

_____. 1959. "The Myth of Functional Analyses." *American Sociological Review* 25:757–72.

DAVIS, KINGSLEY, AND WILBERT E. MOORE. 1945. "Some Principles of Stratification." *American Sociological Review* 10:242–47.

DURKHEIM, ÉMILE. 1893. *The Division of Labor in Society.* New York: Free Press.

_____. 1895. [1930]. *The Rules of Sociological Method.* New York: Free Press.

_____. 1897. [1951]. *Suicide.* New York: Free Press.

_____. 1912. [1915]. *Elementary Forms of the Religious Life.* New York: Free Press.

FREUD, SIGMUND. 1913. [1938]. *Totem and Taboo.* London: Penguin.

GOLDSCHMIDT, WALTER. 1966. *Comparative Functionalism.* Berkeley: University of California Press.

LEVY, MARION J. 1952. *The Structure of Society.* Princeton, N.J.: Princeton University Press.

LUHMANN, NIKLAS. 1982. *The Differentiation of Society.* New York: Columbia.

MALINOWSKI, BRONISLAW. 1913. [1963]. *The Family among the Australian Aborigines.* New York: Schocken.

_____. 1941. "Man's Culture and Man's Behavior." *American Scientist* 29:196–207.

_____. 1944. *A Scientific Theory of Culture and Other Essays.* Chapel Hill: University of North Carolina Press.

MERTON, ROBERT K. 1949. "Manifest and Latent Functions." *Social Theory and Social Structure.* New York: Free Press.

MÜNCH, RICHARD. 1982. *Theorie des Handelns.* Frankfurt: Suhrkamp.

_____. 1989. "The Extension of Parsonian Action Theory Today." Pp. 108–117 in *Theory Building in Sociology,* edited by J.H. Turner. Newbury Park: Sage.

MURDOCK, PETER. 1936. *Our Primitive Contemporaries.* New York: Macmillan.

PARSONS, TALCOTT. 1937. *The Structure of Social Action.* New York: McGraw-Hill.

_____. 1951. *The Social System.* New York: Free Press.

_____. 1966. *Societies: Evolutionary and Comparative Perspectives.* Englewood Cliffs, N.J.: Prentice Hall.

_____. 1971. *The System of Modern Societies.* Englewood Cliffs, N.J.: Prentice Hall.

PARSONS, TALCOTT, ROBERT F. BALES, AND EDWARD A. SHILS. 1953. *Working Papers in the Theory of Action.* New York: Free Press.

PARSONS, TALCOTT, AND NEIL J. SMELSER. 1956. *Economy and Society.* New York: Free Press.

RADCLIFFE-BROWN, A.R. 1913. "Three Tribes of Western Australia." *Journal of Royal Anthropological Institute of Great Britain and Ireland* 43:54–82.

_____. 1952. *Structure and Function in Primitive Society.* London: Cohen and West.

SPENCER, BALDWIN, AND F.J. GILLIAN. 1899. *The Native Tribes of Central Australia.* London: Macmillan.

SPENCER, HERBERT. 1873–1934. *Descriptive Sociology; or, Groups of Sociological Facts,* 16 vols. Various publishers.

_____. 1876. [1966]. *The Works of Herbert Spencer,* 8 vols. Osnabruck: Otto Zeller.

STINCHCOMBE, ARTHUR. 1968. *Constructing Social Theories.* New York: Harcourt.

TURNER, JONATHAN H. 1974. *The Structure of Sociological Theory.* Homewood, Ill.: Dorsey Press.

_____. 1986. *The Structure of Sociological Theory,* 4th edition. Homewood, Ill.: Dorsey Press.

TURNER, JONATHAN H., AND A.R. MARYANSKI. 1978. *Functionalism: An Intellectual Portrait.* Palo Alto: Cummings.

WUTHNOW, ROBERT. 1987. *Meaning and Moral Order: Explorations in Cultural Analysis.* Berkeley: University of California Press.

△▷ CHAPTER 2 ◁△

CONFLICT THEORY

▷━━━━━━━━━━━━━━━━━━━━━━━◁

The *conflict* school of sociology emerged during the late 1950s in American sociology, reflecting a widespread dissatisfaction with the perceived shortcomings of the dominant functionalist paradigm. As mentioned in the introduction to Chapter 1, the criticisms of functionalism fell into three basic categories (Cohen 1968, 47). First, functionalism was seen as untestable; second, it emphasized unity and gave inadequate attention to conflict and competition in society; and third, it was inherently conservative, serving as an apology for the status quo.

Conflict theory, as it emerged in the works of such theorists as Dahrendorf (1958, 1959), Coser (1956, 1967), Lockwood (1956), and Mills (1956, 1959), challenged the functionalist consensus on all three of these counts and offered in its place a model of society radically different from that presented by the functionalists. Whereas the functionalists asserted that societies tended toward functional integration and unity, the conflict theorists argued that societies were inherently dynamic and unstable. Functionalists suggested that soci-

eties were characterized by consensus over fundamental policies and goals, and conflict theorists contended that consensus was often only a mask imposed by force and violence, that in fact societies were torn by fundamental divisions of interest and conflict between rich and poor, men and women, black and white, young and old. Finally, if functionalists showed a conservative attachment to the status quo, conflict theorists argued that conflict and change were not only inevitable, but that they were often beneficial for society, serving to break down archaic and antiquated habits, customs, and systems of power. Conflict was generally seen as a *liberating* and *progressive* force in society.

CLASSICAL CONFLICT THEORY

This attitude was not, of course, an entirely new one to sociology. The basic tenets of the conflict perspective—the emphasis on conflict and change as fundamental properties of society—can be traced back to the earliest social theory. Around 500 B.C. the Greek philosopher Heraclitus propounded the doctrine that instability is the essence of reality—that both physical nature and human nature (including society) are always undergoing transformation and change. The fourteenth-century North African social philosopher Ibn Khaldun (1332–1406)—one of the earliest sociological thinkers—argued that new forms of social and religious life are always established by conflict and strife (Mahdi, 1964). His work marks one of the first systematic attempts to understand the mutually dependent interconnection between social conflict and social solidarity (see Lacoste 1984).

The eighteenth-century European Enlightenment, which marked the rebirth of scientific and secular thought in many areas of intellectual life, gave rise to theories that stressed the role of conflict and competition in bringing about progress in society. In fact, according to Adam Smith (1723–1790), the founder of modern economics, competition was the great "invisible hand" that ordered every aspect of economic and social life. Herbert Spencer combined this economic theory with Charles Darwin's ideas concerning the evolutionary competition of species to create a conservative form of conflict theory known as social Darwinism (see Hofstadter 1955). In social Darwinism society was seen as the arena of an intense struggle for survival, with the biologically fittest achieving wealth and success and the unfit descending into poverty, disease, and extinction.

In this case, as in so many others, social theorists were responding to changing conditions in the larger society in which they lived. Late eighteenth- and early nineteenth-century Europe was being rocked by a series of cataclysmic shocks that dramatically transformed the traditional pastoral feudal way of life. The French Revolution (1789) marked the beginning of more than two decades of constant warfare in Europe, and it placed in motion the social and political forces of a powerful democratic movement that would transform European—and world—politics over the next century. Even more earth-shattering in its effects was the nineteenth-century Industrial Revolution, which, in the space of a few decades, gave rise to the first modern industrial society in England and then spread to the rest of Europe and across the sea to America.

Not all the responses to these revolutionary changes were as sanguine as those of Smith and Spencer. The nineteenth-century French theorist Henri de Saint-Simon (1760–1825), imprisoned during the French Revolution, emerged to become the first sociologist of the new European "industrial" order and the proponent of a form of technocratic socialism. The German philosopher Lorenz von Stein (1815–1890) wrote about the emergent conflict between the industrial classes of capital and labor. His insight was incorporated into the work of the German theorist Karl Marx, arguably the greatest figure of the nineteenth-century "conflict" approach and the founder, in turn, of a new tradition in social theory, Marxism, which we will discuss in more detail in Chapter 3 (see Taylor 1975, von Stein 1964).

The nineteenth-century conflict tradition culminated in the work of the German sociologist Max Weber (1864–1920). In many ways, Weber's work constituted a prolonged engagement with and critique of the work of Karl Marx. Adopting such central Marxian topics as the transition from feudalism to capitalism, the stratification of capitalist society into classes, the role of political ideology, and the political economy of socialism, Weber developed a powerful and distinctive approach to the study of conflict processes in society that avoided the radical commitments of Marx and his followers (see Weber 1968; Mommsen 1989). His approach focused on the concept of *rationalization*, which in many ways functioned in his thought similarly to the concept of capitalism in Marx's writings, as the inexorable force transforming modern society. Yet while Marx believed that capitalism could be successfully resisted and transformed into a more humane form of society called socialism, Weber was profoundly pessimistic about the likelihood of successfully opposing the growing control of society by powerful, efficient, "rational" bureaucracies. The tension between Marx's radical optimism and Weber's conservative pessimism has formed a central unresolved theme in modern conflict sociology.

MODERN CONFLICT THEORY

Much as the emergence of conflict theory in the eighteenth and nineteenth centuries can be interpreted as a response to the impact of the "dual" revolutions, democratization and industrialization, so too the reemergence of conflict theory in American sociology in the middle of the twentieth century can be seen as following upon the onset of real conflicts within American society. Although the McCarthy era of the 1950s had enforced a rigid anticommunist consensus on American society and academic life, by the end of that decade important change had begun with the emergence of the civil rights movement. Indeed, in a seminal article written from the conflict perspective, John Horton (1966) adopted the civil rights movement as his central example of the inadequacy of "order" theory in sociology. The student movement, the "Black power" movement, the emergence of a "New Left," and the anti-Vietnam War movement in the 1960s were so many nails in the coffin of the dominant functionalist perspective, with its emphasis on consensus and order. And for a brief moment, say the late 1960s, conflict theory occupied, if not the whole stage, certainly center stage in the sociological drama.

What is the content of this conflict theory? Conflict theorists such as Lockwood (1956), Giddens (Reading 7), and Dahrendorf (Reading 8) castigated the shortcomings of functionalism; but most conflict theorists were equally critical of orthodox Marxism (see Dahrendorf 1959, ch. 4). Thus, most conflict theorists, following Dahrendorf, preferred to talk about conflict groups, rather than class struggle, dominant elites rather than a ruling class, and management and workers rather than capital and labor. Conflict theorists emphasize the ubiquity of conflict in society, but they do not necessarily evaluate conflict as negative in its consequences. As Coser (Reading 9) points out, conflict, as the mechanism of social change and adjustment, can play a *positive* role, or function, in society. Coser's *The Functions of Social Conflict* (1956)—originally written as his doctoral dissertation under the direction of the functionalist Robert Merton—formed an interesting theoretical bridge between functionalism and conflict theory. While sharing with other conflict theorists a fundamental orientation toward competition and conflict as universal and inevitable social processes, Coser, in focusing on the *integrative* effects of conflict, stated his conclusions in the terminology of orthodox functionalism. His work on the functions of conflict may be read as an effort to incorporate the study of conflict into a radically revised functionalist framework (see Coser 1956, 1967).

Most other conflict theorists, however, following Dahrendorf (Reading 8; see also Dahrendorf 1958), were more emphatic in their rejection of functionalism. For Dahrendorf, functionalism and conflict theory presented mutually exclusive and competing models of society. Dahrendorf's own work, which focused on problems of conflict and order in modern industrial societies, was particularly concerned with authority and authority structures as sources of social conflict.

Whether analyzing the relationship between workers and managers in an industrial enterprise or the exercise of power by a totalitarian state, Dahrendorf characteristically focused on the organization of (or failure to organize) legitimate authority as the major variable explaining the form that conflict relations will take and the intensity of conflict.

Some conflict sociologists have argued that not only should the functionalist theoretical model be rejected, but the orthodox *methodological* program should be abandoned as well. In many cases, such as that of C.Wright Mills (1959), this argument has taken the form of a critique of the "scientific" pretensions of mainstream sociology. One of the early proponents of a conflict approach in the 1950s, Mills called on sociologists to abandon the attempt to construct a functionalist "Grand Theory" and to throw themselves as active participants into the political and social conflicts of the day.

Other conflict sociologists attempted to create a "conflict methodology" that would fulfill Mills' earlier call for a new critical approach to the study of society. In an influential article, Lehmann and Young (1974) argued that—contrary to the scientific pretensions of mainstream sociologists—sociological research is inextricably caught up in the struggles of different groups to impose favorable definitions of reality, interest, and fairness on the rest of society. Traditional sociological research, according to Lehmann and Young, with its methodological assumptions of consensus and order, has invariably been coopted to serve the interests of the powerful at the expense of the powerless. They called on sociologists to actively ally themselves with groups seeking to bring about egalitarian changes in society and to conduct new kinds of social research that are aimed at exposing and disrupting the orderly exercise of power and domination in society

(see also Orenstein and Luken 1978; Young 1971, 1976).

As might be expected, the attempt to reorient sociology toward the study of conflict and change proved to be quite controversial, and the conflict perspective has been subjected to criticisms from other sociological perspectives. Many functionalists have responded to the charge that theirs is a static, order-oriented theory with often intriguing attempts to develop a functionalist theory of change (see Jacobson 1971, W. Moore 1960, Smelser 1959; for more recent efforts, see Colomy, Reading 5 and the essays collected in Alexander and Colomy 1990). Many other sociological critics, standing outside of both theoretical camps, have charged that, to a great degree, the "great debate" in sociology between conflict theorists and functionalists has been rooted in a false and purely semantic opposition between "order" and "conflict." This often heated debate over whether social conflict or social order is the more "natural" state of society is really a philosophical question that more properly belongs in the realm of metaphysics than that of sociology. That both conflict and consensus occur is certain and acknowledged by proponents of both approaches: The real question for sociology then is over prevalence, frequency, relative impact, and the conditions under which each occurs. And this question can be answered only by historically specific empirical research (see McQuarie and Murray 1985).

More important, there is no logical distinction between the functionalist's question, What holds societies together? and the conflict theorist's question, What drives them on? Dahrendorf's (Reading 8) insistence that the response to each constitutes a separate theory of society has been criticized by both functionalists and conflict theorists who have argued that the same factors that compel societies onward can also be sources of societal cohesion (Coser 1956, 1967; Fallding 1972; see Binns 1977). And more recent reformulations of the conflict model, such as those of Collins (1975, 1986, Reading 10), have attempted to overcome the one-sidedness of some of the earlier attempts to explain conflict processes in society.

During the last decade, conflict theorists have been especially active in developing large-scale macrohistorical models of social change. In particular, conflict sociologists have made important contributions to the study of the causes and consequences of political revolutions (see Goldstone 1991, Mann 1986, Skocpol 1979, Tilly 1991). Here, their specific contribution has been to contend with Marxist theorists (such as Barrington Moore [1966] and Perry Anderson [1974]) over the relative importance of *state* actors and institutions as opposed to *class* actors and institutions. These arguments are summarized by Collins (Reading 11), who argues that the recent contributions of conflict theorists to the study of revolution will bring about a fundamental change in the way sociologists look at wars and revolutions, with the state increasingly displacing social class at the center of analysis. (For a review of similar trends among academic historians, see Cannadine 1992).

In summary, the conflict perspective that emerged in the 1950s has proved to be a lasting contribution to sociological theory. With the recent collapse of the U.S.S.R. and the Eastern European socialist states, and the consequent political and ethnic turmoil, conflict theory has reemerged and even gained at the expense of its main rival, Marxist theory, according to one recent essay (Collins 1990). Conflict theorists have made important contributions, primarily in the areas of political sociology, social stratification, criminology, and organizational research (see Chambliss 1973; Collins 1971a, 1971b, 1981; Dahrendorf 1967; Evans, Rueschemeyer, and Skocpol, 1985; Goldstone 1991; Mann 1986; Mills 1956; Murphy 1988; Skocpol 1979; Turk 1966).

REFERENCES

ALEXANDER, JEFFREY, and PAUL COLOMY, eds. 1990. *Differentiation Theory and Social Change: Comparative and Historical Perspectives.* New York: Columbia University Press.

ANDERSON, PERRY. 1974. *Lineages of the Absolutist State.* London: New Left Books.

BINNS, DAVID. 1977. *Beyond the Sociology Conflict.* New York: St. Martins Press.

CANNADINE, DAVID. 1992. "Cutting Classes." *New York Review of Books* 39, no. 21 (December 17): 52–57.

CHAMBLISS, WILLIAM, ed. 1973. *Sociological Readings in the Conflict Perspective.* Reading: Addison-Wesley.

COHEN, PERCY. 1968. *Modern Social Theory.* New York: Basic Books.

COLLINS, RANDALL. 1971a. "A Conflict Theory of Sexual Stratification." *Social Problems* 19 (Summer):3–21.

_____. 1971b. "Functional and Conflict Theories of Educational Stratification. *American Sociological Review* 36 (December):1002–19.

_____. 1975. *Conflict Theory: Toward an Explanatory Science.* New York: Academic Press.

_____. 1981. "Long-Term Social Change and the Territorial Power of States." Pp. 71–106 in *Sociology Since Midcentury: Essays in Theory Cumulation,* Randall Collins. New York: Academic Press.

_____. 1986. *Weberian Sociological Theory.* Cambridge: Cambridge University Press.

_____. 1990. "Conflict Theory and the Advance of Macro-Historical Sociology." Pp. 68–87 in *Frontiers of Social Theory,* ed. George Ritzer. New York: Columbia University Press.

COSER, LEWIS. 1956. *The Functions of Social Conflict.* New York: Free Press.

_____. 1967. *Continuities in the Study of Social Conflict.* New York: Free Press.

DAHRENDORF, RALF. 1958. "Out of Utopia: Towards a Reorientation of Sociological Analysis." *American Journal of Sociology* 64 (September):115–27.

_____. 1959. *Class and Class Conflict in Industrial Society.* Stanford: Stanford University Press.

_____. 1967. *Conflict after Class.* New York: Humanities Press.

EVANS, PETER, DIETRICH RUESCHEMEYER, and THEDA SKOCPOL, eds. 1985. *Bringing the State Back In.* London: Cambridge University Press.

FALLDING, HAROLD. 1972. "Only One Sociology." *British Journal of Sociology* 23 (March): 93–101.

GOLDSTONE, JACK. 1991. *Revolution and Rebellion in the Early Modern World.* Berkeley: University of California Press.

HOFSTADTER, RICHARD. 1955. *Social Darwinism in American Thought.* Boston: Beacon Press.

HORTON, JOHN. 1966. "Order and Conflict Theories of Social Problems as Competing Ideologies." *American Journal of Sociology* 71 (May):701–13.

JACOBSON, A.L. 1971. "A Theoretical and Empirical Analysis of Social Change and Conflict Based on Talcott Parsons' Ideas." Pp. 344–60 in *Institutions and Social Exchange,* ed. Herman Turk and Richard Simpson. New York: Bobbs-Merrill.

LACOSTE, YVES. 1984. *Ibn Khaldun.* London: Verso Editions.

LEHMANN, TIMOTHY, and T.R. YOUNG. 1974. "From Conflict Theory to Conflict Methodology: An Emerging Paradigm for Sociology." *Sociological Inquiry* 44 (Winter):15–28.

LOCKWOOD, DAVID. 1956. "Some Remarks on the Social System." *British Journal of Sociology* 7 (June):134–45.

MAHDI, MUHSIN. 1964. *Ibn Khaldun's Philosophy of History.* Chicago: University of Chicago Press.

MANN, MICHAEL. 1986. *The Sources of Social Power,* vol. 1. New York: Cambridge University Press.

MCQUARIE, DONALD, and MARTIN MURRAY. 1985. "Conflict Theory: An Obituary." Pp. 201–23 in *Current Perspectives in Sociological Theory,* ed. Scott McNall. Greenwich: JAI Press.

MILLS C. WRIGHT. 1956. *The Power Elite.* New York: Oxford University Press.

———. 1959. *The Sociological Imagination.* New York: Oxford University Press.

MOMMSEN, WOLFGANG. 1989. *The Political and Social Theory of Max Weber.* Chicago: University of Chicago Press.

MOORE, BARRINGTON, JR. 1966. *Social Origins of Dictatorship and Democracy.* Boston: Beacon Press.

MOORE, WILBERT. 1960. "A Reconsideration of Theories of Social Change." *American Sociological Review* 25 (December):810–18.

MURPHY, RAYMOND. 1988. *Social Closure: The Theory of Monopolization and Exclusion.* Oxford: Clarendon Press.

ORENSTEIN, DAVID, and PAUL LUKEN. 1978. "Anarchist Methodology." *Sociological Focus* 11 (January):53–68.

SKOCPOL, THEDA. 1979. *States and Social Revolutions.* London: Cambridge University Press.

SMELSER, NEIL. 1959. *Social Change in the Industrial Revolution.* Chicago: University of Chicago Press.

TAYLOR, KEITH, ed. 1975. *Henri Saint-Simon: Selected Writings on Science, Industry, and Social Organization.* New York: Holmes and Meier.

TILLY, CHARLES. 1991. *Coercion, Capital, and European States: A.D. 990–1990.* Oxford: Blackwell.

TURK, AUSTIN. 1966. "Conflict and Criminality." *American Sociological Review* 31 (June):338–52.

VON STEIN, LORENZ. 1964. *The History of the Social Movement in France, 1789–1850.* Totowa: Bedminster Press.

WEBER, MAX. 1978. *Economy and Society.* 1921. Reprint, Berkeley: University of California Press.

YOUNG, T.R. 1971. "The Politics of Sociology: Gouldner, Goffman, and Garfinkel." *The American Sociologist* 6 (November):276–81.

———. 1976. "Some Theoretical Foundations for Conflict Methodology." *Sociological Inquiry* 46:23–29.

▷ READING 7 ◁

TIME AND SPACE IN SOCIAL THEORY: CRITICAL REMARKS UPON FUNCTIONALISM*

ANTHONY GIDDENS

In recent years, there have been fundamental changes in social theory, particularly in the English speaking world. For many years sociology was dominated by a series of assumptions which one could label "the orthodox consensus" (see Atkinson, 1972). This orthodox consensus expressed the dominance of leading trends in American sociology over sociological thinking in Britain. The orthodox consensus, in which writers such as Parsons, Merton, Lipset and others were the major luminaries, can be characterized as follows. On the philosophical side, there was *naturalism*. In the orthodox consensus it was held, in various versions, that sociology shared a broadly similar epistemological framework with the natural sciences. Many writers (not Parsons) adopted *en bloc* logical positivist models of science elaborated by such authors as Carnap, Hempel and Nagel. On the methodological side we had *functionalism*. Those in the ortho-

dox consensus believed that, of all the natural sciences, sociology stood in closest proximity to biology, and that "structural-functional" explanations of the kind favored in macro-biology could constitute the core of sociological explanation. . . .

The orthodox consensus, which reigned from roughly the early fifties to the early seventies, of course, never went unchallenged. Various elements of it were strongly attacked by Marxist writers, and by those who attempted to substitute "conflict theories" for what they saw as an over-concentration—especially by Parsons and his followers—upon consensus in society. Those who advocated entirely different conceptions of sociology . . . went largely unheard.

The decade of the seventies has seen the passing of the orthodox consensus. What was once a consensus has been disowned by almost everybody, including some of its favorite sons. The results are well-known: a fragmentation of social theory into a variety of competing schools, the rise of novel frameworks, such as ethnomethodology, and a massive resurgence of Marxist thought. For a while it

*From Scott G. McNall and Gary Howe, eds. *Current Perspectives in Social Theory*, vol. 2 (Greenwich, CT: JAI Press, 1981), pp. 3–9. Reprinted with permission of JAI Press, Inc.

seemed as though social theory would remain a kaleidoscope of fragmented particles; as though, once the orthodox consensus had been exploded, nothing would hold together any longer, and even dialogue between the varying types of social theory was impossible. We can now see this as a passing phase. Major efforts at the reconstruction of social theory have already been made, and with some considerable success. . . . But it is not enough that the ideas of the orthodox consensus should be quietly forgotten, we have to see just what is defensible, and what must be abandoned, in them. . . .

. . . Now to raise the question of functionalism is almost enough to put everyone to sleep. For has not functionalism been the subject of one of the most protracted and boring debates known to sociology? (See Demerath and Peterson, 1967; and Sztompka, 1974.) Might not the same be said of systems theory, sometimes thought to be closely allied to functionalism? To a certain degree I am prepared to grant these things—especially the somnambulant qualities of the functionalism debate of some fifteen to twenty years ago. What I cannot accept is that the problems raised by functionalist authors can be quietly forgotten. For one thing, this debate did not resolve any of the issues central to the question of the relevance of functionalism to sociology. Nor are they resolved by appeals to information theory or systems theory—even if this is undeniably far more sophisticated than sociological functionalism ever was. I believe that at least some of what I want to argue applies as forcibly to Luhmann's "functional-structuralism" as to American "structural functionalism." Though Luhmann is still prepared to talk of functionalism, there are many who declare themselves to be "nonfunctionalists," and who will have nothing to do with the term. But it is not hard to show that their writings are riddled with functionalist assumptions, often of a very crude kind. I have in

mind here particularly the works of the so-called "structuralist Marxists" who have sought to apply the views of Althusser to contemporary sociology and anthropology.

My argument will be as follows. The term "function" is of no use in sociology: indeed, it would do no harm to *ban it altogether* as a technical term in the social sciences. Most of those who have attacked functionalism, in any interesting way, have on the other hand relapsed into subjectivism. Like those influenced by ordinary language philosophy, or by varieties by phenomenology, they have seen functionalism as a deterministic type of thought, and have attempted to replace it with one which gives primacy to the intending, reasoning agent. In so doing, however, they have moved away from that area where functionalism was strongest: the analysis of institutions and large-scale social processes. In moving away from functionalism we need to be able to recognize *both* what I call the theorem of "knowledgeability" (that all of us are purposeful, knowledgeable agents, who have reasons for our actions), *and* that social processes at the same time work "behind our backs," and affect what we do in ways of which we are unaware. Marx summed this up long ago in the famous aphorism, "Men make history, but not in circumstances of their own choosing." But I do not believe that there is any single school of thought that has managed to successfully spell out the implications of this seemingly banal statement.

Functionalism means many things, but I shall define it as that type of doctrine which holds that: (a) societies, or social systems, have "needs;" and (b) that the identification of the ways in which they meet these needs constitutes an explanation of why particular, given social processes are as they are. This characterization includes both normative functionalism (Parsons) and conflict functionalism (Merton) as well as the various covert functionalisms of Althusser *et alia*.

I shall object to functionalism on several grounds: (1) that (like structuralism) it rests upon a false division between statics and dynamics, or between the synchronic and the diachronic; (2) that, in stressing system needs, functionalist authors have been unable to see human beings as reasoning agents, who know a great deal about what they are doing in the course of day-to-day life; (3) that systems have no needs, except in a sense which is very different from that which functionalist authors believe; (4) that, therefore, to identify system needs is not to explain anything at all: and that there is nothing that counts as functionalist explanation.

I will analyze these soon, but all the points I make can be unfolded in much greater detail, and have a number of very important implications for social theory. (1) One of the most general underlying notions in all my arguments is that time-space relations have to be brought into the heart of social theory. I will not attempt to document the various differing views that functionalist authors have had on the differentiation of synchrony and diachrony. I will simply assert rather dogmatically that this differentiation is *logically*, rather than contingently, associated with functionalism. And, I will claim that it is a division which should be abandoned once and for all. The characteristic view of the synchronic/diachronic distinction is that to study a social system synchronically is to take a sort of "timeless snapshot" of it. By abstracting from time we can identify functional relations; when we study systems diachronically, we analyze how they change over time. But the result of this is an elementary, although crucial error: *time becomes identified with social change.* The identification of time and change has as its obverse the assimilation of "timelessness" and stability: the notion that synchronic analysis allows us to determine the sources of social stability, while diachronic analysis is needed to understand the sources of change in social systems.

The elementary error in this is that time is obviously as logically necessary a component of social stability as it is of change. A stable social order is one in which there is a close similarity between how things are now, and how they used to be. This shows us how misleading it is to suppose that one can take a "timeless snapshot" of a social system, revealing its structure, as one can that of the architecture of a building. For social systems only have structural properties because they function *over time:* the "patterning" of social relations is inseparable from their continual reproduction across time.

(2) My second objection is that functionalist theories have lacked adequate accounts of human *action* in the sense in which much recent philosophy has been preoccupied with that term. I think that this judgment applies to Parsons as much as to anyone in spite of the fact that he labelled his theory "the action frame of reference." This is a complicated issue, but basically I think it is fair to say that human agents appear in Parsons' scheme . . . as, what Garfinkel calls, "cultural dopes;" not as actors who know a great deal (discursively and tacitly) about the institutions they produce and reproduce in and through their actions. Contrast Parsons or Merton with Goffman. Why do Goffman's works have an intuitive appeal for those who have not met with much sociological writing before, while those of authors such as Parsons or Merton do not? This is not simply the result of Goffman's own literary skills, however significant they may be. It is because Goffman treats human beings as skilled and knowledgeable agents, who employ their knowledgeability routinely in the production and reproduction of social encounters. There is a strong phenomenological component in this, which is of central importance in social theory. Goffman shows us many of the things we "know" about social conventions or institutions, and which we must know for their reproduction, but which

we know in a tacit rather than an explicit sense. They become clear to us only when he points them out, but nevertheless we do already know them: and very dazzling and subtle these tacit forms of knowledge turn out to be, however much we ordinarily take them for granted as members of any given society. Functionalists, by contrast, discount agents' reasons in favor of society's reasons believing that a true sociological explanation gets "behind the backs" of the actors themselves. (Reasons, it might be emphasized, are not at all well analyzed as "manifest functions" [Giddens, 1979].)

For the sake of brevity, let me merge (3) and (4). Social systems have no needs—nor even do they have any "functional exigencies." Now there have been functionalists (e.g., Malinowski) who have held that only individuals have needs, not social systems. But most functionalists have attributed needs or requirements to social systems and have believed these have an integral explanatory role in understanding these social systems. But social systems do not have needs, at least in the sense that individual actors do. Let us consider a concrete illustration, Marx's discussion of the reserve army in the capitalist economy. Marx's argument can be read—and frequently has been read—in a functionalist vein. Capitalism has its own "needs," which the system functions to fulfill. Since the system needs a reserve army, one comes into being. The argument is sometimes stated in reverse. Since the operation of capitalism leads to the formation of a reserve army, this must be because it needs one. Neither version of the reserve army argument can be defended. Not even the most deeply sedimented institutional features of societies come about because those societies need them to do so. They come about *historically*, as a result of concrete conditions that have in every case to be directly analyzed; the same holds for their persistence.

There is only *one* logical format in which talk of system needs is viable, but it does not involve attributing empirical needs to social systems. This format on the contrary, is one of *counter-factual argument.* We can quite legitimately pose conjectural questions such as: "What would have to be the case for social system X to come about, or persist, or be transformed?" But we have to be very careful with such propositions, because they readily lend themselves to interpretation in a functionalist mode. Take as an example the statement: "In order to persist in a relatively stable form, the capitalist economy has to maintain a certain overall level of profit." The force of "has to" here is counter-factual: it involves identifying conditions that must be met if certain consequences are to obtain. The "has to" is not a property or "need" of the system.

In my recent writings I have proposed that functionalism should be replaced by what I call a *theory of structuration.* I consider that such a theory meets the criterion I mentioned before, of dispensing with the concept of "function," and with the notion of "functional explanation." It does so, however, without sacrificing the interests of functionalists in institutions, and in long-term, large-scale social processes. I will not attempt to describe this theory in detail here, but merely indicate its outline, because it relates to what I have to say about evolution. According to the theory of structuration, all social action consists of social practices, situated in time-space, and organized in a skilled and knowledgeable fashion by human agents. But human knowledgeability is always "bounded"—by unacknowledged conditions of action on the one side, and unintended consequences of action on the other. A crucial move in this theory is an attempt to transcend the opposition between "action" theories and "institutional" theories mentioned above. This move is accomplished by the concept of what I call the *duality of structure.* By the duality of structure, I mean that the structured properties of social systems are simultaneously the *medium and outcome of social acts.* One way to illustrate this idea is by taking examples from language. The structural properties of language, as qualities of a community of language speakers (e.g., syntactical rules) are drawn upon by a speaker in the production of a sentence. But the very act of speaking that sentence contributes to the reproduction of those syntactical rules as enduring properties of the language. The concept of the duality of structure, I believe, is basic to any account of social reproduction, and has no functionalist overtones at all (Giddens, 1979: Chapter 2). . . .

REFERENCES

ATKINSON, RICHARD. 1972. Orthodox Consensus and Radical Alternative. New York: Basic Books.
DEMERATH, N.J., and RICHARD PETERSON. 1967. System, Change, and Conflict. New York: Free Press.
GIDDENS, ANTHONY. 1979. Central Problems in Social Theory. London: Macmillan.
SZTOMPKA, PIOTR. 1974. System and Function. New York: Academic Press.

TOWARD A THEORY OF SOCIAL CONFLICT*

RALF DAHRENDORF

I

After an interval of almost fifty years, a theme has reappeared in sociology which has determined the origin of that discipline more than any other subject area. From Marx and Comte to Simmel and Sorel, social conflict, especially revolutions, was one of the central themes in social research. The same is true of many early Anglo-Saxon sociologists (although in their work the problem of revolution has been characteristically somewhat neglected), for example, the Webbs in England, Sumner in the United States. However, when Talcott Parsons in 1937 established a certain convergence in the sociological theories of Alfred Marshall, Émile Durkheim, Vilfredo Pareto, and Max Weber,[1] he no longer had in mind an analysis of social conflict; his was an attempt to solve the problem of integration of so-called "social systems" by an organon of interrelated categories. The new question was now "What holds societies together?"—no longer "What drives them on?" The influence of the Parsonian posing of the question on the more recent sociology (and by no means only on American sociology) can be hardly overrated. Thus it is possible that the revival of the study of social conflict in the last decades appears to many not so much a continuation of traditional research paths as a new thematic discovery—an instance of dialectic irony in the development of science.

At this time, approaches toward a systematic study of social conflict are still relatively isolated, compared with the innumerable works on social stratification or on structure and function of specific institutions, organizations, and societies. Still the thesis of a revival of the study of social conflict can be justified with regard to the works of Aron, Philip, Brinton, Kerr, Coser, Brinkmann, Geiger, Gluckmann, and others,[2] as well as an attempt to de-

*From Ralf Dahrendorf, "Toward a Theory of Social Conflict," *Journal of Conflict Resolution* 2:2 (June 1958), 170–79. Reprinted with permission of Sage Publications, Inc. This paper was translated by Anatol Rapaport, Mental Health Research Unit, University of Michigan.

termine a systematic locus and a specific framework for a theory of conflict in sociological analysis.

Types and Varieties of Social Conflict

To begin with a commonplace observation: The problem of conflict is no less complex than that of integration of societies. We now know that the attempt to reduce all actually occurring conflicts among social groups to a common principle, say that of classes, is sterile. It leads either to empty generalizations (such as "Every society experiences social conflicts") or to empirically unjustifiable oversimplifications (such as "The history of all societies so far has been a history of class struggles"). It seems advisable, first, to sort out and to classify the problems which are conceived under the general heading of "social conflict." Even a superficial reflection leads to the distinction of a series of types.

There are wars, and there are conflicts among political parties—evidently two different kinds of struggle. With regard to a given society, A, one could say there are *exogenous* conflicts brought upon or into A from the outside, and there are *endogenous* conflicts generated within A. Of these two categories, which, at least analytically, can be relatively precisely distinguished, there are again several types. Let us confine our attention for the moment—for reasons which will presently be given—to endogenous conflicts. Then further subdivisions are directly perceived: slaves versus freemen in Rome, Negroes versus whites in the United States, Protestants versus Catholics in the Netherlands, Flemings versus Walloons in Belgium, Conservatives versus Laborites in England, unions versus employers in many countries. All these are opposing groups in well-known conflicts. Perhaps each of these examples does not fall into a separate category; but certainly they cannot all be sub-sumed under a single type of social conflict. Whatever criterion one chooses for classification—for example, the objects of contention, the structural origin of the conflicting groups, the forms of conflict—several distinct types result.

The Limits and Goals of a Theory of Social Conflict

An ideal sociology cannot, in principle, exclude any of these categories and types of conflict from analysis. Nevertheless, the types mentioned do not all have the same importance for sociological analysis. A brief recollection of the intent of a sociological theory of conflict reveals that the contribution of sociology to the understanding of conflict (as well as the contribution of conflict to the social process) is in specific instances greater in some cases than in others.

The intent of a sociological theory of conflict is to overcome the predominately arbitrary nature of unexplained historical events by deriving these events from social structural elements—in other words, to explain certain processes by prognostic connections. Certainly it is important to describe the conflict between workers and employers purely as such; but it is more important to produce a proof that such a conflict is based on certain social structural arrangements and hence is bound to arise wherever such structural arrangements are given. Thus it is the task of sociology to derive conflicts from specific social structures and not to relegate these conflicts to psychological variables ("aggressiveness") or to descriptive-historical ones (the influx of Negroes into the United States) or to chance.

In the sense of strict sociological analysis, conflicts can be considered explained if they can be shown to arise from the structure of social positions independently of the orientation of populations and of historical *dei ex machina*. This is necessarily a very abstract formulation; instead of elaborating it, it may be advisable to illustrate its meaning by the following treatment of a form of social conflict. First, however, let us draw a consequence of this formulation which will help to make our problem more precise.

Since the recognition of the inadequacy of the Marxist-Leninist theory of imperialism, the explanation of exogenous conflicts on the basis of the structure of a given society is once again an open problem, the treatment of which has scarcely begun. It seems, moreover, that the explanation of exogenous conflicts by the tools of sociological structure analysis is possible only in a metaphorical sense—namely, only in case the entire societies (or less comprehensive "social systems") are taken to be the units of a new structure, that is, when C is analyzed in terms of the structure of its elements A and B without consideration of the inner structure of A and B. On these grounds it seems sensible to exclude exogenous conflict for the time being from a theory of social conflicts.

On the other hand, the above-mentioned examples of endogenous conflict, if considered from the point of view of their structural significance, fall into two groups. On the one hand, they point to conflicts which arise only in specific societies on the basis of special historical conditions (Negroes or whites in the United States, Protestants versus Catholics in the Netherlands; Flemings versus Walloons in Belgium); on the other hand, however, there are conflicts which can be understood as expressions of general structural features of societies, or of societies in the same stage of development (Conservatives versus Laborites in England; unions versus employers' associations). Certainly in both cases an analysis leading to generalization is possible: a theory of minority or religious conflict is as meaningful as that of class conflict. Nevertheless, their respective weights within a general theory of society are evidently distinguishable. It is not surprising that the "classical" theory of conflict—I mean here primarily the class theory of conflict—has, above all, called attention to such social frictions which can be derived from the structure of societies independently of structurally incidental historical data.

The following approaches toward a theory of conflict also relate themselves to conflicts based on structure. So far, we are by no means considering a general theory of social conflict, although I would undertake to defend the assertion that we are dealing here with one of the most important, if not the most important, type of social conflict. However important as problems of social conflict St. Bartholomew's Night, Crystal Night, and Little Rock may be, the French Revolution and the British General Strike of 1926 and June 17, 1953, seem to me more germane for structural analysis. To put it less dramatically, the sociological theory of conflict would do well to confine itself for the time being to an explanation of the frictions between the rulers and the ruled in given social structural organizations.

II

The explanation of motion requires two separate attacks. We must know the point of departure and the direction of motion or, better yet, the moving force. No theory of social change or of conflict can forego the description of the structural entity which undergoes change or within which conflicts occur. Such a description is offered by the integration theory of society. However, it is erroneous to assume that a description of how the elements of a structure are put together into a stable whole offers, as such, a point of departure for a structural analysis of conflict and change. So far, the claim of the so-called "structural-functional" theory of modern sociology to the status of a general theory of society is demonstrably unjustified.

Toward a Critique of a Structural-Functional Theory

This critique has been led in recent times repeatedly, most effectively by D. Lockwood.[3] It is based on a relatively simple argument. As long as we orient our analysis toward the question as to how the elements of a society are combined into a co-ordinated functioning whole, then the representation of society as a social system is the last point of reference. We are therefore faced with the task of determining certain associations, institutions, or processes within this balanced whole, that is— in Merton's definition—of determining the intentional or unintentional consequences of these associations for the functioning and the preservation of the system. In this way, we come to contentions such as "the educational system functions as a mechanism of assigning social positions," or "religion functions as an agent of integrating dominant values." The majority of sociological investigations in the last years moves in this area of analysis.

However, such an approach leads to difficulties, if we put a question of a different sort. What was the function of the English trade unions in the General Strike of 1926? What was the function of the construction worker in Stalin Allee on June 17, 1953? Without doubt, it can be argued in many cases that militant trade unions or opposition political groups and parties also contribute to the functioning of the existing system. But even when this is the case—and in the two cases cited it would be difficult to establish this—such a conclusion would say little about the role of the group in question. Moreover, it is clear that the intentional, as well as the unintentional, effects of such oppositional groups are in the contribution toward an abolition or destruction of the existing system. The structural-functional position has a comfortable label for such cases: they are "dysfunctional" organizations, institutions, or processes. But this designation again tells us less than nothing. It not only fails to explain the place of these things in the process but actually hinders such explanation by a terminology which seems to be congruent with the system but which, upon closer examination, reveals itself as a residual category. Whatever does not fit is conjured out of the world by word magic.

In every science, residual categories are a fruitful point of departure for new developments. It seems to me that a careful analysis of problems which the term "dysfunction" hides in the structural-functional theory automatically puts us on the trace of a meaningful sociological theory of conflict. At the same time, it offers a remarkable vantage point associated with an attempt of a scientific analysis of society.

Two Models of Society

If we extrapolate the analytical approaches of the structural-functional theory somewhat beyond their boundaries and investigate their implicit postulates, we can construct a model of society which lies at the base of this theory and determines its perspectives. The essential elements of this societal model are these:

1. Every society is a relatively persisting configuration of elements.
2. Every society is a well-integrated configuration of elements.
3. Every element in a society contributes to its functioning.
4. Every society rests on the consensus of its members.

It should be clear that a theory based on this model does not lend itself to the explanation, not even the description, of the phenomena of social conflict and change. For this purpose, one needs a model which takes the diametrically opposite position on all the four points above:

1. Every society is subjected at every moment to change: social change is ubiquitous.
2. Every society experiences at every moment social conflict: social conflict is ubiquitous.
3. Every element in a society contributes to its change.
4. Every society rests on constraint of some of its members by others.

The remarkable nature of our vantage point becomes evident when we examine the two groups of postulates with respect to their truth content, that is, if we ask ourselves which of the two models promises greater utility for cognition of reality. It appears that the juxtaposed pairs of postulates are in no way mutually exclusive with respect to social reality. It is impossible to decide by an empirical investigation which of the two models is more nearly correct; the postulates are not hypotheses. Moreover, it seems meaningful to say that both models are in a certain sense valid and analytically fruitful. Stability and change, integration and conflict, function and "dysfunction," consensus and constraint are, it would seem, two equally valid aspects of every imaginable society. They are dialectically separated and are exhaustive only in combination as a description of the social problems. Possibly a more general theory of society may be thought of which lifts the equivalidity of both models, the coexistence of the uncombinable, onto a higher level of generality. As long as we do not have such a theory, we must content ourselves with the finding that society presents a double aspect to the sociological understanding, each no better, no more valid, than the other. It follows that the criticism of the unapplicability of the structural-functional theory for the analysis of conflict is directed only against a claim of generality of this theory but leaves untouched its competence with respect to the problem of integration. It follows, on the other hand, also that the theory of conflict and change is not a general theory. Comparisons between natural and social sciences always carry the danger of misunder-

standing. However, it may be maintained, without attributing to this analogy more than a logical meaning, that the situation of the sociologists is not unlike that of the physicists with respect to the theory of light. Just as the physicists can solve certain problems only by assuming the wave character of light and others, on the contrary, only by assuming a corpuscular or quantum theory, so there are problems of sociology which can be adequately attacked only with an integration theory and others which require a conflict theory for a meaningful analysis. Both theories can work extensively with the same categories, but they emphasize different aspects. While the integration theory likens a society to an ellipse, a rounded entity which encloses all of its elements, conflict theory sees society rather as a hyperbola which, it is true, has the same foci but is open in many directions and appears as a tension field of the determining forces.

The Tasks of a Theory of Social Conflict

The double aspect of society and the dialectics of the two types of sociological theory are in themselves a most fruitful object of reflection. Nevertheless, another problem seems to be more urgent. The theory of social integration has recently developed to a flourishing state as the structural-functional approach in ethnology and sociology. Our theory of conflict, however, is still in a very rudimentary state. It is an approach based on postulating ubiquitous social change and social conflict, the "dysfunctionality" of all the elements of social structure, and the constraining character of social unity. Our considerations put us in a position to formulate some requirements of such a theory:

1. It should be a scientific theory (as is the theory of social integration), that is, it should be formulated with reference to a plausible and demonstrable explanation of empirical phenomena.

2. The elements of the theory should not contradict the conflict model of society.
3. The categories employed should, whenever possible, agree with those of the integration theory or at least correspond to them.
4. A conflict theory should enable us to derive social conflicts from structural arrangements and thus show these conflicts systematically generated.
5. It should account both for the multiplicity of forms of conflict and for their degrees of intensity.

The last goal of a social theory is the explanation of social change. The integration theory gives us a tool for determining the point of departure of the process. To find the locus of the forces which drive the process and social change is the task of a theory of conflict. It must develop a model which makes understandable the structural origin of social conflict. This seems possible only if we understand conflicts as struggles among social groups, that is, if we make our task precise to the extent that it reduces to the structural analysis of conflicting groups. Under this supposition three questions come especially to the forefront, which conflict theory must answer:

1. How do conflicting groups arise from the structure of society?
2. What forms can the struggles among such groups assume?
3. How does the conflict among such groups effect a change in the social structures?

III

Wherever men live together and lay foundations of forms of social organization, there are positions whose occupants have powers of command in certain contexts and over certain positions, and there are other positions whose occupants are subjected to such commands. The distinction between "up" and "down"—or, as the English say, "Them" and "Us"—is one of the fundamental experiences of most men in society, and, moreover, it appears that

this distinction is intimately connected with unequal distribution of power. The main thesis of the following attempt to construct a model for the structural analysis of conflict is that we should seek the structural origin of social conflict in the dominance relations which prevail within certain units of social organization. For these units I will use Max Weber's concept of "imperatively co-ordinated group." The thesis is not new; it is found (however often with important modifications) in the formulation of many social scientists before and after Marx. But we shall make no attempt to trace the history of this thesis.

Authority and Authority Structures

The concepts of power and authority are very complex ones. Whoever uses them is likely to be accused of lack of precision and of clarity to the extent that he tries to define them "exhaustively." Is the influence of a father on his children, the influence of an industrial combine on the government, or the influence of a demagogue on his followers an instance of an authority relation? Here, as in most other cases, it is basically not a question of a definition but rather a question of an "operational definition," as it is often called today: a method of determination which allows us to identify as such the state of affairs when we are actually confronted with it. However, for the purpose of analysis and identification, Weber's determination of authority is sufficient: "The likelihood that a command of a certain content will be obeyed by given persons."[4] This determination contains the following elements:

1. Authority denotes a relation of supra- and subordination.
2. The supra-ordinated side prescribes to the subordinated one certain behavior in the form of a command or a prohibition.
3. The supra-ordinated side has the right to make such prescriptions; authority is a legitimate relation of supra- and subordination; authority is

not based on personal or situational chance effects but rather on an expectation associated with social position.

4. The right of authority is limited to certain contents and to specific persons.
5. Failure to obey the prescriptions is sanctioned; a legal system (or a system of quasi-legal customs) guards the effectiveness of authority.

This determination of authority makes possible the identification of a cabinet minister, an employer, and a party secretary as occupants of authority positions—in contrast to an industrial syndicate or a demagogue, neither of which satisfies condition 3 above.

It is not the intention of our "definition" of authority to solve all analytical and empirical problems of this category. In fact, the very first step of our model leads us deep into these problems: in each imperatively coordinated group, two aggregates can be distinguished: those which have only general ("civil") basic rights and those which have authority rights over the former. In contrast to prestige and income, a continuum of gradual transition cannot be constructed for the distribution of authority. Rather, there is a clear dichotomy. Every position in an imperatively co-ordinated group can be recognized as belonging to one who dominates or one who is dominated. Sometimes, in view of the bureaucratic large-scale organization of modern societies—under the influence of the state—this assumption may at first sight seem problematic. However, a sharper analysis leaves no doubt that here also the split into the dominating and dominated is valid, even though in reality a considerable measure of differentiation is discernible among those in the dominating group.

The Conflict-Theory Model

The dichotomy of social roles within imperatively co-ordinated groups, the division into positive and negative dominance roles, is a fact of social structure. If and insofar as social conflicts can be referred to this factual situation, they are structurally explained. The model of analysis of social conflict which is developed against a background of an assumption of such a dichotomy involves the following steps:

1. In every imperatively co-ordinated group, the carriers of positive and negative dominance roles determine two quasi-groups with opposite latent interests. We call them "quasi-groups" because we have to do here with mere aggregates, not organized units; we speak of "latent interests," because the opposition of outlook need not be conscious on this level; it may exist only in the form of expectations associated with certain positions. The opposition of interests has here a quite formal meaning, namely, the expectation that an interest in the preservation of the status quo is associated with the positive dominance roles and an interest in the change of the status quo is associated with the negative dominance roles.
2. The bearers of positive and negative dominance roles, that is, the members of the opposing quasi-groups, organize themselves into groups with manifest interests, unless certain empirically variable conditions (the conditions of organization) intervene. Interest groups, in contrast to quasi-groups, are organized entities, such as parties, trade unions; the manifest interests are formulated programs and ideologies.
3. Interest groups which originate in this manner are in constant conflict concerned with the preservation or change in the status quo. The form and the intensity of the conflict are determined by empirically variable conditions (the conditions of conflict).
4. The conflict among interest groups in the sense of this model leads to changes in the structure of the social relations in question through changes in the dominance relations. The kind, the speed, and the depth of this development depend on empirically variable conditions (the conditions of structural change).

The intent of such a model is to delimit a problem area, to identify the factors pertinent to it, to put them into order—that is, to propose fruitful questions—and at the same time to fix precisely their analytical focus. We have delimited our problem area by viewing social conflict as a conflict among groups which emerge from the authority structure of social organizations. We have identified pertinent factors in the conditions of organization, of conflict, and of change. Their order, however, can be expressed on the basis of the model in three functions: interest groups (for example, parties) are a function of conditions of organization if an imperatively co-ordinated group is given; specific forms of conflict (e.g., parliamentary debates) are a function of the conditions of conflict if the interest groups are given; specific forms of change (e.g., revolutions) are a function of the conditions of change if the conflict among interest groups is given. Thus the task of the theory of conflict turns out to be to identify the three sets of conditions and to determine as sharply as possible their respective weight—ideally, by quantitative measure. The following remarks are hardly more than a tentative indication of the sorts of variables in question.

Empirical Conditions of Social Conflict

As far as the conditions of organization are concerned, three groups of factors come to mind. First, we have certain effective social conditions: for example, the possibility of communication among the members of the quasi-group and a certain method of recruitment into the quasi-groups. Next there are certain political conditions which must be fulfilled if interest groups are to emerge. Here, above all, a guaranty of freedom of coalition is important. Finally, certain technical conditions must be fulfilled: an organization must have material means, a founder, a leader, and an ideology.

Under conditions of conflict, two kinds are immediately conspicuous: the degree of social mobility of individuals (or of families) and the presence of effective mechanisms for regulating social conflicts. If we imagine a continuum of intensity of social conflict among interest groups, ranging from democratic debate to civil war, we may conjecture that the presence or absence of social mobility and of regulating mechanisms has considerable influence on the position of specific given conflicts on this continuum. Here, as with the other conditions, the determination of the exact weights of the factors is a task of empirical investigation.

Finally, a third group of conditions or variables determines the form and the extent of social structural changes which arise from the conflict of interest groups. Probably a relatively intimate connection exists between the intensity of the conflict and the change, that is, also between the conditions of conflict and of the structural changes. However, additional factors come into play, such as the capacity of the rulers to stay in power and the pressure potential of the dominated interest group. The sociology of revolutions and especially the unwritten sociology of uncompleted revolutions should contribute considerably to making these factors precise.

It need hardly be re-emphasized that these unsystematic observations can, as such, hardly lay a foundation of a theory of conflict. Nevertheless, we put ourselves in a position to ask meaningful questions both on the theoretical level and with respect to empirical problems. Each of the conditions mentioned offers a fruitful object of theoretically oriented investigations. And in the empirical sphere, the systematic association of factors in such an investigation redirects our questions from a haphazard search for *ad hoc* relations in the world of coincidences to a meaningful study of specific interdependencies, whose locus and meaning are fixed by a general perspective.

By the nature of the subject, our exposition up to this point had to remain somewhat abstract in form. . . .

NOTES

1. Cf. *Structure of Social Action* (New York, 1937; 2d ed., Glencoe, 1949).

2. Raymond Aron, "Social Structure and the Ruling Class," in *Class Status and Power*, ed. Reinhard Bendix and Seymour Martin Lipset (London, 1954); André Philip, *Le Socialisme trahi* (Paris, 1957); Crane Brinton, *The Anatomy of Revolution* (2d ed.; New York, 1952); Clark Kerr, "Industrial Conflict and Its Mediation," *American Journal of Sociology*, Vol. XI, No. 3 (November, 1954); Lewis Coser, *The Functions of Social Conflict* (London, 1956), and "Social Conflict and Social Change," *British Journal of Sociology*, Vol. VIII, No. 3 (September, 1957); Carl Brinkmann, *Soziologische Theorie der Revolution* (Tübingen, 1948); Theodor Geiger, *Klassengesellschaft in Schmelztiegel* (Köln-Hagen, 1949); Max Gluckmann, *Custom and Conflict in Africa* (London, 1957).

3. David Lockwood, "Some Notes on 'The Social System,'" *British Journal of Sociology*, Vol. VII, No. 2 (1956).

4. Max Weber, "Wirtschaft and Gesellschaft," in *Grundriss der Sozialökonomik*, III (3d ed.; Tübingen, 1947), 28.

SOCIAL CONFLICT
AND THE THEORY OF SOCIAL CHANGE*

LEWIS A. COSER

This paper attempts to examine some of the functions of social conflict in the process of social change. I shall first deal with some functions of conflict *within* social systems, more specifically with its relation to institutional rigidities, technical progress and productivity, and will then concern ourselves with the relation between social conflict and the changes *of* social systems.

A central observation of George Sorel in his *Reflections on Violence* which has not as yet been accorded sufficient attention by sociologists may serve us as a convenient springboard. Sorel wrote:

We are today faced with a new and unforeseen fact—a middle class which seeks to weaken its own strength. The race of bold captains who made the greatness of modern industry disappears to make way for an ultracivilized aristocracy which asks to be allowed to live in peace.

The threatening decadence may be avoided if the proletariat hold on with obstinacy to revolu-

tionary ideas. *The antagonistic classes influence each other in a partly indirect but decisive manner.* Everything may be saved if the proletariat, by their use of violence, restore to the middle class something of its former energy.[1]

Sorel's specific doctrine of class struggle is not of immediate concern here. What is important for us is the idea that conflict (which Sorel calls violence, using the word in a very special sense) prevents the ossification of the social system by exerting pressure for innovation and creativity. Though Sorel's call to action was addressed to the working class and its interests, he conceived it to be of general importance for the total social system; to his mind the gradual disappearance of class conflict might well lead to the decadence of European culture. A social system, he felt, was in need of conflict if only to renew its energies and revitalize its creative forces.

This conception seems to be more generally applicable than to class struggle alone. Conflict within and between groups in a society can prevent accommodations and habitual relations from progressively impoverishing creativity. The clash of values and interests,

*From Lewis Coser, "Social Conflict and the Theory of Social Change," *British Journal of Sociology* 8:3 (September 1957), 197–207. Reprinted with permission of the *British Journal of Sociology*.

the tension between what is and what some groups feel ought to be, the conflict between vested interests and new strata and groups demanding their share of power, wealth and status, have been productive of vitality; note for example the contrast between the "frozen world" of the Middle Ages and the burst of creativity that accompanied the thaw that set in with Renaissance civilization.

This is, in effect, the application of John Dewey's theory of consciousness and thought as arising in the wake of obstacles to the interaction of groups. "Conflict is the gadfly of thought. It stirs us to observation and memory. It instigates to invention. It shocks us out of sheep-like passivity, and sets us at noting and contriving. . . . Conflict is a sine qua non of reflection and ingenuity."[2]

Conflict not only generates new norms, new institutions, as I have pointed out elsewhere,[3] it may be said to be stimulating directly in the economic and technological realm. Economic historians often have pointed out that much technological improvement has resulted from the conflict activity of trade unions through the raising of wage levels. A rise in wages usually has led to a substitution of capital investment for labour and hence to an increase in the volume of investment. Thus the extreme mechanization of coal-mining in the United States has been partly explained by the existence of militant unionism in the American coalfields.[4] A recent investigation by Sidney C. Sufrin[5] points to the effects of union pressure, "goading management into technical improvement and increased capital investment." Very much the same point was made recently by the conservative British *Economist* which reproached British unions for their "moderation" which it declared in part responsible for the stagnation and low productivity of British capitalism; it compared their policy unfavourably with the more aggressive policies of American

unions whose constant pressure for higher wages has kept the American economy dynamic.[6] . . .

We have so far discussed change within systems, but changes of systems are of perhaps even more crucial importance for sociological inquiry. Here the sociology of Karl Marx serves us well. Writes Marx in a polemic against Proudhon:

Feudal production also had two antagonistic elements, which were equally designated by the names of *good side* and *bad side* of feudalism, without regard being had to the fact that it is always the evil side which finishes by overcoming the good side. It is the bad side that produces the movement which makes history, by constituting the struggle. If at the epoch of the reign of feudalism the economists, enthusiastic over the virtues of chivalry, the delightful harmony between rights and duties, the patriarchal life of the towns, the prosperous state of domestic industry in the country, of the development of industry organized in corporations, guilds and fellowships, in fine of all which constitutes the beautiful side of feudalism, had proposed to themselves the problem of eliminating all which cast a shadow upon this lovely picture—serfdom, privilege, anarchy—what would have been the result? All the elements which constituted the struggle would have been annihilated, and the development of the bourgeoisie would have been stifled in the germ. They would have set themselves the absurd problem of eliminating history.[7]

According to Marx, conflict leads not only to ever-changing relations within the existing social structure, but the total social system undergoes transformation through conflict.

During the feudal period, the relations between serf and lord, between burgher and gentry, underwent many changes both in law and in fact. Yet conflict finally led to a breakdown of all feudal relations and hence to the rise of a new social system governed by different patterns of social relations.

It is Marx's contention that the negative element, the opposition, conditions the change when conflict between the sub-groups of a system becomes so sharpened that at a certain point this system breaks down. Each social system contains elements of strain and of potential conflict; if in the analysis of the social structure of a system these elements are ignored, if the adjustment of patterned relations is the only focus of attention, then it is not possible to anticipate basic social change. Exclusive attention to wont and use, to the customary and habitual bars access to an understanding of possible latent elements of strain which under certain conditions eventuate in overt conflict and possibly in a basic change of the social structure. This attention should be focused, in Marx's view, on what evades and resists the patterned normative structure and on the elements pointing to new and alternative patterns emerging from the existing structure. What is diagnosed as disease from the point of view of the institutionalized pattern may, in fact, says Marx, be the first birth pang of a new one to come; not wont and use but the break of wont and use is focal. The "matters-of-fact" of a "given state of affairs" when viewed in the light of Marx's approach, become limited, transitory; they are regarded as containing the germs of a process that leads beyond them.[8]

Yet, not all social systems contain the same degree of conflict and strain. The sources and incidence of conflicting behaviour in each particular system vary according to the type of structure, the patterns of social mobility, of ascribing and achieving status and of allocating scarce power and wealth, as well as the degree to which a specific form of distribution of power, resources and status is accepted by the component actors within the different sub-systems. But if, within any social structure, there exists an excess of claimants over opportunities for adequate reward, there arises strain and conflict.

The distinction between changes *of* systems and changes *within* systems is, of course, a rel-

ative one. There is always some sort of continuity between a past and a present, or a present and a future social system; societies do not die the way biological organisms do, for it is difficult to assign precise points of birth or death to societies as we do with biological organisms. One may claim that all that can be observed is a change of the organization of social relations; but from one perspective such change may be considered re-establishment of equilibrium while from another it may be seen as the formation of a new system. . . .

In what follows the distinction between strains, conflicts and disturbances within a system which lead to a re-establishment of equilibrium, and conflicts which lead to the establishment of new systems and new types of equilibria, will be examined. Such an examination will be most profitably begun by considering what Thorstein Veblen has called "Vested Interests."[9]

Any social system implies an allocation of power, as well as wealth and status positions among individual actors and component subgroups. As has been pointed out, there is never complete concordance between what individuals and groups within a system consider their just due and the system of allocation. Conflict ensues in the effort of various frustrated groups and individuals to increase their share of gratification. Their demands will encounter the resistance of those who previously had established a "vested interest" in a given form of distribution of honour, wealth and power.

To the vested interests, an attack against their position necessarily appears as an attack upon the social order. Those who derive privileges from a given system of allocation of status, wealth and power will perceive an attack upon these prerogatives as an attack against the system itself.

However, mere "frustration" will not lead to a questioning of the legitimacy of the position of the vested interests, and hence to conflict. Levels of aspiration as well as feelings of deprivation are relative to institutionalized expectations and are established through comparison.[10] When social systems have institutionalized goals and values to govern the conduct of component actors, but limit access to these goals for certain members of the society, "departures from institutional requirements" are to be expected.[11] Similarly, if certain groups within a social system compare their share in power, wealth and status honour with that of other groups *and* question the legitimacy of this distribution, discontent is likely to ensue. If there exist no institutionalized provisions for the expression of such discontents, departures from what is required by the norms of the social system may occur. These may be limited to "innovation" or they may consist in the rejection of the institutionalized goals. Such "rebellion" "involves a genuine transvaluation, where the direct or vicarious experience of frustration leads to full denunciation of previously prized values."[12] Thus it will be well to distinguish between those departures from the norms of a society which consist in mere "deviation" and those which involve the formation of distinctive patterns and new value systems.

What factors lead groups and individuals to question at a certain point the legitimacy of the system of distribution of rewards, lies largely outside the scope of the present inquiry. The intervening factors can be sought in the ideological, technological, economic or any other realm. It is obvious, moreover, that conflict may be a result just as much as a source of change. A new invention, the introduction of a new cultural trait through diffusion, the development of new methods of production or distribution, etc., will have a differential impact within a social system. Some strata will feel it to be detrimental to their material or ideal interests, while others will feel their position strengthened through its introduction. Such disturbances in the equilibrium of the system lead to conditions in which groups or individual actors no longer do willingly what they have to do and do willingly what they are not supposed to do. Change, no matter what its source, breeds strain and conflict.

Yet, it may be well to repeat that mere "frustration" and the ensuing strains and tensions do not necessarily lead to group conflict. Individuals under stress may relieve their tension through "acting out" in special safety-valve institutions in as far as they are provided for in the social system; or they may "act out" in a deviant manner, which may have serious dysfunctional consequences for the system, and bring about change in this way. This, however, does not reduce the frustration from which escape has been sought since it does not attack their source.

If, on the other hand, the strain leads to the emergence of specific new patterns of behaviour of whole groups of individuals who pursue "the optimization of gratification"[13] by choosing what they consider appropriate means for the maximization of rewards, social change which reduces the sources of their frustration may come about. This may happen in two ways: if the social system is flexible enough to adjust to conflict situations we will deal with change *within* the system. If, on the other hand, the social system is not able to readjust itself and allows the accumulation of conflict, the "aggressive" groups, imbued with a new system of values which threatens to split the general consensus of the society and imbued with an ideology which "objectifies" their claims, may become powerful enough to overcome the resistance of vested interests and bring about the breakdown of the system and the emergence of a new distribution of social values.[14]

In his *Poverty of Philosophy*, Marx was led to

consider the conditions under which economic classes constitute themselves:

Economic conditions have first transformed the mass of the population into workers. The domination of capital created for this mass a common situation and common interest. This mass was thus already a class as against capital, but not for itself. It is in the struggle . . . that the mass gathers together and constitutes itself as a class for itself. The interests which it defends become class interests.[15]

With this remarkable distinction between class *in itself* and class *for itself* (which unfortunately he didn't elaborate upon in later writings though it informs all of them—if not the writings of most latter-day "marxists"), Marx illuminates a most important aspect of group formation: group belongingness is established by an objective conflict situation—in this case a conflict of interests; but only by experiencing this antagonism, that is, by becoming aware of it and by acting it out, does the group (or class) establish its identity.

When changes in the equilibrium of a society lead to the formation of new groupings or to the strengthening of existing groupings that set themselves the goal of overcoming resistance of vested interests through conflict, changes in structural relations, as distinct from simple "maladjustment," can be expected.

What Robert Park said about the rise of nationalist and racial movements is more generally applicable:

They strike me as natural and wholesome disturbances of the social routine, the effect of which is to arouse in those involved a lively sense of common purpose and to give those who feel themselves oppressed the inspiration of a common cause. . . . The effect of this struggle is to increase the solidarity and improve the morale of the "oppressed" minority.[16]

It is this sense of common purpose arising in and through conflict that is peculiar to the behavior of individuals who meet the challenge of new conditions by a group-forming and value-forming response. Strains which result in no such formations of new conflict groups or strengthening of old ones may contribute to bringing about change, but a type of change that fails to reduce the sources of strain since by definition tension-release behaviour does not involve purposive action. Conflict through group action, on the other hand, is likely to result in a "deviancy" which may be the prelude of new patterns and reward systems apt to reduce the sources of frustration.

If the tensions that need outlets are continually reproduced within the structure, abreaction through tension-release mechanisms may preserve the system but at the risk of ever-renewed further accumulation of tension. Such accumulation eventuates easily in the irruption of destructive unrealistic conflict. If feelings of dissatisfaction, instead of being suppressed or diverted are allowed expression against "vested interests," and in this way to lead to the formation of new groupings within the society, the emergence of genuine transvaluations is likely to occur. Sumner saw this very well when he said: "We want to develop symptoms, we don't want to suppress them."[17]

Whether the emergence of such new groupings or the strengthening of old ones with the attendant increase in self-confidence and self-esteem on the part of the participants will lead to a change *of* or *within* the system will depend on the degree of cohesion that the system itself has attained. A well-integrated society will tolerate and even welcome group conflict; only a weakly integrated one must fear it. The great English liberal John Morley said it very well:

If [the men who are most attached to the reigning order of things] had a larger faith in the stability for which they profess so great an anxiety, they would be more free alike in understanding and temper to deal generously, honestly and effectively with those whom they count imprudent innovators.[18]

NOTES

1. George Sorel, *Reflections on Violence*, ch. 2, par. 11.

2. John Dewey, *Human Nature and Conduct*, N.Y., The Modern Library, 1930, p. 300.

3. Lewis A. Coser, *The Functions of Social Conflict*, Glencoe, Ill.; London, Routledge and Kegan Paul, 1956.

4. Cf. McAlister Coleman, *Men and Coal*, N.Y., Farrar and Rinehart, 1943.

5. *Union Wages and Labor's Earnings*, Syracuse, Syracuse Univ. Press, 1951.

6. Quoted by Will Herberg, "When Social Scientists View Labor," *Commentary*, Dec. 1951, XII, 6, pp. 590–6. See also Seymour Melman, *Dynamic Factors in Industrial Productivity*, Oxford, Blackwell, 1956, on the effects of rising wage levels on productivity.

7. Karl Marx, *The Poverty of Philosophy*, Chicago, Charles H. Kerr & Co., 1910, p. 132.

8. For an understanding of Marx's methodology and its relation to Hegelian philosophy, see Herbert Marcuse, *Reason and Revolution*, N.Y., O.U.P., 1941.

9. See especially *The Vested Interests and the State of the Industrial Arts*, N.Y., 1919.

10. See Robert K. Merton and Alice S. Kitt, "Contributions to the Theory of Reference Group Behaviour" Pp. 40–105 in R.K. Merton and P. Lazarsfeld, eds. *Continuities in Social Research* [New York, Free Press, 1950] for a development of the concept of "relative deprivation" (originally suggested by Stouffer et al. in *The American Soldier*) and its incorporation into the framework of a theory of reference groups.

11. This whole process is exhaustively discussed by Merton in his paper on "Social Structure and Anomie," *Social Theory and Social Structure* [Glencoe, Ill., 1949].

12. Ibid., p. 145.

13. Talcott Parsons, *The Social System* [London, Tavistock Publications, 1951], p. 498.

14. R.K. Merton, *Social Theory and Social Structure*, op. cit., pp. 42–3 and 116–17.

15. Karl Marx, *The Poverty of Philosophy*, op. cit., pp. 188–9.

16. Robert E. Park, "Personality and Cultural Conflict," *Publications of the Am. Soc. Soc.*, 25, 1931, pp. 95–110. See p. 107.

17. Wm. G. Sumner, *War and Other Essays*, New Haven, Yale University Press, 1913, p. 241.

18. John Morley, *On Compromise*, London, Macmillan & Co., 1917, p. 263.

THREE FACES OF CRUELTY:
TOWARDS A COMPARATIVE SOCIOLOGY OF VIOLENCE*

RANDALL COLLINS

(margin handwriting: Impersonal nature of history)

To the comparative sociologist, history shows itself on two levels. For the most part it is the site of puzzles and arabesque causalities fascinating to the mind of a theorist. Yet there is another level that occasionally jolts the scholar out of his thoughts—the sense of historical lives as they were actually lived, day by day, moment by moment. Our theories and concepts compress and abstract; to speak of the transformation of the state or the rise of a religion is to look down the decades, if not the centuries, and necessarily to pass over most of the moments and feelings of most of the people involved. To conceive past societies from their great relics of art and literature draws one ever farther from the brutal reality. For to empathize with the human reality of history is to receive a shock, as in the following glimpse of ancient China which brought to an end for me several months of fascinated unravelling of the patterns of Chinese history:

*From Randall Collins, "Three Faces of Cruelty: Towards a Comparative Sociology of Violence," *Theory and Society* 1:4 (Winter 1974), 415–23, 431–40. Reprinted by permission of Kluwer Academic Publishers.

Once a man of Ch'u named Mr. Ho, having found a piece of jade matrix in the Ch'u Mountains, took it to court and presented it to King Li. King Li instructed the jeweler to examine it, and the jeweler reported, "It is only a stone." The king, supposing that Ho was trying to deceive him, ordered that his left foot be cut off in punishment. In time King Li passed away and King Wu came to the throne, and Ho once more took his matrix and presented it to King Wu. King Wu ordered his jeweler to examine it, and again the jeweler reported, "It is only a stone." The King, supposing that Ho was trying to deceive him as well, ordered that his right foot be cut off. Ho, clasping the matrix to his breast, went to the foot of the Ch'u Mountains, where he wept for three days and nights, and when all his tears were cried out, he wept blood in their place. The King, hearing of this, sent someone to question him. "Many people in the world have had their feet amputated—why do you weep so piteously over it?" the man asked. He replied, "I do not grieve because my feet have been cut off. I grieve because a precious jewel is dubbed a mere stone, and a man of integrity is called a deceiver. This is why I weep." The King then ordered the jeweler to cut and polish the matrix, and when he had done so a precious jewel emerged.[1]

The existence of punishment by mutilation is no surprise to the reader in Chinese history.

What shocked, was the blasé question: "Many people in the world have had their feet amputated—why do you weep so piteously over it?" This smug conclusion, redolent with Confucian meritocracy, only underlines the viciousness of the prevailing attitude. Shang bronzes and 800-year cycles lost their charm, and I closed for the time my books on China.

The prevailing reality of world history is violence. "History is a slaughterbench . . . ," cried Hegel, and James Joyce declared, "History is a nightmare from which I am trying to awake." And it is not merely the violence of a machine out of control; the disturbing thing is the viciousness, the vindictiveness, the deliberate torture in so much of it. Beneath the sociologist's patterns lies the personal dimension of evil; the patterns of history are the work of demons.

This is an attempt at exorcising those demons. It is not a theodicy; the problem is not to justify evil, but to explain it. Is there a pattern, a meaning to the cruelty itself? For it is only in isolating a causal theory that we are able to deal with cruelty; the point is not to learn to live with the demons, but to take away their power.

VIOLENCE AND GROUP STRUCTURE

A sociology of violence, in fact, already exists. Above all, we find it in the sociological tradition of France with its emphasis on the logic of emotions. Tocqueville, for instance, was struck by the degree of public benevolence in the America of the 1830's, the extent of personal sympathy and aid to strangers. He attributed this to the condition of political equality, which made it possible for individuals to empathize with one another; to prove his point, he presents a comparison with the moral atmosphere of France in the 17th century:

Aux Rochers, October 30, 1675

Your letter from Aix, my daughter, is droll enough.

At least, read your letters over again before sending them; allow yourself to be surprised by the pretty things that you have put into them and console yourself by this pleasure for the trouble you have had in writing so many. Then you have kissed all of Provence, have you? There would be no satisfaction in kissing all of Brittany, unless one likes to smell of wine . . . Do you wish to hear the news from Rennes? A tax of a hundred thousand crowns has been imposed upon the citizens; and if this sum is not produced within four-and-twenty hours, it is to be doubled and collected by the soldiers. They have cleared the houses and sent away the occupants of the great streets and forbidden anybody to receive them on pain of death; so that the poor wretches (old men, women near their confinement, and children included) may be seen wandering around and crying on their departure from this city, without knowing where to go, and without food or a place to lie in. Day before yesterday a fiddler was broken on the wheel for getting up a dance and stealing some stamped paper. He was quartered after death, and his limbs exposed at the four corners of the city. Sixty citizens have been thrown in prison, and the business of punishing them is to begin tomorrow. This province sets a fine example to the others, teaching them above all that of respecting the governors and their wives, and of never throwing stones into their gardens.

Yesterday, a delightful day, Madame de Tarenté visited these wilds: there is no question about preparing a chamber or a collation; she comes by the gate, and returns the same way . . .

It would be a mistake to suppose that Madame de Sévigné, who wrote these lines, was a selfish or cruel person, she was passionately attached to her children and very ready to sympathize in the sorrows of her friends; nay, her letters show that she treated her vassals and servants with kindness and indulgence. But Madam de Sévigné had no clear notion of suffering in anyone who was not a person of quality.[2] It is the group boundaries that determine the extent of human sympathy; within those boundaries, humanity prevails; outside them, torture is inflicted without a qualm.

The same approach to morality is taken by Durkheim. In his work, Tocqueville's observation becomes a systematic theory. Moral ideas reflect social boundaries; ceremonial observances test group membership and moral worth; God represents society, and changes as society changes shape. Thus, in the world of mutually isolated tribal societies, injunctions on killing, stealing, lying and other offenses extend only up to the boundary of each group; with the extension of the mutual links of an elaborate division of labor, the moral sense expands, becomes more abstract and universal, less concrete and particular. This insight was expanded by Weber, who understood that the abstract, philosophical world religions signified a shift in the social structure, from the mutual moral isolation of kin and ethnic groups, to a cosmopolitan society with universal political and economic possibilities.

Reading this convergence, some theorists such as Talcott Parsons have interpreted history as moral progress, a gradual extension of the collective conscience and an upgrading of moral obligations.[3] From the particularisms and ceremonial concerns of membership in primitive tribal societies, there is an extension of the scope of humanity, emerging into a potential universal brotherhood by the rise of Christianity and the other great world religions, and culminating in the superior mildness and pan-empathy of an advanced division of labor.

An evolutionary interpretation of Durkheim and Tocqueville's insights, however, does not seem warranted. Some of the greatest displays of cruelty in history were carried out by the universal religions, especially Christianity and Islam; one has reason to doubt that the group boundaries focused on in this version are at the center of the matter. It is true that a decline in institutionalized ferociousness can be discerned in the past two hundred years, but this only reminds us that

cruelty comes in more than one form. The concern with alienation in the modern era points to a peculiarly modern form of brutality. Still a third dimension is suggested by the line of thought opened up by Nietzsche and Freud (and echoed in Weber): the migration of cruelty to the interior of the individual mind in the form of psychic repression.

The Durkheimian mechanism takes us in the right direction; we can find a key to cruelty in the connection between morality and the boundaries of group inclusion and exclusion. A moral evolutionism, however, is not a reliable guide. Moreover, additional dimensions must be added to the Durkheimian group mechanism, above all, those of stratification within and among groups. Georges Sorel, yet another of the French analysts of the logic of violent emotions, proposes that not all violence is of the same sort: there is "force" used by dominant classes in a vindictive (and secretly terrified) upholding of their power; and there is "violence" of the rebellious under-class, with its clean moral purity, without viciousness but with the clarity of practical work.[4] It will not do to regard all violence as immoral, in the manner of contemporary pacifists or over-domesticated liberals, for morality not only determines violence in a negative way—in the sense that the boundaries of the group mark the limit outside of which violence is allowed—but also in a positive way. Durkheim saw this clearly enough in his theory of the way in which punishment of transgressors against the group's standards reunifies the group in its righteous indignation. Sorel saw this in the external context as well: the height of morality is in the willingness to endanger oneself in combat for the group against its enemies, and hence violent confrontation is the basis of all the moral virtues.

The key to an understanding of violence, then, is above all the structure of solidary groups and the moralities that reflect their emotional ties. The moral boundaries may set some persons beyond the pale of moral obligation, but they may also organize confrontations that make violence not just morally indifferent but morally motivated. Add to this the internal boundaries of stratification, and we find that moral claims and corresponding forms of violence exist also in the internal struggle for domination or liberation. When we pursue these structures into more complex forms, we find routinized and internalized forms of these moralities and cruelties.

In what follows, an explanation of human cruelty will be sought along three principal dimensions. First ferociousness: *homo lupus homini.* This is the dimension of overt brutality; its explanation leads us along the lines of Tocqueville, Durkheim and Sorel, into a consideration of group boundaries, external and internal. Second, callousness: brutality routinized and bureaucratized, cruelty without passion. Our theoretical leads here extend the Durkeimian model into the themes of Marx and Weber. Third, asceticism: the turning of cruelty against oneself and against others with whom one has solidarity. Here, the leads are provided by Nietzsche and Freud, which we may assimilate into the preceding sociological theory.

I. FEROCIOUSNESS: THE VIOLENCE OF MAN AND ANIMAL

Consider the extremes of overt brutality:

Mutilation: punishment not by death, but by life at its lowest level. The amputation of feet or hands, or ears—so common in ancient Rome, China, Mesopotamia, Palestine and in the Arab societies; the gouging out of eyes. The intent is not merely punishment, but prolonged misery and humiliation. This is especially evident in sexual mutilation, prominent in extremely male-oriented societies: the great Han historian, Ssu-ma Ch'ien, castrated for an honest but unfavorable memorandum to the Emperor; the Turkish sultan of Egypt punishing a rebellion in the Sudan by castrating the men and amputating the breasts of the women.[5] Mutilation might be combined with execution, always in a public form (as in the 17th century European case described by Tocqueville); clearly, public humiliation is at the essence of the phenomenon.

Torture: the deliberate prolongation and refinement of pain, usually dramatized and timed to maximize psychological dread. Torture has been routinely used in many judicial systems as part of the examination of prisoners before trial. Yet as a system for collecting evidence (as has been pointed out by rationalist humanists since Roman times), it is inefficient, precisely because it usually produces whatever reports or fabrications the victims think their torturers wish to hear. Clearly, the purpose of torture is not on this level; it is not to gather evidence, but to enforce submission. The cruelty is not incidental; it is the main purpose.

Peremptory executions: the awesomeness of the powerful lord was usually demonstrated in his death-dealing powers: Attila the Hun with his piles of skulls, King David with the heads of his enemies displayed on a spike.[6] This was the extreme dramatization of arbitrary authority.

Human sacrifices: ritual killing as part of a religious ceremony, with a victim offered to the sacred powers of the other world.[7] These are of two types: sacrifices related to periodic fertility celebrations, especially in advanced horticultural societies (e.g., the Aztecs, the Benin of West Africa, the Dionysian sacrifices that entered Greece from Asia Minor); and funerals of aristocrats (e.g., Shang China or the Hindu suttee) in which slaves and wives follow the dead lord to his grave.

Ritual warhunts: warfare as a ritual frenzy, built up by dancing, drinking or drugs, and culminating in killing patterned after the hunt.[8] The victim is sometimes ritually consumed; in its extreme—cannibalism—he is actually eaten, just like an animal. Not only are the victims treated as animals; the hunters themselves emulate the pack frenzy of carnivorous mammals that hunt their prey in groups.

The explanation of these forms of overt cruelty fits the Durkheim/Tocqueville model. In each case, the violence is practiced by one group against another to dramatize the fact that the human community and its ties extend only to a certain limit, and that persons outside are alien and subordinate. The kinds of group boundaries are not the same in each instance. Ritual warhunts are found almost exclusively in simple horticultural, hunting, or pastoral tribes, where moral ties are very localistic indeed.[9] Human sacrifices, especially in the form of fertility cults, are found primarily in advanced horticultural societies, in which the religion is a divine kingship or a theocracy of priests. The sacrifice supports the gulf between the divine rulers and their subjects; but in fact, the latter are divided into two groups for moral purposes, corresponding to those under the protection of the local gods and those who are not, and hence, it is almost always captives or slaves from other societies who are the victims of human sacrifices.

This is also true to a degree of funeral sacrifices; the Shang rulers, the pre-iron age (advanced horticultural) dynasty of China, raided other groups for slaves precisely in order to sacrifice them (and like the slave-owning Greeks made a very strong distinction between civilized, i.e., literate human beings, and barbarians fit for slavery and sacrifice). Slavery, in general, it should be noted, is based on these same ritual barriers between groups, especially bolstered by religious communities; slavery in Northern Europe died out with the conversion of the Slavs to Christianity, and it is clearly the extension of Christian missionary activity and the decline of African religion among black slaves that gen-

erated the moral sentiments of the anti-slavery movements in America and Britain.

The Hindu suttee—the burning of widows on their husbands' funeral pyres—is in a slightly different category, since Indian society in general has been relatively free from overt violence, for reasons to be considered below. The sacrifice is of women only; and women are in the category of a subordinate but omnipresent group within Hindu society. As such, they are appropriate candidates for human sacrifice.

Peremptory executions, torture, and mutilation are all characteristic of iron-age (agrarian) societies which are highly stratified around a patrimonial form of government. These, indeed, are the most highly stratified societies in world history;[10] and the stratification largely takes the form of external relations of dominance. These are conquest states, often over ethnically diverse areas; administration is tributary rather than intensive, with the local social structure left intact. Hence the moral boundaries along ethnic/religious lines become translated into boundaries along levels of stratification; extreme punishment of the lower by the higher is not only morally neutral, but often is exacerbated into a Sorelian frenzy of defense of the integrity of the dominant group. Hence the public dramatic nature of patrimonial mutilations, tortures, executions: the public is to be impressed that the status community of the aristocracy is not to be infringed in any way, without the most heinous punishment. These cruelties are not only deliberate, they are ceremonially recurrent defenses of the structure of group domination.

In comparing human beings and their activities with those of animals, it appears that the above five types of cruelty constitute a scale. Ritual warhunts are the most animal-like; tortures and mutilations are the most human. That is to say, violence among animals involves a building up of frenzy through an interchange of instinctual gestures. The pack of wolves or rats work each other up into shared ferociousness, which enables them to kill as a team.[11] In this, animals show the same in-group solidarity through arousal against an enemy that Sorel proposed for humans; and indeed their post-kill "celebration" in the form of eating their victim together has its human parallels as well.

The tribal ceremonies designed to stir up the war-frenzy seem to be modeled on those of hunting animals; the fact that these are characteristic of societies with little or no permanent stratification of their own (because of the lack of surplus and permanent wealth) suggests that this democracy of the pack is the only form of group aggression compatible with their usual social organization. It also fits well with the rigid boundaries between tribes often found in this situation; alien tribes may appear as distinct species to each other as do the animals which they often take for their totems.

Compare this relatively direct emotional arousal of the cannibals with the psychology of mutilation or torture. The animal is aroused (the human animal invents ways to do this deliberately), he attacks, he eats. Except for some sense of the fear displayed by his retreating victim, there is no empathy. The torturer or the mutilator, however, could not even attempt his arts without a capacity for taking the role of the other. The torturer does not kill and eat; he concentrates instead on inflicting pain, and above all, in conveying to his victim his intentions and powers for inflicting this pain. For the animal, terror is only an incident in the combat; for the torturer, it is the prime target. Torture and mutilation, then, are distinctively human acts; they are indeed advanced human acts. The boundaries between groups are involved, making possible the detachment that allows (and motivates) a free use of cruelty; but there is a skill at empathizing across the boundary, enough

to be able to gauge the effects of cruelty on its victim. This distinctively human violence becomes symbolic; torture and mutilation are above all forms of communication usable as threats and supports for claims of complete domination. "I can get inside your mind," the torturer boasts: "don't even think of resistance." Mutilation and other public punishments are above all violence to one's social image, and hence are pre-eminently usable for upholding inter-group stratification.

In this perspective, cruelty bears a relation to technological and social evolution. The refined reflexivity of mutilation and torture reflects a more subtle development of human cognitive faculties than the direct emotional arousal of the war-hunt; the human sacrifice is in the middle, organized in a self-consciously religious form but with little attention to refining the pains of the victim. This is borne out by the types of societies in which each of these is commonly found. War-hunts are found primarily in unstratified primitive horticultural, hunting, or pastoral societies; here, external boundaries among groups are very strong, but the external relations are so episodic as to constitute (when they are violent relations) only brief fights, animal-like in their intensity and directness. Human sacrifice is found primarily in advanced horticultural societies, especially around the institution of the divine king or reigning priests, and reflects the gulf between dominant and dominated groups. But such stratification is nevertheless very local in scope; the ruler's power is still very circumscribed by surrounding councils and by the weakness of military technology and administrative organization. Cruelty is now used to uphold the awesomeness of the ruler, but only on limited, highly ceremonial occasions, and without any personal element: a victim is offered to the gods in the name of the society. The extremes of refined cruelty are found in advanced iron-age societies, with their great military powers and their high degree of warfare. Patrimonial administration maintains moral boundaries among groups, but the great territorial extension of such states and the prevailing tone of military conflict bring a great many warrior-contenders into the contest. Domination, unstable as it is under such circumstances, is sought with the refinements that come with a literate mentality; a sharp (if unstable) order of internal stratification appears—indeed, the sharpest in all of history—and ferocious and humiliating extremes of violence are used to maintain it.

If we stop at this point and this level of abstraction, it appears that cruelty actually increases with evolutionary advance.[12] The trend is even stronger if the negative instances are brought in, the examples of societies which show relatively little cruelty and violence. Hunting-and-gathering societies (as far as we can tell) and simple horticultural societies often are relatively peaceful; only a minority are cannibalistic or otherwise warlike, and their violence is very sporadic, external, and unrefined with respect to deliberate cruelty. Compared to this, the height of ferociousness in world history is found among iron-age, agrarian societies, and indeed, among the highly advanced civilizations of this type: ancient Rome, European Christianity, Islam.

The explanation offered here, however, is not an evolutionary one, or even an inverse (or, as we will see, bell-shaped) evolutionary pattern. The variations in group structure that make up the principal explanatory factors are not distributed in a simple way across technological levels. Hence, it is possible to explore this hypothesis into more refined, horizontal comparisons. . . .

The Decline of Ferocious Violence

Modern society has seen an abrupt decline in ferocity. Torture, mutilation, exemplary punishment have disappeared as ideals; while these practices still occur they do so privately and secretly—in the hidden interrogation rooms of police stations, in the personal interaction between guard and prisoner—rather than as the explicit, ceremonial enactments fundamental to the social order. Executions are now to be humane and relatively painless, and are carried out in private; their justification is generally held to be of a rational, educative, warning nature, not passionate vengeance. Ferocity in war becomes atrocity, to be hidden, or even expiated, not gloried in. The heads of malefactors are no longer displayed on spikes, but buried from view.

At what point does the transition come about? We have seen that it does not depend on the universal religions per se, least of all historical Christianity. The movement against ferocity, rather, is a secularizing movement, originating perhaps with Erasmus and the tolerant rationalists who opposed the fanaticisms of the Reformation period; it gained ground with the anti-religious *philosophes* of the French Enlightenment and their British utilitarian counterparts; and began to have a practical effect with the judicial reforms, the anti-slavery campaigns, and other benevolent movements of the 19th century. It is true that a number of liberal (non-ritualist, non-traditionalist) Christian reformers were involved in these movements; but in general, it indicates a break with the ritual boundaries of stratification upheld by traditional religion. This is clearest in the case of the most vehement enemies of religion, the socialists and the communist radicals, who perhaps for the first time extended altruism into a positive concern for universal human happiness, rather than merely a token concern for suffering as an ongoing part of an order of privilege and deference.

In terms of our theoretical principles, the explanation seems to be structural shift. Modern industrial society, for the first time, makes for a shift in patterns of interpersonal interaction that destroy the traditional ceremonial barriers among groups. Above all, the fortified household, with its support for the moral absolutism of the family community and its internal authority structure, gives way to the community of small private households;[13] urbanism, mass transportation, large-scale work and business organizations, mass education, all contribute towards the replacement of older ritual barriers with a new form of ritual co-membership. The social conditions for the human community, in general, emerge for the first time. Along with this, differential resources remain in existence, and the struggle for power, wealth and prestige goes on. But a crucial earlier resource—freely available private violence—is no longer permissible because of the monopolization of violence by the modern state and the ritual barriers that both allowed its use and motivated the retention of a specific deference structure have largely disappeared. With the passing of these conditions, the ceremonial ideal of ferocity has disappeared.

In its place, we have two conflicting tendencies. On the one hand, conditions favor universal movements, including those proclaiming extreme forms of altruism. At the same time, the large-scale and remote organizational forms of modern society do not eliminate the tools of violence and manipulation, but only depersonalize them. Turning from the evil of ferocity, modern social structure delivers us into the hands of another evil: callousness. And in the very mobilization of modern groups there emerges still another side of altruism: demands upon the individual in the form of asceticism.

II. CALLOUSNESS AND BUREAUCRATIZATION

Callousness is cruelty without passion: the kind of hardship or violence people may inflict on others without a special intent to hurt. The subject of the violence is simply an instrument or an obstacle, and his suffering is merely an incidental (usually ignored) feature of some other intention. In this sense, the structural conditions for callousness must be very different from those that produce ferocious violence. Torture, mutilation, and exemplary punishment all involve a certain type of empathy between perpetrator and victim; the victim's subjective life is the target, and his total personality is to be deformed. By comparison, callous violence represents a very restricted contact with the victim, and arises from structures that cut off the possibility of personal empathy.

Callousness is found in all societies throughout history, but it is especially characteristic of certain types. In a sense, the extreme mutual isolation of primitive tribes results in a form of callousness towards each other; but the amount of cruelty done is likely to be severely limited by the very sporadic nature of such external contacts. Where social relationships are organized on a regular basis along impersonal lines, however, callous cruelty is maximal. This of course is the theme of Marx, especially in terms of the callousness of the wage system in an impersonal market economy.

More generally, callous cruelty is especially characteristic of large-scale, bureaucratic organization, the violence of the modern army and state. Indeed, the structural organization of bureaucracy seems uniquely suited to the perpetration of callous violence. Bureaucracy is typically hierarchic, and hence, routinely enforces relationships of domination and submission. But both the means and the ends of bureaucratic action deal not with the individual person and his subjective feelings, but with segmented elements of individual lives. The fundamental principle of bureaucracy, indeed, is the separation of the individual from the position; instead of the charisma of the individual, there is the charisma of office; instead of personal power and personal domination, there is domination by reference to formalities and specialized functions.

Thus, even the application of violence is carried out segmentally; the bureaucrat does not invest his personality and his subjective status in the dominance relationship that results, and the identity and feelings of the victim are not a concern. Bureaucratic violence is the psychological opposite of the ceremonial ferocity of patrimonial society; however painful and terrifying the consequences, they are epiphenomenal to the more general policy being carried out.

The major atrocities of the 20th century are of this sort. The Nazi extermination camps were the epitome of bureaucratic organization. What we find so horrifying about them, above all, is their dramatization of the ultimate Kafka-esque possibilities we have always feared lurked in this organizational form. The very methodical, impersonal, and ritually unthreatening character of most stages of the Nazi extermination procedures are features which no doubt were most responsible for the relative lack of resistance and even the degree of active compliance among the Jewish victims. The secrecy of the camps and gas chambers, the night-time round-ups—all of these stand in sharp contrast to the public, ritual nature of violence in patrimonial societies. For the Nazi participants, the well-known "Eichmann syndrome," the routinized following of orders, eliminated any personal sense of moral responsibility. And it is this, the turning up of the dark side of the bureaucracy that surrounds us, which makes the Nazis an emblem of the specifically modern horror, a horror that dwarfs the personalized cruelties of the Middle Ages.[14]

One prophetic element of the Nazi extermination camps was their use of technology, not only to enhance the bureaucratic efficiency of their callous violence, but to depersonalize and distance it from human contact. The development of high-altitude bombing in the Second World War represents the same sort of atrocity, perhaps extended to even more de-personalized limits. The atomic bombings of Japan are only the most dramatic (because both technically novel and highly publicized) of the atrocities of the fire-bombings of major cities in Japan, Germany, and Britain, with their heavy concentration of civilian casualties. The atrocities of the Vietnam War, again, stem above all from a long-distance bombing policy.[15] Not only were the more publicized incidents—the My Lai massacre and a few others—minor by comparison to the several million casualties of the indiscriminate bombing campaigns throughout South Vietnam, but they are uncharacteristic of the fundamental nature of the atrocities.

Janowitz has argued that modern military organizations have become internally more civilian-like, above all in the air force, because of the emphasis on technological expertise rather than traditional regimentation.[16] But on the external side, the capacity for callous destruction multiplies correspondingly. The traditional deference procedures between officers and men in the military lessen with the modern bureaucratization of their organization, and along with them goes some of the sadism that characterized internal rankings, and perhaps even the personal attitudes characteristic of soldiers towards the outside world. In its place, though, we find an increase in callousness when the men use instruments of unsurpassed destructiveness. In guerilla warfare, as in Vietnam, where guerillas are not only mingled with the civilian population, but very often *are* the civilians, including the women and children, it is not surprising that the use of long-distance, bureaucratically administered weapons should produce appalling atrocities. The long chain of information reporting and the very impersonality of communications categories served to keep much of the human consequences from the awareness of not only the American public, but of the soldiers themselves; but enough leaked through to create the most extreme sense of schizophrenia between the low-key personal relationships within the modern military and their vicious consequences for its victims.

III. ASCETICISM AND ENFORCED COMMUNITY MEMBERSHIP

Asceticism, at its extreme, is a turning inwards of cruelty, directing it towards oneself. In its origins, asceticism was purely personal, a form of self-denial valued for its supposed key mystical experience. Insofar as asceticism became a part of social organization in religions like Buddhism, it was the social organization of voluntary drop-outs from ordinary social experience; hence, violence towards outsiders was shunned as simply one more ordinary social tie to be cut in the interest of entering the Void.

Asceticism becomes organized social cruelty when an ascetic religion becomes part of the on-going, secular social structure. In this, Christianity is the prime example. The ascetic ideal, the mark of holiness for the religious specialist, takes on wider significance when a church is organized, and its leaders become the exemplars of ordinary life. What Weber called "inner-worldly asceticism" (i.e., asceticism in the world) may be viewed not only as a motivating force for economic activities, but also as the transformation of self-denial, even positive self-cruelty, into a dominant social ideal. Such a status hierarchy in itself generally constitutes an increase in social cruelty by its effect on others through emulation. Moreover, when religion becomes an important administrative and ceremonial adjunct to the state, as well as the basis for community organization, then the influence of ascetic cruelty becomes coercive. Not only is the ascetic individual rewarded with high status (and certain opportunities for power and wealth), but asceticism becomes a mark of membership in the community, and is enforced upon everyone by external authority.

The first level of cruelty in asceticism is the cruelty of deprivation, especially of those forms of happiness that are most private and individual. These include, above all, sexuality (especially in forms that have not been ceremonially justified by the group); the focusing of attention on one's own body and on the private moods of one individual or two (or perhaps a small group), is the attitude most to be combatted by an ascetic mode of social organization. Hence the ban on vanity and display in clothes and decor—precisely because they are individualizing, and because they celebrate the particularism of the body. Light-hearted, trivial, individualized games are banned for the same reason; games are acceptable only if they are made serious, contestlike, above all requiring the mobilization of the individual into the collective cause. Alcohol and drugs, one the subject of battles for control by advocates of traditional community structures in the early 20th century, the other the focus of a similar battle today, are above all privatizing agents, hence anathema to the ascetic representative of group controls and duties.[17]

Asceticism may be extended to more symbolic manifestations of individualism. The labor camps and insane asylums of the Soviet Union are used to enforce political conformity, even along lines which do not involve real substantive disagreements with the program of socialism but only with the principle of individual discussion of policy matters. These punishments (although *perhaps* a more extreme example) are representative of the form that ascetic controls take everywhere. The punishment is regarded as a form of purgatory; the offender is not simply the inadvertent victim of callous violence, nor a low-status creature to be humiliated or mutilated. His identity as a deviant is not conceived of as permanent; the punishment, rather, is to change his soul, to strip him of individualist tendencies and to reintegrate him into the ascetic standards of the group.

We can now see the distinctive social organization underlying ascetic violence. It implies a ceremonially united community, and one which places the strongest possible emphasis on individual membership and commitment. It is, moreover, a community which ceremonially emphasizes the equality and equal participation of all members within it. Such an organization is characteristic of universal religions and universal moral reform movements. It should be especially intense during those times when the group makes the greatest demands on its individual members, above all, in times of war or conflict with outside forces. It should reach a maximum during periods of struggle over the very nature of the group's boundaries, which are defined ideologically as periods of struggle against heresies. Thus, we find the height of ascetic atrocities—purgatorial actions—during the Reformation and Counterreformation in medieval Christianity;[18] comparable outbreaks of ascetic violence were characteristic of the Sunni-Shi'ite battles in Islam. There [are] also the milder, less violent upsurges of asceticism found when groups within a society fight to maintain or raise their social status, putting pressure on all individual members to maintain a united front. An example of this defensive sort of asceticism is found at the height of the anti-alcohol crusade in the U.S.; of the offensive sort, the "Victorian revolution" in sexual mores that accompanied the mobilization of modern women in their first effort to raise their social status.[19]

Ascetic cruelty remains important in the modern secular world because the issues of community membership and individual obligation to the group continue in the struggles of status groups, and political mobilization of any conflict groups in society—including both intellectual factions and larger social classes—is a continual phenomenon. We cannot escape the fact that most of the major humanitarian reform movements of the modern era, above all Marxism, but also to a lesser degree piece-meal reformisms, are especially prone to ascetic cruelty. Their very universalism and their intense mobilization makes it easy; wherever their gaze is turned outwards towards their enemies, and not inwards towards their own dangers, it becomes all the more likely.

CONCLUSION

In our contemporary society, ferocious cruelty is no longer structurally induced; it is no longer part of the dominant ceremonial order, although we still find individual cases. In this sense, modern society appears more humane. But at the same time, the dangers of callousness increase; and the technological efficiency of modern instruments of destruction makes its consequences all the more appalling while it hides them from view. Between these opposing trends, ascetic cruelty has had its ups and downs, cresting during periods of mobilized conflict.

There is no evolutionary trend towards kindness and happiness. Ferociousness once increased, then declined; callousness and asceticism now oppose each other as defenders and challengers of the status quo. And the institutionalized asceticism of a victorious revolutionary movement easily amalgamates with the callousness of an established bureaucratic regime.

The demons can be exorcised, but only by

seeing them for what they are. Those who claim that the demons can be exorcised only by action in the world, not by theorizing about them, seem to be possessed by demons of their own, especially the demon of asceticism; one senses here the communal hostility of the ascetic to the individual luxury of intellectual contemplation. And here is the danger. Those who deny everything for the self deny it as well for others; our altruism, taken too exclusively, is an infinite regress, passing a bucket from hand to hand that never reaches the fire. When we act, we call out the demons to meet us. Be careful: they are ourselves.

NOTES

1. Han Fei Tzu, *Basic Writings*, New York: Columbia University Press, 1964, p. 80. Original ca. 235 B.C.

2. Alexis de Tocqueville, *Democracy in America*, volume 2, New York: Vintage Books, 1960, pp. 174–175; originally published 1840.

3. Talcott Parsons, "Evolutionary Universals in Society," in *Sociological Theory and Modern Society*, New York: Free Press, 1967; *Societies, Evolutionary and Comparative Perspectives*, Englewood Cliffs: Prentice Hall, 1966; *The System of Modern Societies*, Englewood Cliffs: Prentice Hall, 1971.

4. Georges Sorel, *Reflections on Violence*, New York: Free Press, 1970. Originally published 1908.

5. Alan Moorehead, *The Blue Nile*, New York: Harper and Row, 1963, p. 192.

6. 1 Samuel 17: 51–54; 2 Samuel 4: 7–12.

7. Gerhard Lenski, *Power and Privilege: A Theory of Social Stratification*, New York: McGraw-Hill, 1966, pp. 155–159.

8. Gerhard Lenski, *Human Societies*, New York: McGraw-Hill, 1970, pp. 225–227.

9. Lenski, *Human Societies*, p. 139; *Power and Privilege*, pp. 122–123.

10. Lenski, *Power and Privilege*, p. 437.

11. Konrad Lorenz, *On Aggression*, New York: Harcourt, Brace, 1966, pp. 133–158.

12. Lenski, *Human Societies*, pp. 138–139, 474–475.

13. Phillipe Aries, *Centuries of Childhood*, New York: Random House, 1962, pp. 365–404; Lawrence Stone, *The Crisis of the Aristocracy*, New York: Oxford University Press, 1967, pp. 96–134.

14. Cf. Hannah Arendt, *Eichmann in Jerusalem: A Report on the Banality of Evil*, New York: Viking Press, 1963.

15. Frank Harvey, *Air War: Vietnam*, New York: Bantam Books, 1967.

16. Morris Janowitz, *The Professional Soldier*, New York: Free Press, 1960.

17. Joseph R. Gusfield, *Symbolic Crusade*, Urbana: University of Illinois Press, 1963.

18. H.R. Trevor-Roper, *Religion, Reformation, and Social Change*, London: Macmillan, 1967, pp. 90–192; cf. Keith Thomas, *Religion and the Decline of Magic*, New York: Scribner's, 1971.

19. Randall Collins, "A Conflict Theory of Sexual Stratification," *Social Problems* 19 (Summer, 1971), pp. 3–21.

MATURATION OF THE STATE-CENTERED THEORY OF REVOLUTION AND IDEOLOGY*

RANDALL COLLINS

Once upon a time we had a theory of revolution and ideology. The basic outlines of the theory were set by Marx and Engels, but the general frame of analysis was widely accepted. Revolutions were class conflicts: a privileged class faced increasing pressure from a discontented rising class. The revolutionary transfer of power eventually broke through the block, setting off a new period of social change. This process was synchronized with a succession of ideological hegemonies. The ruling ideas were those of the ruling elite; as class challengers emerged, their change in consciousness acted as a barometer as well as a mobilizer for the coming revolution.

For Marxists, the class actors in the drama were the owners of the means of production versus the suppliers of labor power and the owners of rival means of production. Non-Marxists also made use of the scheme. The English and French revolutions typically were

*From Randall Collins, "Maturation of the State-Centered Theory of Revolution and Ideology," *Sociological Theory* 11:1 (March 1993), 117–28. Reprinted with permission of the American Sociological Association and the author.

attributed to the "rise of the bourgeoisie," or sometimes to the "rise of the gentry." The wave of nineteenth-century European revolutions and many of the "modernizing" revolutions of the twentieth century also were described as "bourgeois revolutions," and the resulting institutions and ideologies typically were referred to as "bourgeois" or "middle-class" democracy.

The general model of rising and falling classes was separated from a class basis while preserving its structural features. In U.S. sociology since the time of Sorokin in the 1920s, the emphasis has shifted to the mobility of individuals; revolutions were attributed to the blockage of mobility by persons of talent and ambition, whereas open mobility according to merit was regarded as the safety valve that relieved pressure and prevented revolutionary conditions from occurring. The study of social mobility (later called "status attainment") that dominated sociological research through the 1960s was largely the result of accepting the underlying model whereby the blocking of "rising social classes" causes revolutions, together with a preference for the piecemeal and gradualist reform that mobility was believed to represent.

The theory of ideology also was modified, although it stayed within the framework of the original Marxian/Hegelian model. There was nothing explicitly Marxist about Crane Brinton's (1938) natural history of the great revolutions, but the ideological desertion of the intellectuals was taken as the first harbinger of upheaval. Mannheim's famous theory of ideology extended the Marxian model to incorporate the utopian ideology of the revolutionaries themselves. Mannheim aimed to step outside the historical process by locating a free-floating group of intellectuals who could play the role of liberal social engineers; they, in turn, needed a social base—if outside the class structure—and Mannheim's later work turned to the sociology of education and the sociology of intellectual communities themselves.

C. Wright Mill's work in the 1950s and Gouldner's work on ideology in the 1970s followed a Mannheimian line. In Gouldner's (1976) studies on what he called "the dark side of the dialectic," Marxism was tagged as the ideology of the intellectuals, surreptitiously exalting their indispensability in the processes of revolution and postrevolutionary rule. Gouldner made explicit what was claimed implicitly by the student-based "New Left" of the 1960s: that education and the mass media rather than old class conflicts were the route to power; in short, the ideology-producing institutions now were taken to be the center of the political dynamic.

In contrast, mainstream Marxians continued to view the ideological thrust of revolutions as hinging on class culture. Dispute went on between the line descending from Gramsci and that descending from Lukacs. The Gramscian line was that the rulers hold ideological hegemony; thus control of the media of culture prevents revolutionary mobilization. The Lukacians, on the contrary, stressed the autonomous class culture of the working class (as in E.P. Thompson's famous work on the English working class), and thus argued for at least a potential basis for revolt. This position was undermined when Calhoun (1982) demonstrated that the rebellious English workers in Marx's day came not from the factories but from the dying traditional handcrafts, and that their ideology was a conservative return to the past. The postmodernism popular today is in effect the triumph of an extremely pessimistic version of the Gramscian line; the hyperactive cultural marketplace of late capitalism makes revolution and its ideology not only impossible but meaningless.

In recent decades, the old class-conflict paradigm of revolution has broken down; vestiges remain in current thinking about ideology, rather like a flywheel spinning after the drive shaft has broken off. Meanwhile a new theory of revolution has developed, based on the wealth of historical data now available. We know a great deal more than our predecessors about the actual participation of social classes in revolutionary politics, and we have a picture of state finance, military structures, economic development, and population patterns that was completely unavailable in the time of Marx, or even of Mannheim and Brinton. And we have become much less Europe-centered, so that we have come to pay attention to the crises of China, Japan, and Turkey and to what they had in common with Western revolutions as well as what was distinctive. This maturation of comparative historical sociology is the key to our increasing sophistication in the theory of revolution.

The turning point was Barrington Moore's (1966) *Social Origins of Dictatorship and Democracy*. In some ways this work might be regarded as the last shot of the old theory because Moore emphasizes class conflict as a driving force; but now the conflicts emerge from the property systems of capitalist agriculture rather than from industry. Peasant revolts become more central; so do the interests of government bureaucrats. From here it is only a step to Theda Skocpol's (1979) *States and Social Revolutions*; Skocpol marks the full-fledged revolution in the theory of revolutions, for now the state, with its military and fiscal interests, is the central actor and the location of crisis.

By the beginning of the 1990s, the new state-centered theory of revolutions had matured visibly. Jack Goldstone's (1991) *Revolution and Rebellion in the Early Modern World* is an intellectual descendant of Skocpol's theory; in fact, Goldstone is a former student of Skocpol, just as Skocpol was a student of Moore. Goldstone's work is the state of the art; in the sophistication of its model, and in the thorough use of historical materials and comparisons, it is surely the best work on revolutions yet produced. This is no idiosyncratic development, for the state-centered theory has been advancing on a broad front. Robert Wuthnow's (1989) *Communities of Discourse* makes an excellent companion to Goldstone; it also is the state of the art, the best book yet written on the theory of ideology. Wuthnow too draws on the richness of historical materials and adopts the strategy of comparisons to isolate causes; he too is an heir to the Skocpolian theoretical revolution. Examining these works together, we can see how far we have come.

GOLDSTONE AND THE THEORY OF STATE BREAKDOWN

The original title of Goldstone's manuscript was "State Breakdown in the Early Modern World"; this captured the main theme of the new theory better than his current title. Revolutions occur because of a breakdown from above rather than insurgence from below. No matter how deprived popular groups are, they cannot overthrow the state as long as the elites and their military apparatus of repression hold together. Other variants on the social psychology of rebellion are equally impotent in the absence of state breakdown; rising expectations will not do the job either. This point has become one of the most solid findings of the social sciences; it is bolstered, for instance, by Tilly's (1978) research, which shows that rebellious mobilization will go as far as is allowed by the condition of intra-elite conflict and the demobilization of the repressive resources of the state.

Goldstone describes three components of state breakdown: (1) fiscal strain, the inability of the state to pay its own functionaries and, above all, its soldiers; (2) elite conflicts, an internecine warfare that divides the rulers and paralyzes their ability to act; and (3) popular revolt, which coincides with the other two processes and leads to the destruction of the state and the formation of new centers of power. All three must be present to permit a full-scale state breakdown and thus a successful revolution.

This model brings together various processes that have been researched separately. One cannot say that popular grievances have nothing to do with revolution; they are one of the factors that flow into popular revolts, along with the conditions spelled out in resource mobilization theory. Similarly, conflicts within the elite have been noted since Marx's *Eighteenth Brumaire.* Much of the revisionist research of the last few decades, documenting the large degree of internal division within the elites (for instance, in the English and French revolutions), has concluded that class conflict could have nothing to do with revolution because the same classes were represented on both sides. Goldstone transforms this weakness of the old class conflict theory into a feature of the breakdown theory: a situation becomes revolutionary precisely because structural conditions split the elite into warring factions. Goldstone shows further that the old "pressure-cooker" theory of blocked mobility is wrong; it is precisely in periods of high social mobility that intra-elite conflict is highest.

The core of Goldstone's model is essentially the core of Skocpol's theory. She too presented a theory of state breakdown, combining a fiscal-administrative crisis of the state, conflicts within the ruling elite, and popular revolt. Skocpol specified the antecedents and character of these three components somewhat differently than Goldstone. In her view, the source of fiscal/administrative crisis was military strain resulting from geopolitical conditions. The pattern jumps out from her cases: the French revolution followed on the debts incurred by the American wars, and the Russian and Chinese revolutions occurred in the aftermath of the world wars of the twentieth century. Following Barrington Moore, Skocpol identified the prime intra-elite conflict as that between rural landowners and state bureaucrats, essentially a battle over who was to be taxed to pay the expenses of the state. Skocpol's popular revolts were those of peasants; here again she follows Moore because it is the various patterns of class relations within capitalist agriculture that determine how the peasantry are mobilized and how the elites respond.

Goldstone changes not the core of the theory, but the antecedents of the three components of crisis. He demonstrates that in the early modern period, population growth was responsible for all three aspects of breakdown. (1) In a predominantly agricultural economy, when population grows faster than cultivation, the price of food and of most other staple goods increases. This price increase places great pressure on state budgets, above all because the state needs to feed its army; this fiscal strain typically is exacerbated because the size of armies increases enormously (the so-called "military revolution") as population growth makes more soldiers available for contemporary arms races. The fiscal crisis hits full-bore if the state has tied its taxation policies to agricultural output, because it is taxing the sector in which relative resources are shrinking in real terms.

(2) Population growth generates conflict within the elite, again via several mutually reinforcing paths. Rising prices make it more expensive for elites to support themselves and their dependents. At the same time, elite families are bigger; there are more daughters to be dowered and married off, more sons seeking preferment in military or government posts. And rising prices create profits for some families situated in the most advantageous positions in production or trade, so there are more families aspiring to enter the elite; their successful mobility intensifies the competition among the existing elite.

(3) As a result of population growth, more peasants are dividing the soil; hence increasing numbers are driven into poverty or into the nonagricultural labor force. The wages of urban workers decline because there is a labor glut; their real income falls still further because of rising prices. Thus real grievances mount, and with them the incidence of popular revolt. Notice, incidentally, that Goldstone finds a real immiseration of the workers that Marx projected for the final crisis of capitalism. Goldstone, however, finds it earlier, in the previous round of revolution—including the workers' movements of the 1820s that Marx knew from his youth.

Skocpol and Goldstone are variants on the same model, although they disagree on some points. Goldstone criticizes Skocpol's military emphasis as a misinterpretation of the evidence. He points out that the breakdown of the French state in 1789 came six years after the American revolutionary wars against England, in which France was victorious. Those six years of war (1778–1783) were surrounded by a period of peace dating back to 1763;

moreover, this war was inexpensive compared to the Seven Years' War of 1756–1763. The French state was in a far worse fiscal situation as the result of the continuous wars under Louis XIV during 1689–1714; yet at that time there was no breakdown and no revolution. The difference, Goldstone argues, is that Louis XIV and his successors benefited from a period in which population pressure had ceased; the state's real income caught up, and the war debts were liquidated. After 1750, though, population surged to new heights; the resulting concatenation of problems made the smaller military burden into the catalyst of state breakdown. Goldstone makes a similar comment on the role of the Scottish war in 1637–1639 in precipitating England's state crisis, which led to the civil war.

Goldstone's population-driven model and the geopolitical strain model need not be construed as opposites, however. As Goldstone himself emphasizes, the key process in breakdown is a structural relationship between state obligations and state resources, not population pressure per se. It would be a caricature to regard Goldstone's model as merely neo-Malthusian. Goldstone notes that the Meiji Restoration in Japan was a full-fledged state breakdown with revolutionary consequences for the structure of Japanese society. Japanese population, however, had been stable for the previous century; how then did the Japanese state enter the fiscal crisis that led to the breakdown? In this case, the Japanese elites drew their income in kind rather than in cash; hence the falling price of rice, combined with growth in productivity and population stability, had effects similar to those in the European crises: government budgetary crisis, elite distress and infighting, and pressures leading to popular rebellions. It is the structural relationships that matter, not population growth per se.

By the same logic, the key is the balance between military costs and government re-source-extracting capability rather than the absolute level of either element. In late eighteenth-century France, war debts, together with the costs of the standing army, had been building up for 40 years. By the 1780s the treasury was spending most of its income merely to service the debts of earlier wars (Goldstone 1991, p. 211); the American war, though not particularly severe, came at just the wrong time and broke the camel's back. One could show a similar pattern of cumulative military debts in the case of the English crown in the early 1600s, and indeed in the crises of the Ottomans and the various Chinese dynasties. Because current or past military expense was the largest part of state budgets for premodern states everywhere (documented, for instance, in Mann 1986), one side of Goldstone's balance between state obligations and resources always would be determined by the size of military expenses.

In more extreme cases, the state collapses not merely from long-term military expenditure but because the military apparatus is broken apart by defeat in war. Here we have the Russian and the Chinese revolutions of the twentieth century as well as the Turkish revolution of 1920–1922. Goldstone does a path-breaking job in analyzing the recurrent state breakdowns of the Ottoman empire between 1590 and 1660, during periods of strain resulting from population growth, and the Ottoman recovery after 1660 when population leveled off. Because of the point where he stops the story, he leaves out the long-term decline in Ottoman territory under geopolitical pressures, which culminated at the turn of the twentieth century. Kemal Ataturk's nationalist revolution was a direct result of the Ottoman defeat in World War I; with the British army holding the Sultan as a puppet in Constantinople and Greek armies invading the coast of Asia Minor, the army command revolted in the Anatolian interior, threw off the delegitimated Muslim rule, and carried out a secularizing revolution. Revolutions of this sort fit the model of geopolitical strain quite directly; so does the 1989–1991 collapse of the Soviet empire in the culminating strains of an expensive arms race under conditions of geopolitical disadvantage (Collins 1986, pp. 186–209; Collins and Waller 1992).

The point is not that we have two rival theories of revolution. Rather, there exists a core model of state breakdown—fiscal/administrative strain, elite conflict, popular revolt—plus a number of pathways towards crisis conditions in these factors. Population growth sometimes can play a very large role in building up crisis; at other times geopolitical conditions can have overwhelming effects. In many cases, population and geopolitics interact. This is especially likely to be the case in premodern states, where the state budget is overwhelmingly military and where population is so vulnerable to shifts in mortality from disease, while the economy is not very flexible in absorbing population growth.

This observation gives us another reason why it is preferable to view Goldstone's work as an extension of a core model of state breakdown which can be activated in various ways. If we insist strongly on the population/resource strain dynamic, Goldstone's model is limited to a particular historical period. The "early modern state" is an "in-between" kind containing a widespread market economy for agricultural products, so that prices can make a difference for state budgets; at the same time there is a weak central bureaucracy, big enough to be expensive but too inefficient to extract what it needs without giving in to the interests of the landed elites. In addition, mortality drives large population swings because diseases spread widely through social networks, without the medical technology to control them. What happens, then, as the state and the economy modernize further? Goldstone himself makes the point that the population/resource dynamic ended when states entered a strongly growing capitalist economy. England in the 1820s was still in trouble from the multiplying effects of population growth, but in the 1830s, capitalist growth was able to absorb an even more rapidly accelerating population. Under Goldstone's model, if we construe this point strictly, revolutions are possible only in those parts of the world where capitalist growth is not yet underway.

Surely this claim is unrealistic; nor does it seem to be Goldstone's intention. It is more valuable to treat Goldstone's argument as a very sophisticated statement of the core theory of state breakdown, along with an application of this model to conditions under which population is the driving force in the background variables. Yet even when the effects of population are mitigated, a state breakdown can be activated if geopolitical strains are severe enough. I seriously doubt that the age of revolutions is now over, even for the industrial-capitalist world, despite its ability to control or absorb population growth. Geopolitical strain is possible for any state as long as it builds its legitimation around the organization of force upon a territory; some political rulers always will be tempted to expand their legitimation through military exploits, and will run the endless risk of becoming militarily overmatched, outpositioned, or overextended. The theory of state breakdowns will not become a relic of the past; no doubt we will see it enacted again in the future.

THE AFTERMATH OF STATE BREAKDOWNS AND THE QUESTION OF CULTURE

Goldstone explicitly overturns Marxian theory at a number of points, although some continuity remains insofar as state breakdown theory is materialistic and structural. In fact, one might describe this whole line of theory as "political materialism"; economics is still very important, but most important of all is the fiscal economics of the state. Geopolitical conditions pose a particular problem in coordinating the physical resources of threat and destruction. The rise of the state itself now is shown as various ways of extracting economic resources to support the growing and centralizing military machinery; Tilly's (1991) *Coercion, Capital and European States* reaps another harvest of comparative history in showing how the fates of different state structures depended on which flows of resources supported them.

Goldstone is very much a "political materialist" until the point at which states break down. In analyzing what happens next, however, he begins to waffle. One part of his analysis here remains ruthlessly materialist: states will be able to pull themselves back together if they can regain a favorable flow of resources. This may happen if they have the good fortune to enter an era in which the population declines (as in France, England, and the Ottoman empire in the late 1600s). The struggles of the breakdown period themselves may kill off enough of the population to relieve the pressure; Goldstone believes this happened in the stabilizing transition from the Ming to the Qing dynasty in China.

Goldstone also considers why state breakdowns have such different structural results. England and (at a slower pace) France were rescued from the population pressure dynamic by the takeoff of capitalism; but Spain merely stagnated, as did the Ottomans and China. Goldstone finds Meiji Japan especially puzzling because it carried out very extensive reforms, leading to rapid economic growth and expansion of military power, although under an ideology proclaiming restoration of old traditions. At this point Goldstone suggests that material conditions determine state breakdowns, but ideology becomes an independent factor in defining where the society goes from there. This part of Goldstone's

book lacks the depth of his earlier chapters, and his line of argument is not very convincing. He suggests that the European states, because they inherited a religious eschatology of linear progress, were able to innovate consciously, and thus arrived at modern democracy and capitalism. Asian societies, on the other hand, were dominated by a cultural imagery of eternal cycles, whether deriving from Ibn Khaldun for Islam or from Confucianism and Buddhism for East Asia; as a result, conservative movements followed state breakdowns and cut off the possibility of structural change.

Neither the comparisons nor the specifics of this argument hold up very well. Spain was as much the inheritor of a Christian eschatology as the rest of Europe, while Japan was dominated ideologically by Buddhism and Confucianism, very much like China. The Ottoman empire was Muslim, and Islam is as eschatological as Christianity, complete with a creator God and a Last Judgment; Ibn Khaldun was simply one philosopher, and his views had no religious significance. Even within particular regions, the ideological correlation doesn't work; Islamic Egypt and Syria had a booming economy that peaked in the twelfth and thirteenth centuries (Abu-Lughod 1989); China had a veritable capitalist takeoff during the Sung Dynasty (eleventh and twelfth centuries), when conservative neo-Confucianism flourished. Attributing capitalist growth to ideological causes is too simple; a great deal of work has been done on the larger question, and I would say that the more adequate models are predominantly structural. (For a review of this subject from a Weberian point of view, see Collins 1986; from another angle, see Jones 1988).

Moreover, Goldstone does not stick to his "culture determines aftermaths" theme across the board. In discussing the effects of revolutions on democracy, he comes up with the formulation that democracy is determined not by revolutions but by defeats in war, which delegitimate an authoritarian elite. This can hardly be a very complete theory of democracy, but at any rate it is structural. If one wanted to push this idea further, one would have to consider Barrington Moore's argument that the alternatives—democracy, socialism, and fascism—are branches of the property relations of capitalist agriculture and the coalitions that arise in periods of state breakdown. Goldstone's own intellectual lineage will yield an even better structural theory of the political consequences of revolutions when someone carefully puts all these pieces together.

In the last few years it has become fashionable to proclaim the autonomy of culture; it appears that Goldstone, deciding to swim with that tide a bit, tacked on the comparatively brief remarks in which he makes a place for culture as determining the part of history that he himself has not analyzed. Of course there are plenty of interesting things to be done in the sociology of culture, but there are two ways to go about doing them. One is to continue to be a sociologist in the tradition of the sociology of knowledge; in this case we look for the social conditions that underlie how culture is produced. The other approach seems to carry an antisociological animus: it is bent on showing that sociology cannot explain culture, and that instead culture autonomously shapes society. One way to reach the latter conclusion is by coming to the end of one's tether; that is, a researcher analyzes things as far as time and energy permit. Whatever arbitrary features of history remain on the horizon, one describes as culture. Thus Goldstone sees that capitalist growth makes a crucial difference in the aftermath of state breakdowns; having devoted enormous scholarly energy to the meticulous analysis of causes of breakdowns, he lacks the time to embark on a similar project on the causes of capitalist trajectories in Japan, China, Turkey,

and the various parts of Europe; so he rests on his oars and calls it "culture."

The scholarly world is a cooperative enterprise; what one person doesn't do can sometimes be supplied somewhere else. If the missing piece of Goldstone's argument is really the cause of capitalism, some answers, heavily structural, can be found in other research. If we are really concerned here with the production of culture and its connection to state breakdowns, we have gone back to the theory of ideology. For this we have an excellent counterpoint in Wuthnow's recent work.

WUTHNOW
AND THE POLITICAL MEANS
OF IDEOLOGICAL PRODUCTION

Like Goldstone's volume, Wuthnow's book is not described well by its title. "*Communities of Discourse*" no doubt was chosen to indicate the concern with the inner dynamics of culture, but it gives a misleading impression by conjuring the image of warm, fuzzy discussion groups. Make no mistake; Wuthnow's is a book about social conflicts, and its underlying argument reminds me of Marx and Engels in *The German Ideology*, transmuted into the terms of the state-centered theory of today. The theme of the book comes across more clearly in its subtitle: *Ideology and Social Structure in the Reformation, the Enlightenment, and European Socialism.* These are the ideologies of the three great waves of modern revolutions; the first included the English revolution; the second, the French and American revolutions and most of the nineteenth-century revolutions; the third, the revolutionary wave of the twentieth century until about 1965. This is such a book as Marx's ghost might have written in collaboration with the ghost of Georg Simmel.

In keeping with today's scholarship, Wuthnow overturns the traditional class-actor dynamic. Nevertheless a version of class conflict is important in his model. This is the conflict of economic interests emphasized by Moore and Skocpol: the conflict of government officials with landowners over revenues. Wuthnow's is a conflict theory of coalitions. In all three of his cases, new political/economic resources strengthen the state sector; then, if a stalemate or a prolonged balance of power occurs between the state actors and the major property-owning conservatives, room is opened up for a "third party" of cultural entrepreneurs, who eventually will benefit from the struggle, *tertius gaudens*. In the Reformation, the stalemate is between the landed aristocrats and the urban/trade-based state structures; in the Enlightenment, it is between the central bureaucracy and the independent representative bodies dominated by the aristocracy; in the socialist movements of the nineteenth century, it is between the landowning and the bourgeois parties. Class interests continue to operate, but they do not determine ideology directly, and the most important class actors are on the reactionary side.

In the context of these conflicts, Wuthnow documents the shifting material bases of cultural production. In the Reformation period, a split occurred over what might be called the "ritual economy" of the church. In the rural parishes, everyday life was organized by a round of religious assemblies that placed the local aristocrats in the center of ceremonial attention. It is small wonder that the country landowners were the bulwarks of traditional Catholicism, because they patronized its priests directly and received in return an emotional and symbolic legitimation of their status. Protestantism, in pruning away rituals and substituting sermons and vernacular books, was attacking the social as well as the religious status order.

Protestant reforms grew for a variety of reasons; Wuthnow does not focus on this point but concentrates instead on the period from 1519 to 1559, during which the various states of Europe decided whether to adopt the reforms. No doubt one could refer back to the schisms in church government in the 1300s, the failure of the Conciliar movement in the 1400s (which would have turned the centralized papacy into a republic of bishops), and the crisis in papal finances that led to Luther's repudiation of the revenue-raising sale of indulgences. Here one senses another complementarity between Wuthnow's and Goldstone's concerns, for the medieval papacy underwent a variant of state breakdown. Wuthnow concentrates on the aftermath—analytically, the phase in which Goldstone is weakest. In Wuthnow's model, the Reformation was successful in those places where the state was able to tap new sources of revenue, based on the growth of trade. These states— above all the free cities and independent principalities of Germany, Switzerland, and the Netherlands, and to a lesser degree the kingdoms of Scandinavia and England—were able to build up their own staffs of officials without depending on the rural economy, the province of the aristocracy. We see here a superior resource mobilization on the part of these states, which enabled them to challenge the aristocracy for control of the church, its property, and its revenues. Religious reformers proliferated in the midst of this struggle; some were selected and institutionalized where the balance of resources most favored the state. Where these conditions were lacking—Spain, France, eastern Europe—the Reformation failed.

The outburst of secularizing intellectuals that constituted the Enlightenment was produced by another shift in the means of cultural production. Here the state was even more important, for the new printing industries depended heavily on government licensing as well as on government-sponsored publications. Intellectuals acquired a new basis for careers as publicists for political factions in parliamentary regimes such as England, or in the salons that sprang up around burgeoning governmental centers such as Paris. In the background we find a further round of expansion of the state, in tandem with expansion of the capitalist economy; the fusion of these two provided a patronage base for the new intellectuals, independent of the older intellectual basis in the church. If the intellectuals were to embark on a round of creativity in their own right, a second ingredient was required: a division of authority, so that the central bureaucracy was challenged by an independent judiciary, parliaments, or plural religious institutions. These gave multiple bases for patronage, partly independent of the crown; intellectuals enjoyed a favorable market and could choose among rival patrons. It appears to follow (although Wuthnow does not develop the point explicitly) that the Enlightenment concern for the supremacy of "Reason" was the ideology of intellectual autonomy, a reflection of the intellectuals on their new situation, where they had become the cultural mediators in a political balance of power.

Wuthnow's third case is the rise of socialist ideologies during 1864–1914. Here the most favorable circumstance was a centralized state, intervening strongly to shape economic growth. The industrialization of Bismarck's Germany is an archetypal example; that country became the site of the strongest and intellectually most active socialist movement in Europe. The shape of political coalitions was crucial. Where an authoritarian state was highly interventionist, the party of the conservative landowners was forced into alliance with the industrial bourgeoisie; the working class; excluded from power, was pushed to the left. In contrast, where bourgeois republicans had won political victories against the conservatives (as in England, France, Italy, and Spain), all the parties of the "left" tended to ally themselves against right-wing resurgence. Bourgeois liberals gave some support to working-class interests, thereby imparting a moderate character to reformist politics, and socialist ideology was weak.

The immediate material bases for socialist intellectuals were editorial positions in the mass newspapers and magazines sponsored by their political parties. This base was strongest in Germany, where trade unions and parliamentary politicians formed a virtual state within the state. Not surprisingly, this is where socialist ideas were elaborated most professionally, under the leadership of Engels (publishing Marx's manuscripts in the 1880s and 1890s), Bebel, Kautsky, Bernstein, Hilferding, Luxemburg, and others. Germany was the place foreign revolutionaries such as Lenin looked to as the center of the world socialist movement. Russia, which Wuthnow omits from his comparisons, also appears to fit well with the underlying structural pattern of class coalitions, although there the material resources for socialist intellectuals were more constricted.

In Wuthnow's comparisons, the continuity with Moore, Skocpol, and Goldstone is remarkably strong. In some respects Wuthnow resembles Moore most strongly; though history is no longer based on the old Marxian scheme of rising social classes, class conflicts still provide the balance of forces into which intellectuals then move with their own creativity. The expansion of capitalism plays a causal role throughout, although farther back in the explanatory chain. No one has yet made a grand synthesis of all the parts of the picture, but there is considerable coherence around the fateful consequences of the commercialization of agriculture (Moore), the material economy of the state (Skocpol, Goldstone, Wuthnow, Tilly), the patterns of intra-elite conflict generated by the foregoing (all of these theorists), and the provision of an autonomous space for intellectuals (Wuthnow).

In Wuthnow's treatment of the Reformation, a key factor is the ability of the state to tap sources of revenue that do not place it into competition over landed wealth; Goldstone shows that the failure to do just this was one of the main paths leading to state breakdown in England in 1640 and France in 1789. The Reformation failed in France because of the state's dependence on the aristocracy; for geopolitical reasons this dependence was particularly acute during the Reformation period, when the French King was defeated in war and had to be ransomed by the nobles in 1525. In England, as Wuthnow (1989, p. 154) notes in rather Goldstonean fashion, rising agricultural prices in the late 1500s caused a resurgence of the landed aristocracy and an attempt to reestablish Catholicism; the nominal Protestantism of the Church of England thus was caught in the middle of a long conflict between religious traditionalists and sectarian Protestants. The ideological mobilization that Wuthnow explains thus supplies much of the discourse that surrounded Goldstone's state breakdowns.

Wuthnow's analysis of the conditions under which socialist movements prevailed meshes with Barrington Moore's model of coalition patterns. Moore pointed out that where landowners go directly into the market by selling their agricultural products and coercing rural labor through traditional controls, the aristocratic interest becomes tied to that of the authoritarian state. Subsequently, when industrialization from above promotes the class alliance of landowners and industrial bourgeoisie, a "marriage of iron and rye," the workers have nowhere to go except into revolutionary opposition. If Germany is at one pole, the United States is at the other, although Wuthnow does not elaborate on the latter case. Moore argued that the disappearance of the conservative labor-coercing landowners, due to the end of the slave plantations, eliminated the aristocracy as a faction in American class coalitions. The bourgeoisie (including the small commercial farmers) dominated American politics; in the absence of an authoritarian class, for a long period there was no party in favor of a strongly centralized state. Because state patronage directly or indirectly is the basis of politicized intellectual movements, the absence of both a strong working-class party and a centralized state accounts for the privatized condition of American intellectuals.

Wuthnow's analysis is concerned with the material bases of cultural production and with the political/economic configurations that give intellectuals a breathing space. He does not do much with the contents of their ideas themselves; especially in the case of the Reformation, he emphasizes the process by which ideas are selected and institutionalized. Some reviewers have regarded this emphasis as a weakness, a failure to give ideas their autonomous significance. Before we are swept to conclusions by the force of contemporary rhetoric, however, let us consider what Wuthnow shows. When material and structural conditions are favorable, the result is an outpouring of intellectual productivity. This entails a proliferation of ideas, including a wide range of disagreements. Unanimity among creative intellectuals is almost a contradiction in terms; they make their mark by saying something different from the others. For this reason intellectuals as a group cannot produce a structural change; they disagree too much about what direction to take.

As Goldstone recognizes well enough at some points, a proliferation of critical ideologies adds to the atmosphere of state breakdown, but some selection must be made among those ideas if they are to acquire any coherence in the period of postrevolutionary reconstruction. This point is apparent in the huge array of critical stances regarding Catholic dogma and practice at the end of the Middle Ages; beginning in 1300, there were all manner of mystics, occultists, Platonists, scripturalists, pietists, ascetics, and others, not to mention many specific plans for reforming the church organization. Luther became central not because his doctrine was somehow more penetrating than any of the others, but because his rebellion in the patchwork of German states began a series of political upheavals that finally succeeded in unraveling the centralized authority of the Pope. Similar patterns seem to hold in the case of other revolutions. Whether we like it or not, the creativity of intellectuals is highlighted selectively by upheavals in political structures; in itself it does not determine the direction in which structures change.

How, then, do we explain the contents of ideas in their own right? In one important sense culture is autonomous, but that does not mean that it is socially undetermined. Wuthnow points out that cultural production expands creatively when the political/economic structure gives it a breathing space, a well-supported but competitive market for ideas. The historically constructed autonomy of that space constitutes the autonomy of culture. This is not to say that sociologists can say nothing about the internal organization of the competitive space among intellectuals; in fact, the history of creative ideas is the history of the successive rearrangements of the networks of intellectuals and their alliances and conflicts with each other. But that is another story, which can be pursued elsewhere; it is not the mainspring of political or economic history.

SOCIOLOGY AFTER THE FALL

Yes, there is a macro sociology after the fall of the traditional Marxist paradigm. The state-centered revolution in the theory of political and ideological change has given us a coherent model, capable of explaining the many variants that make up the richness of modern history. Of course there are contentions over points of emphasis; loose ends are left dangling; gaps and frontiers lie open, where speculation runs ahead of solid analysis. The state-centered model may yet turn out to have some serious flaws. But the points of overlap and coherence among the works of Moore, Skocpol, Goldstone, and Wuthnow, as well as of Tilly, Calhoun, geopolitical theorists, and other researchers, strongly implies that something very solid has been accomplished here at the core of a general theory. By building on this new sociological tradition, perhaps even by radical modifications—such as Goldstone has done by adding population dynamics to the state breakdown model—scholars no doubt will create further great works of macro sociology in the years to come. . . .

REFERENCES

ABU-LUGHOD, JANET L. 1989. *Before European Hegemony: The World System A.D. 1250–1350.* New York: Oxford University Press.

BRINTON, CRANE. 1938. *The Anatomy of Revolution.* New York: Random House.

CALHOUN, CRAIG. 1982. *The Question of Class Struggle.* Chicago: University of Chicago Press.

COLLINS, RANDALL. 1986. *Weberian Sociological Theory.* Cambridge, UK: Cambridge University Press.

COLLINS, RANDALL, and DAVID V. WALLER. 1992. "What Theories Predicted the State Breakdowns and Revolutions of the Soviet Bloc?" Pp. 1–20 in *Research in Social Movements, Conflicts and Change,* Vol. 14, edited by Louis Kriesberg. Greenwich, CT: JAI.

GOLDSTONE, JACK A. 1991. *Revolution and Rebellion in the Early Modern World.* Berkeley: University of California Press.

GOULDNER, ALVIN W. 1976. *The Dialectic of Ideology and Technology.* New York: Seabury.

JONES, ERIC L. 1988. *Growth Recurring: Economic Change in World History.* Oxford: Clarendon.

MANN, MICHAEL. 1986. *The Sources of Social Power,* Vol. 1. New York: Cambridge University Press.

MOORE, BARRINGTON, Jr. 1966. *Social Origins of Dictatorship and Democracy.* Boston: Beacon.

SKOCPOL, THEDA. 1979. *States and Social Revolutions.* New York: Cambridge University Press.

TILLY, CHARLES. 1978. *From Mobilization to Revolution.* Reading, MA: Addison-Wesley.

_____. 1991. *Coercion, Capital, and European States: AD 990–1990.* Oxford: Blackwell.

WUTHNOW, ROBERT. 1989. *Communities of Discourse: Ideology and Social Structure in the Reformation, the Enlightenment, and European Socialism.* Cambridge, MA: Harvard University Press.

CHAPTER 3

MARXISM AND NEO-MARXISM

Contemporary Marxism includes diverse approaches to social theory. They all bear in common an allegiance to the theoretical legacy of the nineteenth-century German socialist Karl Marx (1818–1883), whose work lies in the general tradition of conflict theory. Indeed, Marx's work may be seen as one of the more elaborate and sophisticated attempts to construct a general conflict theory of society. Such a reading, however, overlooks much that is distinctive in Marx. For example, his theory of society also bears a close relationship to functionalism (see Cohen 1978). Many scholars have attempted to derive from Marx's work a social psychology or a theory of human nature, often basing their interpretations on his early writings such as the 1844 *Economic and Philosophical Manuscripts* (see Geras 1983, Ollman 1971, Séve 1978). And his work has also been claimed as lying in the mainstream of contemporary systems theory (Ludz 1975, McQuarie and Amburgey 1978).

The very theoretical richness and diversity of Marx's work have given rise to a variety of contemporary interpretations. Nonetheless, there seems to be general agreement over many aspects, and, indeed, the fundamental elements of Marx's theory can be stated easily and clearly (for a general introduction to Marx's thought, see Lichtheim 1965, McLellan 1973, McQuarie 1978, Suchting 1983).

CLASSICAL MARXISM

Marxism is a remarkable synthesis of elements of the social and economic theory and philosophy of Marx's time. Marx's interest was in developing a critical social theory, one that not only sought to understand society but that also would work toward the active transformation of society in an egalitarian and democratic direction. According to Marx, "The philosophers have only *interpreted* the world, in various ways; the point, however, is to *change* it" (Marx 1968, 30).

The theoretical foundations of Marx's attempt to construct such a theory lay in his insight into the central role played by economic conditions in molding social life. Whereas other social theorists had stressed philosophy and morality or religion or the state as the central institution in society, Marx pointed to the importance of economic, or "material," life. Explaining the development of his ideas, Marx wrote:

My inquiry led me to the conclusion that neither legal relations nor political forms could be comprehended whether by themselves or on the basis of a so-called general development of the human mind, but on the contrary they originate in the material conditions of life. (Marx 1970, 20)

Marx was especially interested in the particular *form* that economic or material production takes in different societies. The development of different historical forms of economic enterprise, or *modes of production*, as Marx called them, leads to the development of new and different forms of religion, politics, family life, and so on. Indeed, Marx argued that the very ways in which people think about themselves and their society are determined by this ongoing development of forces of production. Thus, in contrasting the development of European feudal society to that of modern capitalism, Marx wrote: "The hand-mill gives you society with the feudal lord; the steam-mill, society with the industrial capitalist" (Marx 1963, 109). And if social relations in a society using the handmill are different from those in a society using the steam-mill, then the political systems, religious organizations, law, science, and philosophy must also be different in the two societies.

Assume a particular state of development in the productive faculties of man and you will get a particular form of commerce and consumption. Assume particular stages of development in production, commerce, and consumption and you will have a corresponding organization of the family, of orders or of classes, in a word, a corresponding civil society. Assume a particular civil society and you will get particular political conditions which are but the official expression of civil society. (Marx to Annenkov, 1846, in Marx and Engels 1955, 35)

The application of this approach enabled Marx to identify different historical "modes of production," or forms of society—primitive communalism, ancient society, feudalism, capitalism, and others—each based on a particular level of development of the forces of economic production and the organization of those forces—tools, skills, and equipment—in a characteristic form of economic enterprise.

A second major aspect of Marx's theory involves the role that social conflict plays in this ongoing process of social and economic development. Social conflict, for Marx, is a result of the exploitation of some groups in society by others. In general, the ability to exploit others in any society is a result of control over the economic resources needed to make a livelihood. In fact, it is the very labor of the poor and exploited that creates the wealth and power of the exploiting group or class. Thus, Marx saw history as a succession of conflicts pitting the "haves" against the "have-nots," with the former using their wealth and power to exploit the latter. Marx wrote:

The history of all hitherto existing society is the history of class struggles. Freeman and slave, patrician and plebian, lord and serf, guildmaster and jouneyman, in a word oppressor and oppressed, stood in constant opposition to one another, carried on an uninterrupted, now hidden, now open fight, a fight that each time ended either in a revolutionary reconstitution of society at large, or in the common ruin of the contending classes. (Marx and Engels 1968, 35–36)

Marx's most important achievement was to combine these two insights concerning the importance of (1) *economic conditions* and (2) *class conflict* in the determination of social life into a unified general theory of society. This general theory has come to be known as "historical materialism."

It was, of course, capitalism that most intrigued Marx and was the object of his most intensive theorizing. This research culminated in the publication in 1867 by Marx of his masterwork, *Capital: Vol. I* (Marx 1867). In it, Marx applied the principles of his historical materialism to the analysis of the new modern industrial economy and society that had emerged in Europe during his lifetime. Marx was not the first theorist to examine the structure of this new, dynamic society, which had sprung from the ruins of European feudalism. He had been preceded by the Scottish and French political economists of the eighteenth and early nineteenth centuries, who had already preached the doctrine of the free market and international trade (see Therborn 1976, ch. 2). Nor was Marx the first theorist to morally critique the harsh consequences of industrialization that had befallen the displaced peasant farmers, the unemployed laborers, and the overworked and underpaid industrial workforce. Nor was he even the first to call for socialism as the remedy to those evils (see Lichtheim 1969).

Marx's unique accomplishment was to mold these three together into a theory that at one and the same time (1) offered a "scientific" analysis of capitalism's structure and development, (2) showed that the inherent structure of capitalism itself necessarily generated the evils of poverty and unemployment, and (3) demonstrated that the development of capitalism led inevitably to social revolution and its replacement by socialism. This theory—which with all of its admitted weaknesses and inadequacies has retained a powerful influence even over many non-Marxist thinkers—is the single most impressive amalgam of theoretical analysis, moral critique, and social prediction in the history of the social sciences. How did Marx bring this off?

For Marx, capitalism was a specific historical mode of production, which had emerged in Europe during the seventeenth and eighteenth centuries. The development of urban life and of commerce and trade, the despoila-

tion by the Europeans of their colonies in Asia and the New World, the breakdown of the traditional feudal landholding system based on inheritance and status, and the introduction of national economies based on accepted national currencies—these were all important preconditions leading to the rise of capitalism. Marx enumerated the essential elements of the capitalist mode of production as follows: (1) private ownership of the economic wealth of society; (2) the free utilization of that wealth by its owners—capitalists, in Marx's terminology—to create more wealth through investment in industry and trade; (3) the employment by the capitalists of wage-laborers, workers who were legally free and yet bound by economic necessity and poverty to sell their ability to work to the capitalist in exchange for a wage; and (4) the sale by the capitalists of the goods produced by their workers on the market, out of which sale they would realize the cost of their original investment in equipment, land, and raw materials, the cost of the wages paid to their workers, and—most important—an additional sum, profit. It was this final element, the pursuit of profit, which Marx believed was the wheel that drove capitalism onward. Once established, the pursuit of profit became the major transformative force in society, leading to the building of roads, dams, factories, cities—the entire infrastructure of our modern industrial society.

But, Marx believed, there was an inner flaw, or contradiction, that underlay all the dynamism of this new capitalist order. This flaw was the fact that, in the long run, the ability of capitalists to realize a profit was based on their ability to exploit the labor of their workers, to realize more from their workers' contribution in labor than they paid out in wages. In short, just as had been the case in all precapitalist social orders, Marx believed that capitalism was founded upon exploitation—not the direct exploitation by the lash and the whip, but the indirect exploitation by poverty and economic hardship. And, indeed, looking at the terrible poverty, disease, and squalor of nineteenth-century Europe's industrial cities, it was hard not to reach this conclusion. The feudal peasants and laborers had escaped one form of bondage only to fall into another even more deadly form—wage slavery—in which their wages and standard of living were slowly pushed down to or even below the bare minimum level to sustain life (see Hobsbawm 1962, 238–57).

At the very moment of its triumph, however, capitalism had created the conditions of its own destruction. Throughout his writings, Marx gives several different accounts of the underlying forces that will lead from capitalism to socialism. Two major and related reasons are the following.

First, capitalism, as a form of economy, inevitably produces major economic crises. Recessions, depressions, inflation—these are, Marx believed, the inevitable hallmarks of capitalist economy. One reason for these crises is that capitalists in a sense have a contradictory set of interests: They wish to produce as many consumption goods as possible and sell them on the market—to other capitalists, but also to workers, who, of course, make up the majority of the population—yet they also wish to pay their own workers the minimum possible wage. The result, on a societywide or even international scale, is periodic crises of *overproduction*, in which more goods are produced by the efficient machinery of capitalist industry than can be absorbed by the market. Overproduction reflects the even more fundamental problem of capitalism, for Marx, which is that under capitalism, economic production is not geared toward *human need* but rather is governed by considerations of *profitability*. Thus, in times of economic crisis, it is quite possible to have many poor people homeless, short of food and

clothing, and lacking the basic necessities of life while, at the same time, the wealthy are consuming vast amounts of society's resources in the form of frivolous luxuries, conspicuous consumption, and needless waste.

Second, the progress of capitalism, achieved under the harsh lash of competition, results in the centralization of wealth and industry. Weak and inefficient enterprises are crowded out of the market by larger, more efficient firms. Increasingly, the capitalist market tends toward monopoly conditions in which large, highly mechanized and highly efficient factories produce vast amounts of goods. In these factories, hundreds and then thousands of workers are thrown together in work, learn the value of cooperation, and together actually control the day-to-day operation of capitalist industry.

The central contradiction of capitalism, Marx concluded, is that in its most advanced state, economic production has been completely *socialized*. The capitalist is now a meaningless cipher, buying and selling stocks and bonds but making no meaningful contribution to the production process, which is carried on entirely by paid managers and workers, while the appropriation of profit from this highly socialized production process remains *private*, that is, in the hands of the capitalist owners. In such societies, Marx believed, all that remained was for the workers to recognize the injustice of this system and overthrow the capitalists in a workers' revolution. This revolution would be followed by a natural transition to a socialist form of economy, or mode of production, in which the socialized production system created by capitalism would be redistributed in a socialized—or socialist—manner that would guarantee to each member of society a fair share of the society's wealth. Marx wrote:

Along with the constantly diminishing number of the magnates of capital, who usurp and monopolize all the advantages of this process of transformation, grows the mass of misery, oppression, slavery, degradation, and exploitation; but with this too grows the revolt of the working-class, a class always increasing in numbers, and disciplined, united, organized by the mechanism of the process of capitalist production itself. The monopoly of capital becomes a fetter upon the mode of production, which has sprung up and flourished along with, and under it. Centralization of the means of production and socialization of labor at last reach a point where they become incompatible with their capitalist integument. This integument is burst asunder. The knell of capitalist private property sounds. The expropriators are expropriated. (Marx 1967, 763)

CONTEMPORARY MARXISM

After Marx's death, Marxism continued to develop, contributing to new approaches and schools in the social sciences. This proliferation of approaches had, by the middle of the twentieth century, given rise to competing interpretations Marx's work. In addition to the social-democratic interpretation of Marxism developed by Marx's close friend and co-author Friedrich Engels and Marx's other German followers, there were Soviet Marxism (or Communism, founded by Lenin and Trotsky, two leaders of the Russian Revolution), Austro-Marxism, existential Marxism, French structural-Marxism, humanist-Marxism, and critical Marxism, just to mention a few of the many approaches (see Benton 1984, Bottomore and Goode 1978, Jordan 1967, Poster 1975, Salvadori 1979, Shroyer 1973, Stojanovic 1973).

One of the more interesting approaches to emerge out of this proliferation of "Marxisms" was the body of theory produced by the German "Frankfurt School," established in the 1920s by Max Horkheimer, Theodor Adorno, and other well-known German scholars (see Held 1980, Jay 1973). Critical of the dogmatism of much of "orthodox" Marxism, both in its social-democratic and

Communist guises, the Frankfurt School Marxists attempted to expand Marxist theorizing beyond the usual realms of economics and politics. This expansion included a special emphasis on the role of culture, including brilliant studies in art, literature, music, and popular culture, as well as attempts to integrate Marxism and psychoanalysis and investigations of the philosophical underpinnings of modern industrial society (Adorno 1967, Benjamin 1969, Fromm 1941, Horkheimer 1972, Horkheimer and Adorno 1972; Lowenthal 1961, Marcuse 1955—for an introduction to this literature, see Bronner and Kellner, 1989).

Common to the works of these theorists was a pessimistic and critical tone. Writing during the Nazi conquest of power in Germany (from which many of these theorists emigrated to the United States), the seizure of power in Russia by Stalin and his bloody strangulation of the radical promise of the Russian Revolution, and the holocaust of World War II, most of the Frankfurt School Marxists were skeptical of the prospects for a worker-led socialist revolution. This profound pessimism led them to a heightened critical awareness of the obstacles in Western capitalism and in human nature, as well, that prevented the easy realization of the Marxian emancipatory project. But this despair of socialism did not lead, for most, to an acceptance of the values of capitalist culture. For example, Herbert Marcuse (Reading 12), one of the more eminent members of the Frankfurt School, believed that the lack of immediate prospects for a transition to socialism led instead to (1) a heightened critical sense concerning the culture and institution of modern capitalism, coupled with (2) a reaffirmation of an emancipatory vision of human freedom. In Reading 12, we can see the considerable theoretical distance Frankfurt School Marxism had traveled from Marx's original work. Far from identifying rationality and technology with the advance of human freedom, as had Marx in his more optimistic passages, Marcuse—adopting a theme typical of Frankfurt School Marxism—identified the technical sophistication of modern society with the loss of human individuality and freedom. In his later masterwork, *One-Dimensional Man,* Marcuse developed these themes into a sustained and savage attack on the mindlessness of the modern affluent society, a society that smothers dissent and rebellion in what Marcuse called "a comfortable, smooth, reasonable, democratic unfreedom" (1964, 1).

In one way or another, all schools of contemporary Marxist thought have been forced to come to grips with the failure of socialist revolutions to materialize in the advanced capitalist societies of Western Europe and North America. Two important themes that have emerged in works attempting to account for this failure have been (1) the development of the interventionist welfare state as a "regulator" of the capitalist economy and society and (2) the emergence of intermediary social strata between capital and labor, unanticipated by Marx (see Abercrombie and Urry 1983; Carchedi 1977; Gramsci 1971; Miliband 1969; Poulantzas 1973, 1975; Walker 1979; for a general discussion, see Carnoy 1984, Spaulding and McQuarie 1984). In Reading 13, Philip Kasinitz reviews recent contributions to the Marxist theory of the state, concluding that the expanding role of the state in both its military and welfare functions in capitalist societies makes it an increasingly important object of analysis.

Kasinitz's essay draws especially on the work of Nicos Poulantzas (1975), perhaps the leading Marxist scholar of his generation and one of the leading contributors to the debate on the role of the expanding "white-collar" stratum of managers, scientists, and technicians in capitalist societies (which has been estimated at about 25 percent of the workforce in the United States today). Poulantzas argued that this group indeed constitutes a "new" middle class, or "petty bourgeoisie" whose interests can be assumed to coincide neither with those of the working class nor with those of the capitalist class. According to Poulantzas, this important class can be won over to the struggle for socialism only by a strategy that recognizes the interests and rights of non-working-class groups in the population. In later works, Poulantzas argued that this task especially necessitates a respect by socialists for the values of political democracy and civil liberties, without which socialism cannot exist (see Poulantzas 1978; see also Bobbio 1987, Laclau and Mouffe 1985).

This increased interest in the role of the state and political struggle has led some Marxists to note a fundamental contradiction between two primary tasks of the capitalist state. On the one hand, it must sustain the process of private capital accumulation or, put more directly, it must act to promote the interests of the capitalist class. On the other hand, in order to preserve social stability and order in society, the state must also act to preserve the loyalty of the dominated classes in society. This means that the state must contrive to appear as a *neutral arbiter* of class (and all other) conflicts. "Legitimation" theorists such as Claus Offe (1984), Jürgen Habermas (1975), and Alan Wolfe (1977) see these two goals as incompatible in the long run.

According to these theorists, the capitalist state has shouldered increasing economic and social welfare functions during the twentieth century in order to avoid economic crises. But these state actions have not been based on purely—or even largely—economic criteria. Instead, the general thrust of the twentieth-century welfare state has been to ensure an acceptable level of "mass loyalty." Moreover, as the state expands its actions into areas previously considered to belong to the "private" sphere of capital, increasing public attention and debate is drawn to issues of public choice, planning, and control, which reveal the state's preference for capital and the one-sided nature of its functioning (Habermas 1975, 68–73; Offe 1984, 155–57).

Different legitimation theorists have emphasized different aspects of this crisis. Some have argued that the growth of the welfare state has derailed anticapitalist politics to the extent that workers may find it "rational" to choose to struggle within capitalism for further reforms rather than seek to overthrow it as a system (Offe 1984, Przeworski 1985). Others have emphasized the degree to which the legitimation crisis of the modern state has displaced struggles for socialism to the level of struggles for democracy (Bowles and Gintis 1986, Wolfe 1977). All these theorists agree that the state can no longer be assumed to act solely and unambiguously in the interests of capital. Instead, state agencies and policies have become part of the field of class struggle, subject to cross-cutting and contradictory class-based pressures and influences. In Reading 14, Jürgen Habermas, a leading exponent of the legitimation thesis—and the most important contemporary figure associated with the Frankfurt School's approach (Habermas 1984, 1987), develops this argument in the context of a discussion of the nature of crises in contemporary "late" capitalism.

Another important theme that has emerged in Marxist theory in recent years is a displacement of analysis from the advanced capitalist societies of Western Europe and North America to a wider focus on capitalism as an integrated *world system* (Chase-Dunn 1990; Frank 1967, 1979; Wallerstein 1974; Wolf 1982). This "world-system perspective" (see Wallerstein, Reading 15) has developed an important, if often overlooked, strand in Marx's thought that links the historical development of Western capitalism with the underdevelopment of the "Third World" of Africa, Asia, and Latin America through the mechanisms of colonialism, economic trade, direct

investment, and extraction of raw materials. The development of capitalism and its eventual supersession by socialism, these theorists argue, cannot be understood in terms of national economies but must be studied as an interdependent worldwide phenomenon.

As Marxism has become absorbed into academic sociology, increasingly, academic Marxists find themselves influenced by intellectual currents prevalent in the larger sociological discipline. For many, this influence has led to a redefinition of their work as neo-Marxist, rather than Marxist, indicating a more eclectic and less orthodox approach to classical Marxist theory. The incorporation of new approaches and non-Marxist intellectual influences into Marxism has led to several new, and often unexpected, developments in contemporary neo-Marxist theory. Since the 1980s the leading problem in sociological theory has been to develop linkages between large-scale theories of social structure and social change and social-psychological theories of individual behavior, values, and motivation (see Chapter 5). This general interest in the "macro-micro link" has led neo-Marxists to reexamine the psychological and motivational basis of Marxist theory (see Geras 1983, Séve 1978).

For one group of neo-Marxists, this search has resulted in an attempt to incorporate the analytical model of *game theory*, which has been widely used in the social sciences as a paradigm of rational human behavior, into Marxist theory (see Carling 1986, Lash and Urry 1984, Roemer 1986). For these "analytical Marxists," as Erik Olin Wright (Reading 16) explains, greater attention to the microfoundations of Marxist theory are essential in order to clarify and extend the general explanatory power of the Marxian model as well as to confront the crisis of Marxist theory occasioned by the general failure of the socialist political project during the 1980s. The relevance of the rational choice model implicit in such game-theoretic Marxism has, however, been the subject of considerable controversy within Marxism and will continue to generate a great deal of debate in the future (see Wood 1989).

Another example of the fruitful cross-fertilization of Marxist theory by other theoretical traditions has been the increasing attention paid by neo-Marxists to feminist theory. The feminist critique of Marxism that emerged during the 1970s demonstrated convincingly that the classical Marxist paradigm had produced a male-centered discourse that ignored and denigrated the problems, contributions, and specific role of women (see Firestone 1970). The 1980s and 1990s, however, have seen the development of an impressive body of *socialist-feminist* literature, which has sought to blend the insights of Marxism and feminism to create new, more inclusive theories of women's oppression and male privilege in capitalism (see Eisenstein 1979, Hamilton and Barrett 1986, Hartsock 1983, Sargent 1981, Vogel 1983). In Reading 17, Lise Vogel surveys this literature and offers a perceptive assessment of several dominant themes in this socialist-feminist literature.

Neo-Marxism, over the last decade, has become established as one of the important theoretical schools in American sociology. Although it is a theory (or set of theories) that has been developed largely outside of the academic context, and despite the historical weakness of socialist thought in America, neo-Marxism has become increasingly accepted by American sociologists as an important and valid theoretical approach. Neo-Marxists have made important contributions in recent years in the sociology of law, political sociology, urban sociology, sociology of race relations, sociology of the family, and many other areas of sociological analysis (see Balbus 1977, Block 1987, Bonacich 1976, McNall, Levine, and Fantasia 1991, O'Connor 1973, Tabb and Sawyers 1978, Wiener 1978; for a recent general assessment, see the essays collected in McGuire and McQuarie 1994).

REFERENCES

ABERCROMBIE, NICHOLAS, AND JOHN URRY. 1983. *Capital, Labour and the Middle Class.* London: George Allen and Unwin.

ADORNO, THEODOR. 1967. *Prisms.* London: Neville Spearman.

BALBUS, ISAAC. 1977. *The Dialectics of Legal Repression.* New Brunswick: Transaction Books.

BENJAMIN, WALTER. 1969. *Illuminations.* New York: Schocken Books.

BENTON, TED. 1984. *The Rise and Fall of Structural Marxism.* New York: St. Martins Press.

BLOCK, FRED. 1987. *Revising State Theory.* Philadelphia: Temple University Press.

BOBBIO, NORBERTO. 1987. *Which Socialism?* Minneapolis: University of Minnesota Press.

BONACICH, EDNA. 1976. "Advanced Capitalism and Black-White Relations in the United States: A Split Labor Market Interpretation." *American Sociological Review* 41 (February):34–51.

BOTTOMORE, TOM, AND PATRICK GOODE, eds. 1978. *Austro-Marxism.* London: Oxford University Press.

BOWLES, SAMUEL, AND HERBERT GINTIS. 1986. *Democracy and Capitalism.* New York: Basic Books.

BRONNER, STEPHEN, AND DOUGLAS KELLNER, eds. 1989. *Critical Theory and Society.* New York: Routledge.

CARNOY, MARTIN. 1984. *The State and Political Theory.* Princeton: Princeton University Press.

CARCHEDI, GUGLIELMO. 1977. *On the Economic Identification of Social Classes.* London: Routledge and Kegan Paul.

CARLING, ALAN. 1986. "Rational Choice Marxism." *New Left Review* 160 (November–December:24–62.

CHASE-DUNN, CHRISTOPHER. 1990. *Global Formation: Structures of the World Economy.* Cambridge: Basil Blackwell.

COHEN, G.A. 1978. *Karl Marx's Theory of History: A Defense.* Princeton: Princeton University Press.

EISENSTEIN, ZILLAH, ed. 1979. *Capitalist Patriarchy and the Case for Socialist Feminism.* New York: Monthly Review Press.

FIRESTONE, SHULAMITH. 1970. *The Dialectic of Sex.* New York: Bantam Books.

FRANK, ANDRE GUNDER. 1967. *Capitalism and Underdevelopment in Latin America.* New York: Monthly Review Press.

_____. 1979. *Dependent Accumulation and Underdevelopment*. New York: Monthly Review Press.

FROMM, ERICH. 1941. *Escape from Freedom*. New York: Holt, Rinehart and Winston.

GERAS, NORMAN. 1983. *Marx and Human Nature*. London: New Left Books.

GRAMSCI, ANTONIO. 1971. *Selections from the Prison Notebooks*. New York: International Publishers.

HABERMAS, JÜRGEN. 1975. *Legitimation Crisis*. Boston: Beacon Press.

_____. 1984, 1987. *The Theory of Communicative Action*, vols. 1 and 2. Boston: Beacon Press.

HAMILTON, ROBERTA, AND MICHELE BARRETT, eds. 1986. *The Politics of Diversity*. London: Verso.

HARTSOCK, NANCY. 1983. *Money, Sex, and Power: Towards a Feminist Historical Materialism*. London: Longman.

HELD, DAVID. 1980. *Introduction to Critical Theory*. Berkeley: University of California Press.

HOBSBAWM, E.J. 1962. *The Age of Revolution, 1789–1848*. New York: World Publishing.

HORKHEIMER, MAX. 1972. *Critical Theory*. New York: Seabury Press.

HORKHEIMER, MAX, AND THEODOR ADORNO. 1972. *Dialectic of Enlightenment*. New York: Seabury Press.

JAY, MARTIN. 1973. *The Dialectical Imagination*. Boston: Little, Brown.

JORDAN, Z.A. 1967. *The Evolution of Dialectical Materialism*. New York: St. Martins Press.

LACLAU, ERNESTO, AND CHANTAL MOUFFE. 1985. *Hegemony and Socialist Strategy: Toward a Radical Democratic Politics*. London: Verso.

LASH, SCOTT, AND JOHN URRY. 1984. "The New Marxism of Collective Action: A Critical Analysis". *Sociology* 18 (February:34–50.

LICHTHEIM, GEORGE. 1965. *Marxism: An Historical and Critical Study*. New York: Praeger.

_____. 1969. *The Origins of Socialism*. New York: Praeger.

LOWENTHAL, LEO. 1961. *Literature, Popular Culture, and Society*. Englewood Cliffs: Prentice Hall.

LUDZ, PETER. 1975. "Marxism and Systems Theory." *Social Research* 42 (Winter):661–74.

MARCUSE, HERBERT. 1955. *Eros and Civilization*. Boston: Beacon Press.

_____. 1964. *One-Dimensional Man*. Boston: Beacon Press.

MARX, KARL. 1963. *The Poverty of Philosophy*. 1847. Reprint, New York: International Publishers.

_____. 1967. *Capital: Vol. I*. 1867. Reprint, New York: International Publishers.

_____. 1968. "Theses on Feuerbach." Pp. 28–30 in *Marx and Engels: Selected Works*. New York: International Publishers.

_____. 1970. *A Contribution to the Critique of Political Economy*. 1859. Reprint, New York: International Publishers.

MARX, KARL, AND FRIEDRICH ENGELS. 1955. *Selected Correspondence*. Moscow: Progress Publishers.

_____. 1968. "Manifesto of the Communist Party." Pp. 35–63 in *Marx and Engels: Selected Works*. New York: International Publishers.

MCGUIRE, PATRICK, AND DONALD MCQUARIE, eds. 1994. *From the Left Bank to the Mainstream: Historical Debates and Contemporary Research in Marxist Sociology*. New York: General Hall.

MCLELLAN, DAVID. 1973. *Karl Marx: His Life and Thought*. New York: Harper and Row.

MCNALL, SCOTT, RHONDA LEVINE, AND RICK FANTASIA, eds. 1991. *Bringing Class Back In*. Boulder: Westview Press.

MCQUARIE, DONALD, ed. 1978. *Marx: Sociology, Social Change, Capitalism*. London: Quartet Books.

MCQUARIE, DONALD, AND TERRY AMBURGEY. 1978. "Marx and Modern Systems Theory." *Social Science Quarterly* 59 (June):3–19.

MILIBAND, RALPH. 1969. *The State in Capitalist Society*. New York: Basic Books.

O'CONNOR, JAMES. 1973. *The Fiscal Crisis of the State*. New York: St. Martin's Press.

OFFE, CLAUS. 1984. *Contradictions of the Welfare State*. Cambridge: MIT Press.

OLLMAN, BERTELL. 1971. *Alienation: Marx's Conception of Man in Capitalist Society*. London: Cambridge University Press.

POSTER, MARK. 1975. *Existential Marxism in Postwar France*. Princeton: Princeton University Press.

POULANTZAS, NICOS. 1973. *Political Power and Social Class*. London: New Left Books.

_____. 1975. *Classes in Contemporary Capitalism*. London: New Left Books.

_____. 1978. *State, Power, Socialism*. London: New Left Books.

PRZEWORSKI, ADAM. 1985. *Capitalism and Social Democracy*. Cambridge: Cambridge University Press.

ROEMER, JOHN, ed. 1986. *Analytical Marxism*. Cambridge: Cambridge University Press.

SALVADORI MASSIMO. 1979. *Karl Kautsky and the Socialist Revolution (1880–1938)*. London: New Left Books.

SARGENT, LYDIA, ed. 1981. *Women and Revolution*. Boston: South End Press.

SCHROYER, TRENT. 1973. *The Critique of Domination*. New York: George Braziller.

SÉVE, LUCIEN. 1978. *Man in Marxist Theory.* Atlantic Highlands, New Jersey: Humanities Press.

SPAULDING, MARC, AND DONALD MCQUARIE. 1984. "Recent Developments in the Marxist Theory of Classes: Considerations on the 'New Middle Class'." *Social Science Journal* 21 (April):83–98.

STOJANOVIC, SVETOZAR. 1973. *Between Ideals and Reality.* New York: Oxford University Press.

SUCHTING, W.A. 1983. *Marx: An Introduction.* New York: New York University Press.

TABB, WILLIAM, AND LARRY SAWYERS, eds. 1978. *Marxism and the Metropolis.* New York: Oxford University Press.

THERBORN GÖRAN. 1976. *Science, Class and Society.* London: New Left Books.

VOGEL, LISE. 1983. *Marxism and the Oppression of Women.* New Brunswick: Rutgers University Press.

WALKER, PAT, ed. 1979. *Between Labor and Capital.* Boston: South End Press.

WALLERSTEIN, IMMANUEL. 1974. *The Modern World-System.* New York: Academic Press.

WIENER, JONATHAN. 1978. *Social Origins of the New South.* Baton Rouge: Louisiana State University Press.

WOLF, ERIC. 1982. *Europe and the People without History.* Berkeley: University of California Press.

WOLFE, ALAN. 1977. *The Limits of Legitimacy.* New York: Free Press.

WOOD, ELLEN MEIKSINS. 1989. "Rational Choice Marxism: Is the Game Worth the Candle?" *New Left Review* 177 (September–October):41–88.

SOME SOCIAL IMPLICATIONS
OF MODERN TECHNOLOGY*

HERBERT MARCUSE

In this article, technology is taken as a social process in which technics proper (that is, the technical apparatus of industry, transportation, communication) is but a partial factor. We do not ask for the influence or effect of technology on the human individuals. For they are themselves an integral part and factor of technology, not only as the men who invent or attend to machinery but also as the social groups which direct its application and utilization. Technology, as a mode of production, as the totality of instruments, devices and contrivances which characterize the machine age is thus at the same time a mode of organizing and perpetuating (or changing) social relationships, a manifestation of prevalent thought and behavior patterns, an instrument for control and domination.[1]

Technics by itself can promote authoritarianism as well as liberty, scarcity as well as abundance, the extension as well as the abolition of toil. National Socialism is a striking ex-ample of the ways in which a highly rationalized and mechanized economy with the utmost efficiency in production can operate in the interest of totalitarian oppression and continued scarcity. The Third Reich is indeed a form of "technocracy": the technical considerations of imperialistic efficiency and rationality supersede the traditional standards of profitability and general welfare. In National Socialist Germany, the reign of terror is sustained not only by brute force which is foreign to technology but also by the ingenious manipulation of the power inherent in technology: the intensification of labor, propaganda, the training of youths and workers, the organization of the governmental, industrial and party bureaucracy—all of which constitute the daily implements of terror—follow the lines of greatest technological efficiency. This terroristic technocracy cannot be attributed to the exceptional requirements of "war economy"; war economy is rather the normal state of the National Socialist ordering of the social and economic process, and technology is one of the chief stimuli of this ordering.[2]

In the course of the technological process a new rationality and new standards of individu-

*From Herbert Marcuse, "Some Social Implications of Modern Technology," *Studies in Philosophy and Social Science* 9:3 (1941), 414–23, 433, 435–39. Reprinted with permission of the heirs of Herbert Marcuse.

ality have spread over society, different from and even opposed to those which initiated the march of technology. These changes are not the (direct or derivative) effect of machinery on its users or of mass production on its consumers; they are rather themselves determining factors in the development of machinery and mass production. In order to understand their full import, it is necessary to survey briefly the traditional rationality and standards of individuality which are being dissolved by the present stage of the machine age.

The human individual whom the exponents of the middle class revolution had made the ultimate unit as well as the end of society stood for values which strikingly contradict those holding sway over society today. If we try to assemble in one guiding concept the various religious, political and economic tendencies which shaped the idea of the individual in the sixteenth and seventeenth century, we may define the individual as the subject of certain fundamental standards and values which no external authority was supposed to encroach upon. These standards and values pertained to the forms of life, social as well as personal, which were most adequate to the full development of man's faculties and abilities. By the same token, they were the "truth" of his individual and social existence. The individual, as a rational being, was deemed capable of finding these forms by his own thinking and, once he had acquired freedom of thought, of pursuing the course of action which would actualize them. Society's task was to grant him such freedom and to remove all restrictions upon his rational course of action.

The principle of individualism, the pursuit of self-interest, was conditioned upon the proposition that self-interest was rational, that is to say, that it resulted from and was constantly guided and controlled by autonomous thinking. The rational self-interest did not coincide with the individual's immediate self-interest, for the latter depended upon the standards and requirements of the prevailing social order, placed there not by his autonomous thought and conscience but by external authorities. In the context of radical Puritanism, the principle of individualism thus set the individual against his society. Men had to break through the whole system of ideas and values imposed upon them, and to find and seize the ideas and values that conformed to their rational interest. They had to live in a state of constant vigilance, apprehension, and criticism, to reject everything that was not true, not justified by free reason. This, in a society which was not yet rational, constituted a principle of permanent unrest and opposition. For false standards still governed the life of men, and the free individual was therefore he who criticised these standards, searched for the true ones and advanced their realization. The theme has nowhere been more fittingly expressed than in Milton's image of a "wicked race of deceivers, who . . . took the virgin Truth, hewd her lovely form into a thousand peeces, and scatter'd them to the four winds. From that time ever since, the sad friends of Truth, such as durst appear, imitating the careful search that Isis made for the mangl'd body of Osiris, went up and down gathering up limb by limb still as they could find them. We have not yet found them all, . . . nor ever shall do, till her Master's second coming . . . —To be still searching what we know not, by what we know, still closing up truth to truth as we find it (for all her body is homogeneal and proportionall)," this was the principle of individualistic rationality.[3]

To fulfill this rationality presupposed an adequate social and economic setting, one that would appeal to individuals whose social performance was, at least to a large extent, their own work. Liberalist society was held to be the adequate setting for individualistic rationality. In the sphere of free competition, the tangible achievements of the individual which made his products and performances a part of society's need, were the marks of his individuality. In the course of time, however, the process of commodity production undermined the economic basis on which individualistic rationality was built. Mechanization and rationalization forced the weaker competitor under the dominion of the giant enterprises of machine industry which, in establishing society's dominion over nature, abolished the free economic subject.

The principle of competitive efficiency favors the enterprises with the most highly mechanized and rationalized industrial equipment. Technological power tends to the concentration of economic power, to "large units of production, of vast corporate enterprises producing large quantities and often a striking variety of goods, of industrial empires owning and controlling materials, equipment, and processes from the extraction of raw materials to the distribution of finished products, of dominance over an entire industry by a small number of giant concerns. . . . " And technology "steadily increases the power at the command of giant concerns by creating new tools, processes and products."[4] Efficiency here called for integral unification and simplification, for removal of all "waste," the avoidance of all detours, it called for radical coordination. A contradiction exists, however, between the profit incentive that keeps the apparatus moving and the rise of the standard of living which this same apparatus has made possible. "Since control of production is in the hands of enterprisers working for profit, they will have at their disposal whatever emerges as surplus after rent, interest, labor, and other costs are met. These costs will be kept at the lowest possible minimum as a matter of course."[5] Under these circumstances, profitable employment of the apparatus dictates to a great extent the quantity, form and kind of commodities to be produced, and through this mode of production and distrib-

ution, the technological power of the apparatus affects the entire rationality of those whom it serves.

Under the impact of this apparatus, individualistic rationality has been transformed into technological rationality. It is by no means confined to the subjects and objects of large scale enterprises but characterizes the pervasive mode of thought and even the manifold forms of protest and rebellion. This rationality establishes standards of judgment and fosters attitudes which make men ready to accept and even to introcept the dictates of the apparatus.

Lewis Mumford has characterized man in the machine age as an "objective personality," one who has learned to transfer all subjective spontaneity to the machinery which he serves, to subordinate his life to the "matter-of-factness" of a world in which the machine is the factor and he the factum.[6] Individual distinctions in the aptitude, insight and knowledge are transformed into different quanta of skill and training, to be coordinated at any time within the common framework of standardized performances.

Individuality, however, has not disappeared. The free economic subject rather has developed into the object of large-scale organization and coordination, and individual achievement has been transformed into standardized efficiency. The latter is characterized by the fact that the individual's performance is motivated, guided and measured by standards external to him, standards pertaining to predetermined tasks and functions. The efficient individual is the one whose performance is an action only insofar as it is the proper reaction to the objective requirements of the apparatus, and his liberty is confined to the selection of the most adequate means for reaching a goal which he did not set. Whereas individual achievement is independent of recognition and consummated in the work itself, efficiency is a rewarded performance and consummated only in its value for the apparatus.

With the majority of the population, the former freedom of the economic subject was gradually submerged in the efficiency with which he performed services assigned to him. The world had been rationalized to such an extent, and this rationality had become such a social power that the individual could do no better than adjust himself without reservation. Veblen was among the first to derive the new matter-of-factness from the machine process, from which it spread over the whole society: "The share of the operative workman in the machine industry is (typically) that of an attendant, as assistant, whose duty it is to keep pace with the machine process and to help out with workmanlike manipulation at points where the machine process engaged is incomplete. His work supplements the machine process rather than makes use of it. On the contrary the machine process makes use of the workman. The ideal mechanical contrivance in this technological system is the automatic machine."[7] The machine process requires a knowledge oriented to "a ready apprehension of opaque facts, in passably exact quantitative terms. This class of knowledge presumes a certain intellectual or spiritual attitude on the part of the workman, such an attitude as will readily apprehend and appreciate matter of fact and will guard against the suffusion of this knowledge with putative animistic or anthropomorphic subtleties, quasi-personal interpretations of the observed phenomena and of their relations to one another."[8]

As an attitude, matter-of-factness is not bound to the machine process. Under all forms of social production men have taken and justified their motives and goals from the facts that made up their reality, and in doing so they have arrived at the most diverging philosophies. Matter-of-factness animated ancient materialism and hedonism, it was responsible in the struggle of modern physical science against spiritual oppression, and in the revolutionary rationalism of the enlightenment. The new attitude differs from all these in the highly rational compliance which typifies it. The facts directing man's thought and action are not those of nature which must be accepted in order to be mastered, or those of society which must be changed because they no longer correspond to human needs and potentialities. Rather are they those of the machine process, which itself appears as the embodiment of rationality and expediency.

Let us take a simple example. A man who travels by automobile to a distant place chooses his route from the highway maps. Towns, lakes and mountains appear as obstacles to be bypassed. The countryside is shaped and organized by the highway: what one finds en route is a byproduct or annex of the highway. Numerous signs and posters tell the traveler what to do and think; they even request his attention to the beauties of nature or the hallmarks of history. Others have done the thinking for him, and perhaps for the better. Convenient parking spaces have been constructed where the broadest and most surprising view is open. Giant advertisements tell him when to stop and find the pause that refreshes. And all this is indeed for his benefit, safety and comfort; he receives what he wants. Business, technics, human needs and nature are welded together into one rational and expedient mechanism. He will fare best who follows its directions, subordinating his spontaneity to the anonymous wisdom which ordered everything for him.

The decisive point is that this attitude—which dissolves all actions into a sequence of semi-spontaneous reactions to prescribed mechanical norms—is not only perfectly rational but also perfectly reasonable. All protest is senseless, and the individual who would insist on his freedom of action would become a crank. There is no personal escape from the apparatus which has mechanized and standardized the world. It is a rational apparatus, combining utmost expediency with utmost convenience, saving time and energy, removing waste, adapting all means to the end, anticipating consequences, sustaining calculability and security.

In manipulating the machine, man learns that obedience to the directions is the only way to obtain desired results. Getting along is identical with adjustment to the apparatus. There is no room for autonomy. Individualistic rationality has developed into efficient compliance with the pregiven continuum of means and ends. The latter absorbs the liberating efforts of thought, and the various functions of reason converge upon the unconditional maintenance of the apparatus. It has been frequently stressed that scientific discoveries and inventions are shelved as soon as they seem to interfere with the requirements of profitable marketing.[9] The necessity which is the mother of inventions is to a great extent the necessity of maintaining and expanding the apparatus. Inventions have "their chief use . . . in the service of business, not of industry, and their great further use is in the furtherance, or rather the acceleration, of obligatory social amenities." They are mostly of a competitive nature, and "any technological advantage gained by one competitor forthwith becomes a necessity to all the rest, on pain of defeat," so that one might as well say that, in the monopolistic system, "invention is the mother of necessity."[10]

Everything cooperates to turn human instincts, desires and thoughts into channels that feed the apparatus. Dominant economic and social organizations "do not maintain their power by force . . . They do it by identifying themselves with the faiths and loyalties of the people," [11] and the people have been trained to identify their faiths and loyalties with them. The relationships among men are increasingly mediated by the machine process. But the mechanical contrivances which facilitate intercourse among individuals also intercept and absorb their libido, thereby diverting it from the all too dangerous realm in which the individual is free of society. The average man hardly cares for any living being with the intensity and persistence he shows for his automobile. The machine that is adored is no longer dead matter but becomes something like a human being. And it gives back to man what it possesses: the life of the social apparatus to which it belongs. Human behavior is outfitted with the rationality of the machine process, and this rationality has definite social content. The machine process operates according to the laws of physical science, but it likewise operates according to the laws of mass production. Expediency in terms of technological reason is, at the same time, expediency in terms of profitable efficiency, and rationalization is, at the same time, monopolistic standardization and concentration. The more rationally the individual behaves and the more lovingly he attends to his rationalized work, the more he succumbs to the frustrating aspects of this rationality. He is losing his ability to abstract from the special form in which rationalization is carried through and is losing his faith in its unfulfilled potentialities. His matter-of-factness, his distrust of all values which transcend the facts of observation, his resentment against all "quasi-personal" and metaphysical interpretations, his suspicion of all standards which relate the observable order of things, the rationality of the apparatus, to the rationality of freedom,—this whole attitude serves all too well those who are interested in perpetuating the prevailing form of matters of fact. The machine process requires a "consistent training in the mechanical apprehension of things," and this training, in turn, promotes "conformity to the schedule of living," a "degree of trained insight and a facile strategy in all manner of quantitative adjustments and adaptations . . ."[12] The "mechanics of conformity" spread from the technological to the social order; they govern performance not only in the factories and shops, but also in the offices, schools, assemblies and, finally, in the realm of relaxation and entertainment.

Individuals are stripped of their individuality, not by external compulsion, but by the very rationality under which they live. Industrial psychology correctly assumes that "the dispositions of men are fixed emotional habits and as such they are quite dependable reaction patterns."[13] True, the force which transforms human performance into a series of dependable reactions is an external force: the machine process imposes upon men the patterns of mechanical behavior, and the standards of competitive efficiency are the more enforced from outside the less independent the individual competitor becomes. But man does not experience this loss of his freedom as the work of some hostile and foreign force; he relinquishes his liberty to the dictum of reason itself. The point is that today the apparatus to which the individual is to adjust and adapt himself is so rational that individual protest and liberation appear not only as hopeless but as utterly irrational. The system of life created by modern industry is one of the highest expediency, convenience and efficiency. Reason, once defined in these terms, becomes equivalent to an activity which perpetuates this world. Rational behavior becomes identical with a matter-of-factness which teaches reasonable submissiveness and thus guarantees getting along in the prevailing order. . . .

The idea of compliant efficiency perfectly illustrates the structure of technological rationality. Rationality is being transformed from a critical force into one of adjustment and compliance. Autonomy of reason loses its meaning in the same measure as the thoughts, feelings, and actions of men are shaped by the technical requirements of the apparatus which they have themselves created. Reason has found its resting place in the system of standardized control, production and consumption. There it reigns through the laws and mechanisms which insure the efficiency, expediency and coherence of this system.

As the laws and mechanisms of technological rationality spread over the whole society, they develop a set of truth values of their own which hold good for the functioning of the apparatus—and for that alone. Propositions concerning competitive or collusive behavior, business methods, principles of effective organization and control, fair play, the use of science and technics are true or false in terms of this value system, that is to say, in terms of instrumentalities that dictate their own ends. These truth values are tested and perpetuated by experience and must guide the thoughts and actions of all who wish to survive. Rationality here calls for unconditional compliance and coordination, and consequently, the truth values related to this rationality imply the subordination of thought to pregiven external standards. We may call this set of truth values the technological truth, technological in the twofold sense that it is an instrument of expediency rather than an end in itself, and that it follows the pattern of technological behavior.

By virtue of its subordination to external standards, the technological truth comes into striking contradiction with the form in which individualistic society had established its supreme values. The pursuit of self-interest now appears to be conditioned upon heteronomy, and autonomy as an obstacle rather than stimulus for rational action. The originally identical and "homogenous" truth seems to be split into two different sets of truth values and two different patterns of behavior: the one assimilated to the apparatus, the other antagonistic to it; the one making up the prevailing technological rationality and governing the behavior required by it, the other pertaining to a critical rationality whose values can be fulfilled only if it has itself shaped all personal and social relationships. The critical rationality derives from the principles of autonomy which individualistic society itself had declared to be its self-evident truths. Measuring these principles against the form in which individualistic society has actualized them, critical rationality accuses social injustice in the name of individualistic society's own ideology. The relationship between technological and critical truth is a difficult problem which cannot be dealt with here, but two points must be mentioned. (1) The two sets of truth values are neither wholly contradictory nor complementary to each other; many truths of technological rationality are preserved or transformed in critical rationality. (2) The distinction between the two sets is not rigid; the content of each set changes in the social process so that what were once critical truth values become technological values. For example, the proposition that every individual is equipped with certain inalienable rights is a critical proposition but it was frequently interpreted in favor of efficiency and concentration of power. . . .

The spreading hierarchy of large scale enterprise and the precipitation of individuals into masses determine the trends of technological rationality today. What results is the mature form of that individualistic rationality which characterized the free economic subject of the industrial revolution. Individualistic rationality was born as a critical and oppositional attitude that derived freedom of action from the unrestricted liberty of thought and conscience and measured all social standards and relations by the individual's rational self-interest. It grew into the rationality of competition in which the rational interest was superseded by the interest of the market, and individual achievement absorbed by efficiency. It ended with standardized submission to the all-embracing apparatus which it had itself created. This apparatus is the embodiment and resting place of individualistic rationality, but the latter now requires that individuality must go. He is rational who most efficiently accepts and executes what is allocated to him, who entrusts his fate to the large scale enterprises and organizations which administer the apparatus. . . .

The elements of restraint and resignation which became increasingly strong in the individualist philosophy of the nineteenth century elucidate the connection between individualism and scarcity. Individualism is the form liberty assumes in a society wherein the acquisition and utilization of wealth is dependent on competitive toil. Individuality is a distinct possession of "pioneers"; it presupposes the open and empty spaces, the freedom of "hewing out a home" as well as the need to do so. The individual's world is a "world of labor and the march," as Walt Whitman says, one in which the available intellectual and material resources must be conquered and appropriated through incessant struggle with man and nature, and in which human forces are released to distribute and administer scarcity.

In the period of large scale industry, however, the existential conditions making for individuality give way to conditions which render individuality unnecessary. In clearing the ground for the conquest of scarcity, the technological process not only levels individuality but also tends to transcend it where it is concurrent with scarcity. Mechanized mass production is filling the empty spaces in which individuality could assert itself. The cultural standardization points, paradoxically enough, to potential abundance as well as actual poverty. This standardization may indicate the extent to which individual creativeness and originality have been rendered unnecessary. With the decline of the liberalistic era, these qualities were vanishing from the domain of material production and becoming the ever more exclusive property of the highest intellectual activities. Now, they seem to disappear from this sphere too: mass culture is dissolving the traditional forms of art, literature and philosophy together with the "personality" which unfolded itself in producing and consuming them. The striking impoverishment which characterizes the dissolution of these forms may involve a new source of enrichment. They derived their truth from the fact that they represented the potentialities of man and nature which were excluded or distorted in the reality. So far were those potentialities from their actualization in the social consciousness that much cried out for unique expression. But today, *humanitas,* wisdom, beauty, freedom and happiness can no longer be represented as the realm of the "harmonious personality" nor as the remote heaven of art nor as metaphysical systems. The "ideal" has become so concrete and so universal that it grips the life of every human being, and the whole of mankind is drawn into the struggle for its realization. Under the terror that now threatens the world the ideal constricts itself to one single and at the same time common issue. Faced with Fascist barbarism, everyone knows what freedom means, and everyone is aware of the irrationality in the prevailing rationality.

Modern mass society quantifies the qualitative features of individual labor and standardizes the individualistic elements in the activities of intellectual culture. This process may bring to the fore the tendencies which make individuality a historical form of human existence, to be surpassed by further social development. This does not mean that society is bound to enter a stage of "collectivism." The collectivistic traits which characterize the development today may still belong to the phase of individualism. Masses and mass culture are manifestations of scarcity and frustration, and the authoritarian assertion of the common interest is but another form of the rule of particular interests over the whole. The fallacy of collectivism consists in that it equips the whole (society) with the traditional properties of the individual. Collectivism abolishes the free pursuit of competing individual interests but retains the idea of the common interest as a separate entity. Historically, however, the latter is but the counterpart of the former. Men experience their society as the objective embodiment of the collectivity as long as the individual interests are antagonistic to and competing with each other for a share in the social wealth. To such individuals, society appears as an objective entity, consisting of numerous things, institutions and agencies: plants and shops, business, police and law, government, schools and churches, prisons and hospitals, theaters and organizations, etc. Society is almost everything the individual is not, everything that determines his habits, thoughts and behavior patterns, that affects him from "outside." Accordingly, society is noticed chiefly as a power of restraint and control, providing the framework which integrates the goals, faculties and aspirations of men. It is this power which collectivism retains in its picture of society, thus perpetuating the rule of things and men over men.

The technological process itself furnishes no justification for such a collectivism. Technics hampers individual development only insofar as they are tied to a social apparatus which perpetuates scarcity, and this same apparatus has released forces which may shatter the special historical form in which technics is utilized. For this reason, all programs of an anti-technological character, all propaganda for an anti-industrial revolution serve only those who regard human needs as a by-product of the utilization of technics. The enemies of technics readily join forces with a terroristic technocracy. The philosophy of the simple life, the struggle against big cities and their culture frequently serves to teach men distrust of the potential instruments that could liberate them. We have pointed to the possible democratization of functions which technics may promote and which may facilitate complete human development in all branches of work and administration. Moreover, mechanization and standardization may one day help to shift the center of gravity from the necessities of material production to the arena of free human realization. The less individuality is required to assert itself in standardized social performances, the more it could retreat to a free "natural" ground. These tendencies, far from engendering collectivism, may lead to new forms of individualization. The machine individualizes men by following the physiological lines of individuality: it allocates the work to finger, hand, arm, foot, classifying and occupying men according to the dexterity of these organs. The external mechanisms which govern standardization here meet a "natural" individuality; they lay bare the ground on which a hitherto suppressed individualization might develop. On this ground, man is an individual by virtue of the uniqueness of his body and its unique position in the space-time continuum. He is an individual insofar as this natural uniqueness molds his thoughts, instincts, emotions, passions and desires. This is the "natural" *principium individuationis*. Under the system of scarcity, men developed their senses and organs chiefly as implements of labor and competitive orientation: skill, taste, proficiency, tact, refinement and endurance were qualities molded and perpetuated by the hard struggle for life, business and power. Consequently, man's thoughts, appetites and the ways of their fulfillment were not "his," they showed the oppressive and inhibitive features which this struggle imposed upon him. His senses, organs and appetites became acquisitive, exclusive and antagonistic. The technological process has reduced the variety of individual qualities down to this natural basis of individualization, but this same basis may become

the foundation for a new form of human development.

The philosophy of individualism established an intrinsic connection between individuality and property. According to this philosophy, man could not develop a self without conquering and cultivating a domain of his own, to be shaped exclusively by his free will and reason. The domain thus conquered and cultivated had become part and parcel of his own "nature." Man removed the objects in this domain from the state in which he found them, and made them the tangible manifestation of his individual labor and interest. They were his property because they were fused with the very essence of his personality. This construction did not correspond to the facts and lost its meaning in the era of mechanized commodity production, but it contained the truth that individual development, far from being an inner value only, required an external sphere of manifestation and an autonomous concern for men and things. The process of production has long dissolved the link between individual labor and property and now tends to dissolve the link between the traditional form of property and social control, but the tightening of this control counteracts a tendency which may give the individualistic theory a new content. Technological progress would make it possible to decrease the time and energy spent in the production of the necessities of life, and a gradual reduction of scarcity and abolition of competitive pursuits could permit the self to develop from its natural roots. The less time and energy man has to expend in maintaining his life and that of society, the greater the possibility that he can "individualize" the sphere of his human realization. Beyond the realm of necessity, the essential differences between men could unfold themselves: everyone could think and act by himself, speak his own language, have his own emotions and follow his own passions. No longer chained to competitive efficiency, the self could grow in the realm of satisfaction. Man could come into his own in his passions. The objects of his desires would be the less exchangeable the more they were seized and shaped by his free self. They would "belong" to him more than ever before, and such ownership would not be injurious, for it would not have to defend its own against a hostile society.

Such a Utopia would not be a state of perennial happiness. The "natural" individuality of man is also the source of his natural sorrow. If the human relations are nothing but human, if they are freed from all foreign standards, they will be permeated with the sadness of their singular content. They are transitory and irreplaceable, and their transitory character will be accentuated when concern for the human being is no longer mingled with fear for his material existence and overshadowed by the threat of poverty, hunger, and social ostracism.

The conflicts, however, which may arise from the natural individuality of men may not bear the violent and aggressive features which were so frequently attributed to the "state of nature." These features may be the marks of coercion and privation. "Appetite is never excessive, never furious, save when it has been starved. The frantic hunger we see it so often exhibiting under every variety of criminal form, marks only the hideous starvation to which society subjects it. It is not a normal but a morbid state of the appetite, growing exclusively out of the unnatural compression which is imposed upon it by the exigencies of our immature society. Every appetite and passion of man's nature is good and beautiful, and

destined to be fully enjoyed. . . . Remove, then, the existing bondage of humanity, remove those factitious restraints which keep appetite and passion on the perpetual lookout for escape, like steam from an overcharged boiler, and their force would instantly become conservative instead of destructive."[14]

NOTES

1. Cf. Lewis Mumford, *Technics and Civilization*, New York 1936, p. 364.

2. Cf. A.R.L. Gurland. "Technological Trends and Economic Structure under National Socialism," *Studies in Philosophy and Social Science* IX (1941), No. 2, pp. 226ff.

3. *Areopagitica*, in Works, New York 1931, 4, pp. 338–339.

4. *Temporary National Committee*, Monograph No. 22, "Technology in Our Economy," Washington, 1941, p. 195.

5. *Temporary National Economic Committee, Final Report of the Executive Secretary*, Washington 1941, p. 140.

6. L. Mumford, op. cit., pp. 361ff.

7. *The Instinct of Workmanship*, New York 1922, p. 306f.

8. Ibid., p. 310.

9. Florian Znaniecki, *The Social Role of the Man of Knowledge*, New York 1940, p. 54f. Bernard J. Stern, *Society and Medical Progress*, Princeton 1941, Chapter IX, and the same author's contribution to *Technological Trends and National Policy*, U.S. National Resources Committee, Washington 1937.

10. Thorstein Veblen, op. cit., p. 315f.

11. Thurman Arnold, *The Folklore of Capitalism*, New York 1941, p. 193f.

12. Thorstein Veblen, op. cit., p. 314.

13. Albert Walton, *Fundamentals of Industrial Psychology*, New York 1941, p. 24.

14. Henry James, "Democracy and Its Issues," in *Lectures and Miscellanies*, New York 1852, p. 47f.

NEO-MARXIST VIEWS OF THE STATE*

PHILIP KASINITZ

The revolution is not at hand. Although this fact is no surprise to anyone, it does merit some reflection. At the very moment when the industrialized West faces something akin to those "crises of capitalism" that Marxists have talked about for so long, almost everyone is finally admitting the obvious. Capitalism, for all its profound current difficulties, has outlived the Marxist predictions of its demise. This has not led to the progressive "immerseration" of the masses (at least in the industrialized nations)—and while capitalist societies may have changed greatly since Marx's day, reform, not revolution, has been the primary force in that transformation.

In light of these facts, it is not surprising that "theories of the state" now are the major growth industry in Marxist and neo-Marxist scholarship. As Marxist writers shift their attention from the question of how revolutions come about to that of why capitalist societies endure, the structure, history, and current problems of the welfare state take on a new importance. Yet while many scholars look to

the expanding role of the state as an explanation of the persistence of capitalism, few agree on what that role is or exactly how it is played. Even reference to scripture is of little help; for, like all holy texts, Marx bears a variety of interpretations. The notion of the state as the "executive committee" of the bourgeoisie has been interpreted to mean both that members of the bourgeoisie must participate directly in the governance of the state—and also that they need not do so because the state by its nature "functions" as an arm of the proprietary class. Still other analysts have pointed to the *Eighteenth Brumaire of Louis Bonaparte* as evidence that Marx himself, when not committed to the angry polemics of the *Manifesto,* saw the state as something more than an executive committee.

What follows, then, is a review of the major trends in recent neo-Marxist discussions of the state in advanced capitalism. Following John Mollenkopf and Theda Skocpol,[1] I shall describe the writers I consider "instrumentalists" or "structuralists," with the "structuralists" further divided between the functionalist approach of the late Nicos Poulantzas and the class-struggle approach in the recent work of Fred Block.

*From Philip Kasinitz, "Neo-Marxist Views of the State," *Dissent* 30:3 (Summer 1983), 337–46. Reprinted with permission of the Foundation for the Study of Independent Social Ideas and the author.

INSTRUMENTALISM

"Instrumental" views are those that tend to describe the state as the instrument of a specific social class. The common starting point for this loose grouping of writers is the refutation of pluralist theories of politics. All instrumentalists seek to demonstrate the continuing tendency of the upper class to dominate the state apparatus, while conceding that in "normal times" this class may be somewhat disunited and its members at cross purposes. Control of the state apparatus is maintained, nevertheless, through the formal and informal ties of the upper class to the state. Further, in times of crises members of this class use state intervention in the economy to maintain their position.

It is, therefore, the task of these theorists to demonstrate that the welfare-state reforms of post-New Deal America and Western Europe have not only served the long-run interests of capital but were instigated for that very purpose by the elite or, at least, by a farsighted vanguard of that elite. As Fred Block points out, "the heart of the theory is the idea that enlightened capitalists recognize that the crises of capitalism can be resolved through an extension of the state's role."[2]

Beyond this, the instrumentalists take widely different, though overlapping approaches. For the sake of discussion, they may be loosely subdivided into two groups. Both these groups address similar issues. The first consists of the historians of "corporate liberalism," notably James Weinstein and Ronald Radosh, who are concerned with tracing the evolution of the "corporate capitalist state" as a structure for mediating the contradictions of capitalism. (This approach has recently been criticized on historical grounds by Theda Skocpol.[3]) The second group contains such power-structure researchers as G. William Domhoff. This second group has concerned itself with teasing out elite influences on the governmental process as well as documenting class cohesion among the elites, something that more orthodox Marxists take for granted. The power-structure researchers also differ from the orthodox Marxists in that their definition of "elite" (they differ greatly among themselves on the particulars of this definition[4]) tends to be based on a combination of status characteristics, such as social-club membership and educational and ethnic background, as well as neo-Weberian common consumption and life-style characteristics. . . .

The power-structure theorists have consciously set out to challenge the pluralists on the latters' turf, examining the ways in which concrete decisions are made rather than the structural conditions that keep some issues from being raised.[5] Their task is to show exactly where and how a cohesive elite comes to dominate political decision-making.

William Domhoff, in response to criticism on this point, protests that while he is philosophically committed to the idea of "class hegemony," he views his role as "accepting the challenge" of the "dominant social science paradigm" and demonstrating upper-class dominance as a matter of "process." Given this, he maintains somewhat ambiguously that upper-class overrepresentation in positions of political power is a significant "indicator" of upper-class power, not that overrepresentation is power itself.[6] Ironically, while Domhoff has been criticized for his somewhat haphazard methodology even by his fellow instrumentalists,[7] he defends his stance by asserting that he is a level-headed empiricist using "the tried and true methods of sociological empiricism—operational definitions, network analysis, context analysis, disproportionate representation, and so forth."[8]

While the instrumentalists draw on Weberian sociology, their initial concepts are firmly within the Marxist tradition. Unlike Mills, they presume the existence of a "ruling class." (Domhoff, like Mills, generally uses the terms "elite" or "power elite." However, his work differs from Mills's precisely in that he maintains he has "grounded the power elite in a social class." Domhoff defines the "power elite as the leadership group or operating arm of the ruling class."[9] This enables him to describe the operation of the elite while remaining theoretically committed to class analysis.)

The instrumentalists' method is basically to tease out the workings of this "ruling class." The central difference between Domhoff and the pluralists is that while they share a method, they tend to look for evidence in different places. Domhoff, informed by his assumptions about what is important in American politics, expands his notion of the state to include interest groups, policy advisory councils, and the candidate-selection process. Pluralists have tended to focus discussion on more manifestly political events and decisions. Both have, not surprisingly, generally found what they were looking for.

Much power-structure research was inspired and in many cases directly undertaken by groups associated with the New Left. As might be expected, this research is sometimes crude and generally "action-oriented." The implicit political agenda accounts for both the theoretical strengths and weaknesses of the approach. Domhoff and his associates have done much to pin down exactly what and whom they mean by "the state." This pragmatic orientation is politically useful (for, as Saul Alinsky has pointed out, it is much easier to organize people to fight Mr. Jones's brutal oppression than to fight "social conditions prevalent under late capitalism"). It also has some scholarly merit. Power-structure research tends to avoid many of the muddled generalizations and sweeping assertions that obscure much structural Marxism.

However, as I will attempt to demonstrate, this is also a central theoretical weakness—for two reasons. First, power-structure research has tended to reduce class relations to those of individuals. Second, the instrumentalists have tended to accept a highly deterministic long-run view of history. For example, the mere absence of a socialist labor movement in the contemporary U.S. is seen as evidence that labor must have been somehow co-opted by class-conscious capitalists. The research question then becomes "when" and "how." This demonstrates a view of historical causation that is mainly a matter of faith. . . .

STRENGTH OF THE INSTRUMENTALIST ARGUMENT

Despite these problems, there are a number of appealing aspects to the instrumentalist argument as exemplified by Domhoff's work. Most central is a willingness to deal with flesh-and-blood people and real political events rather than with conceptual categories and scholastic abstractions.

Rather than presume a community of "real interests" based solely on class position, Domhoff attributes collective interests only to groups where a collective identity can be clearly demonstrated. Hence he is defining his "Higher Circles" as those people who belong to certain clubs, are listed in the *Social Register,* attend specific prep schools, or have both a father who was a millionaire entrepreneur or a high-level executive or lawyer *and* appropriate educational credentials. It follows that not all capitalists are elite members, nor are all elite members capitalists. Domhoff also describes the mechanisms through which elites circulate and the social practices by which new members are initiated into the elite's world view. While one may question the significance of the details of his anthropology, he certainly grounds his notions about class cohesion in demonstrable instances of mutual association.

Hence, for Domhoff, a professor who is both a millionaire's brother and a millionaire's son, remains a member of the elite, rather than becoming merely another wage slave. On the other hand, the first-generation entrepreneur, raised in poverty, who has no elite trappings and few elite associates, is not a member of the elite, regardless of how large a share of the means of production he may own (although he can later buy his children a place within the elite).

Rather than speak of "the state" in general terms, as if all capitalist states were the same, Domhoff deals specifically with certain agencies of the American government and describes how they are influenced by the specific needs of specific members of the elite. By thus restricting himself (primarily) to the American case, he is able to avoid the all too common error of imposing European theoretical notions on American reality. Again, while we may disagree with him on the significance of his findings, we must credit him for providing us with the grounds for this disagreement: his work lends itself to testing more readily than does the work of most structural Marxists. Power-structure researchers have localized the concept of upper-class power. For them, classes are not only national entities cut off from local roots, but also local elites with locatable needs and regional interests.

While the presumption that a ruling class exists and needs only to be found colors many of the instrumentalists' findings, their approach has generated a great deal of marvelous data. This material can be useful even to those who do not accept the instrumentalists' premises. For example, one need not accept that an elite consciously "dominates" the state apparatus in order to appreciate the importance of policy councils, industry groups, and even social clubs. Domhoff and others have discovered a great deal about upper-class definition, cohesion, and crystallization. We do not need to accept the whole argument in order to learn profitably from various pieces of it.

Domhoff recently complained that critics and friends alike have tended to trivialize certain aspects of his work, most notably the fascinating description of social clubs in *The Bohemian Grove and Other Resorts* (Harper and Row, 1974). He blames himself for paying too much attention to the anthropological exotica of the ruling class. But this flair for detail would be universally applauded were he investigating the Kikuyu or the contemporary urban "underclass." Americans exhibit a remarkable tendency to condescension toward the upper strata of society. Popular culture frequently portrays the rich as frivolous remnants of a dying class or as "eccentric" millionaires. As the media's enormous coverage of the recent Pulitzer divorce attests, Americans tend to look to the wealthy for entertainment—a view asserting that they are amusing precisely because they are not very important.

Domhoff's critics reflect this tendency. There is, however, nothing trivial about his findings. Indeed, that some of America's wealthiest people share summer retreats with conservative political leaders, that nonelected policy councils dominated by big business continue to have high-level input into foreign-policy decisions, and that 25 percent of our cabinet members in the 20th century have been listed in the Social Register—all these are significant observations.[10] They tell us a great deal about the real distribution of power in America. They do not, however, demonstrate *conscious elite domination* of the state. Power-structure research would tell us a great deal more were its proponents not out to prove so much.

WEAKNESSES OF THE INSTRUMENTALIST APPROACH

Instrumentalists argue that since state intervention in the economy and social welfare reforms did occur, and socialism did not, therefore state intervention prevented the otherwise "inevitable" transition to socialism. These reforms, they maintain, not only "saved" capitalism but were instituted by self-interested capitalists. The first point is pure conjecture, although it may be reasonable enough. One need not accept any "inevitable" teleologies to assert that reforms such as the New Deal turned out to be highly functional for U.S. capitalism. However, it does not follow that . . . Domhoff's "elite" . . . realized this at the time.

Skocpol shows not only that a large part of the capitalist class was dragged into the New Deal reforms, but that many aspects of the New Deal (most notably the Wagner Act) were in fact profoundly dysfunctional for capitalism in the first few years. Instrumentalist researchers credit capitalists with being incredibly long-sighted (could they have anticipated World War II or the position of labor in the prosperous 1950s?), and the resulting research systematically confuses function and intent. Today, many of us on the left are struck by the fact that a probusiness administration is enthusiastically dismantling regulations we long assumed to be in the interests of business. This does not necessarily mean that we were wrong in our original assumption; but it does mean that we cannot explain the function of these regulations by reference to what individual capitalists think of them.

Instrumentalists also assume that the mere presence of capitalists (or "elite members") or experts sponsored by capitalists within the state proves that those capitalists must rule in their own interests. Even were one to prove that the state was staffed exclusively by those on the payroll of the corporate elite, it does not follow that they would rule in the interests of the elite. As Skocpol points out, one might as well assert that the *Communist Manifesto* was in the interests of capitalism since at the time he wrote it, Marx was being "sponsored" by the son of a wealthy capitalist, one Friedrich Engels.

Since history is full of examples of men and women who led revolutionary struggles against their own class interests, why should we assume that contemporary capitalists are different? Domhoff never documents how many graduates of elite prep schools went on to become SDS activists or Marxist professors. Since in our society many sorts of political involvement are effectively restricted to those who are not pressed by the requirements of making a living, it should not be surprising to find the elite overrepresented throughout the political spectrum, and not merely on the side of the status quo.

The fact is that power-structure researchers, most notably Domhoff, actually are arguing two separate points: elite overrepresentation and elite domination. These are not at all the same thing. While Domhoff sets out to prove the latter, he in fact proves only the former. But who would be surprised by the fact that the wealthiest members of society are disproportionately represented in positions of power? Or, for that matter, who would be surprised by the corresponding fact that the poor and the working class are underrepresented? Does anyone today really maintain that power is equally distributed among U.S. citizens? Unequal distribution of political resources is the very cornerstone of the pluralist argument that Domhoff is supposedly trying to refute. The question is, at what point does overrepresentation constitute potential *domination,* that is, the real ability to control the outcome of all or at least of the most significant political disputes? By disproving the existence of equal representation in the U.S., instrumentalists have won a victory over a straw man.

Further, as both Block and Poulantzas have pointed out, the instrumentalists have tended to reduce the whole relationship of state and economy to that of capitalists and bureaucrats. Domhoff is so wedded to the notion of a self-conscious ruling class that he recently responded to criticism by asserting:

> . . . it seems highly unlikely that leaders within the ruling class, especially given the uncertainties of a capitalist economy, would be content to trust their fate to the workings of invisible structural restraints stressed by the structuralists. . . . [11]

Clearly, Domhoff assumes that the decision to delegate authority is a decision that capitalists are able to make; they hold the power to decide whether or not they will "trust" someone else. The model here is of a collection of individual decision-makers, not of a class in the Marxian sense. From Domhoff's point of view the question of how the ruling class might lose political battles and be *forced* into arrangements that turn out to help it in the long run cannot even come up.

This concept of power—power as always exercised at the pleasure of an elite that makes necessary concessions but remains firmly in control—underestimates the amount of real struggle by which reforms have been forced upon the state from below. By focusing entirely on upper-class concessions rather than working-class victories, Domhoff underestimates the power to force changes, or at least to disrupt the system, that labor and other interest groups may exert, particularly in times of economic and social upheaval.

If the state is an instrument of a given social class, it is difficult to conceive of other groups using control of the state apparatus to exact concessions over the vocal objections of that class. Yet in the history of urban American politics, this often has happened. The political machines were not, to be sure, any real threat to capitalism. But it would be a gross misreading of history to assert that Domhoff's self-conscious "higher circles" ever *perceived* the governments of William Marcy Tweed or James Michael Curley, for example, as being in their interests. In fact, the Social Register set was conspicuous in its attempts to "reform" and otherwise combat the immigrant machines. Many of these efforts were successful but, significantly, many were not.

Finally, instrumentalists have also tended to underestimate the autonomous bureaucracy as an independent force in the administration of the state. The real power of unionized civil service workers to shape policy and even bring the state to a point of fiscal crisis (as in New York City in 1975) cannot be explained by the instrumentalists' approach—for it is a strange "tool" that starts to exact its own demands of the user.

If, then, the instrumentalists' view of the state cannot facilitate an understanding of American politics, we must examine the more "structuralist" views. While these are extremely diverse, I will follow Skocpol's analysis and describe two distinct trends within the structuralist argument: what Skocpol terms "political functionalism," best exemplified by the early works of Nicos Poulantzas, and the "class struggle" position best seen in the recent works of Fred Block. While hardly representative of the total of structuralist arguments, they provide a useful contrast. While both share the structural starting point of the autonomous state, they represent extremes within the structuralist camp—from the most deterministic (Poulantzas) to the least (Block).

POLITICAL FUNCTIONALISM: A RELATIVELY AUTONOMOUS STATE

The late Nicos Poulantzas, whose debate with Ralph Miliband was the starting point for much of the instrumentalist vs. structuralist debated, viewed the state as a "relatively autonomous" institution: "autonomous," because state policy is seen as independent of the wills of capitalists; "relative" because of the ultimately "determinant role of relations of production."[12]

Poulantzas criticizes Miliband (he could have made an even stronger case against Domhoff) for not seeing classes as "objective structures and their relations as an objective system of regular connections, a structure and a system whose agents, men, are in the words of Marx 'bearers' of it. . . . "[13] For Poulantzas, the central difficulty in the work of modern Marxists is the confusion between men as actors and men as bearers of structural relations larger than themselves. The view that credits too much agency to individual actors, is, he argues, a non-Marxist view. In his reading of Marx, it is the structure of capitalist society and its culture that makes the state an executive committee of the bourgeoisie, not the decisions or actions of individuals.

Power for Poulantzas is the "capacity of a social class to realize its specific objective interests."[14] The state's interests correspond to those of the dominant class and hence, since classes are in constant struggle, must be in opposition to the interests of all classes other than the dominant one. Since the capitalist state was created by capitalists, the state's structural interests simply are the interests of capitalism, whether or not contemporary capitalists and contemporary bureaucrats realize the identity.

This means that direct participation of capitalists in the state, while possible, is not at all necessary for capitalist control of the state: this is only one possible arrangement and, moreover, a "chance and contingent one." Indeed, Poulantzas goes on to assert that under the modern capitalist system the state is likely to function best when capitalists are *not* directly involved. State bureaucrats must transcend the short-sighted interests of individual capitalists in favor of the general interests of capitalism. Hence the state may enforce necessary concessions, engage in long-term plan-

ning, and defend the interests of capitalism over those of particular capitalists. In addition, such an "autonomous" state serves to disunite workers, promote the privatized citizen and undermine the politics of class struggle. It is, in short, best for capitalism "when the ruling class is not the politically governing class."[15]

The major strength of this approach is that it separates the question of capitalist domination of society (Marx's question) from that of elite domination of the state apparatus (Domhoff's question). Hence Poulantzas is able to explain what happens in those situations where state intervention in the economy is needed to accomplish things that the nature of the competitive market prevents capitalists from accomplishing for themselves.

However, to call Poulantzas' notion of the state "autonomous" is quite misleading. For while he grants autonomy from class domination, he nevertheless paints a picture of a state utterly determined by structural imperatives, where all outcomes other than "revolution" are entirely predictable. For all his Marxist faith, Poulantzas is in many ways profoundly conservative. Anything other than "revolution" will "inevitably" be co-opted by capital. How is one to know when one places pressure on the state whether one is creating the groundwork for revolution or merely allowing the state to mediate social contradictions? In the long run, all nonrevolutionary change seems to be functional for the owning class. This view is problematic on two important counts.

First, if it is so, all history is predictable, so why bother to analyze specific situations (as Marx did)? Second, it negates as counterproductive all the very real progress that production workers have made without revolution in bettering their lives. It ignores the possibility of outcomes that are neither desirable for capital *nor* revolutionary.

Poulantzas' emphasis on objective structures implies an actorless notion of power and an ahistorical notion of the state. Men and women are cut out of the picture entirely, and the state has no specific history of its own—as if capitalists one day simply called it into being. His theory is so huge that we are left asking, "What state?" "When?" "By whom?" He ignores the unique character of the American, the French, or the German state. His formulation is based more upon its own internal logic than upon any concrete history.

Ironically, while Poulantzas can accept the fact of division within the capitalist class, he postulates the state as a unified whole that acts in a unified manner. But this surely contradicts what we know of the history of state intervention in the economy. While he denies that short-sighted capitalists understand their own long-run interests, he gives a remarkable crystal ball to short-sighted bureaucrats. He denies that their interests are ever at odds with those of the dominant class. He changes the state from the "tool" of conspirators to the "tool" of structures, and this is equally unacceptable.

A FULLY AUTONOMOUS STATE

Fred Block—while acknowledgding the contributions both of the instrumentalists and of Poulantzas—attempts to come up with a theory of the state capable of explaining class domination without reducing the state to a permanent conspiracy or a wholly determined structure. He still needs to explain what he perceives as the dominance of capital. But he has enough of a sense of history to want to leave room for struggles whose outcomes are not known in advance. Following Marx's *Eighteenth Brumaire,* he also wants to explain division *within* the capitalist class.

Block starts from the idea that modern capitalism consists of a division of labor between the rulers and the accumulators. He sees these two spheres as autonomous with no "inherent" reason why the state should serve the class of accumulators. Hence the question is reversed. Rather than ask whether the state can ever act against capitalist interests, Block asks why it tends to act in those interests. What structural factors reduce the likelihood of state managers turning against the dominant class? Why do state managers, who do not hesitate to intervene in the economy in the face of capitalist resistance, still tend to rationalize and reform capitalism rather than eliminate it?

Like Poulantzas, Block sees capitalists as concerned primarily with short-term profits. Unlike Poulantzas, he recognizes that these same capitalists are under constant pressure from workers who have their own goals. And the state, rather than simply refereeing the contest, is itself a third interested party. State officials also have their own goals: the maintenance of their rule, political stability, the steady collection of revenue, and the expansion of their own domain.

Both capital and labor apply pressure on the state to do their bidding and to "mediate the contradictions" of the system in ways favorable to them. Thus the state in the modern world is in a uniquely vulnerable position: if the economic sector fails, it is the government, not generally the economic system, that will fall. If taxes cannot be collected or if a fiscal crisis develops, it is the state that will have to cut back, its officials who will lose jobs and power.

The state therefore seeks economic stability not because of any mythical structural "needs," but because of simple self-interest on the part of politicians and bureaucrats. Either capital or labor (even movements of poor people outside the mainstream economy) can disrupt the economy. A large enough disruption can force the state to act or bring about the collapse of a particular administration or government. Capital, however, can disrupt the economy far more easily than labor. All capital needs to do is to refuse to invest. This requires no conspiracy. It is merely the aggregate of the individual capitalist responses to what is perceived to be a poor climate for investment. This aggregate response constitutes an effective veto over state policies that are interpreted as "bad for business." This is true for all capitalist states, but the veto works best in peripheral ones from which investors can easily shift their assets to other countries (witness Chile under Allende). More generally, however, the refusal to invest does not mean that the capitalists will themselves suffer from the resulting economic stagnation; they merely shift investment from productive, job-creating, stability-producing areas to savings and luxuries: Krugerrands, paintings, or rare wines.

Normally, this capital veto cannot be matched by labor. It is very difficult for labor to disrupt the system since this requires putting thousands of workers out on the streets and keeping up a sustained pressure. However, during certain exceptional periods, such as a depression or a war, when popular unrest runs high or when conscientious, willing workers are necessary to national safety, the labor veto becomes easier to apply. Under these special conditions, the state must respond to labor rather than to capital because labor can bring down the state much faster than capital can. Therefore, the state will intervene to restore economic stability, if necessary, at the expense of capital. But this does not lead to socialism because the same need for economic stability that forces the state to mediate on behalf of labor during a crisis will also force it to structure its intervention so as to appease capital as soon as the workers have left the streets and the crisis has passed.

State managers are always aware, as Block writes, that "exceptional periods are generally of a limited duration" and that they "will return to their earlier dependence on capitalist cooperation."[16] This explains for Block the "tendency" of state intervention to aid capital without denying the importance of conflict or "the continuous possibility of other outcomes."[17] Further, while arguing that the state will endeavor to restore business confidence, Block denies Poulantzas' claim that the state always does what is "necessary" toward this end:

This pattern is not a smoothly working functional process always producing the same result [Block writes]. State managers can make all kinds of mistakes, including excessive concessions to the working class. State managers have no special knowledge of what is necessary to make capitalism more rational. They grope toward effective action as best they can within existing political constraints. . . . [18]

Up to this point, Block is postulating a state that (as in Poulantzas' model) can intervene on behalf of a "a more general rationality." State bureaucrats "unlike the individual capitalist . . . do not have to operate on the narrow basis of a profit maximizing rationality."[19] At the same time, he gives these bureaucrats no crystal ball in which to perceive the "perfect" capitalist future. He describes the tendency of capital to prevail without resorting to hypothetical "real" interests (knowable only by astute social scientists) or to any mumbo-jumbo about structure. This much of his analysis I find quite appealing. But Block must be feeling a bit far from home by now because he adds an epicycle to his formulation to give it a touch of conventional Marxist teleology.

Class struggle is also, Block maintains, functional for capital in that every workers' victory forces capital to improve methods of production and control. If wages go up, capitalists have to develop more capital-intensive technology. This "diminishes the capacity of workers to win wage gains." In short, "class struggle is responsible for much of the economic dynamism of capitalism."[20] Changes in the relations of production produce changes in the means of production.

Every step of this cycle pushes capitalism forward. It also humanizes and at the same time rationalizes and reinforces capitalist domination. This account gives to Block's theory an uncomfortable determinism of its own. For, where is this spiral leading? Is social democracy the highest form (and hence the "last stage") of capitalism? Is it a step toward liberation or a more insidious form of oppression? Is incremental reform necessary and progressive, or does it merely rationalize the system that must be smashed by a vanguard party of some sort? I remain uncertain as to whether Block is an advocate of social democracy or Leninism, and whether he believes that the second must follow the first.

Block's commitment to the class struggle as the motor of history mars his otherwise admirable attempt to develop a neo-Marxist theory that has real explanatory value for modern capitalist policies. Perhaps he feels that to abandon this notion would place him outside the Marxian tradition. (It would certainly make his work substantially more "neo" than "Marxist"!) This would be unfortunate, for if the arguments I have reviewed teach us anything, it is the futility of explaining the contemporary state by fitting it into worn-out teleologies.

What is needed, it seems to me, is an analysis of the state that continues to ask vital "Marxist questions"—What is the relationship between economic inequality and political domination? How can we change the status quo? At the same time we must acknowledge the indeterminate nature of politics and the unpredictability of history. Given the expanding role of the state in capitalist societies (not to mention the overwhelming and often terrifying role of the state in noncapitalist societies), we can hardly afford to underestimate the state's independence or to conceive of it as a reflection of anything. For neo-Marxist political analysis to move forward, it must not rely on old formulations about the necessary interconnectedness of state, economy, and society. It must view these interconnections afresh in light of the dynamic nature of capitalism as it is today. It must abandon theoretical tools that obscure more than they elucidate—which is, after all, exactly what Marx himself did.

NOTES

1. See John Mollenkopf. "Theories of the State and Power Structure Research," *Insurgent Sociologist* 4 (Spring 1975). Also Theda Skocpol. "Political Response to Capitalist Crises: Neo-Marxist Theories of the State and the New Deal," *Politics and Society* 10, no. 12 (1980), pp. 155–201.

2. Fred Block, "Beyond Corporate Liberalism," *Social Problems* 24 (February 1977), p. 355.

3. Skocpol, "Political Response."

4. For an analysis of various definitions of the term "elite," see Harold Kerbo and Richard Della Fave, "The Empirical Side of the Power Elite Debate," *Sociological Quarterly* 20, no. 1 (1979), pp. 5–22.

5. This "decisionist" view of power, emphasizing the ability of actors to effect political decisions, is best exemplified in Robert Dahl, *Who Governs?* (New Haven: Yale University Press, 1961). It is criticized in Steven Lukes, *Power: A Radical View* (London and New York: Macmillan, 1974), as a "one-dimensional view of power."

6. G. William Domhoff, *The Powers That Be* (New York: Vintage, 1979), pp. 9 and 23.

7. Kerbo and Della Fave, "The Empirical Side." Also Ted George Goertzel, *Political Sociology* (New York: Rand McNally, 1976).

8. G. William Domhoff, "Provincial in Paris: Finding the French Council on Foreign Relations," *Social Policy*, March–April 1981.

9. Domhoff, *The Powers That Be*, pp. 14 and 13.

10. G. William Domhoff, *Bohemian Grove and Other Resorts* (New York: Harper & Row, 1974), and Domhoff, *The Powers That Be*; see also Richard Zweigenhaft, "Who Represents America?" *Insurgent Sociologist* 4, no. 3 (1975).

11. Domhoff, "Provincial in Paris," p. 6.

12. Nicos Poulantzas, interviewed by Stuart Hall and Alan Hunt, in *Socialist Review* 48 (Nov.–Dec. 1979), p. 67.

13. Nicos Poulantzas, "The Problem of the Capitalist State," *New Left Review* 58 (Nov.–Dec. 1969).

14. Nicos Poulantzas, *Political Power and Social Classes* (London: Verso, 1973), pp. 104 and 120.

15. Poulantzas, "Problem of the Capitalist State," p. 73.

16. Fred Block. "Beyond Relative Autonomy: State Managers as Historical Subjects," *New Political Science* 2 (Fall 1981), p. 39.

17. Fred Block, "The Ruling Class Does Not Rule," *Socialist Revolution* 33 (1977), p. 23.

18. Ibid., p. 26.

19. Ibid., p. 20.

20. Ibid., p. 21.

WHAT DOES A CRISIS MEAN TODAY?
LEGITIMATION PROBLEMS IN LATE CAPITALISM*

JÜRGEN HABERMAS

The expression "late capitalism" implicitly asserts that, even in state-regulated capitalism, social developments are still passing through "contradictions" or crises. I would therefore like to begin by elucidating the concept of *crisis.*

Prior to its use in economics, we are familiar with the concept of crisis in medicine. It refers to that phase of a disease in which it is decided whether the self-healing powers of the organism are sufficient for recovery. The critical process, the disease, seems to be something objective. A contagious disease, for instance, affects the organism from outside. The deviations of the organism from what it should be—i.e., the patient's normal condition—can be observed and, if necessary, measured with the help of indicators. The patient's consciousness plays no part in this. *How* the patient feels and *how* he experiences his illness is at most a symptom of events that he himself can barely influence. Nevertheless, we

would not speak of a crisis in a medical situation of life or death if the patient were not trapped in this process with all his subjectivity. A crisis cannot be separated from the victim's inner view. He experiences his impotence toward the objectivity of his illness only because he is a subject doomed to passivity and temporarily unable to be a subject in full possession of his strength.

Crisis suggests the notion of an objective power depriving a subject of part of his normal sovereignty. If we interpret a process as a crisis, we are tacitly giving it a normative meaning. When the crisis is resolved, the trapped subject is liberated.

This becomes clearer when we pass from the medical to the dramaturgical notion of crisis. In classical aesthetics from Aristotle to Hegel, crisis signifies the turning point of a fateful process which, although fully objective, does not simply break in from the outside. There is a contradiction expressed in the catastrophic culmination of a conflict of action, and that contradiction is inherent in the very structure of the system of action and in the personality systems of the characters. Fate is revealed in conflicting norms that destroy

*From Jürgen Habermas, "What Does a Crisis Mean Today? Legitimation Problems in Late Capitalism," *Social Research* 40:4 (Winter 1973), 643–60, 667. Reprinted with permission of *Social Research* and the author.

the identities of the characters unless they in turn manage to regain their freedom by smashing the mythical power of fate.

The notion of crisis developed by classical tragedy has its counterpart in the notion of crisis to be found in the doctrine of salvation. Recurring throughout the philosophy of history in the eighteenth century, this figure of thought enters the evolutionary social theories of the nineteenth century. Marx is the first to develop a sociological concept of system crisis. It is against that background that we now speak of social or economic crises. In any discussion of, say, the great economic crisis in the early 'thirties, the Marxist overtones are unmistakable.

Since capitalist societies have the capacity of steadily developing technological productive forces, Marx conceives an economic crisis as a *crisis-ridden process of economic growth*. Accumulation of capital is tied to the acquisition of surplus. This means for Marx that economic growth is regulated by a mechanism that both establishes and conceals a power relationship. Thus the model of rising complexity is contradictory in the sense that the economic system keeps creating new and more problems as it solves others. The total accumulation of capital passes through periodic devaluations of capital components: this forms the cycle of crises, which Marx in his time was able to observe. He tried to explain the classical type of crisis by applying the theory of value with the help of the law of the tendential fall of the rate of profit. But that is outside my purpose at the moment. My question is really: Is late capitalism following the same or similar self-destructive pattern of development as classical—i.e., competitive—capitalism? Or has the organizing principle of late capitalism changed so greatly that the accumulation process no longer generates any problems jeopardizing its existence?

My starting point will be a rough descriptive model of the most important structural features of late-capitalist societies. I will then mention three crisis tendencies which today, though not specific to the system, are major topics of discussion. And finally, I will deal with various explanations of the crisis tendencies in late capitalism.

STRUCTURAL FEATURES OF LATE-CAPITALIST SOCIETIES

The expression "organized or state-regulated capitalism" refers to two classes of phenomena both of which can be traced back to the advanced stage of the accumulation process. One such class is the process of economic concentration (the creation of national and by now even multinational corporations) and the organization of markets for goods, capital, and labor. On the other hand, the interventionist state keeps filling the increasing functional gaps in the market. The spread of oligopolistic market structures certainly spells the end of competitive capitalism. But no matter how far companies may see into the future or extend their control over the environment, the steering mechanism of the market will continue to function as long as investments are determined by company profits. At the same time, by complementing and partially replacing the market mechanism, government intervention means the end of liberal capitalism. But no matter how much the state may restrict the owner of goods in his private autonomous activity, there will be no political planning to allocate scarce resources as long as the overall societal priorities develop naturally—i.e., as indirect results of the strategies of private enterprise. In advanced capitalist societies, the economic, the administrative, and the legitimation systems can be characterized as follows.

The Economic System. During the 1960s, various authors, using the example of the United States, developed a three-sector model based on the distinction between the private and public areas. Private production is market-oriented, one sector still regulated by competition, another by the market strategies of the oligopolies that tolerate a competitive fringe. However, the public area, especially in the wake of armament and space-travel production, has witnessed the rise of great industries which, in their investment decisions, can operate independently of the market. These are either enterprises directly controlled by the government or private firms living on government contracts. The monopolistic and the public sectors are dominated by capital-intensive industries; the competitive sector is dominated by labor-intensive industries. In the monopolistic and the public sectors, the industries are faced with powerful unions. But in the competitive sector, labor is not as well organized, and the salary levels are correspondingly different. In the monopolistic sector, we can observe relatively rapid progress in production. However, in the public sector, the companies do not *need* to be, and in the competitive sector they *cannot* be, that efficient.

The Administrative System. The state apparatus regulates the overall economic cycle by means of global planning. On the other hand, it also improves the conditions for utilizing capital.

Global planning is limited by private autonomous use of the means of production (the investment freedom of private enterprises cannot be restricted). It is limited on the other hand by the general purpose of crisis management. There are fiscal and financial measures to regulate cycles, as well as individual measures to regulate investments and overall demand (credits, price guarantees, subsidies, loans, secondary redistribution of income, government contracts based on business-cycle policies, indirect labor-market policies, etc.). All these measures have the reactive character of avoidance strategies within the context of a well-known preference system. This system is determined by a didactically demanded compromise between competing imperatives: steady growth, stability of money value, full employment, and balance of trade.

Global planning manipulates the marginal conditions of decisions made by private enterprise. It does so in order to *correct* the market mechanism by neutralizing dysfunctional side effects. The state, however, *supplants* the market mechanism wherever the government creates and improves conditions for utilizing excess accumulated capital. It does so:

- by "strengthening the competitive capacity of the nation," by organizing supranational economic blocks, by an imperialistic safeguarding of international stratification, etc.;
- by unproductive government consumption (armament and space-travel industry);
- by politically structured guidance of capital in sectors neglected by an autonomous market;
- by improving the material infrastructure (transportation, education and health, vocation centers, urban and regional planning, housing, etc.);
- by improving the immaterial infrastructure (promotion of scientific research, capital expenditure in research and development, intermediary of patents, etc.);
- by increasing the productivity of human labor (universal education, vocational schooling, programs of training and reeducation, etc.);
- by paying for the social costs and real consequences of private production (unemployment, welfare; ecological damage).

The Legitimation System. With the functional weaknesses of the market and the dysfunctional side effects of the market mechanism, the basic bourgeois ideology of fair exchange also collapsed. Yet there is a need for even greater legitimation. The government apparatus no longer merely safeguards the prerequisites for the production process. It also, on its own initiative, intervenes in that process. It must therefore be legitimated in the growing realms of state intervention, even though there is now no possibility of reverting to the

Arguable - A univ. idea/?

traditions that have been undermined and worn out in competitive capitalism. The universalistic value systems of bourgeois ideology have made civil rights, including suffrage, universal. Independent of general elections, legitimation can thus be gotten only in extraordinary circumstances and temporarily. The resulting problem is resolved through formal democracy.

A wide participation by the citizens in the process of shaping political will—i.e., genuine democracy—would have to expose the contradiction between administratively socialized production and a still private form of acquiring the produced values. In order to keep the contradiction from being thematized, one thing is necessary. The administrative system has to be sufficiently independent of the shaping of legitimating will. This occurs in a legitimation process that elicits mass loyalty but avoids participation. In the midst of an objectively politicized society, the members enjoy the status of passive citizens with the right to withhold their acclaim. The private autonomous decision about investments is complemented by the civil privatism of the population.

Class Structure. The structures of late capitalism can be regarded as a kind of reaction formation. To stave off the system crisis, late-capitalist societies focus all socially integrative strength on the conflict that is structurally most probable. They do so in order all the more effectively to keep that conflict latent.

In this connection, an important part is played by the quasi-political wage structure, which depends on negotiations between companies and unions. Price fixing, which has replaced price competition in the oligopolistic markets, has its counterpart in the labor market. The great industries almost administratively control the prices in their marketing territories. Likewise, through wage negotiations, they achieve quasi-political compromises with their union adversaries. In those industrial branches of the monopolistic and public sectors that are crucial to economic development, the commodity known as labor has a "political" price. The "wage-scale partners" find a broad zone of compromise, since increased labor costs can be passed on into the prices, and the middle-range demands made by both sides against the government tend to converge. The main consequences of immunizing the original conflict zone are as follows: (1) disparate wage developments; (2) a permanent inflation with the corresponding short-lived redistribution of incomes to the disadvantage of unorganized wage earners and other marginal groups; (3) a permanent crisis in government finances, coupled with public poverty—i.e., pauperization of public transportation, education, housing, and health; (4) an insufficient balance of disproportionate economic developments, both sectoral (e.g., agriculture) and regional (marginal areas).

Since World War II, the most advanced capitalist countries have kept the class conflict latent in its essential areas. They have extended the business cycle, transforming the periodic pressures of capital devaluation into a permanent inflationary crisis with milder cyclical fluctuations. And they have filtered down the dysfunctional side effects of the intercepted economic crisis and scattered them over quasi-groups (such as consumers, school children and their parents, transportation users, the sick, the elderly) or divided groups difficult to organize. This process breaks down the social identity of the classes and fragments class consciousness. In the class compromise now part of the structure of late capitalism, nearly everyone both participates and is affected as an individual—although, with the clear and sometimes growing unequal distribution of monetary values and power, one can well distinguish between those belonging more to the one or to the other category.

THREE DEVELOPING CRISES

The rapid growth processes of the late-capitalist societies have confronted the system of world society with new problems. These problems cannot be regarded as crisis phenomena specific to the system, even though the possibilities of coping with the crises *are* specific to the system and therefore limited. I am thinking of the disturbance of the ecological balance, the violation of the personality system (alienation), and the explosive strain on international relations.

The Ecological Balance. If physically economic growth can be traced back to the technologically sophisticated use of more energy to increase the productivity of human labor, then the societal formation of capitalism is remarkable for impressively solving the problem of economic growth. To be sure, capital accumulation originally pushes economic growth ahead, so there is no option for the conscious steering of this process. The growth imperatives originally followed by capitalism have meanwhile achieved a global validity by way of system competition and worldwide diffusion (despite the stagnation or even retrogressive trends in some Third World countries).

The mechanisms of growth are forcing an increase of both population and production on a worldwide scale. The economic needs of a growing population and the productive exploitation of nature are faced with material restrictions: on the one hand, finite resources (cultivable and inhabitable land, fresh water, metals, minerals, etc.); on the other hand, irreplaceable ecological systems that absorb pollutants such as fallout, carbon dioxide, and waste heat. Forrester and others have estimated the limits of the exponential growth of population, industrial production, exploitation of natural resources, and environmental pollution. To be sure, their estimates have rather weak empirical foundations. The mechanisms of population growth are as little known as the maximum limits of the earth's potential for absorbing even the major pollutants. Moreover, we cannot forecast technological development accurately enough to know which raw materials will be replaced or renovated by future technology.

However, despite any optimistic assurances, we are able to indicate (if not precisely determine) *one* absolute limitation on growth: the thermal strain on the environment due to consumption of energy. If economic growth is necessarily coupled with increasing consumption of energy, and if all natural energy that is transformed into economically useful energy is ultimately released as heat, it will eventually raise the temperature of the atmosphere. Again, determining the deadline is not easy. Nevertheless, these reflections show that an exponential growth of population and production—i.e., an expanded control over external nature—will some day run up against the limits of the biological capacity of the environment.

This is not limited to complex societal systems. Specific to these systems are the possibilities of warding off dangers to the ecology. Late-capitalist societies would have a very hard time limiting growth without abandoning their principle of organization, because an overall shift from spontaneous capitalist growth to qualitative growth would require production planning in terms of use-values.

The Anthropological Balance. While the disturbance of the ecological balance points out the negative aspect of the exploitation of natural resources, there are no sure signals for the capacity limits of personality systems. I doubt whether it is possible to identify such things as psychological constants of human nature that inwardly limit the socialization process. I do, however, see a limitation in the kind of socializing that societal systems have been using to create motives for action. Our behavior is oriented by norms requiring justification and by interpretative systems guaranteeing identity. Such a communicative organization of behavior can become an obstacle in complex societies for a simple reason. The adaptive capacity in organizations increases proportionately as the administrative authorities become independent of the particular motivations of the members. The choice and achievement of organization goals in systems of high intrinsic complexity have to be independent of the influx of narrowly delimited motives. This requires a generalized willingness to comply (in political systems, such willingness has the form of legitimation). As long as socialization brings inner nature into a communicative behavioral organization, no legitimation for norms of action could conceivably secure an unmotivated acceptance of decisions. In regard to decisions whose contents are still undetermined, people will comply if convinced that those decisions are based on a legitimate norm of action. If the motives for acting were no longer to pass through norms requiring justification, and if the personality structures no longer had to find their unity under interpretative systems guaranteeing identity, then (and only then) the unmotivated acceptance of decisions would become an irreproachable routine, and the readiness to comply could thus be produced to any desirable degree.

The International Balance. The dangers of destroying the world system with thermonuclear weapons are on a different level. The accumulated potential for annihilation is a result of the advanced stage of productive forces. Its basis is technologically neutral, and so the productive forces can also take the form of destructive forces (which has happened because international communication is still undeveloped). Today, mortal damage to the natural substratum of global society is quite possible. International communication is therefore governed by a historically new imperative of self-limitation. Once again, this is not limited to all highly militarized societal systems, but the possibilities of tackling this problem have limits specific to the systems. An actual disarmament may be unlikely because of the forces behind capitalist and postcapitalist class societies. Yet regulating the arms race is not basically incompatible with the structure of late-capitalist societies if it is possible to increase technologically the use-value of capital to the degree that the capacity effect of the government's demand for unproductive consumer goods can be balanced.

DISTURBANCES SPECIFIC TO THE SYSTEM

I would now like to leave these three global consequences of late-capitalist growth and investigate disturbances specific to the system. I will start with a thesis, widespread among Marxists, that the basic capitalist structures continue unaltered and create economic crises in altered manifestations. In late capitalism, the state pursues the politics of capital with other means. This thesis occurs in two versions.

Orthodox state-theory maintains that the activities of the interventionist state, no less than the exchange processes in liberal capitalism, obey economic laws. The altered manifestations (the crisis of state finances and permanent inflation, growing disparities between public poverty and private wealth, etc.) are due to the fact that the self-regulation of the realization process is governed by power rather than by exchange. However, the crisis tendency is determined, as much as ever, by the law of value, the structurally forced asymmetry in the exchange of wage labor for capital. As a result, state activity cannot permanently compensate for the tendency of falling rates of profit. It can at best mediate that trend—i.e., consummate it with political means. The replacement of market functions by state functions does not alter the unconscious nature of the overall economic process. This is shown by the narrow limits of the state's possibilities for manipulation. The state cannot substantially intervene in the property structure without causing an investment strike. Neither can it manage to permanently avoid cyclical stagnation tendencies of the accumulation process—i.e., stagnation tendencies that are created endogenously.

A revisionist version of the Marxist theory of the state is current among leading economists in the German Democratic Republic. According to this version, the state apparatus, instead of naturally obeying the logic of the law of value, is consciously supporting the interests of united monopoly capitalists. This agency theory, adapted to late capitalism, regards the state not as a blind organ of the realization process but as a potent supreme capitalist who makes the accumulation of capital the substance of his political planning. The high degree of the socialization of production brings together the individual interests of the large corporations and the interest in maintaining the system. And all the more so because its existence is threatened internally by forces transcending the system. This leads to an overall capitalist interest, which the united monopolies sustain with the aid of the state apparatus.

I consider both versions of the theory of economic crises inadequate. One version underestimates the state, the other overestimates it.

In regard to the orthodox thesis, I wonder if the state-controlled organization of scientific and technological progress and the system of collective bargaining (a system producing a class compromise, especially in the capital- and growth-intensive economic sectors) have not altered the mode of production. The state, having been drawn into the process of production, has modified the determinants of the process of utilizing capital. On the basis of a partial class compromise, the administrative system has gained a limited planning capacity. This can be used within the framework of the democratic acquisition of legitimation for purposes of reactive avoidance of crises. The cycle of crises is deactivated and rendered less harmful in its social consequences. It is replaced by inflation and a permanent crisis of public finances. The question as to whether these surrogates indicate a successful halting of the economic crisis or merely its temporary shift into the political system is an empirical one. Ultimately, this depends on whether the indirectly productive capital invested in research, development, and education can continue the process of accumulation. It can manage to do so by making labor more productive, raising the rate of surplus value, and cheapening the fixed components of capital.

The revisionist theory has elicited the following reservations. For one thing, we cannot empirically support the assumption that the state apparatus, no matter in whose interest, can actively plan, as well as draft and carry through, a central economic strategy. The theory of state-monopoly capitalism (akin to Western theories of technocracy) fails to recognize the limits of administrative planning in late capitalism. Bureaucracies for planning always reactively avoid crises. The various bureaucracies are not fully coordinated, and because of their limited capacity for perceiving and steering, they tend to depend largely on the influence of their clients. It is because of this very inefficiency that organized partial interests have a chance to penetrate the administrative apparatus. Nor can we empirically support the other assumption that the state is active as the agent of the united monopolists.

The theory of state-monopoly capitalism (akin to Western elite theories) overrates the significance of personal contacts and direct influence. Studies on the recruiting, make-up, and interaction of the various power elites fail to cogently explain the functional connections between the economic and administrative systems.

In my opinion, the late-capitalist state can be properly understood neither as the unconscious executive organ of economic laws nor as a systematic agent of the united monopoly capitalists. Instead, I would join Claus Offe in advocating the theory that late-capitalist societies are faced with two difficulties caused by the state's having to intervene in the growing functional gaps of the market. We can regard the state as a system that uses legitimate power. Its output consists in sovereignly executing administrative decisions. To this end, it needs an input of mass loyalty that is as unspecific as possible. Both directions can lead to crisislike disturbances. Output crises have the form of the efficiency crisis. The administrative system fails to fulfill the steering imperative that it has taken over from the economic system. This results in the disorganization of different areas of life. Input crises have the form of the legitimation crisis. The legitimation system fails to maintain the necessary level of mass loyalty. We can clarify this with the example of the acute difficulties in public finances, with which all late-capitalist societies are now struggling.

The government budget, as I have said, is burdened with the public expenses of an increasingly socialized production. It bears the costs of international competition and of the demand for unproductive consumer goods (armament and space travel). It bears the costs for the infrastructural output (transportation and communication, scientific and technological progress, vocational training). It bears the cost of the social consumption in-directly concerned with production (housing, transportation, health, leisure, general education, social security). It bears the costs of providing for the unemployed. And finally, it bears the externalized costs of environmental damage caused by private production. Ultimately, these expenses have to be met by taxes. The state apparatus thus has two simultaneous tasks. It has to levy the necessary taxes from profits and income and employ them so efficiently as to prevent any crises from disturbing growth. In addition the selective raising of taxes, the recognizable priority model of their utilization, and the administrative performance have to function in such a way as to satisfy the resulting need for legitimation. If the state fails in the former task, the result is a deficit in administrative efficiency. If it fails in the latter task, the result is a deficit in legitimation.

THEOREMS OF THE LEGITIMATION CRISIS

I would like to restrict myself to the legitimation problem. There is nothing mysterious about its genesis. Legitimate power has to be available for administrative planning. The functions accruing to the state apparatus in late capitalism and the expansion of social areas treated by administration increase the need for legitimation. Liberal capitalism constituted itself in the forms of bourgeois democracy, which is easy to explain in terms of the bourgeois revolution. As a result, the growing need for legitimation now has to work with the means of political democracy (on the basis of universal suffrage). The formal democratic means, however, are expensive. After all, the state apparatus does not just see itself in the role of the supreme capitalist facing the conflicting interests of the various capital factions. It also has to consider the generalizable interests of the population as far as necessary to retain mass loyalty and prevent a conflict-ridden withdrawal of legitimation. The state has to gauge these three interest areas (individual capitalism, state capitalism, and generalizable interests), in order to find a compromise for competing demands. A theorem of crisis has to explain not only why the state apparatus encounters difficulties but also why certain problems remain unsolved in the long run.

First, an obvious objection. The state can avoid legitimation problems to the extent that it can manage to make the administrative system independent of the formation of legitimating will. To that end, it can, say, separate expressive symbols (which create a universal willingness to follow) from the instrumental functions of administration. Well known strategies of this sort are: the personalizing of objective issues, the symbolic use of inquiries, expert opinions, legal incantations, etc. Advertising techniques, borrowed from oligopolistic competition, both confirm and exploit current structures of prejudice. By resorting to emotional appeals, they arouse unconscious motives, occupy certain contents positively, and devalue others. The public, which is engineered for purposes of legitimation, primarily has the function of structuring attention by means of areas of themes and thereby of pushing uncomfortable themes, problems, and arguments below the threshold of attention. As Niklas Luhmann put it: The political system takes over tasks of *ideology planning*.

The scope for manipulation, however, is narrowly delimited, for the cultural system remains peculiarly resistant to administrative control. There is no administrative creation of meaning, there is at best an ideological erosion of cultural values. The acquisition of legitimation is self-destructive as soon as the mode of acquisition is exposed. Thus, there is a systematic limit for attempts at making up for legitimation deficits by means of well aimed manipulation. This limit is the structural dissimilarity between areas of administrative action and cultural tradition.

A crisis argument, to be sure, can be constructed out of these considerations only with the viewpoint that the expansion of state activity has the side effect of disproportionately increasing the need for legitimation. I regard such an overproportionate increase as likely because things that are taken for granted culturally, and have so far been external conditions of the political systems, are now being drawn into the planning area of administration. This process thematizes traditions which previously were not part of public programming, much less of practical discourse. An example of such direct administrative processing of cultural tradition is educational planning, especially the planning of the curriculum. Hitherto, the school administration merely had to codify a given naturally evolved canon. But now the planning of the curriculum is based on the premise that the tradition models can also be different. Administrative planning creates a universal compulsion for justification toward a sphere that was actually distinguished by the power of self-legitimation.

In regard to the direct disturbance of things that were culturally taken for granted, there are further examples in regional and urban planning (private ownership of land), health planning ("classless hospital"), and family planning and marriage-law planning (which are shaking sexual taboos and facilitating emancipation).

An awareness of contingency is created not just for contents of tradition but also for the techniques of tradition—i.e., socialization. Among preschool children, formal schooling is already competing with family upbringing. The new problems afflicting the educational routine, and the widespread awareness of these problems, are reflected by, among other indications, a new type of pedagogical and psychological writing addressed to the general public.

On all these levels, administrative planning has unintentional effects of disquieting and publicizing. These effects weaken the justification potential of traditions that have been forced out of their natural condition. Once they are no longer indisputable, their demands for validity can be stabilized only by way of discourse. Thus, the forcible shift of things that have been culturally taken for granted further politicizes areas of life that previously could be assigned to the private domain. However, this spells danger for bourgeois privatism, which is informally assured by the structures of the public. I see signs of this danger in strivings for participation and in models for alternatives, such as have developed particularly in secondary and primary schools, in the press, the church, theaters, publishing, etc.

These arguments support the contention that late-capitalist societies are afflicted with serious problems of legitimation. But do these arguments suffice to explain why these problems cannot be solved? Do they explain the prediction of a crisis in legitimation? Let us assume the state apparatus could succeed in making labor more productive and in distributing the gains in productivity in such a way as to assure an economic growth free of crises (if not disturbances). Such growth would nevertheless proceed in terms of priorities independent of the generalizable interests of the population. The priority models that Galbraith has analyzed from the viewpoint of "private wealth vs. public poverty" result from a class structure which, as always, is still being kept latent. This structure is ultimately the cause of the legitimation deficit.

We have seen that the state cannot simply take over the cultural system and that, in fact, the expansion of areas for state planning creates problems for things that are culturally taken for granted. "Meaning" is an increasingly scarce resource. Which is why those expectations that are governed by concrete and identifiable needs—i.e., that can be checked by their success—keep mounting in the civil population. The rising level of aspirations is proportionate to the growing need for legitimation. The resource of "value," siphoned off by the tax office, has to make up for the scanty resource of "meaning." Missing legitimations have to be replaced by social rewards such as money, time, and security. A crisis of legitimation arises as soon as the demands for these rewards mount more rapidly than the available mass of values, or if expectations come about that are different and cannot be satisfied by those categories of rewards conforming with the present system.

Why, then, should not the level of demands keep within operable limits? As long as the welfare state's programming in connection with a widespread technocratic consciousness (which makes uninfluenceable system-restraints responsible for bottlenecks) maintains a sufficient amount of civil privatism, then the legitimation emergencies do not have to turn into crises. To be sure, the democratic form of legitimation could cause expenses that cannot be covered if that form drives the competing parties to outdo one another in their platforms and thereby raise the expectations of the population higher and higher. Granted, this argument could be amply demonstrated empirically. But we would still have to explain why late-capitalist societies even bother to retain formal democracy. Merely in terms of the administrative system, formal democracy could just as easily be replaced by a variant—a conservative, authoritarian welfare state that reduces the political participation of the citizens to a harmless level: or a Fascist authoritarian state that keeps the population toeing the mark on a relatively high level of permanent mobilization. Evidently, both variants are in the long run less compatible with developed capitalism than a party state based on mass democracy. The sociocultural system creates demands that cannot be satisfied in authoritarian systems. . . .

THE PRESENT STATE OF THE DEBATE ON WORLD INEQUALITY*

IMMANUEL WALLERSTEIN

It has never been a secret from anyone that some have more than others. And in the modern world at least, it is no secret that some countries have more than other countries. In short, world inequality is a phenomenon about which most men and most groups are quite conscious.

I do not believe that there has ever been a time when these inequalities were unquestioned. That is to say, people or groups who have more have always felt the need to justify this fact, if for no other reason than to try to convince those who have less that they should accept this fact with relative docility. These ideologies of the advantaged have had varying degrees of success over time. The history of the world is one of a constant series of revolts against inequality—whether that of one people or nation vis-à-vis another or of one class within a geographical area against another.

This statement is probably true of all of recorded history, indeed of all historical events, at least since the Neolithic Revolution.

*From Immanuel Wallerstein, ed. *World Inequality* (Montreal: Black Rose Books, 1975), pp. 12–26. Reprinted with permission of Black Rose Books.

What has changed with the advent of the modern world in the 16th century is neither the existence of inequalities nor of the felt need to justify them by means of ideological constructs. What has changed is that even those who defend the "inevitability" of inequalities in the present feel the need to argue that eventually, over time, these inequalities will disappear, or at the very least diminish considerably in scope. Another way of saying this is that of the three dominant ideological currents of the modern world—conservatism, liberalism, and Marxism—two at least (liberalism and Marxism) are committed in theory and the abstract to egalitarianism as a principle. The third, conservatism, is not, but conservatism is an ideology that has been very much on the defensive ever since the French revolution. The proof of this is that most conservatives decline to fly the banner openly but hide their conservative ideas under the mantle of liberalism or occasionally even Marxism.

Surely it is true that in the universities of the world in the 20th century, and in other expressions of intellectuals, the contending ideologies have been one variant or another of liberalism and Marxism. (Remember at this

How about multinationals?

point we are talking of ideologies and not of political movements. Both "Liberal" parties and Social-Democratic parties in the 20th century have drawn on liberal ideologies.)

One of the most powerful thrusts of the 18th-century Enlightenment, picked up by most 19th and 20th century thought-systems, was the assumption of progress, reformulated later as evolution. In the context of the question of equality, evolution was interpreted as the process of moving from an imperfect, unequal allocation of privileges and resources to some version of equality. There was considerable argument about how to define equality. (Reflect on the different meanings of "equality of opportunity" and "to each according to his needs.") There was considerable disagreement about who or what were the obstacles to this desired state of equality. And there was fundamental discord about how to transform the world from its present imperfection to the desired future, primarily between the advocates of gradualism based on education to advocates of revolution based on the use at some point in time of violence.

I review this well-known history of modern ideas simply to underline where I think our current debates are simply the latest variant of now classic debates and where I think some new issues have been raised which make these older formulations outdated.

If one takes the period 1945–1960, both politically and intellectually, we have in many ways the apogee of the liberal-Marxist debate. The world was politically polarized in the so-called cold war. There were two camps. One called itself the "free world" and argued that it and it alone upheld the first part of the French Revolution's trilogy, that of "liberty." It argued that its economic system offered the hope over time of approximating "equality" through a path which it came to call "economic development" or sometimes just "development." It argued too that it was gradually achieving "fraternity" by means of education

and political reform (such as the 1954 Supreme Court decision in the United States, ending the legality of segregation.)

The other camp called itself the "socialist world" and argued that it and it alone represented the three objectives of the French Revolution and hence the interests of the people of the world. It argued that when movements inspired by these ideas would come to power in all non-"socialist" countries (and however they came to power) each would enact legislation along the same lines and by this process the whole world would become "socialist" and the objective would be achieved.

These somewhat simplistic ideological statements were of course developed in much more elaborate form by the intellectuals. It has become almost traditional (but I think nonetheless just) to cite W.W. Rostow's *The Stages of Economic Growth* as a succinct, sophisticated, and relatively pure expression of the dominant liberal ideology which informed the thinking of the political leadership of the United States and its Western allies. Rostow showed no modesty in his subtitle: which was "a non-Communist Manifesto."

His basic thesis is no doubt familiar to most persons interested in these problems. Rostow saw the process of change as a series of stages through which each national unit had to go. They were the stages through which Rostow felt Great Britain had gone, and Great Britain was the crucial example since it was defined as being the first state to embark on the evolutionary path of the modern industrial world. The inference, quite overtly drawn, was that this path was a model, to be copied by other states. One could then analyze what it took to move from one stage to another, why some nations took longer than others, and could prescribe (like a physician) what a nation must do to hurry along its process of "growth." I will not review what ideological function such a formulation served. This has been done repeatedly and well. Nonetheless, this viewpoint, somewhat retouched, still informs the developmentalist ideas of the major Western governments as well as that of international agencies. I consider Lester Pearson's "Partners in Progress" report in the direct line of this analytic framework. . . .

There is another perspective that has slowly pushed its way into public view during the 1960's. It has no commonly-accepted name, in part because the early formulations of this point of view have often been confused, partial, or unclear. It was first widely-noticed in the thinking of the Latin American structuralists (such as Prebisch and Furtado) and those allied to them elsewhere (such as Dudley Seers). It later took the form of arguments such as the "development of underdevelopment" (A.G. Frank, in the heritage of Baran's *The Political Economy of Growth*), the "structure of dependence" (Theotonio Dos Santos), "unequal exchange" (Arghiri Emmanuel), "accumulation of world capital" (Samir Amin), "subimperialism" (Ruy Mauro Marini). It also surfaced in the Chinese Cultural Revolution as Mao's concept of the continuity of the class struggle under socialist regimes in single countries. . . .

I would like to designate this point of view the "world-system perspective." I mean by that term that it is based on the assumption, explicitly or implicitly, that the modern world comprises a single capitalist world-economy, which has emerged historically since the sixteenth century and which still exists today. It follows from such a premise that national states are *not* societies that have separate, parallel histories, but parts of a whole reflecting that whole. To the extent that stages exist, they exist for the system as a whole. To be sure, since different parts of the world play and have played differing roles in the capitalist world-economy, they have dramatically different internal socio-economic profiles and hence distinctive politics. But to understand the internal class contradictions and political struggles of a particular state, we must first situate it in the world-economy. We can then understand the ways in which various political and cultural thrusts may be efforts to alter or preserve a position within this world-economy which is to the advantage or disadvantage of particular groups located within a particular state.

What thus distinguishes the developmentalist and the world-system perspective is not liberalism versus Marxism nor evolutionism vs. something else (since both are essentially evolutionary). Rather I would locate the distinction in two places. One is in mode of thought. To put it in Hegelian terms, the developmentalist perspective is mechanical, whereas the world-system perspective is dialectical. I mean by the latter term that at every point in the analysis, one asks not what is the formal structure but what is the consequence for both the whole and parts of maintaining or changing a certain structure at that particular point in time, given the totality of particular positions of that moment in time. Intelligent analysis demands knowledge of the complex texture of social reality (historical concreteness) within a long-range perspective that observes trends and forces of the world-system, which can explain what underlies and informs the diverse historically concrete phenomena. If synchronic comparisons and abstracted generalizations are utilized, it is only as heuristic devices in search of a truth that is ever contemporary and hence ever-changing.

This distinction of scientific methodology is matched by a distinction of praxis, of the politics of the real world. For what comes through as the second great difference between the two perspectives (the developmentalist and the world-system) is the prognosis for action. This is the reason why the latter perspective has emerged primarily from the intellectuals of the Third World. The developmentalist perspective not only insists that the model is to be found in the old developed countries (whether Great Britain—U.S.A. or U.S.S.R.) but also that the fundamental international political issues revolve around the relations among the hegemonic powers of the world. From a world-system perspective, there are no "models" (a mechanical notion) and the relations of the hegemonic powers are only one of many issues that confront the world-system.

The emergence of the world-system perspective is a consequence of the dramatic challenge to European political domination of the world which has called into question all Europo-centric constructions of social reality. But intellectual evolution itself is seldom dramatic. The restructuring of the allocation of power in the world has made itself felt in the realm of ideas, particularly in the hegemonic areas of the world, via a growing malaise that intellectuals in Europe (including of course North America) have increasingly felt about the validity of their answers to a series of "smaller" questions—smaller, that is, than the nature of the world-system as such.

Let us review successively six knotty questions to which answers from a developmentalist perspective have increasingly seemed inadequate.

Why have certain world-historical events of the last two centuries taken place where and when they have? The most striking "surprise," at the moment it occurred and ever since, is the Russian Revolution. As we all know, neither Marx nor Lenin nor anyone else thought that a "socialist revolution" would occur in Russia earlier than anywhere else. Marx had more or less predicted Great Britain as the likely candidate, and after Marx's death, the consensus of expectation in the international socialist movement was that it would occur in Germany. We know that even after 1917 almost all the leading figures of the CPSU [Communist Party of the Soviet Union] expected that the "revolution" would have to occur quickly in Germany if the Soviet regime was to survive. There was however no socialist revolution in Germany and nonetheless the Soviet regime did survive.

We do not want for explanations of this phenomenon, but we do lack convincing answers. Of course, there exists an explanation that turns Marx on his head and argues that socialist revolutions occur not in the so-called "advanced capitalist" countries but precisely in "backward" countries. But this is in such blatant contradiction with other parts of the developmentalist perspective that its proponents are seldom willing to state it baldly, even less defend it openly.

Nor is the Russian Revolution the only anomaly. There is a long-standing debate about the "exceptionalism" of the United States. How can we explain that the U.S.A. replaced Great Britain as the hegemonic industrial power of the world, and in the process managed to avoid giving birth to a serious internal socialist movement? And if the U.S.A. could avoid socialism, why could not Brazil or Russia or Canada? Seen from the perspective of 1800, it would have been a bold social scientist who would have predicted the particular success of the U.S.A.

Again there have been many explanations. There is the "frontier" theory. There is the theory that underlines the absence of a previously entrenched "feudal" class. There is the theory of the U.S. as Britain's "junior partner" who overtook the senior. But all of these theories are precisely "exceptionalist" theories, contradicting the developmentalist paradigm. And furthermore, some of these variables apply to other countries where they did not seem to have the same consequences.

We could go on. I will mention two more briefly. For a long time, Great Britain's primacy (the "first" industrial power) has been unquestioned. But was Britain the "first" and if so why was she? This is a question that only recently has been seriously adumbrated. In April 1974 at another international colloquium held here in Montreal on the theme of "Failed Transitions to Industrialism: The Case of 17th Century Netherlands and Renaissance Italy," one view put forward quite strongly was that neither Italy nor the Netherlands was the locus of the Industrial Revolution precisely because they were too far *advanced* economically. What a striking blow to a developmentalist paradigm.

And lastly one should mention the anomaly of Canada: a country which economically falls into a category below that of the world's leading industrial producers in structural terms, yet nonetheless is near the very top of the list in per capita income. This cannot be plausibly explained from a developmentalist perspective.

If the world has been "developing" or "progressing" over the past few centuries, how do we explain the fact that in many areas things seem to have gotten worse, not better? Worse in many ways, ranging from standard of living, to the physical environment, to the quality of life. And more to the point, worse in some places but better in others. I refer not merely to such contemporary phenomena as the so-called "growing gap" between the industrialized countries and the Third World, but also to such earlier phenomena as the deindustrialization of many areas of the world (starting with the widely-known example of the Indian textile industry in the late 18th and early 19th century).

You may say that this contradicts the liberal version of the developmentalist perspective but not its Marxist version, since "polarization" was seen as part of the process of change. True enough, except that "polarization" was presumably within countries and not between them. Furthermore, it is not clear that it is "polarization" that has occurred. While the rich have gotten richer and the poor have gotten poorer, there is surely a fairly large group of countries now somewhere in between on many economic criteria, to cite such politically diverse examples as Mexico, Italy, Czechoslovakia, Iran, and South Africa.

Furthermore, we witness in the 1970's a dramatic shift in the distribution of the profit and the international terms of trade of oil (and possibly other rare materials). You may say it is because of the increased political sophistication and strength of the Arab world. No doubt this has occurred, but is this an explanation? I remind this group that the last moment of time in which there was a dramatic amelioration of world terms of trade of primary products was in the period 1897–1913, a moment which represented in political terms the apogee of European colonial control of the world.

Once again it is not that there are not a large number of explanations for the rise in oil prices. It is rather that I find these explanations, for what they're worth, in contradiction with a developmentalist perspective.

Why are there "regressions"? In 1964, S.N. Eisenstadt published an article entitled "Breakdowns of Modernization," in which he discussed the fact that there seemed to be cases of "reversal" of regimes to a "a lower, less flexible level of political and social differentiation. . . . "[1]

In seeking to explain the origins of such "reversals," Eisenstadt restricted himself to hesitant hypotheses:

The problem of why in Turkey, Japan, Mexico, and Russia there emerge in the initial stages of modernization elites with orientations to change and ability to implement relatively effective policies, while they did not develop in these initial phases in Indonesia, Pakistan, or Burma, or why elites with similar differences tended to develop also in later stages of modernization, is an extremely difficult one and constitutes one of the most baffling problems in comparative sociological analysis. There are but four available indications to deal with this problem. Very tentatively, it may perhaps be suggested that to some extent it has to do with the placement of these elites in the preceding social structure, with the extent of their internal cohesiveness, and of the internal transformation of their own value orientation.[2]

As is clear, Eisenstadt's tentative explanation is to be found in anterior factors operating internally in the state. This calls into question the concept of stages through which all not only must pass but all *can* pass, but it leaves intact the state framework as the focus of analysis and explanation. This of course leads us logically to ask how these anterior factors developed. Are they pure historical accident?

Similarly after the political rebellion of Tito's Yugoslavia against the U.S.S.R., the latter began to accuse Yugoslavia of "revisionism" and of returning to capitalism. Later, China took up the same theme against the U.S.S.R.

But how can we explain how this happens? There are really two varieties of explanation from a developmentalist perspective. One is to say that "regression" seems to have occurred, but that in fact "progress" had never taken place. The leaders of a movement, whether a nationalist movement or a socialist movement, only pretended to favor change. In fact they were really always "neocolonialist" stooges or "revisionists" at heart. Such an explanation has partial truth, but it seems to me to place too much on "false consciousness" and to fail to analyze movements in their immediate and continuing historical contexts. The second explanation of "regression" is a change of heart—"betrayal." Yes, but once again, how come sometimes, but not always? Are we to explain large-scale social phenomena on the basis of the accident of the biographic histories of the particular leaders involved? I cannot accept this, for leaders remain leaders in the long run only if their personal choices reflect wider social pressures.

If the fundamental paradigm of modern history is a series of parallel national processes, how do we explain the persistence of nationalism, indeed quite often its primacy, as a political force in the modern world? Developmentalists who are liberals deplore nationalism or explain it away as a transitional "integrating" phenomenon. Marxists who are developmentalists are even more embarrassed. If the class struggle is primary—that is, implicitly the intra-national class struggle—how do we explain the fact that the slogan of the Cuban revolution is "Patria o muerte—venceremos"? And how could we explain this even more astonishing quotation from Kim Il Sung, the leader of the Democratic People's Republic of Korea:

The homeland is a veritable mother for everyone. We cannot live nor be happy outside of our homeland. Only the flourishing and prosperity of our homeland will permit us to go down the path to happiness. The best sons and daughters of our people, all without exception, were first of all ardent patriots. It was to recover their homeland that Korean Communists struggled, before the Liberation, against Japanese imperialism despite every difficulty and obstacle.[3]

And if internal processes are so fundamental, why has not the reality of international workers' solidarity been greater? Remember the First World War.

As before, there are many explanations for the persistence of nationalism. I merely observe that all of these explanations have to *explain away* the primacy of internal national processes. Or to put it another way, for developmentalists nationalism is sometimes good, sometimes bad. But when it is the one or the other, it is ultimately explained by developmentalists in an ad hoc manner, adverting to its meaning for the world-system.

An even more difficult problem for the developmentalists has been the recrudescence of nationalist movements in areas smaller than that of existing states. And it is not Biafra or Bangladesh that is an intellectual problem, because the usual manner of accounting for secessionist movements in Third World countries has been the failure to attain the stage of "national integration."

No, the surprise has been in the industrialized world: Blacks in the U.S.A., Québec in Canada, Occitania in France, the Celts in Great Britain, and lurking in the background the nationalities question in the U.S.S.R. It is not that any of these "nationalisms" is new. They are all long-standing themes of political and cultural conflict in all these countries. The surprise has been that, as of say 1945 or even 1960, most persons in these countries, using a developmentalist paradigm, regarded these movements or claims as remnants of a dying past, destined to diminish still further in vitality. And lo, a phoenix reborn. . . .

One last question, which is perhaps only a reformulation of the previous five. How is it that the "ideal types" of the different versions of the developmentalist perspective all seem so far from empirical reality? Who has not had the experience of not being quite certain which party represents the "industrial proletariat" or the "modernizing elite" in Nigeria, or in France of the Second Empire for that matter? Let us be honest. Each of us, to the extent that he has ever used a developmentalist paradigm, has stretched empirical reality to a very Procrustean bed indeed.

Can the world-system perspective answer these questions better? We cannot yet be sure. This point of view has not yet been fully thought through. But let me indicate some possible lines of argument.

If the world-system is the focus of analysis, and if in particular we are talking of the capitalist world-economy, then divergent historical patterns are precisely to be expected. They are not an anomaly but the essence of the system. If the world-economy is the basic economic entity comprising a single division of labor, then it is natural that different areas perform different economic tasks. Anyway it is natural under capitalism, and we may talk of the core, the periphery and the semi-periphery of the world-economy. Since however political boundaries (states) are smaller than the economic whole, they will each reflect different groupings of economic tasks and strengths in the world-market. Over time, some of these differences may be accentuated rather than diminished—the basic inequalities which are our theme of discussion.

It is also clear that over time the loci of economic activities keep changing. This is due to many factors—ecological exhaustion, the impact of new technology, climate changes, and the socio-economic consequences of these "natural" phenomena. Hence some areas "progress" and others "regress." But the fact that particular states change their position in the world-economy, from semi-periphery to core say, or vice versa, does not in itself change the nature of the system. These shifts will be registered for individual states as "development" or "regression." The key factor to note is that within a capitalist world-economy, all states cannot "develop" simultaneously by definition, since the system functions by virtue of having unequal core and peripheral regions.

Within a world-economy, the state structures function as ways for particular groups to affect and distort the functioning of the market. The stronger the state-machinery, the more its ability to distort the world-market in favor of the interests it represents. Core states have stronger state-machineries than peripheral states.

This role of the state machineries in a capitalist world-economy explains the persistence of nationalism, since the primary social conflicts are quite often between groups located in different states rather than between groups located within the same state-boundaries. Furthermore, this explains the ambiguity of class as a concept, since class refers to the economy which is world-wide, but class consciousness is a political, hence primarily national, phenomenon. Within this context, one can see the recrudescence of ethno-nationalisms in industrialized states as an expression of class consciousness of lower caste-class groups in societies where the class terminology has been preempted by nation-wide middle strata organized around the dominant ethnic group.

If then the world-system is the focus of analysis rather than the individual states, it is the natural history of this system at which we must look. Like all systems, the capitalist world-economy has both cyclical and secular trends, and it is important to distinguish them.

On the other hand, the capitalist world-economy seems to go through long cycles of "expansion" and "contraction." I cannot at this point go into the long discussion this would require. I will limit myself to the very brief suggestion that "expansion" occurs when the totality of world production is less than world effective demand, as permitted by the existing social distribution of world purchasing power, and that "contraction" occurs when total world production exceeds world effective demand. These are cycles of 75–100 years in length in my view and the downward cycle is only resolved by a political reallocation of world income that effectively expands world demand. I believe we have just ended an expansionary cycle and we are in the beginning of a contractual one.

These cycles occur within a secular trend that has involved the physical expansion and politico-structural consolidation of the capitalist world-economy as such, but has also given birth to forces and movements which are eating away at these same structural supports of the existing world-system. In particular, these forces which we call revolutionary forces are calling into question the phenomenon of inequality so intrinsic to the existing world-system.

The trend towards structural consolidation of the system over the past four centuries has included three basic developments:

The first has been the capitalization of world agriculture, meaning the ever more efficient use of the world's land and sea resources in large productive units with larger and larger components of fixed capital. Over time, this has encompassed more and more of the earth's surface, and at the present we are probably about to witness the last major physical expansion, the elimination of all remaining plots restricted to small-scale, so-called "subsistence" production. The counterpart of this process has been the steady concentration of the world's population as salaried workers in small, dense pockets—that is, proletarianization and urbanization. The initial impact of this entire process has been to render large populations more exploitable and controllable.

The second major structural change has been the development of technology that maximizes the ability to transform the resources of the earth into useable commodities at "reasonable" cost levels. This is what we call industrialization, and the story is far from over. The next century should see the spread of industrial activity from the temperate core areas in which it has hitherto been largely concentrated to the tropical and semi-tropical peripheral areas. Industrialization too has hitherto tended to consolidate the system in providing a large part of the profit that makes the system worth the while of those who are on top of it, with a large enough surplus to sustain and appease the world's middle strata. Mere extension of industrial activity will not change a peripheral area into a core area, for the core areas will concentrate on ever newer, specialized activities.

The third major development, at once technological and social, has been the strengthening of all organizational structures—the states, the economic corporate structures, and even the cultural institutions—vis-à-vis both individuals and groups. This is the process of bureaucratization, and while it has been uneven (the core states are still stronger than the peripheral states, for example), all structures are stronger today than previously. Prime ministers of contemporary states have the power today that Louis XIV sought in vain to achieve. This too has been stabilizing because the ability of these bureaucracies physically to repress opposition is far greater than in the past.

But there is the other side of each of these coins. The displacement of the world's population into urban areas has made it easier ultimately to organize forces against the power structures. This is all the more so since the ever-expanding market-dependent, property-less groups are simultaneously more educated, more in communication with each other, and hence *potentially* more politically conscious.

The steady industrialization of the world has eaten away at the political and hence economic justifications for differentials in rewards. The technological advances, while still unevenly distributed, have created a new military equality of destructive potential. It is true that one nation may have 1000 times the fire power of another, but if the weaker one has sufficient to incur grievous damage, of how much good is it for the stronger to have 1000 times as much strength? Consider not merely the power of a weaker state with a few nuclear rockets but the military power of urban guerillas. It is the kind of problem Louis XIV precisely did *not* need to worry about.

Finally, the growth of bureaucracies in the long run has created the weakness of topheaviness. The ability of the presumed decision-makers to control not the populace but the bureaucracies has effectively diminished, which again creates a weakness in the ability to enforce politico-economic will.

When then in this picture do the forces of change, the movements of liberation, come in? They come in precisely as not totally coherent pressures of groups which arise out of the structural contradictions of the capitalist world-economy. These groups seem to take organizational form as movements, as parties, and sometimes as regimes. But when the movements become regimes, they are caught in the dilemma of becoming part of the machinery of the capitalist world-economy they are presuming to change. Hence the so-called "betrayals." It is important neither to adulate blindly these regimes, for inevitably they "betray" in part their stated goals, nor to be cynical and despairing, for the movements which give birth to such regimes represent real forces, and the creation of such regimes is part of a long-run process of social transformation. . . .

NOTES

1. S.N. Eisenstadt, "Breakdowns of Modernization," *Economic Development and Cultural Change*, XII, 4, July 1964, 367.

2. Ibid., pp. 365–366.

3. *Activité Révolutionnaire du Camarade Kim Il Sung* (Pyongyang: Ed. en langues étrangères, 1970). Livre illustré, 52nd page (edition unpaginated). Translation mine—I.W.

WHAT IS ANALYTICAL MARXISM?*

ERIK OLIN WRIGHT

It is commonplace these days to speak of a crisis of Marxism. The evidence is easy enough to find:

First, there are the extraordinary changes taking place in societies ruled by communist parties under the ideological banner of Marxism. A decade ago it seemed that Marxist orthodoxy in one form or another was firmly in place as the ruling ideology of these societies. Now, with the success of Solidarity in Poland, the development of *perestroika* in the USSR and the emergence of widespread private enterprise in China, it is no longer clear what set of ideological principles actually guides the development of these societies.

Second, when we look at the policies and practices of communist, socialist, and social democratic parties in the advanced capitalist world, it is often very difficult to discern co-

herent programs for progressive social reform, let alone for revolutionary transformation. And it is certainly unclear whether or not the politics of most of these parties have even vestigial linkages to Marxism as a social theory.

Finally, when we look more narrowly at Marxist theory itself, one is struck both by the rapid exit of many radical intellectuals from Marxism in recent years towards something that is often called post-Marxism, as well as by the decline in consensus among the remaining Marxist intellectuals over the core theoretical postulates of Marxism itself.

Of course, there has always been deep and often bitter debate within the Marxist tradition. Such divisions in the past, however, generally revolved around a common core of theoretical, if not political, agreement—the labor theory of value as the basis for analyzing capitalism; historical materialism as the basis for analyzing epochal historical development; class structure and class struggle as the basis for understanding the state and ideology. At

*From Erik Olin Wright, "What Is Analytical Marxism?" *Socialist Review* 19:4 (October–December 1989), 35–49. Reprinted with permission of Duke University Press.

the present this core itself is much harder to discern, and there is certainly sharp disagreement over every one of its elements. There are now many theorists who consider themselves to be Marxists who nevertheless reject the labor theory of value as a satisfactory way of understanding capitalism, who are skeptical that historical materialism constitutes a plausible theory of history, and who see classes as only one of a variety of determinants of the state and ideology.

Now, one might argue that those who reject these classical core elements of Marxist theory should not rightfully call themselves Marxist. There is, after all, a venerable tradition in the history of Marxism to draw lines of demarcation between true Marxists and phony Marxists. The latter might use Marxist rhetoric, but they have abandoned Marxism itself. Alternatively, and I think more constructively, it could simply be recognized that Marxism is not a unified theory with well-defined boundaries, but a family of theories united by a common terrain of debate and questions. There have always been a plurality of Marxisms; what is new, perhaps, is the degree of theoretical and methodological heterogeneity that exists on this intellectual terrain.

Given this decline in intellectual consensus among Marxists over many of the core elements of their own theoretical tradition, it is certainly easy to see why many commentators consider this a period of profound theoretical crisis within Marxism, if not necessarily of the kind of mortal crisis proclaimed by the right. However, it is equally a period of considerable theoretical vitality and innovation in which significant progress is being made in clarifying a whole set of problems. While it may at times be difficult to distinguish "crisis" from "dynamic change," I believe that the Marxism which will emerge from the present period of theoretical transformation will not

only be more powerful theoretically than the Marxism of the heyday of the New Left, but also of more political relevance as well.

In this paper I want to look at one particular strand of new theoretical development that has emerged rather forcefully as a tendency in the context of this internal turmoil in the Marxist tradition, particularly in the United States and Great Britain. This is a tendency that has come to be known as "Analytical Marxism." While Analytical Marxism is by no means the only vibrant intellectual current in contemporary Marxism, it does offer, in my judgment, the most promising general strategy for reconstructing Marxism.

THE EMERGENCE OF ANALYTICAL MARXISM

In the aftermath of the student movement and radical politics of the 1960s and early 1970s, Marxism entered the university in the developed capitalist democracies in an unprecedented way. Although with few exceptions Marxism never became a dominant perspective in academic departments, nevertheless it gained intellectual influence and even a measure of respectability in a wide variety of academic fields—history, sociology, education, political science, and economics, among others.

Analytical Marxism emerged in the late 1970s as one intellectual tendency within this newly influential academic Marxism. It grew out of a belief that Marxism continued to constitute a productive intellectual tradition within which to ask questions and formulate answers, but that this tradition was frequently burdened with a range of methodological and metatheoretical commitments that seriously undermined its explanatory potential. The motivation for trying to rid Marxism of this burden was the conviction that the core ideas of Marxism, embodied in concepts like class, exploitation, the theory of history, capitalism, socialism, and so on, remained essential for any emancipatory political project.[1] . . .

WHAT IS "ANALYTICAL" ABOUT ANALYTICAL MARXISM?

There are four specific commitments that I think characterize Analytical Marxism and justify considering it a distinct "school" of contemporary Marxist thought:

1. A commitment to *conventional scientific norms* in the elaboration of theory and the conduct of research.

2. An emphasis on the importance of *systematic conceptualization,* particularly of concepts that are at the core of Marxist theory. This involves careful attention to both definitions of concepts and the logical coherence of interconnected concepts.

3. A concern with a relatively *fine-grained specification of the steps in the theoretical arguments linking concepts,* whether the arguments be about causal processes in the construction of explanatory theories or about logical connections in the construction of normative theories.

4. The importance accorded to *the intentional action of individuals* within both explanatory and normative theories.

It would be arrogant to suggest that Marxism lacked these elements prior to the emergence of Analytical Marxism as a self-conscious school. There have certainly been Marxists attentive to each of these issues, and there are Marxists attentive to them today who for one reason or another distance themselves from Analytical Marxism. What makes Analytical Marxism distinctive, then, is the extent to which these principles are brought to the forefront and systematically

applied to the construction and reconstruction of theory.

In what follows, we will look at each of these points in turn, illustrating them with examples of specific work by Analytical Marxists. This will help to clarify what is analytical about Analytical Marxism. . . .

The Commitment to Conventional Scientific Norms

Marxism as a theoretical tradition has always had a rather peculiar relation to "science." On the one hand, there has always been a strong current within Marxism which is quite hostile to the canons of conventional science. Particularly in the strand of Marxism associated with the tradition of critical theory, positivism and claims to scientificity are often looked upon as instruments of ideological domination rather than emancipatory knowledge. On the other hand, the type of Marxism that has enthusiastically embraced the label "scientific socialism" and claimed the status of a full-fledged "science of society" has often been guilty of the most serous abuses of scientific norms. Self-styled "Scientific Marxism" has often taken the form of a rigid ideology with pregiven answers to all questions, functioning more like a secular theology than a scientific discipline: Marxism became Marxology; classical texts were canonized; and the central arguments of the "science" were impervious to transformation. Instead of constituting a theoretical apparatus capable of learning new things about the world—the hallmark of a scientific theory—scientific Marxism has often been a closed system of thought continually reaffirming itself through its own selective observations and interpretations. Marxism has thus either been hostile to science or adopted a particularly distorted and unscientific identification with science.

Analytical Marxists are committed to the view that Marxism should, without embarrassment, aspire to the status of a genuine social science. Marxism should not be absolved from the standards of science even if it accepts other standards of evaluation and relevance in addition to strictly scientific ones.

Such a commitment to scientificity leaves unspecified exactly what is meant by "science," and this is, of course, a hotly contested issue in philosophy. Generally speaking, I think, most Analytical Marxists adopt what can be loosely described as a *realist* view of science. This involves the following basic view of the scientific enterprise: science attempts to identify the *mechanisms* which generate the empirical phenomena we experience in the world. Our observations of those phenomena are simultaneously shaped by two kinds of mechanisms: mechanisms internal to the process of observation and mechanisms which directly generate the phenomenon in question. Because of this duality, it is in general impossible to inductively discover truths about mechanisms simply from raw empirical "facts," since those facts are necessarily selected by the observation process itself. This implies a rejection of what might be called the naive empiricist view that we can gather facts about the world and use them to generate scientific knowledge without theoretically informed principles of selecting the objects of our observation. In this specific sense, observations cannot be theory-neutral, and therefore our theories cannot simply be inductive generalizations from raw "facts." But Analytical Marxists would also reject the anti-realist view that our observations are wholly constituted by the categories of thought, by the discourses we use in describing the world. Scientific theories attempt to construct explanations based on real mechanisms that exist in the world independently of our theories even though the selection of observations of those

mechanisms and their effects depend in part upon the theories themselves.

There are three important implications of the general acceptance of conventional scientific norms by Analytical Marxists: first, Analytical Marxists tend to be quite skeptical of traditional Marxist claims to a distinctive "Marxist Methodology"; second, they tend to emphasize the importance of empirical research joined to systematic theoretical models for the advance of scientific knowledge; and third, they try to be open to continual reassessment of their own theoretical positions, acknowledging their theoretical failures as well as arguing for their successes.

There is a long tradition among Marxists which claims that Marxism has a distinctive method which differentiates it radically from "bourgeois social science." Such claims involve a familiar list of contrasts: Marxism is dialectical, historical, materialist, antipositivist, holist, while bourgeois social theory is undialectical, ahistorical, idealist, positivist, and individualist. Analytical Marxists are quite skeptical of the value of such claims. This is not to say that all of the specific elements that are traditionally subsumed under the expression "Marxist methods" are rejected out of hand. Analytical Marxists, for example, have found ways of including notions of contradiction and even dialectics in their arguments. But when they do so they are generally quite careful to show how these complex ideas can be translated into a language of causes, mechanisms, and effects.

Take the notion of "contradiction." One way of explicating this concept is to treat it as a situation in which there are multiple conditions for the reproduction of a system which cannot all be simultaneously satisfied. Or, alternatively, a contradiction can be viewed as a situation in which the unintended consequences of a strategy subvert the accomplishment of its intended goals. In either case, "contradiction" is not treated as a philosophically driven way of interpreting the essence of a process, but as a way of explicating the interactions among a set of causal mechanisms. This kind of translation of an element of Marxist method into a language of causal mechanisms would be characteristic of Analytical Marxism.

The second implication of the embrace of conventional scientific norms is a commitment to the importance of systematic empirical research. This is not to say that all Analytical Marxists are themselves directly engaged in empirical research. Some are primarily concerned with normative political theory and do not engage in empirical research at all. Others are concerned with explanatory models, but are primarily preoccupied with the elaboration of the logic of the models themselves. Nevertheless, most Analytical Marxists feel that an essential element in the elaboration of theories is the systematic confrontation with empirical research. This has led to the development of a number of substantial research projects by Analytical Marxists. My own research, for example, has involved conducting closely replicated social surveys on class structure, class biography, and class consciousness in eleven capitalist democracies: the United States, Sweden, Norway, Finland, Denmark, Britain, West Germany, Canada, Australia, New Zealand, and Japan. The central objective of this research has been to develop strictly comparable micro-level data on class and its effects in this set of countries so that we could systematically explore variations in the causal interconnections among class related variables across different macro-historical contexts. Other empirical research projects by Analytical Marxists include Robert Brenner's research on the transition from feudalism to capitalism; Adam Przeworski's project on social democratic party politics; Joel Rogers's research on the interaction of the state and the labor movement in American history. While none

of these projects are based on a belief in simple empirical "tests" of complex theoretical ideas, they all affirm the conventional scientific view that theoretical advances depend in part on their engagement with relevant data from empirical research.

Finally, one of the striking properties of the work of Analytical Marxists is the extent to which they take seriously the problem of revising their own theoretical positions in the light of debate and criticism. Cohen's work on the Marxist theory of history has gone through a number of significant transformations in the light of issues raised in discussions of his original formulations. Roemer first developed a comprehensive concept of exploitation and then, in the context of critical discussions of his framework, moved on to questions the very relevance of exploitation so defined for understanding and criticizing capitalism. And in my own work, my treatment of class structure has gone through at least two significant reconstructions in response to debates within class analysis. The commitment to science, therefore, means that Analytical Marxists treat their arguments as needing to be continually subjected to criticism and revision rather than as constituting definitive embodiments of "truth."

Conceptualization

One of the distinctive signatures of work by Analytical Marxists is the amount of energy devoted to the elaboration of basic concepts. A great deal of time is spent defending specific definitions, discussing alternative criteria, examining the logical interconnections of concepts, puzzling over inconsistencies, and so on. Let me give an example from my own work, the definition of the "middle class," to illustrate this concern with conceptualization.

Here is the problem: Marxian class concepts are built around a polarized notion of class relations. There are capitalists and workers, lords and serfs. What does it mean to occupy a middle-class location within such polarized relations? Traditionally, Marxists have dealt with this problem by treating the "middle" class as a residual—any location that cannot be firmly situated within the bourgeoisie or the proletariat is, by default, in the "middle class." I wanted a positive specification of this kind of class location. In my work, I proposed two basic solutions. The first was to treat the middle class as those locations in the class structure which were simultaneously in two or more classes. Managers, for example, could be thought of as simultaneously in the bourgeoisie and the proletariat. I referred to such positions as "contradictory class locations." The second solution argued that capitalist societies consisted of multiple forms of exploitation, not simply capitalist exploitation proper. For example, following the work of John Roemer, I argued that the control over certain kinds of skills could constitute a mechanism of exploitation. The middle class, then, was defined as locations which were exploited capitalistically but were exploiters through some subordinate mechanism of exploitation.

Many other examples of this kind of intensive work on concept formation could be given: John Roemer's work on exploitation; G.A. Cohen's analysis of forces of production or the meaning of "proletarian unfreedom"; Jon Elster's discussion of the concept of "solidarity"; Joel Rogers and Joshua Cohen's analysis of "democracy"; Andrew Levine's analysis of "freedom."[2] In each case there is the assumption that a necessary condition for the development of powerful theories is the elaboration of logically coherent concepts. It is in part from this preoccupation that Analytical Marxism gets it name: the analytical coherence of concepts is essential for the explanatory power of theories.

Elaboration of Explicit Models

One of the striking characteristics of Analytical Marxism has been the use of explicit abstract models, sometimes highly formalized as in game theory, other times somewhat less formalized as causal models. Many Marxists (as well as non-Marxist radicals) find such models objectionable on the grounds that they involve such dramatic simplifications of the complexity of real world situations that they cannot possibly deepen our knowledge of the world. Analytical Marxists counter such objections on several grounds:

First, the fact that models constitute simplifications of complexity is not in and of itself a failing, but a virtue. This is precisely what we want a good theory to do: to get to the heart of a complex problem by identifying the central mechanisms involved.

Second, the essential structure of a formal model is to create a thought experiment of some process. That is, one is forced to specify the underlying assumptions of the model, the conditions which are treated as parameters, and the ways in which the mechanisms work. The clarity forced upon a theorist by making explicit such assumptions and arguments is desirable. Furthermore, since in real-life social situations it is generally hard to construct real experimental conditions for revealing the operation of causal mechanisms (or even, through comparative methods, quasi-experimental designs), thought experiments are essential to give plausibility to the causal claims we actually make about any concrete problem.

Finally, it is generally the case that lurking behind every informal causal explanation is a tacit formal model. All explanatory theories contain assumptions, claims about the conditions under which the explanations hold, claims about how the various mechanisms fit together. The difference between what Analytical Marxists do and what many historical and empirical Marxist researchers do, then, may be basically a question of the extent to which they are prepared to put their cards on the table and articulate the causal models in their theories.

To get a sense of how Analytical Marxists actually use these kinds of models to engage Marxist questions, it will be useful to look in some detail at two prominent examples: Adam Przeworski's analysis of social democracy, which relies on elements of rational-choice theory, and G.A. Cohen's reconstruction of Marx's theory of history, which is built around functional explanations.[3]

Adam Przeworski develops a general theoretical model of the historical trajectory of social-democratic politics in capitalist societies. He argues that once bourgeois democratic institutions are in place, social-democratic parties face a series of dilemmas when selecting a political strategy. The first dilemma is whether or not to participate in elections at all. If they participate, they risk incorporation into the machine of state domination; if they abstain from participation, they risk political marginalization. Second, if they decide to participate, they face a dilemma rooted in their electoral base. If they attempt to be a pure working-class party, then they can adopt a consistent set of pro-working-class policies, but they will never get an electoral majority (since the working class is never a majority of the population); if they seek alliances with various segments of the middle class, then they dilute their working-class base and ultimately alienate their working class support.

Przeworski then shows, using formal mathematical models, that: (a) given the distribution of the population into the class structure, and (b) the historical legacy of past strategies on the patterns of loyalty to and defection from parties by people in different classes, then (c) it is possible to define the maximum

and minimum levels of the total vote that are available to the social-democratic party at any given time. These define what could be called the "Gramsci bounds" on electoral strategies: the limits of what is possible under the historically embodied constraints. The cumulative effect of past strategies and current structures, then, is an historical trajectory of changing possibilities. Przeworski develops both mathematical models of this trajectory of limits for various countries, and then an empirical investigation of the actual trajectory of electoral outcomes that occur within these limits.

A second example is G.A. Cohen's analysis of classical historical materialism. Cohen's task is to try to see what kind of explanation is represented by the Marxist theory of history. He wants to reconcile a number of distinct theses: (1) the level of development of the forces of production determines the form of social relations of production; (2) the economic structure (the totality of all relations of production) determines the political superstructure; (3) the relations of production explain the development of the forces of production; (4) the superstructure explains the persistence of the economic structure. Cohen argues that these propositions can be made consistent only if they are linked together through a series of functional explanations. Thus, for example, he argues that for statements (2) and (4) above both to be true, the word "determines" in statement (2) must mean "functionally explains." The superstructure must be functionally explained by the economic base in the following way: the superstructure takes the form that it does because the economic base needs it in order to be reproduced. This may or may not, of course, be a plausible theory either of the relationship between economic and noneconomic institutions or of historical development; but it is the necessary form of the argument if the specific elements of the theory as developed by Marx are to be internally consistent.

What is striking in both of these examples is not mainly the abstract substantive claims which they make. After all, Przeworski's argument could be basically viewed as an example of Marx's famous statement that "Men make their own history, but under circumstances not of their choosing," applied to the specific problem of socialist electoral politics. And Cohen's analysis is directly based on Marx's analysis of the "dialectical relation" between forces and relations of production. What is novel in this work is the rigor of the effort at specifying the details of the mechanisms which underlie these more abstract claims. This not only enhances the depth of our understanding of the abstract arguments themselves, but makes it much easier to identify their weaknesses and reconstruct them in light of empirical research.

The Importance of Choice

The feature of Analytical Marxism that has caused the most controversy, perhaps, is the self-conscious use by certain Analytical Marxists of rational-actor models, including mathematical game theory. This has led some people to rename Analytical Marxism "Rational-Choice Marxism,"[4] and to characterize it as embodying a general commitment to methodological individualism (i.e., to the methodological claim that all social phenomena are in principle explainable exclusively with reference to individuals and their attributes).

This identification of Analytical Marxism with methodological individualism is, I believe, mistaken. Indeed, a number of Analytical Marxists have been explicitly critical of methodological individualism and have argued against the exclusive reliance on models

of abstract rationality as a way of understanding human action.[5] What is true, however, is that most Analytical Marxists take quite seriously the problem of understanding the relationship between individual choice and social processes. This does not imply that social processes can be *reduced* to problems of individual intentionality, nor does it imply that instrumental rationality is the ubiquitous basis for intentional action; but it does mean that social theory should systematically incorporate a concern with conscious choice. One way of doing this is through rational-actor models of various kinds.

Now, it is certainly possible to acknowledge the usefulness of the intellectual discipline of constructing formal models, and yet reject rational-choice models as simply being stupid models. Particularly given the historical identification of rational-actor theory with neoclassical economics, what is the attraction of this particular kind of model to many Analytical Marxists? I think the attraction lies in the importance most Analytical Marxists give to a particular analytical task, namely elaborating what is sometimes called the *micro-foundations* of macro-structural theory—that is, analyzing the mechanisms through which individuals come to act the way they do within a set of structurally defined social relations. Whatever else one might want of a social theory, if we want to understand the mechanisms through which a given social cause generates its effects, we must try to understand why individuals act the way they do. And in this context, rational-actor models and game theory provide a systematic strategy for analyzing one particularly salient aspect of individual action: action that results from conscious choices in which the costs and benefits are assessed over a range of feasible alternatives within a set of social constraints. If you believe (a) that at least in some important social contexts actors make conscious choices, and (b) that when they make choices they take into consideration the expected consequences of their actions, and finally, (c) that in assessing such consequences they take into consideration the choices of other actors—that is, that they act strategically, not just rationally—then something like game theory and rational-choice theory would be an appropriate part of one's repertoire of analytical techniques.

The difference between the way Analytical Marxists deploy these kinds of models and the way neoclassical economists and political scientists deploy them lies not in the internal logic of the models themselves, but in the kinds of problems they are used to address and the ways in which the "conditions of existence" of the models are specified. Thus, for example, John Roemer uses rational-choice theory to explore the problem of exploitation. In his analysis, the central conditions faced by actors are particular systems of property relations which give different actors monopolies over particular kinds of resources. He then uses the formal mathematical models of rational-choice theory to show how exploitation is generated out of such conditions. Thus, while Roemer adopts the formal mathematical apparatus of "bourgeois" models in his work, he asks different questions from neoclassical economists and he characterizes the environment of rational choice in a very different way. As a result, he comes to very different conclusions: far from generating optimal distributional consequences in a market environment, Roemer concludes that individual optimizing strategies systematically generate exploitation and classes.

To be sure, there are limits to the explanatory capacity of formal models built around rational action. Thus, most Analytical Marxists would agree that these kinds of models need to be supplemented in a variety of ways with other kinds of explanations in the construction of social theory. Examples include such things as functional explanations in G.A. Cohen's analysis of the theory of history; subintentional causal explanations in Jon Elster's analysis of the cognitive underpinnings of ideology; and institutional-structural explanations in my work on class formation and Robert Brenner's work on economic crisis. One of the innovations of Analytical Marxism, then, is the attempt to systematically link, within a Marxist theoretical agenda, these sorts of explanatory strategies with the analysis of individual rationality and choice. . . .

NOTES

1. Some of the most important works published by this cast of characters would include: G.A. Cohen, *Karl Marx's Theory of History: A Defense* (Princeton: Princeton University Press, 1978); John Roemer, *A General Theory of Exploitation and Class* (Cambridge, MA: Harvard University Press, 1982); Adam Przeworski, *Capitalism and Social Democracy* (Cambridge: Cambridge University Press, 1985); Erik Olin Wright, *Classes* (London: Verso, 1985); Bob Brenner, "The Agrarian Roots of European Capitalism," in *The Brenner Debate*, T.H. Aston and C.H.E. Philpon, eds. (Cambridge: Cambridge University Press, 1985), pp. 213–327; Jon Elster, *Making Sense of Marx* (Cambridge: Cambridge University Press, 1985); Phillippe Van Parijs, *Evolutionary Explanation in the Social Sciences: An Emerging Paradigm* (Totawa, NJ: Rowman & Littlefield, 1981); Samuel Bowles and Herbert Gintis, *Democracy and Capitalism* (New York: Basic Books, 1986).

2. Roemer, *A General Theory of Class*, Cohen, *Karl Marx's Theory of History*, ch. 2, and "The Structure of Proletarian Unfreedom," in Roemer, ed., *Analytical Marxism*, (Cambridge: Cambridge University Press, 1986); Elster, *Making Sense of Marx*, ch. 6.2; Joshua Cohen and Joel Rogers, *On Democracy*, (New York: Penguin, 1983); Andrew Levine, *Arguing for Socialism.* (London: Routledge and Kegan Paul, 1984).

3. See Przeworski, *Capitalism and Social Democracy*, and Adam Przeworski and John Sprague, *Pa-*

per *Stones* (Chicago: University of Chicago Press, 1986); Cohen, *Karl Marx's Theory of History*.

4. See for example Alan Carling, "Rational Choice Marxism," *New Left Review*, 160 (1986).

5. See, in particular, Andrew Levine, Elliott Sober, and Erik Olin Wright, "Marxism and Methodological Individualism," *New Left Review*, 162 (1987). See also the exchange in *Socialist Review* (89/1, 89/2, 89/3) between Michael Burawoy and Adam Przeworski over the problem of microfoundations of macro-theory.

MARXISM AND SOCIALIST-FEMINIST THEORY:
A DECADE OF DEBATE*

LISE VOGEL

INTRODUCTION

The 1960s marked the appearance of move-ments for the liberation of women in virtually every capitalist country, a phenomenon that had not been seen for half a century. Begin-ning in North America, this "second wave" of militant feminism spread quickly. Great Britain and the nations of Europe reacted first to the North American catalyst, and a new feminist consciousness emerged as well in such places as Japan, India, Iran and Latin America. Although reminiscent of earlier feminism, the women's liberation movement of the 1960s and 1970s in Europe and North America necessarily constituted a specific re-sponse to new social conditions. Not the least of its peculiarities was the existence of a sig-nificant trend within it known as socialist fem-inism or Marxist feminism, which sought to merge the two traditions so self-consciously linked together. Socialist feminism, argued its proponents, represents "a unique politics that

*From Scott G. McNall and Gary Howe, eds. *Current Perspectives in Social Theory*, vol. 2 (Greenwich, CT: JAI Press, 1981), pp. 209–18, 221–31. Reprinted with permission of JAI Press, Inc.

addresses the interconnection of patriarchy and capitalism, with the goal of dealing with sexism, class conflict, and racism" (Red Apple Collective, 1978:39).

Socialist feminists shared a general strate-gic and organizational perspective. They ar-gued that the participation of women, con-scious of their own oppression as a group, is critical to the success of any revolutionary struggle. They asserted that the key oppres-sions of sex, class, and race are interrelated and that the struggles against them must be coordinated—although the precise character of that coordination remained unspecified. In any case, socialist feminists agreed on the ne-cessity of an autonomous women's movement throughout the revolutionary process, in or-der to guarantee socialist commitment to women's liberation, particularly in the areas of ideological and psychological relations and in the "private" sphere. Autonomy, they main-tained, is a political as well as a tactical princi-ple. Finally, socialist-feminist theorists argued that the movement shares with much of the new left "a totalistic view of the socialist trans-formation, an emphasis on subjective factors in the revolutionary process, and a rejection of mechanical stage-ism" (Ehrenreich, 1975:87). For most activists, however, the essence and strength of the socialist-feminist movement lay not in its view of socialism but in its particular interpretation of the feminist insights that sisterhood is powerful and that the personal is political.

Theory did not play a large role in the development of the women's liberation movement in its first stages. Indeed, the very ability to exist and grow without firm theoretical or organizational bearings testified to the movement's strength as a real social force. By the early seventies, however, the movement began to reevaluate its practice, and to examine more closely the theoretical framework implicitly guiding its activity. In turning to theoretical work, participants in the women's liberation movement addressed practical issues arising out of their political experience. Nowhere was this new commitment to theory stronger than among socialist feminists. Their interest in theory responded, in large part, to a sense that the already established socialist-feminist strategic orientation needed a more adequate foundation.

Socialist feminists quite naturally looked to the socialist tradition for a theoretical starting point. As they soon discovered, however, the tradition fails to provide adequate or consistent answers to the so-called woman question. In the gloomy wake of this failure, socialist feminists refused to accept traditional answers. If the problem of women's oppression and women's liberation are ever to be resolved, they argued, a number of difficult questions must be confronted more successfully. At the theoretical level, these questions centered on three interrelated areas:

First, all women, not just working-class women, are oppressed in capitalist society. Women occupy a subordinate place, moreover, in all class societies, and some would argue that women are subordinated in every society, including socialist society. What is the root of women's oppression? How can its cross-class and transhistorical character be understood theoretically?

Second, women's biological capacity to bear children acquires different social expression in the sex division of labor of each particular society. Generally speaking, however, the sex division of labor represents a stubborn barrier to women's full social participation in every society. How is it possible, then, for women to be truly equal? Shouldn't the very notion of equality be transcended in order for women to be liberated?

Third, women's oppression bears strong analogies to the oppression of racial and national groups, as well as to the exploitation of subordinate classes. Are sex, race, and class parallel oppressions of essentially similar kind, requiring parallel organizational forms? Is there any other way to grasp this phenomenon in theoretical terms?

Explicitly or implicitly, socialist feminism set itself the task of developing a better set of answers to these questions than the socialist tradition had been able to offer.

Like the movement to which it owes its existence, socialist-feminist theory is far from monolithic. In general, socialist feminists argue that socialist theory must be extended or even entirely transformed by means of the insights offered by feminist theory and practice. A variety of attempts to execute this transformation have been made, although no consensus yet exists on their adequacy. If anything, socialist feminists increasingly recognize the difficulty of the theoretical task. "We have been excessively impatient for finished products, answers, and total theories," comments one group. "We have not allowed for the tremendous amount of work involved in clearing new paths and dealing with new questions" (Red Apple Collective, 1978:43). Nonetheless, more than ten years of theoretical efforts in the name of socialist feminism have left their mark. Despite weaknesses, which sometimes function as obstacles to further progress, the socialist-feminist movement has made some of the most important advances in the development of socialist theory on the question of women since the nineteenth century.

MITCHELL AND THE STRUCTURES OF WOMEN'S OPPRESSION

Initial efforts to develop a socialist-feminist theoretical perspective focused on the family unit and the labor of housework in contemporary capitalist societies. The opening argument, an article on "Women: The Longest Revolution," by Juliet Mitchell, actually appeared well before the development of the socialist-feminist movement proper. First printed in 1966 in *New Left Review*, a British Marxist journal, Mitchell's piece began to circulate widely in the United States two years later. It rapidly became a major theoretical influence on the emerging socialist-feminist trend within the women's liberation movement. The 1971 publication of Mitchell's book, *Woman's Estate*, based on the earlier article, reinforced its impact.

Mitchell begins "Women: The Longest Revolution" with what was, at the time, the first intelligent critique of the classical Marxist literature on the question of women. She comments briefly on the schematic view of woman's liberation held by Marx, Engels, Bebel, and Lenin, locating its failures in the absence of an appropriate strategic context. And she observes that De Beauvoir's *The Second Sex*, while an important contribution, remains limited by the crudity of its attempt to meld idealist psychological explanation with an economistic interpretation of socialist construction.

What, then, is Mitchells' alternative? Her discussion situates women with respect to four distinct structures in which they are inte-grated: production, reproduction, socialization, and sexuality. Each structure, she claims, develops separately and requires its own analysis; together, they form the "complex unity" of woman's position. Under production, Mitchell includes various activities external to what we might intuitively call the domestic or family sphere, for example, participation in wage labor in capitalist society. Conversely, the remaining three categories, oppressively united in the institution known as the family, encompass woman's existence outside of production, as wife and mother. In an effort to reach general strategic conclusions, Mitchell then surveys the current state of each of the four structures. Production, reproduction, and socialization show little dynamism, she says, and indeed have not for years. The structure of sexuality, by contrast, is presently undergoing severe strain, and constitutes the strategic weak link—that is, the structure most vulnerable to immediate attack.

While one structure may be the weak link, Mitchell argues that socialist strategy will have to confront all four structures in the long run. Furthermore, "economic demands are still primary" in the last instance. In this context, Mitchell makes a number of sensitive strategic observations. The left must reject both reformism and voluntarism on the woman question, for they always lead to inadequate strategic programs. The reformist tendency manifests itself as a set of modest ameliorative demands divorced from any fundamental critique of women's position. The voluntarist approach takes the more belligerent form of maximalist demands concerning the abolition of the family, total sexual freedom, collective childrearing, and the like. Although these demands appear radical, they "merely serve as a substitute for the job of theoretical analysis or practical persuasion. By pitching the whole subject in totally intransigent terms, voluntarism objectively helps to maintain it outside the framework of normal political discussion." In place of such abstract programs, the socialist movement requires a practical set of demands that address all four structures of woman's position. For instance, in the area of wage labor, Mitchell observes, quite correctly, that "the most elementary demand is not the right to work or receive equal pay for work—the two traditional reformist demands—but *the right to equal work itself.*" As for the abolition of the family, the strategic concern should rather be the liberation of women and the equality of the sexes. The consequences of this concern are "no less radical, but they are concrete and positive, and can be integrated into the real course of history. The family as it exists at present, is, in fact, incompatible with either women's liberation or the equality of the sexes. But equality will not come from its administrative abolition, but from the historical differentiation of its functions. The revolutionary demand should be for the liberation of these functions from an oppressive monolithic fusion" (Mitchell, 1971:150). . . .

Even with its problems, easier to recognize at a distance of more than ten years, Mitchell's 1966 article played an extremely positive role within the developing socialist-feminist movement. Its differentiation of the content of women's lives into constituent categories helped women's liberationists to articulate their experience and begin to act on it. Its perceptive overview of the classical Marxist literature on women provided a base from which to confront both dogmatist versions of Marxism and the growing influence of radical feminism. Its insistence, within a Marxist framework, on the critical importance of social phenomena not easily characterized as economic anticipated the socialist-feminist critique of economic determinism. And the political intelligence of its specific strategic comments set a standard which remains a model. Theoretically, Mitchell's central contribution was to legitimate a perspective which recognizes the ultimate primacy of the economic level, yet allows for the fact that other aspects of women's situation not only have importance but may play key roles at certain junctures.

BENSTON, MORTON, AND DALLA COSTA: A MATERIALIST FOUNDATION

By 1969, the North American women's liberation movement had reached a high point of activity, its militance complemented by a flourishing literature, published and unpublished. In this atmosphere, two Canadians, Margaret Benston and Peggy Morton, circulated and then published important essays. Each piece offered an analysis in Marxist terms of the nature of womens' unpaid work within the family household and discussed its relationship to existing social contradictions and the possibilities for change.

Benston (1969) starts from the problem of specifying the root of women's secondary status in capitalist society. She maintains that this root is "economic" or "material," and can be located in women's unpaid domestic labor. Women undertake a great deal of economic activity—they cook meals, sew buttons on garments, do laundry, care for children, and so forth—but the products and services which result from this work are consumed directly and never reach the marketplace. That is, these products and services have use-value but no exchange-value. For Benston, then, women stand in a definite relationship to the means of production, distinct from that of men. Women constitute the "group of people which is responsible for the production of simple use-values in those articles associated with the home and family." Hence, the family is an economic unit whose primary function is not consumption, as was generally held at the time by feminists, but production. "The family should be seen primarily as a production unit for housework and child-rearing." Moreover, because women's unpaid domestic labor is technologically primitive and outside the money economy, Benston argues that each family household represents an essentially pre-industrial and pre-capitalist entity. While noting that women also participate in wage labor, she regards such production as transient and not central to women's definition as a group. It is women's responsibility for domestic work which provides the material basis for their oppression and enables the capitalist economy to treat them as a massive reserve army of labor. Equal access to jobs outside the home will remain a woefully insufficient precondition for women's liberation if domestic labor continues as private and technologically backward. Benston's strategic suggestions, therefore, center on the need to provide a more important precondition by converting work now done in the home into public production. That is, society must move towards the socialization of housework and childcare. In this way, she revives a traditional socialist theme, not as dogma but as forceful argument made in the context of a developing discussion within the contemporary women's movement.

Peggy Morton's article (1970), published a year after Benston's, deepened as well as sharpened the analysis of the family as an economic unit in capitalist society. For Morton, Benston's discussion of unpaid household labor as the material basis for women's oppression leaves open a number of questions: Do women form a class? Should women be organized only through their work in the household? How and why has the nature of the family as an economic institution in capitalist society changed? Morton proposes a more precise definition of the family: It is the economic unit whose function is the maintenance and reproduction of labor power, meaning the labor power of the working class.

In this way, she ties the argument more closely to the workings of the capitalist mode of production, and focuses on the contradictions experienced by working-class women within the family, in the labor force, and between the two roles. In particular, she shows that as members of the reserve army of labor, women are central, not peripheral, to the economy, for they make possible the functioning of those manufacturing, service and state sectors where low wages are a priority. While the strategic outlook in the several versions of Morton's paper bears only a loose relationship to its analysis, and fluctuates from workers' control to revolutionary cadre-building, her discussion of the contradictory tendencies in women's situation introduces a dynamic element that had been missing from Benston's approach.

Both Benston's and Morton's articles have a certain simplicity that even at the time invited critique. In the bright glare of hindsight, their grasp of Marxist theory and their ability to develop an argument appear painfully limited. Benston's facile dismissal of women's participation in wage labor requires correction, as Morton and others quickly pointed out. Moreover, her delineation of women's domestic labor as a remnant from pre-capitalist modes of production, which had somehow survived into the capitalist present, cannot be sustained theoretically. Morton's position, while analytically more precise, glosses over the question of the special oppression of all women as a group, and threatens to convert the issue of women's oppression into a purely working-class concern. None of these problems should obscure, however, the theoretical advances made by Benston and Morton. Taken together, their two articles established the material character of women's unpaid domestic labor in the family household. Each offered an analysis of the way this labor functioned as the material basis for the host of contradictions in women's experience in capitalist society. Morton, in addition, formulated the issues in terms of a concept of the reproduction of labor power, and emphasized the specific nature of contradictions within the working class. These theoretical insights had a lasting impact on subsequent socialist-feminist work and remain an important contribution. Moreover, they definitively shifted the framework in which discussion of women's oppression had to be located. Where Mitchell had analyzed women's situation in terms of roles, functions, and structures, Benston and Morton focused on the issue of women's unpaid labor in the household and its relationship to the reproduction of labor power. In this sense, they rooted the question of women in the theoretical terrain of materialism.

Mariarosa Dalla Costa, writing from Italy less than two years later, took the argument several steps further (Dalla Costa, 1972). Agreeing that women constitute a distinct group whose oppression is based on the material character of unpaid household labor, she maintains that on a world level, all women are housewives. Whether or not a woman works outside the home, "it is precisely what is particular to domestic work, not only measured as number of hours and nature of work, but as quality of life and quality of relationships which it generates, that determines a woman's place wherever she is and to whichever class she belongs." At the same time, Dalla Costa concentrates her attention on the working-class housewife, whom she sees as indispensable to capitalist production.

As housewives, working-class women find themselves excluded from socialized production, isolated in routines of domestic labor which have the technological character of pre-capitalist labor processes. Dalla Costa disputes the notion that these housewives are mere suppliers of use-values in the home and, therefore, essentially external to the workings of capitalism and to the class struggle. Polemicizing against both traditional left views and the literature of the women's movement, she argues that housework only appears to be a personal service outside the arena of capitalist production. In reality, it produces not just use-values for direct consumption in the family, but the commodity labor power. Moreover, housework produces surplus-value, and housewives are therefore "productive workers" in the strict Marxist sense. Appropriation of this surplus value is organized by the capitalist's payment of a wage to the working-class husband, who thereby becomes the instrument of woman's exploitation. The survival of the working class depends on the working-class family, "but *at the woman's expense against the class itself.* The woman is the slave of a wage slave, and her slavery ensures the slavery of her man ... And that is why the struggle of the woman of the working class against the family is crucial."

Since working-class housewives are productive laborers who are peculiarly excluded from socialized production, demystification of domestic work as a "masked form of productive labor" becomes a central task. Dalla Costa proposes two major strategic alternatives. First, socialize the struggle—not the work—of the isolated domestic laborer by mobilizing working-class housewives around community issues, the wagelessness of housework, the denial of sexuality, the separation of family from outside world, and the like. "We must discover forms of struggle which immediately break the whole structure of domestic work, rejecting it absolutely, rejecting our role as housewives and the home as the ghetto of our existence, since the problem is not only to stop doing this work, but to smash the entire role of housewife." Second, reject work altogether, especially in a capitalist economy which increasingly draws women into the wage-labor force. In opposition to the left's traditional view of this tendency as progressive, Dalla Costa maintains that the modern women's movement constitutes a rejection of this alternative. Economic independence through performing social labor in a socialized structure is no more than a sham reform. Women have worked enough, and they must "refuse the myth of liberation through work."

The polemical energy and political range of Dalla Costa's article had a substantial impact on the women's movement on both sides of the Atlantic. Unlike Benston, Morton, and other North American activists, Dalla Costa seemed to have a sophisticated grasp of Marxist theory and politics. Her arguments and strategic proposals struck a responsive chord in a movement already committed to viewing women's oppression mainly in terms of their family situation. Few noticed that Dalla Costa, like Morton, talked only of the working class, and never specified the relationship between the oppression of working-class housewives and that of *all* women. What was most important was that Dalla Costa, even more than Benston and Morton, seemed to have situated the question of women's oppression within an analysis of the role of their unpaid domestic labor in the reproduction of capitalist social relations. Moreover, since her article functioned as the theoretical foundation for a small but aggressive movement to demand wages for housework, which flourished briefly in the early 1970s, it acquired an overtly political role denied to most women's liberation theoretical efforts. . . .

PATRIARCHY AND THE MODE OF REPRODUCTION

While Juliet Mitchell had advised that "we should ask the feminist questions, but try to come up with some Marxist answers" (1971:99), by the early 1970s, many socialist feminists disagreed. They argued that the quest for Marxist answers to their questions led down a blind alley, where the feminist struggle becomes submerged in the socialist struggle against capitalism. To move forward, then, socialist feminism had to construct new theoretical categories.

At first, socialist feminists turned to the radical feminism of the late sixties for concepts that could account for the depth and pervasiveness of women's oppression in all societies. Radical feminists typically considered the struggle between the sexes to be universal, and, indeed, the essential dynamic underlying all social development. At the same time, some radical feminist writings seemed to be extensions or deepenings of the insights offered by Marx and Engels. Shulamith Firestone's *Dialectic of Sex*, for instance, claimed to go beyond the merely economic level addressed by Marx and Engels, in order to uncover the much larger problem of sex oppression. "The class analysis is a beautiful piece of work," Firestone wrote, "but limited." In proposing a dialectic of sex, she hoped "to take the class analysis one step further to its roots in the biological division of the sexes. We have not thrown out the insights of the socialists; on the contrary, radical feminism can enlarge their analysis, granting it an even deeper basis in objective conditions and thereby explaining many of its insolubles" (Firestone, 1970:4, 11). Similarly, Kate Millett's *Sexual Politics* acknowledged Engels as a major theorist, but her presentation of Engels' work transformed it almost beyond recognition into a subordinate contribution to the sexual revolution. The limitation of Marxist theory, she maintained, was that it "failed to supply a sufficient ideological base for a sexual revolution, and was remarkably naive as to the historical and psychological strength of patriarchy" (Millett, 1970:169). In broad strokes, Millett depicted Nazi Germany, the Soviet Union, and Freudian psychology as comparable instances of reactionary patriarchal policy and ideology, arguing that patriarchy will survive so long as psychic structures remain untouched by social programs. For

Millett, the sexual revolution requires not only an understanding of sexual politics but the development of a comprehensive theory of patriarchy.

Firestone's and Millett's books, both published in 1970, had a tremendous impact on the emerging socialist-feminist trend within the women's movement. Their focus on sexuality, on psychological phenomena, and on the stubborn persistence of social practices oppressive to women struck a responsive chord. The concept of patriarchy entered socialist-feminist discourse virtually without objection. Those few critiques framed within a more orthodox Marxist perspective, such as Juliet Mitchell's, went unheard. Although acknowledging the limitations of radical feminism, many socialist feminists, particularly in the United States, simply assumed that "the synthesis of radical feminism and Marxist analysis is a necessary first step in formulating a cohesive socialist feminist political theory, one that does not merely add together these two theories of power but sees them as interrelated through the sexual division of labor" (Eisenstein, 1978:6). No longer was the problem one of using Marxist categories to build a theoretical framework for the analysis of women's oppression. Like the radical feminists, these socialist feminists took Marxism more or less as a given, and did not seek to elaborate or deepen it.

The task, then, was to develop the synthesis which is socialist feminism—or, as one writer put it, to dissolve the hyphen (Petchesky, 1978). To accomplish this task, socialist feminists explored two related themes: patriarchy, and the mode of reproduction. The notion of patriarchy, taken over from radical feminism, required appropriate transformation. Millett had used the term to indicate a universal system of political, economic, ideological and, above all, psychological structures through which men subordinate women. Socialist feminists had to develop a concept of patriarchy capable of linkage with the theory of class struggle, which posits each mode of production as a specific system of structures through which one class exploits and subordinates another. In general, socialist feminists suggested, as Heidi Hartmann and Amy Bridges put it, that "Marxist categories, like capital itself, are sex-blind; the categories of patriarchy as used by radical feminists are blind to history" (1981:11). From this point of view, the concept of patriarchy provides a means for discussing social phenomena that somehow escape Marxist categories. Some argued that the theory of patriarchy could explain why certain individuals, men as well as women, are in particular subordinate or dominant places within the social structure of a given society. Others believed that issues of interpersonal dominance and subordination could best be addressed by a theory of patriarchy. Although socialist feminists often focused on the psychological aspects of these hierarchical relations, they argued that patriarchy is not just an ideological superstructure. "Patriarchal authority," wrote Sheila Rowbotham, "is based on male control over the woman's productive capacity, and over her person" (1973:117). That is, patriarchy has a material foundation in men's ability to control women's labor, access to resources, and sexuality. Through these formulations, socialist-feminist theory began to extend what was actually a traditional Marxist understanding of patriarchy as a form of household labor organization and property control, in order to encompass the sex division of labor. The origin of sex divisions of labor, and the relationship between patriarchal structures and the workings of a given mode of production continue to be key problems for socialist-feminist theorists. The precise nature of the autonomy which socialist feminists claim for patriarchy also remains to be specified. In this connection, some socialist feminists have begun to focus on a new concept, the mode of reproduction—comparable to, but relatively autonomous from, the mode of production which characterizes a given society.

As with the concept of patriarchy, there is little agreement on the substance of the mode of reproduction. Some simply identify the mode of reproduction with what appears to be the obvious functions of the family. Despite the empiricism of this approach, it clarifies the analytical tasks which socialist feminists confront. In Renate Bridenthal's words, "the relationship between production and reproduction is a dialectic within a larger historical dialectic. That is, changes in the mode of production give rise to changes in the mode of reproduction," and this dialectic must be analyzed (1976:5). Similarly, some participants in the domestic labor debate have postulated the existence of a "housework mode of production" alongside the capitalist mode of production, but subordinate to it. The socialist-feminist concept of a mode of reproduction converges, moreover, with recent suggestions by Marxist anthropologists that the contemporary family, as well as some primitive domestic community, acts as a perpetual source of human labor power. An analogous concept of the mode of reproduction is often implicit in the work of socialist feminists who study the relationship between imperialism and the family in dependent third-world countries.

The concept of a mode of reproduction seems to offer a way to incorporate the notion of patriarchy into a more rigorous Marxist framework. Indeed, a quite similar concept of an autonomous, family-based mode of production—"simple commodity production"—has a long history within Marxist studies of social development. Largely in ignorance of this history, socialist feminists have partially recreated it. At the same time, the effort to delineate the mode of reproduction as an explanation of women's oppression and of the relationship between family and society has brought socialist-feminist theory closer to current developments in Marxism.

TOWARDS A UNITARY THEORY OF WOMEN'S OPPRESSION

In reviewing the theoretical work produced in the context of the socialist-feminist movement, certain major themes and leading ideas stand out. Taken together, they indicate the important contribution made by socialist feminism to the development of theory on the question of women. Simultaneously, they suggest some of its limitations.

Socialist-feminist theory starts from a correct insistence that behind the serious social, psychological, and ideological phenomena of women's oppression lies a material root. It points out that Marxism has never adequately analyzed the nature and location of that root. And it hypothesizes that the family constitutes a major if not the major terrain which nourishes it. With this position, socialist feminism implicitly rejects two fallacious, as well as contradictory, currents in the legacy of socialist theory and practice on the so-called woman question. First, the socialist-feminist emphasis on the material root of oppression counters an idealist tendency within the left, which trivializes the woman question as a mere matter of lack of rights and ideological chauvinism. Second, socialist feminists' special concern with psychological and ideological issues, especially those arising within the family, stands opposed to the crudities of economic determinist views of women's oppression. These perspectives—which make up the implicit theoretical content of the slogan "the personal is political"—establish guidelines for socialist-feminist consideration of women's oppression and women's liberation. Through them, socialist feminism returns, wittingly or not, to the best of Marx and Engels' work on the woman question. At the same time, it promises to take that work beyond its still rudimentary form.

Socialist feminists recognize the inadequacies as well as the contributions of Engels' discussion of the family and property relations in the *Origin of the Family, Private Property and the State*. Like Engels, they locate the oppression of women within the dynamic of social development, but they seek to establish a more dialectical phenomenon as its basis than Engels was able to identify. Such a phenomenon must satisfy several implicit criteria. It must be a material process which is specific to a particular mode of production. Its identification should nevertheless suggest why women are oppressed in all class societies—or, for some socialist feminists, in all known societies. Most important, it must offer a better understanding of women's oppression in subordinate as well as ruling classes than does Engels' critique of property. Socialist-feminist analyses share the view that child-bearing, child-raising and housework fit these criteria, although they offer a wide variety of theoretical interpretations of the relationship between these activities and women's oppression.

Some socialist feminists try to situate domestic labor within broader concepts covering the processes of maintenance and reproduction of labor power. They suggest that these processes have a material character, and that they take place, furthermore, *within*, not outside of, social production. For elaboration of this position, which shifts the immediate focus away from women's oppression per se, and on to wider social phenomena, they turn to Marx's writings, and especially to *Capital*. At the same time, they resist, as best they can, the contradictory pulls of economic determinism and idealism inherited from the socialist tradition.

The relationship between the capitalist wage and the household it supports represents yet another major theme. Socialist feminists point out that Marxism has never been clear on the question of whom the wage covers. The concept of the historical subsistence level of wages refers, at times, to individuals, and at other times, to the worker "and his family." Sensitivity to this ambiguity has inspired a series of attempts to reformulate and answer questions concerning divisions of labor according to sex in both the family and wage labor. While some such efforts stress concepts of authority and patriarchy, others focus on questions involving the determination of wage levels, competition in the labor market, and the structure of the industrial reserve army. Whatever the approach, the identification of the problem in itself constitutes a significant theoretical step forward.

Socialist-feminist theory also emphasizes that women in capitalist society have a double relation to wage labor, as both paid and unpaid workers. It generally regards women's activity as consumers and unpaid domestic laborers as the dominant factor shaping every woman's consciousness, whether or not she participates in wage labor. This position accompanies on important strategic orientation. Socialist feminists maintain, against some opinions on the left, that women can be successfully organized and they point to the long history of militant activity by women in the labor movement, in communities and in social revolution. They observe, however, that mobilization demands a special sensitivity to women's experience as women, and they quite properly assert the legitimacy and importance of organizations comprised of women only. Socialist-feminist theory takes on the political task of developing a framework to guide such organizing efforts.

Finally, socialist-feminist theory links its theoretical outlook to a passage from Engels's Preface to the *Origin* (1972:71–72):

According to the materialistic conception, the determining factor in history, is, in the final instance, the production and reproduction of immediate life. This, again, is of a twofold character: on the one side, the production of the means of existence, of food, clothing and shelter and the tools necessary for that production; on the other side, the production of human beings themselves, the propagation of the species. The social organization under which the people of a particular historical epoch and a particular country live is determined by both kinds of production: by the stage of development of labor on the one hand and of the family on the other.

The citation of these sentences, repeated in article after article, accomplishes a number of purposes. It affirms the socialist-feminist commitment to the Marxist tradition. It suggests that Marx and Engels had more to say about the question of women than the later socialist movement was able to hear. It seems to situate the problem of women's oppression in the context of a theory of general social reproduction. It emphasizes the material essence of the social processes for which women hold major responsibility. And it implies that the production of human beings constitutes a process which has not only an autonomous character, but a theoretical weight equal to that of the production of the means of existence. In short, Engels' remarks appear to offer authoritative Marxist backing for the socialist feminist focus on the family, sex divisions of labor, and unpaid domestic work, for its strategic commitment to the autonomous organization of women, and for its theoretical dualism. Yet, the passage actually reflects Engels at his theoretical weakest (Brown, 1978; Vogel, 1983:ch. 5). Socialist-feminist insights into the role of women in social reproduction need a more solid basis.

Despite the strengths, richness and real contributions of socialist-feminist theoretical work, its development has been constrained by loyalty to an already established strategic perspective, as well as by its practitioners' insufficient grasp of Marxist theory. With their roots in a practical commitment to women's liberation and to the development of an autonomous women's movement, participants in the socialist-feminist movement have only recently begun to explore their relationship to trends and controversies within the left. At the theoretical level, the exploration has taken the form of a new wave of publications seeking, on the one hand, to delineate the substance of socialist feminism more clearly, and on the other, to situate women's oppression more precisely within, rather than alongside, a Marxist theory of social reproduction. These efforts are important, although they continue to suffer from a theoretical outlook shaped by a preexisting strategic orientation. If theoretical work is to have any significance, however, it must be as a guide to, not a simple reflection of, social practice.

REFERENCES

BENSTON, MARGARET. 1969. "The political economy of women's liberation." Monthly Review 21 (September):13–27.

BRIDENTHAL, RENATE. 1976. "The dialectics of production and reproduction in history." Radical America 10 (March–April):3–11.

BROWN, BEVERLY. 1978. "Natural and social division of labour: Engels and the domestic labour debate." m/f 1:25–47.

DALLA COSTA, MARIAROSA. 1972. "Women and the subversion of the community." Radical America 6 (January–February):67–102.

EHRENREICH, BARBARA. 1975. "Speech at national conference on socialist feminism." Socialist Revolution 5 (October–December):85–93.

EISENSTEIN, ZILLAH (ed.). 1978. Capitalist Patriarch and the Case for Socialist Feminism. New York: Monthly Review.

ENGELS, FREDERICK. [1884] 1972. The Origin of the Family, Private Property and the State. New York: International.

FIRESTONE, SHULAMITH. 1970. The Dialectic of Sex. New York: Morrow.

HARTMANN, HEIDI. 1981. "The unhappy marriage of Marxism and feminism." Pp. 1–41 in L. Sargent (ed.) Women and Revolution. Boston: South End.

MILLETT, KATE. 1970. Sexual Politics. New York: Doubleday.

MITCHELL, JULIET. 1966. "Women: the longest revolution." New Left Review 40 (November–December):11–37.

———. 1971. Woman's Estate. Baltimore: Penguin.

MORTON, PEGGY. 1970. "A woman's work is never done, or: the production, maintenance and reproduction of labor power." Leviathan (May).

PETCHESKY, ROSALIND. 1978. "Dissolving the hyphen: a report on Marxist-feminist groups 1–5." Pp. 373–89 in Z. Eisenstein (ed.), Capitalist Patriarchy and the Case for Socialist Feminism. New York: Monthly Review.

RED APPLE COLLECTIVE. 1978. "Socialist-feminist women's unions: past and present." Socialist Review 38 (March–April):37–57.

ROWBOTHAM, SHEILA. 1973. Women's Consciousness, Man's World. Baltimore: Penguin.

VOGEL, LISE. 1983. Marxism and the Oppression of Women: Toward a Unitary Theory. New Brunswick: Rutgers University Press.

CHAPTER 4

MICROSOCIOLOGY

The term *microsociology* refers to a variety of approaches in contemporary sociology. In general, these approaches share a general dissatisfaction with the more structural theories that have been dominant throughout most of the history of sociology. Thus, microsociologists tend to be equally critical of both functionalism and the radical structural approaches such as conflict and neo-Marxian theories. They argue that structurally oriented, or *macro*, theory, with its emphasis on large-scale social structures and processes, has lost sight of the actual behaviors of individuals in society. Thus, in a famous 1964 essay, George Homans argued for a return to a more psychologically oriented sociology. Homans wrote:

If a serious effort is made to construct theories that will even begin to explain social phenomenon it turns out that their general propositions are not about the equilibrium of societies but about the behavior of men. This is true even of some good functionalists, though they will not admit it. They keep psychological explanations under the table and bring them out furtively like a bottle of whiskey, for use when they really need help. What

I ask is that we bring what we say about theory into line with what we actually do, and so put an end to our intellectual hypocrisy. (Homans 1964, 818)

CLASSICAL MICRO THEORY

The debate over the incorporation of psychological explanations in sociology has a long history, dating back to Emile Durkheim's 1895 *The Rules of Sociological Method,* considered by many to be the most important text on methodology in classical sociology (see Nisbet 1974, vii). Durkheim was especially concerned to distinguish his emerging discipline of sociology from the already existing academic subject of psychology. In fact, he was concerned for the practical reason that if sociology was to be accepted as a subject in French universities, it had to be demonstrated that it was indeed a new field of study and did not simply duplicate other well-established disciplines.

For Durkheim, psychology was concerned with the study of *psychological facts,* that is, states "internal" to the individual. Sociology should take as its subject matter the study of *social facts,* which Durkheim defined as "external to" and "coercive of" the individual (Durkheim 1982, ch. 1).

There was, however, a second, more political aspect to Durkheim's rejection of psychological theorizing in sociology. For Durkheim, societies were held together by powerful collective beliefs and norms that found expression in common cultural, religious, and political practices. Durkheim believed that the development of modern industrial society in late-nineteenth-century Europe had weakened those ties. In his view, the weakening of such ties had led to the emergence of a "cult of the individual" that was reflected in a weakening of the moral order, loss of respect for authority, and increasing rates of antisocial behavior of various types, including suicide, a topic that Durkheim studied in depth (Durkheim 1951). In Durkheim's view, sociology could be a powerful antidote to the excessive individualism of the modern age by emphasizing the collective and social causes of such apparently individual pathologies as divorce and suicide. This, then, in Durkheim's view, was another powerful argument against psychological individualism in sociology.

Durkheim's views were not universally accepted by other classical sociologists. For example, the German sociologist Max Weber (1864–1920) developed his sociology on the basis of a conception of *social action* that emphasized the subjective meaning of collective action for individual social actors (Weber 1949). But the work of another German theorist, Georg Simmel (1858–1918), proved to be even more important for the development of a micro orientation in sociology.

Simmel, a contemporary of his more famous colleague Weber, shared Weber's interest in exploring the subjective, personal meaning of social action. Whereas Weber, however, was interested in constructing ty-

pologies of social action primarily as a means for explaining large-scale historical conditions, Simmel sought to explore the microlevel of social interaction as an end in itself.

Simmel, primarily an essayist, wrote brilliantly insightful studies of different cultural "types," such as the stranger, the poor, the miser, and the spendthrift, and of specific arenas of social interaction, such as the modern city or metropolis (see Simmel 1971). But the main thrust of his work on *sociation,* or the forms of social interaction, was to attempt to construct a formal "geometry" of social relations. This social geometry was based on close, detailed analyses of small-scale social interactions. Its major variables were such concepts as group size and social distance. Simmel's studies resulted in highly abstract analyses of the properties of interaction processes. These studies examined, among other things, the effects of group size on interactions in groups of two (a dyad), three (a triad), or larger social groups (see Simmel 1950, 87–177). In addition, Simmel's analyses of these interaction processes in terms of their social setting, or form, gave rise to essays on superordination and subordination, conflict, exchange, prostitution, and sociability.

SYMBOLIC INTERACTIONISM

Simmel's microlevel approach to sociology was introduced into the United States during the early twentieth century through his influence on Robert Park (1864–1944) and other members of the "Chicago School," the influential early department of sociology at the University of Chicago. For the first three decades of the twentieth century, the University of Chicago was the home of the most innovative sociology program in the United States. Park, one of the department's central members, had attended Simmel's lectures in

Berlin and had been profoundly influenced by his work. Simmel's emphasis on close study of the "forms" of social interaction fit well with the Chicago School's characteristic emphasis on detailed analyses ("scientific reporting" in Park's words) of the various communities and subcultures of urban Chicago (Park 1973). But the most important scholar at the University of Chicago in the reformulation of Simmel's microsociological approach for an American audience was not Park or any other member of the department of sociology; it was the philosopher George Herbert Mead (1863–1931). Mead's work is remarkable in many respects. Although he was not a sociologist—and, indeed, held no graduate degree in *any* discipline—his teaching influenced generations of sociology students at Chicago. Although today he is perhaps the most widely read of the American sociologists of his generation, he did not publish a single book during his lifetime. Mead was a firm believer in the scientific method, but the theory that he founded, *symbolic interactionism,* has been understood by several generations of sociologists to be a humanistic alternative to the scientistic approaches of more macro-oriented sociological theories.

From 1894 to 1931, Mead taught courses in social psychology at the University of Chicago, using these to develop his own approach to the study of human behavior. From the accounts of Mead's students (see Cottrell, Reading 18), we know that Mead was a powerful and compelling lecturer, often using the classroom as a laboratory for the development of his theories. At the time of his death in 1931, little of Mead's theoretical work had been published; most of it lay buried in the lecture notes taken by his students. In one of the more remarkable collaborations in the history of sociology, several of his former students brought together their notes from Mead's class in social psychology, using these as the basis for the first full presentation of

Mead's views in *Mind, Self, and Society,* which was published in 1934 (Mead 1962).

The intellectual starting point for Mead was the psychological perspective of *behaviorism,* which, developed in the work of psychologist John B. Watson (an early student of Mead's) and others, had proved to be a powerful tool for the explanation of animal behavior (see Watson 1924). Central to the behaviorist perspective was a rigid insistence on controlled experiment and observation. Behaviorists would utilize the experimental environment to manipulate various stimuli to the organism and then observe the organism's response. In this way, behaviorists set out to produce a strict science of animal behavior that could, in principle, include human behavior as well.

Mead's criticism of this perspective stemmed from the refusal of behaviorists to study the mental processes of the organisms under study. In the case of radical behaviorists, this position would occasionally lead to a denial that such "invisible" processes were important in explaining the organisms's behavior or, in some cases, to the denial that such processes played any role at all in the stimulus-response nexus.

Mead believed that, although this approach might be applied successfully to the study of animal behavior, it was clearly inadequate to capture the distinctive *symbolic* character of human thought and behavior. In Mead's words, "John B. Watson's attitude was that of the Queen in *Alice in Wonderland*—'Off with their heads!'—There were no such things" (Mead 1962, 2–3). Even more critically, the radical behaviorist approach, with its characteristic methodological focus on controlled experimentation, ignored the distinctive *social context* in which all human behavior is embedded and which gives it meaning.

The form in which Mead's work had been published as posthumously collected lecture notes led (and has continued to lead) to disputes over the precise interpretation of his thought. Thus, there are today several different "schools" of Meadian theory, known today as *symbolic interactionism* (see Meltzer, Petras, and Reynolds 1975, Fine 1990, Reynolds 1990). Probably the most prominent of Mead's later interpreters has been Herbert Blumer who, in a series of articles published over three decades and eventually collected in 1969, coined the term *symbolic interactionism* (Blumer 1937, 1969). Blumer's work (see Reading 19) marks an attempt to systematize Mead's theory and to give it a more clearly sociological orientation. The academic context in which Blumer was writing had changed considerably from that of Mead. For Blumer, the major opponent to be faced was no longer Watsonian behaviorism, which by this time had already begun to be eclipsed in its own field of psychology. Rather, the main threat was seen by Blumer to now reside in the then-dominant macrosociological theory of structural functionalism (Ritzer 1988, 293–94).

To Blumer, while operating from different premises, functionalism had repeated many of the errors of Watsonian behaviorism. Like behaviorism, the functionalist model, especially in the work of Talcott Parsons (see Reading 3), assumed that social actors are motivated to act by forces that are largely beyond their conscious control. For Parsons, the mainsprings of social action are either socially imposed *values* and *attitudes* that are learned in childhood socialization and are ever after reinforced by the application of socially imposed sanctions and rewards or even more fundamental innate biological drives (Parsons and Shils 1951, 111). Blumer, like Mead before him, opposed any theory that ignores the process by which social actors *construct* meaning and values and that reduces human behavior to determination by outside forces—either social or natural.

In Blumer's view, the functionalist model of human behavior was just as rigid and mechanistic as the behaviorist approach criticized by Mead. But there was a further challenge here. The behaviorists had been primarily psychologists interested in explaining the behavior of individual organisms. The challenge posed by functionalism to the symbolic interactionist model was that it was a theory of social order or social structure that, like symbolic interactionism, sought to account for human behavior in its specifically *social* context. In response, Blumer sought to extend Mead's insights into the social origins of human behavior to show that the symbolic interactionist perspective could, in fact, be used to explain the genesis and nature of social structure itself (see Blumer, Reading 19).

In keeping with Mead's insights, Blumer developed an interactionist model of society that emphasizes the symbolically mediated and flexible nature of social structure. For Blumer, as for Mead, society is not something that exists a priori outside the individual, but is something that is continually negotiated and reinvented by social actors attempting to define and act in their own social world.

ETHNOMETHODOLOGY

This concern with the ways in which ordinary people creatively act to "invent" social order in their everyday lives is the focus of a second important microtheory, *ethnomethodology*. This perspective was developed during the turbulent 1960s by sociologists who were critical of what they saw as the scientistic and manipulative pretensions of mainstream sociology. Geographically, ethnomethodology was a product of California sociology and was centered around the work of Harold Garfinkel (1967) at UCLA. Ethnomethodology may be interpreted as an attempt to apply the insights of the European philosophy of *phenomenology* to sociology (see Schutz 1970, Wolff 1978). Phenomenologists and ethnomethodologists are particularly interested in the process whereby individuals go about "constructing" their social reality through interaction with others (see Berger and Luckmann 1966, Button 1991, Douglas 1980, Heritage 1987, Turner 1974).

This process is the focus of various "experiments" carried out by ethnomethodologists that attempt to expose or disrupt the functioning of everyday norms and procedures in order to observe how people respond to the disorganization of their taken-for-granted social world. As George Psathas (Reading 20) points out, in many respects the work of ethnomethodologists is similar to the "ethnoscience" practiced by cultural anthropologists who study an alien culture. Such study demands close attention to the details of social life and a fundamental respect for the ways in which individuals creatively construct and interpret their social world.

This ethnomethodological (quite literally, the word means "the study of peoples' methods"—the methods or means by which everyday social actors construct their social environment) perspective is captured nicely in Ryave and Schenkein's study of "doing walking" (Reading 21), which undertakes to construct an ethnomethodological account of one of the most common everyday experiences. Like the best ethnomethodological work, "Notes on the Art of Walking" challenges its readers to look at the everyday world of social interaction in a new and sometimes surprising light.

EXCHANGE THEORY

The 1960s and 1970s saw a dramatic turn toward this focus on the subjective experience of social actors at the micro level in sociology. For many sociologists, the new micro-orientation in social theory was a badly needed corrective to the conformist assumptions about the nature of individual socialization and behavior characteristic of the dominant functionalist model. In a survey of contemporary theory, one sociologist wrote:

The novelty of the constructionist turn of the 1960s and 1970s was that reality construction, for the first time, *came to be treated as a process and a variable in its own right.* Several micro theory groups turned in this direction at about the same time, Herbert Blumer and Harold Garfinkel being perhaps the key theoretical figures. (Wiley 1985, 190)

There was, however, an important rival to the social constructionist mainstream during this period that proved to be equally influential in the sociology of the 1970s and 1980s; this rival was *exchange theory.* Primarily associated with the work of George Homans (1961, 1962, 1967), Peter Blau (1964), and Richard Emerson (1976, 1981; see also Cook 1987), the exchange model was developed from the same theoretical roots as symbolic interactionism in psychological behaviorism. Its earliest and most trenchant expression in sociology was in the work of George Homans, who first outlined the propositions of an *exchange approach to social behavior* in a famous 1958 article (Reading 22).

Like Mead, Homans began with the behaviorist model and its characteristic focus on breaking complex behaviors down into their simple components and subjecting these components to rigorous observation and experiment. Like Mead, Homans rejected the strict behaviorist injunction against imputing subjective motives to human actors. At this point, however, the theoretical strategies adopted by Mead and Homas differed radically. Whereas Mead sought to root human subjectivity in a dialectical process of interaction between the individual and society, Homans sought to base his theory of human motivation in a model of calculating *interest.*

The concept of interest has a long history

in social science. Perhaps its earliest formulation was in the liberal eighteenth-century European Enlightenment's scientific rationalism, which proclaimed *reason* as the most basic human quality. But its most systematic development occurred in the work of the economists, who enthroned a concept of rational, calculating interest as the fundamental motive underlying all economic behavior (see Hirschman 1977). In summary, the economic paradigm describes economic actors, in their roles as both producers and consumers, as entering the market attempting to maximize their economic gains (profits) and minimize their costs (losses). In the words of the famous eighteenth-century economic theorist Adam Smith, the object of all economic activity is to "sell high and buy dear" (Smith 1937).

Homans believed this model of rational, self-interested motivation could not only be used to explain economic behavior, but it could also be extended to explain the full range of human behaviors in society. For Homans, the equation Profit = Reward – Cost is not just an economic formula for calculating the most satisfactory line of behavior in the market, it is a fundamental calculation engaged in by social actors continuously in pursuit of their goals in everyday life. *All* human behavior, according to Homans, can be analyzed as a form of *social exchange* in which social actors trade favors, influence, rewards, and punishments in an intricate ballet of negotiation, bluff, and compromise.

Even more than Meadian symbolic interactionism, Homans' exchange theory is focused on the level of the individual social actor. Throughout his career, Homans has resolutely maintained that sociological explanation should be couched at the level of the individual and his or her beliefs, values, and sentiments (Homans 1964, 1987). Of all contemporary theorists, Homans has been the most forthright defender of methodological individualism and the harshest critic of the classical Durkheimian program of restricting the use of psychological explanations in sociology. In fact, for Homans, *all* sociological explanations, insofar as they are valid, are reducible in principle to the basic psychological principles of his exchange model (Homans 1967, 1987).

Homans' model is quite powerful and convincing when applied to the analysis of simple models of face-to-face interaction within small groups. This is the social environment from which Homans drew all of his examples in his most important theoretical work (see Homans 1961). Thus, the famous exchange of assistance for thanks and approval between Person and Other in Homans' *Social Behavior: Its Elementary Forms* has long served as a paradigm of the exchange model. But social life in modern industrial (and postindustrial) societies is in fact much more complex than this simple model of face-to-face interaction allows. Under conditions of indirect mediated exchange, questions about what constitutes a "fair" exchange, how we decide what is equitable, and how we deal with inequity are important questions for any model that seeks to treat social life as exchange.

Elaine Hatfield's article (Reading 23) exemplifies a body of literature that has developed within exchange theory that attempts to unravel the social conditions under which equitable exchanges are defined, conducted, and enforced. The notions of justice, equity, and fair exchange are important for the exchange model, for they form the normative consensus that makes exchange processes in general possible in society, much as prior agreement on the norms of market behavior makes possible the conduct of market exchange—buying and selling—in the economic system.

The general application of market models in sociology by the proponents of exchange theory has drawn criticism from other perspectives in sociology, most especially from conflict and neo-Marxist theorists (see Gouldner 1970, 395–96; see also Abrahamsson 1970, Molm 1981). In Reading 24, Nancy Hartsock presents a critique of exchange theory written from the perspective of women's experience. For Hartsock, the model's emphasis on competitive exchange and its consequent denial of the role of cooperation in society is a serious distortion of the range of human experience. Hartsock argues that exchange theory's preoccupation with the concepts of equity and fair exchange and its assumption of normative balancing mechanisms in society have led the theory's proponents to overlook the role of power, force, and inequality in social life. She finds that exchange theory offers, rather than a value-neutral model of social life, a gender- and class-biased model constructed from the perspective of the powerful, a model that ignores and devalues the experience of the powerless.

THE DRAMATURGICAL MODEL

A central division among microsociologists has developed over the issue of whether microsociology should aim at the development of general explanatory theories (Homans, Blumer) or whether it should focus on the detailed description and analysis of individual microprocesses in society (Garfinkel, the ethnomethodologists). As we have seen, the work of George Herbert Mead and early symbolic interactionism was intended as a method for combining these two goals into a single research program. Perhaps no modern sociologist has more closely pursued this goal than Erving Goffman. In a series of studies published during the 1950s and 1960s, Goffman developed a *dramaturgical* model of society (see Goffman 1959, 1961a, 1963a, 1967; Brissett and Edgley, 1990). This dramaturgical model takes quite seriously William Shakespeare's epigram "All the world's a stage." That is, for Goffman, social interaction can be understood as a massive drama, a pageant of life, with stage, actors, audience, and props. The play itself is constantly improvised and transformed as actors interact. Indeed, each actor's own sense of self is itself the product of the dramatic interaction between actor and audience. It is the resourceful utilization of this dramaturgical model that gives coherence to Goffman's varied studies of mental asylums, stigmatization, and interaction in public places (Goffman 1961b, 1963a, 1963b).

In his later work, Goffman moved toward a closer analysis of social structure and structuration processes that arise from interaction (see Goffman 1974). Goffman argues (Reading 25) that society should be understood as a relatively stable and structured "interaction order." Goffman's conception of an interaction order marks his attempt to integrate the study of the emergence and persistence of larger-scale forms and processes of social life with the characteristic microsociological focus on the individual and face-to-face interaction. Goffman's dramaturgical approach has been extended through sociological studies that have examined a wide range of social settings and activities, from crowds at a football game to the medical profession to war and diplomacy (Haas and Shaffir 1982, Kitahara 1986, Snow, Zurcher, and Peters 1984, Zurcher 1985).

In conclusion, the microsociological perspective has remained vigorous and innovative throughout the past three decades (see Ritzer 1985). It has both extended the theoretical arguments of such traditional theories as symbolic interactionism and exchange theory and has seen the development of new perspectives and approaches such as phenomenology, ethnomethodology, and dramaturgical sociology. Although much new theoretical work continues to be done within the microsociological paradigm, increasingly, attention is being focused on the linkage between the micro and macro levels of analysis. We will turn to that topic in Chapter 5.

REFERENCES

ABRAHAMSSON, BENGT. 1970. "Homans on Exchange." *American Journal of Sociology* 76: 273–85.

BERGER, PETER, AND THOMAS LUCKMAN. 1966. *The Social Construction of Reality: A Treatise in the Sociology of Knowledge*. New York: Doubleday.

BLAU, PETER. 1964. *Exchange and Power in Social Life*. New York: Wiley.

BLUMER, HERBERT. 1937. "Social Psychology." Pp. 144–98. in *Man and Society*, ed. E.P. Schmidt. New York: Prentice Hall.

_____. 1969. *Symbolic Interaction: Perspective and Method*. Englewood Cliffs: Prentice Hall.

BRISSETT, DENNIS, AND CHARLES EDGLEY, eds. 1990. *Life as Theater: A Dramaturgical Sourcebook*. New York: Aldine de Gruyter.

BUTTON, GRAHAM, ed. 1991. *Ethnomethodology and the Human Sciences*. London: Cambridge University Press.

COOK, KAREN, ed. 1987. *Social Exchange Theory*. Beverly Hills: Sage Publications.

DOUGLAS, JACK, ed. 1980. *Introduction to the Sociologies of Everyday Life*. Boston: Allyn and Bacon.

DURKHEIM, EMILE. 1951. *Suicide: A Study in Sociology*. New York: Free Press.

_____. 1982. *The Rules of Sociological Method*. New York: Free Press.

EMERSON, RICHARD. 1976. "Social Exchange Theory." Pp. 335–62 in *Annual Review of Sociology*, vol. 2, ed. Alex Inkeles et al. Palo Alto: Annual Reviews.

_____. 1981. "Social Exchange Theory." Pp. 30–65 in *Social Psychology: Sociological Perspectives*, ed. Morris Rosenberg and Ralph H. Turner. New York: Basic Books.

FINE, GARY. 1990. "Symbolic Interactionism in the Post-Blumerian Age." Pp. 117–57 in *Frontiers of Social Theory*, ed. George Ritzer. New York: Columbia University Press.

GARFINKEL, HAROLD. 1967. *Studies in Ethnomethodology*. Englewood Cliffs: Prentice Hall.

GOFFMAN, ERVING. 1959. *The Presentation of Self in Everyday Life*. New York: Anchor Press.

_____. 1961a. *Encounters: Two Studies in the Sociology of Interaction*. Indianapolis: Bobbs-Merril.

_____. 1961b. *Asylums*. New York: Anchor Press.

_____. 1963a. *Behavior in Public Places*. New York: Free Press.

_____. 1963b. *Stigma: Notes on the Management of Spoiled Identity*. Englewood Cliffs: Prentice Hall.

_____. 1967. *Interaction Ritual: Essays on Face-to-Face Behavior*. New York: Anchor Press.

_____. 1974. *Frame Analysis: An Essay on the Organization of Experience*. New York: Harper Colophon.

GOULDNER, ALVIN. 1970. *The Coming Crisis of Western Sociology*. New York: Basic Books.

HAAS, JACK, AND WILLIAM SHAFFIR. 1982. "Taking on the Role of the Doctor: A Dramaturgical Analysis of Professionalization." *Symbolic Interaction* 5:187–203.

HERITAGE, JOHN. 1987. "Ethnomethodology." Pp. 224–72 in *Social Theory Today*, ed. Anthony Giddens and Jonathan Turner. Stanford: Stanford University Press.

HIRSCHMAN, ALBERT. 1977. *The Passions and the Interests*. Princeton: Princeton University Press.

HOMANS, GEORGE. 1961. *Social Behavior: Its Elementary Forms*. New York: Harcourt, Brace, and World.

_____. 1962. *Sentiments and Activities*. New York: Free Press.

_____. 1964. "Bringing Men Back In." *American Sociological Review* 29 (December):809–18.

_____. 1967. *The Nature of Social Science*. New York: Harcourt, Brace, and World.

_____. 1987. "Behaviorism and After." Pp. 58–81 in *Social Theory Today*, ed. Anthony Giddens and Jonathan Turner. Stanford: Stanford University Press.

KITAHARA, MICHIO. 1986. "Commodore Perry and the Japanese: A Study in the Dramaturgy of Power." *Symbolic Interaction* 9:53–65.

MEAD, GEORGE HERBERT. 1962. *Mind, Self, and Society*. 1934. Reprint, Chicago: University of Chicago Press.

MELTZER, BERNARD, JOHN PETRAS, and LARRY REYNOLDS. 1975. *Symbolic Interactionism: Genesis, Varieties, and Criticism*. London: Routledge and Kegan Paul.

MOLM, LINDA. 1981. "The Legitimacy of Behavioral Theory as a Sociological Perspective." *The American Sociologist* 16:153–66.

NISBET, ROBERT. 1974. *The Sociology of Emile Durkheim*. New York: Oxford University Press.

PARK, ROBERT. 1973. "Life History." *American Journal of Sociology* 79:251–60.

PARSONS, TALCOTT, AND EDWARD SHILS, eds. 1951. *Toward a General Theory of Action*. Cambridge: Harvard University Press.

REYNOLDS, LARRY. 1990. *Interactionism: Exposition and Critique*. New York: General Hall.

RITZER, GEORGE. 1985. "The Rise of Micro-Sociological Theory." *Sociological Theory* 3 (Spring): 88–98.

_____. 1988. *Sociological Theory*. New York: Alfred A. Knopf.

SCHUTZ, ALFRED. 1970. *On Phenomenology and Social Relations*. Chicago: University of Chicago Press.

SIMMEL, GEORG. 1950. *The Sociology of Georg Simmel*. Ed. Kurt Wolff. New York: Free Press.

_____. 1971. *On Individuality and Social Forms*. Ed. Donald Levine. Chicago: University of Chicago Press.

SMITH, ADAM. 1937. *An Inquiry into the Nature and Causes of the Wealth of Nations*. 1776. Reprint, New York: Modern Library.

SNOW, DAVID, LOUIS ZURCHER, AND ROBERT PETERS. 1984. "Victory Celebrations as Theater: A Dramaturgical Approach to Crowd Behavior." *Symbolic Interaction* 8:21–42.

TURNER, ROY, ed. 1974. *Ethnomethodology*. New York: Penguin Books.

WATSON, JOHN. 1924. *Behaviorism*. New York: W.W. Norton.

WEBER, MAX. 1949. *The Methodology of the Social Sciences*. New York: Free Press.

WILEY, NORBERT. 1985. "The Current Interregnum in American Sociology." *Social Research* 52 (Spring):179–207.

WOLFF, KURT. 1978. "Phenomenology and Sociology." Pp. 499–556 in *A History of Sociological Analysis*, ed. Tom Bottomore and Robert Nisbett. New York: Basic Books.

ZURCHER, LOUIS. 1985. "The War Game: Organizational Scripting and the Expression of Emotion." *Symbolic Interaction* 8:191–206.

GEORGE HERBERT MEAD:
THE LEGACY OF SOCIAL BEHAVIORISM*

LEONARD S. COTTRELL, JR.

There may be special point in having one of his relatively few surviving students reflect upon the ideas of George Herbert Mead and upon the ways in which they came into being and were communicated to a succession of student-cohorts at the University of Chicago. As I shall soon tell, I write only from the vantage point of having sat in his famous course, Advanced Social Psychology, almost half a century ago and from a subsequent deep interest in what I take to be the essential Mead. On that basis, I shall try to convey a sense of Mead the teacher. I shall examine his theoretical orientation as I understood it then and as I have come to understand it since. I shall then go on to say something about the continuing relevance of his ideas and I shall report on that influence as I know it best—upon my own work. And, finally, I shall suggest

*From Robert K. Merton and Matilda White Riley, eds., *Sociological Traditions from Generation to Generation* (Norwood, NJ: Ablex Publishing Company, 1980), pp. 45–59. Reprinted with permission of Ablex Publishing Corporation.

some promising lines of inquiry for the further development of Mead's seminal ideas.

All of us tend to revise the past to fit our current beliefs and the imperious realities of our lives. It is a hazardous undertaking, therefore, to try to parcel out the details of how I, as a student, saw Mead's work and how I understand him today. To reduce the hazards of reading the present into the past, I shall move freely between them and, not infrequently, check my own estimates against those of others.

DISCLAIMERS AND CAVEATS

At the outset I wish to enter certain disclaimers lest I appear to be sailing under false colors.

In the first place I never experienced the close working relationship with Professor Mead that so frequently occurs between a graduate student and a teacher whom he greatly admires and is strongly influenced by. He was in the Philosophy Department and I was in the Sociology Department, and, while there was a reasonably good working relationship between the two departments, there were few occasions of interdepartmental contacts. I took only the one course I have mentioned with Professor Mead, the large lecture course, Advanced Social Psychology, in the winter quarter of 1930. There was no class discussion, and I never had a personal conference with him. I can recall no contact with him outside of class. It has been a matter of keen regret and a sense of loss that has increased over the years that I did not seize the opportunity to take additional courses and seminars with him and thus gain a firmer grasp of his thought and a more intimate acquaintance with him as a person. But remote and transient as the contact was, there is no question that Professor Mead has had a profound impact on my thinking and on my career as a social psychologist.

Secondly, I wish to make clear that I do not qualify as a Meadian scholar. He was a philosopher of central importance as well as a social psychologist. His writings and lectures cover a wide range in pragmatic philosophy and social psychology as well as in practical matters such as education, crime and punitive justice, problems of the urban community, the societal functions of play and recreation, war and international relations. Nor do I pretend to an adequate grasp of Mead's philosophic position, though with the prodding of my young friends David Lewis of Notre Dame and Richard Smith of Charleston College (1980), and Charles Varela of Union College (1973 and 1978) I am only now beginning to get some glimpse of Mead's central importance in the current drive for a more adequate metaphysic for social theory and philosophy of science.

However, it is as a social psychologist that I am fascinated, not to say obsessed, by the social behaviorism of Professor Mead. And if I, as I shouldn't, do say so myself, I believe I have a better understanding of Meadian social behaviorism and have used his system more consistently in my research and theorizing than most contemporary behavioral scientists, and certainly more consistently than most symbolic interactionists. Having voiced such a deplorably immodest sentiment, let me hasten to balance it with the admission that I find many regrettable instances in some of my own work of what I now recognize as misperceptions and misinterpretations of Mead's conceptualizations. Let me then, with all due apologies, urge the caveat that what I report here is Mead as perceived and experienced by Cottrell the 1930 student and not necessarily as he is understood by his more learned and competent students.

With disclaimers and apologies out of the way we can now turn to consider Mead's impact on my thinking and career and my assessment of his place in our discipline. . . .

MEAD AS TEACHER

For me, the course with Professor Mead was a unique and unforgettable experience. The class was large. We met in the moot courtroom of the Law School. Professor Mead was a large, amiable-looking man who wore a magnificent mustache and a Van Dyke beard. He characteristically had a benign, rather shy smile matched with a twinkle in his eyes as if he were enjoying a secret joke he was playing on his audience. He always entered the classroom at the stroke of the bell, tossed his overcoat, cap and long copious scarf on the railing in front of the judge's bench and took his seat in the swivel chair behind the bench. He then reached behind him and picked up a good-sized piece of chalk from the blackboard that covered the wall behind the bench. He cast a benevolent smile over the heads of the class, who sat with notebooks and pencils ready, and without more ado launched into his lecture. His lectures always started with a summarization of what had been previously presented. As the course moved on, these summaries took a substantial segment of the class hour, but they seemed useful as a way of giving him a running jump into the new material.

As he lectured—always without notes—Professor Mead would manipulate the piece of chalk and watch it intently. From time to time he would scribble something on the bench, look at it and rub it out with his sleeve. When he made a particularly subtle point in his lecture he would glance up and throw a shy, almost apologetic smile over our heads—never looking directly at anyone. His lectures flowed and we soon learned that questions or comments from the class were not welcome. Indeed, when someone was bold enough to raise a question there was a murmur of disapproval from the students. They objected to any interruption of the golden flow. I have mentioned Professor Mead's intent focus on the gyrations of his piece of chalk as he lectured. One day an irreverent miscreant removed all the chalk from the chalk shelf. Professor Mead came in, tossed his cloak, etc., etc. on the rail, sat down and reached for his chalk. Not feeling any, he turned around to look. Not finding any, he momentarily lost his benevolent expression and appeared a bit disturbed. He obviously had difficulty in getting his lecture underway and it was only after a rather labored ten or twelve minutes that he hit his usual stride. For some time after that I carried some chalk in my pocket and as I entered the classroom glanced over to see that chalk was in the proper place.

His expectations of students were modest. He never gave exams. The main task for each of us students was to write as learned a paper as one could. These Professor Mead read with great care and what he thought of your paper was your grade for the course. One might suppose that students would read materials for the paper rather than attend his lectures but that was not the case. Students always came. They couldn't get enough of Mead.

By the time I became a student in Professor Mead's course I considered myself a behaviorist. J.B. Watson's experiments in conditioning so-called instinctive responses of infants were for me quite convincing evidence of the modifiability of human behavior. My undergraduate major had been in biology where genetic determinism was stressed, and when I ran head on into the sociological challenge to that perspective I found it quite exciting. However, the sociological evidence lacked explicit description of the processes by which human behavior patterns were implanted. J.B. Watson's behaviorism seemed to point the way to closing the gap. But I had serious reservations about his dismissal of what he called mentalistic phenomena as irrelevant to the objective analysis of behavior. It seemed to me he was ruling out much that was distinctive of and essential to an understanding of human behavior. Imagine, then, my excitement and delight to discover a thoroughgoing behaviorist, trained in physiological psychology, who proceeded to treat intrapersonal processes such as empathic responses, the self, mind, thinking and all their elaborations as behavior and legitimate objects of behavioral analysis. Early in the course, Mead (1934) sharply distinguished between his social behaviorism and the behaviorism of Watson (1919). The juxtaposition of these two positions, however, was one of the highlights of my student days with Mead.

As some of you know, Watson had studied, did research and taught at the University of Chicago during the period of 1900–1908. He took several courses in philosophy—some of them with Professor Mead. During the first 15 years or so of his career at Chicago, Professor Mead had taught courses in general psychology, comparative psychology and methodology of psychology, in addition to his course in social psychology. Watson also took some of these courses and I believe that for a time he was Mead's assistant. There can be little doubt that he got a good deal of stimulation from Professor Mead to make behavioral research his focal interest. While, as Watson reported in his autobiography (1961), he could never make much sense out of Mead's philosophy courses, the two men were good friends and spent many Sunday afternoons in the animal psychology laboratory discussing Watson's experimental work with rats and monkeys. The young behaviorist apparently found peace of mind away from the confusion and ambiguity of philosophic discourse when he could make objective observations of the behavior of his animals. Unfortunately, in this interaction, Watson either rejected or never grasped the possibility and crucial significance of behavioral analysis of the covert processes that are of such central importance to the understanding of human behavior.

To leap from my student days to my current estimate of Mead's behaviorism, Watson, of course, was not alone in his failure to grasp the significance of Mead's system. By and large the American psychological establishment has neither understood nor cared to understand or test Meadian social behaviorism. Sociologists likewise have largely failed to grasp the full significance of Mead for their discipline. I believe it can be shown that these disciplines are paying and will continue to pay a high price for their failure to make full use of Meadian social behaviorism. An inability to achieve a satisfactory theory of the distinctive nature of the human being and of the integration of human societies is a substantial part of this price. In my opinion there are rather strong practical, ideological, economic and political reasons for this strange resistance to Meadian theory. . . .

BASIC CONCEPTS OF MEADIAN SOCIAL BEHAVIORISM

But what is this Meadian mystery that I claim so many are failing to comprehend and utilize? While we cannot here undertake a complete examination of Meadian social behaviorism, I must clarify what appear to me to be certain unique and critical features of his system. In attempting to do this, I shall rely heavily upon my own recollections and upon my own student notes, although I shall not hesitate to draw upon the critiques and writings of others. In that way, I hope to substantiate to some degree my estimate of Mead as of central and enduring importance for achieving a more adequate social science (Mead, 1913, 1922, 1932, 1934, 1938, 1964.)

Social Interaction: The Central Process

Even those having only a limited acquaintance with Mead's work will know that the central focus of his theory is the analysis of the processes and emergent products of social interaction. Obviously a key to understanding Mead is to know what he means by social interaction. Not many have an adequate grasp of the term and its implications. It is ironic that, as Charles Varela (1973) has so well demonstrated, sociological theorists have pretty generally failed to give a satisfactory behavioral account of the concept of social interaction. Thus what is regarded as a central concept and assumed to be universally understood, remains a rather ambiguous catch-bag of doubtful theoretical or practical value.

The term *interpenetrative interaction* indicates more precisely an essential part of the process as conceived in the Meadian (1934) theory. It points to the crucial assumption that, behaviorally speaking, in any given social interact the participants become parts of one another. Thus a basic proposition can be stated as follows:

When two human organisms A and B become involved in a series of reciprocally interdependent interacts, each participant in the interaction not only learns his own act part, but also learns the act part of the other *as he perceives or experiences that other.*

This learning of the act part of the other as it is perceived is usually learned covertly and not manifested overtly. It should be emphasized that this is not a metaphorical statement. The act parts covertly acquired are assumed to be actually enacted behaviorally in incipient neuromuscular or attitudinal mobilizations. The interchanges may be in gestural form, verbal or nonverbal. These are covertly learned and the actions they signify are assumed to be evoked in incipient form. It should also be recognized that misperceptions and distortions of various kinds may complicate the process. However, continued interaction will move the perceptions toward greater shared commonality. The proposition stated above is addressed to the dyadic situation. It can be extended to apply to more than two participants and to symbolized collectivities or "generalized others," as Mead (1934) called them. As Mead's student in 1930, I can remember these arguments coming through to me with little or no ambiguity.

If, then, one can get a firm grasp on this basic process and see social behavior in terms of it, one will have no trouble in understanding the rest of Meadian social behaviorism. Otherwise, one will not get to first base—assuming that one wants to get to first base.

At this point, you are undoubtedly asking how does Mead or Cottrell or anyone else know what goes on in this so-called interpenetrative interaction? A good question. You should also be impressed by now by the difficulties confronting any attempt to demonstrate experimentally that what the theory claims does in fact happen.

Those whose perceptions are sensitized by a reasonably good understanding of the concept of interpenetrative interaction will find a certain amount of confirmatory evidence in observational, anecdotal, clinical and other qualitative case-study material. (For illustrations see Cottrell, 1933; Burgess & Cottrell, 1939; Cottrell, 1941, 1942, 1969.) Much rarer are controlled experimental demonstrations such as these: An exploratory study by Cottrell and Dymond (1949) in measuring variations in role-taking accuracy, reported in Dymond (1949); an experimental study of role-taking by O'Toole and Dubin (1968 & 1976); an electromyographic study of covert role-taking in interpersonal interaction by Cottrell (1971); an experimental study by Richard Smith (1971) of Mead's treatment of vocal gestures; a study of electrophysiology of mental activities by Jacobson (1932). A helpful summary and discussion of these and other experimental studies will be found in O'Toole, Smith and Cottrell (1978). Also relevant to this type of research is David Lewis's discussion of the social behaviorist's conception of the Meadian "I" (1979).

As technology for precise observation and recording of overt as well as covert behavior improves, more experimental testing of the central concepts of social behaviorism can be undertaken. Considerable progress is being made in this technology by those interested in nonverbal communication. Unfortunately, most of the research on this kind of interaction is being done without regard to the kinds of questions posed by the hypothesis of interpenetrative interaction. For example, Duncan and Fiske (1979) in their study of face-to-face conversational interaction, have developed precise methods of observation and recording of even the most detailed bits of verbal and nonverbal behavior. Although their identification of regularities in action sequences is of considerable interest, their results indicate to me that their theory and method need to be greatly enriched by the conceptualizations of Meadian social behaviorism and methods which permit observations of covert behavior if they are to make much progress in understanding social interaction. It is, incidentally, ironic that these investigators, based at the University of Chicago, write as if they had never heard of George Herbert Mead.

I have spoken at some length about the concept of interpenetrative interaction as I understood it as a student and as I have perceived its development since then because, in my opinion, it is the central component in Meadian social behaviorism. If the processes indicated by that central concept can be shown to be real, then the remaining components of the Meadian system follow as natural behavioral emergents. Obviously, this is not the place for a detailed examination of the entire conceptual framework, but I do propose to touch briefly on the essential elements in an effort to show why I regard it as a coherent, straightforward and strategic formulation, well worth careful and persistent testing and application. Of critical significance are the following:

1. The emergence of what Mead calls the significant symbol and its function in communication
2. The self process and the nature of identity
3. Thinking and the mind as a social behavioral process
4. Social integration

All these can be shown to be behavioral processes and emergent products of the basic processes of interpenetrative interaction. As Mead's student, I glimpsed all these processes and products. While my understandings have obviously developed and deepened since 1930, the foundation was clearly laid down during those early years in Chicago.

Act, Gesture and the Significant Symbol

Complex social interaction is greatly facilitated by the fact that small movements in the early stages of an act come to stand as signs or signals of the oncoming act. These signals, which we call gestures, evoke responses to the whole act that the gesture signals. These responses themselves, in turn, are indicated by gestures of the respondent. Thus, complex social interacts can be conducted in shorthand, as it were, by a conversation of gestures. In these gestural transactions, taking the role of the others is accomplished by responding to one's own gestures with the gestured responses of the others. Now, when an actor is able to respond to his own gesture with the response of the other, that is, in the role of the other, Mead (1922 & 1934) states that the gesture has become a significant symbol. It has the same meaning to both participants. The meaning of a gesture is the response it evokes. It has a common meaning to the extent that it evokes the same response in the actor and his respondent. Vocal gestures have a special efficiency for significant communication since the participant who makes the sounds that evoke responses in the hearer also hears his own vocal gesture and can take the role of his hearer and respond to his own gesture as the other responds to it. Thus, when we speak, we know what we are saying to the degree that we can respond to our words in the role of the hearer. It is only when this condition is met through interactive learning that we communicate meaningfully. It is regrettable that much contemporary communication theory and practice is relatively weak and sterile because of failure to utilize this kind of Meadian contribution to the understanding of communicative behavior.

But the social behaviorist concept for the significant symbol is not only relevant for understanding communication; it is also of critical importance in the analysis of basic intra-personal behavioral processes: the self, identity and mind.

The Self and Identity

Over the years, the self has, by and large, been something of an embarrassment to most psychologists. They use the term, but when called upon to define it they resort to tautologies or catch-bag lists of descriptive attributes that tend to become so extended as to be unmanageable. The so-called objective psychologists prefer to do without the concept altogether.

The social behaviorists, on the other hand, regard the self as an emergent of the inter-penetrative interact. Actions of participant A are responded to by actions of participant B. A takes the role of B and responds to his own acts with the incorporated responses of B. A's acts become objects to himself, or he knows or experiences their meaning through reacting to them in the role of B. It is this reflexive behavioral process that constitutes the experience of self. A self, therefore, is not a given, an endowment of the organism, but an emergent. The subjective experience of what we refer to as *myself* or *me* arises when an action in its initial or incipient or attitudinal stage evokes the incorporated attitudinal responses of the relevant significant others. Thus, the self is a dynamic process rather than a static morphological entity.

Describing the self in this way may make it appear ephemeral and of no substance. However, we know that the person's very sense of being depends on incorporation of this dyadic process. As the human being matures and experiences broader, more stabilized interactive contexts or situations in which he achieves roles or positions, he develops what we call identities. An identity, as subjectively experienced, is an established pattern of an-ticipated other-responses to one's acts. If these anticipated acts are not confirmed in reality or at least in fantasy, the person suffers the pain and panic of a disastrous loss of identity or sense of self. The self-conception or identity becomes more stabilized as the person interacts in stable group settings that make up his life situations. In these he develops what Mead (1913 & 1934) refers to as "generalized others" with whom he interacts. Thus I heard it said in 1930.

Language as a system of significant symbols facilitates both the overt interaction of the person with respondent-others and the intrapersonal covert interaction processes through which the person finds his concept of himself and his self-evaluations.

Mind and Thinking as Social Interaction

Professor Mead once remarked in a lecture to our class that, "Mind is the presence in behavior of significant symbols." This rather enigmatic comment had me stumped for quite some time. It is unintelligible unless one goes back to a social behavioral statement of what a significant symbol is. Remember what was said about it? A significant symbol is a gesture—a bit of behavior that signals an oncoming act—that evokes in the maker of the gesture the responding gestures of the other to whom the gesture is made. Now, keeping in mind that these gestured acts can be experienced as covert act mobilizations or attitudinal postures, we can say that thinking is a social interactional process conducted by means of significant symbols. Mind is not, therefore, something apart from behavior. So far as we know, the human organism is unique in its capacity to import the social interactional process and thus be capable of the behavior we experience and describe as thinking. This enables the organism to anticipate responses of the environment to alternate proposed lines of action and to select those which permit resolution of the problematic situation and completion of the blocked social act.

Social Integration

A social interactional account of how aggregates of separate organisms become an integrated collectivity capable of functioning as such was one of Mead's early theoretical concerns. For his students it was a challenging problem, indeed. Among nonhuman species, there are numerous instances of the precise and intricate integration of complementary actions necessary for the life of the collectivity. But in these species, the separate collaborating actors appear to be genetically programmed for their parts in the communal act. No such principle of integration appears to be operative in human social units except in the bisexual and parent-offspring relations, and here only in a rather limited determination of specific behavioral patterning.

From the foregoing discussion, I am sure you will anticipate that the processes of interpenetrative interaction and the capability of the human organism to incorporate the roles of the other participants in the interact were seen by the social behaviorists as making possible the integration of functioning collective entities. The individual member's action can be guided by his expectations of the acts of the others and his perception of their expectations of him. Moreover, in the course of collective activity and in the course of determining and achieving group goals, the individual develops a generalized concept, a personification of the group or community. As we have seen, Mead (1934) termed this a "generalized other" and regarded it as functioning as a symbolically represented "other" in the interactional situational field as perceived by the participant. Thus, the person's reference to what his family would say or what his platoon or his community would do is a reference to a behaviorally real, generalized other—whose role can be taken in response to his own acts and intentions. Can you imagine the excitement of Mead's lectures when he dealt with such topics?

Alternative Interpretations of Social Behaviorism

So here we have what, in my view, is an elegantly lucid and coherent account of the behavioral processes through which emerges that amazing creation, man—the human person and the human society. Through their capacity for interpenetrative interaction, by incorporating the responses of the objects of their environment, these organisms become objects to themselves, develop reflexive selves, symbolic communicative processes, minds and societies. These profoundly important realities are not given; they are emergents of an ongoing process. I hold that Meadian social behaviorism still offers a far more promising conceptual framework for a basic social psychology than any of the currently competing conceptualizations.

The widely utilized conceptual framework of the various conditioning theories and the practices based on them can in no way account for or produce the emergence of the basic and distinctive human characteristics that must be of central concern to any adequate social psychology. This is not to underestimate the highly effective technology of conditioning and its behavior-modification procedures. Man is an animal and like rats, pigeons, monkeys, etc., his overt behavior can be conditioned by procedures developed by highly competent scientists (Skinner, 1953). But behavior molded in this manner will not result in significant symbolic communication, reflexive selves, minds or societies based on interpenetrative interaction. The conditioning procedures can produce an aggregate of individuals appropriately conditioned to respond to controlling stimuli. But such mass-conditioned behavior is more like that of mindless lemmings than of collaborative-minded participant-selves. Indeed, it is a matter of serious concern that the rapid rise of electronic technology has put the means of widespread mass conditioning, manipulation and control in the hands of powerful interests. To the extent that persons and groups become subject to such conditioning they become dehumanized. Fortunately, the social behavioral capabilities and processes continue to operate sufficiently to constitute a threat to the manipulative controls and make possible a recovery of the important human competencies. Sometimes this recovery is a slow, painful and costly process, for example, after the apathy and nonparticipation in political processes which appear when people feel they have been taken for a ride by their government, or, to take another example, after the costly loss in productivity by workers following the perception that their employers have manipulated them through various simulations of concern for their welfare. For an interesting discussion of the recent literature on this problem, I recommend Richard Sennett's (1979) article entitled "The Boss's New Clothes" in the *New York Review of Books.* Speaking as one who has always regarded himself as a student of Mead, I can assure you that we were innocent of all such questions in 1930.

I do not propose to review here the other competing conceptual frameworks used by sociologists as social psychological foundations of their discipline. It would be an interesting exercise to use the Meadian system as a touchstone for examining the more widely used theoretical systems to determine their relative adequacy for use as the social psychological foundations for sociological theory. In my own limited efforts in this respect I have,

as you will anticipate, become quite convinced that Meadian social behaviorism comes closer to meeting the requirements of our discipline than any other system of social psychology. It is disconcerting, therefore, to realize that most sociologists appear to prefer almost any conceptual framework except that of Meadian social behaviorism.

In 1940 I was quite optimistic about the signs of a trend in the behavioral disciplines toward an interactional orientation; my colleague, Ruth Gallagher, and I (Cottrell & Gallagher, 1941) predicted an acceleration of that trend for the next decade with the result that Meadian social behaviorism would be a predominant theoretical base. We were wrong. In recent years, however, it has been encouraging to note the apparent renaissance of Meadian theory and research among an increasing number of sociologists who refer to themselves as symbolic interactionists. This increasing interest has provided the impetus for the formation of a Society for the Study of Symbolic Interaction. Unfortunately, the term symbolic interaction has become something of an umbrella covering a rather wide range of theoretical orientations. The literature (Manis & Meltzer, 1978) being generated frequently describes attempts to effect syntheses of some aspect of Meadian theory with operant conditioning theory, psychoanalysis or some of its off-shoots, cognitive theory, phenomenology and numerous others.

Now while one must applaud these efforts to broaden the theoretical base of a social psychology fit to serve as a foundation for sociological theory and practice, it is also the case that, by and large, this literature is quite confusing and sometimes actually misleading for anyone seeking to comprehend Meadian social behaviorism. Even when the objective is to clarify Meadian theory there is frequently evidence of a lack of grasp of significant aspects of the theory. I have found it advisable to caution students to avoid this literature until they have gained a firm hold on Mead's own ideas. . . .

REFERENCES

BURGESS, E.W., AND COTTRELL, L.S., JR. *Predicting success or failure in marriage.* Englewood Cliffs, N.J.: Prentice Hall, 1939, Chapter 11.

COTTRELL, L.S., JR. "Roles and Marital Adjustment." *Publications of the American Sociological Association,* 1933. *27,* 107–115.

COTTRELL, L.S., JR. "The Case-Study Method in Prediction." *Sociometry,* 1941, *4,* 358–370.

COTTRELL, L.S., JR. "The Analysis of Situational Fields in Social Psychology." *American Sociological Review,* 1942, *7,* 370–382.

COTTRELL, L.S., JR. "Interpersonal Interaction and the Development of the Self." In D.A. Goslin (ed.), *Handbook of socialization theory and practice.* Chicago: Rand McNally, 1969, 543–570.

COTTRELL, L.S., JR. "Covert Behavior in Interpersonal Interaction." *Proceedings of the American Philosophical Society* Vol. 115 No. 6, 1971, 462–469.

COTTRELL, L.S., JR. AND DYMOND, R.F. "The Empathic Responses: A Neglected Field for Research." *Psychiatry* 1949, *12,* 355–359.

COTTRELL, L.S., JR., AND GALLAGHER, R. *Developments in social psychology 1930–1940.* New York: Beacon House, Inc., 1941.

DUNCAN, S., JR., AND FISKE, D.W., "Dynamic Patterning in Conversation." *American Scientist,* 1979, *67,* 90–98.

DYMOND, R.F. "A Scale for the Measurement of Empathic Ability." *Journal of Consulting Psychology,* 1949, *13,* 127–133.

JACOBSON, E. "Electrophysiology of Mental Activities." *American Journal of Psychology,* 1932, *44,* 677–694.

LEWIS, D. "A Social Behaviorist Interpretation of the Meadian 'I'." *American Journal of Sociology,* 1979, *85,* 261–87.

LEWIS, D. and SMITH, R.L. *American sociology and pragmatism: Mead, Chicago sociology, and symbolic interaction.* Chicago: University of Chicago Press, 1980.

MANIS, J.G., AND MELTZER, B.N. *Symbolic interaction: A reader in social psychology.* Third Edition. Boston: Allyn and Bacon, Inc., 1978.

MEAD, G.H. "The Social Self." *Journal of Philosophy,* 1913, *10,* 374–380.

MEAD, G.H. "A Behavioristic Account of the Significant Symbol." *Journal of Philosophy,* 1922, *19,* 157–163.

MEAD, G.H. *The philosophy of the present.* Chicago: Open Court, 1932.

MEAD, G.H. *Mind, self and society.* Chicago: University of Chicago Press, 1934.

MEAD, G.H. *The philosophy of the act.* Chicago: University of Chicago Press, 1938.

MEAD, G.H. *Selected writings,* A.J. Reck (ed.). Indianapolis: The Bobbs Merrill Co., 1964.

O'TOOLE, R., AND DUBIN, R. "Baby Feeding and Body Sway: An Experiment in George Herbert Mead's 'Taking the Role of the Other'." *Journal of Personality and Social Psychology,* 1968, *10,* 59–65.

O'TOOLE, R., SMITH, R.L., AND COTTRELL, L.S., JR. "Interpenetrative Interaction: Some Implications of a Neglected Approach." Unpublished Manuscript, 1978.

SENNETT, R. "The Boss's New Clothes." *New York Review of Books,* 1979, *26,* 42–46.

SKINNER, B.F. *Science and human behavior.* New York: Macmillan, 1953.

SMITH, R.L. *Reflexive behavior: An experimental examination of George Herbert Mead's treatment of vocal gesture.* Unpublished M.A. dissertation, University of South Carolina, 1971.

VARELA, C. *The crisis of western sociology: The problem of social interaction, the self, and unawareness for sociological theory.* Unpublished Ph.D. dissertation, New York: New York University, 1973.

VARELA, C. *How is sociology impossible?: The distrust of reason and the conceptual reformation.* Unpublished manuscript, Cranford, N.J.: Union College, 1978.

WATSON, J.B. *Psychology from the standpoint of a behaviorist.* New York: J.B. Lippincott, 1919.

WATSON, J.B. "Autobiography." In C. Murchison (ed.), *A history of psychology in autobiography.* New York: Russell and Russell, 1961.

SOCIETY AS SYMBOLIC INTERACTION*

HERBERT BLUMER

A view of human society as symbolic interaction has been followed more than it has been formulated. Partial, usually fragmentary, statements of it are to be found in the writings of a number of eminent scholars, some inside the field of sociology and some outside. Among the former we may note such scholars as Charles Horton Cooley, W.I. Thomas, Robert E. Parks, E.W. Burgess, Florian Znaniecki, Ellsworth Faris, and James Mickel Williams. Among those outside the discipline we may note William James, John Dewey, and George Herbert Mead. None of these scholars, in my judgment, has presented a systematic statement of the nature of human group life from the standpoint of symbolic interaction. Mead stands out among all of them in laying bare the fundamental premises of the approach, yet he did little to develop its methodological implications for sociological study. Students who seek to depict the posi-

tion of symbolic interaction may easily give different pictures of it. What I have to present should be regarded as my personal version. My aim is to present the basic premises of the point of view and to develop their methodological consequences for the study of human group life.

The term "symbolic interaction" refers, of course, to the peculiar and distinctive character of interaction as it takes place between human beings. The peculiarity consists in the fact that human beings interpret or "define" each other's actions instead of merely reacting to each other's actions. Their "response" is not made directly to the actions of one another but instead is based on the meaning which they attach to such actions. Thus, human interaction is mediated by the use of symbols, by interpretation, or by ascertaining the meaning of one another's actions. This mediation is equivalent to inserting a process of interpretation between stimulus and response in the case of human behavior.

The simple recognition that human beings interpret each other's actions as the means of

*From Rose, Arnold M. (Editor), *Human Behavior and Social Processes.* Copyright © 1962 by Houghton Mifflin Company. Used with permission.

acting toward one another has permeated the thought and writings of many scholars of human conduct and of human group life. Yet few of them have endeavored to analyze what such interpretation implies about the nature of the human being or about the nature of human association. They are usually content with a mere recognition that "interpretation" should be caught by the student, or with a simple realization that symbols, such as cultural norms or values, must be introduced into their analyses. Only G.H. Mead, in my judgment, has sought to think through what the act of interpretation implies for an understanding of the human being, human action, and human association. The essentials of his analysis are so penetrating and profound and so important for an understanding of human group life that I wish to spell them out, even though briefly.

The key feature in Mead's analysis is that the human being has a self. This idea should not be cast aside as esoteric or glossed over as something that is obvious and hence not worthy of attention. In declaring that the human being has a self, Mead had in mind chiefly that the human being can be the object of his own actions. He can act toward himself as he might act toward others. Each of us is familiar with actions of this sort in which the human being gets angry with himself, rebuffs himself, takes pride in himself, argues with himself, tries to bolster his own courage, tells himself that he should "do this" or not "do that," sets goals for himself, makes compromises with himself, and plans what he is going to do. That the human being acts toward himself in these and countless other ways is a matter of easy empirical observation. To recognize that the human being can act toward himself is no mystical conjuration.

Mead regards this ability of the human being to act toward himself as the central mechanism with which the human being faces and deals with his world. This mechanism enables the human being to make indications to himself of things in his surroundings and thus to guide his actions by what he notes. Anything of which a human being is conscious is something which he is indicating to himself—the ticking of a clock, a knock at the door, the appearance of a friend, the remark made by a companion, a recognition that he has a task to perform, or the realization that he has a cold. Conversely, anything of which he is not conscious is, ipso facto, something which he is not indicating to himself. The conscious life of the human being, from the time that he awakens until he falls asleep, is a continual flow of self-indications—notations of the things with which he deals and takes into account. We are given, then, a picture of the human being as an organism which confronts its world with a mechanism for making indications to itself. This is the mechanism that is involved in interpreting the actions of others. To interpret the actions of another is to point out to oneself that the action has this or that meaning or character.

Now, according to Mead, the significance of making indications to oneself is of paramount importance. The importance lies along two lines. First, to indicate something is to extricate it from its setting, to hold it apart, to give it a meaning or, in Mead's language, to make it into an object. An object—that is to say, anything that an individual indicates to himself—is different from a stimulus; instead of having an intrinsic character which acts on the individual and which can be identified apart from the individual, its character or meaning is conferred on it by the individual. The object is a product of the individual's disposition to act instead of being an antecedent stimulus which evokes the act. Instead of the individual being surrounded by an environment of pre-existing objects which play upon him and call forth his behavior, the proper picture is that he constructs his objects on the basis of his on-going activity. In any of his countless acts—whether minor, like dressing himself, or major, like organizing himself for a professional career—the individual is designating different objects to himself, giving them meaning, judging their suitability to his action, and making decisions on the basis of the judgment. This is what is meant by interpretation or acting on the basis of symbols.

The second important implication of the fact that the human being makes indications to himself is that his action is constructed or built up instead of being a mere release. Whatever the action in which he is engaged, the human individual proceeds by pointing out to himself the divergent things which have to be taken into account in the course of his action. He has to note what he wants to do and how he is to do it; he has to point out to himself the various conditions which may be instrumental to his action and those which may obstruct his action; he has to take account of the demands, the expectations, the prohibitions, and the threats as they may arise in the situation in which he is acting. His action is built up step by step through a process of such self-indication. The human individual pieces together and guides his action by taking account of different things and interpreting their significance for his prospective action. There is no instance of conscious action of which this is not true.

The process of constructing action through making indications to oneself cannot be swallowed up in any of the conventional psychological categories. This process is distinct from and different from what is spoken of as the "ego"—just as it is different from any other conception which conceives of the self in terms of composition or organization. Self-indiction is a moving communicative process in which the individual notes things, assesses them, gives them a meaning, and decides to act on the basis of the meaning. The human being stands over against the world, or against "alters," with such a process and not with a mere ego. Further, the process of self-indication cannot be subsumed under the forces, whether from the outside or inside, which are presumed to play upon the individual to produce his behavior. Environmental pressures, external stimuli, organic drives, wishes, attitudes, feelings, ideas, and their like do not cover or explain the process of self-indication. The process of self-indication stands over against them in that the individual points out to himself and interprets the appearance or expression of such things, noting a given social demand that is made on him, recognizing a command, observing that he is hungry, realizing that he wishes to buy something, aware that he has a given feeling, conscious that he dislikes eating with someone he despises, or aware that he is thinking of doing some given thing. By virtue of indicating such things to himself, he places himself over against them and is able to act back against them, accepting them, rejecting them, or transforming them in accordance with how he defines or interprets them. His behavior, accordingly, is not a result of such things as environmental pressures, stimuli, motives, attitudes, and ideas but arises instead from how he interprets and handles these things in the action which he is constructing. The process of self-indication by means of which human action is formed cannot be accounted for by factors which precede the act. The process of self-indication exists in its own right and must be accepted and studied as such. It is through this process that the human being constructs his conscious action.

Now Mead recognizes that the formation of action by the individual through a process of self-indication always takes place in a social context. Since this matter is so vital to an understanding of symbolic interaction it needs to be explained carefully. Fundamentally, group action takes the form of a fitting together of individual lines of action. Each individual aligns his action to the action of others by ascertaining what they are doing or what they intend to do—that is, by getting the meaning of their acts. For Mead, this is done by the individual "taking the role" of others—either the role of a specific person or the role of a group (Mead's "generalized other"). In taking such roles the individual seeks to ascertain the intention or direction of the acts of others. He forms and aligns his own action on the basis of such interpretation of the acts of others. This is the fundamental way in which group action takes place in human society.

The foregoing are the essential features, as I see them, in Mead's analysis of the bases of symbolic interaction. They presuppose the following: that human society is made up of individuals who have selves (that is, make indications to themselves); that individual action is a construction and not a release, being built up by the individual through noting and interpreting features of the situations in which he acts; that group or collective action consists of the aligning of individual actions, brought about by the individuals' interpreting or taking into account each other's actions. Since my purpose is to present and not to defend the position of symbolic interaction I shall not endeavor in this essay to advance support for the three premises which I have just indicated. I wish merely to say that the three premises can be easily verified empirically. I know of no instance of human group action to which the three premises do not apply. The reader is challenged to find or think of a single instance which they do not fit.

I wish now to point out that sociological views of human society are, in general, markedly at variance with the premises which I have indicated as underlying symbolic inter-

action. Indeed, the predominant number of such views, especially those in vogue at the present time, do not see or treat human society as symbolic interaction. Wedded, as they tend to be, to some form of sociological determinism, they adopt images of human society, of individuals in it, and of group action which do not square with the premises of symbolic interaction. I wish to say a few words about the major lines of variance.

Sociological thought rarely recognizes or treats human societies as composed of individuals who have selves. Instead, they assume human beings to be merely organisms with some kind of organization, responding to forces which play upon them. Generally, although not exclusively, these forces are lodged in the make-up of the society, as in the case of "social system," "social structure," "culture," "status position," "social role," "custom," "institution," "collective representation," "social situation," "social norm," and "values." The assumption is that the behavior of people as members *of a society* is an expression of the play on them of these kinds of factors or forces. This, of course, is the logical position which is necessarily taken when the scholar explains their behavior or phases of their behavior in terms of one or another of such social factors. The individuals who compose a human society are treated as the media through which such factors operate, and the social action of such individuals is regarded as an expression of such factors. This approach or point of view denies, or at least ignores, that human beings have selves—that they act by making indications to themselves. Incidentally, the "self" is not brought into the picture by introducing such items as organic drives, motives, attitudes, feelings, internalized social factors, or psychological components. Such psychological factors have the same status as the social factors mentioned: they are regarded as factors which play on the individual to produce his action. They do not constitute the process of self-indication. The process of self-indication stands over against them, just as it stands over against the social factors which play on the human being. Practically all sociological conceptions of human society fail to recognize that the individuals who compose it have selves in the sense spoken of.

Correspondingly, such sociological conceptions do not regard the social actions of individuals in human society as being constructed by them through a process of interpretation. Instead, action is treated as a product of factors which play on and through individuals. The social behavior of people is not seen as built up by them through an interpretation of objects, situations, or the actions of others. If a place is given to "interpretation," the interpretation is regarded as merely an expression of other factors (such as motives) which precede the act, and accordingly disappears as a factor in its own right. Hence, the social action of people is treated as an outward flow or expression of forces playing on them rather than as acts which are built up by people through their interpretation of the situations in which they are placed.

These remarks suggest another significant line of difference between general sociological views and the position of symbolic interaction. These two sets of views differ in where they lodge social action. Under the perspective of symbolic interaction, social action is lodged in acting individuals who fit their respective lines of action to one another through a process of interpretation; group action is the collective action of such individuals. As opposed to this view, sociological conceptions generally lodge social action in the action of society or in some unit of society. Examples of this are legion. Let me cite a few. Some conceptions, in treating societies or human groups as "social systems," regard group action as an expression of a system, either in a state of balance or seeking to achieve balance.

Or group action is conceived as an expression of the "functions" of a society or of a group. Or group action is regarded as the outward expression of elements lodged in society or the group, such as cultural demands, societal purposes, social values, or institutional stresses. These typical conceptions ignore or blot out a view of group life or of group action as consisting of the collective or concerted actions of individuals seeking to meet their life situations. If recognized at all, the efforts of people to develop collective acts to meet their situations are subsumed under the play of underlying or transcending forces which are lodged in society or its parts. The individuals composing the society or the group become "carriers," or media for the expression of such forces; and the interpretative behavior by means of which people form their actions is merely a coerced link in the play of such forces.

The indication of the foregoing lines of variance should help to put the position of symbolic interaction in better perspective. In the remaining discussion I wish to sketch somewhat more fully how human society appears in terms of symbolic interaction and to point out some methodological implications.

Human society is to be seen as consisting of acting people, and the life of the society is to be seen as consisting of their actions. The acting units may be separate individuals, collectivities whose members are acting together on a common quest, or organizations acting on behalf of a constituency. Respective examples are individual purchasers in a market, a play group or missionary band, and a business corporation or a national professional association. There is no empirically observable activity in a human society that does not spring from some acting unit. This banal statement needs to be stressed in light of the common practice of sociologists of reducing human society to social units that do not act—for example, social classes in modern society. Obviously, there are ways of viewing human society other than in terms of the acting units that compose it. I merely wish to point out that in respect to concrete or empirical activity human society must necessarily be seen in terms of the acting units that form it. I would add that any scheme of human society claiming to be a realistic analysis has to respect and be congruent with the empirical recognition that a human society consists of acting units.

Corresponding respect must be shown to the conditions under which such units act. One primary condition is that action takes place in and with regard to a situation. Whatever be the acting unit—an individual, a family, a school, a church, a business firm, a labor union, a legislature, and so on—any particular action is formed in the light of the situation in which it takes place. This leads to the recognition of a second major condition, namely, that the action is formed or constructed by interpreting the situation. The acting unit necessarily has to identify the things which it has to take into account—tasks, opportunities, obstacles, means, demands, discomforts, dangers, and the like; it has to assess them in some fashion and it has to make decisions on the basis of the assessment. Such interpretative behavior may take place in the individual guiding his own action, in a collectivity of individuals acting in concert, or in "agents" acting on behalf of a group or organization. Group life consists of acting units developing acts to meet the situations in which they are placed.

Usually, most of the situations encountered by people in a given society are defined or "structured" by them in the same way. Through previous interaction they develop and acquire common understandings or definitions of how to act in this or that situation. These common definitions enable people to act alike. The common repetitive behavior of people in such situations should not mislead the student into believing that no process of interpretation is in play; on the contrary, even though fixed, the actions of the participating people are constructed by them through a process of interpretation. Since ready-made and commonly accepted definitions are at hand, little strain is placed on people in guiding and organizing their acts. However, many other situations may not be defined in a single way by the participating people. In this event, their lines of action do not fit together readily and collective action is blocked. Interpretations have to be developed and effective accommodation of the participants to one another has to be worked out. In the case of such "undefined" situations, it is necessary to trace and study the emerging process of definition which is brought into play.

Insofar as sociologists or students of human society are concerned with the behavior of acting units, the position of symbolic interaction requires the student to catch the process of interpretation through which they construct their actions. This process is not to be caught merely by turning to conditions which are antecedent to the process. Such antecedent conditions are helpful in understanding the process insofar as they enter into it, but as mentioned previously they do not constitute the process. Nor can one catch the process merely by inferring its nature from the overt action which is its product. To catch the process, the student must take the role of the acting unit whose behavior he is studying. Since the interpretation is being made by the acting unit in terms of objects designated and appraised, meanings acquired, and decisions made, the process has to be seen from the standpoint of the acting unit. It is the recognition of this fact that makes the research work of such scholars as R.E. Park and W.I. Thomas so notable. To try to catch the interpretative process by remaining aloof as a so-called "objective" observer and refusing to take the role of the acting unit is to risk the worst kind of subjectivism—the objective observer is likely to fill in the process of interpretation with his own surmises in place of catching the process as it occurs in the experience of the acting unit which uses it.

By and large, of course, sociologists do not study human society in terms of its acting units. Instead, they are disposed to view human society in terms of structure or organization and to treat social action as an expression of such structure or organization. Thus, reliance is placed on such structural categories as social system, culture, norms, values, social stratification, status positions, social roles and institutional organization. These are used both to analyze human society and to account for social action within it. Other major interests of sociological scholars center around this focal theme of organization. One line of interest is to view organization in terms of the functions it is supposed to perform. Another line of interest is to study societal organization as a system seeking equilibrium; here the scholar endeavors to detect mechanisms which are indigenous to the system. Another line of interest is to identify forces which play upon organization to bring about changes in it; here the scholar endeavors, especially through comparative study, to isolate a relation between causative factors and structural results. These various lines of sociological perspective and interest, which are so strongly entrenched today, leap over the acting units of a society and bypass the interpretative process by which such acting units build up their actions.

These respective concerns with organization on one hand and with acting units on the other hand set the essential difference between conventional views of human society and the view of it implied in symbolic interaction. The latter view recognizes the presence of organization to human society and respects its importance. However, it sees and treats organization differently. The difference is along two major lines. First, from the standpoint of symbolic interaction the organization of a human society is the framework inside of which social action takes place and is not the determinant of that action. Second, such organization and changes in it are the product of the activity of acting units and not of "forces" which leave such acting units out of account. Each of these two major lines of difference should be explained briefly in order to obtain a better understanding of how human society appears in terms of symbolic interaction.

From the standpoint of symbolic interaction, social organization is a framework inside of which acting units develop their actions. Structural features, such as "culture," "social systems," "social stratification," or "social roles," set conditions for their action but do not determine their action. People—that is, acting units—do not act toward culture, social structure or the like; they act toward situations. Social organization enters into action only to the extent to which it shapes situations in which people act, and to the extent to which it supplies fixed sets of symbols which people use in interpreting their situations. These two forms of influence of social organization are important. In the case of settled and stabilized societies, such as isolated primitive tribes and peasant communities, the influence is certain to be profound. In the case of human societies, particularly modern societies, in which streams of new situations arise and old situations become unstable, the influence of organization decreases. One should bear in mind that the most important element confronting an acting unit in situations is the actions of other acting units. In modern society, with its increasing criss-crossing of lines of action, it is common for situations to arise in which the actions of participants are not previously regularized and standardized. To this extent, existing social organization does not shape the situations. Correspondingly, the symbols or tools of interpretation used by acting units in such situations may vary and shift considerably. For these reasons, social action may go beyond, or depart from, existing organization in any of its structural dimensions. The organization of a human society is not to be identified with the process of interpretation used by its acting units; even though it affects that process, it does not embrace or cover the process.

Perhaps the most outstanding consequence of viewing human society as organization is to overlook the part played by acting units in social change. The conventional procedure of sociologists is (a) to identify human society (or some part of it) in terms of an established or organized form, (b) to identify some factor or condition of change playing upon the human society or the given part of it, and (c) to identify the new form assumed by the society following upon the play of the factor of change. Such observations permit the student to couch propositions to the effect that a given factor of change playing upon a given organized form results in a given new organized form. Examples ranging from crude to refined statements are legion, such as that an economic depression increases solidarity in the families of workingmen or that industrialization replaces extended families by nuclear families. My concern here is not with the validity of such propositions but with the methodological position which they presuppose. Essentially, such propositions either ignore the role of the interpretive behavior of acting units in the given instance of change, or else regard the interpretative behavior as coerced by the factor of change. I wish to point out that any line of social change, since it involves change in human action, is necessarily mediated by interpretation on the part of the people caught up in the change—the change appears in the form of new situations in which people have to construct new forms of action. Also, in line with what has been said previously, interpretations of new situations are not predetermined by conditions antecedent to the situations but depend on what is taken into account and assessed in the actual situations in which behavior is formed. Variations in interpretation may readily occur as different acting units cut out different objects in the situation, or give different weight to the objects which they note, or piece objects together in different patterns. In formulating propositions of social change, it would be wise to recognize that any given line of such change is mediated by acting units interpreting the situations with which they are confronted.

Students of human society will have to face the question of whether their preoccupation with categories of structure and organization can be squared with the interpretative process by means of which human beings, individually and collectively, act in human society. It is the discrepancy between the two which plagues such students in their efforts to attain scientific propositions of the sort achieved in the physical and biological sciences. It is this discrepancy, further, which is chiefly responsible for their difficulty in fitting hypothetical propositions to new arrays of empirical data. Efforts are made, of course, to overcome these shortcomings by devising new structural categories, by formulating new structural hypotheses, by developing more refined techniques of research, and even by formulating new methodological schemes of a structural character. These efforts continue to ignore or to explain away the interpretative process by which people act, individually and collectively, in society. The question remains whether human society or social action can be successfully analyzed by schemes which refuse to recognize human beings as they are, namely, as persons constructing individual and collective action through an interpretation of the situations which confront them.

ETHNOMETHODS AND PHENOMENOLOGY*

GEORGE PSATHAS

There are two approaches in the social sciences which have developed in recent years, one in anthropology called ethnoscience, the other in sociology called ethnomethodology. Both have the potential for making a great impact on research in anthropology and sociology. In this paper, I would like to examine these approaches, show some of the similarities and differences between them, comment on their significance, and indicate their relation to phenomenological approaches.

ETHNOSCIENCE

Ethnoscience has been defined by Sturtevant[1] as "the system of knowledge and cognition typical of a given culture." He says that, from this point of view, "a culture amounts to the sum of a given society's folk classifications, all of that society's ethnoscience, its particular ways of classifying its material and social universe."

Following this approach, the task of the social scientist it to discover how members of a culture perceive, define and classify, how they actually perform their activities and what meanings they assign to acts occurring in the context of their culture.

Despite the fact that ethnoscience has been called the New Ethnography,[2] there is much in it that is old. Malinowski, some years ago, stated that the aim of the ethnographer is "to grasp the native's point of view, his relation to life, to realize his vision of the world."[3] Anthropologists would agree that this has been a central task of anthropology. Ethnoscience may simply be providing a more recent statement of that aim within a framework of new methodology and research techniques.

With reference to the method for determining what the native has "in mind," Malinowski stated:

... we cannot expect to obtain a definite, precise and abstract statement from a philosopher, belonging to the community itself. The native takes his fundamental assumptions for granted, and if he reasons or inquires into matters of belief, it would be always in regard to details and concrete

*From George Psathas, "Ethnomethods and Phenomenology," *Social Research* 35:3 (Autumn 1968), 500–503, 508–20. Reprinted with permission of *Social Research* and the author.

applications. Any attempts on the part of the ethnographer to induce his informant to formulate such a general statement would have to be in the form of leading questions of the worst type because in these leading questions he would have to introduce words and concepts essentially foreign to the native. Once the informant grasped their meaning, his outlook would be warped by our own ideas having been poured into it. Thus, the ethnographer must draw the generalizations for himself, must formulate the abstract statement without the direct help of a native informant.[4]

The ethnoscientist would agree that the phrasing of questions must be carefully done so as not to introduce ideas to the native which were not part of *his* cognitive system. Borrowing from methods in linguistics, he would attempt more systematic (and possibly replicable) questioning procedures to elicit data adequate to the development of a more complete analysis of that aspect of the culture which he is studying. . . .

Goodenough, in a more recent statement of the aim of the New Ethnography, repeats that the aim is to grasp the native's view:

A society's culture consists of whatever it is one has to *know* or believe in order to operate in a manner acceptable to its members, and to do so in any role that they accept for any one of themselves. . . . It is the forms of things that people have in mind, their models for perceiving, and otherwise interpreting them . . . Ethnographic description, then, requires methods of processing observed phenomena such that we can inductively construct a theory of how our informants have organized the same phenomena. It is the theory, not the phenomena alone, which ethnographic descriptions aim to present.[5]

As this last quotation indicates, the task of the ethnographer is not merely to describe events as he might see them from his observer's perspective, but also to get "inside" those events to see what kind of theory it is that the natives themselves inductively use to organize phenomena in their daily lives. In terms used in phenomenology, the task is to discover how natives "constitute" the phenomena which exist for them in their lives.

From a slightly different perspective, the task of the social scientist is to construct a theory of natives' theories, or as Schutz has put it, "a typification of their typifications." (I think that Goodenough's use of the term "theory" can be interpreted in the sense of Schutz's notion of typification.)

ETHNOMETHODOLOGY

Ethnomethodology is the term coined by Garfinkel and his students[6] to refer to their work. Garfinkel has defined ethnomethodology as: "the investigation of the rational properties of indexical expressions and other practical actions as contingent ongoing accomplishments of organized artful practices of everyday life."[7] An elaboration of the particular meanings of these terms, as Garfinkel defines them, is beyond the scope of this paper. We shall only note that he is concerned with the practical, everyday activities of men in society as they make accountable, to themselves and others, their everyday affairs, and with the methods they use for producing and managing those same affairs. He sees similarity in the activities of producing and making accountable. His concern with the everyday, routine and commonplace activities as phenomena in their own right, deserving of detailed study, is certainly consistent with the views of phenomenology.[8]

The ethnomethodologist seeks to discover the "methods" that persons use in their everyday life in society in constructing social reality and also to discover the nature of the realities they have constructed. In studying, for example, the way that jurors recognize the "correctness" of a verdict, he would focus on how the jurors make their activities "normal," on how the moral order of their world is created. They are seen as creating, through their activities, familiar scenes and procedures which are recognizable to them as the world they know in common and take for granted, by

example !

which and within which "correctness" of a verdict is determined. Only by examining their procedures and discovering what they consist of, can one fully understand what they mean by correctness, as *correctness is decided by those who construct it.* Further, as Garfinkel shows, some understanding of decision-making in daily life, i.e., in situations other than the jury-room, is also achieved.

In common with ethnoscience is the ethnomethodologist's effort to understand the world as it is interpreted by men in daily life. For example, Natanson, in his introduction to Schutz's collected papers, states, "the social scientist's task is the reconstruction of the way in which men in daily life interpret their own world."[9] This is a basic position in the work of ethnomethodologists and in Schutz's own work.

The distinction between natural science and social science, as Natanson, Schutz and others clearly point out, is based on the fact that men are not only objects existing in the natural world to be observed by the scientist, but they are creators of a world, a cultural world, of their own. In creating this world, they interpret their own activities. Their overt behavior is only a fragment of their total behavior. Any social scientist who insists that he can understand all of man's behavior by focusing only on that part which is overt and manifested in concrete, directly observable acts is naive, to say the least. The challenge to the social scientist who seeks to understand social reality, then, is to understand the meaning that the actor's act has for him. If the observer applies only his own categories or theories concerning the meanings of acts, he may never discover the meanings these same acts have for the actors themselves. Nor can he ever discover how social reality is "created" and how subsequent acts by human actors are performed in the context of *their* understandings.

This, it seems to me, is similar to the problem of bracketing in phenomenological analysis. The scientist must bracket his own pre-suppositions concerning the phenomena and seek to discover the suppositions which human actors, in situ, adopt and use. Further he must also bracket these suppositions in an effort to analyze the phenomena themselves.[10]

Both ethnoscience and ethnomethodology are involved in the problem of cultural relativism, but ethnomethodology, in my estimation, may come closer to escaping the bounds of the particular culture that is studied because of the phenomenological sophistication which aids it. For example, the ethnoscientist in studying one culture's classification system has no reason to expect that another culture's classification system will be the same. His emic analysis refers to one society's culture, i.e., he may discover how the Subanun classify disease but he does not claim that any other culture will have the same system of classification. Certainly he can do cross-cultural comparisons to see if emic systems of different cultures share common elements. But he does not take the position that an emic analysis will produce a system which is universally true or valid. Similarly, the ethnomethodologist studying particular actors in particular groupings in a particular society cannot claim that what he discovers will be true generally for all men. Some aspects of decision-making by jurors, for example, may change depending on changes in legal rules and procedures at a later historical point, may differ from one culture to another depending on how the legal system is structured, etc.

However, the grounding of ethnomethodology in phenomenology implies that research problems will be defined and approached in such a way as to result in the discovery of the essential features of the social phenomena being studied. This may appear to be a contradiction. In one sense it is, but at another level it may not be. For example, if one looks at the problem of jurors making decisions as a study of the general phenomenon of decision-making, an analysis of their procedures has implications for the understanding of the essence of the process of decision-making, of how groups, in contrast to individuals, make decisions, and of the rules of decision-making in everyday life. By taking a phenomenological position in which one tries to discover the basic essence of the process, it is possible for the ethnomethodologist to discover that which is more generally true and not be limited to culturally and temporally relative conclusions. As an example from what is more clearly a phenomenological analysis, the "natural attitude" and the "inter-subjective world of everyday life"[11] are presented as being characteristic not only of Western man, but probably of all men living in society. They are part of the basic human condition, so to speak. For example, that men assume, and assume that others assume, that if "I change places with the other, so that his 'here' becomes mine, I shall be at the same distance from things and see them with the same typicality that he does; moreover, the same things would be in my reach which are actually in his (and that the reverse is also true)" (Ibid, p. 12); that the world is taken for granted to be an inter-subjective world; that the world existed yesterday and will exist tomorrow; that my actions are based on my believing that others can interpret those actions as intelligible, given their understanding of what we know in our culture, etc. If we take the position that the basic features of the "natural attitude" and of the "inter-subjective world of everyday life" may represent essences of the human condition which are universally true—and there is certainly much to indicate in Schutz's analysis that the natural attitude is a taken-for-granted aspect of everyday life—then it is on this background or within this frame that men perform meaningful acts in their everyday activities. The meanings which are then added to behavior are based on the pre-suppositions of the natural attitude. If this is so, then it is possible to look for those common elements in a variety of cultures, based on the natural attitude and the inter-subjectivity of knowledge, that may affect the meanings assigned to activities. What I am saying here is that it is possible that, given this background, some restrictions are placed on how men can perceive and interact. The use of drugs to "escape" the taken-for-granted aspects of everyday life and throw these into sharp question is some indication that men are somehow tied down, bound by, the "facts" of human existence. It is only with some effort, such as the taking of drugs, that one can escape the bounds of the world of everyday life and enter other realities.

Given this grounding in phenomenology (of Schutz and others), the ethnomethodologist's approach to problems, it seems to me, is somewhat different from that of the ethnoscientist's. One contrast is that the former is directed more towards problems of *meaning* in everyday life situations. But even more basic is his concern with discovering those basic features (essences, perhaps) of everyday interaction so that the problem of how meanings are constructed and how social reality is created out of the interlocked activity of human actors becomes an important and critical topic for examination.

Starting from the taken-for-granted, everyday world analyzed by the phenomenologist, the ethnomethodologist takes the position that this is the basis for all other strata of man's reality. This is the ground on which all other realities are constructed. If so, it is important to know what it is that is basic, since one is concerned with the reality of everyday-life-as-seen-by-men-in-society, and one wants to learn how men perceive, experience, and construct the social reality in which they live. This represents, in a real sense, I believe, a phenomenological position of "going to the things themselves," to the social phenomena rather than to previously developed theories to be tested by the formulation of deductive hypotheses.

Both approaches emphasize the importance of investigating the taken-for-granted aspects of man's existence in the world. The ethnoscientists investigate what they call components and the ethnomethodologists what they call background expectancies. Both are concerned with the "methods" which men use to make their world meaningful. The difference between the two approaches is that ethnoscience tends to emphasize the static thingness of the phenomena being studied, whereas ethnomethodology is concerned with the active processes whereby things (mainly activities) are constituted in the world of social action.

It is important to note, in this connection, the effort by Garfinkel in his article "Studies of the Routine Grounds of Everyday Activities"[12] to demonstrate the existence of the natural attitude and the intersubjectivity of knowledge drawing from Schutz's analysis. In what Garfinkel calls "demonstration experiments," the technique used was that of disturbing or introducing a "nasty surprise" in interacting with others in order to demonstrate the presence of much that was taken for granted. The technique is simple though limited, and if imaginative variation were used,[13] would possibly not be necessary. Garfinkel disturbed others by simply not performing those acts which they expected—or by performing acts which others did not have any "reason" to expect. For example, his students were instructed to treat their parents at home as though they, the students, were guests in the home rather than the sons or daughters of the parents. The politeness and small acts of kindness they performed were then taken by their parents to be signs of hostility, antagonism or fatigue. For example, to ask one's parents if one may be allowed to look in the

refrigerator or the pantry for something to eat—or to ask permission to eat in the first place—was greeted with perplexity, confusion and surprise.

Garfinkel reports going up to a customer standing in line in a restaurant and treating him as though he were the waiter, or revealing to a friend during a conversation that he, Garfinkel, had a tape recorder and was recording the entire conversation. What can be learned from such demonstrations? A great deal, though I would not wish to recommend these procedures to others since I do not feel that these are necessarily the only, or even the best, ways of obtaining data concerning the taken-for-granted assumptions of the common sense world of everyday life. They may certainly reveal the variety and complexity of the pre-suppositions or taken-for-granteds that exist in everyday life. The grounds of man's social existence can be discovered. Such discovery can have tremendous possibilities not only for understanding particular social worlds but also for changing or even destroying them altogether. . . .

The last point I want to make concerns the importance of understanding subjective reality. It is indeed significant that the problem of understanding the *manner* by which men understand other men's minds has not been solved in social science. It is a basic fact of everyday life, however, that men claim to and act as though they can and do understand others, i.e., that they can "know others' minds." They can, at least, know that which is relevant to be known, given the interaction in which they are engaged. Men in everyday society do not doubt that they can know others' minds. They further assume that other men can know their minds, as well.

For the social scientist, a major task in any study is to discover the understandings that the actor and the other have *of one another*. His task is to explicate those understandings. It is

example—

not his concern to analyze, in all their detail, the subjective aspects of the actor's behavior, nor of his own (the scientist's) perceptions. His task is to form objective, ideal constructs relating to the understandings and the typifications that men have of one another. (Ethnomethodology, more than ethnoscience, is involved in this task.) In so doing he need not elaborate all of the variations that are involved in some of these typifications. Rather, it is his task to make typifications of those typifications; to make abstractions, to make constructs, and to determine the essences of the typifications which actors make. It is significant that phenomenologists are also undertaking the analysis of some of these problems and have discussed methods whereby men can determine how other men perceive. For example, Spiegelberg[14] shows that "imaginative self transposal" can occur, and sets out some of the elements of this process. One of these elements is what he calls "imaginative projection in thought"[15] in which one begins to "construct the other in his world on the basis of the clues which we find in the situation into which we have put ourselves imaginatively . . . and try to build, from these elements, his self and the world as he is likely to see it." The aim, as stated by Spiegelberg, is one which could not have been stated better by sociologists or anthropologists. It is to "see the world through another person's eyes" and consider the "whole 'frame' of existence which the other occupies."[15]

The other method, that of cooperative encounter or cooperative exploration, involves exploring the other's world with his helpful cooperation in a prolonged and extended dialogue involving the sympathetic probing, exploring and interrogation of the other. Anthropologists who have used native informants for long periods of time have experienced the phenomenon of coming to see the world through the other's eyes aided by the checks and qualifications introduced by the other in response to questions and comments. A better example, though it is a model which has not been extensively used for the development of scientific or phenomenological accounts of the other's world, is that of the patient-therapist relationship. Here the psychiatrist can achieve an encounter in which he comes to understand the other "in his entirety."

The method of participant observation in the social sciences has some of these possibilities also. The extension of this method into *disguised* participation observation, in which the observer actually becomes a member of the group and performs a role within the group which others take to be his real identity rather than a role "put on" for the sake of collecting data, enables the observer-researcher to experience the role from within. That is, by having to perform *in that world*, he must develop and adopt the perspective that goes with that world. An example from my own experience is that of being a person who was asking others for directions in order to experience the receiving of directions; also vice versa—offering others directions in order to experience the giving of directions. This could be extended to many roles which I as a sociologist could take, even to that of being a sociologist presenting a paper to a sociological convention. By then examining my own feelings, ideas, behavior, etc., I can construct possible typifications of the social role and the perspective which it provides for *me*. I can then use myself as a model of what others who perform this role are like, i.e., what the world is as seen by typical others from this perspective.

It is to be hoped that ethnomethodologists will turn their attention to methods whereby it is possible to "know other men's minds." It is often taken for granted in research done by those in the symbolic interactionist tradition in social psychology (influenced by G.H. Mead, C.H. Cooley, W.I. Thomas and others) and ethnomethodologists that it is possible for the researcher to "know the mind" of the subjects studied. A necessary extension is the determination of how members of society know other members' minds. What ethnoscientists are doing is calling our attention to the possibility of devising strict and rigorous procedures for the determination of the other's "mind" and furthermore making possible the replication of results. However, their methodology may have built-in limitations stemming from the assumption that linguistic categories and their underlying components can provide adequate understanding of men in society. It remains to be seen whether more "imaginative," "introspective" and "subjective" approaches to the understanding of others can produce *replicable* results in a manner similar to the methods used in linguistic and semantic analysis.

There is much to be expected from these approaches. Phenomenology has a great deal to offer the social scientist. We may hope that attention now being directed to phenomenology by the ethnomethodologists will stimulate the selection of those aspects of phenomenological methods and insights which are most relevant and significant for the social scientist's endeavor.

Both approaches promise to affect the course of research by focusing attention on the world of everyday life. Since the world is so vast and complex, they virtually guarantee that scientific activity will never end. More important, however, than guaranteeing us jobs forever is that they guarantee a better understanding of human behavior-in-society, which I take to be the main aim of social science, that is, not an understanding of behavior-in-the-laboratory, or behavior-in-the-sociologists' society, but rather behavior where it occurs, in everyday life.

NOTES

1. W.C. Sturtevant, "Studies in Ethnoscience," *American Anthropologist*, Special Publication, 66, Part 2; Romney, A.K., and D'Andrade, R.G. (eds.), "Transcultural Studies in Cognition," Report of a Conference sponsored by the Social Sciences Research Council, 1964.

2. Sturtevant, ibid, p. 99.

3. B. Malinowski, *Argonauts of the Western Pacific*, New York: E.P. Dutton and Company, 1950, p. 396.

4. Ibid., p. 396.

5. W. Goodenough, "Cultural Anthropology and Linguistics," in Garvin, P.L. (ed.). *Monograph Series on Languages and Linguistics*, No. 9, Institute of Languages and Linguistics, Washington: Georgetown University, 1957, pp. 167–173.

6. For representative works see the following: H. Garfinkel, "Studies of the Routine Grounds of Everyday Activities," *Social Problems*, 11, 1964, pp. 225–250; Garfinkel *Studies in Ethnomethodology*, Englewood Cliffs, N.J.: Prentice Hall, 1967; E. Bittner, "The Police on Skid-Row," *American Sociological Review*, 32, 1967, pp. 669–715; A. Cicourel, *Method and Measurement in Sociology*, New York: The Free Press, 1964; D. Sudnow, "Normal Crimes," *Social Problems*, 12, 1965, pp. 255–276; L. Churchill, "Everyday Quantitative Practices," paper presented to meetings of the American Sociological Association, August, 1966.

7. Garfinkel, *Studies in Ethnomethodology*, p. 11.

8. For an elaboration of the notion of accounts, see M. Scott and S.M. Lyman, "Accounts," *American Sociological Review*, 33, 1968, pp. 46–62.

9. M. Natanson, in A. Schutz, *Collected Papers*, Vol. 1. The Hague: Martinus Nijhoff, 1962, Editor's Introduction. p. ixvi.

10. H. Spiegelberg, *The Phenomenological Movement, II*. The Hague: Martinus Nijhoff, 1965, p. 690.

11. A. Schutz, *Collected Papers*, Vol. I, The Hague: Martinus Nijhoff, 1962.

12. Garfinkel, op. cit.

13. Spiegelberg, op. cit., p. 680.

14. H. Spiegelberg, "Phenomenology through Vicarious Experience," in E. Strauss, *Phenomenology: Pure and Applied*, Pittsburgh: Duquesne University Press, 1964.

15. H. Spiegelberg, "Toward a Phenomenology of Imaginative Understanding of Others," *Proceedings of XIIth International Congress of Philosophy*, Brussels, 1953, p. 237.

NOTES ON THE ART OF WALKING*

A. LINCOLN RYAVE AND JAMES N. SCHENKEIN

It can be observed that the transportation of our bodies is a commonplace feature of our everyday experience of the world; to be sure, when such is not the case, we have certain warrant for noting those details of our circumstances rendering bodily transportation unlikely. While we of course have a variety of devices to achieve our transportation (automobiles, tricycles, elevators, donkeys, and so on), the body itself is regularly used for its own self-transportation. Using the body in this way can take many forms, and some of these can be pointed to with readily understood glosses in our native discourses: crawling, hopping, running, cartwheeling, jumping, skipping, walking, and so on.

The substantive focus of this discussion shall be the phenomenon of "doing walking." We use the verb "doing" to underscore a conception of walking as the concerted accomplishment of members of the community involved as a matter of course in its production and recognition. We hope to indicate that these members rely upon an elaborated collection of methodic practices in the conduct of doing walking, and we want to sketch out one sort of analytic technology to gain access to the details of these methodic practices. In treating this commonplace phenomenon as the problematic achievement of members, we hope to build towards a greater understanding of social phenomena as on-going situated accomplishments. It is, after all, these methodic practices that make the phenomenon of doing walking so utterly unnoteworthy at first glance to both lay and professional social analysts alike; indeed, it is through these methodic practices that the commonplace presents itself to us as ordinary, and the exotic as extraordinary.

ON THE ISSUE OF DATA

For the purposes of inquiring into the phenomenon of doing walking, two eight-minute segments of videotape were filmed on a public pavement travelled primarily by students. In order to capture a number of instances of the phenomenon, and in order to observe a variety of situations that confront walkers ne-

*From Roy Turner, ed. *Ethnomethodology* (New York: Penguin Books, 1974), pp. 265–74. Reproduced by permission of Penguin Books Ltd.

gotiating their progress among other walkers, we filmed at a time when students are routinely negotiating their ways from class to class. The setting was additionally selected for the sorts of "natural boundaries" within which walkers on this pavement must conduct their progress: on one side walkers are confronted with an eight-foot high concrete wall, and on the other with a continuous row of parked cars; along the length of curb were also typically spaced telephone poles and parking regulation signs.

It is worth noting, although it will not be greatly developed, that the sense in which we speak of the environment as constituted by "natural boundaries" is itself a members' ongoing accomplishment. While the constraint of "natural boundaries" may be an omnipresent contingency realized and realizable on occasions of doing walking, the content of those boundaries is both varied and variable within a single setting and across different settings. So the "natural boundaries" members cooperate to maintain while doing walking include not merely the physical conditions of the scene, but also the encircling space accompanying other walkers as they conduct themselves along their respective paths, their trajectories, the space between those seen as walking together, and the like. We will later offer some remarks on the way in which altering or violating some "natural boundary" will unavoidably suggest "something special"; but for now, let us observe that walking on the tops of parked cars, down the middle of the street, or through a hand-holding couple becomes the extraordinary event it does in contrast to the ordinary concerted maintenance of those boundaries seen as constituting the environment.

One last comment on the collection of the data with videotape seems appropriate. It is plain enough that the use of videotape affords us the opportunity to review a given instance of the phenomenon innumerable times without relying on a single observation of an essentially transitory phenomenon. In addition, since a key focus of our inquiry is how an instance of the phenomenon presents itself, we require intimate study of actual instances of walking and cannot be satisfied with the study of reports *on* those instances. So while we seek to study the issue of producing and recognizing instances of doing walking, we want our inquiry to be based on data representing actual instances of doing walking, and not second-order reports which are distinct from the thing we want to treat as problematic.

THE NAVIGATIONAL PROBLEM

The ways in which doing walking is an on-going members' accomplishment can be initially appreciated by considering what we shall refer to as the "navigational problem." We take it that our data captures utterly routine occasions of walking under circumstances of heavy walking traffic, and that there occur in our data no instances of bumping into one another is no freak happening. The avoidance of collision is a basic index to the accomplished character of walking: that participants to the setting "manage" not to collide with one another or with some other (e.g. physical) natural boundary is to be viewed as the product of concerted work on the part of those co-participants.

This concerted work is not a particularly troublesome matter for participants. The conduct of walking is not experienced as an activity of worry, requires no exotic forethought for its successful management, and can be achieved without viewing the prospect of collision as some likely yet prescribable happening; indeed, the converse of any of these observations provides members reasonable evidence for their "trouble" in now having to attend to such matters.

There is, none the less, a treatment of this

accomplishment as a navigational problem that recommends our attention to the structures relied upon and manipulated by participant walkers as they "solve" their navigational problem routinely in the normal conduct of their walking. The "problem" to which we shall address ourselves is an analytic one: what is the nature of the work executed routinely by participant walkers? An articulation of this work will represent a description of the members' solution to what is analytically treatable as the "navigational problem" of walking.

TOWARD DESCRIBING THE MEMBERS' SOLUTION

A further focus of our investigation is provided by the observation that members have the ability to distinguish between "walking-together" and "walking-alone." In the course of this discussion we hope to provide a foundation for a disciplined investigation of the social-interactional relevance this distinction has for members' achieved solutions to the navigational problem. Our interests will involve us in an examination of members' methods for the *production* and *recognition* of walking-alone and of walking-together as on-going situated accomplishments. The notions of "production" and "recognition" are invoked to take note of the fact that doing "walking-together" involves setting co-participants both in doing the activity (production) and in observing the activity (recognition).

We shall begin and guide our investigation by addressing the matter of how it is that we, as members, are able to do "recognizing walking-together"; it is this recognition that provides co-participant walkers a basic constituent of their achieved solution to the navigational problem.

Our interest in the production and recognition of walking-together and walking-alone is informed by the fact that members, in the conduct of their walking, attend to this dimension of the phenomenon; that attention, or lack of it, has interactional consequences for the navigational problem. For a lone walker, the noticing of some collection of approaching walkers decidedly walking-together has particular navigational relevance: (a) without some alteration of the opposing trajectories, collision would recognizably occur, and (b) for the culture we are describing, it is expected, it is proper, for the lone walker to do walking-around those decidedly doing walking-together. This constraint seems also to be operative in cases where a lone walker (or a series of lone walkers) is confronted by a collection of walkers decidedly walking-together in the same direction but at a slower pace: the constraint is upon the lone walker, again, not to walk-between but to walk-around.

We must be clear about the nature of what we mean by "constraint." It is not that someone cannot walk between an on-going group walking-together when that group is met head on or employs too slow a pace in the same direction, but that to do so has definite social consequences and meanings. For example, a way of being demonstrably "rude" is by violating the above mentioned constraint, a way young male adults have of "choosing off" is by violating the constraint, a way one comes to build a reputation for "absent-mindedness" is by preferring absorption in one's books over attention to one's navigational responsibilities while walking, and so on.

The constraint we mention is also properly attended to by those walkers party to a large group that is walking-together, where, in order not to prevent others from walking-around them, they will break up into smaller groups of two-abreast instead of four-abreast, for example, lest approaching or following others be forced to walk-between their ranks. The sorts of interactional possibilities occasioned by the routine two-by-two formation of walkers instead of a four-abreast formation surely deserve additional investigation. It is, of course, well known that maintaining a large group walking-together (and thereby forcing other walkers either to step aside or break the ranks of the approaching ensemble) is a classic street challenge. The point is: both those walking-together and those walking-alone can and do orient to this dimension of the phenomenon of doing walking.

PRODUCTION AND RECOGNITION

To put the matter another way, an integral feature of the achieved members' solution to the navigational problem is the production and recognition of walking-together and walking-alone. That is to say, contained in our noticing of the interactional relevances of walking-alone and walking-together is an implicit claim to the members' capacities and practices in both producing and recognizing, as a matter of course, that aspect of the conduct of walking. Let us now treat that aspect problematically in an effort to indicate the sort of investigation into members' solutions that is here recommended for the study of walking. We shall, of course, be devoting ourselves to an inquiry into the procedures out of which both the production and recognition of walking-alone and walking-together are fashioned.

The task of determining the procedures by which members can decide who is walking with whom in some setting was initiated by the observation that we were able, when relevant to do so, in various degrees of agreement, to come to determinations about the matter. It became apparent that what was essentially involved was some membership ability to distinguish between "alone" and "together." If these are then available and situationally relevant categorization devices for members, the primary concern becomes discovering the procedures for applying these categories by member observers.

Our task then becomes one of demonstrating some attributes of what might be called "togetherings" and "alonings"; that is, we now could focus upon combinations of setting and activities of which a constituent feature is "togetherness" and "aloneness"; the procedures we may uncover in an analysis of how members achieve their observations of walking-alone and walking-together then, have particular use in later studies of parties, restaurants, movies, libraries, and other settings where the dimension revealed by the categories "alone" and "together" is prominent. For now, however, this more general phenomenon shall be approached with special focus on the togethering displayed in doing walking-together and on the aloning displayed in doing walking-alone.

Naturally, the application of these categories by members is a double task involving both (a) production work on the part of those members doing the walking-together or doing the walking-alone, and (b) recognition work on the part of those members observing the distribution of those categories among walkers. Let us now turn to a consideration of these two reflexive features of the phenomenon.

RECOGNITION WORK

A togethering, for example doing walking-together, is a settinged activity. By that we mean the propriety and relevance of a togethering is a function of such factors as time, place, and participants: there are, clearly, proper and/or expectable occasions for a togethering. This observation is rather fundamental in a consideration of recognition work for such factors as time, place, and participants are invoked by members to see, notice, and account for some others *as a togethering* without having to approach them to determine by interview if such is, in fact, the case. Plainly, walking-together cannot be properly done anytime, anywhere, with anybody. What are some features that are provided by a setting and invoked by members in order to recognize the propriety of, for example, walking-together?

A pervasive feature of the culture we are dealing with is the use of members' identification categories (e.g. family, stranger, friend, Bill, Oriental, boy, etc.) as mechanisms for the establishment of who can expectably be engaging in a togethering, or whatever. It can be noted that members attend to the fact that certain category relations obligate the occasion of a togethering, as with the walking-together that might be occasioned on the meeting of a friend who is going in the same direction. The obligatory status of certain category relations can be noted by the consequent availabilities of such things as "making excuses," "begging-off," "changing direction of one's body movement," "apologies," and other avoidance or circumventing arrangements to an expected walking-together. Similarly, the constraints of certain category relations provide for the impropriety of walking-together as when "strangers" find themselves "following one another" or "walking side by side"; here the consequences of "rudeness," "picking-up," "misidentifications," "spying," and suspicions of other pretexts become relevant.

That there is work involved in prescribing the propriety of both the when and who of a togethering, then, provides one important basis from which members devise and invoke recognition procedures. These are attentive to what might be called proper "togethering sets"; for example, that some people can be seen as walking-together may turn on their identifiability as a proper togethering. A child walking ten feet ahead of an adult woman may be seeable as mother-and-child, and they thereby can be taken as walking-together, whereas a uniformed policeman and teenage girl walking in a similar arrangement may present us with no recognizable togethering set,

and each thereby can be taken as walking-alone.

So, recognition work can inhere in the settinged character of walking-together, which provides for the recognizability of a togethering on the basis of availability, relevance, or properness of some togetherness set. Again, this is not a matter in which one has to interrogate in order to find out if such is the case; rather one takes-it-for-granted until "informed" otherwise.

In order to provide a more complete picture of some of the features of recognition work we need to anticipate our discussion of production work, for part and parcel of recognition is the participant's knowledge and reliance upon the accomplishment of walking-alone and walking-together. For example, members who can be seen as involved in the maintenance of spatial proximity can properly be seen as walking-together. Our data instance two members observed walking in spatial proximity, approaching a disrupting obstacle (a telephone pole) which upsets the on-going maintenance of co-present spatial proximity; when they re-establish their former co-presence after the obstacle has been passed, the sense of seeing them as a togethering was secured. Another illustration from our data is an instance in which three members were observed walking-together while making a left turn from the street-crossing onto the pavement; in that each adjusted his pace so as to make the turning non-disruptive of the established spatial proximity, the sense of seeing them as a togethering was secured.

Relatedly, those members who can be seen as involved in some togethering-bound-activity can properly be seen as walking-together. For example, in two instances from our data the sense of seeing walking-together was secured by the observations that, in the first, two members were holding hands and exchanging sustained reciprocal glances while, in the second, two members maintained an extended interchange of verbal remarks. The fact of producing walking-together provides for the propriety or relevance of certain social activities, and the recognizability of these activities will inform on the status of walkers as alone or together.

These rough examples are intended to suggest the delicacy with which our recognition work operates. The noticing of potential category relations among persons distributed along the pavement, the noticing of spatial patterns not merely as features of the scene but as patterns re-established by walkers after passing some obstacle, the noticing of paces being adjusted to achieve a harmonious collective turning while walking, the noticing of various degrees of body contact among those walking, and the noticing of various activities walkers are engaged in besides their walking—all of these involve rather fine attentions to the progressively revealed and changing setting in which the walking and its recognition occur. We are recommending here that an analysis of doing walking must be prominently energetic in its treatment of these attentions by members. And we are recommending as well that topics such as the identification of collectivities, features of being together and of being alone, the normative and moral constitution of social phenomena, and so on, can be richly generated by detailed study of members' mundane activities (such as walking). Perhaps this will become more clear in a consideration of the production work of walking-together and walking-alone.

PRODUCTION WORK

We have noted that walking-together can be recognized on the basis of various cues by an observer (pace, direction, spatial proximity, physical contact, talking, greetings and partings, head direction, etc.). It is evident that these "cues" must be continually produced by the parties to the togetherings in order to make the activity continually available and accountable. Being together, as a fact, provides constraints and instructs a programme of actions, which in turn provides the basis for the doing and seeing, the producing and recognizing, of a togethering such as walking-together. It takes some effort, for example, to "keep up" or to manage to "take the right turn," and it takes some attention to the doing of a parting upon dissolution of walking-together, and so on. How then do members go about producing walking-together?

The on-going production of walking-together involves the participants in at least maintaining spatial proximity in some recognizable pattern. By this we intend to take note of the fact that definitive to walking-together is some physical co-presence, and that one who claims to be walking-together with someone who is absent is considered to suffer from some kind of longing or some kind of madness. The requirement of spatial proximity is illustrated by the observations that (a) participants who have lost some proximity will engage in repair work ranging from hurrying or slowing to calling out or later explaining the separation, (b) relatedly, violation of the maintenance of spatial proximity fundamentally undermines the enterprise of walking-together and can be seen as a serious interactional breach, and (c) similarly related, spatial proximity is a requisite for the production of some of the togethering-bound-activities like body contact and verbal exchanges. These observations deserve some explication.

Two features related to the maintenance of proximity in walking-together are direction and pace. Clearly, as direction and/or pace of those walking-together vary, the maintenance of spatial proximity becomes problematic for the participants. The strength of maintaining spatial proximity and, thereby, physical co-presence as non-problematic features of walking-together can be seen in such things as the propriety of announced changes in direction or pace. To do such body movements unannounced provides members with, and constrains members to see, such activities as "showing disapproval," "cold-shouldering," "humorous disappearance," etc. It regularly occurs that before members engage in the activity of walking-together they will formulate those problems of direction, pace, destination, etc., that can be potentially problematic for the anticipated enterprise; of course, such a matter might interestingly differ if one joins a walk-in-progress where direction and pace are already in action.

As we have noted, part and parcel of the production of the activity of walking-together and contingent upon the maintenance of spatial proximity, are certain walking-together-bound-activities. In walking-together, for example, such activities as conversing, being available for conversation, touching, laughing, offering of offerables such as cigarettes or sweets, parting, and so on, are made relevant, and expectable, by the sheer fact of walking-together. That is, the fact of walking-together provides for the propriety and expectation of these activities. They are both cause and consequence (again, the phenomenon of reflexivity) of the production of the walking-together. These observations are demonstrable, in part, by taking note of the fact that members can excuse themselves from doing walking-together with accounts that, for example, they don't want to or cannot talk right now; indeed when someone joins a walk-in-progress, he can be informed that he has intruded by not being engaged in any walking-together-bounded-activities.

The production procedures prescribing the how of walking-together provide the basis or resource by which members accomplish the fact of recognizing that some other members are doing walking-together. That some members can be seen as walking-together turns on their appearance as producing that particular togethering.

It should be perfectly well understood that walking-alone is likewise through and through a member's achievement—both in its production and in its recognition. For example, the relevance of the dimension of spatial proximity in doing walking-alone is dramatically illustrated in our data when a lone walker embarks on a passing of some other walker: direction, pace, and body attitude were all mobilized to ensure that the moment when the passer was in precise physical co-presence with the one he was passing would only be a fleeting one; and we have previously taken note of the work a lone walker must do in avoiding "following," "joining," or in other ways violating others in the street. We might also mention that members who are in fact alone can sometimes affect behaviour to suggest that they are "with" someone when, for example, their unattached status makes them open to unwanted interactions. But the thrust of these observations is to suggest that doing walking-alone and doing walking-together are both the achievements of members engaged in producing their enterprises.

CONCLUDING REMARKS

This discussion should of course be treated as only a sketch of one sort of analytic technology for gaining access to the methodic practices of members engaged in doing walking. It may be useful now to review briefly the thread of the discussion.

1. Beginning with a treatment of doing walking as the problematic accomplishment of members, we first took note of the relevance for members of achieving a solution to the "navigational problem" occasioned by doing walking—repeated observations of the data revealed that members managed to avoid collisions under circumstances of heavy two-way walking traffic.

2. In attempting to gain access to some salient details of the members' solution, our

observations of the data revealed that determinations of who was walking with whom appeared relevant for the accomplishment of such things as who and when and where to pass, how and why to adjust pace or bodily attitude, with whom which activities besides doing walking might be additionally engaged in, and the like—the fact of walking-alone and of walking-together provided members both a constraint and a resource in navigating their progress while doing walking.

3. We then took note of the reflexive character of producing and recognizing the accomplishments of walking-alone and of walking-together—our observations of the data provided us with some prominent features of both the "recognition work" of member observers and of the "production work" of members engaged in achieving walking-alone or walking-together.

We are now at the point of suggesting that these methodic practices of the "art of walking" are indeed accessible to disciplined investigation. It would be no injustice to this report to say that we have taken the phenomenon of doing walking as an occasion to explore the interestingness of findings generated by a particular analytic framework that might well be applied to any commonplace activity of everyday life.

So while the substantive focus has been on the phenomenon of doing walking, we have not been concerned here with descriptively detailing this activity. Rather, our aim has been to recommend the fruitfulness of investigating the ordinary activities of everyday life under the auspices of an analytic apparatus treating those activities as the problematic accomplishments of members. We hope to have pointed to a treatment of doing walking that will expose and take as its central topic the methodic practices of members engaged as a matter of course in its production and recognition. But in the end, the promise of researches such as this is not merely that they may make accessible to rigorous inquiry the accomplished character of the mundane activities of everyday life; for the promise also resides in the fact that such researches treat as their topic of inquiry those features of social life taken for granted by lay and professional social analysts alike.

SOCIAL BEHAVIOR AS EXCHANGE*

GEORGE C. HOMANS

THE PROBLEMS OF SMALL GROUP RESEARCH

. . . As I survey small-group research today, I feel that, apart from just keeping on with it, three sorts of things need to be done. The first is to show the relation between the results of experimental work done under laboratory conditions and the results of *quasi*-anthropological field research on what those of us who do it are pleased to call "real-life" groups in industry and elsewhere. If the experimental work has anything to do with real life—and I am persuaded that it has everything to do—its propositions cannot be inconsistent with those discovered through the field work. But the consistency has not yet been demonstrated in any systematic way.

The second job is to pull together in some set of general propositions the actual results,

*From George C. Homans, "Social Behavior as Exchange," *American Journal of Sociology* 63:6 (May 1958), 597–606. Reprinted with permission of The University of Chicago Press.

from the laboratory and from the field, of work on small groups—propositions that at least sum up, to an approximation, what happens in elementary social behavior, even though we may not be able to explain why the propositions should take the form they do. A great amount of work has been done, and more appears every day, but what it all amounts to in the shape of a set of propositions from which, under specified conditions, many of the observational results might be derived, is not at all clear—and yet to state such a set is the first aim of science.

The third job is to begin to show how the propositions that empirically hold good in small groups may be derived from some set of still more general propositions. "Still more general" means only that empirical propositions other than ours may also be derived from the set. This derivation would constitute the explanatory stage in the science of elementary social behavior, for explanation *is* derivation.[1] (I myself suspect that the more general set will turn out to contain the propositions of behavioral psychology. I hold myself to be an "ultimate psychological reductionist," but I cannot know that I am right so long as the reduction has not been carried out.)

I have come to think that all three of these jobs would be furthered by our adopting the view that interaction between persons is an exchange of goods, material and non-material. This is one of the oldest theories of social behavior, and one that we still use every day to interpret our own behavior, as when we say, "I found so-and-so rewarding"; or "I got a great deal out of him"; or, even, "Talking with him took a great deal out of me." But, perhaps just because it is so obvious, this view has been much neglected by social scientists. So far as I know, the only theoretical work that makes explicit use of it is Marcel Mauss's *Essai sur le don*, published in 1925, which is ancient as social science goes.[2] It may be that the tradition of neglect is now changing and that, for instance, the psychologists who interpret behavior in terms of transactions may be coming back to something of the sort I have in mind.[3]

An incidental advantage of an exchange theory is that it might bring sociology closer to economics—that science of man most advanced, most capable of application, and, intellectually, most isolated. Economics studies exchange carried out under special circumstances and with a most useful built-in numerical measure of value. What are the laws of the general phenomenon of which economic behavior is one class?

In what follows I shall suggest some reasons for the usefulness of a theory of social behavior as exchange and suggest the nature of the propositions such a theory might contain.

AN EXCHANGE PARADIGM

I start with the link to behavioral psychology and the kind of statement it makes about the behavior of an experimental animal such as the pigeon.[4] As a pigeon explores its cage in the laboratory, it happens to peck a target, whereupon the psychologist feeds it corn. The evidence is that it will peck the target again; it has learned the behavior, or, as my friend Skinner says, the behavior has been reinforced, and the pigeon has undergone *operant conditioning*. This kind of psychologist is not interested in how the behavior was learned: "learning theory" is a poor name for his field. Instead, he is interested in what determines changes in the rate of emission of learned behavior, whether pecks at a target or something else.

The more hungry the pigeon, the less corn or other food it has gotten in the recent past, the more often it will peck. By the same token, if the behavior is often reinforced, if the pigeon is given much corn every time it pecks, the rate of emission will fall off as the pigeon gets *satiated*. If, on the other hand, the behavior is not reinforced at all, then, too, its rate of emission will tend to fall off, though a long time may pass before it stops altogether, before it is *extinguished*. In the emission of many kinds of behavior the pigeon incurs *aversive stimulation*, or what I shall call "cost" for short, and this, too, will lead in time to a decrease in the emission rate. Fatigue is an example of a "cost." Extinction, satiation, and cost, by decreasing the rate of emission of a particular kind of behavior, render more probable the emission of some other kind of behavior, including doing nothing. I shall only add that even a hard-boiled psychologist puts "emotional" behavior, as well as such things as pecking, among the unconditioned responses that may be reinforced in operant conditioning. As a statement of the propositions of behavioral psychology, the foregoing is, of course, inadequate for any purpose except my present one.

We may look on the pigeon as engaged in an exchange—pecks for corn—with the psychologist, but let us not dwell upon that, for the behavior of the pigeon hardly determines the behavior of the psychologist at all. Let us turn to a situation where the exchange is real, that is, where the determination is mutual. Suppose we are dealing with two men. Each is emitting behavior reinforced to some degree by the behavior of the other. How it was in the past that each learned the behavior he emits and how he learned to find the other's behavior reinforcing we are not concerned with. It is enough that each does find the other's behavior reinforcing, and I shall call the reinforcers—the equivalent of the pigeon's corn—*values*, for this, I think, is what we mean by this term. As he emits behavior, each man may incur costs, and each man has more than one course of behavior open to him.

This seems to me the paradigm of elementary social behavior, and the problem of the elementary sociologist is to state propositions relating the variations in the values and costs of each man to his frequency distribution of behavior among alternatives, where the values (in the mathematical sense) taken by these variables for one man determine in part their values for the other.[5]

I see no reason to believe that the propositions of behavioral psychology do not apply to this situation, though the complexity of their implications in the concrete case may be great indeed. In particular, we must suppose that, with men as with pigeons, an increase in extinction, satiation, or aversive stimulation of any one kind of behavior will increase the probability of emission of some other kind. The problem is not, as it is often stated, merely, what a man's values are, what he has learned in the past to find reinforcing, but how much of any one value his behavior is getting him now. The more he gets, the less valuable any further unit of that value is to him, and the less often he will emit behavior reinforced by it.

THE INFLUENCE PROCESS

We do not, I think, possess the kind of studies of two-person interaction that would either bear out these propositions or fail to do so. But we do have studies of larger numbers of persons that suggest that they may apply, notably the studies by Festinger, Schachter, Back, and their associates on the dynamics of influence. One of the variables they work with they call *cohesiveness*, defined as anything that attracts people to take part in a group. Cohesiveness is a value variable; it refers to the degree of reinforcement people find in the activities of the group. Festinger and his colleagues consider two kinds of reinforcing activity: the symbolic behavior we call "social approval" (sentiment) and activity valuable in other ways, such as doing something interesting.

The other variable they work with they call *communication* and others call *interaction*. This is a frequency variable; it is a measure of the frequency of emission of valuable and costly verbal behavior. We must bear in mind that, in general, the one kind of variable is a function of the other.

Festinger and his co-workers show that the more cohesive a group is, that is, the more valuable the sentiment or activity the members exchange with one another, the greater the average frequency of interaction of the members.[6] With men, as with pigeons, the greater the reinforcement, the more often is the reinforced behavior emitted. The more cohesive a group, too, the greater the change that members can produce in the behavior of other members in the direction of rendering these activities more valuable.[7] That is, the more valuable the activities that members get, the more valuable those that they must give. For if a person is emitting behavior of a certain kind, and other people do not find it particularly rewarding, these others will suffer their own production of sentiment and activity, in time, to fall off. But perhaps the first person has found their sentiment and activity rewarding, and, if he is to keep on getting them, he must make his own behavior more valuable to the others. In short, the propositions of behavioral psychology imply a tendency toward a certain proportionality between the value to others of the behavior a man gives them and the value to him of the behavior they give him.[8]

Schachter also studied the behavior of members of a group toward two kinds of other members, "conformers" and "deviates."[9] I assume that conformers are people whose activity the other members find valuable. For conformity is behavior that coincides to a degree with some group standard or norm, and the only meaning I can assign to *norm* is "a verbal description of behavior that many members find it valuable for the actual behavior of themselves and others to conform to." By the same token, a deviate is a member whose behavior is not particularly valuable. Now Schachter shows that, as the members of a group come to see another member as a deviate, their interaction with him—communication addressed to getting him to change his behavior—goes up, the faster the more cohesive the group. The members need not talk to the other conformers so much; they are relatively satiated by the conformers' behavior: they have gotten what they want out of them. But if the deviate, by failing to change his behavior, fails to reinforce the members, they start to withhold social approval from him: the deviate gets low sociometric choice at the end of the experiment. And in the most cohesive groups—those Schachter calls "high cohesive-relevant"—interaction with the deviate also falls off in the end and is lowest among those members that rejected him most strongly, as if they had given him up as a bad job. But how plonking can we get? These findings are utterly in line with everyday experience.

PRACTICAL EQUILIBRIUM

At the beginning of this paper I suggested that one of the tasks of small-group research was to show the relation between the results of experimental work done under laboratory conditions and the results of field research on real-life small groups. Now the latter often appear to be in practical equilibrium, and by this I mean nothing fancy. I do not mean that all real-life groups are in equilibrium. I certainly do not mean that all groups must tend to equilibrium. I do not mean that groups have built-in antidotes to change: There is no homeostasis here. I do not mean that we assume equilibrium. I mean only that we sometimes *observe* it, that for the time we are with a group—and it is often short—there is no great change in the values of the variables we choose to measure. If, for instance, person A is intereacting with B more than with C both at the beginning and at the end of the study, then at least by this crude measure the group is in equilibrium.

Many of the Festinger-Schachter studies are experimental, and their propositions about the process of influence seem to me to imply the kind of proposition that empirically holds good of real-life groups in practical equilibrium. For instance, Festinger et al. find that, the more cohesive a group is, the greater the change that members can produce in the behavior of other members. If the influence is exerted in the direction of conformity to group norms, then, when the process of influence has accomplished all the change of which it is capable, the proposition should hold good that, the more cohesive a group is, the larger the number of members that conform to its norms. And it does hold good.[10]

Again, Schachter found, in the experiment I summarized above, that in the most cohesive groups and at the end, when the effort to influence the deviate had failed, members interacted little with the deviate and gave him little in the way of sociometric choice. Now two of the propositions that hold good most often of real-life groups in practical equilibrium are precisely that the more closely a member's activity conforms to the norms the more interaction he receives from other members and the more liking choices he gets from them too. From these main propositions a number of others may be derived that also hold good.[11]

Yet we must ever remember that the truth of the proposition linking conformity to liking may on occasion be masked by the truth of other propositions. If, for instance, the man that conforms to the norms most closely also exerts some authority over the group, this may render liking for him somewhat less than it might otherwise have been.[12]

Be that as it may, I suggest that the laboratory experiments on influence imply propositions about the behavior of members of small groups, when the process of influence has worked itself out, that are identical with propositions that hold good of real-life groups in equilibrium. This is hardly surprising if all we mean by equilibrium is that all the change of which the system is, under present conditions, capable has been effected, so that no further change occurs. Nor would this be the first time that statics has turned out to be a special case of dynamics.

PROFIT AND SOCIAL CONTROL

Though I have treated equilibrium as an observed fact, it is a fact that cries for explanation. I shall not, as structural functional sociologists do, use an assumed equilibrium as a means of explaining, or trying to explain, why

the other features of a social system should be what they are. Rather, I shall take practical equilibrium as something that is itself to be explained by the other features of the system.

If every member of a group emits at the end of, and during a period of time much the same kinds of behavior and in much the same frequencies as he did at the beginning, the group is for that period in equilibrium. Let us then ask why any one member's behavior should persist. Suppose he is emitting behavior of value A_1. Why does he not let his behavior get worse (less valuable or reinforcing to the others) until it stands at $A_1 - \Delta A$? True, the sentiments expressed by others toward him are apt to decline in value (become less reinforcing to him), so that what he gets from them may be $S_1 - \Delta S$. But it is conceivable that, since most activity carries cost, a decline in the value of what he emits will mean a reduction in cost to him that more than offsets his losses in sentiment. Where, then, does he stabilize his behavior? This is the problem of social control.[13]

Mankind has always assumed that a person stabilizes his behavior, at least in the short run, at the point where he is doing the best he can for himself under the circumstances, though his best may not be a "rational" best, and what he can do may not be at all easy to specify, except that he is not apt to think like one of the theoretical antagonists in the *Theory of Games*. Before a sociologist rejects this answer out of hand for its horrid profit-seeking implications, he will do well to ask himself if he can offer any other answer to the question posed. I think he will find that he cannot. Yet experiments designed to test the truth of the answer are extraordinarily rare.

I shall review one that seems to me to provide a little support for the theory, though it was not meant to do so. The experiment is reported by H.B. Gerard, a member of the Festinger-Schachter team, under the title "The

Anchorage of Opinions in Face-to-Face Groups."[14] The experimenter formed artificial groups whose members met to discuss a case in industrial relations and to express their opinions about its probable outcome. The groups were of two kinds: high-attraction groups, whose members were told that they would like one another very much, and low-attraction groups, whose members were told that they would not find one another particularly likable.

At a later time the experimenter called the members in separately, asked them again to express their opinions on the outcome of the case, and counted the number that had changed their opinions to bring them into accord with those of other members of their groups. At the same time, a paid participant entered into a further discussion of the case with each member, always taking, on the probable outcome of the case, a position opposed to that taken by the bulk of the other members of the group to which the person belonged. The experimenter counted the number of persons shifting toward the opinion of the paid participant.

The experiment had many interesting results, from which I choose only those summed up in Tables 4.1 and 4.2. The three different agreement classes are made up of people who, at the original sessions, expressed different degrees of agreement with the opinions of other members of their groups. And the figure 44, for instance, means that, of all members of high-attraction groups whose initial opinions were strongly in disagreement with those of other members, 44 per cent shifted their opinion later toward that of others.

In these results the experimenter seems to have been interested only in the differences in the sums of the rows, which show that there is more shifting toward the group, and less shifting toward the paid participant, in the high-attraction than in the low-attraction condition. This is in line with a proposition suggested earlier. If you think that the members of a group can give you much—in this case, liking—you are apt to give them much—in this case, a change to an opinion in accordance with their views—or you will not get the liking. And, by the same token, if the group can give you little of value, you will not be ready to give it much of value. Indeed, you may change your opinion so as to depart from agreement even further, to move, that is, toward the view held by the paid participant.

So far so good, but, when I first scanned these tables, I was less struck by the difference between them than by their similarity. The

TABLE 4.1

Percentage of Subjects Changing toward Someone in the Group

	Agreement	Mild Disagreement	Strong Disagreement
High attraction	0	12	44
Low attraction	0	15	9

TABLE 4.2

Percentage of Subjects Changing toward the Paid Participant

	Agreement	Mild Disagreement	Strong Disagreement
High attraction	7	13	25
Low attraction	20	18	8

same classes of people in both tables showed much the same relative propensities to change their opinions, no matter whether the change was toward the group or toward the paid participant. We see, for instance, that those who change least are the high-attraction, agreement people and the low-attraction, strong-disagreement ones. And those who change most are the high-attraction, strong-disagreement people and the low-attraction, mild-disagreement ones.

How am I to interpret these particular results? Since the experimenter did not discuss them, I am free to offer my own explanation. The behavior emitted by the subjects is opinion and changes in opinion. For this behavior they have learned to expect two possible kinds of reinforcement. Agreement with the group gets the subject favorable sentiment (acceptance) from it, and the experiment was designed to give this reinforcement a higher value in the high-attraction condition than in the low-attraction one. The second kind of possible reinforcement is what I shall call the "maintenance of one's personal integrity," which a subject gets by sticking to his own opinion in the face of disagreement with the group. The experimenter does not mention this reward, but I cannot make sense of the results without something much like it. In different degrees for different subjects, depending on their initial positions, these rewards are in competition with one another: they are alternatives. They are not absolutely scarce goods, but some persons cannot get both at once.

Since the rewards are alternatives, let me introduce a familiar assumption from economics—that the cost of a particular course of action is the equivalent of the foregone value of an alternative[15]—and then add the definition: Profit = Reward – Cost.

Now consider the persons in the corresponding cells of the two tables. The behavior of the high-attraction, agreement people gets them much in the way of acceptance by the group, and for it they must give up little in the way of personal integrity, for their views are from the start in accord with those of the group. Their profit is high, and they are not prone to change their behavior. The low-attraction, strong-disagreement people are getting much in integrity, and they are not giving up for it much in valuable acceptance, for they are members of low-attraction groups. Reward less cost is high for them, too, and they change little. The high-attraction, strong-disagreement people are getting much in the way of integrity, but their costs in doing so are high, too, for they are in high-attraction groups and thus foregoing much valuable acceptance by the group. Their profit is low, and they are very apt to change, either toward the group or toward the paid participant, from whom they think, perhaps, they will get some acceptance while maintaining some integrity. The low-attraction, mild-disagreement people do not get much in the way of integrity, for they are only in mild disagreement with the group, but neither are they giving up much in acceptance, for they are members of low-attraction groups. Their rewards are low; their costs are low too, and their profit—the difference between the two—is also low. In their low profit they resemble the high-attraction, strong-disagreement people, and, like them, they are prone to change their opinions, in this case, more toward the paid participant. The subjects in the other two cells, who have medium profits, display medium propensities to change.

If we define profit as reward less cost, and if cost is value foregone, I suggest that we have here some evidence for the proposition that change in behavior is greatest when perceived profit is least. This constitutes no direct demonstration that change in behavior is least when profit is greatest, but if, whenever a man's behavior brought him a balance of reward and cost, he changed his behavior away from what got him, under the circumstances, the less profit, there might well come a time when his behavior would not change further. That is, his behavior would be stabilized, at least for the time being. And, so far as this were true for every member of a group, the group would have a social organization in equilibrium.

I do not say that a member would stabilize his behavior at the point of greatest conceivable profit to himself, because his profit is partly at the mercy of the behavior of others. It is a commonplace that the short-run pursuit of profit by several persons often lands them in positions where all are worse off than they might conceivably be. I do not say that the paths of behavioral change in which a member pursues his profit under the condition that others are pursuing theirs too are easy to describe or predict; and we can readily conceive that in jockeying for position they might never arrive at any equilibrium at all.

DISTRIBUTIVE JUSTICE

Yet practical equilibrium is often observed, and thus some further condition may make its attainment, under some circumstance, more probable than would the individual pursuit of profit left to itself. I can offer evidence for this further condition only in the behavior of subgroups and not in that of individuals. Suppose that there are two subgroups, working close together in a factory, the job of one being somewhat different from that of the other. And suppose that the members of the first complain and say: "We are getting the same pay as they are. We ought to get just a couple of dollars a week more to show that our work is more responsible." When you ask them what they mean by "more responsible," they say that, if they do their work wrong, more damage can result, and so they are under more pressure to take care.[16] Something

like this is a common feature of industrial behavior. It is at the heart of disputes not over absolute wages but over wage differentials—indeed, at the heart of disputes over rewards other than wages.

In what kind of proposition may we express observations like these? We may say that wages and responsibility give status in the group, in the sense that a man who takes high responsibility and gets high wages is admired, other things equal. Then, if the members of one group score higher on responsibility than do the members of another, there is a felt need on the part of the first to score higher on pay too. There is a pressure, which shows itself in complaints, to bring the *status factors,* as I have called them, into line with one another. If they are in line, a condition of *status congruence* is said to exist. In this condition the workers may find their jobs dull or irksome, but they will not complain about the relative position of groups.

But there may be a more illuminating way of looking at the matter. In my example I have considered only responsibility and pay, but these may be enough, for they represent the two kinds of thing that come into the problem. Pay is clearly a reward; responsibility may be looked on, less clearly, as a cost. It means constraint and worry—or peace of mind foregone. Then the proposition about status congruence becomes this: If the costs of the members of one group are higher than those of another, distributive justice requires that their rewards should be higher too. But the thing works both ways: If the rewards are higher, the costs should be higher too. This last is the theory of *noblesse oblige,* which we all subscribe to, though we all laugh at it, perhaps because the *noblesse* often fails to *oblige.* To put the matter in terms of profit: though the rewards and costs of two persons or the members of two groups may be different, yet the profits of the two—the excess of reward over cost—should tend to equality. And more than "should." The less-advantaged group will at least try to attain greater equality, as, in the example I have used, the first group tried to increase its profit by increasing its pay.

I have talked of distributive justice. Clearly, this is not the only condition determining the actual distribution of rewards and costs. At the same time, never tell me that notions of justice are not a strong influence on behavior, though we sociologists often neglect them. Distributive justice may be one of the conditions of group equilibrium.

EXCHANGE AND SOCIAL STRUCTURE

I shall end by reviewing almost the only study I am aware of that begins to show in detail how a stable and differentiated social structure in a real-life group might arise out of a process of exchange between members. This is Peter Blau's description of the behavior of sixteen agents in a federal law-enforcement agency.[17]

The agents had the duty of investigating firms and preparing reports on the firms' compliance with the law. Since the reports might lead to legal action against the firms, the agents had to prepare them carefully, in the proper form, and take strict account of the many regulations that might apply. The agents were often in doubt what they should do, and then they were supposed to take the question to their supervisor. This they were reluctant to do, for they naturally believed that thus confessing to him their inability to solve a problem would reflect on their competence, affect the official ratings he made of their work, and so hurt their chances for promotion. So agents often asked other agents for help and advice, and, though this was nominally forbidden, the supervisor usually let it pass.

Blau ascertained the ratings the supervisor made of the agents, and he also asked the agents to rate one another. The two opinions agreed closely. Fewer agents were regarded as highly competent than were regarded as of middle or low competence; competence, or the ability to solve technical problems, was a fairly scarce good. One or two of the more competent agents would not give help and advice when asked, and so received few interactions and little liking. A man that will not exchange, that will not give you what he has when you need it, will not get from you the only thing you are, in this case, able to give him in return, your regard.

But most of the more competent agents were willing to give help, and of them Blau says:

A consultation can be considered an exchange of values: both participants gain something, and both have to pay a price. The questioning agent is enabled to perform better than he could otherwise have done, without exposing his difficulties to his supervisor. By asking for advice, he implicitly pays his respect to the superior proficiency of his colleague. This acknowledgment of inferiority is the cost of receiving assistance. The consultant gains prestige, in return for which he is willing to devote some time to the consultation and permit it to disrupt his own work. The following remark of an agent illustrates this: "I like giving advice. It's flattering, I suppose, if you feel that others come to you for advice."[18]

Blau goes on to say: "All agents liked being consulted, but the value of any one of very many consultations became deflated for experts, and the price they paid in frequent interruptions became inflated."[19] This implies that, the more prestige an agent received, the less was the increment of value of that prestige; the more advice an agent gave, the greater was the increment of cost of that advice, the cost lying precisely in the foregone value of time to do his own work. Blau suggests that something of the same sort was true of an agent who went to a more competent colleague for advice: the more often he went, the more costly to him, in feelings of inferiority, became any further requests. "The repeated admission of his inability to solve his own problems . . . undermined the self-confidence of the worker and his standing in the group."[20]

The result was that the less competent agents went to the more competent ones for help less often than they might have done if the costs of repeated admissions of inferiority had been less high and that, while many agents sought out the few highly competent ones, no single agent sought out the latter much. Had they done so (to look at the exchange from the other side), the costs to the highly competent in interruptions to their own work would have become exorbitant. Yet the need of the less competent for help was still not fully satisfied. Under these circumstances they tended to turn for help to agents more nearly like themselves in competence. Though the help they got was not the most valuable, it was of a kind they could themselves return on occasion. With such agents they could exchange help and liking, without the exchange becoming on either side too great a confession of inferiority.

The highly competent agents tended to enter into exchanges, that is, to interact with many others. But, in the more equal exchanges I have just spoken of, less competent agents tended to pair off as partners. That is, they interacted with a smaller number of people, but interacted often with these few. I think I could show why pair relations in these more equal exchanges would be more economical for an agent than a wider distribution of favors. But perhaps I have gone far enough. The final pattern of this social structure was one in which a small number of highly competent agents exchanged advice for prestige with a large number of others less competent and in which the less competent agents exchanged, in pairs and in trios, both help and liking on more nearly equal terms.

Blau shows, then, that a social structure in equilibrium might be the result of a process of exchanging behavior rewarding and costly in different degrees, in which the increment of reward and cost varied with the frequency of the behavior, that is, with the frequency of interaction. Note that the behavior of the agents seems also to have satisfied my second condition of equilibrium: the more competent agents took more responsibility for the work, either their own or others', than did the less competent ones, but they also got more for it in the way of prestige. I suspect that the same kind of explanation could be given for the structure of many "informal" groups.

SUMMARY

The current job of theory in small-group research is to make the connection between experimental and real-life studies, to consolidate the propositions that empirically hold good in the two fields, and to show how these propositions might be derived from a still more general set. One way of doing this job would be to revive and make more rigorous the oldest of theories of social behavior—social behavior as exchange.

Some of the statements of such a theory might be the following. Social behavior is an exchange of goods, material goods but also non-material ones, such as the symbols of approval or prestige. Persons that give much to others try to get much from them, and persons that get much from others are under pressure to give much to them. This process of influence tends to work out at equilibrium to a balance in the exchanges. For a person engaged in exchange, what he gives may be a cost to him, just as what he gets may be a reward, and his behavior changes less as profit, that is, reward less cost, tends to a maximum. Not only does he seek a maximum for himself, but he tries to see to it that no one in his group makes more profit than he does. The cost and the value of what he gives and of what he gets vary with the quantity of what he gives and gets. It is surprising how familiar these propositions are; it is surprising, too, how propositions about the dynamics of exchange can begin to generate the static thing we call "group structure" and, in so doing, generate also some of the propositions about group structure that students of real-life groups have stated.

In our unguarded moments we sociologists find words like "reward" and "cost" slipping into what we say. Human nature will break in upon even our most elaborate theories. But we seldom let it have its way with us and follow up systematically what these words imply.[21] Of all our many "approaches" to social behavior, the one that sees it as an economy is the most neglected, and yet it is the one we use every moment of our lives—except when we write sociology.

NOTES

1. See R.R. Braithwaite, *Scientific Explanation* (Cambridge: Cambridge University Press, 1953).

2. Translated by I. Cunnison as *The Gift* (Glencoe, Ill.: Free press, 1954).

3. In social anthropology D.L. Oliver is working along these lines, and I owe much to him. See also T.M. Newcomb, "The Prediction of Interpersonal Attraction," *American Psychologist*, XI (1956), 575–86.

4. B.F. Skinner, *Science and Human Behavior* (New York: Macmillan Co., 1953).

5. Ibid., pp. 297–329. The discussion of "double contingency" by T. Parsons and E.A. Shils could easily lead to a similar paradigm (see *Toward a General Theory of Action* [Cambridge, Mass.: Harvard University Press. 1951], pp. 14–16).

6. K.W. Back, "The Exertion of Influence through Social Communication," in L. Festinger, K. Back, S. Schachter, H.H. Kelley, and J. Thibaut (eds.), *Theory and Experiment in Social Communication* (Ann Arbor: Research Center for Dynamics, University of Michigan, 1950), pp. 21–36.

7. S. Schachter, N. Ellerston, D. McBride, and D. Gregory, "An Experimental Study of Cohesiveness and Productivity," *Human Relations,* IV (1951), 229–38.

8. Skinner, op. cit., p. 100.

9. S. Schachter, "Deviation, Rejection, and Communication," *Journal of Abnormal and Social Psychology,* XI, VI (1951), 190–207.

10. L. Festinger, S. Schachter, and K. Back, *Social Pressures in Informal Groups* (New York: Harper & Bros., 1950), pp. 72–100.

11. For propositions holding good of groups in practical equilibrium see G.C. Homans, *The Human Group* (New York: Harcourt, Brace & Co., 1950), and H.W. Riecken and G.C. Homans, "Psychological Aspects of Social Structure," in G. Lindzey (ed.), *Handbook of Social Psychology* (Cambridge, Mass.: Addison-Wesley Publishing Co., 1954), II, 786–832.

12. See Homans, op. cit., pp. 244–48, and R.F. Bales, "The Equilibrium Problem in Small Groups," in A.P. Hare, E.F. Borgatta, and R.F. Bales (eds.), *Small Groups,* (New York: A.A. Knopf, 1953), pp. 450–56.

13. Homans, op cit., pp. 281–301.

14. *Human Relations,* VII (1954), 313–25.

15. G.J. Stigler, *The Theory of Price* (rev. ed.; New York: Macmillan Co., 1952), p. 99.

16. G.C. Homans, "Status among Clerical Workers," *Human Organization,* XII (1953), 5–10.

17. Peter M. Blau, *The Dynamics of Bureaucracy* (Chicago: University of Chicago Press, 1955), 99–116.

18. Ibid., p. 108.

19. Ibid., p. 108.

20. Ibid., p. 109.

21. *The White-Collar Job* (Ann Arbor: Survey Research Center, University of Michigan, 1953), pp. 115–27.

EQUITY THEORY AND RESEARCH:
AN OVERVIEW*

ELAINE HATFIELD

EQUITY: THE THEORY

Propositions I–IV

Equity theory is a strikingly simple theory. It is composed of four interlocking propositions:

PROPOSITION I: Individuals will try to maximize their outcomes (where outcomes equal rewards minus punishments).

PROPOSITION IIa: Groups (or rather the individuals comprising these groups) can maximize collective reward by evolving accepted systems for equitably apportioning resources among members. Thus, groups will evolve such systems of equity, and will attempt to induce members to accept and adhere to these systems.

PROPOSITION IIB: Groups will generally reward members who treat others equitably and generally punish members who treat each other inequitably.

*From H.H. Blumberg, A.P. Hare, V. Kent, and M. Davies, eds., *Small Groups and Social Interaction*, vol. 2 (New York: John Wiley and Sons, 1983), pp. 401–412. Reproduced by permission of John Wiley and Sons Limited.

PROPOSITION III: When individuals find themselves participating in inequitable relationships, they will become distressed. The more inequitable the relationship, the more distress they will feel.

PROPOSITION IV: Individuals who discover they are in inequitable relationships will attempt to eliminate their distress by restoring equity. The greater the inequity that exists, the more distress they will feel, and the harder they will try to restore equity. . . .

Who Decides Whether a Relationship Is Equitable?

According to the theory, equity is in the eye of the beholder. Observers' perceptions of how equitable a relationship is will depend on their assessment of the value and relevance of the participants' inputs and outcomes. If different observers assess participants' inputs and outcomes differently, and it is likely that they will, it is inevitable that they will disagree about whether or not a given relationship is equitable. For example, a wife—focusing on the fact that she works long hours, is trapped with no one to talk to all day, and is constantly engulfed by noise, mess, and confusion—may feel that her relative gains are extremely low. Her husband—focusing on the fact that she gets up in the morning whenever she pleases, and can see whom she wants, when she wants—may disagree; he thinks she "has it made." Moreover, an "objective" observer may calculate the couple's relative gains still differently.

The Psychological Consequences of Inequity

According to Proposition III, when individuals find themselves participating in inequitable relationships, they feel distress—regardless of whether they are the beneficiaries or the victims of inequity. The overbenefited may label their distress as guilt, dissonance, empathy, fear of retaliation, or conditioned anxiety. The underbenefited may label their distress as anger or resentment. Essentially, however, both the overbenefited and the underbenefited share certain feelings—they feel "distress" accompanied by physiological arousal (see Austin and Walster, 1974a, b).

Techniques by Which Individuals Reduce Their Distress

Proposition IV states that individuals who are distressed by their inequitable relations will try to eliminate such distress by restoring equity to their relationship. There are only two ways by which participants can restore *actual equity*—by altering their own or their partners' relative gains. For example, imagine that an unskilled laborer discovers that a contractor has been paying him less than the minimum wage. He can re-establish actual equity in four different ways: he can neglect his work (thus lowering his inputs); he can start his work (thus lowering his inputs); he can start

to steal equipment from the company (thus raising his own outcomes); he can make mistakes so that the contractor will have to work far into the night undoing what he has done (thus raising the employer's inputs); or he can damage company equipment (thus lowering the contractor's outcomes). (The ingenious ways people contrive to bring equity to inequitable relationships are documented by Adams, 1965.)

Participants can restore *psychological equity* to their relationship by changing their perceptions of the situation. They can try to convince themselves and others that the inequitable relationship is, in fact, perfectly fair. For example, suppose that the exploitative contractor starts to feel guilty about underpaying his unskilled laborers. He can try to convince himself that his relationship is equitable in four ways: he can restore psychological equity by minimizing his workers' inputs ("You wouldn't believe how useless they are"); by exaggerating his own inputs ("Without my creative genius the company would fall apart"); by exaggerating his workers' outcomes ("They really work for the variety the job provides"); or by minimizing his own outcomes ("The tension on this job is giving me an ulcer").

Actual versus Psychological Equity Restoration

At this point, equity theorists confront a crucial question: Can one specify when people will try to restore actual equity to their relationships, versus when they will settle for restoring psychological equity? From Equity theory's Propositions I and IV, one can make a straightforward derivation: people may be expected to follow a cost–benefit strategy in deciding how they will respond to perceived inequity. Whether individuals respond to injustice by attempting to restore actual equity, by distorting reality, or by doing a little of both has been found to depend on costs and benefits participants think they will derive from each strategy (see Berscheid and Walster, 1967; Berscheid et al., 1969; or Weick and Nesset, 1968).

EQUITY: THE RESEARCH

Researchers have applied the Equity framework to four major areas of human interaction—exploiter/victim relationships, philanthropist/recipient relationships, business relationships, and intimate relationships. (See Walster et al., 1978; Hatfield and Traupmann, 1980 for review of this voluminous research.)

Let us consider a sampling of the kind of research that Equity theorists have conducted in the first of these areas—exploiter/victim relationships.

Exploiter/Victim Relationships

People have always been concerned with promoting social justice. It is not surprising, then, that early Equity theorists, who could have begun by investigating any of the four Equity propositions, in fact, focused on a single question: "How do exploiters and their victims respond to injustice?"

Definition of terms. Researchers began by defining terms. They defined *exploiters* (or *harm-doers*) as "People who commit acts that cause their relative gains to exceed their partners'." The *exploited* (or *victims*) are "People whose relative gains fall short of their partners'."

Reactions of exploiters and their victims to inequity. (a) *Distress:* According to Equity theory (see Hatfield et al., 1979):

Proposition III: When individuals find themselves participating in inequitable relationships, they will become distressed. The more inequitable the relationship, the more distress they will feel. (p. 101)

According to the theory, then, any time people take more than they deserve ... or accept less, they should feel distress. On first glance one might think that people who receive far more than they deserve should be delighted, not distressed. The theory, however, predicts that they will feel both delight at receiving such a large reward ... mixed with the distress they feel at finding themselves caught up in an inequitable relationship. If inequitable relationships are distressing to exploiters, they should be doubly distressing to their victims. ...

Compelling evidence exists to support the contention that both exploiters and their victims *do* feel intense distress after an inequitable exchange. (See Austin and Walster, 1974a, b; Walster et al., 1978; and Utne et al., 1984, for a review of this research.) In one study, for example, Austin and Walster (1974b) investigated workers' cognitive, affective, and physiological reactions to equity and inequity. They tested the dual predictions that (1) workers will be more content (and less distressed) when they are fairly rewarded than when they are either over-rewarded or under-rewarded. Further (2) participants will be less distressed when they are over-rewarded than when they are under-rewarded.

Austin invited college students to participate in a psychological study of decision making. Each student was assigned to work on a task with a partner (actually an experimental accomplice). A third student (also an experimental accomplice) was designated "decision maker" and told to pay the two students on the basis of their task performance. Since both students performed equally well, the "decision" should have been a simple one—each student should have received $2.00. Sometimes, the decision maker did pay the student an equitable $2.00. Sometimes, however, by prearrangement, he did the unexpected: sometimes he overpaid her (i.e. gave her $3.00; $1.00 more than she deserved); other times he underpaid her (i.e. gave her $1.00; $1.00 less than she deserved). The student was then quizzed about how she felt about the way she had been treated. As predicted, equitably paid students were more cognitively and emotionally content than either overpaid or underpaid individuals. Also as predicted, overbenefited students were more content than underbenefited ones. The women who received $1.00 more than they deserved were slightly upset, those who received $1.00 less than they deserved were extremely upset.

Physiological data tended to substantiate the women's reports of how they felt about the decision. *Galvanic Skin Response* measures revealed that equitably treated workers were the most tranquil. Overbenefited women were slightly aroused; deprived women were even more aroused. (Additional evidence in support of this contention comes from Austin and Walster, 1974a, b; Walster et al., 1978; Hatfield and Traupmann, 1980; and Utne et al., 1984.)

(b) *Restoration of Equity:* According to Equity theory (see Hatfield et al., 1979):

Proposition IV: Individuals who discover they are in inequitable relationships will attempt to eliminate their distress by restoring equity. The greater the inequity that exists, the more distress they will feel, and the harder they will try to restore equity. (p. 101)

Theoretically, an exploiter/victim could be taught to perform *any* action that reduces his or her anxiety. Aronfreed (1961) has demonstrated the wide variety of ways transgressors can learn to reduce their anxiety: they may find relief by confessing their sins, in self-criticism, by apologizing and making reparation to their victim, or in promising to modify their future behavior.

When we look at exploiters'/victims' be-havior, however, we find that two classes of responses seem to occur most commonly (perhaps because they reduce anxiety most effectively). There is compelling evidence to support the Proposition IV contention that exploiters and victims try to eliminate their distress by restoring either actual or psychological equity to their relationships.

Restoration of actual equity. People can restore actual equity to a relationship in a straightforward way—exploiters can compensate their victims; victims can insist on restitution. Cynics such as Junius have acidly observed that even "a death bed repentance seldom reaches to restitution." Such pessimism is not always warranted. Recent studies verify the fact that *harm-doers often do voluntarily compensate their victims* (see, for example, Berscheid and Walster, 1967; Berscheid et al., 1969; Brock and Becker, 1966; Carlsmith and Gross, 1969; Freedman et al., 1967; Walster and Prestholdt, 1966; Walster et al., 1970).

Demands for compensation. Undoubtedly the victim's first response to exploitation is to seek restitution (see Leventhal and Bergman, 1969, and Marwell et al., 1970). If victims secure compensation, they have "set things right" and benefited materially. It is easy to see why this is a popular response.

Restoration of psychological equity. As we noted earlier, people can restore equity in a second way—they can distort reality and convince themselves that their unjust relationship is, in fact, perfectly fair. If exploiters and victims can minimize the exploiter's relative gains, or can aggrandize the victim's gains, they can convince themselves and perhaps others that their relationship is, in fact, equitable. Some distortions that harm-doers and victims use include: blaming the victim, minimization of the victim's suffering, or denial of responsibility for the victim's suffering.

Let us focus first on the exploiter's responses:

Blaming the victim. It is not unfair to exploit others if they deserve to be exploited. Thus, an obvious way by which exploiters can persuade themselves that their acts were equitable is by devaluing their victim's inputs. That harm-doers will often derogate their victims has been demonstrated by a number of researchers (see Berkowitz, 1962; Davidson, 1964; Davis and Jones, 1960; Glass, 1964; Katz et al., 1973, Sykes and Matza, 1957; and Walster and Prestholdt, 1966). In a typical experiment, Davis and Jones (1960) found that students who were recruited to insult other students, as part of a research project, generally ended up convincing themselves that the students deserved to be ridiculed. Sykes and Matza (1957) found that juvenile delinquents often defended their victimization of others by arguing that their victims are really homosexuals, bums, or possess other traits that make them deserving of punishment. In tormenting others, then, the delinquents can claim to be the restorers of justice rather than harm-doers.

Minimization of the victim's suffering. If exploiters can deny that their victims were harmed, they can convince themselves that their relationship with the victim is an equitable one. Sykes and Matza (1957) and Brock and Buss (1962) demonstrate that harm-doers will consistently underestimate how much harm they have done to another. Brock and Buss, for example, found that college students who administer electric shock to other students soon come to underestimate markedly the painfulness of the shock.

Denial of responsibility for the act. If exploiters can convince themselves that it was not their own behavior, but rather the action of someone else (e.g. the experimenter or fate) that caused the victim's suffering, then their relationship with the victim becomes an equitable one. (The person who is unjustly assigned responsibility for reducing the victim's outcomes will now be perceived as the harm doer, and it will be this third party's relationship with the victim, not the original harm-doer's relationship, that is perceived as inequitable.)

That harm-doers will often deny their responsibility for harm-doing has been documented by Sykes and Matza (1957) and by Brock and Buss (1962, 1964). In daily life, the denial of responsibility seems to be a favorite strategy of those who are made to feel guilty about exploiting others. War criminals protest vehemently that they were "only following orders."

But, it is not just exploiters who justify their unjust acts. Victims, too, have been found to justify their own exploitation. Sometimes, victims find that it is impossible to elicit restitution. Under such circumstances, the impotent victims are then left with only two options—they can acknowledge the exploitations and their inability to do anything about it, or they can justify their own exploitation. Often, victimized individuals find it less upsetting to distort reality and justify their victimization than to acknowledge that the world is unjust and that they are too impotent to elicit fair treatment (see Lerner and Matthews, 1967).

Victimized individuals have been found to restore psychological equity to the exploiter/victim relationship in several ways:

Concluding it was all for the best. Sometimes victims console themselves by imagining that they were not really exploited, or by insisting that exploitation has brought compensating benefits. For example, there is evidence that when things are arranged so that people cannot win, they often convince themselves that they do not want to win. For example, Solomon (1957) set up an experimental game. A powerful player treated some players benevolently (benefiting them whenever he could) and others malevolently (depriving them whenever he could). As we would expect, the benefited players were more content than the frustrated ones. More interestingly, the players who were treated benevolently attached far more importance to doing well in the game than did the malevolently treated ones.

It will all come out in the wash. Sometimes victims console themselves by concluding that in the long run the exploiter will be punished as he deserves ("The mill of the Lord grinds slowly, but it grinds exceedingly fine").

He who has deserves to get. Or, victims may convince themselves that their exploiters actually deserved the enormous benefits they received. Recent data demonstrate that the exploited are inclined to justify their exploiter's excessive benefits. Jecker and Landy (1969), Walster and Prestholdt (1966), and Hastorf and Regan (personal communication, 1962) pressured individuals into performing a difficult favor for an unworthy recipient. They found that the abashed favor-doers tried to justify the inequity by convincing themselves that the recipient was especially needy or worthy.

Reformers who work to alleviate social injustice are often enraged to discover that the exploited themselves are sometimes vehement defenders of the status quo. Black militants encounter "Uncle Toms" who defend white supremacy. Women's liberation groups lobbying for the Equal Rights Amendment must face angry housewives who threaten to defend to death the inferior status of women. Reformers might have more sympathy for such "Uncle Toms" if they understood the psychological underpinnings of such reactions. When one is treated inequitably, but has no hope of altering the situation, denying reality is often less degrading than facing up to one's humiliating position.

SUMMARY

The Theory

Equity theorists agree that people try to maximize their outcomes (Proposition I). A group of individuals can maximize its collective outcomes by devising an equitable system for sharing resources. Thus, groups try to induce members to behave equitably: that is, they try to ensure that all participants receive equal relative outcomes.

They can do this in only one way: by making it more profitable to be good than to be greedy. They can reward members who behave equitably and punish members who behave inequitably (Proposition II). When socialized persons find themselves enmeshed in inequitable relationships, they experience distress (Proposition III) and are motivated to reduce such distress either by restoring actual equity or by restoring psychological equity to their relationships (Proposition IV).

The Data

Equity theorists have collected evidence in support of Proposition III, namely, they have shown that:

1. Men and women feel most content when they are engaged in equitable relationships. Both the overbenefited and the underbenefited feel ill at ease. The more inequitable the relationship, the more uncomfortable participants feel. Participants are less distressed by inequity when they gain from it than when they lose from it.
2. People who discover they are in an inequitable relationship (and become distressed) try to reduce their distress by restoring either actual equity or psychological equity to their relationships.

Cynics have expressed skepticism that exploiters will voluntarily compensate their victims to restore equity . . . but the data suggest that they often do. It probably comes as no surprise that victims are generally eager to be compensated.

If compensation does not occur, both exploiter and victim have been found to restore psychological equity by aggrandizing the exploiter, minimizing the victim's suffering, or assuming that some outside power will intervene and set things right.

REFERENCES

ADAMS, J.S. (1965). "Inequity in social exchange," in L. Berkowitz (ed.), *Advances in Experimental Social Psychology*, Vol. II, pp. 267–299, Academic Press, New York.

ARONFREED, J. (1961). "The nature, variety and social patterning of moral responses to transgression." *Journal of Abnormal and Social Psychology*, 63, 223–240.

AUSTIN, W., AND WALSTER, E. (1974a). "Participants' reactions to 'Equity with the World'," *Journal of Experimental Social Psychology*, 10, 528–548.

AUSTIN, W., AND WALSTER, E. (1974b). "Reactions to confirmations and disconfirmations of expectancies of equity and inequity," *Journal of Personality and Social Psychology*, 30, 208–216.

BERKOWITZ, L. (1962). *Aggression: A Social Psychological Analysis*, McGraw-Hill, New York.

BERSCHEID, E., AND WALSTER, E. (1967). "When does a harm-doer compensate a victim?" *Journal of Personality and Social Psychology*, 6, 435–441.

BERSCHEID, E., WALSTER, E., AND BARCLAY, A. (1969). "Effect of time on tendency to compensate a victim," *Psychological Reports*, 25, 431–436.

BROCK, T.C., AND BECKER, L. (1966). "Debriefing and susceptibility to subsequent experimental manipulations," *Journal of Experimental Social Psychology*, 2, 314–323.

BROCK, T.C. AND BUSS, A.H. (1962). "Dissonance, aggression and evaluation of pain," *Journal of Abnormal and Social Psychology*, 65, 197–202.

BROCK, T.C., AND BUSS, A.H. (1964). "Effects of justification for aggression in communication with the victim on post-aggression dissonance," *Journal of Abnormal and Social Psychology*, 68, 403–412.

CARLSMITH, J.M., AND GROSS, A.E. (1969). "Some effects of guilt on compliance," *Journal of Personality and Social Psychology*, 11, 232–239.

DAVIDSON, J. (1964). "Cognitive familiarity and dissonance reduction," in L. Festinger (ed.), *Conflict, Decision, and Dissonance*, pp. 45–60, Stanford University Press, Stanford, Calif.

DAVIS, K.E., AND JONES, E.E. (1960). "Changes in interpersonal perception as a means of reducing cognitive dissonance," *Journal of Abnormal and Social Psychology*, 61, 402–410.

FREEDMAN, J.L., WALLINGTON, S.A., AND BLESS, E. (1967). "Compliance without pressure: The effect of guilt," *Journal of Personality and Social Psychology*, 7, 117–124.

GLASS, D.C. (1964). "Changes in liking as a means of reducing cognitive discrepancies between self-esteem and aggression," *Journal of Personality*, 32, 520–549.

HATFIELD, E., AND TRAUPMANN, J. (1980). "Intimate relationships: A perspective from Equity theory," in Steve Duck and Robin Gilmour (eds.), *Personal Relationships I: Studying Personal Relationships*, pp. 165–178, Academic Press, London.

HATFIELD, E., UTNE, M.K., AND TRAUPMANN, J. (1979). "Equity theory and intimate relationships," in Robert L. Burgess and Ted L. Huston (eds.), *Social Exchange in Developing Relationships*, pp. 99–133, Academic Press, New York.

JECKER, J., AND LANDY, D. (1969). "Liking a person as a function of doing him a favor," *Human Relations*, 22, 371–378.

KATZ, I., GLASS, D.D., AND COHEN, S. (1973). "Ambivalence, guilt, and the scapegoating of minority group victims," *Journal of Experimental Social Psychology*, 9, 432–436.

LERNER, M.J., AND MATTHEWS, GALE (1967). "Reactions to the suffering of others under conditions of indirect responsibility," *Journal of Personality and Social Psychology*, 5, 319–325.

LEVENTHAL, G.S., AND BERGMAN, J.T. (1969). "Self-depriving behavior as a response to unprofitable inequity," *Journal of Experimental Social Psychology*, 5, 153–171.

MARWELL, G., SCHMITT, D.R. AND SHOTOLA, R. (1970). "Sex differences in a cooperative task," *Behavioral Science*, 15, 184–186.

SOLOMON, L. (1957). "The influence of some types of power relationships and motivational treatments upon the development of interpersonal trust," Research Center for Human Relations, New York University, New York.

SYKES, G.M., AND MATZA, D. (1957). "Techniques

of neutralization: A theory of delinquency," *American Sociological Review*, 22, 664–670.

UTNE, M.K., HATFIELD, E., TRAUPMANN, J., AND GREENBERGER, D. (1984). "Equity, marital satisfaction and stability," *Journal of Social and Personal Relationships*, 1, 323–32

WALSTER, E., BERSCHEID, E., and WALSTER, G.W. (1970). "The exploited: Justice or justification?" in J. Macaulay and L. Berkowitz (eds.), *Altruism and Helping Behavior*, pp. 179–204, Academic Press, New York.

WALSTER, E., AND PRESTHOLDT, P. (1966). "The effect of misjudging another: Overcompensation or dissonance reduction?" *Journal of Experimental Social Psychology*, 2, 85–97.

WALSTER, E., WALSTER, G.W., AND BERSCHEID, E. (1978). *Equity: Theory and Research*, Allyn and Bacon, Boston.

WEICK, K.E., and NESSET, B. (1968). "Preferences among forms of equity," *Organizational Behavior and Human Performance*, 3, 400–416.

EXCHANGE THEORY:
CRITIQUE FROM A FEMINIST STANDPOINT*

NANCY C. M. HARTSOCK

Market models are widely popular among analysts of social life. Some have attempted to explain politics by means of the model of the market (Downs, 1957; Buchanan and Tullock, 1965). Others have argued that the behavior of elected officials is best understood on the model of money-seekers in the market (Mayhew, 1974). The model appears as well in such disparate locations as studies of family violence, sexual relations, and the construction of kinship (Goode, 1971; Allen and Strauss, 1980; Vance, 1980; Lévi-Strauss, 1969).

I have argued elsewhere that the popularity of these models is due to the fact that we live in a society in which the market is a central institution, and that taking the market as the most important social institution expresses the reality of only the ruling economic class (Hartsock, 1983; Part I). Here, however, I want to argue that theories such as

this also operate from the experience of a group privileged by gender. I will argue that the use of this experience as the basis of a social theory both justifies and obscures relations of gender domination.

I can best support this claim by examining the most explicit and well-worked-out of the theories which treat social life on the model of the market—those which claim that all social behavior should be seen as an exchange of goods. Homans and Blau have been identified as two of the most central theorists in this tradition (Hingers and Willer, 1979:170). In their work, the assumptions of exchange as a model for social life are explicit and the consequences of this theoretical choice are most apparent.

My remarks here are not intended to constitute a balanced or complete analysis of the work of either scholar, nor do I wish to involve myself in the many polemical debates about their work. My interest here is simply to follow out the logic of the exchange theories they put forward in order to: (1) describe the fundamental features of exchange as they un-

*From Scott G. McNall, ed., *Current Perspectives in Social Theory*, vol. 6 (Greenwich, CT: JAI Press, 1985), pp. 57–70. Reprinted with permission of JAI Press, Inc.

derstand it; and, (2) examine the theoretical consequences of the market model, and thereby to highlight its gender assumptions.

EXCHANGE THEORIES: CONCEPTIONS OF COMMUNITY

Blau and Homans take commodity exchange in a capitalist economy as their model for social theory. Use of this model points to the theoretical conclusion that competition in exchange results in relations of domination. At the same time these theories legitimize this domination either by denying it or by treating it as inevitable but unimportant. David Baldwin has explicitly remarked on this property of exchange: because "exchange relations . . . tend to be depicted as cooperative, positive, beneficial, voluntary, and pleasant," such a focus would emphasize the relational and reciprocal nature of power relations rather than their hierarchical and asymmetrical nature and would decrease the tendency to view power relations as "conflictual, negative, and exploitative, coercive, and unpleasant from the standpoint of the one who is influenced" (Baldwin, 1978:1240–1241). The utility of exchange theory is further illustrated by the fact that Baldwin went on to construct a situation in which the statement, "your money or your life" could be viewed as other than coercive.

The basic assumptions of exchange theory are nowhere more boldly stated than by Homans. Social behavior, he argues, is an exchange of goods, both material and non-material. It is a set of interactions which tends to work out to a balance. What each person gives "may be a cost to him, just as what he gets may be a reward, and his behavior changes less as profit, that is, reward less cost, tends to a maximum. It is surprising how familiar these propositions are. . . . Human nature will break in upon even our most elaborate theories. Of all our many 'approaches' to social

behavior, the one that sees it as an economy is the most neglected, and yet it is the one we use every moment of our lives—except when we write sociology" (1958:606).

Homans has taken rational economic man out of the realm of economics and molded him into man in general. He reiterates many assumptions made by neoclassical economists. He ignores the institutions in which his actors are embedded and focuses instead on the interaction between Person and Other— two individuals who meet in a disembodied transaction independent of social structure, based only on mutual desire. Because their desire is mutual, they are assumed to be equals. Indeed, when Homans considers power, he suggests that in repeated exchanges "power differences tend to disappear," thus once again reinforcing his postulate of human equality (1967, cited in Zeitlin, 1973:7–8).

Second, Homans' rational economic men engage only in the production and consumption of help and social approval. Even their tasks and positions in the office hierarchy are ignored. Because each individual is assumed to be equal to every other, each unit of approval is exactly equal to every other, no matter who gives or receives it. Perhaps most important, since both parties gain, no one can be said to be exploited in any reasonable sense. Thus, exchange behavior represents an uncoerced choice. The mutual interdependence of assumption and conclusion is obvious: Exchange is voluntarily engaged in, and therefore must be mutually profitable and nonexploitative.

But at the same time, the account of human interaction they represent indicates the centrality of conflict. As Homans summarizes it, "conflict lies at the marrow of our view of human behavior. . . ." (1961:57). The situation Homans constructed between Person and Other both reveals this fundamental conflict and underscores the fact that it is inherent in the interaction based on mutual gain. Despite the interdependence of Person and Other, the latter remains Other—someone to whom Person has only instrumental and extrinsic ties and to whom he relates only to gain his own ends. Thus Homans' account of the situation emphasizes the extent to which community is problematic for him: It represents the fundamental dilemma to be resolved. His attempt at a solution, however, makes clear that the conflict between buyer and seller, the prototype for all human interaction, blocks the creation of a strong and lasting community.

Blau's more sophisticated account of social exchange and the nature of power explicitly differentiates social from economic exchange. Thus, his analysis is not open to some of the more obvious objections that may be lodged against those who take economic behavior as the model for all human action. Blau defines exchange behavior as behavior directed toward ends achievable only through interaction with other persons (rather than the natural world) and aimed at eliciting rewarding reactions. Moreover, this behavior must employ appropriate means to these ends; irrational conduct is excluded, but expressive, goal-oriented actions are included, since he characterizes social exchange as lying midway between economic exchange and the diffuse and intrinsic rewards of a love relationship (1964:5, 95, 112). In addition, his work is especially useful because he is explicitly concerned both with the creation of community and with what he seems to see as the inevitably concomitant formation of patterns of dominance.

He, unlike Homans, recognizes that communities have emergent properties that are not commensurate with the properties of individuals. Indeed, in his view, the utility of the concept of exchange is that it directs attention to precisely this feature of social life (1964:3–4). Blau's analysis expands, strength-ens, and makes more plausible the account of social relations as exchange. He moves from a simple model of individual exchange to one in which exchange and competition for scarce goods lead to class differentiation and even the accumulation of capital, a model in which one group provides continuous services to the other in return for dependence and future compliance. His work, then, can be very useful in demonstrating how the conflict and competition embodied in relations of exchange lead to the systematic appropriation of the resources of some by others.

The characteristics of social exchange appear in striking form in Blau's extraordinary discussion of the courtship market. In it, we meet isolated individuals associating on a voluntary basis for the purpose of mutual gain. Blau, operating of course from the masculine perspective, notes that when a man makes a decision to associate with a woman, he engages in comparison shopping by comparing her traits to those of other females—their "looks, and their charm, their supportiveness, and the congeniality of their emotional makeup" (1964:31, 35). The "love object's" popularity with other men functions as a kind of market pricing system (1964:79).

The commodities exchanged in the courtship market are "sexual gratification" and "firm commitments," (presumably marriage). Conflicting interests are present, since the girl wants to keep the price of sexual favors high and the boy wants to obtain sexual gratification at the lowest possible price. She withholds sex to create a scarcity, but in the end, must deliver the goods in return for proper payment. Blau holds, then, that if most girls kissed boys on the first date, and offered sexual favors soon afterward, they would "depreciate the price of these rewards in the community, making it difficult for a girl to use the promise of sexual intercourse to elicit a firm commitment from a boy. . . " (1964:80).

Most of the features of the neo-classical economist's account of rational economic man and his world are clearly present in this account. The actors are isolated individuals; they come together in the context of unspecified social institutions that appear to set no limits on the forms of their interactions; they join together voluntarily—indeed, Blau's definition of social exchange rules out involuntary relations—and meet in an atmosphere of mutual distrust for the purpose of maximum individual gain.

The circulating medium—whether money, social approval, or sexual gratification (though probably not firm commitments)—is the translator and bearer of the relation between the individuals involved in the exchange. In the market, the Other's status as Other is maintained. Both solidarity and rivalry play important roles, and community is only the by-product of actions directed at disparate ends. Although the fundamental interests of the participants conflict, each has a common interest in maintaining the association. As Blau has tellingly put it, their last choices are identical, but the first choice of each is the second last of the other (1964:114). Each wants to strike the best bargain, but since both want to complete the transaction, their last choices are identical. In such a community the paradigmatic connections between people are instrumental, or extrinsic and conflictual, and relations of competition and domination come to be substitutes for a more substantial and encompassing community. It is in such a false community that the very social character of activity can appear as something alien and puzzling. And individuals can appear to be subordinated to social relations "which subsist independently of them and which arise out of collisions of mutually indifferent individuals" (Marx, 1973:157).

Marx's sarcastic summary of the classical economists' account of relations in the market highlights all these features of exchange theory. The market

. . . is in fact a very Eden of the innate rights of man. There alone rule Freedom, Equality, Property, and Bentham. Freedom, because both buyer and seller of a commodity, say of labour-power, are constrained only by their own free will. They contract as free agents, and the agreement they come to is but the form in which they give legal expression to the other, as with a simple owner of commodities, and they exchange equivalent for equivalent. Property, because each looks only to himself. The only force that brings them together and puts them in relation with each other, is the selfishness, the gain and the private interests of each. Each looks to himself only, and no one troubles himself about the rest, and just because they do so, do they all, in accordance with the pre-established harmony of things, or under the auspices of an all-shrewd providence, work together for their mutual advantage, for the common wealth, and in the interest of all (Marx, 1967: 176).

One can raise a large number of questions about this account and those given by Homans and Blau. Here however I want to ask a different question—one similar to that posed by Marx himself, who noted that on leaving Eden and on moving into the realm of production, one notices a change in the appearance of the actors. "He who before was the money-owner, now strides in front as capitalist; the possessor of labour power follows as his labourer. The one with an air of importance, smirking, intent on business; the other timid and holding back, like one who is bringing his own hide to market and has nothing to expect but—a hiding" (Marx, 1967:176). I propose to leave the Eden of the market in company of a different actor, the female participant in the courtship market who has exchanged "sexual gratification" for "firm commitments." And rather than follow capitalist and worker into the factory, let us follow them home at the end of the day. Our female participant in the courtship market may of course have spent her day at work for wages, but on leaving the sphere of production, we once again see a change in the appearance of the actors. He who before followed behind as worker now strides in front, while she now follows timidly behind, carrying groceries, baby, and diapers.

Marx argued forcefully and persuasively that humans are not what they eat but what they do, especially what they do in the course of producing subsistence. Moreover, each means of producing subsistence can be expected to carry with it both social relations and relations to the world of nature that express the social understanding contained in that mode of production. Given the systematically divergent practical activities of workers and capitalists, one should expect the growth of logically divergent world views. Here I propose to explore both the nature of women's activities and to develop the critique of exchange theory women's life activities can generate.

THE FEMINIST STANDPOINT AND THE SEXUAL DIVISION OF LABOR

Let us begin by noticing that women's lives differ structurally from those of men, that the categories developed from men's experience frequently do not work for women.

Women's work in every society differs systematically from men's. And if Marx was right that existence produces consciousness, then on the basis of an account of the sexual division of labor, one should be able to begin to explore the oppositions and differences between women's and men's activity and their consequences for consciousness. Here, on the basis of a schematic and simplified account of the sexual division of labor, I sketch out a kind of ideal type of the social relations and world view characteristic of men's and women's activity in order to explore the epistemology and assumptions contained in the institutionalized sexual division of labor.

Women's activity as institutionalized in the West has a double aspect: their contribution to subsistence and their contribution to childrearing. Whether or not all women do both, women as a sex are institutionally responsible for producing both goods and human beings, and all women are expected to become the kinds of persons who can do both. In capitalism, women contribute both production for wages and production of goods in the home.

There are similarities with the work of some men, but also important differences. First, women as a group work more than men We are all familiar with the phenomenon of the "double day," and with indications that women work many more hours per week than men. Second, a larger proportion of women's labor time is devoted to the production of use values than men's. Only some of the goods women produce are commodities (however much they live in a society structured by commodity production and exchange).

Thus the man, in the process of production, is involved in contact with necessity and interchange with nature as well as with other human beings, but the process of production or work does not consume his whole life. The activity of a woman in the home as well as the work she does for wages keeps her continually in contact with a world of qualities and change. Her immersion in the world of use—in concrete, many-qualitied, changing material processes—is more complete than his. And if life itself consists of sensuous activity, the vantage point available to women on the basis of their contribution to subsistence represents an intensification and deepening of the materialist world view available to the producers of commodities in capitalism, in fact an intensification of class consciousness. The availability of this outlook to even nonworking-class women has been strikingly formulated by the novelist Marilyn French: "Washing the toilet used by three males, and the floor and walls around it, is, Mira thought, coming face to face with necessity. And that is why women were saner than men, did not come up with the mad, absurd schemes men developed: they were in touch with necessity, they had to wash the toilet bowl and floor" (1978:214).

Women's contribution to subsistence, however, represents only a part of women's labor. Women also produce/reproduce men (and other women) on both a daily and a long-term basis. This aspect of women's "production" exposes the deep inadequacies of the concept of production as a description of women's activity. Much more than production is involved; their activity cannot easily be dichotomized into play or work. Helping another to develop, the gradual relinquishing of control, the experiencing of the human limits of one's actions—all these are important features of women's activity as mothers. Women, as mothers, even more than as workers, are institutionally involved in processes of change and growth, and more than workers, must understand the importance of avoiding excessive control in order to help others grow. The activity involved is far more complex than instrumentally working with others to transform objects. (Interestingly, much of women's wage work—nursing, social work, and some secretarial jobs in particular—requires and depends on the relational and interpersonal skills women learned through being mothered by someone of the same sex.)

It is here that the opposition between feminist and masculinist experience and outlook is most clearly rooted, and it is here that features of the proletarian vision are enhanced and modified for the woman and diluted for the man. Women's experience in reproduction represents a unity with nature that goes beyond the worker's experience of interchange with nature. As Mary O'Brien has put it "reproductive labor might be said to combine the functions of the architect and the bee: Like the architect, parturitive woman

knows what she is doing; like the bee, she cannot help what she is doing." And just as the worker's acting on the eternal world changes both the world and the worker's nature, so too "a new life changes the world and the consciousness of the woman" (1978:108). In addition, in the process of producing human beings, relations with others may take a variety of forms with deeper significance than simple cooperation with others for common goals—forms that range from a deep unity with another through the many-leveled and changing connections mothers experience with growing children.

Motherhood in the large sense, that is, motherhood as an institution rather than an experience, including pregnancy and the preparation for motherhood almost all female children receive in being raised by a woman, results in the construction of female existence as centered within a complex relational nexus. In turn, the fact that women but not men are primarily responsible for young children means that the infant first experiences itself as not fully differentiated from the mother and then as an I in relation to an It that it later comes to know as female. Chodorow and Flax have argued that the object-relations school of psychoanalytic theory puts forward a materialist psychology, much of it compatible with a Marxian account of social relations. According to object-relations theory, the process of differentiation from a woman by both boys and girls reinforces boundary confusion in women's egos and boundary strengthening in men's. Individuation is far more conflictual for male than for female children, in part because both mother and son experience the other as a definite "other" (Chodorow, 1978:105–109).

The complex relational world inhabited by women has its start in the experience and resolution of the oedipal crisis, cleanly resolved for the boy, whereas the girl is much more likely to retain both parents as love objects.

The nature of the crisis itself differs by sex: The boy's love for the mother is an extension of mother-infant unity and thus essentially threatening to his ego and independence. In contrast, the girl's love for the father is less threatening both because it occurs outside this unity and because it occurs at a later stage of development. For boys, the central issue to be resolved concerns gender identification; for girls, the issue is psychosexual development (Chodorow, 1978:127–131, 163). Chodorow concludes that girls' gradual emergence from the oedipal period takes place in such a way that empathy is built into their primary definition of self, and they have a variety of capacities for experiencing another's needs or feelings as their own (1978:166).

The more complex female relational world is reinforced by the process of socialization. Girls learn roles from watching their mothers; boys must learn roles from rules that structure the life of an absent male figure. Girls can identify with a concrete example present in daily life; boys must identify with an abstract set of maxims only occasionally concretely present in the form of the father. As a result, masculinity is idealized for boys, whereas femininity is concrete for girls (1978: 174–178). Women and men, then, grow up with personalities affected by different boundary experiences, differently constructed and experienced inner and outer worlds, and preoccupations with different relational issues. This early experience forms an important ground for the feminine sense of self as connected to the world and the masculine sense of self as separate, distinct, and even disconnected.

This excursion into psychoanalytic theory has served to point to the differences in men's and women's experience of self resulting from the sexual division of labor in childrearing. These different psychic experiences both structure and are reinforced by the differing patterns of men's and women's activity required by the sexual division of labor, and are thereby replicated as epistemology and ontology.

Women's construction of self in relation to others leads in general toward opposition to dualisms of any sort; valuation of concrete, everyday life; a sense of a variety of connectednesses and continuities both with other persons and with the natural world. If material life structures consciousness, women's relationally defined existence, bodily experience of boundary challenges, and activity of transforming both physical objects and human beings must be expected to result in a world view to which dichotomies are foreign. Women experience others and themselves along a continuum whose dimensions are evidenced in Rich's argument that the child carried for nine months can be defined "neither as me or as not-me," and she argued that inner and outer are not polar opposites but a continuum (1976:64, 167).

Let us use this perspective as a vantage point from which to examine the assumptions and contentions of exchange theories of social life. Women's activities as defined by the sexual division of labor stand as an implicit critique of both the assumptions exchange theories require and the conclusions to which they lead. Let us make this critique explicit.

If we re-examine the claims and conclusions of exchange theories, it becomes evident that they fail to describe women's experience. Women's experience of existence in a complex, relational world, coupled with the importance of empathy in women's self-definition counter the claim that individuals are fundamentally separate and isolated from each other. Second, women's experience fails to confirm the view that all social relations can be understood on the model of the voluntary and freely chosen interchanges which appear to characterize the market. Particularly in the case of womens' work as mothers, the idea that all interactions with others are voluntary and freely chosen is obviously false. While co-workers in an office may choose to interact or not, those in charge of small children have little choice. Moreover, one should remember that while the decision to bear and/or rear children is now a voluntary choice for many women, it has not been so historically.

Third, exchange theory rests on the claim that social relations are relations with conflict at the base, that the interests of individuals are necessarily opposed to each other. Thus, while each profits in exchange, the first choice of each is the next to last of the other. Yet, if one looks at women's lives both as partners in the courtship market and as mothers, this claim does not describe their experience. Parents and children, of course, come into conflict. But the conflict is not at the core of their relation. Indeed, in the light of the psychoanalytic theory alluded to in this paper, one could argue that the relation is conflictual especially, and perhaps only, from the perspective of the male child for whom the task of differentiation is central. Helping another to grow, gradually relinquishing control: these are not the activities of someone whose goal is simply the gaining of maximum profit from a set of interactions.

Fourth, exchange theory ignores social institutions, and in so doing ignores the fact that different types of social actors are produced by social institutions and interact within the framework of these institutions. Some of the problems which result from ignoring institutions show up in Blau's account of the courtship market. His disregard for the role of institutions makes his analysis of the courtship market a period piece which says more about Blau's insensitivity to the effects of institutions on human behavior than about the courtship market itself. His own two-person example, simple as it is, reflects a second sort of problem as well. Not only do institutions structure social interactions, but they also give rise to different types of social actors. The boy and girl in his courtship market are not interchangeable exchangers who might change places at will. Blau assumes that sexual gratification is worth something to the boy, but not to the girl. He assumes it is a commodity she possesses and can exchange, but not he. He is the buyer, she the seller— not vice versa.

The only aspect of women's lives which would lend even some credibility to an account of social life as exchange is the area most like the lives of men, that devoted to wage work. But it must be remembered that exchange theories express the reality only of the dominant economic class, whereas most women's experience in the world of wage work coincides with the experience of the producers, or the dominated class. And for wage-workers in general, exchange theories have only the surface plausibility provided by the counterfactual assumption that individuals freely and voluntarily choose to sell their labor power. One effect, then, of adopting a feminist perspective on exchange theories of social life is to make visible their fundamental implausibility and their roots in the experience of only one gender.

But the difficulties pointed to as yet are simply markers for still deeper problems. Exchange theories present a vision of the human community as arbitrary and fragile, structured fundamentally by competition and domination. The community is based on the brief coincidence of the perceived interests of individuals with no intrinsic connections to each other; it is a community composed of competitors whose only commonality is their opposition to each other; it is temporary because subjective interests may change; and ultimately it is false, since it is only a by-product of the individuals' pursuit of private gain. Being a woman mothered by a woman makes such a world foreign to women's experience of the social world.

Of the problems faced by exchange theories, however, the most important is the fact that these theories obscure relations of domination by insisting that at least initially, each individual is equal to every other, is the same kind of social actor, and interacts with others in a context unstructured by institutions. Thus, there is no reason to think that society coerces anyone. Second, these theories assume that all interactions are entered voluntarily with a view to individual gain. Thus, if an interchange occurs at all, one must assume that both parties are profiting. Third, even if the individuals in the transaction can be shown to possess unequal resources, the exercise of power by some over others is held to be justifiable since the compliance of the former gives them a currency to pay their debts. The result is that relations of domination and submission must be understood as not only beneficial for the community as a whole (increasing collective output and efficiency) but also as making a positive contribution to the equality of members of the community. Exchange theories suggest that because we already live in the best possible community—given the imperfections of human nature—there is no ground to argue for change. The Panglossian nature of this reasoning cannot be overemphasized: No matter the apparent inequality and harm occasioned by relations of domination and hierarchy, in reality all is for the best.

CONCLUSION

In sum, exchange theories populated by fictive independent, isolated individuals who take no actions other than those they wish, are clearly populated by men, and not women, men to whom connection with others and dependence are both threatening and denied. Their "rationality" carries the ring of the set of formal maxims learned by the boy, maxims separate from the total reality of daily life.

Such a contention gains support from the exchange theories extant in anthropology—especially the theories of Mauss (1967) and Lévi-Strauss (1969). In their theories the actors are not rational economic men, but much more hostile and threatening others. They engage in exchange not for mutual and private gain but rather for rivalry, show, and a desire for greatness. To accept a gift is to accept a challenge to one's honor and prestige (Mauss, 1967:39–40). To refuse to participate is the equivalent of a declaration of war (Mauss, 1967:11).

Two features of these theories (and of the societies which they purport to describe) should be particularly noted. The first is the presence of women as items of exchange. Mauss lists them along with other objects which are passed back and forth. Levi-Strauss (1969) argues that the exchange of women is what makes the human community human. Second, these exchange theories were developed in reference to societies in which the sexual division of labor was the only division of labor. One might suggest, then, that exchange theories most fundamentally describe masculine experience, and only secondarily describe the experience of the ruling class in capitalism, or indeed, that this latter experience is a variant or sub-type of masculine experience.

If exchange theories express not just the experience of the ruling class but also that of the ruling gender, then a re-examination of exchange theories, whatever forms they take, is in order. Such a re-examination could help clarify the relation between social systems structured by a sexual division of labor as opposed to those structured as well by the division between mental and manual labor.

REFERENCES

ALLEN, CRAIG, AND MURRAY STRAUS. 1980. "Resources, power and husband-wife violence." In Murray Straus and Gerald Hotaling (eds.), The Social Causes of Husband-Wife Violence. Minneapolis: University of Minnesota Press.

BALDWIN, DAVID. 1978. "Power and social exchange." American Political Science Review 72:1229-42.

BLAU, PETER. 1964. Exchange and Power in Social Life. New York: Wiley.

BUCHANAN, JAMES, AND GORDON TULLOCK. 1965. The Calculus of Consent. Ann Arbor: University of Michigan Press.

CHODOROW, NANCY. 1978. The Reproduction of Mothering. Berkeley: University of California Press.

DOWNS, ANTHONY. 1957. An Economic Theory of Democracy. New York: Harper and Row.

FRENCH, MARILYN. 1978. The Women's Room. New York: Jove.

GOODE, WILLIAM. 1971. "Force and violence and the family." Journal of Marriage and the Family 33:624-636.

HARTSOCK, NANCY C.M. 1983. Money, Sex, and Power: Toward a Feminist Historical Materialism. Boston: Northeastern University Press.

HINGERS, R.H., AND DAVID WILLER. 1979. "Prevailing postulates of exchange theory." Pp. 169-186 in Scott G. McNall (ed.). Theoretical Perspectives in Sociology. New York: St. Martin's Press.

HOMANS, GEORGE. 1958. "Social behavior as exchange." American Journal of Sociology 62:597-606.

_____. 1961. Social Behavior: Its Elementary Forms. New York: Harcourt, Brace, and World.

_____. 1967. "Fundamental social processes." Pp. 549-594 in Neil Smelser (ed.), Sociology: An Introduction. New York: Wiley.

LÉVI-STRAUSS, CLAUDE. 1969. The Elementary Structures of Kinship. Boston: Beacon Press.

MAUSS, MARCEL. 1967. The Gift. New York: Harper and Row.

MARX, KARL. 1967. Capital, I. New York: International Publishers.

_____. 1973. Grundrisse. Middlesex, England: Penguin.

MAYHEW, DAVID. 1974. Congress: The Electoral Connection. New Haven: Yale University Press.

O'BRIEN, MARY. 1978. "Reproducing Marxist man." Pp. 99-116 in Lorenne Clark and Lynda Lange (eds.), The Sexism of Social and Political Thought. Toronto: University of Toronto Press.

RICH, ADRIENNE. 1976. Of Woman Born. New York: Norton.

VANCE, CAROLE S. 1980. "Gender systems, ideology, and sex research: an anthropological analysis." Feminist Studies 6:129-43.

ZEITLIN, MAURICE. 1973. Rethinking Sociology: A Critique of Contemporary Theory. Englewood Cliffs, NJ: Prentice Hall.

THE INTERACTION ORDER*

ERVING GOFFMAN

III

In speaking of the interaction order I have so far presupposed the term "order," and an account is called for. I mean to refer in the first instance to a domain of activity—a particular kind of activity, as in the phrase, "the economic order." No implications are intended concerning how "orderly" such activity ordinarily is, or the role of norms and rules in supporting such orderliness as does obtain. Yet it appears to me that *as* an order of activity, the interaction one, more than any other perhaps, is in fact orderly, and that this orderliness is predicated on a large base of shared cognitive presuppositions, if not normative ones, and self-sustained restraints. How a given set of such understandings comes into being historically, spreads and contracts in geographical distribution over time, and how at any one place and time particular individu-

*From Erving Goffman, "The Interaction Order," *American Sociological Review* 48:1 (January 1983), 5–13. Reprinted with permission of the American Sociological Association.

als acquire these understandings are good questions, but not ones I can address.

The workings of the interaction order can easily be viewed as the consequences of systems of enabling conventions, in the sense of the ground rules for a game, the provisions of a traffic code or the rules of syntax of a language. As part of this perspective one could press two accounts. First, the dogma that the overall effect of a given set of conventions is that all participants pay a small price and obtain a large convenience, the notion being that any convention that facilitates coordination would do, so long as everyone could be induced to uphold it—the several conventions in themselves having no intrinsic value. (That, of course, is how one defines "conventions" in the first place.) On the second account, orderly interaction is seen as a product of normative consensus, the traditional sociological view that individuals unthinkingly take for granted rules they nonetheless feel are intrinsically just. Incidentally, both of these perspectives assume that the constraints which apply to others apply to oneself also, that other selves take the same view regarding constraints on their behavior, and that everyone understands that this self-submission obtains.

These two accounts—social contract and social consensus—raise obvious questions and doubts. Motive for adhering to a set of arrangements need tell us nothing about the effect of doing so. Effective cooperation in maintaining expectations implies neither belief in the legitimacy or justice of abiding by a convention contract in general (whatever it happens to be), *nor* personal belief in the ultimate value of the particular norms that are involved. Individuals go along with current interaction arrangements for a wide variety of reasons, and one cannot read from their apparent tacit support of an arrangement that they would, for example, resent or resist its change. Very often behind community and consensus are mixed motive games.

Note also that individuals who systematically violate the norms of the interaction order may nonetheless be dependent on them most of the time, including some of the time during which they are actively engaged in violations. After all, almost all acts of violence are mitigated by the violator proffering an exchange of some kind, however undesired by the victim, and of course the violator presupposes the maintenance of speech norms and the conventions for gesturing threat to accomplish this. So, too, in the case of unnegotiated violence. Assassins must rely on and profit from conventional traffic flow and conventional understanding regarding normal appearances if they are to get into a position to attack their victim and escape from the scene of the crime. Hallways, elevators, and alleys can be dangerous places because they may be hidden from view and empty of everyone except victim and assailant; but again, behind the opportunity that these arrangements provide the miscreant, is his reliance on understandings regarding normal appearances, these understandings allowing him to enter and leave the area in the guise of some-

one who does not abuse free passage. All of which should remind us that in almost all cases, interaction arrangements can withstand systematic violation, at least over the short run, and therefore that although it is in the interests of the individual to convince others that their compliance is critical to the maintenance of order, and to show apparent approval of their conformity, it will often not be in that individual's interests (as variously defined) to personally uphold the niceties.

There are deeper reasons to question the various dogmas regarding the interaction order. It might be convenient to believe that individuals (and social categories of individuals) always get considerably more from the operation of various aspects of the interaction order than the concomitant restraints cost them. But that is questionable. What is desirable order from the perspective of some can be sensed as exclusion and repression from the point of view of others. It does not raise questions about the neutrality of the term order to learn of tribal councils in West Africa that orderly speaking reflects (among other things) adherence to a rule of rank. Nor that (as Burrage and Corry have recently shown) in orderly ceremonial processions through London, from Tudor to Jacobean times, representatives of the trades and crafts maintained a traditional hierarchy both with respect to their place as marchers and as watchers. But questions do arise when we consider the fact that there are categories of persons— in our own society very broad ones—whose members constantly pay a very considerable price for their interactional existence.

Yet, over the short historic run at least, even the most disadvantaged categories continue to cooperate—a fact hidden by the manifest ill will their members may display in regard to a few norms while sustaining all the rest. Perhaps behind a willingness to accept the way things are ordered is the brutal fact of one's place in the social structure and the real or imagined cost of allowing oneself to be singled out as a malcontent. Whatever, there is no doubt that categories of individuals in every time and place have exhibited a disheartening capacity for overtly accepting miserable interactional arrangements.

In sum, then, although it is certainly proper to point to the unequal distribution of rights in the interaction order (as in the case of the segregative use of the local communities of a city), and the unequal distribution of risk (as, say, across the age grades and between the sexes), the central theme remains of a traffic of use, and of arrangements which allow a great diversity of projects and intents to be realized through unthinking recourse to procedural forms. And of course, to accept the conventions and norms as given (and to initiate one's action accordingly), is, *in effect,* to put trust in those about one. Not doing so, one could hardly get on with the business at hand; one could hardly have any business at hand.

The doctrine that ground rules inform the interaction order and allow for a traffic of use raises the question of policing, and policing, of course, once again raises political considerations.

The modern nation state, almost as a means of defining itself into existence, claims final authority for the control of hazard and threat to life, limb, and property throughout its territorial jurisdiction. Always in theory, and often in practice, the state provides standby arrangements for stepping in when local mechanisms of social control fail to keep breakdowns of interaction order within certain limits. Particularly in public places but not restricted thereto. To be sure, the interaction order prevailing even in the most public places is not a creation of the apparatus of a state. Certainly most of this order comes into being and is sustained from below as it were, in some cases in spite of overarching au-

thority not because of it. Nonetheless the state has effectively established legitimacy and priority here, monopolizing the use of heavy arms and militarily disciplined cadres as an ultimate sanction.

In consequence, some of the standard forms of interaction life—podium addresses, meetings, processions—not to speak of specialized forms like picket lines or sit-down strikes—can be read by governing officials as an affront to the security of the state and forcibly disbanded on these grounds although, indeed, no appreciable threat to public order in the substantive sense may be involved. And on the other side, breaches of public order may be performed not only for self gain, but as a pointed challenge to the authority of the state—symbolical acts read as a taunt and employed in anticipation of this reading. . . .

V

I speak no further of the forms and processes of social life specific to the interaction order. Such talk might only have relevance for those interested in human ethology, collective behavior, public order, and discourse analysis. I want instead to focus my concluding remarks on one general issue of wider bearing: the interface between the interaction order and the more traditionally considered elements of social organization. The aim will be to describe some features of the interaction order, but only those that directly bear upon the macroscopic worlds beyond the interaction in which these features are found.

From the outset a matter that is so obvious as to be taken for granted and neglected: the direct impact of situational effects upon social structures. Three examples might be cited.

First, insofar as a complex organization

comes to be dependent on particular personnel (typically personnel who have managed to acquire governing roles), then the daily sequence of social situations on and off the job—that is, the daily round—in which these personages can be injured or abducted are also situations in which their organizations can suffer. Corner businesses, families, relationships, and other small structures are similarly vulnerable, especially those stationed in high crime-rate areas. Although this issue can acquire great public attention in various times and places, it seems to me of no great conceptual interest; analytically speaking, unexpected death from natural causes introduces much the same embarrassment to organizations. In both cases one deals with nothing more than risk.

Second, as already implied, there is the obvious fact that a great deal of the work of organizations—decision making, the transmission of information, the close coordination of physical tasks—is done face-to-face, requires being done in this way, and is vulnerable to face-to-face effects. Differently put, insofar as agents of social organizations of any scale, from states to households, can be persuaded, cajoled, flattered, intimidated, or otherwise influenced by effects only achievable in face-to-face dealings, then here, too, the interaction order bluntly impinges on macroscopic entities.

Third, there are people-processing encounters, encounters in which the "impression" subjects make during the interaction affects their life chances. The institutionalized example is the placement interview as conducted by school counselors, personnel department psychologists, psychiatric diagnosticians, and courtroom officials. In a less candid form, this processing is ubiquitous: everyone is a gatekeeper in regard to something. Thus, friendship relationships and marital bonds (at least in our society) can be

traced back to an occasion in which something more was made of an incidental contact than need have been.

Whether made in institutionalized settings or not, what is situational about such processing encounters is clear: Every culture, and certainly ours, seems to have a vast lore of fact and fantasy regarding embodied indicators of status and character, thus appearing to render persons readable. By a sort of prearrangement, then, social situations seem to be perfectly designed to provide us with evidence of a participant's various attributes—if only to vividly re-present what we already know. Further, in social situations, as in other circumstances, deciders, if pressed, can employ an open-ended list of rationalizations to conceal from the subject (and even from themselves) the mix of considerations that figure in their decision and, especially, the relative weight given to these several determinants.

It is in these processing encounters, then, that the quiet sorting can occur which, as Bourdieu might have it, reproduces the social structure. But that conservative impact is not, analytically speaking, situational. The subjective weighting of a large number of social attributes, whether these attributes are officially relevant or not, and whether they are real or fanciful, provides a micro-dot of mystification; covert value given, say, to race, can be mitigated by covert value given to other structural variables—class, gender, age, co-memberships, sponsorship network—structures which at best are not fully congruent with each other. And structural attributes, overtly or covertly employed, do not mesh fully with personal ones, such as health or vigor, or with properties that have all of their existence in social situations—looks, personality, and the like. What is situational, then, about processing encounters is the evidence they so fully provide of a participant's real or apparent attributes while at the same time allowing life chances to be determined through an inaccessible weighting of this complex of evidence. Although this arrangement ordinarily allows for the surreptitious consolidation of structural lines, the same arrangement can also serve to loosen them.

One can point, then, to obvious ways in which social structures are dependent on, and vulnerable to, what occurs in face-to-face contacts. This has led some to argue reductively that all macrosociological features of society, along with society itself, are an intermittently existing composite of what can be traced back to the reality of encounters—a question of aggregating and extrapolating interactional effects. (This position is sometimes reinforced by the argument that whatever we do know about social structures can be traced back to highly edited summaries of what was originally a stream of experience in social situations).

I find these claims uncongenial. For one, they confuse the interactional format in which words and gestural indications occur with the import of these words and gestures, in a word, they confuse the situational with the merely situated. When your broker informs you that he has to sell you out or when your employer or your spouse informs you that your services are no longer required, the bad news can be delivered through a sequestered talk that gently and delicately humanizes the occasion. Such considerateness belongs to the resources of the interaction order. At the time of their use you may be very grateful for them. But the next morning what does it matter if you had gotten the word from a wire margin call, a computer readout, a blue slip at the time clock, or a terse note left on the bureau? How delicately or indelicately one is treated during the moment in which bad news is delivered does not speak to the structural significance of the news itself.

Further, I do not believe that one can learn about the shape of the commodities market,

or the distribution of a city's land values, or the ethnic succession in municipal administrations, or the structure of kinship systems, or the systematic phonological shifts within the dialects of a speech community by extrapolating or aggregating from particular social encounters among the persons involved in any one of these patterns. (Statements about macroscopic structures and processes can reasonably be subjected to a microanalysis but of the kind that digs behind generalizations to find critical differences between, say, different industries, regions, short-term periods, and the like, sufficiently so to fracture overall views, and not because of face-to-face interactions.)

Nor do I subscribe to the notion that face-to-face behavior is any more real, any less of an arbitrary abstraction, than what we think of as the dealings between two corporations, or the distribution of felonies across the weekly cycle and subregions of a New York borough; in all these cases what we get is somebody's crudely edited summaries. I claim merely that forms of face-to-face life are worn smooth by constant repetition on the part of participants who are heterogeneous in many ways and yet most quickly reach a working understanding; these forms thus seem more open to systematic analysis than are the internal or external workings of many macroscopic entities. The forms themselves are anchored in subjective feelings, and thus allow an appreciable role for empathy. The very brief span in space and time of the phenomenal side of many of these events facilitates recording (and replaying), and one has, of course, the comfort of being able to keep one's own eyes on particular instances throughout the full course of their occurrence. Yet one must see that even within the domain of face-to-face interaction, what some students accept as the smallest (and in that sense, ultimate) units of personal experience, others see as already a hopelessly complex matter requiring a much more refined application of microanalysis.

In sum, to speak of the relatively autonomous forms of life in the interaction order (as Charles Tilly has nicely done in connection with a special category of these forms) is not to put forward these forms as somehow prior, fundamental, or constitutive of the shape of macroscopic phenomena. To do so is akin to the self-centering game of playwrights, clinical psychologists, and good informants—all of whom fit their stories out so that forces within individual characters constitute and govern the action, allowing individual hearers and readers to identify gratefully with the result. Nor is it to speak of something immutable. All elements of social life have a history and are subject to critical change through time, and none can be fully understood apart from the particular culture in which it occurs. (Which is not to say that historians and anthropologists can often provide us with the data we would need to do a realistic analysis of interaction practices in communities no longer available to us.)

VI

I have mentioned direct connections between social structures and the interaction order not because of having anything new or principled to say about them, but only to establish the appropriate contrast for those interface effects that are most commonly considered, namely, the Durkheimian ones. You all know the litany. A critical feature of face-to-face gatherings is that in them and them alone we can fit a shape and dramatic form to matters that aren't otherwise palpable to the senses. Through costume, gesture, and bodily alignment we can depict and represent a heterogeneous list of immaterial things, sharing only the fact that they have a significance in our lives and yet do not cast a shadow: notable events in the past, beliefs about the cosmos and our place in it, ideals regarding our various categories of persons, and of course social relationships and larger social structures. These embodiments are centered in ceremonies (in turn embedded in celebrative social occasions) and presumably allow the participants to affirm their affiliation and commitment to their collectivities, and revive their ultimate beliefs. Here the celebration of a collectivity is a conscious reason for the social occasion which houses it, and naturally figures in the occasion's organization. The range in scale of such celebrative events is great: at one end, coronations, at the other, the two-couple dine-out—that increasingly common middle-class network ritual, to which we all give, and from which we all gain, so much weight.

Social anthropology claims these various ceremonies as its province, and indeed the best treatment of them in modern communities is Lloyd Warner's *The Living and the Dead*. Secular mass societies, it turns out, have not proven hostile to these celebrations—indeed Soviet society, as Crystal Lane has recently documented, is rife with them. Benedictions may be on the decline in number and significance, but not the occasions on which they once would have been offered.

And presumably these occasions have consequences for macrostructures. For example, Abner Cohen tells us that the steel-band carnival that began in the Notting Hill area of London as a multi-ethnic block party ended up as the beginning of the political organization of London's West Indians; that what started out as an annual Bank Holiday social affair—quintessentially a creature having merely an interactional life—ended up as an expression of a politically self-conscious group, the expression itself having helped considerably to create the structural context in which it would come to be seen. So the carnival was more the cause of a social movement and its group-formative effects than an expression thereof. Similarly, Simon Taylor tells us that the calendar of political celebrations developed by the national socialist movement in Germany—the calendar being a Hitler-centric version of basic Christian ceremonies—played an important role in consolidating the hold of the Party upon the nation. The key occasion in this annual cycle, apparently, was the Nuremberg Reichspartyday held in the Zeppelinfield. This place could concentrate almost a quarter of a million people while affording all of them direct visual access to the stage. That number of people responding in unison to the same platform event apparently had lasting influence on some participants; certainly we have here the limiting case of a situational event, and certainly the interesting issue is not how the ritual reflected Nazi doctrines regarding the world, but how the annual occasion itself clearly contributed to the political hegemony of its impresarios.

In these two examples—admittedly both somewhat extreme—one has a direct leap from interactional effect to political organization. Of course, every rally—especially ones involving collective confrontation with authority—can have some long-standing effect upon the political orientation of the celebrants.

Now although it seems easy enough to identify the collectivities which ceremony projects on to a behavioral screen, and to cite, as I have just done, evidence of the critical contribution the shadow may make to the substance, it is quite another matter to demonstrate that *in general* anything macroscopically significant results from ceremony—at least in contemporary society. Those individuals who are in a position to authorize and organize such occasions are often the ones who star in them, and these functionaries always seem to be optimistic about the result. But in fact, the ties and relation-ships that we ceremonialize may be so attenuated that a periodic celebration is all that we are prepared to commit to them; so what they index is not our social reality but our nostalgia, our bad conscience, and our lingering piety in regard to what is no longer binding. (When friends remove to another town, the celebration of chance conjunctions can become the substance of the relationship not its expression.) Furthermore, as Moore and Myerhoff have suggested, the categories of persons that come together in a ceremony (and thus the structures that are involved) may never come together again, ceremonially or otherwise. A one-time intersection of variously impinging interests may be represented, and nothing beyond that. Certainly celebrative occasions such as this presidential address don't necessarily have the effect of recommitting the members of the audience to the discipline and profession under whose name they foregather. Indeed, all one can hope for is that memory of how the hour was passed will fade quickly, allowing everyone to attend again the following year, willing once again to not not come. In sum, sentiments about structural ties serve more as an involvement or resource—serve more to carry a celebrative occasion—than such affairs serve to strengthen what they draw from.

VII

If we think of ceremonials as narrative-like enactments, more or less extensive and more or less insulated from mundane routines, then we can contrast these complex performances with "contact rituals," namely, perfunctory, brief expressions occurring incidental to everyday action—in passing as it were—the most frequent case involving but two individuals. These performances have not been handled very well by anthropology even though they seem much more researchable than the more complex sequences. Indeed, ethology and the ethological conception of ritual, at least in the sense of intention display, turn out to be as germane as the anthropological formulation. The question, then, becomes: what principles inform the bearing of social structures on contact rituals? It is this issue I want to consider in closing.

The events occurring for incidental reasons when individuals are in one another's immediate presence are well designed to serve as micro-ecological metaphors, summaries and iconic symbols of structural arrangements—whether wanted or not. And should such expressions not occur incidentally, local environments can easily be manipulated so as to produce them. Given the selective sensibilities in a particular culture—for example, concern over relative elevation, value placed on right- over left-sidedness, orientation to the cardinal directions—given such cultural biases, some depictive, situated resources will of course be exploited more than others. The question, then, is how will these features of the interaction order be geared or linked into, connected up with, tied into social structures, including social relationships? Here the social sciences have been rather easygoing, sufficiently so on occasion to be content with the phrase "an expression of." Minor social ritual is not an expression *of* structural arrangements in any simple sense; at best it is an expression advanced *in regard* to these arrangements. Social structures don't "determine" culturally standard displays, merely help select from the available repertoire of them. The expressions themselves, such as priority in being served, precedence through a door, centrality of seating, access to various public places, preferential interruption rights in talk, selection as addressed recipient, are interactional in substance and character; at best they are likely to have only loosely coupled relations to anything by way of social structures that might be associated with them. They are sign vehicles fabricated from depictive materials at hand, and what they come to be taken as a "reflection" of is necessarily an open question.

Look, for example, at the bit of our ritual idiom frequently treated in term papers: license to employ reciprocal first-naming as an address formula. Pairs of persons licensed to greet and talk to each other through reciprocal first name can't be taken by evidence of this fact alone to be in a particular structural relation, or to be co-members of a particular social organization or group or category. There is great variation by region, class, and epoch, and these variations do not correspond closely to variation in social structure. But there are other issues. Take persons like ourselves for a moment. We are on reciprocal first name terms with sibs, relatives of same generation, friends, neighbors, early school mates, the newly introduced to us at domestic social gatherings, our office mates, our car salesman, our accountant, and when we gamble privately, the cronies we do it with. I regret to say that in some cases we are also on such terms with our parents and children. The very fact, that in some cases (sibs and spouses for example) first-name terms (as opposed to other proper names) are obligatory and in other relationships optional, suggests the looseness of the usage. The traditional term "primary ties" addresses the issue, but optimistically; it reflects the psychological reductionism of our sociological forefathers, and their wistful memories of the neighborhoods they were raised in. In fact, reciprocal first naming is a culturally established resource for styling immediate dealings: reduced formality is implied and the abjuring of a tone-setting opportunity to stand on one's claim to ritual circumspection. But informality is constituted out of interactional materials (as is formality), and the various social relations and social circles that draw on this resource merely share some affinities.

Which is not to say, of course, that a full catalogue of the symmetrical and asymmetrical forms of interactional regard and disregard, of circumspection and ritual ease, that two individuals routinely extend to each other would not appreciably inform us about their structural ties. Nor is it to say that convention can't link some displays to social structures in exclusive ways; in our society the wedding ceremony, for example, employs some forms that advertise the formation of an instance of a particular class of social structure and this alone. Nor is it to say that forms of interaction can't themselves be responsible to the institutional setting in which they occur. (Even apart from *what* is said, turn-taking rules in informal talk differ somewhat from those in family therapy sessions, which are different in turn from those in classroom teaching, and these in turn differ from the practices found in court hearings. And these differences in form are partly explicable in terms of the special tasks undertaken in these several settings, which in turn are determined by extrasituational concerns.)

In general, then (and qualifications apart) what one finds, in modern societies at least, is a nonexclusive linkage—a "loose coupling"—between interactional practices and social structures, a collapsing of strata and structures into broader categories, the categories themselves not corresponding one-to-one to anything in the structural world, a gearing as it were of various structures into interactional cogs. Or, if you will, a set of transformation rules, or a membrane selecting how various externally relevant social distinctions will be managed within the interaction.

One example. From the perspective of how women in our society fare in informal cross-sexed talk, it is of very small moment that (statistically speaking) a handful of males, such as junior executives, have to similarly wait and hang on other's words—albeit in each case not many others. From the point of view of the interaction order, however, the issue is critical. For one, it allows us to try to formulate a role category that women and junior executives (and anyone else in these interactional circumstances) share, and this will be a role that belongs *analytically* to the interaction order, which the categories women and junior executives do not.

I need only remind you that the dependency of interactional activity on matters outside the interaction—a fact characteristically neglected by those of us who focus on face-to-face dealings—doesn't in itself imply dependency on social structures. As already suggested, a quite central issue in all face-to-face interaction is the cognitive relation of the participants, that is, what it is each can effectively assume the other knows. This relationship is relatively context-free, extending beyond any current social situation to all occasions when the two individuals meet. Pairs constituting intimate structures, by definition, will know considerable about each other, and also know of many experiences they exclusively share—all of which dramatically affects what they can say to each other and how laconic they can be in making these references. But all this exclusive information pales when one considers the amount of information about the world two barely acquainted individuals can assume it is reasonable to assume in formulating their utterances to each other. (Here, once again, we see that the traditional distinction between primary and secondary relations is an insight sociology must escape from.)

The general formulation I have suggested of the relation between the interaction order and the structural ones allows one (I hope) to proceed constructively. First, as suggested, one is encouraged to treat as a matter for discovery just who it is that does it to whom, the assumption being that in almost every case the categories that result will not quite coincide with any structural division. Let me press yet another example. Etiquette books are full of conceptualizations concerning the courtesies that men owe women in polite society. Less clearly presented, of course, is an understanding concerning the kinds of women and the kinds of men who would not be looked to as expected participants in these little niceties. More germane here, however, is the fact each of these little gestures turns out to be also prescribed between other categories: an adult in regard to an old person, an adult in regard to a young person, a host for a guest, an expert for a novice, a native for a visitor, friends in regard to the celebrant of a life turning-point, a well person for a sick one, a whole person for an incapacitated one. And, as suggested, it turns out that what all these pairings share is not something in the social structure but something that a scene of face-to-face interaction allows for. (Even if one were to restrict oneself to one sphere of social life—say activity within a complex organization—a loose coupling between the interaction order and social structure would remain. The precedence one gives one's immediate boss one gives to his or her immediate boss too, and so on to the head of the organization; for precedence is an interactional resource that speaks to ordinal ranking, not to the distance between the rungs.) It is easy enough, then, and even useful, to specify in social structural terms who performs a given act of deference or presumption to whom. In the study of the interaction order, however, after saying that, one must search out who else does it to whom else, then categorize the doers with a term that covers them all, and similarly with the done to. And one must provide a technically detailed description of the forms involved.

Second, a loose-coupling approach allows one to find a proper place for the apparent power of fads and fashions to effect change in ritual practices. A recent example, known to you all, was the rapid and somewhat temporary shift to informal dress in the business world during the latter phases of the hippie movement, accompanied sometimes by a change in salutational forms, all without much corresponding change in social structure.

Third, one can appreciate the vulnerability of features of the interaction order to direct political intervention, both from below and above, in either case bypassing socioeconomic relationships. Thus, in recent times blacks and women have concertedly breached segregated public places, in many cases with lasting consequence for access arrangements, but, all in all, without much change in the place of blacks and women in the social structure. And one can appreciate the purpose of a new regime in introducing and enforcing a practice that strikes at the manner in which broad categories of persons will appear in public, as, for example, when the National Socialists in Germany required Jews to wear identifying arm bands when in public places, or the Soviet government took official action to discourage the wearing of veils by women of the Siberian Khanty ethnic group, or the Iranian government took veils in exactly the opposite direction. And one can appreciate, too, the effectiveness of efforts directly to alter contact interchanges, as when a revolutionary salute, verbal greeting, or address term is introduced from above, in some cases rather permanently.

And finally, one can appreciate the leverage those in an ideological movement can obtain by concentrating their efforts upon salutations and farewells, address terms, tact and indirection, and other junctures for politeness in the management of social contacts and verbal intercourse. Or the fuss that can be made by a doctrine that leads to systematic breaching of standards for seemly public dress. In these matters, American Hippies, and later, "The Chicago Seven," were interesting amateurs; the great terrorists of contact forms were the mid-17th century Quakers in

Britain, who managed, somehow (as Bauman has recently described it) to design a doctrine that struck directly at the then settled arrangements through which social structures and broad official values were given polite due in social intercourse (To be sure other religious movements of the period employed some of these recalcitrancies too, but none so systematically.) That sturdy band of plain speakers should always stand before us as an example of the wonderfully disruptive power of systematic impoliteness, reminding us once again of the vulnerabilities of the interaction order. There is no doubt: Fox's disciples raised to monumental heights the art of becoming a pain in the ass. . . .

CHAPTER 5

MICRO VERSUS MACRO APPROACHES

For much of the history of sociology, the division between *macro* theories—theories of large-scale social structures—and *micro* theories—theories of individual personality and consciousness—has been a fundamental divide separating two distinct approaches to theory. The division has historically formed one of the key categorical oppositions of European—and much non-European—philosophy (see Alexander et al. 1987, 3). Although classical sociology offers several examples of theorists who combined these two approaches in their work—one thinks, especially, of Max Weber's theory of social action and Karl Marx's theory of alienation—until the last few years, modern sociology seemed to have erected an unbridgeable gulf between the micro order of individual social actors and the macro order of social structure.

One of the consequences of the emergence of this theoretical divide was the development of an extreme sense of rivalry between practitioners of these two styles of sociological theory. Reading 26 by George Homans and Reading 27 by Bruce Mayhew give a good sense of the degree of mutual hostility often felt by theorists writing within the two camps. Both Homans and Mayhew are excellent writers and debaters; each stakes out his position in a stark and belligerent manner, and each argues his position in blunt, straightforward prose.

Homans, of course, has long been associated with the micro-orientation of exchange theory, which he developed in a series of articles and books published in the 1950s and 1960s (see Reading 22; Homans 1961). He has also been a vigorous defender over the years of the micro approach in sociology (see Homans 1964, 1967, 1987). His position is that all sociological theories are reducible to propositions about the behavior of individuals—or else they are nonsense. This position is known in the philosophy of science as *methodological individualism,* and Homans defends it fiercely.

The opposing position is represented in this reader by Mayhew, who cites Karl Marx's dictum that "Society does not consist of individuals, but expresses the sum of interrelations in which individuals stand with respect to one another" (Marx 1973, 265). For Mayhew, this view points to the fact that sociologists should be concerned about social structures, networks, and organization; the individual has no place in sociology, either as the object of social research or as the focus of theory construction. Mayhew offers an interpretation of modern sociology as having been almost completely consumed by the resort to inappropriate individualistic explanations of social life. (It is interesting to note in this regard that Homans believes just the opposite—that is, modern sociology has been largely dominated by meaningless *structural* theories.)

Mayhew purports that the "individualist perspective" is reducible to the trite proposition "*people do things because they want to*"— which is not meaningful as a sociological explanation—or even as an interpretation—of human behavior. Mayhew opposes to this "individualist" principle, the "structuralist" principle that 95 percent of the variation in human society is caused by such structural variables as population, environment, ideology, and technology. Mayhew calls for a reorientation of American sociology toward this "new" structuralist perspective.

THE MOVE TOWARD SYNTHESIS

If the predominant mood of the sociology of the 1960s and the 1970s was to polarize the split between macro- and microlevel analyses, the spirit of the 1980s and 1990s has been to move toward a synthesis of the two levels of theoretical analysis (Ritzer 1990). Increasingly, debate has taken place, not over whether such a synthesis should take place, but rather over *what form* such a synthesis should take. In particular, theorists have undertaken the search for micro foundations for macrosociology (see Hechter 1983). This

quest is not entirely new to sociological theory. In fact, from Max Weber to Talcott Parsons, many classical and modern theorists have sought to anchor their macro theorizing in a micro theory of social action. George Homans' exchange theory was especially clear about its programmatic status as a theory building from the micro to the macro level of analysis—a project that was most fully carried out in Peter Blau's (1964) brilliant study *Exchange and Power in Social Life*.

Recent rational-choice perspectives, developed from an exchange theory background, claim that the kind of rational-choice calculation characteristic of economic theory can be used as a microtheoretical premise for macrosociological theory (Coleman 1987, 1990; Coleman and Fararo 1992; Friedman 1983). Again, the approach is not completely novel to sociology—Weber's theory of social action was rooted in early neoclassical economic theory, with its emphasis on rational social action as the basis for evaluating all human action. Even Marx, perhaps the classical macrotheorist *par excellence,* was quite ready to understand the cyclical movements of the capitalist mode of production as the result of the market-oriented, self-interested behavior of capitalists and workers. As Friedman and Hechter (Reading 28) show, rational-choice models have demonstrated a wide degree of applicability in sociological research.

But most theorists exploring the micro-macro link see rational-choice theory as investigating a limited set of behaviors and offering an excessively narrow range of explanations. Perhaps the best-known proponent of a general microfoundations strategy is Randall Collins, who, in a series of papers (1981, 1987, 1988), has developed an argument for microreduction (that is, the *reduction* of large-scale theories to their underlying principles of human behavior) as a strategy for constructing macrolevel theory. In Reading 29, Collins surveys and assesses the debate between proponents of micro and macro approaches to theory construction. He then proposes that sociologists pursue a model of macrosocial theory created by the aggregation of smaller-scale theories functioning at the micro level. He concludes that the reduction of macro theories, to demonstrate the underlying causal micro principles of human interaction at work, strengthens macro theories by increasing their explanatory plausibility. While not seeking to ban macrolevel theorizing (as, for example, would Homans), Collins argues that theoretical reduction *completes* the arguments of macrolevel theory by adding the explanatory *why* that can be found only in microlevel theories of human behavior and motivation.

Most sociologists interested in the micro-macro issue have moved in the direction of closer synthesis; one interesting exception has been Peter Blau, the sociologist whose work in exchange theory was so important in framing the debate over micro-macro synthesis. In *Exchange and Power in Social Life*, Blau had argued for a microfoundations approach, but in one of his last published essays (Reading 30), written more than thirty years later, Blau took a much more skeptical stand on the possibility of a unified sociological theory. In his earlier work, Blau had championed the approach taken by Collins—that macrosociological theory should be built on the basis of microlevel theory. Blau opted (in Reading 30) for the view that the two levels of theorizing require different theoretical assumptions, perspectives, and approaches (see Calhoun, Meyer, and Scott 1990). Still, Blau did not reject the ultimate goal of a unified sociological theory, arguing that even now, although this final vision is not yet a practical undertaking, the two levels of theory are complementary and each will gain by recognizing and utilizing the accomplishments of the other.

The micro-macro link has been a focus of attention in the work of both Pierre Bourdieu and Anthony Giddens, two prominent European sociological theorists. Although Bourdieu, a French sociologist, has long enjoyed a reputation for his work in stratification and educational theory, his work in recent years has taken on a broader focus as he has developed his concepts of "social space" and "habitus" (see Bourdieu 1979, 1985, 1990, Bourdieu and Wacquant 1992; see also Wacquant 1989, Calhoun, LiPuma, and Postone 1993). Bourdieu uses these terms as a means to address and, he hopes, go beyond the traditional dichotomization of macro and micro as levels of analysis (see Brubaker 1985). In Reading 31, Bourdieu proposes that sociologists rethink the concept of "social reality" by focusing on the ways in which the world is symbolically made and remade in everyday life. He argues that the social world is, above all, a world of symbolically structured meaning. Bourdieu proposes that an appreciation of the social power inherent in control over symbols and discourse leads us to a resolution of many traditional sociological dichotomizations, such as macro/micro and objective/subjective, that have plagued sociological analysis.

"Structuration theory," which has been developed in recent years by Anthony Giddens is, very much like Bourdieu's work, an attempt to get beyond the dichotomized categories of traditional sociological thought. Beginning, again like Bourdieu, with an initial attachment to Marxism in his early work, Giddens' work has become over the years more distinctive and difficult to categorize in terms of traditional paradigms (see Bryant and Jary 1991). The central sociological problem in Giddens' later writings, of which Reading 32 is a good example, has been the attempt to overcome the gap between social structure and social action—with structure denoting the macrolevel of analysis, and action, the microlevel.

The culmination of Giddens' work on this

problem is the theoretically dense *The Constitution of Society* (1984). Giddens breaks with the traditional sociological conception of structure as something external to and coercive over social actors, affirming instead what he calls the "duality of structure." That is, social structure is *both* a set of rules that constrain the behavior of social actors and a resource upon which actors draw to achieve their goals. In Giddens' words: "Structure is not to be equated with constraint but is always both constraining and enabling" (1984, 25). In Giddens' view, sociological theory has tended to emphasize one of these characteristics of structure while neglecting the other. Thus, macrostructural theory has utilized the concept of structure as constraint, and microaction theory has emphasized the goal-oriented activities of social actors.

As Cohen (1987; see also Giddens 1987, Held and Thompson 1989) noted, Giddens' structuration theory is very much a theory still under construction. Along with Bourdieu's still-evolving theory of social space, however, it gives us an insight into the future of sociological theorizing on the micro-macro dimension. The fact that so many important theorists have placed this problem at the heart of their recent work indicates that the search for micro-macro linkages will lead to the development of more sophisticated and powerful theoretical syntheses over the next few decades.

REFERENCES

ALEXANDER, JEFFREY, BERNHARD GIESON, RICHARD MÜNCH, AND NEIL SMELSER, eds. 1987. *The Micro-Macro Link.* Berkeley: University of California Press.

BLAU, PETER. 1964. *Exchange and Power in Social Life.* New York: Wiley.

BOURDIEU, PIERRE. 1979. "Symbolic Power." *Critique of Anthropology* 13–14 (Summer): 77–85.

_____. 1985. "The Social Space and the Genesis of Groups." *Theory and Society* 14 (November):723–44.

_____. 1990. *The Logic of Practice.* Stanford: Standford University Press.

BOURDIEU, PIERRE AND LOÏC WACQUANT. 1992. *An Invitation to Reflexive Sociology.* Chicago: University of Chicago Press.

BRUBAKER, ROGERS. 1985. "Rethinking Classical Theory: The Sociological Vision of Pierre Bourdieu." *Theory and Society* 14 (November):745–75.

BRYANT, CHRISTOPHER, AND DAVID JARY. 1991. "Coming to Terms with Anthony Giddens." Pp. 1–31 in *Giddens' Theory of Structuration,* ed. Christopher Bryant and David Jary. London: Routledge.

CALHOUN, CRAIG, EDWARD LIPUMA, AND MOISHE POSTONE, eds. 1993. *Bourdieu: Critical Perspectives.* Chicago: University of Chicago Press.

CALHOUN, CRAIG, MARSHALL MEYER, AND W. RICHARD SCOTT. 1990. "Introduction: Peter Blau's Structuralism." Pp. 1–36 in *Structures of Power and Constraint,* ed. Craig Calhoun, Marshall Meyer, and W. Richard Scott. Cambridge: Cambridge University Press.

COHEN, IRA. 1987. "Structuration Theory and Social Praxis." Pp. 273–308 in *Social Theory Today,* ed. Anthony Giddens and Jonathan Turner. Stanford: Stanford University Press.

COLEMAN, JAMES. 1987. "Microfoundations and Macrosocial Behavior." Pp. 153–73 in *The Micro-Macro Link,* ed. Jeffrey Alexander et al. Berkeley: University of California Press.

_____. 1990. *Foundations of Social Theory.* Cambridge: Harvard University Press.

COLEMAN, JAMES, AND THOMAS FARARO, eds. 1992. *Rational Choice Theory: Advocacy and Critique.* Newbury Park, Cal.: Sage Publications.

COLLINS, RANDALL. 1981. "On the Microfoundations of Macrosociology." *American Journal of Sociology* 5 (March):984–1014.

_____. 1987. "Interaction Ritual Chains, Power and Property: The Micro-Macro Connection as an Empirically Based Theoretical Problem." Pp. 193–206 in *The Micro-Macro Link,* ed. Jeffrey Alexander et al. Berkeley: University of California Press.

_____. 1988. "The Micro Contribution to Macro Sociology." *Sociological Theory* 6 (Fall):242–53.

FRIEDMAN, DEBRA. 1983. "Normative and Rational Explanations of a Classic Case: Religious Specialization in Academia." Pp. 90–114 in *The Microfoundations of Macrosociology,* ed. Michael Hechter. Philadelphia: Temple University Press.

GIDDENS, ANTHONY. 1984. *The Constitution of Society: Outline of the Theory of Structuration.* Berkeley: University of California Press.

_____. 1987. "Time and Social Organization." Pp. 140–65 in *Social Theory and Modern Sociology,* by

Anthony Giddens. Stanford: Stanford University Press.

HECHTER, MICHAEL, ed. 1983. *The Microfoundations of Macrosociology*. Philadelphia: Temple University Press.

HELD, DAVID, AND JOHN THOMPSON 1989. *Social Theory of Modern Societies: Anthony Giddens and His Critics*. London: Cambridge University Press.

HOMANS, GEORGE, 1961. *Social Behavior: Its Elementary Forms*. New York: Harcourt, Brace and World.

_____. 1964. "Bringing Men Back In." *American Sociological Review* 29 (December): 809–18.

_____. 1967. *The Nature of Social Science*. New York: Harcourt, Brace and World.

_____. 1987. "Behaviorism and After." Pp. 58–81 in *Social Theory Today,* ed. Anthony Giddens and Jonathan Turner. Stanford: Stanford University Press.

MARX, KARL. 1973. *Grundrisse: Introduction to the Critique of Political Economy*. 1858. Reprint, London: Penguin Books.

RITZER, GEORGE. 1990. "The Current Status of Sociological Theory: The New Syntheses." Pp. 1–30 in *Frontiers of Social Theory,* ed. George Ritzer. New York: Columbia University Press,

WACQUANT, LOÏC. 1989. "Towards a Reflexive Sociology: A Workshop with Pierre Bourdieu." *Sociological Theory* 7 (Spring):26–63.

THE PRESENT STATE
OF SOCIOLOGICAL THEORY*

GEORGE C. HOMANS

Intellectually, sociology is in greater disarray than usual. In the sixties it looked as if the discipline might rally around the so-called structural-functional school. It did not. Instead it fractured into a number of different schools: symbolic interactionism, ethnomethodology, Goffmanesque dramaturgy, conflict theory, exchange theory, various Marxist schools, and others. Each claimed to be distinct from the rest and each to have its own "theory," which it did not, except perhaps for exchange theory. The curious thing is that all of them held the same theory, but that fact did not become apparent, because none of them, again with the exception of exchange theory, made its theory explicit. All were well employed stating and testing empirical propositions. But these do not make a theory. What passed for theory in all the schools were discussions of what

*Abridged from George Homans, "The Present State of Sociological Theory," *The Sociological Quarterly* 23:3 (Summer 1982), 285–93, 297–99. Reprinted with permission of *The Sociological Quarterly*.

they intended to do. But such discussions are metatheoretical, not theoretical.

WHAT IS THEORY?

Theory is a word to which people have given a number of meanings. Here I shall use it in what I believe to be its classical sense in science. A theory of a phenomenon is an explanation of the phenomenon. But like *theory* itself, *explanation* is just another word, so it looks as if I had made no advance. Again I shall use it as I believe it has been used in much classical science and in some philosophies of science, especially those of Braithwaite (1953) and Nagel (1961). In doing so I hope to make its meaning more specific.

An explanation consists of a set of at least three propositions. (An example is the Aristotelian syllogism.) To be allowed to take part in an explanation, a proposition must meet at least two conditions. It must state a relationship between at least two variables and it must begin to state what that relationship is. It is not enough to say there is *some* relationship between the variables—a very frequent kind of statement in sociology. It must say, for instance, that if x is present, y is also present, or that if x increases in numerical value, y also increases. In sociological explanation let us not insist on premature rigor, though of course in cases where it is now within our power we should not abandon it. When it is not, we shall be satisfied with propositions stating that if x increases, y increases, even if we do not know by just how much.

One of the propositions, usually one of a low order of generality, such as I call an empirical proposition, is the one to be explained, and therefore in Latin called the *explicandum*. There must be two other kinds of propositions in the set. There must be at least one general proposition, and what that is I shall describe later, and one proposition that states the given condition or conditions to which the general proposition is to be applied. When the *explicandum* follows in logic from the other propositions in the set, it is said to be explained. Thus an explanation forms a deductive system. The deductions may be made with the help of the nonempirical (or noncontigent) propositions of mathematics.

The test of a general proposition is that it cannot itself be logically derived from the other propositions in the set, as the *explicandum* can be derived from the general propositions and the others. Some scholars forget that in explanation general propositions do not operate in a vacuum. They must be applied to given conditions. Both the general propositions and the givens may themselves become the *explicanda* of further deductive systems. Where the theorist chooses to stop depends partly on his convenience—has he enough space and time?—partly on his information—for instance, the historical information necessary to explain some given conditions runs out sooner or later—and partly on whether he can borrow or invent propositions relevant to his deductive system that are still more general than the ones he has used. Some general propositions have remained such for long periods of time, but experience shows that they will not do so forever. It is the general proposition (or propositions) that gives its name to the model of explanation put forward here: it is called the "covering-law" model.

Usually we do not dignify the explanation of a single empirical proposition with the name of a theory. What we call a theory is the explanation of a number of propositions in a single field, when all the explanations share some of the same general propositions. Thus we speak of thermodynamics as a single theory, because its propositions are all concerned with heat, and its explanations have in common at least one general proposition, together of course with others that differ. I claim that the covering-law model of explanation applies to all the sciences, including the social sciences. Naturally the actual propositions differ from science to science, but the process of explanation is the same for all. Not all philosophers agree that this is an adequate model for explanation (Suppe, 1974). But until the dissidents have agreed on what a better model would be, I shall stick to one that seems to me to embody classical practice.

Many departments of sociology offer courses on "theory construction." I am not now talking about theory construction but about what a completed theory looks like—not that any theory is ever more than provisionally completed. What it looks like we can specify pretty clearly: it is a deductive system. What we cannot do is specify how a scholar arrives at a theory. Of course he needs long familiarity with the data in the field, that is, a prepared mind. But even that is not enough.

At some point he must move from empirical propositions to general ones; that requires a "leap of the imagination," and we do not know how to produce at will such a leap (Holton, 1978). Of course if one is lucky, one may apply an already developed theory to new empirical propositions. Still, somebody must have originally invented the theory.

WHAT ARE THE COVERING LAWS IN SOCIOLOGY?

If one adopts the covering-law model of explanation, one is forced to ask what the covering laws in one's subject should be. When I reached this stage in my thinking, I decided that the laws must be those of behavioral psychology, so-called to distinguish it from physiological psychology. What are psychological laws? First, they are those usually stated and tested by persons who call themselves psychologists. Second, they refer to the behavior of individual human beings not, so to speak, in their individual idiosyncrasies—for the propositions themselves can be used to explain some of the variation in individual personalities—but as members in common of the same human species. The propositions are the laws of what we used to call human nature, and of much animal nature too. What they are definitely not is propositions about groups, organizations, or human aggregates as such.

The first reason for taking psychological propositions as the covering laws of psychology is general. J.S. Mill stated this reason early and well (1843, bk. 6, chap. 7, sec. 1):

The laws of the phenomena of society are, and can be, nothing but the laws of the actions and passions of human beings united together in the social state. Men, however, in a state of society are still men; their actions and passions are obedient to the laws of individual human nature. Men are not, when brought together, converted into another kind of substance, with different properties. . . . Human beings in society have no properties but those which are derived from, and may be resolved into, the laws of the nature of individual man. In social phenomena the Composition of Causes is the universal law.

Watkins (1959, in Gardiner, 1959:505) has called this position "methodological individualism." By the "Composition of Causes" Mill was referring to the fact that the consciously or unconsciously combined actions of many persons—and that is what we mean by social behavior—may have resultants that are different from what the outcomes of the actions of the individuals, taken in isolation, would have been.

But general considerations are not enough. To produce explanations, the covering laws must at some point be explicitly stated. Otherwise no deductions, however crude, can be made from them. The chief difficulty with the current schools of sociology is just this: they do not come right out and state their covering laws explicitly. For myself I decided to take the other course. But I also decided to follow the advice of my old teacher Professor L.J. Henderson. He urged that at the beginning of a science one should not attempt more than first approximations to the complexity of fact. Accordingly in my attempts to explain social behavior I did not use all of the known laws of behavioral psychology but only such as I could not do without in trying to accomplish what I wished. (For a summary see Homans, 1974:15–50.)

The propositions of behavioral psychology are propositions about feedback, about the effects of a person's present and past behavior on his future behavior. In this sense, they are historical. If a person's action results in his getting something that rewards him, he is likely to repeat it. The more valuable the reward to the person in question, the more likely he is to repeat it. The reward includes the avoidance of, or escape from punishment. The repetition upon some new occasion of the circumstances (usually called stimuli or cues) attending the performance of a person's rewarded action, the more likely he is to repeat it. If a person's repeated action is rewarded at a rate higher than some threshold, he is apt to become satiated with it. The value for him of some new unit of the reward goes down, and hence he performs less often the action that gets him the reward. Finally I added a couple of propositions about the determinants and results of emotional behavior such as aggression and approval. The interesting thing about these behaviors is that while they may begin as pure reflexes—which behavioral psychology does not deal with—they may be learned and used as ordinary actions (or operants as they are sometimes called). Thus a person may learn to repeat aggressive behavior because it brings him reward, as it often does.

Some scholars make a sharp distinction between behavioral and cognitive psychology. I believe that we should include perceptions among actions. Few perceptions are given us at birth. We learn to perceive the world by acting on it. If, by perceiving it in a certain way, we are rewarded by being better able to cope with it, we are likely to maintain our perception. But that is just the way we learn and repeat other kinds of actions.

The action resulting from these propositions must always be assessed in relation to some alternative action open to the person in question. If a person takes an action whose expected reward (usually considered to be the expected value of the result multiplied by the expected probability of success in getting it) is greater than the expected value of the action not taken (forgone), the difference is usually called the *cost* of the action taken. Expectations are precipitates of a persons's past experience.

I took my formulation of the propositions

of behavioral psychology from B.F. Skinner (1953). Some people think it makes a difference which behavioral psychologist one takes them from. It does not, though of course different psychologists emphasize different aspects of behavior. For instance, Albert Bandura (1969) emphasizes, quite rightly, model or vicarious learning. If a person observes another taking an action that obviously rewards the other, the observer himself is likely to *acquire* the action in the sense of being able to perform it when similar circumstances present themselves to him. Skinner does not stress model learning, though he certainly agrees that behavior may be acquired in this way (personal communication). But no matter how the behavior is *acquired,* the person who then performs it must be *rewarded* by the result before he is likely to repeat it. Acquisition without success is not likely to have much effect. On this point Skinner and Bandura are in agreement, and it makes no difference to explanation whose formulation one uses.

Much more important, the propositions of behavioral psychology, as Mill was aware, hold good whether the person is acting on the human or on the nonhuman environment. Naturally, when he is acting toward another person and the other acting toward him according to the same propositions, the concrete results may be different from what happens when he is, say, chopping down a tree. But the propositions themselves do not change. When the action of a person is rewarded by the action of another and the other responds with an action rewarding to the first, their combined behavior looks very much like an exchange of rewards. Accordingly some sociologists call the social theory that uses psychological general propositions by the name of "exchange theory." Sociologists will add the word "theory" to almost any subject. In this case I have been an accessory to this behavior. I entitled the first article in which I adumbrated my approach "Social Behavior as Exchange" (1958, 1962). What my approach represents in fact is something more general: the use of the propositions of behavioral psychology in explaining human social behavior. What they will explain is not limited to exchange.

THE DIFFERENT SCHOOLS
OF SOCIOLOGY USE
THE SAME COVERING LAWS

I believe it is quite easy to show that all the current schools of sociology, with the exception of what I shall call "societal functionalism," use propositions of behavioral psychology to explain the phenomena they happen to be interested in. That is, if one reconstructs in full their explanatory arguments, one finds that a proposition or propositions of behavioral psychology must occupy the position of general propositions. (Note that if one anticipates what usually happens in science, these propositions will ultimately be shown to follow from still more general ones, but that is not true now.) The question is why sociologists in general do not recognize that their general propositions are those of behavioral psychology. My answer is that they leave the general principles unstated. These are the "unstated major premises" that Mr. Justice Holmes often said were common in legal arguments. In the technical language of philosophy such arguments are *enthymematic.*

Consider some of the statements in a useful book by Mitchell, which reviews some of the work in the relatively new schools of social exchange, dramaturgy (Goffman), and ethnomethodology, for example, a statement from the discussion of Goffman's approach (Mitchell, 1978:112): "An effective actor then is not only one who is rewarded for good performances by the acceptance of his audience, but also is one who comes to see a continuity

of essentials in his performances and is able to account for himself as more than a mere shell." Let me try to turn this into a more nearly complete explanatory argument, though I do not claim to have included every possible step:

1. A person is more likely to take an action, the more valuable to him is the result of the action.
2. (Given) The person in question is a dramatic actor on a stage and has before him some kind of an audience.
3. (Given) A person's good stage performance leads to results that are valuable to him in two ways: (a) by the acceptance (applause or equivalent) of the audience and (b) an increase in psychological well-being. (I put the matter in this way, because it is not clear just what "to account for himself as more than a mere shell" means.)
4. Therefore, the person in question will try to perform well; if he succeeds, he is likely to continue to offer stage performances and improve his skill in his special style.

Goffman apparently makes no mention of proposition 1, though in fact it is essential to his argument. There are dozens of other examples in the book. Let me take just one more (Mitchell, 1978:148). Mitchell is talking about the work of Harold Garfinkel: "The issues of ethnomethodology are the issues of communication exchange in that the ethnomethodological search is for the communication processes that lead to a sense of common understanding among people." Here I shall not try to spell out the argument in something like complete form. But "common understanding" *rewards* people: social life is impossible without it. Therefore proposition 1 must take its place in the full argument. It does not: it is implied but never explicitly stated. If one were to be rigorous, one should make the above arguments, comparing the expected rewards of the actions in question with those of alternative actions open to the actor. For a brief but excellent reference to the problem of making general propositions explicit in explanation, see Singer (1981, in Rosenberg and Turner, 1981:72): "For the moment, the reader is invited to consider whether, for example, explaining attitude change in terms of changes in reference groups really explains much of anything at all, or whether it gives the illusion of explanation while simply pushing the crucial explanatory task one step further back." The proposition is in fact an *explicandum* without any deductive system to explain it. Would that we had more sociologists like Singer!

WHY DO SOCIOLOGISTS REJECT BEHAVIORAL PSYCHOLOGY IN EXPLANATION?

The next question is why many social scientists reject making their general propositions explicit or at least do not make them so in fact. It is true, and a good sign, that more and more of the concepts of behavioral psychology are finding their way into the discourse of sociology: reward (or reinforcement), punishment, outcome, cost. But to produce an argument that even begins to be logical, one must not just use some of the right words: one must actually state the propositions that relate the words to one another. One cannot have it both ways: one must not talk so much about theory in social science, unless one is prepared at some time to produce real theories. Only then can one tell whether the theories are the same—as I believe they are in sociology with respect to general propositions—or different. No propositions, no theories.

One reason for the rejection is that some social scientists believe the propositions of behavioral psychology to be obvious. Indeed most people know and can state the propositions, though seldom in just the way psychologists do. They even learn to use the proposi-

tions to get outcomes favorable to themselves, as when they increase the rewards they offer others for the goods and services they themselves need. How else could it be? Over the millennia human beings have had more experience with their own behavior than with any other class of phenomena. How could they fail to learn about it? And what if the propositions are obvious? They are still true, and we are as much concerned with truth in explanation as in any other aspect of science.

Some social scientists dislike the alleged hedonistic implications of behavioral psychology: all those individuals pursuing rewards, apparently for themselves alone. But behavioral psychology has no such implications, not even at its very base in social behavior. Social exchange is unlikely to continue unless each party rewards the other. And people can and do learn values, including the value of altruism. Some persons may even possess genes that facilitate their learning altruistic behavior, at least toward some kinds of others. And they can learn altruistic behavior by getting in return for it rewards that in themselves are just as individualistic and hedonistic as can be. For instance, their altruistic behavior may be rewarded by an increase in status accorded them by others.

James Coleman (1975, in Blau, 1975:79) rejects behavioral psychology because he believes it eliminates from the analysis of human behavior the crucial concept of purpose. It does no such thing. All it does is to say that most human purposes do not spring into being out of the blue. (Some drives of course are inborn, but purposes are learned.) If I say it is my purpose to go down to the corner postbox to post a letter, I must first have gone through at least one of a large class of previous experiences. For instance, my mother may have asked me to post the letter, and I may well have found obedience to my mother rewarding, in experiences going back to my earliest childhood. According to behavioral psychology, I am then more likely to comply with her requests again. And if the letter is my own; it reaches its destination—an event increasingly unlikely in the present U.S. Postal Service—and I receive a reply, my action (and my action *is* my purpose) is further reinforced. Look not just at different words but to the processes they refer to.

One reason the position I take here is unpopular is that it is "reductionist," and scientific reduction does not enjoy a good reputation in the social sciences. In the eyes of the vulgar—and I *mean* the vulgar—it seems to have the connotation of saying that some phenomenon is really "nothing but" something else, usually considered in some sense lower than the phenomenon reduced. If we get rid of these emotional connotations, reduction really seems to mean the explanation of a proposition from some named science with the help of a proposition from some other science in some sense more general. The classic example is Willard Gibbs' demonstration that the propositions of thermodynamics follow from those of statistical mechanics. (There are some tricky problems I shall not go into here concerning the definitions of the concepts of the reduced science in terms of the concepts of the more general science. Thus temperature in thermodynamics is defined as the mean kinetic energies of molecules in statistical mechanics.)

Reduction is going on all the time in the physical sciences and does not seem to arouse any hostility. Often it is of more intellectual than practical interest. But it does arouse hostility among sociologists. Here reduction seems to imply the explanation of empirical sociological propositions with the use of psychological covering laws, such as proposition 1 in the example I have given above. Apparently a sociological proposition is one that applies to groups or aggregates as such, but not to the individuals composing them, whereas psychological propositions certainly do apply to individuals, though the individuals in question may sometimes be many and anxious to secure the same rewards. The example of an explanation that I used above, is absurdly simple, and I should not have called the *explicandum* sociological if it had not been stated by a sociologist. Later I shall perhaps state a truly sociological *explicandum*. As a discipline, sociology never stops emphasizing its youth, and it certainly feels insecure. It fears that, were it reduced to psychology, it would lose its identity, than which nothing is more precious. I shall later suggest a further reason for this fear.

Sociology ought not to be so afraid, for were it to be reduced to psychology, it would be in good company. Economics is the most prestigious of the social sciences, even though it is not very successful. The propositions of at least microeconomics, such as the theory of price, can certainly be reduced to behavioral psychology, as those of sociology can. This does not mean that sociology will merge with microeconomics. People always forget that general propositions must always be applied to given conditions, and if the givens differ, the propositions that can be explained differ too. The basic given condition of classical economics is the market, in which none of the participants need enter into repeated exchanges with any one of the others. Under these conditions economics can explain many things, but not everything.

Much sociology, such as that of small groups, is concerned with a very different given condition. It is concerned with explaining empirical propositions that hold good under the given condition that the participants do hold regular exchanges with one another for a significant period of time. Under this condition behavioral psychology can explain the emergence, for instance, of a status system, which economics cannot (Homans, 1974:68; Emerson, 1981:36). Of course there are other areas where the two disciplines overlap. See particularly Olson (1965) on the "free rider" problem.

I shall not deal at length here with the question whether one of the propositions of behavioral sociology, such as proposition 1 in the example I used above, is a tautology. If the only way one has of telling how valuable a person finds a reward is to observe how much action he will take to get it, the proposition looks tautological indeed. Practically we observe how much action various kinds of people take to get it, and under what circumstances, and then explain or predict by the proposition the behavior of some new person, if he is similar in other respects to the persons we already know about. But the matter is trickier than that. The same problem arises in other sciences, including physics. Braithwaite shows that if their theories did not contain this tautological element, their theories would not be flexible enough to expand (Braithwaite, 1953:1–114). The argument is too long and intricate to reproduce here (see also Homans, 1974:33–37).

Nor shall I now deal with the claim that behavioral psychologists in their explanations do not take sufficient account of the social-structural conditions within which the behavior they explain occurs. Such conditions are represented by the given condition, proposition 2, in my little model explanation above. Of course we could have explained this condition, and treated it as still another *explicandum*, but did not, simply because to do so would have taken too much space. So-called social structure raises other issues, which I shall try to deal with later.

THE ADVANTAGES
TO SOCIOLOGY OF ACCEPTING
BEHAVIORAL PSYCHOLOGY

Sociology uses in its explanations the propositions of behavioral psychology but does not recognize that it does so because it hardly ever makes them explicit. Such a recognition would have several advantages. It would produce real, instead of enthymematic, theories. It would get rid of much of the time we now waste in "theoretical" disputes. It would help unify what now appears to be a hopelessly divided discipline. It would help clarify its relationships with other social-science disciplines. It would open the way for more rigorous solutions of old problems and for getting into new and interesting ones (see Emerson, 1981, and Opp, 1978, for examples).

But let me be practical. If sociological texts should spell out in full, beginning with their covering laws, the explanations of *all* the phenomena they are interested in, they would become too long for publication. They would also become unreadable, because the covering laws would have to be repeated over and over again. The texts are unreadable enough as it is. For myself I should be satisfied if a sociologist at least began his text by stating explicitly what his covering laws were, and applied them in some detail to at least one *explicandum*. Then the reader could be trusted to apply them to others. That is what I try to do (Homans, 1974). The practice is not common. One problem at least we shall never have to face. We shall never be able to explain every social phenomenon, not because we do not have the covering laws, but because we do not have enough knowledge of the given conditions we must apply them to. This is especially true of historical explanations. . . .

SOCIAL STRUCTURE:
THE TWO SOCIOLOGIES

I propose to end by talking about *social structure*, not because I think sociology has any strictly structural theory, unless the "pattern" type of theory is one, but because the idea helps account for some of the attitudes sociologists take toward the theories of other sociologists. No phrase is more often used nor defined in more varied or vaguer ways than *social structure*. Raymond Boudon is right in saying (1968:26) that some of the words used to define *structure* are at least as obscure as what is being defined. For me the phrase refers to relatively enduring—which may not endure very long—relationships between individuals or groups, including the endurance of certain kinds of social distributions, such as socioeconomic status. Others would add to the definition that all the elements of a social structure are related to one another in a system in such a way that if one element of the system changes all the rest must do so too. I myself have come to the conclusion that most social systems are much less organic and much looser than that. But things that claim to be called social structures in some sense certainly do exist.

The question then becomes one of explaining the origins, maintenance, and effects of social structures. Here sociologists tend to fall into roughly two groups. One, the smaller, to which I and, for instance, Joseph Berger and his colleagues belong (see Meeker, 1981) is largely concerned with explaining, using the propositions of behavioral psychology, how social structures arise and are maintained. Structure is, so to speak, the dependent variable. Often these sociologists explain the phenomena, such as the development of status systems, as they appear in small groups, where they can be closely observed and even experimented with. For the development of larger and more enduring social structures, sociologists must have recourse to the data of history, though no new general propositions are required. Large numbers of people, some acting in concert, some at odds with one another, and often without being aware of what the others are doing, regularly produce structures that are different from what any single one of the individuals or

groups would have intended. Sociologists critical of the approach persons like myself take are never tired of pointing out that we explain some of the phenomena appearing in small groups while simply taking as given the larger social structures within which these phenomena occur and which condition their existence. Our critics are quite right, but one never has space or information enough to explain everything. What is much more important, our critics forget that these social structures themselves did not appear out of thin air but were the product of human beings, often as I have said, many human beings all acting in accordance with behavioral principles. The larger structures often developed earlier than did the small ones, but they developed in the same way. The existence of social structures does nothing to overthrow the position taken here.

The other type of sociologists, and I believe their numbers are larger, tend to start with social structures as their independent variables and look at the effects of structures on the behavior of groups, categories, and individuals. They examine, for instance, the effect of racial segregation, surely a structural feature of some societies, on the quality of education received by individual children. One of the earliest and most distinguished leaders of this type of approach was the French sociologist Emile Durkheim. The trouble with his thinking and that of many of his followers is that they often talked as if the structures directly affected the behavior of groups, categories, and individuals (see esp. Durkheim, 1927). Remember that groups and categories themselves consist of individuals. But structures never act in this way. To explain their effects we need further propositions.

Consider a law, which is surely a structural feature of a society. It may act as a stimulus to a person's behavior. If it is enforced, a process that is always carried out by individuals and never by the law itself, it affects the behavior of those subject to the law through the rewards and punishments brought to bear by the enforcing officers. All of these mechanisms are mechanisms of behavioral psychology.

Yet it seems to me somehow natural that the sociologists who start from social structure would be less sympathetic with behavioralism than would the other group. Social structures often seem so strong and so enduring that it is difficult to bear constantly in mind that they are still the products of individual human actions. The distinction between the two kinds of sociologists has sometimes led to the argument that there are two sociologies, an *individualist* (the former group) and a *collectivist* (the latter). I confess I do not like the political connotations of the word *collectivist* (see esp. Vanberg, 1975; Opp, 1979).

Of course I have made the differences between the two sociologies too sharp, and some sociologists practice both kinds. Indeed that is what I myself try to do. After showing by the laws of behavioral psychology how a status system might arise and maintain itself in a small group, that is, how it might become a structure, I then turn around and show, by the same laws, how a person's position in this structure might affect his further behavior (Homans, 1974:319–39).

Some of the things that I have said in this paper I have said before, and I shall continue to do so in other publications so long as I am able or so long as I think their acceptance by sociologists is necessary to bring order out of the present chaos of our discipline.

REFERENCES

BANDURA, ALBERT. 1969. Principles of Behavior Modification. New York: Holt, Rinehart and Winston.

BLAU, PETER M., ed. 1975. Approaches to the Study of Social Structure. New York: Free Press.

BOUDON, RAYMOND, 1968. A quoi sert la notion de "Structure"? Paris: Gallimard.

BRAITHWAITE, RICHARD B. 1953. Scientific Explanation. Cambridge: Cambridge University Press.

COLEMAN, JAMES S. 1975. "Social structure and a theory of action." Pp. 76–93 in Blau, ed., Approaches to the Study of Social Structure. New York: Free Press.

DURKHEIM EMILE. 1927. Les Règles de la Méthode sociologique. Paris: Alcan.

EMERSON, RICHARD M. 1981. "Social exchange theory." Pp. 30–65 in Rosenberg and Turner, eds. Social Psychology: Sociological Perspectives. New York: Basic Books.

GARDINER, PATRICK, ed. 1959. Theories of History, Glencoe, Ill.: Free Press.

HOLTON, GERALD, 1978. The Scientific Imagination. Cambridge: Cambridge University Press.

HOMANS, GEORGE C.
_____. 1958. "Social behavior as exchange." American Journal of Sociology 63:597–606.

_____. 1962. Sentiments and Activities. Glencoe, Ill.: Free Press.

_____. 1974. Social Behavior. Rev. ed. New York: Harcourt Brace Jovanovich.

MEEKER, BARBARA F. 1981. "Expectation states and interpersonal behavior." Pp. 290–319 in Rosenberg and Turner, eds., Social Psychology: Sociological Perspectives. New York: Basic Books.

MILL, JOHN STUART. [1843]. A System of Logic. New York: Harper, 1881.

MITCHELL, JACK N. 1978. Social Exchange, Dramaturgy and Ethnomethodology. New York: Elsevier.

NAGEL, ERNEST. 1961. The Structure of Science. New York: Harcourt, Brace and World.

OLSON, MANCUR, JR. 1965. The Logic of Collective Action. Cambridge, Mass.: Harvard University Press.

OPP, KARL-DIETER. 1978. Theorie sozialer Krisen. Hamburg: Hoffman and Campe.

_____. 1979. Individualistische Sozialwissenschaft. Stuttgart: Ferdinand Enke.

ROSENBERG, MORRIS, AND RALPH H. TURNER, eds. 1981. Social Psychology: Sociological Perspectives. New York: Basic Books.

SINGER, ELEANOR. 1981. "Reference groups and social evaluations." Pp. 66–93 in Rosenberg and Turner, eds., Social Psychology: Sociological Perspectives. New York: Basic Books.

SKINNER, B.F. 1953. Science and Human Behavior. New York: Macmillan.

SUPPE, FREDERICK, ed. 1974. The Structure of Scientific Theories. Urbana: University of Illinois Press.

VANBERG, VIKTOR. 1975. Die Zwei Soziologien. Tübingen: Mohr.

WATKINS, J.W.N. 1959. "Historical explanation in the social sciences." Pp. 503–14 in Gardiner, ed., Theories of History, Glencoe, Ill.: Free Press.

STRUCTURALISM VERSUS INDIVIDUALISM: SHADOWBOXING IN THE DARK*

BRUCE H. MAYHEW

One wonders sometimes if science will not grind to a stop in an assemblage of walled-in hermits, each mumbling to himself words in a private language that only he can understand (Kenneth E. Boulding, 12).

In recent years, I have heard from one source and another that there are several structuralisms around. There are varieties of both Marxist and non-Marxist structuralism (Sahlins; Sebag). These include French structuralism, British structuralism, and—difficult to believe though it may be—even an American structuralism. Similarly, under a plethora of names, there are several varieties of "methodological individualism," such as symbolic interactionism, ethnomethodology, behavioral sociology, etc. There is, however, nothing new in this spectrum.

Sociology has always contained a marked variety of metatheoretical positions. Individualism and structuralism, as I shall define

*Reprinted from *Social Forces* (59:2, December 1980). "Structuralism versus Individualism: Shadowboxing in the Dark" by Bruce H. Mayhew. Copyright © The University of North Carolina Press.

them, are only two voices in a wider, many-sided conversation. The larger din provides a background of noise making discussion of this one difference difficult to comprehend. There is a tendency to confuse the individualism-structuralism dispute with the disagreements between the subjectivist and objectivist camps, the humanist and naturalist camps, the conflict and consensus camps, the voluntarist and mechanist camps, the idealist and materialist camps, the essentialist and analyst camps, etc. The confusion is compounded by the fact that there is some truth to the view that individualism, on the one hand, and structuralism, on the other, have tended to cluster with particular end points of these other axes, somewhat along the lines suggested in Table 1. But the clustering is never complete, and we can find an odd man out for any of these comparisons. Durkheim, for example, was a structuralist, but he could hardly be called a conflict theorist. Similarly, Homans is an individualist, but his style of explanation is nomothetic.

Some theorists contend that all the differ-

ences I have listed in Table 1 are false oppositions (e.g., Bourdieu). What they mean, however, is that only one side is correct. Bourdieu
solves the opposition between voluntarism
and mechanism by embracing free will.

Excluding the differences for unit of analysis, I could have constructed two tables with
the same axes shown in Table 1: one for the
individualists and one for the structuralists.
Within these new tables, the left-hand side
would correspond to "soft" individualism and
"soft" structuralism, while the right-hand side
would correspond to "hard" individualism
and "hard" structuralism. Such a pair of tables
would make it easier to locate Durkheim and
Homans, but it would still show significant
discrepancies. If I went on to construct four
tables, then eight, etc., the kaleidoscope of sociological assumptions and concerns would
be more accurately revealed. But an expanded number of tables would need more
axes than I have indicated in Table 1.

Table 1 is no more than the tip of an ice-
berg. One need only consider the varieties of
Marxist sociology, which Rodinson has estimated to number possibly thousands, to appreciate the fragmented nature of sociology's
intellectual domain. I am referring to academic Marxism (Legros and Copans). Doctri-
naire Marxism (cf. Assmann and Stollberg) is

of no interest here. Structuralists would agree
with Varga (3–4) that "dogmatic Marxists"
pose a barrier to sound Marxian analysis, for
the same reason that militant enthusiam
poses a barrier to *any* analysis (Rodinson, 14).

Further complicating matters is the fact
that sociologists are not only speaking from
different camps, they are speaking different
languages. Shall I discuss individualism and
structuralism with a subjectivist definition of
terms or an objectivist definition of terms?
Shall my syntax be in the humanist or naturalist mode? Actually, I have no choice: time
compels me to glide over the terminiological
squabble. My biases fall more on the right-
hand side of Table 1, so I will speak from
there. I like to believe that I can appreciate
some hypotheses offered by the left-hand
side, but my appreciation has limits. Unlike
the individualists, I do not believe that one
can jump overboard while swimming under-
water. Nor do I imagine that anything I say
here will diminish the controversy. Most
American sociologists listen in the language
of individualism. They have, as the structuralists say, cultivated a trained incapacity to hear
any other point of view.

Most of what I have to say about structuralism does not derive from sources in American
sociology. The reasons for this are numerical.

TABLE 1
Some Differences in Metatheoretical Positions Adopted by Schools (Factions) in Sociology

Differences in Assumptions and Concerns Corresponding Roughly to:		
Psychologism		Sociologism
Individual (individualism)	(Unit of analysis)	Social network (structuralism)
Inside (subjectivism)	(Location of observer)	Outside (objectivism)
Essentialist	(Construction of phenomena)	Analyst
Ideal	(Prime movers are)	Material
Voluntarism (free will)	(Dynamic assumed)	Mechanism (impersonal constraint)
Ideographic (interpretation; humanist)	(Understanding mode)	Nomothetic (explanation; natural-ist)
Consensus	(Basis for association)	Conflict
The present	(Time frame for study)	All history & prehistory
Parochial	(Location of inquiry)	Cross-cultural

Within American sociology, structuralists have always been a tiny minority, a minority that is seldom heard. Partly for this reason, individualists in American sociology do not have a marked familiarity with the concerns of structural sociology. But, even more to the point, within the United States most structuralists are not in sociology. They are found largely in anthropology, geography, economics, and history. For this reason, structural sociologists in America spend most of their time talking to people outside sociology (Blau, b). They talk to other sociologists only on very rare occasions. Since, on these rare occasions, structuralists have to switch to the language of individualism in order to be understood, structuralists generally regard these conversations as a waste of time. Finally, the structuralists in the United States are a tiny minority of all structuralists in the world. Most structural sociology—regardless of the academic field which develops it—is done outside the United States. This is partly because many Marxists are structuralists (however, some structuralists are not Marxists). There are very few Marxists in the United States in any field of social science. Furthermore, most Marxists in American sociology are actually individualists who have adopted only those elements of dogmatic Marxism which they see as consistent with their individualist assumptions (e.g., Flacks and Turkel). Within American sociology, the number of Marxists concerned with explanation (as distinguished from preaching) can probably be counted on one finger.

The brevity of this essay will require that I speak in caricatures, rather than in detailed qualifications. For this reason, among others, some structuralists would not agree with what I have to say about structuralism and some individualists would not agree with what I have to say about individualism. Although I will be critical of individualism, I will at least emulate one of its high priests by speaking *ex cathedra* (Freud).

STRUCTURALISM

From the holist or totalist point of view, everything happens at the population level, so that the individual is nothing but a passive reflection or, at best, a partial one, of processes which are quite independent of him and belong to a quite different genetic scale (Jean Piaget, 393).

Writing in 1857, Karl Marx formulated the view of society which I take to be fundamental: "Society does not consist of individuals, but expresses the sum of interrelations in which individuals stand with respect to one another" (176). In this view, the individual is never the unit of analysis in either research or theory construction. Rather, in this *structuralist* conception of social life, sociologists are studying a communication network mapped on some human population. That network, the interaction which proceeds through it, and the social structures which emerge in it are the subject matter of sociology. Sociology is therefore the study of this network's *organization*. It is an attempt to construct and test explanations of variation in social organization.

Of course, structuralists conceive of their task in somewhat broader terms than "social organization" alone would suggest. They are also concerned with determining how social organization is related to other forms of organization. At a minimum, the latter include (1) the *organization of information* (symbols)—commonly called the cultural or ideological system—and (2) the *organization of materials* (tools)—commonly called the technological system. Most structuralists (see Duncan) would also insist that explaining social organization presupposes a knowledge of the social network's underlying demographic structure as well as its ecological context (biophysical and social environment).

In studying organization, structuralists are concerned with at least two kinds of phenomena: (1) aggregate properties of populations and (2) *emergent* (purely structural) properties of organization itself. An aggregate property is one which can be used to construct a variable by simple addition of bio-physical characteristics of individual population elements, e.g., population size. However, an emergent property can only be constructed from relations between population elements. In the case of social organization, an emergent property is one defined on the overall connectivity of the network, and is not, therefore, derived from characteristics of individual population elements (Krippendorff). The division of labor and the degree of stratification are emergent properties of social organization.

Structuralists do not study human behavior. The behavior they do study is that of the variables which define various aspects of social organization, its population, environment, ideological and technological subsystems. For structuralists, a general sociological theory is a set of theorems stated in terms of these variables, theorems which will predict and explain the structure and dynamics of societal phenomena. This is a rather large task—coextensive with sociology itself—and it has few workers in the United States.

Most American sociologists do not study sociology in the structuralist sense of the term indicated above. Rather, they merely assume the existence of social structures in order to study their impact on *individuals,* that is, in order to study *social psychology* (the study of the behavior and experience of individuals in social stimulus situations: see Mead; Sherif; Sherif and Sherif). In this subfield of psychology (Sherif and Sherif) the objectives are expected to be aligned with those of general psychology (Asch; Mead; Sherif; Sherif and Sherif) not necessarily with the objectives of sociology (see Blau, a). In other words, most American sociologists adopt the *individualist* perspective in that the individual is their unit of analysis and so-called "human behavior"

(in both its subjective and objective aspects) is the individual level phenomena they seek to explain or interpret.

To a very large degree, this means that structuralists and individualists are asking different questions. They are attempting to explain different things. I would not say (as individualists often do) that structuralists and individualists are merely studying different aspects of the same phenomena. This may happen in a few instances, but generally their paths of inquiry diverge to such a marked degree that no shared language and no line of communication unites them in any common discourse. From my structuralist point of view, the psychological concerns of American sociologists do not bear on questions of social structure and organization, and at best would have only a secondary relevance to them (Blau, a). The reason for this is quite simple (say the structuralists). If one assumes the structure of society in order to examine its impact on the immediate acts, thoughts, and feelings of individuals, one has assumed most of what has to be explained (indeed, about 95 percent of the variation in human society) in order to study a small part of human activity and experience (about 5 percent—and as such, difficult to distinguish from random noise). Whereas, in the structuralist view, the primary task of sociology (Blau, a) is not to assume the empirical conditions of social structure, but to explain its existence in the first place (the opposite of social psychology's concerns). The reason for this, of course, is that structural sociologists are interested in explaining most of what happens in human society, not some minute fraction of it. . . .

A DIALOGUE OF THE DEAF

The predictability of academic debates is less depressing than their emptiness (Gail T. Parker, 43).

Since structuralists are interested in explaining organization and individualists are interested in interpreting the acts of individuals, it surprises no one that they make radically different assumptions, conceive of social phenomena in radically different terminologies, and generally approach any topic from opposite directions. It would only be surprising to find one of them who understands what the other is saying.

The differences between structuralist and individualist modes of apprehending social phenomena could only be enumerated in a lengthy monograph. I will mention only a few of them here.

Individualists may speak of certain social characteristics of individuals, such as an individual's ethnicity, or of certain psychological characteristics of individuals, such as an individual's self-concept. Structuralists do not speak of individuals in these terms (except when trying to communicate with an individualist). Structuralists do not attribute social or psychological characteristics to individual humans. Rather, structuralists view individual human beings as biological organisms. Hence, individual characteristics might include pulse rate, blood pressure, height, metabolic rate and so on. But there are no social characteristics of individuals. To structuralists, social phenomena are properties of social networks (properties of organization); they are never characteristics of biological individuals. Furthermore, for structuralists, psychological phenomena do not exist (they are not defined).

What individualists call psychology is for the structuralist either a part of biology, or it is an item of data in a culture which posits psychic phenomena (in the same sense that witchcraft is an item of data in a culture which posits witches). To the structuralist, people who talk about self-concepts are like people who talk about witches.

To the structuralist, psychology is contemporary civilization's witchcraft and psychologists are its corresponding witchdoctors. This refers, of course, to psychology as the study of the psyche (mind). Behavioral psychology is a contradiction in terms, and structuralists relegate it to the field of biology. Structuralists generally consider that there are two fields of study relevant to understanding human society: biology and (the structuralists version of) sociology. They fail to see any psychic (mental) phenomena falling in between these two, for much the same reasons as are implied in van den Berge's statement: "Several brands of social psychology, notably psychoanalysis, symbolic interactionism, and the currently fashionable 'ethnomethodology' rely heavily on a conceptual apparatus that presupposes questionable inferences from people's behavior, rather than being directly derived from readily observable behavior" (19). Structuralists tend to agree with Kunkel that sociologists have made too many unwarranted assumptions about human beings.

Structuralists consider that the human brain is a biological phenomenon and that its electro-chemical processes are the subject matter of biology, most particularly of what may be called "machine biology." Human organisms are conceived as information and energy processing machines, much as one finds them treated in the writings of von Bertalanffy (a, b) and Broadbent. To structuralists, the human central nervous system is a biological computer.

Accordingly, structuralists do not assume that people think, that people are conscious, or have a mind as these terms are defined by individualists—e.g., Ritzer et al. claim that "To the sociologist, the mind is not viewed as a physical entity, but as a mental process" (25). The sociologist in question is not a structuralist. From the structuralist point of view, what individualists call "being conscious" is an electrochemical configuration not unlike the one projected on a television screen. To structuralists, this configuration is a "simulation function" of the central nervous system (Monod). From the structuralist point of view, differences between the biological computers in grasshoppers and humans is a difference in the structure of nervous systems as empirically determined by biologists. It is not a difference to be endowed with divine qualities.

Hence, one of the largest differences between structuralists and individualists occurs in their treatment of the organization of information. Initially, I indicated that this organization was in terms of symbols. I said that to avoid creating a panic. To structuralists, information fills a much broader category along the lines conceived in the mathematical theory of information (Meyer-Eppler), whereas individualists generally include only symbols processed by the human central nervous system. Because they are interested in population structure and ecological context, structuralists include the information transmitted in light waves (von Foerster), through the genetic code (Monod), and even in the viral diseases of epidemiological systems (Weidl).

Needless to say, structuralists distinguish cultural information from these other forms and do not minimize the importance of symbol systems organized into social ideologies. Rather, exactly that form of information organization is of paramount importance to structuralists. But they do not suffer from the conceptual restrictions of individualism. Structuralists find symbols stored in either the biological memory banks of humans or in the external memory banks of material culture: writing in books (Febvre and Martin), numbers in computers (Janco and Furjot), paintings on cave walls (Leroi-Gourhan), etc.

Whereas individualism, with its emphasis on "minded" individuals, wanders off into

free will (Robertson) and random behavior (Blumer), structuralists study the organization of information at the societal level, including the relations of information transfer between social networks and their environments (social and bio-physical). For example, structuralists see the development of "artificial memory" in material culture as a crucial shift in social history, leading to the structural transformations into urban civilizations (Lévi-Strauss), bureaucratic empires (Loewe), and on to the bustle of information levels in industrial societies (Blute; Segraves). These developments in information processing technology are used to explain changes in the organization of information itself (Goody).

Thus, while some sociologists have insisted that humans are fundamentally non-logical or irrational (Pareto, a, b) and others have treated them as rational (Heath), structuralists see these phenomena as functions of information processing technology. As Goody noted, only with the development of external memory banks in the form of writing was it possible to develop the logic underlying Western science. Without external representations of statements, syllogisms could not be systematically articulated by humans. Their biological computers were too frail—hence Lévy-Bruhl's thesis. Communication among humans in the absence of material aids, and even with a few, is notoriously prone to every kind of distortion (cf. Campbell, a; DeFleur). The human central nervous system can perform logical operations when it can cultivate that form of information organization through external props, through material information processing technology. Piaget appears to be one of the few biologists to have grasped the significance of these material developments.

Structuralists do not assume that humans are logical or non-logical, rational or non-rational, per se. They see logic and rationality as aspects of the organization of information, as properties of sociocultural systems, not as characteristics of individuals (cf. Godelier). An integral part of the structuralist argument rests on the extension of the *material bases* of communication in society (Østerberg, a, b). But, structuralists are not committed to a view that technology alone alters information structure. They see forms of social organization as being of critical importance in transforming and sustaining particular systems of ideas (cf. Foucault).

All this discussion of machine biology and material technology makes it easier to see why structuralists do not employ subjectivist concepts such as purposes or goals in their analyses. What these vague notions were presumed to accomplish by individualists are, in the structuralist view, accomplished in a more parsimonious fashion by blind variation (Campbell, b) and equifinality (von Bertalanffy, a).

In a word, even in looking at some very limited aspects of sociocultural phenomena—such as the organization of information—we find that the differences between structuralists and individualists are enormous.

Another point at which there is a nearly perfect distinction between structuralist and individualist conceptions is the distinction drawn between micro- and macro-level social phenomena (Duverger). The differentiation has to be made primarily in the way they treat micro-level phenomena, because most individualists fail to mention (or even deny the existence of) macro-level social phenomena. If individualists mention macro-level phenomena, they usually see it as a direct extension of micro-level activity (e.g., Homans, a, b).

That is, for most individualists micro-level phenomena are the only social phenomena: the individual is the unit of analysis and "human behavior" in relatively small face-to-face aggregates is the object of inquiry. Macro-aggregates are merely additive collections of mi-

cro-aggregates: human behavior is simply summed over a larger number of individuals. The social aspect of the human behavior studied is usually an incidental feature—it merely indicates the presence of others. Individualists seldom study social interaction itself, even when provided with the opportunity to do so (e.g., Homans, c). On those rare occasions when behavior involves some kind of social interaction, it is seen at both levels of aggregation as a direct function of subjective states, such as attitudes (Sakoda). Generally, however, interaction is ignored, and the focus of inquiry is on the individual's subjectively defined "experiences" (cf. Smith; Smith-Lovin).

In the structuralist view, micro- and macro-level social phenomena are distinguished by the nature of the *population elements* on which social networks are defined. Micro-level phenomena are defined on networks of relations between individual human organisms, usually, but not invariably, in face-to-face groups. Macro-level social phenomena, on the other hand, are defined on networks of relations between groups, communities, organizations, societies or any other set of supra-individual population elements selected for study. The variables defined on these two levels may, therefore, be the same: social inequality, division of labor, network vulnerability, etc. Some differences occur, however, because there is usually a more restricted range for each variable in micro-level networks. Micro-level networks seldom include more than forty to fifty population elements and usually range in size from two to thirty people. This restricted size range places definite upper limits on the range of structural variables defined on micro-level networks. Also, some kinds of social relations can be defined between individual organisms which cannot be defined between groups and vice versa. In any case, the structuralist concern is the same for both levels: the organization of the network. Structuralists are particularly concerned with determining whether the same or different processes and structures occur at these two levels and especially with whether the same or different theoretical considerations apply to them.

Accordingly, for structuralists, the shift from macro- to micro-level phenomena does not involve a change in the unit of analysis; it involves a change in the kind of population elements on which the unit of analysis is defined. In structural sociology the unit of analysis is always the social network, *never the individual.* I have already stated the reason for this: structuralists see human organisms and their behavior as *biological,* not social phenomena.

. . . What I have said here—incomplete though it may be as a catalogue of diversity—should be sufficient to make it clear that any conversation between a structuralist and an individualist is a dialogue of the deaf. They are speaking different languages even when they employ the same terms.

REFERENCES

ASCH, SOLOMON. 1952. *Social Psychology.* Englewood Cliffs: Prentice Hall.

ASSMANN, GEORG, AND RUHARD STOLLBERG (eds.). 1977. *Grundlagen der marxistischleninistischen Soziologie.* Berlin: Dietz.

BERTALANFFY, LUDWIG, VON. a:1940. "Der Organismus als physikalisches System betrachtet." *Die Naturwissenschaffen* 28:521–31.

_____. b:1951. *Theoretische Biologie.* Bern: Francke.

BLAU, PETER M. a:1969. "Objectives of Sociology." In Robert Bierstedt (ed.), *A Design for Sociology.* Philadelphia: American Academy of Political and Social Science.

_____. b:1977. *Inequality and Heterogeneity.* New York: Free Press.

BLUMER, H. 1962. "Society as Symbolic Interaction." In Arnold M. Rose (ed.), *Human Behavior and Social Processes.* Boston: Houghton Mifflin.

BLUTE, M. 1972. "The Growth of Science and Economic Development." *American Sociological Review* 37:455–64.

BOULDING, K.E. 1956. "General Systems Theory." *General Systems* 1:11–17.

BOURDIEU, PIERRE. 1972. *Esquisse d'une théorie de la pratique.* Genève: Droz.

BROADBENT, DONALD E. 1971. *Decision and Stress.* New York: Academic Press.

CAMPBELL, D.T. a:1958. "Systematic Error on the Part of Human Links in Communication Systems." *Information and Control* 1:334–69.

_____. b:1960. "Blind Variation and Selective Survival as a General Strategy in Knowledge-Processes." In M.C. Yovits and S. Cameron (eds.), *Self-organizing Systems.* London: Pergamon.

DEFLEUR, M.L. 1962. "Mass Communication and the Study of Rumor." *Sociological Inquiry* 32:51–70.

DUNCAN, O.D. 1964. "Social Organization and the Ecosystem." In Robert E.L. Faris (ed.), *Handbook of Modern Sociology.* Chicago: Rand McNally.

DUVERGER, MAURICE. 1964. *Méthodes des sciences sociales.* (3. ed.) Paris: PUF.

FEBVRE, LUCIEN, AND HENRI-JEAN MARTIN. 1958. *L'Apparition du livre.* Paris: Albin Michel.

FLACKS, R., AND G. TURKEL. 1978. "Radical Sociology." *Annual Review of Sociology* 4:193–238.

FOERSTER, H., VON. 1966. "From Stimulus to Symbol." In George Kepes (ed.), *Sign, Image, and Symbol.* New York: Braziller.

FOUCAULT, MICHEL. 1975. *Surveiller et punir.* Paris: Gallimard.

FREUD, SIGMUND. 1940. "Abriss der Psychoanalyse." *Imago* 25:7–67.

GODELIER, MAURICE. 1966. *Rationalité et irrationalité en économie.* Paris: Maspero.

GOODY, J. 1973. "Evolution and Communication." *British Journal of Sociology* 24:1–12.

HEATH, ANTHONY. 1976. *Rational Choice and Social Exchange.* Cambridge: Cambridge University Press.

HOMANS, GEORGE C. a:1946. "The Small Warship." *American Sociological Review* 11: 294–300.

_____. b:1950. *The Human Group.* New York: Harcourt, Brace.

_____. c:1954. "The Cash Posters." *American Sociological Review* 19:724–33.

JANCO, MANUEL, AND DANIEL FURJOT. 1972. *Informatique et capitalisme.* Paris: Maspero.

KRIPPENDORFF, K. 1971. "Communication and the Genesis of Structure." *General Systems* 16:171–85.

KUNKEL, J.H. 1969. "Some Behavioral Aspects of Systems Analysis." *Pacific Sociological Review* 12:12–22.

LEGROS, D. AND J. COPANS. 1976. "Est-il possible de synthétiser formalisme, substantivisme et marxisme en anthropologie économique?" *Revue canadienne de sociologie et d'anthropologie* 113:373–86.

LEROI-GOURHAN, ANDRÉ. 1965. *Préhistoire de l'art occidental.* Paris: Mazenod.

LÉVI-STRAUSS, CLAUDE. 1949. *Les Structures élémentaires de la parenté.* Paris: Plon.

LÉVY-BRUHL, LUCIEN. 1910. *Les Fonctions mentales dans les sociétés inférieurs.* Paris: Alcan.

LOEWE, MICHAEL. 1966. *Imperial China.* New York: Praeger.

MARX, KARL. 1939. *Grundrisse der Kritik der politischen Okonomie (Rohentwurf 1857–1858).* Moskau: Verlag für fremdsprache Literatur.

MEAD, GEORGE H. 1934. *Mind, Self, and Society.* Chicago: University of Chicago Press.

MEYER-EPPLER, WERNER. 1959. *Grundlagen und Anwendung der Informationstheorie.* Berlin: Springer.

MONOD, JACQUES. 1970. *Le Hasard et la nécessité.* Paris: Seuil.

ØSTERBERG, DAG. a:1971. *Makt og materiell.* Oslo: Pax.

———. b:1977. *Sosiologiens nøkkelbegreper.* Oslo: Cappelen.

PARETO, VILFREDO. a:1909. *Manuel d'économie politique.* Paris: Giard et Brière.

———. b:1923. *Trattato di Sociologia generale.* Seconda edizione. Firenze: Barbèra. Vol. I.

PARKER, G.T. 1976. "While Alma Mater Burns." *Atlantic* 238:39–47.

PIAGET, JEAN. 1967. *Biologie et connaissance.* Paris: Gallimard.

RITZER, GEORGE, KENNETH C.W. KAMMEYER, AND NORMAN R. YETMAN. 1979. *Sociology.* Boston: Allyn Bacon.

ROBERTSON, IAN. 1977. *Sociology.* New York: Worth.

RODINSON, MAXIME. 1966. *Islam et capitalisme.* Paris: Seuil.

SAHLINS, MARSHALL D. 1976. *Culture and Practical Reason.* Chicago: University of Chicago Press.

SAKODA, J.M. 1971. "A Checkerboard Model of Social Interaction." *Journal of Mathematical Sociology* 1:119–32.

SEBAG, LUCIEN. 1964. *Marxisme et structuralisme.* Paris: Payot.

SEGRAVES, B.A. 1974. "Ecological Generalization and Structural Transformation of Sociocultural Systems." *American Anthropoligist* 76:530–52.

SHERIF, MUSAFER. 1948. *An Outline of Social Psychology.* New York: Harper.

SHERIF, MUSAFER, AND CAROLYN W. SHERIF. 1956. *An Outline of Social Psychology.* 2D ed. New York: Harper & Row.

SMITH, T.W. 1979. "Happiness." *Social Psychology Quarterly* 42:18–30.

SMITH-LOVIN, L. 1979. "Behavioral Settings and Impressions Formed from Social Scenarios." *Social Psychology Quarterly* 42:31–43.

VAN DEN BERGE, PIERRE L. 1975. *Man in Society.* New York: Elsevier.

VARGA, EUGEN. 1964. *Ocherki po problemam politekonomii kapitalizma.* Moskva: Izdatel'stvo politicheskoi literatury.

WEIDL, WOLFHARD. 1964. *Virus und Molekularbiologie.* (2. Auflage) Berlin: Springer.

THE CONTRIBUTION
OF RATIONAL CHOICE THEORY
TO MACROSOCIOLOGICAL RESEARCH*

DEBRA FRIEDMAN AND MICHAEL HECHTER

Until recently, microsociologists and macro-sociologists have fundamentally disagreed about the proper level of analysis for sociological inquiry. As members of these two camps increasingly have come to appreciate the theoretical and empirical payoffs of joint venture, however, there is a new call for micro-macro research (Collins 1981; Hechter 1983; Coleman 1986; Alexander, Giesen, Munch, and Smelser 1987). One of the (several) starting points from which it is possible to generate explanations that provide for micro-macro links is rational choice theory. Beyond its reliance on the concept of purposive action (the idea that all action is intentional) and its commitment to methodological individualism (the doctrine that all social phenomena are, in principle, only explicable in

*From Debra Friedman and Michael Hechter, "The Contribution of Rational Choice Theory to Microsociological Research," *Sociological Theory* 6:2 (Fall 1988), 201–204, 212–18. Reprinted with permission of the American Sociological Association and the authors.

terms of the action of individuals), the properties of rational choice theory are poorly appreciated by many sociologists.

Our aims in this paper are threefold: (1) to provide the bare skeleton of all rational choice arguments; (2) to demonstrate their applicability to a range of macrosociological concerns; and (3) to discuss the weaknesses of rational choice and the possibilities for its future development.

A case for rational choice theory could be made on epistemological grounds, but we shall not make it; such philosophical discussions have flowered at least since the time of Thomas Hobbes. Nor will we argue for its merits in accounting for social-psychological and small group processes; in sociology this has been the province of exchange theory (Heath 1976; Emerson 1981; Cook 1987). Nor will we argue for the development of the theory merely for theory's sake; the search for Nash equilibria and for saddle points we leave to others. Instead, we shall argue that rational choice offers an alternative theory to explain, and sometimes to predict, *empirical* observations that have traditionally been of concern to *macrosociologists*. In future contests with other kinds of explanations of these same phenomena, we will be content to let empirical analyses tip the balance in favor of one theory or the other.

I. A SKELETAL RATIONAL CHOICE MODEL

What follows ia a basic skeleton of all rational choice models, inclusive of the bones found in nearly every rational choice argument, and exclusive of the flesh of any specific rational choice model. For the moment, the work of those who would rearrange the skeletal frame will be set aside. A diagram of the main points of the argument that follows is to be found in Figure 1.

Figure 1 is intended to be a heuristic device to accompany the discussion in the first and second sections of the paper. The solid lines represent the explanatory paths of typical rational choice theories. Some theories, for example, link purposive actors to social outcomes through the mechanism of opportunity costs, while others link purposive actors with social outcomes through the mechanism of institutional constraints, or preferences. The paths are numbered for the purpose of identification. The aggregation mechanism is enclosed in broken lines to indicate that it is often implicit in these theories.

Basic Assumptions

Rational choice models always rely on conceptions of actors as purposive and intentional. These actors are conceived to have given preferences, values or utilities (here-

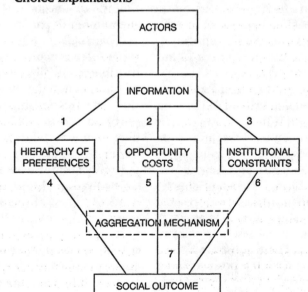

FIGURE 1

The Various Paths to Social Outcomes in Rational Choice Explanations

after termed *preferences* in this essay). They act with the express purpose of attaining ends that are consistent with their hierarchy of preferences. In general, rational choice theory is mute about what these preferences might be and where they come from. In any specific rational choice theory, however, actors' ends (and the preferences implied by those ends) must be specified in advance. Without such prespecification of actors' ends, rational choice explanations are liable to be tautological.

Yet individual action is not solely the product of intentions. It is also subject to constraints that derive from at least two independent sources. The first set of constraints is due to a scarcity of resources. Differential possession of and access to resources make some ends easy for individuals to attain, some more difficult, and preclude the attainment of others altogether. On account of scarcity, then, the *opportunity costs*—those costs associated with foregoing the next most attractive course of action—will vary considerably for different actors. Hence, actors will not always choose that course of action which satisfies their most valued ends. In seeking to reap maximum benefit, actors keep a wary eye on opportunity costs, for these lower the net benefit of any contemplated action.

Social institutions can be a second source of constraints. The modal individual will find his or her actions checked from birth to death by familial and school rules; laws and ordinances; firm policies; churches, synagogues and mosques; and hospitals and funeral parlors. By restricting the feasible set of courses of action available to individuals, enforceable rules of the game—including norms, laws, agendas, and voting rules—systematically affect social outcomes. These constraints serve to provide sanctions of both a positive and a negative kind that raise or lower the net benefit of any contemplated course of action.

Therefore, within rational choice models, variations in outcomes can be due logically to variations in preferences, in opportunity costs, and/or in institutional constraints. We will discuss examples of research demonstrating each of these three sources of variation. For example, Thomas Schelling's (1978) model of residential segregation is based on the assumption that individuals have a weak *preference* for living with their own kind (this kind of explanation corresponds to path 4 in Figure 1). This low level preference, he shows, rapidly results in a chain of actions that leads to extreme segregation—a social outcome that is unintended by any of the individual actors who participate in the system. Take away the weak preference assumption and Schelling's predicted outcome disappears. Another example of a model in which variation in social outcomes is attributed to variations in preferences is illustrated in Anthony Downs's (1957:118–25) discussion of the causes of two-party as against multi-party systems. For Downs, the distribution of single-peaked voter preferences across a left/right political dimension is a major determinant of the number of parties in a given society.

Opportunity costs also can be the source of variation in outcomes (path 5). These are not distributed equally, either over every category of actor, or for the same sort of action. Consider the relationship between age and opportunity costs. Older people (especially older women) tend to attend church more frequently than younger people do: the opportunity costs associated with foregoing possible salvation rise as the prospect of death nears (Azzi and Ehrenberg 1975). In general, these costs drop in the post-child-rearing, post-retirement phase of life. Young people engage in crime more often than their elders (Gottfredson and Hirschi 1986) because, in general, they have less to lose if they are apprehended (that is, they have lower opportunity costs). Finally, it has often been observed that hard science is a young person's game. This is because the opportunity costs associated with retooling each time a technological advance occurs are often prohibitively high.

The third major source of variation in outcomes is due to *institutional constraints* (path 6). It is by now well appreciated that different voting rules—majority, plurality, or unanimity—can influence both the time it takes to arrive at a decision as well as the actual decision itself (Buchanan and Tullock 1962). As any member of an academic department knows, the order of items on an agenda may have implications for which items hold the day (Riker 1986).

Opportunity costs and institutional constraints are more often the cause of variation in rational choice explanations than are preferences. Less is known about preferences—about their origin, persistence, or malleability—than about either opportunity costs or institutional constraints. There are several reasons that the role of preferences tends to be slighted in rational choice models. First, opportunity costs and institutional constraints are more reliably measured than are internal states. Second, while price theory undergirds opportunity cost arguments, and a multitude of empirical generalizations support institutional constraint arguments, no comparable theoretical or empirical structure supports arguments based on preferences. Until we have a robust theory of preference-formation, or a rich body of data, the persuasiveness of explanations based upon preferences will hinge on reader's perceptions of their intuitive appeal.

There are two other elements common to all rational choice models. The first is an *aggregation mechanism* by which the separate individual actions are combined to produce the social outcome. Often rational choice theories read as if there were no aggregation problem. This is because in most of the original applications the market is taken to be the mechanism that aggregates preferences. In non-market applications there is an assumption, which is frequently hidden, that all actors have similar preference orderings over a given set of choices. The usual defense of this assumption relies on the law of large numbers (Stinchcombe 1968:67–8; Hechter 1987: 31–3).

The alternative to making an assumption of homogeneous preference orderings is to specify an aggregation mechanism that reflects the preferences of the constituent actors. It has been difficult to formulate such a mechanism: when actors have heterogeneous preference orderings, no determinate collective outcome may be able to be predicted (Arrow 1951). The most extensive work on this problem has been done as part of the scholarship on voting. The work on the Condorcet paradox is relevant here (for an overview, see Mueller 1979: Ch. 3).

The final element is *information*. Initially, rational choice models assumed that actors had perfect or sufficient information necessary for making purposive choices among alternative courses of action. In much of the most recent work, however, the quantity and quality of available information is taken to be a variable, and a highly significant one at that (Hirschleifer and Riley 1979)....

III. LIMITATIONS OF CURRENT RATIONAL CHOICE EXPLANATIONS

Despite their ability to explain a variety of empirical phenomena, rational choice models are by no means exempt from criticism. Criticism comes from many different sources. The advocates of interpretive analysis (phenomenologists, hermeneuticists, and neofunctionalists, among others) often argue for a social science that is antipositive; as noted earlier, we shall not deal with their work here. Some Durkheimians, network analysts, Marxists and other structuralists object on principle to *any* approach that is based on methodological individualism. A consideration of this objection is also beyond the scope of this paper. What we discuss here are the criticisms levelled at rational choice either from those who work within the tradition, or from those who explicitly advocate an alternative to it without, however, rejecting methodological individualism out of hand (see Hogarth and Reder [1978] for a state-of-the-art collection of papers critical to various aspects of rational choice).

Most of the critics object to the highly unrealistic behavioral assumptions of rational choice models. Especially in the earliest models, most real-world complexities were suppressed in order to derive determinate solutions. That which could not be modelled was not considered. Thus, heterogeneity of preferences and interests among groups of actors, strategic interaction (such as sophisticated voting), and the costs of information all were assumed away.

It was no surprise that the inadequacy of these simple models was revealed as empirical tests proceeded. One famous example was that Americans vote in much greater numbers than Downs could account for under any extension of his, or (for that matter) any other plausible rational choice voting model. It was terribly clear to analysts and voters alike that hardly any given individual voters ever would feel themselves to be casting the deciding ballot, which is the only readily allowable motivation in rational choice models of voting. Why then did they bear opportunity costs to take an action that could not materially affect the outcome? Another famous example was that there is far more collective action than Olson (1965)—or any other rational

choice theorist of collective action—could easily explain. While the lack of selective incentives seemed to provide a powerful explanation for the failure of collective action to occur, collective action sometimes did occur in the absence of sufficient selective incentives. So strikes, riots, anti-apartheid demonstrations in South Africa and in New York City, civil rights marches, and even contributions to public goods in laboratory settings, all took place with a frequency that defied explanation in strict rational choice terms.

Resolving the growing disjuncture between theory and data became a problem of paramount importance. Three tacks to more successfully account for real world phenomena seemed promising. The first was to fiddle with the behavioral assumptions of rational choice theory—especially those of its most testable form, expected utility theory (see Arrow 1987:204–206). The second was to maintain the standard behavioral assumptions of rational choice, but to explore in depth the effects of incomplete information on subsequent action. The third was to elaborate the contribution of structural constraints in determining social outcomes.

Fiddling with the Behavioral Assumptions of Rational Choice Theory

A growing body of research has indicated that there are significant and systematic empirical deviations from the hypotheses of expected utility theory that underlie standard rational choice behavioral assumptions (as conceived of and formalized by von Neumann and Morgenstern 1947; see also Allais and Hagen 1979; Kahneman and Tversky 1979; Machina 1983; and Hogarth and Reder 1987). For economists interested in accounting for market-oriented behavior, these findings are not so troubling, for in the market setting wealth maximization can be realistically substituted for utility maximization: any participant in a perfectly competitive market whose behavior is not motivated by wealth maximization will not long survive. Yet for social scientists interested in accounting for non-market-oriented behavior, these results were both distressing and intriguing.

They were distressing because the kinds of predictions that could be derived from the simplistic assumptions of expected utility theory all became suspect; they were intriguing because some of these findings provided a basis for explanations of empirical findings that otherwise seemed to fly in the face of some of rational choice theory's key predictions.

For example, the work of Tversky and Kahneman (1987), which demonstrates the inconstancy of preferences about risk (the same people are risk-seeking when choosing among losses and risk-averse when choosing among gains), may be used to account for hitherto mystifying behavior about gambling and insurance (see also Brenner 1983: Ch. 1; Einhorn and Hogarth 1985). Thus, what had seemed to be clearly non-rational behavior could, in fact, be accounted for when simplistic assumptions about risk preferences were modified.

While improving the fit of the theory to the data, complicating the behavioral assumptions nonetheless begs a fundamental question. Where do preferences come from? If people are said to act rationally to pursue their most preferred ends, what are these ends and why do individuals hold these ends dear as against others? As long as the behavior in question is market-oriented behavior, this question can be skirted simply by inserting wealth-maximization for the "most preferred ends" part of the model. With any kind of non-market-oriented behavior such a substitution can be made, but only in a post-hoc fashion, and only with considerable qualification. For instance, in Friedman's (1987)

model of collective action, it is assumed that people prefer certainty to uncertainty. She can provide a theoretical reason for this particular assumption (e.g., people cannot act rationally under conditions of uncertainty), and can assemble considerable supportive empirical evidence, yet it is quite conceivable that a different logic and a different body of evidence might be mustered to support the opposite claim.

That there is no theory of preference formation has implications not only for the behavior of individuals and groups, but also for social outcomes. The nature of any social outcome clearly depends upon the set of underlying preferences. For instance, if people are wealth-maximizers, they will desire social outcomes that provide for the greatest economic efficiency. Even so, there are a multitude of possible Pareto-efficient equilibria, depending upon the initial distribution of resource endowments across individuals. Other kinds of behavioral assumptions lead to different social outcomes, however. These outcomes might emphasize certainty, fairness, or justice, as against efficiency. Such outcomes are not at all far-fetched from rational choice premises, for no single individual stands to benefit from efficiency as a state of affairs (because it is a public good), whereas all individuals may well find that fairness is in their own self-interest.

Until the time that significant progress is made toward an understanding of preferences, the scope or power of rational choice analyses is clearly limited. Since preferences are given rather than explained in rational choice analyses, these analyses are far better suited for social phenomena that are the outgrowth of individual preferences that are strong (relative to competing), stable (over time), and uniform (across actors). Hence, social outcomes dependent on preferences that result from fundamental biological drives or from strongly sanctioned social conventions are good candidates for rational choice analyses. Social outcomes dependent on unstable, weak, or variable preferences—consumer behavior, for example—are by this token poor subjects for rational choice analyses.

Elaborating the Role of Information

Yet another way to increase the empirical fit of rational choice models is to appreciate that variable amounts and types of information will have systematic effects on outcomes. These models typically require some assumption of "sufficient information" in order for individuals to choose successfully among alternatives. This assumption is increasingly regarded as problematic, however. To illustrate, consider a situation in which two people who are subject to the same structural constraints behave differently. We can account for this by saying that they have different preferences, or that they have different information about the consequences of their actions. To claim that behavior is explicable by reference to different preferences is tautological, and undermines the standard methodology of rational choice. The second explanation is more satisfying: the amount of information that agents have can affect behavior *independently* of constraints or preferences. It may well be that information is the crucial intervening variable in all rational choice explanations.

Indeed, information has become an increasingly key variable in studies of contracting, bargaining, and organization. Both principal agent and transaction-cost models start with the assumption that informational asymmetries are significant. What seems to be missing in these literatures, however, is a theory of optimal information investment. Such a theory would have to answer a host of questions. How much information is it rational to collect and use in making a specific decision?

How does the agent decide when to stop searching? How do we understand the case in which two individuals have precisely the same information but draw different conclusions from it? Finally, suppose that the information that is required to make a decision rationally is inherently unavailable (that is, the situation is marked by uncertainty). What then should we expect rational actors to do?

Elaborating the Contribution of Structural Constraints

In addition to modifying behavioral assumptions to increase their verisimilitude, it is also possible to introduce other structural constraints than purely institutional ones explicitly into these models (we refer here to constraints such as those produced by macroeconomic fluctuations, wars, and even the size of one's generational birth cohort). All structural constraints affect behavior by determining the objective probabilities that an individual's most preferred end can be realized. In this way they act as inducements to the pursuit of one end as against another.

Not a great deal of effort has gone into this area of rational choice analysis (see, however, Easterlin 1980), but sociologists know a great deal about how it is that locations within social structures limit individual choices. One cannot marry an Eskimo if there are none around (Blau 1987:79). Among those who wish to work full-time, everyone would clearly prefer to work in a primary rather than a secondary labor market. That not everyone does is often explicable by race, class, and/or gender position. Much of the new work by sociologists using rational choice theory to understand macrosociological problems falls into this category (Brustein 1988; Brinton 1988; Kiser 1987).

Another way to elaborate the role of structural constraints in determining outcomes is to inquire as to the origins of the institutions that produce such constraints. This line of research is just beginning (Coleman 1989; Hechter 1989; Kliemt 1989).

CONCLUSION

Rational choice provides a number of discrete benefits to researchers who work within its confines. Once scholars can identify the appropriate problem to which their research question belongs, they are assured of finding a determinate solution. Armed with a given theory, the investigator knows which facts are critical for the solution and which facts are largely irrelevant. Since this often leads to a demand to collect new kinds of data, rational choice has a built-in tendency to create new research agendas out of old ones. Further, researchers beginning from rational choice premises never need to build their theory anew, starting from first principles and defining and justifying the use of each concept. Not only does this save a good deal of intellectual energy, but it also enables scholars with quite different substantive interests and areas of expertise to communicate with one another. All of these conditions combine to help sustain a research program in which knowledge cumulates relatively efficiently and progress is swift.

Debates about the merits or demerits of rational choice theories often take on an ideological cast, and sometimes rational choice theories are rejected because they seem to have unpalatable political implications. In this regard we think that it is important to note two characteristics of rational choice theories. First, in these theories, individuals are accorded significantly more respect than in most other sociological models. Rational choice theories of collective action, for instance, take into account contextual constraints on action but also leave room for the informed choices of actors. This is in contrast to those who would argue that participants are merely sheep heeding the call of the shepherd, or individuals who ignore reason when their sensibilities are excited. Second, arguing that individuals will often follow their self-interest in choosing among actions is not the same thing as saying that they ought to do so. While this was the position of Bentham and the utilitarians, positive and normative analyses have no necessary connection.

As rational choice explanations come to include more realistic behavioral assumptions, more knowledge about the effects of social structures, and greater appreciation of the role of information, they cannot fail to provide more satisfactory empirical accounts. Scholarship is required on all of these separate fronts. Sociologists have a comparative advantage in contributing to at least one aspect of this work, namely, to the study of the effects of social structural constraints on social outcomes. Sociologists also know a great deal about how organizations control information. At the same time, cognitive scientists enjoy a comparative advantage in the search for more realistic behavioral assumptions, and indeed much research on this subject is already underway. Together these two strands of research may well contribute to the development of positive theory in social science.

REFERENCES

ALEXANDER, JEFFREY C., BERNHARD GIESEN, RICHARD MUNCH, AND NEIL J. SMELSER, EDS. 1987. *The Micro-Macro Link*. Berkeley: University of California Press.

ALLAIS, M., AND O. HAGEN, 1979. *Expected Utility Hypotheses and the Allais Paradox: Contemporary Discussions of Decision under Uncertainty with Allais' Rejoinder*. Dordrecht: D. Reidel.

ARROW, KENNETH J. 1951. *Social Choice and Individual Values.* New Haven: Yale University Press.

ARROW, KENNETH J. 1987. "Rationality of Self and Others in an Economic System." Pp. 201–16 in Robin M. Hogarth and Melvin W. Reder. eds., *Rational Choice: The Contrast between Economics and Psychology.* Chicago: University of Chicago Press.

AZZI, CORRY, and RONALD EHRENBERG. 1975. "Household Allocation of Time and Church Attendance." *Journal of Political Economy*, 83, 1:27–55.

BLAU, PETER. 1987. "Constrasting Theoretical Perspectives." Pp. 71–86 in J.C. Alexander, B. Giesen, R. Munch, and N. Smelser, eds., *The Micro-Macro Link.* Berkeley: University of California Press.

BRENNER, REUVEN. 1983. *History: The Human Gamble.* Chicago: University of Chicago Press.

BRINTON, MARY. 1988. "The Social-Institutional Bases of Gender Stratification: Japan as an Illustrative Case." *American Journal of Sociology* 94:330–34.

BRUSTEIN, WILLIAM. 1988. *Social Origins of Political Regionalism: France 1849–1981.* Berkeley: University of California Press.

BUCHANAN, JAMES, AND GORDON TULLOCK. 1962. *The Calculus of Consent.* Ann Arbor: University of Michigan Press.

COLEMAN, JAMES, S. 1986. "Social Theory, Social Research, and a Theory of Action." *American Journal of Sociology* 86(5):984–1014.

COLEMAN, JAMES, S. 1989. "The Emergence of Norms." in M. Hechter, K.D. Opp, and R. Wippler, *Social Institutions: Their Emergence Maintenance and Effects.* New York: Aldine de Gruyter.

COLLINS, RANDALL. 1981. "On the Microfoundations of Macrosociology." *American Journal of Sociology*, 86, 5:984–1014.

COOK, KAREN, ed. 1987. *Social Exchange Theory.* Beverly Hills: Sage Publications.

DOWNS, ANTHONY. 1957. *An Economic Theory of Democracy.* New York: Harper & Row.

EASTERLIN, RICHARD A. 1980. *Birth and Fortune: The Impact of Numbers on Personal Welfare.* New York: Basic Books.

EINHORN, HILLEL J., AND ROBIN M. HOGARTH. 1985. "Ambiguity and Uncertainty in Probabilistic Inference." *Psychological Review*, 92, 4:433–61.

EMERSON, RICHARD M. 1981. "Social Exchange Theory." Pp. 30–65 in Morris Rosenberg and Ralph H. Turner. eds., *Social Psychology: Sociological Perspectives.* New York: Basic Books.

FRIEDMAN, DEBRA. 1987. "Uncertainty and Collective Action." Unpublished paper.

GOTTFREDSON, MICHAEL, AND TRAVIS HIRSCHI. 1986. "The True Value of Lambda Would Appear to Be Zero: An Essay on Career Criminals, Criminal Careers, Selective Incapacitation, Cohort Studies, and Related Topics." *Criminology*, 24, 2:213–234.

HEATH, ANTHONY. 1976. *Rational Choice and Social Exchange.* Cambridge: Cambridge University Press.

HECHTER, MICHAEL, ed. 1983. *The Microfoundations of Macrosociology.* Philadelphia: Temple University Press.

HECHTER, MICHAEL. 1987. *Principles of Group Solidarity.* Berkeley and London: University of California Press.

HECHTER, MICHAEL. 1989. "The Emergence of Cooperative Social Institutions." In M. Hechter, K.D. Opp. and R. Wippler, eds., *Social Institutions: Their Emergence, Maintenance and Effects.* New York: Aldine de Gruyter.

HIRSCHLEIFER, J., AND JOHN G. RILEY. 1979. "The Analytics of Uncertainty and Information—An Expository Survey." *Journal of Economic Literature*, 27:1375–1421.

HOGARTH, ROBIN M., AND MELVIN W. REDER, eds. 1987. *Rational Choice: The Contrast between Economics and Psychology.* Chicago: University of Chicago Press.

KAHNEMAN, DANIEL, AND AMOS TVERSKY. 1979. "Prospect Theory: An Analysis of Decision under Risk." *Econometrica*, 21:263–91.

KISER, EDGAR. 1987. *Kings and Classes: Crown Autonomy, State Policies and Economic Development in Western European Absolutisms.* PhD Dissertation. Department of Sociology, University of Arizona.

KLIEMT, HARTMUT. 1989. "The Costs of Organizing Social Cooperation: Some Remarks about the Game of Creating a Game." In M. Hechter, K.D. Opp, and R. Wippler, eds., *Social Institutions: Their Emergence, Maintenance and Effects.* New York: Aldine de Gruyter.

MACHINA, MARK J. 1983. "Generalized Expected Utility Analysis and the Nature of Observed Violations of the Independence Axiom." Pp. 263–293 in B.P. Stigum and F. Wenstop, eds., *Foundations of Utility and Risk Theory with Applications.* Dordrecht: D. Reidel.

MUELLER, DENNIS C. 1979. *Public Choice.* Cambridge: Cambridge University Press.

OLSON, MANCUR. 1965. *The Logic of Collective Action.* Cambridge: Harvard University Press.

RIKER, WILLIAM H. 1986. *The Art of Political Manipulation.* New Haven: Yale University Press.

SCHELLING, THOMAS C, 1978. *Micromotives and Macrobehavior.* New York: W.W. Norton.

STINCHCOMBE, ARTHUR. 1968. *Constructing Social Theories.* New York: Harcourt and Brace.

TVERSKY, AMOS, AND DANIEL KAHNEMAN. 1987. "Rational Choice and the Framing of Decisions." Pp. 67–94 in Robin M. Hogarth and Melvin W. Reder, eds., *Rational Choice: The Contrast between Economics and Psychology* Chicago: University of Chicago Press.

VON NEUMANN, JOHN, AND OSKAR MORGANSTERN. 1947. *Theory of Games and Economic Behavior.* Princeton: Princeton University Press.

Micro-translation
as a Theory-Building Strategy*

Randall Collins

A debate has been emerging in recent years between micro-and macro-sociology. Earlier versions of this debate went on between symbolic interactionism and various forms of macro-sociology; for a time a compromise seemed available by such linking devices as role theory, exchange theory, and Parsonian action theory. But the debate has revived in much stronger terms, with the development of radical forms of micro-sociology, above all ethnomethodology. And this newer micro-sociology faces a strong critique from the macro-side, especially from contemporary structuralism and Marxism.

In the following, I will argue pragmatically that we cannot do without either micro- or macro-sociology. But the most recent round of the debate does not leave us at the earlier point of compromise. For the newer, radical micro-sociology is epistemologically and empirically much more thorough than any previous sociological method; and it claims a number of important discoveries about the ways in which social realities are constructed. The task of micro-research has hardly been finished, and many of the key micro-discoveries are doubtless yet to be made. But I would suggest that the effort coherently to reconstitute macro-sociology upon radically empirical micro-foundations is the crucial step toward a more successful sociological science.

I shall review the micro-and macro-critiques of each other, and attempt to resolve the debate by locating in time and space the types of sociological concepts usable in causal explanations, and by undertaking micro-translations of these concepts. This effort at translation enables us to see what elements of macro-concepts are irreducible and which are not; and it prompts a search for the mechanisms by which long-term and large scale social processes are reproduced in micro-situations.

Recent micro-sociology has become increasingly "radical" in several senses. Through the use of audio and now video recordings, it has been able to concentrate on much finer

*From K. Knorr-Cetina and A.V. Cicourel, eds., *Advances in Social Theory and Methodology: Toward an Integration of Micro- and Macro-Sociologies* (London: Routledge and Kegan Paul, 1981), pp. 81–95. Reprinted with permission of Routledge.

detail empirically than previous micro-sociologies. Instead of loose participant observation of a chain of situations, we get carefully scrutinized analyses of interaction in segments as small as "the first five seconds."[1] This shift, moreover, has been away from the more idiosyncratic or dramatic events that occasionally occur in behind-the-scenes maneuvering, to the mundane routine that is apparent throughout everyday life. All previous sociological theories and research methods are called into question from this radically *empirical* stance.

Micro-sociology has also become *philosophically* radical. Where the symbolic interactionists have generally accepted the pragmatist version of an ongoing construction of a conventional world, the ethnomethodologists have imported the stance of Husserlian phenomenology. Thus radical micro-sociology brackets the ordinary pragmatic assumptions in order to examine their foundations. Unlike in the practice of philosophers, however, this is done empirically. Instead of examining only the observer's own philosophical subjectivity, the micro-sociologist now examines cognitive and epistemological issues via the close analysis of conversation,[2] and of the construction and use of written texts in social organizations.[3]

The unique thrust of recent, "radical" micro-sociology is in its combination of an extreme micro-empiricism with a stance which attempts to question all sociological as well as philosophical presuppositions. This questioning is not necessarily relativistic, although it can be that. It is at its most useful, I would claim, where it aims at discovering the fundamental grounds for the topics with which other social analysts concern themselves. Its concerns cut in two directions: towards the grounds of all social structures, and towards the grounds of cognition, especially as displayed in commonsense social reasoning. The two concerns are sometimes brought together, as when radical empiricism is turned upon the sociological research process itself, to show the ways in which the world as portrayed by sociologists has been constructed by observers relying implicitly upon their own use of ordinary practical reasoning. The problems of reality-construction begin at home, and the observer's own cognitive strategies are a first order of materials to be examined in any truly radical empiricism: they are topic as well as resource.

For the present, however, I would like to consider only one of these issues: the implication for conventional macro-sociology of having a vigorous new research tradition which concentrates on ordinary social activity in second-by-second detail.

1 THE MICRO-CRITIQUE OF MACRO-SOCIOLOGY

Micro-sociology has a strong claim to be considered the only directly empirical form of sociology, with materials that are the only empirical reality there is. Empirical reality is that which is given in experience; as such, it is always experience in a particular time and place and by a particular observer. Human experience is always a *selection* from the totality of sensory experience, since the total amount in all modalities can easily overload the perceptual and information-processing capacities of the human organism. One task of micro-sociology is to discover the structure of the "filters" and the semantic memory by which actors in particular situations experience what is empirical for them. But even before we have fully uncovered this inner organization of the individual, it is possible to criticize the conventional notion of empirical reality as held in macro-sociology. For empirical evidence is necessarily bounded by the time-span of the observer's presence; any "evidence" that is more than a report on the observer's flow of attention becomes indirect and introduces elements which are cognitive constructions of a different sort from the primary empirical materials.

The term "empirical" has often been used misleadingly in social science to mean numerical evidence or "hard data," although the latter is actually several removes from empirical in the experiential sense.[4] What is the empirical reality underlying a numerical measure of social mobility, for example? First, there is the actual empirical situation in which an interviewer confronts a subject with a question. Micro-sociologists concerned to be strictly empirical examine this situation to see just in what senses the procedures of formally asking and answering such questions create the kind of data produced. Beyond this, there is the process by which the subjects transform an enormous amount of their previous social experience into a few words: their "father's occupation" and their "own occupation" can be rendered in two words, but they summarize materials that empirically, minute by minute in their previous lives, consisted of a variety of social interactions, negotiations, efforts, cognitions. The processual detail by which their career was actually made is compressed into a few nouns, given a hard and object-like form, and thence enters into the sociologist's fund of "data."

There are further transformations that a micro-sociologist can observe in applying micro-analysis to the research process: the practical and cognitive contingencies of the coder's actions, the juxtaposing and rearranging of many subjects' answers, reflections upon these arrangements in the form of counting, and then various operations upon these numbers according to theories of statistics, mathematical exposition, and substantive sociology. The final product depicting "social mobility" in tabular form on the printed page has the appearance of thing-like reality. However, it is, in fact, the product of numerous

transformations of the basic empirical materials—the long sequences of social behaviour which alone have sensory, time-and-space reality.[5] Many radical micro-sociologists have thus tended to despair of the problems of arriving at any general explanation of large-scale social processes. Under these circumstances, all sociology can do is examine its own processes; at most, it might be able to uncover the universal micro-mechanisms by which people deal with the daily epistemological problem of producing or at least negotiating ordinary reality.

From this perspective, macro-sociology fails in several regards. It misses the actual here-and-now, enacted nature of social life behind it ignores its own reality-constructing activities, especially the artificial bias given by the practical contingencies of research and by the bias given by the practical contingencies of research and by the forcing of social reality into the alien mould of numerical categories. It ignores the limited cognitive mechanism that sociologists share with all other social actors. The most important of these are *indexicality* (the embeddedness of any communicative reference in some unexplicated, taken-for-granted aspect of the situation), and *reflexivity* (the potentially infinite regress of self-regarding viewpoints that an observer may enter upon when attempting completely to account for the possibility of understanding any situation). In both cases, the empirical inference is that everyday thinkers do *not* act because they have a full and self-conscious view of the grounds for their inferences, but precisely because they avoid questioning what is taken for granted. It is from this point of view that the cognitive presuppositions of symbolic interactionism and other traditional micro-sociologies have been questioned. For none of them assumes there is any fundamental problem in taking the role of the other, recognizing an exchange, or applying a norm (whatever the case may be with particular theories), whereas ethnomethodology claims that ordinary social action could not be carried out if people continuously and explicitly had to recognize these cognitive objects. In fact, social action can be carried out at all only because people do not usually have to think about such things.[6]

Radical micro-sociology applies this type of criticism not only to the standard forms of empirical macro-sociology, into which category it fits not only large-scale research but virtually all quantitative research of any scale, but also to historical sociology and macro-level theorizing in general, and especially to structural-functionalism. Moreover, it claims that macro-theoretical concepts are not only empirically ungrounded and inaccurate, hence at best *glosses* on the underlying reality, but that there is a crucial element of ideology or *reification* in macro-sociology. A *gloss* may be potentially unfolded to reveal a fuller description, albeit an infinitely expandable one; a *reification*, however, is not a failed effort to expound reality but a successful effort to construct a particular mental reality that can constrain people who accept it as true. Hence ethnomethodologists[7] may claim that social researchers and theorists have no superiority to the people they study, since they all use the same fundamental cognitive procedures, such as avoiding explication of glosses because this is an endless and hence impractical task, and one which is usually ignored lest cognitive chaos result from realizing this predicament. And if ultimate reality can never be reached, sociologists had better turn to another task, puncturing dangerous illusions in everyday life such as stratifying practices which create the sense of "social classes."

In so far, then, as people take the "state" to be not an intermittent collection of actions by certain people, some of whom have weapons, but as an expression of the collective will of the people, or a manifestation of God, or simply as a self-subsistent entity, they bolster the power of those who enact the "state." The same can be said of concepts of "property," or "position," or "organization," or "culture," or "society" itself. Actors in everyday life and sociologists in their analytical constructions are alike, from this viewpoint, in using reifications and thereby contributing to the privilege of those individuals who benefit from the deference they thereby receive in real-life micro-situations. In this critical stance, radical micro-sociology can be very radical indeed.

2 THE MACRO-CRITIQUE OF MICRO-SOCIOLOGY

A number of criticisms have been made in the other direction, some of them expounded against earlier versions of micro-sociology, some directed at contemporary phenomenological versions. Schematically, these are the criticisms of subjectivism, triviality, historical and structural situatedness, and reductionism.[8]

It can be claimed that micro-sociology is simply another form of subjective idealism, an incursion of long-standing philosophical positions into sociology, a clever argument by which hard material realities and the constraints of social organization are reduced to phantoms in the mind. Such an argument focuses on the human being only as thinker, rather than actor, and leaves out the surrounding physical world and its constraints. The fact that such arguments, taken to the extreme, end in solipsism or mysticism is in itself a refutation of them by reduction to absurdity.

It has also been charged that micro-sociology is trivial. It is a method without substance, or at best a focus upon the minor details and surface appearances of encounters. In either case, it is trivial because it misses the important sociological issues—stratification, politics, social conflicts and movements, social change—all located on the macro-level.

Further, the patterns of behaviour studied in micro-sociology are themselves the results of macro-patterns. For micro-sociologists study styles of interaction and cognition which are specific to a particular social class or ethnic group, or at least to a particular society at a particular time in history. Micro-sociologists are oblivious to the situatedness of their own observations, and hence they not only overgeneralize their findings to the entire social universe, but fail to see how their patterns are themselves the results of larger historical and structural patterns. Gouldner,[9] for example, sees the ethnomethodologists as symptoms of the youth world of the 1960s, in which all was uncertain: drugs, sex, school, family, religion. He argues that Garfinkel's breaching experiments were a kind of hippie happening, expressing not only the underlying normlessness of the youth culture, but a sadistic pleasure in disrupting people's ordinary lives. This particular interpretation may be rather speculative, to be sure, as well as rather anachronistic about the timing of Garfinkel's work; but the more general point does have force, that micro-behaviour is not necessarily an historical constant, but itself varies in a larger historical context.

Finally, there is a long-standing argument against micro-reductionism. Durkheim[10] pointed out, in opposition to individual, psychological explanations of social behaviour, that the individual is constrained by the entire structure of interaction; one's location in a particular type of division of labour, for instance, is an externally constraining force upon the individual. Just as physiology is an independently organized level of analysis above chemistry, sociology is a level of organization above psychology—and by extension, macro-sociology is independent of micro-sociology. The reductionist error is to miss the structure of relationships among the parts, and its determining influence upon the parts, by focusing only upon the parts. This critique

has subsequently been applied to Homans's attempt explicitly to reduce sociology to the principles of behavioural psychology,[11] and it may be applied equally to radical micro-sociology. Contemporary structuralist Marxism in particular[12] has been adamant in proclaiming that the economic and other formal structures of a society are independent of any subjective, individual level of experience.

3 A CONFRONTATION

Micro-sociology produces five main criticisms of macro-sociology. Macro-sociological research (and to some degree, theory) is criticized: (1) as unexplicated gloss; (2) as false construction because it forces social reality into an inappropriate mould though bureaucratic research procedures and/or numerical concepts; (3) as impossible in principle because it shares a mode of everyday cognition that can never fully account for its tacit grounds; (4) macro-concepts are criticized as reifications; (5) micro-events *are* the empirical reality of human actors, and hence situational reductionism *is* appropriate—in a sex-neutral version of Homans's dictum, "bringing people back in."

Macro-sociology makes four main criticisms. It claims that micro-sociology is: (1) idealistic; (2) trivial; (3) causally contingent; (4) reductionist.

Only the last point in each series confronts the other directly. Let us examine the others seriatim.

The first four micro-criticisms do not seem to me impediments to doing valid macro-sociology, at least in some sophisticated fashion.

(1) Macro-evidence as presented may be a set of unexplicated glosses, but this fact can be taken not as a condemnation but as an invitation to unpack those concepts into their constituent parts. Micro-sociology, though, points to several different directions in which

explication could proceed: *externally*, into the details of subjects' real-life situations that are usually referred to cryptically as a "career," or even more abstractly (i.e., after several more cognitive operations) as a "mobility rate," etc.; and *internally*, into the processes by which researchers construct their data as finally presented. Of these two types of explication, the former (external explication) is more directly important for rebuilding macro-concepts on a firm foundation. The latter, internal explication of the research process itself, may have some corrective value (see the following point), but as a substantive issue it cuts in a different, and far more general, direction than the effort at external explication of glosses. Internal explications, as a substantive (rather than methodological) concern, can contribute to the discovery of universally present micro-mechanisms of cognition, which must be one component of any total explanation of a macro-pattern. But they are one component only, and they may be discovered from other types of analysis than an explication of macro-research procedures. Hence to lead all efforts to explicate the glosses in micro-research in this internal direction would be to miss the more useful type of explication that can be supplied here.

(2) Micro-sociology also contributes a methodological critique of macro-research. Such a critique does not destroy macro-research. It shows instead how crude an approximation is being tendered, in some instances; in other instances, it proposes that particular types of methods or concepts may be entirely inappropriate to certain phenomena. In either case, it clears the road to improved macro-research.[13]

(3) The most extreme micro-criticism is that absolute truth is never possible on the macro-level (or any level) because research and theory can never escape from such properties of everyday cognition as unexplicated glosses and other tacit grounds of communi-

cation. No matter how much explicating one does, there is always more to do. Yet to dismiss macro-sociology on these grounds would be to make a choice for an absolute ideal of truth, while it is quite possible to live with a pragmatic ideal of truth which recognizes successive approximations rather than some final resting point as its aim. The importance of pragmatic approximations can be seen by the following example. What would be required to give a relatively full explication of every gloss involved in a macro-concept such as a mobility rate? It would require, to begin with, an explication of every cognitive moment in the lives of every individual referred to in the mobility rate. To do this, even without adding much analysis, and leaving the analyst's reflexivity at each point out of the question entirely, would take at least as long as the sum of the times of all the lives involved. To say anything in this fashion about world history would take many times longer than the length of world history itself. Given these stringent requirements, it is no wonder radical micro-sociologists often confine themselves to very small slices of data. More practically, one must conclude that typifications (glosses) by means of strategic samplings and summaries are inescapable. The task of micro-sociological critique should not be to prevent us from doing it, but to enable us to do it better; indeed, to point us to the crucial junctures at which macro-institutions are reproduced or changed.

(4) Micro-sociology charges that macro-concepts are reifications. This is a suggestion worth following, above all as a direction for research. For it is not only the practice of sociological *theorists* that may contribute to reifying the social world, but the practice of people in everyday conversations, and the effects of the latter are by far the more important. It is a research question, though, rather than a theoretical given, because everyday usage may vary a good deal in how much reification it in-

volves, and locating these variations among particular people and particular situations may go a long way towards demonstrating the ways in which a stratified world is produced.

Macro-sociology, then, seems possible, and in a fashion that is consistent with the enhanced sophistication and empirical precision of radical micro-sociology.

In the opposite direction, several of the macro-critiques of micro-sociology can also be disposed of.

(1) Although some micro-sociology resembles idealist philosophy, and much of it owes historical debts to this philosophical tradition, many versions are not susceptible to this critique. Indeed, radical micro-sociology is highly empirical—on its own terms, arguably more so than macro-sociology. Micro-sociology certainly need not slight the external side of experience, for all its frequent emphasis upon the problems of the internal processes of cognition. It is true that some versions of ethnomethodological hyper-empiricism stay entirely within the cognitive constructs by which actors experience concrete situations. In the history of philosophy, such analysis has been the gateway to idealist systems, which concentrate upon supposedly universal and transcendent mental categories, and end by denying the reality of concrete moments in time and space. Phenomenologically inspired sociologies are in danger of traveling the same route.

As a corrective, I am suggesting that radical micro-sociology should hold fast to the concrete experience of individuals in time and space, and not jump immediately to the categories or alleged "rules" by which they cognitively structure their situations. There is no doubt that the bare physical encounter of human bodies in some particular place is an abstraction—a construct by a theorist such as myself. My argument, however, is that this is the most fruitful starting-point for sociological explanation. It is the touchstone by which

we may test the reality of various kinds of cognitive constructions, both those of theorists and those of everyday actors. Only in this way can we avoid the path of trying to explain what people do by accepting commonsense ideologies. This error has vitiated much of previous sociological theory of a more conventional sort, such as functionalism, and it threatens to reappear in a new form in so far as phenomenological micro-sociology takes an exclusively cognitive stance. This is not to say that cognitions play no part in social life. But we need to show realistically just what part they do play: they are parts of chains of the experiences and of the speech actions of particular people at particular times and places, and are to be understood as part of people's efforts to deal with *that situation,* not as the rules of the social structure itself. In short, radical micro-sociology can avoid idealism by locating people's cognitions in their concrete, lived experience, instead of cognitivizing the entire social world.

(2) Micro-sociology, like any other form of specialized research, may appear trivial to outside observers who do not see the theoretical issues with which it deals. I would suggest that not all microsociologists themselves are aware of the theoretical issues for which their materials are relevant, but these issues are certainly there. Micro-materials touch on every important issue in sociology, in so far as every macro-theoretical concept is a gloss upon a series of micro-events. And even without this effort at translation, the leading work in micro-sociology aims explicitly at a crucial theoretical issue for the entire field, whether one couches it as "the basis of social order" or the "the construction of social realities."

(3) It is unfortunately true that virtually all micro-sociology is oblivious to the historical and often the class context of its materials. Nevertheless, this critique of micro-sociology is not as devastating as it might seem. For if one claims that micro-interactions are caused

by historical and structural patterns, the question arises: what are those historical and structural patterns themselves? *Empirically,* they are made up of long sequences and aggregates of other micro-situations. At most, then, this critique states that micro-behaviour in certain situations is due to micro-behaviour in other situations. For example, the social class variable invoked to explain micro-conversational styles may be translated into previous micro-situations involving interaction in the realm of work, handling money and other property, etc.[14] One may still ask: why do these working and property-handling situations exist, and why do particular individuals get into those situations? In so far as one is unwilling to admit that these questions may be answered by citing still further chains of micro-events, one is claiming structural irreducibility of the larger pattern. Hence the whole of the macro-critique of micro-sociology devolves upon the crucial question of (4) reductionism.

4 MICRO-REDUCTION AS A THEORY-BUILDING STRATEGY

The issue of reductionism has generally evoked extreme positions. On one side, reduction is declared to be impossible, seeking for explanations of structural phenomena on a level where the phenomena cannot even be found. Thus the term reductionism itself is taken as epithet, and pinning it on an opponent is taken as sufficient disproof. On the other side, rather strong stands have been taken in favour of reduction by several types of micro-sociologists. Ethnomethodology and Homansian behaviourism alike have usually stressed that the micro-situation alone is empirically real, and that explanations which are not grounded in real people in real places are false conceptualizations. If one seeks for causal explanations, then Homan's dictum

applies: the analyst must bring people back in every instance, for only real physical people can actually make social events happen. The radical side of symbolic interactionism expresses the point even more strongly: in Blumer's[15] terms, there is only a series of ongoing situations, and there are no larger sociological laws or patterns because situations can always be created anew.

Yet the case for or against reductionism is not logically either all or nothing. One can make (at least) three different claims against reduction: that it cannot be done at all; that it cannot be done in an important number of cases; that it is not necessary or desirable for the progress of sociology.

The third claim is the mildest and the most defensible. It holds that work on the macro-level of analysis does not depend on work on the micro-level; one does not need to have a successful explanation of individuals' situational behaviour in order to make progress in analysing, for example, stratification patterns or long-term social changes. In the same way, Durkheim[16] pointed out that research in physiology is not dependent upon research in chemistry, even though the empirical components of a living body are chemical; physiology could move ahead at its own pace and by generating its own explanatory concepts. But this argument, although acceptable, is not a decisive reason not to attempt micro-reduction. For although physiology did indeed progress without reduction to chemistry, the more recent developments of biochemistry and molecular biology show that a more advanced theory can usefully proceed by seeking for the micro-mechanisms that produce the larger pattern.

The question, then, remains: is micro-reduction generally impossible, sometimes impossible, or always possible? I would suggest the question has never been conclusively settled, but only argued programmatically for one extreme or the other. Yet it is not a hypothetical question but an operational one. The only way we will know the answer is to attempt micro-reduction systematically across the range of sociological conceptualizations and explanations. The answer, as we can see, may not be conclusively yes or no: some aspects of sociology may prove irreducible, while others are not.

There are several advantages of attempting micro-reduction, and these advantages hold whether reduction proves to be fully possible or not. Reduction produces an empirically stronger theory, on any level of analysis, by displaying the real-life situations and behaviours that make up its phenomena. In particular, it introduces empirically real causal forces in the shape of human beings expending energy. It enables us to discover which macro-concepts and explanations are empirically groundable, and which are not, thus enabling us by a strict criterion to separate out hypostatizations. And to the extent that hypostatizations are part of people's social realities, we can clearly situate them in people's cognitive usages in particular times and places.

These advantages appear to be entirely formal, the micro-sociologist forcing an increased degree of empirical and conceptual accountability from the macro-sociologist. But we may see advantages from the opposite direction. Micro-reduction increases the plausibility of macro-theories. For although I do not wish to discourage anyone from producing macro-analyses of any degree of historical and theoretical scope, I would suggest that such analyses are almost always merely plausible in a general way. They are pictures of the world that make sense but are rarely demonstrated rigorously. This is especially true of analyses of entire societies or of large historical events such as the Industrial Revolution or the rise of world capitalism, for here one cannot sample randomly from a large universe of cases or make a full range of controlled comparisons for all important variables. History simply does not provide enough cases. In my view, this is not a reason for abandoning large macro-analyses; surely one learns more from an analysis of world history, even if it comprises only one case, than from ignoring that wealth of material. Sampling procedures of a given kind (like any other methodological device) are not a *sine qua non* of valid sociological research; they are merely a device for increasing the plausibility of an empirical argument. There are other means of increasing plausibility. In the case of a large-scale macro-theory (such as Weber's or Wallerstein's theories of the rise of capitalism),[17] one may improve its plausibility by showing that it involves a network of explanatory principles, which we have reason to believe are true because there is evidence for them in other contexts. In other words, a macro-analysis, like any analysis, is strengthened when its implicit structure can be made coherent with the rest of social theory. In so far as macro-theoretical principles can be tightly knit together with micro-principles in a single explanatory web, the macro-analysis has a stronger claim to being correct. In arguing among rival macro- or macro-historical explanations, then, the theory that can be better micro-grounded is much more plausible than one that cannot.

My argument, then, is not that macro-sociologists should cease their work and become micro-sociologists, but only that they should realize that their work is theoretically incomplete. No macro-analysis is a strong argument until it can show not only that a particular historical pattern exists, but why that particular pattern exists rather than another. The requisite cases to compare may not be available on that macro-level, but systematic theory linking micro and macro can provide empirical substitutes as a repository of principles whose plausibility has been more strongly demonstrated in other, smaller contexts.

There is a final advantage in attempting micro-reduction across the entire range of sociological theory, precisely in the event that there are genuinely irreducible macro-components of explanation. In this case, micro-reduction should give us a clearer idea of just what irreducible macro-concepts may consist of. We will be able to distinguish among different types of macro-usages in sociology, and macro-variables, if they genuinely exist, may be economically reduced to a finite and possibly quite small number. Let us call this process "micro-translation," to avoid the negative connotations of the term "reduction"; it should be thought of as a revisualization of social theory in micro-terms, a sort of X-ray vision of the micro-components and linkages that make up macro-structure. . . .

NOTES

1. Emmanuel Schegloff, "The First Five Seconds," unpublished PhD dissertation (University of California, 1967).

2. Harvey Sacks, Emmanuel Schegloff, and Gail Jefferson, "A Simplest Systematics for the Organization of Turn-taking in Conversation," *Language*, 50 (1974), pp. 696–735; Jo Ann Goldberg, "A System for the Transfer of Instructions in Natural Settings and the Amplitude Shift Mechanism: a Procedure for Utterance Affiliation in Sequence Construction," unpublished PhD dissertation (University of California, 1977).

3. Aaron V. Cicourel, *The Social Organization of Juvenile Justice* (New York: Wiley, 1968); Stewart Clegg, *Power, Rule, and Domination: A Critical and Empirical Understanding of Power in Sociological Theory and Everyday Life* (London: Routledge and Kegan Paul, 1975).

4. Aaron V. Cicourel, *Method and Measurement in Sociology* (New York: Free Press, 1964).

5. This point has also been made by George Homans, "Bringing Men Back in," *American Sociological Review*, 29 (1964), pp. 809–18; and by Herbert Blumer, *Symbolic Interactionism* (Englewood Cliffs: Prentice Hall, 1969), although without as great an emphasis upon micro-detail as by the ethnomethodologists.

6. Harold Garfinkel, *Studies in Ethnomethodology* (Englewood Cliffs: Prentice Hall, 1967).

7. Hugh Mehan and Houston Wood, *The Reality of Ethnomethodology* (New York: Wiley, 1975).

8. A sampling of the many expressions of these criticisms may be found in Guy E. Swanson, Anthony F.C. Wallace, and James S. Coleman, "Review Symposium on Harold Garfinkel's *Studies in Ethnomethodology*," *American Sociological Review*, 33 (1968), pp. 122–30; and Lewis A. Coser, "Two Methods in Search of a Substance," *American Sociological Review*, 40 (1975), pp. 691–700.

9. Alvin W. Gouldner, *The Coming Crisis of Western Sociology* (New York: Basic Books, 1970), pp. 390–5.

10. Émile Durkheim, *Sociology and Philosophy* (New York: Free Press, 1974; originally published 1924).

11. Robert R. Blain. "On Homans' Psychological Reductionism," *Sociological Inquiry*, 41 (1971), pp. 3–25; Jonathan H. Turner, *The Structure of Sociological Theory* (Homewood: Dorsey Press, 1974), pp. 242–57; George C. Homans, "Reply to Blain," *Sociological Inquiry*, 41 (1971), pp. 21–3.

12. Nicos Poulantzas, *Classes in Contemporary Capitalism* (London: New Left Books, 1975); Louis Althusser, *For Marx* (New York: Pantheon, 1970).

13. Aaron V. Cicourel, *Theory and Method in a Study of Argentine Fertility* (New York: Wiley, 1974); Randall Collins, *Conflict Sociology: Towards an Explanatory Science* (New York: Academic Press, 1975), pp. 450–6.

14. Randall Collins, *Conflict Sociology*, pp. 49–160.

15. H. Blumer, *Symbolic Interactionism*.

16. E. Durkheim, *Sociology and Philosophy*.

17. Max Weber, *General Economic History* (New York: Collier, 1961; originally published 1924); I. Wallerstein, *The Modern World System*, vol. 1 (New York: Academic Press, 1974).

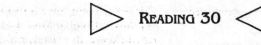
MICROPROCESS AND MACROSTRUCTURE*

PETER M. BLAU

Microsociology and macrosociology involve contrasting theoretical perspectives on social life and consequently explain it in different terms. The units of analysis are different—individuals in the first case and populations in the second—and so are the concepts and variables—attributes of human beings in microsociology, emergent properties of population structures in macrosociology. Individuals can be rich or poor, but only collectivities can exhibit more or less economic inequality. The two are not alternative theories, however, and corroborating one does not entail falsifying the other, because they deal with different aspects of social life and each seeks to explain phenomena the other assumes to be given, takes for granted, or ignores.

Thus microsociology and macrosociology employ different concepts and seek to formulate different theories to explain social relations and the more complex social patterns

based on social relations. Microsociology analyzes the underlying social processes that engender relations between persons. The focus is on social interaction and communication, and important concepts are exchange, reciprocity, significant symbols, obligations, investment, and dependence. Macrosociology analyzes the structure of different positions in a population and their constraints on social relations. The focus is on the external limitations of the social environment on people's relations, and important concepts are differentiation, institutions, inequality, heterogeneity, and crosscutting circles. In short, microsociology dissects the internal dynamic processes underlying social relations, whereas macrosociology analyzes the influences on social relations exerted by external structural constraints and opportunities—Durkheim's social facts. . . .

. . . What I plan to do in this chapter is first to review briefly the version of exchange theory I developed, . . . then to discuss the macrostructural theory on which I have centered attention in recent years, and to conclude by examining the nexus between

*From Karen S. Cook, ed., *Social Exchange Theory* (Newbury Park, CA: Sage Publications, 1987), pp. 83–87, 92–100. Reprinted with permission of Sage Publications, Inc.

microsociological and macrosociological schemes.

EXCHANGE THEORY

... The main reason for my interest in social exchange is that I consider it a strictly social phenomenon and thus particularly well suited for investigation by sociologists. This is not the case for most of the subjects we study in surveys. People's attitudes, votes in elections, education, career achievements, and work satisfaction, for example, are certainly socially conditioned and influenced, and many are oriented toward other people, but these factors themselves refer to the acting and thinking of individuals and not to a social process. Social exchange, in contrast, centers attention directly on the social process of give-and-take in people's relations and analyzes how ego's behavior depends, not on ego's prior conditioning, or experiences, or attributes, but on alter's behavior that in turn is contingent on ego's behavior. The behavior of each is, of course, psychologically motivated, but exchange theory does not seek to explain why each individual participates in the exchange in terms of these motives but, instead, dissects the transaction process to explain the interdependent contingencies in which each response is dependent on the other's prior action and is simultaneously the stimulus evoking the other's further reaction. Thus, the motivation of participants is taken as given, and concern is with the alternating reciprocities underlying the social interaction. My disagreement with Homans's (1961) theory stems from this conception of mine of the distinctly social nature of exchange. To be sure, exchange can be analyzed in terms of the motives of the partners to the transactions, just as conflict can be analyzed in terms of the motives of the adversaries. But such psychological reductionism ignores the social

process presumably under investigation, the repeated reciprocities implicit in exchange, or the seemingly inevitable growth of conflict potential resulting from threats and counterthreats as illustrated by an arms race.

In terms of substantive conceptions, the most important difference of my scheme from Homans's is that I do not confine the analysis to reciprocal transactions but lay great stress on unilateral exchanges, in which prestige and power become differentiated because ego receives benefits from alter but has no resources alter wants with which to reciprocate and consequently becomes dependent on and subordinate to alter. This analysis of unilateral transactions generating differentiation of status is strongly influenced by Emerson's (1962:35) analysis of alternatives to dependence. To be sure, he starts with a relation of dependence and then stipulates the operations required to restore balance, whereas I (1964:118–125) reconceptualize his principles to specify what the alternatives to dependence are and then conclude that the absence of any of these alternatives makes imbalances, dependence, and subordination in interpersonal relations inevitable. Nevertheless, the basic principles of my analysis are directly derived from Emerson's scheme.

There are a number of additional reasons for sociologists to be interested in the analysis of social exchange. It is one of the few subject matters, outside of mathematical sociology, that lends itself to the development of systematic axiomatic theory. Such concepts as marginal utility, borrowed from economics, can be adapted to explain noneconomic observations—for example, the declining significance of social approval with the increasing number of persons from whom social approval has already been received—and hence can serve as building stones for constructing rigorous, hypothetico-deductive theory. Indeed, Homans's exchange theory and Emerson's analysis of power and exchange are two of the rather rare attempts in sociology to devise such a theory, and whereas I disagree with the psychological reductionism of Homans's theory I fully agree with his emphasis on the importance for sociology to develop more systematic deductive theories that yield testable predictions.

Another advantage of exchange theory is that its basic ideas and concepts are widely applicable and give new meaning to everyday observations, for example, why people do favors even to strangers, or why they often fight over who pays the check in a restaurant. A final attraction exchange theory had for me is that I hoped that it could serve as a microsociological foundation for building a macrosociological theory of social structure. This is what I attempted to do in my book on the subject 20 years ago. But I was more successful in the microsociological analysis of exchange processes than in employing the micro principles as the groundwork for building a rigorous macrostructural theory. This is the main reason why my interest shifted away from social exchange to a different approach to macrosociological theorizing.

But before I returned to primarily theoretical analysis I spent more than a decade conducting empirical research on bureaucratic organizations of various kinds. I had a longstanding interest in the organizational principles of Weber's analysis of bureaucracy, and this interest motivated my early case studies of government offices, but I could deal with bureaucratic principles there only inferentially and not directly, because general principles of organizations require comparing many and cannot be based on case studies. Homans noted this in a book review of my early research that, though generally favorable, indicated that the title (*The Dynamics of Bureaucracy*) is misleading, because the book deals essentially with informal relations in work groups of officials and not with bureaucracy. To attack problems of organizational structure directly, I carried out a series of studies, each of which involved the quantitative analysis of data collected from a large number of comparable organizations, for example, many government agencies, many academic institutions, or many factories. This research does address the macrosociological issues of bureaucratic structure with which Weber's theory is concerned. Although not devoid of theoretical inferences and implications, these studies concentrated on the analysis of empirical findings. I became increasingly eager to escape being submerged in empirical data and to try to develop a deductive macrosociological theory of social structure.

An important issue in constructing macrosociological theory is the linkage with microsociological theory. One approach is to start with microsociological principles and use these as the foundation for building macrosociological theory. The alternative approach rests on the assumption that different perspectives and conceptual frameworks are necessary for micro and macro theories, primarily because the major terms of macrosociological theories refer to emergent properties of population structures that have no equivalent in microsociological analysis. I have come to the conclusion that the second approach is the only viable one, at least at this stage of sociological development....

MACROSTRUCTURAL THEORY

People's cultural values and psychological preferences affect, of course, their choices of associates in social relations, particularly in profound and lasting relations like marriage. But they are not the only factors that affect social bonds. People's options are also limited by their social environments, that is, by the population composition of the place where they live. (I shall ignore migration in the interest of brevity, except to say that it merely alters and does not eliminate the constraints the population structure exerts on choices of associates.) The issue of free will is completely irrelevant for these external social influences. Whether our choices are fully determined by our constitution and background and experiences or we are entirely free to marry anyone who is willing to marry us, we cannot marry Eskimos if there are none around. These limits on options are much more severe when large numbers are under consideration than when single individuals are. For example, it is impossible for most white Americans to have close friends who are blacks, because this would require that the average black American has about ten close friends who are whites.

A domain assumption, in Gouldner's (1970:31–35) phrase, implicit in the theory is that the structural constraints and opportunities created by the population composition in a place exert a dominant influence on social relations that counteracts the influences of social values, psychological dispositions, and ingroup preferences. These influences are the external contraints of social facts Durkheim emphasized, notably in his earlier works. The major theorems reflect this structural assumption, and empirical evidence corroborating them provides indirect evidence for the assumption. To illustrate the theory, three major theorems will be deduced from two higher-order premises that are assumptions postulated as valid, but for which there is also substantial empirical evidence from previous research.

The first assumption is that people tend to associate disproportionately with others proximate to them in social space, that is, with others who belong to the same group or whose social status is close to their own, whatever the dimension under consideration. There is much empirical support for this proposition that associations between persons in similar social positions exceed chance expectations.

Thus, disproportionate numbers of marriages involve spouses of the same race, religion, and national origin (Kennedy, 1944; Hollingshead, 1950; Carter and Glick, 1970; Abramson, 1973; Heer, 1974; Alba, 1976). Similarities in education, occupation, and social class have also been observed to enhance the likelihood of marriage (Centers, 1949; Hollingshead, 1950; Blau and Duncan, 1967; Carter and Glick, 1970; Tyree and Treas, 1974). Friendships, too, have been found to be promoted by shared social positions. The second assumption postulates that the extent of social associations depends on opportunities for contact. Aside from the fact that this is virtually self-evident, it implies that physical propinquity, which engenders contact opportunities, is expected to increase the likelihood of marriages and friendships, and empirical studies found this is to be the case (Abrams, 1943; Festinger et al., 1950; Caplow and Foreman, 1950).

One major theorem stipulates that heterogeneity promotes intergroup relations. This seems paradoxical, inasmuch as it appears to contradict the first assumption that people tend to associate with others of their own group. Nevertheless, the theorem can be deduced from the two assumptions jointly with the definition of heterogeneity. Because it is assumed that people tend to select ingroup associates, intergroup relations are rare in homogeneous places; and because it is also assumed that associations depend on contact opportunities; and because heterogeneity is defined as the chance expectation that two randomly chosen persons belong to different groups; it follows that heterogeneity increases the chances that fortuitous encounters involve members of different groups, which reduces opportunities for ingroup associations and increases probabilities of intergroup associations. The greater a city's ethnic heterogeneity, for example, the more likely are interethnic marriages.

Another main theorem is that inequality fosters status-distant social relations. The originally published formulation of this theorem was incorrect (Blau, 1977:55). My reasoning then was that because status distance inhibits social associations, by assumption, and because inequality refers to average status distance, inequality should also discourage status-distant associations. But this argument completely ignores the external constraints of the population composition that acts as a counteracting influence in the case of inequality, just as it does in the case of heterogeneity. Therefore, the theorem was reformulated: Because inequality, as defined, increases the likelihood that chance encounters involve two persons relatively distant in status, it constrains individuals to modify their preferences for status-proximate associates and makes status-distant associations more likely. Thus, the theorem predicts that much income inequality in a neighborhood tends to increase the difference in income between friends.

The final theorem to be presented is that many intersecting social differences promote intergroup relations. This central proposition of my theory incorporates Simmel's concept of crosscutting circles. If people tend to associate with others in their ingroup in various dimensions, as is assumed; and if the various dimensions intersect (are weakly related); people's very tendencies to associate with others in their ingroup on any one dimension (for instance, race) involve many of them in intergroup associations with respect to other dimensions (for instance, class, and age). The multiform heterogeneity generated by many crosscutting social circles creates compelling constraints to associate with persons outside one's own groups, because most of one's ingroup associates in any one dimension are outsiders belonging to different groups in several other dimensions. The greater our ingroup bias in some respects, the more we re-strict our choices in others, increasing the constraints to maintain intergroup relations in these other respects. A corollary of this theorem is that consolidated social differences that reinforce one another and strengthen the barriers between different social positions, discourage intergroup relations. For example, the more closely race is related to occupation and income, the rarer are associations between persons in different social strata.

After the deductive theory had been formulated, a research project was designed to test the three theorems outlined and some others (Blau and Schwartz, 1984). The research was based on data from the 1970 U.S. Census on the 125 largest metropolitan areas in the United States, ranging in population from one-quarter to eleven million. The objective was to ascertain whether the theorems correctly predict the influence of the structural parameters specified on rates of intermarriage. Data on intermarriage provided a severe test of the theory and its structural assumptions. The domain assumption is that structural conditions limit options and influence intergroup relations even in the face of opposite influences exerted by cultural values and psychological predispositions (that are reflected in the ingroup assumption). The observation of such opposite structural influences is most plausible for casual acquaintances in small places, inasmuch as one would expect opportunities for chance encounters to influence superficial associations in a neighborhood. Marriage, in contrast, is an enduring relation that people do not enter lightly merely as the result of casual meetings but that is undoubtedly much affected by cultural values and personal attitudes, ranging from religious beliefs and racial bias to tastes in music and movies. Besides, in a metropolis with many thousands of people, it should be relatively easy to escape the constraints imposed by the population composition and find a spouse of one's own choosing. If marriage in large metropolitan areas is subject to the structural influences implied by the theorems, casual social relations in smaller places are still more likely to be so.

The first theorem discussed was tested with six forms of heterogeneity (using nine different measures), ranging from racial to occupational heterogeneity and intermarriage. The second was tested with inequality in education, occupational status, and earnings (using four measures). The last theorem was tested with eight forms of the intersection of one kind of social differences with several others (using ten measures). The empirical findings corroborate the theorems; all conform to the predictions when proper controls are introduced, and most do so also without any controls (that is, employing simple correlations). In sum, macrostructural constraints apparently exert substantial influence on social relations and the integration of diverse segments in a large community.

CLOSING THE CIRCLE

This macrostructural theory seems to be far removed from microsociological exchange theory. Indeed, the two are fundamentally different because they look at social relations from opposite perspectives. One might say, speaking metaphorically, that exchange theory examines social relations from within whereas macrostructural theory examines them from without. The former dissects the exchange processes assumed to underlie all social relations and gives them their features and dynamics, whatever the broader social system in which they are embedded; it is a micro but a general theory, like microeconomics. Macrostructural theory analyzes the structural framework consisting of the population composition that limits and governs the social relations that can develop, regardless of cultural norms and individual desires, and thereby shapes the patterns or structures of social relations in communities and other large collectivities. The contrasting perspectives yield quite different explanations, but not contradictory ones. An analogy would be that the clotting of blood can be explained chemically by its contact with oxygen or biologically by its preventing loss of life from small wounds. There is no conflict between these explanations; they simply examine a phenomenon from different standpoints.

Exchange theory and macrostructural theory are complementary, not contradictory. Merton (1975) has stressed the significance of pluralistic theories in a discipline for the advancement of knowledge. Different subject matters often require explanations by different theories, at least in the early stages of the development of a discipline, notwithstanding the ultimate goal of integrating the various theories, in accordance with the principle of Occam's razor. What I mean by saying that the two theories are complementary is that what the one takes as given and postulates as an assumption without trying to explain it, the other treats as problematic and seeks to explain. The macrosociological focus is appropriate for the study of entire societies or other large collectivities, because it is impossible to trace and dissect the interpersonal relations of many thousands or millions of people, and neither would it be meaningful if all were described. In this case, the minutiae of daily social life must be neglected and the major regularities and patterns must be abstracted from them, which the macrostructural approach does by ignoring the social interaction between individuals and analyzing the rates of social interaction between social positions, that is, persons classified on the basis of various social dimensions.

However, we are also interested in the social processes implicit in all human relations and essential for understanding them. The macrosociological approach, painting a large canvas in bold strokes, cannot explain these processes because it does not investigate interpersonal relations in depth. For example, the existence of ingroup tendencies is assumed by the macrostructural theory but the processes producing them are not explained. Exchange theory seeks to explain them by noting how similarities in background, experiences, and social position make it likely that people exchange mutual support for their opinions and conduct, furnishing incentives for social interaction. Moreover, ingroup preferences, such as people's values generally, have two manifestations: They induce persons to associate with members of their own group themselves, and they also induce them to approve of others who choose ingroup associates and to disapprove of those who choose outsiders. These exchange processes sustain and reinforce the ingroup pressures, assumed to exist by macrostructural theory. According to this theory, however, structural conditions may constrain persons to engage increasingly in intergroup relations, as we have seen. Such greater prevalence of intergroup relations implies that ingroup pressures are weakened, because when many persons are involved in intergroup relations these are no longer widely disapproved. Here again exchange theory can explain the diminished ingroup pressures by the lesser approval people earn for confining their relations to the ingroup.

Exchange theory is not concerned with the structure of social relations that develop in the larger social environment and with the significance of that structure for the nature of social exchange. Macrostructural theory directly addresses the first issue and has implications for the second. An increase in intergroup relations, as the result of new and different social conditions, alters the nature of the prevalent exchange transactions, because social exchange in intergroup relations tends to differ from that in ingroup relations. (Although most social relations are simultaneously ingroup and intergroup on different dimensions, social exchange usually centers either on the shared or on the different attributes of the dyad.) Exchange theory dissects the processes in different social relations, but takes these differences as given, whereas macrostructural theory seeks to explain why some social relations are more prevalent than others.

Social exchange between members of the same ingroup, who tend to share views and opinions, often involves mutual support and approval. But exchange in intergroup relations usually involves different benefits or services, owing to differences in experience and resources. One person may advise another about gardening, and the other discharges his or her obligation by helping the first to repair the family car. Social differences also create the possibility that one person can advise and help another but the second has nothing to return except his respect, gratitude, and deference. In this way, status differences are generated in intergroup relations. But these informal differences in prestige and influence between associates are quite different from formal authority or power, like that of the manager over the workers. The personal element in informal status differences resulting from unilateral exchange makes it less inescapable and oppressive than the formal authority of the boss or the coercive power of the police officer. . . .

The ultimate aim, to be sure, is to develop a unified sociological theory that encompasses explanations of the significance of both macrostructures and microprocesses for social life. But the day we can achieve this is still far off, just as microeconomics and macroeconomics have not yet been able to develop a unified rigorous theory. Indeed, not even physics, surely a far more advanced science than sociology, has been successful in developing a unified theory, notwithstanding the endeavors to do so of as great a genius as Einstein. This is the reason that I think that theories of microprocesses and theories of macrostructure require different approaches at the present stage of sociological theorizing and probably will for a long time. But I also think that the two approaches are complementary and that each is enriched by taking cognizance of the other. Acknowledgment of the importance of the opportunity structure for microprocesses, and the illustrations in the last few pages of the significance of microprocesses for fully understanding macrostructures, help to close a circle by narrowing the gap between these two contrasting theoretical perspectives. A further step in narrowing this gap is contextual analysis that explicitly investigates how the structural context modifies and shapes the processes of social exchange that govern and reflect social relations.

To conclude, let me indicate why I changed my mind since I wrote the book on exchange and power, in which I suggested that macrosociological theory should be built on the basis of microsociological theory, whereas I now believe that the two theories require different, if complementary, perspectives and approaches. One major reason is that the two involve incommensurate conceptual schemes. Basic concepts of microanalysis, such as reciprocity, obligation, network density, or multiplexity, are not relevant for macroanalysis because the latter does not dissect social interaction and role relations between individuals. At the same time, basic concepts of macroanalysis, such as heterogeneity, inequality, and the degree to which various social differences are related, are emergent properties of collectivities that cannot refer to individuals and thus are not appropriate for the study of role relations between individuals. Even when the same term is used, its meaning in micro- and macro-

analysis is quite different. Imbalanced obligations and dependence in exchange relations give rise to interpersonal power, but this superordination is neither the same as nor the source of the power of concern in macrosociological analysis—like that of the corporation executive, the general, the dictator—which rests on resources and authority positions. Both involve dependence, but interpersonal dependence and power are confined to relatively narrow circles of persons with whom one has direct or, at least, indirect contact, whereas large resources enable a person to make very large numbers dependent and hence to exercise power over them without even indirect contact with them.

Another reason for my now thinking that macrosociological analysis cannot be built on microsociological analysis but requires a distinct perspective is that the sociopyschological processes with which microanalysis is concerned are not the foundation of the conditions that produce the social structures analyzed in macrosociological studies. To investigate why societies or communities differ in various kinds of heterogeneity, of inequality, and of degrees of intersection, it is necessary to analyze comparatively and historically the influences of economic and political conditions and the patterns of social and geographical mobility that influence the development of the existing variations in social structure. The observed differences in structures of social positions can then be used to explain differences in the structures of social relations, which is what I endeavored in my macrosociological theory. No microanalysis of exchange processes involving direct social associations, even if it were feasible to carry it out for an entire society, can explain these macrostructures. However, the study of microprocesses, albeit not based on representative samples, complements the study of macrostructures, not by explaining these structures but by deepening our understanding of them by helping to account for some of the assumptions made in macroanalysis, just as the latter contributes to microanalysis by accounting for the structural context that tends to be taken as given in microsociological studies. For all these reasons, I consider the microsociological study of interpersonal processes and the macrosociological study of large structures of social positions and relations to require different perspectives but that they provide complementary interpretations of social life and thereby deepen our understanding of it.

REFERENCES

ABRAMS, R.H. 1943. "Residual propinquity as a factor in marriage selection." American Sociological Review 8:288–294.

ABRAMSON, H.J. 1973. Ethnic Diversity in Catholic America. New York: John Wiley.

ALBA, R.D. 1976. "Social assimilation among American Catholic groups." American Sociological Review 41:1030–1046.

BLAU, P.M. 1964. Exchange and Power in Social Life. New York: John Wiley.

———. 1977. Inequality and Heterogeneity: A Primitive Theory of Social Structure. New York: Free Press.

BLAU, P.M., AND O.D. DUNCAN. 1967. The American Occupational Structure. New York: John Wiley.

BLAU, P.M., AND J.E. SCHWARTZ. 1984. Crosscutting Social Circles. Orlando: Academic Press.

CAPLOW, T., AND R. FORMAN. 1960. "Neighborhood interaction in a homogeneous community." American Sociological Review 15: 357–366.

CARTER, H., AND P. GLICK. 1970. Marriage and Divorce. Cambridge, MA: Harvard University Press.

CENTERS, R. 1949. "Marital selection and occupational strata." American Journal of Sociology 54:508–519.

EMERSON, R.M. 1962. "Power-dependence relations." American Sociological Review 27:31–41.

FESTINGER, L., S. SCHACHTER, AND K. BACK. 1950. Social Pressures in Informal Groups. New York: Harper and Row.

GOULDNER, A.W. 1970. The Coming Crisis of Western Sociology. New York: Basic Books.

HEER, D.M. 1974. "The prevalence of black-white marriage in the United States." Journal of Marriage and the Family 36:246–258.

HOLLINGSHEAD, A.B. 1950. "Cultural factors in the selection of marriage mates." American Sociological Review 15:619–627.

HOMANS, G.C. 1961. Social Behavior: Its Elementary Forms. New York: Harcourt Brace Jovanovich.

KENNEDY, R.J. 1944. "Single or triple melting pot?" American Journal of Sociology 39: 331–339.

MERTON, R.K. 1975. "Structural analysis in sociology," pp. 21–52 in P.M. Blau (ed.) Approaches to the Study of Social Structure. New York: Free Press.

TYREE, A., AND J. TREAS. 1974. "The occupational and marital mobility of women." American Sociological Review 39:293–302.

SOCIAL SPACE AND SYMBOLIC POWER*

PIERRE BOURDIEU

★ ★ ★

I

Speaking in the most general terms, social science, be it anthropology, sociology or history, oscillates between two seemingly incompatible points of view, two apparently irreconcilable perspectives: objectivism and subjectivism or, if you prefer, between physicalism and psychologism (which can take on various colorings, phenomenological, semiological, etc.). On the one hand, it can "treat social facts as things," according to the old Durkheimian precept, and thus leave out everything that they owe to the fact that they are objects of knowledge, of cognition—or misrecognition—within social existence. On the other hand, it can reduce the social world to the representations that agents have of it, the task of social science consisting then in

producing an "account of the accounts" produced by social subjects.

Rarely are these two positions expressed and above all realized in scientific practice in such a radical and contrasted manner. We know that Durkheim is no doubt, together with Marx, the one who expressed the *objectivist* position in the most consistent manner. "We believe this idea to be fruitful, he wrote (Durkheim 1970, p. 250), that social life must be explained, not by the conception of those who participate in it, but by deep causes which lie outside of consciousness." However, being a good Kantian, Durkheim was not unaware of the fact that this reality can only be grasped by employing logical instruments, categories, classifications. This being said, objectivist physicalism often goes hand in hand with the positivist proclivity to conceive classifications as mere "operational" partitions, or as the mechanical recording of breaks or "objective" discontinuities (as in statistical distributions for instance).

It is no doubt in the work of Alfred Schutz and of the ethnomethodologists that one would find the purest expression of the *subjec-*

*From Pierre Bourdieu, "Social Space and Symbolic Power," *Sociological Theory* 7:1 (Spring 1989), 14–25. Reprinted with permission of the American Sociological Association and the author.

tivist vision. Thus Schutz (1962, p. 59) embraces the standpoint exactly opposite to Durkheim's: "The observational field of the social scientist—social reality—has a specific meaning and relevance structure for the human beings living, acting, and thinking within it. By a series of common-sense constructs, they have pre-selected and pre-interpreted this world which they experience as the reality of their daily life. It is these thought objects of theirs which determine their behavior by motivating it. The thought objects constructed by the social scientist in order to grasp this social reality have to be founded upon the thought objects constructed by the common-sense thinking of men, living their daily life within their social world. Thus, the constructs of the social sciences are, so to speak, constructs of the second degree, that is, constructs of the constructs made by the actors on the social scene." The opposition is total: in the first instance, scientific knowledge can be obtained only by means of a break with primary representations—called "pre-notions" in Durkheim and "ideologies" in Marx—leading to unconscious causes. In the second instance, scientific knowledge is in continuity with common sense knowledge, since it is nothing but a "construct of constructs."

If I have somewhat belabored this opposition—one of the most harmful of these "paired concepts" which, as Reinhard Bendix and Bennett Berger (1959) have shown, pervade the social sciences—it is because the most steadfast (and, in my eyes, the most important) intention guiding my work has been to overcome it. At the risk of appearing quite obscure, I could sum up in one phrase the gist of the analysis I am putting forth today: on the one hand, the objective structures that the sociologist constructs, in the objectivist moment, by setting aside the subjective representations of the agents, form the basis for these representations, and constitute the structural constraints that bear upon interac-

tions; but, on the other hand, these representations must also be taken into consideration particularly if one wants to account for the daily struggles, individual and collective, which purport to transform or to preserve these structures. This means that the two moments, the objectivist and the subjectivist, stand in a dialectical relationship (Bourdieu 1977) and that, for instance, even if the subjectivist moment seems very close, when taken separately, to interactionist or ethnomethodological analyses, it still differs radically from them: points of view are grasped as such and related to the positions they occupy in the structure of agents under consideration.

In order to transcend the artificial opposition that is thus created between structures and representations, one must also break with the mode of thinking which Cassirer (1923) calls *substantialist* and which inclines one to recognize no reality other than those that are available to direct intuition in ordinary experience, i.e., individuals and groups. The major contribution of what must rightly be called the structuralist revolution consists in having applied to the social world the *relational* mode of thinking which is that of modern mathematics and physics, and which identifies the real not with substances but with relations (Bourdieu 1968). The "social reality" which Durkheim spoke of is an ensemble of invisible relations, those very relations which constitute a space of positions external to each other and defined by their proximity to, neighborhood with, or distance from each other, and also by their relative position, above or below or yet in between, in the middle. Sociology, in its objectivist moment, is a social topology, an *analysis situs* as they called this new branch of mathematics in Leibniz's time, an analysis of relative positions and of the objective relations between these positions.

This relational mode of thinking is at the point of departure of the construction presented in *Distinction* [Bourdieu 1984a]. It is a fair bet, however, that the space, that is, the system of relations, will go unnoticed by the reader, despite the use of diagrams (and of correspondence analysis, a very sophisticated form of factorial analysis). This is due, first, to the fact that the substantialist mode of thinking is easier to adopt and flows more "naturally." Secondly, this is because, as often happens, the means one has to use to construct social space and to exhibit its structure risk concealing the results they enable one to reach. The groups that must be constructed in order to objectivize the positions they occupy hide those positions. Thus the chapter of *Distinction* devoted to the different fractions of the dominant class will be read as a description of the various lifestyles of these fractions, instead of an analysis of locations in the space of positions of power—what I call the field of power. (Parenthesis: one may see here that changes in vocabulary are at once the condition and the product of a break with the ordinary representation associated with the idea of "ruling class").

At this point of the discussion, we can compare social space to a geographic space within which regions are divided up. But this space is constructed in such a way that the closer the agents, groups or institutions which are situated within this space, the more common properties they have; and the more distant, the fewer. Spatial distances—on paper—coincide with social distances. Such is not the case in real space. It is true that one can observe almost everywhere a tendency toward spatial segregation, people who are close together in social space tending to find themselves, by choice or by necessity, close to one another in geographic space; nevertheless, people who are very distant from each other in social space can encounter one another and interact, if only briefly and intermittently, in physical space. Interactions, which bring immediate gratification to those with empiricist

dispositions—they can be observed, recorded, filmed, in sum, they are tangible, one can "reach out and touch them"—mask the structures that are realized in them. This is one of those cases where the visible, that which is immediately given, hides the invisible which determines it. One thus forgets that the truth of any interaction is never entirely to be found within the interaction as it avails itself for observation. One example will suffice to bring out the difference between structure and interaction and, at the same time, between the structuralist vision I defend as a necessary (but not sufficient) moment of research and the so-called interactionist vision in all its forms (and especially ethnomethodology). I have in mind what I call strategies of condescension, those strategies by which agents who occupy a higher position in one of the hierarchies of objective space symbolically deny the social distance between themselves and others, a distance which does not thereby cease to exist, thus reaping the profits of the recognition granted to a purely symbolic denegation of distance ("she is unaffected," "he is not highbrow" or "stand-offish," etc.) which implies a recognition of distances. (The expressions I just quoted always have an implicit rider: "she is unaffected, for a duchess," "he is not so highbrow, for a university professor," and so on.) In short, one can use objective distances in such a way as to cumulate the advantages of propinquity and the advantages of distance, that is, distance and the recognition of distance warranted by its symbolic denegation.

How can we concretely grasp these objective relations which are irreducible to the interactions by which they manifest themselves? These objective relations are the relations between positions occupied within the distributions of the resources which are or may become active, effective, like aces in a game of cards, in the competition for the appropriation of scarce goods of which this social universe is the site. According to my empirical investigation, these fundamental powers are economic capital (in its different forms), cultural capital, social capital, and symbolic capital, which is the form that the various species of capital assume when they are perceived and recognized as legitimate (Bourdieu 1986a). Thus agents are distributed in the overall social space, in the first dimension, according to the overall volume of capital they possess and, in the second dimension, according to the structure of their capital, that is, the relative weight of the different species of capital, economic and cultural, in the total volume of their assets.

The misunderstanding that the analyses proposed particularly in *Distinction* elicit are thus due to the fact that classes on paper are liable to being apprehended as real groups. This realist (mis)reading is objectively encouraged by the fact that social space is so constructed that agents who occupy similar or neighboring positions are placed in similar conditions and subjected to similar conditionings, and therefore have every chance of having similar dispositions and interests, and thus of producing practices that are themselves similar. The dispositions acquired in the position occupied imply an adjustment to this position, what Goffman calls the "sense of one's place." It is this sense of one's place which, in interactions, leads people whom we call in French "*les gens modestes,*" "common folks," to keep to their common place, and the others to "keep their distance," to "maintain their rank," and to "not get familiar." These strategies, it should be noted in passing, may be perfect.y unconscious and take the form of what is called timidity or arrogance. In effect, social distances are inscribed in bodies or, more precisely, into the relation to the body, to language and to time—so many structural aspects of practice ignored by the subjectivist vision.

Add to this the fact that this sense of one's place, and the affinities of habitus experienced as sympathy or antipathy, are at the basis of all forms of cooptation, friendships, love affairs, marriages, associations, and so on, thus of all the relationships that are lasting and sometimes sanctioned by law, and you will see that everything leads one to think that classes on paper are real groups—all the more real in that the space is better constructed and the units cut into this space are smaller. If you want to launch a political movement or even an association, you will have a better chance of bringing together people who are in the same sector of social space (for instance, in the northwest region of the diagram, where intellectuals are) than if you want to bring together people situated in regions at the four corners of the diagram.

But just as subjectivism inclines one to reduce structures to visible interactions, objectivism tends to deduce actions and interactions from the structure. So the crucial error, the theoreticist error that you find in Marx, would consist in treating classes on paper as real classes, in concluding from the objective homogeneity of conditions, of conditionings, and thus of dispositions, which flows from the identity of position in social space, that the agents involved exist as a unified group, as a class. The notion of *social space allows us to go beyond the alternative of realism and nominalism* when it comes to social classes (Bourdieu 1985): the political work aimed at producing social classes as *corporate bodies,* permanent groups endowed with permanent organs or representation, acronyms, etc., is all the more likely to succeed when the agents that it seeks to assemble, to unify, to constitute into a group, are closer to each other in social space (and therefore belonging to the same theoretical class). Classes in Marx's sense have to be made through a political work that has all the more chance of succeeding when it is armed with a theory that is well-founded in reality, thus more capable of exerting a *theory ef-*

fect—theorein, in Greek, means to see—that is, of imposing a vision of divisions.

With the theory effect, we have escaped pure physicalism, but without foresaking the gains of the objectivist phase: groups, such as social classes, are *to be made*. They are not given in "social reality." The title of E.P. Thompson's (1963) famous book *The Making of the English Working Class* must be taken quite literally: the working class such as it may appear to us today, through the words meant to designate it, "working class," "proletariat," "workers," "labor movement," and so on, through the organizations that are supposed to express its will, through the logos, bureaus, locals, flags, etc., is a well-founded historical artefact (in the sense in which Durkheim said that religion is a well-founded illusion). But this in no way means that one can construct anything anyhow, either in theory or in practice.

II

We have thus moved from social physics to social phenomenology. The "social reality" objectivists speak about is also an object of perception. And social science must take as its object both this reality and the perception of this reality, the perspectives, the points of view which, by virtue of their position in objective social space, agents have on this reality. The spontaneous visions of the social world, the "folk theories" ethnomethodologists talk about, or what I call "spontaneous sociology," but also scientific theories, sociology included, are part of social reality, and, like Marxist theory for instance, can acquire a truly real power of construction.

The objectivist break with pre-notions, ideologies, spontaneous sociology, and "folk theories," is an inevitable, necessary moment of the scientific enterprise—you cannot do without it, as do interactionism, ethnomethodol-

ogy, and all these forms of social psychology which rest content with a phenomenal vision of the social world, without exposing yourself to grave mistakes. But it is necessary to effect a *second and more difficult break with objectivism*, by reintroducing, in a second stage, what had to be excluded in order to construct objective reality. Sociology must include a sociology of the perception of the social world, that is, a sociology of the construction of visions of the world which themselves contribute to the construction of this world. But, having constructed social space, we know that these points of view, as the word itself suggests, are views taken from a certain point, that is, from a determinate position within social space. And we also know that there will be different or even antagonistic points of view, since points of view depend on the point from which they are taken, since the vision that every agent has of the space depends on his or her position in that space.

By doing this, we repudiate the universal subject, the transcendental ego of phenomenology that ethnomethodologists have taken over as their own. No doubt agents do have an active apprehension of the world. No doubt they do construct their vision of the world. But this construction is carried out under structural constraints. One may even explain in sociological terms what appears to be a universal property of human experience, namely, the fact that the familiar world tends to be "taken for granted," perceived as natural. If the social world tends to be perceived as evident and to be grasped, to use Husserl's (1983) expression, in a doxic modality, this is because the disposition of agents, their habitus, that is, the mental structures through which they apprehend the social world, are essentially the product of the internalization of the structures of that world. As perceptive dispositions tend to be adjusted to position, agents, even the most disadvantaged ones, tend to perceive the world as natural and to accept it much more readily than one might imagine—especially when you look at the situation of the dominated through the social eyes of a dominant.

So the search for invariant forms of perception or of construction of social reality masks different things: firstly, that this construction is not carried out in a social vacuum but subjected to structural constraints; secondly, that structuring structures, cognitive structures, are themselves socially structured because they have a social genesis; thirdly, that the construction of social reality is not only an individual enterprise but may also become a collective enterprise. But the so-called microsociological vision leaves out a good number of other things: as often happens when you look too closely, you cannot see the wood from the tree; and above all, failing to construct the space of positions leaves you no chance of seeing the point from which you see what you see.

Thus the representations of agents vary with their position (and with the interest associated with it) and with their habitus, as a system of schemes of perception and appreciation of practices, cognitive and evaluative structures which are acquired through the lasting experience of a social position. Habitus is both a system of schemes of production of practices and a system of perception and appreciation of practices. And, in both of these dimensions, its operation expresses the social position in which it was elaborated. Consequently, habitus produces practices and representations which are available for classification, which are objectively differentiated; however, they are immediately perceived as such only by those agents who possess the code, the classificatory schemes necessary to understand their social meaning. Habitus thus implies a "sense of one's place" but also a "sense of the place of others." For example, we say of a piece of clothing, a piece of furniture, or a book: "that looks pretty bourgeois" or "that's intellectual." What are the social conditions of possibility of such a judgment? First, it presupposes that taste (or habitus) as a system of schemes of classification, is objectively referred, via the social conditionings that produced it, to a social condition: agents classify themselves, expose themselves to classification, by choosing, in conformity with their taste, different attributes (clothes, types of food, drinks, sports, friends) that go well together and that go well with them or, more exactly, suit their position. To be more precise, they choose, in the space of available goods and services, goods that occupy a position in this space homologous to the position they themselves occupy in social space. This makes for the fact that nothing classifies somebody more than the way he or she classifies. Secondly, a classificatory judgment such as "that's petty bourgeois" presupposes that, as socialized agents, we are capable of perceiving the relation between practices or representations and positions in social space (as when we guess a person's social position from her accent). Thus, through habitus, we have a world of common sense, a world that seems self-evident.

I have so far adopted the perspective of the perceiving subject and I have mentioned the principal cause of variations in perception, namely, position in social space. But what about variations whose principle is found on the side of the object, in this space itself? It is true that the correspondence that obtains, through habitus (dispositions, taste), between positions and practices, preferences exhibited, opinions expressed, and so on, means that the social world does not present itself as pure chaos, as totally devoid of necessity and liable to being constructed in any way one likes. But this world does not present itself as totally structured either, or as capable of imposing upon every perceiving subject the principles of its own construction. The social world may be uttered and constructed in different ways according to different principles of vision and division—for example, economic divisions and ethnic divisions. If it is true that, in advanced societies, economic and cultural factors have the greatest power of differentiation, the fact remains that the potency of economic and social differences is never so great that one cannot organize agents on the basis of other principles of division—ethnic, religious, or national ones, for instance.

Despite this potential plurality of possible structurings—what Weber called the *Vielseitigkeit* of the given—it remains that the social world presents itself as a highly structured reality. This is because of a simple mechanism, which I want to sketch out briefly. Social space, as I described it above, presents itself in the form of agents endowed with different properties that are systematically linked among themselves: those who drink champagne are opposed to those who drink whiskey, but they are also opposed, in a different way, to those who drink red wine; those who drink champagne, however, have a higher chance than those who drink whiskey, and a far greater chance than those who drink red wine, of having antique furniture, playing golf at select clubs, riding horses or going to see light comedies at the theater. These properties, when they are perceived by agents endowed with the pertinent categories of perception—capable of seeing that playing golf makes you "look" like a traditional member of the old bourgeoisie—function, in the very reality of social life, as signs: *differences function as distinctive signs* and as signs of distinction, positive or negative, and this happens outside of any intention of distinction, of any conscious search for "conspicuous consumption." (This is to say, parenthetically, that my analyses have nothing in common with those of Veblen—all the more so in that distinction as I construe it, from the point of view of indigenous criteria, excludes the de-

liberate search for distinction). In other words, through the distribution of properties, the social world presents itself, objectively, as a symbolic system which is organized according to the logic of difference, of differential distance. Social space tends to function as a symbolic space, a space of lifestyles and status groups characterized by different lifestyles.

Thus the perception of the social world is the product of a *double structuring*: on the objective side, it is socially structured because the properties attributed to agents or institutions present themselves in combinations that have very unequal probabilities: just as feathered animals are more likely to have wings than furry animals, so the possessors of a sophisticated mastery of language are more likely to be found in a museum than those who do not have this mastery. On the subjective side, it is structured because the schemes of perception and appreciation, especially those inscribed in language itself, express the state of relations of symbolic power. I am thinking for example of pairs of adjectives such as heavy/light, bright/dull, etc., which organize taste in the most diverse domains. Together, these two mechanisms act to produce a common world, a world of commonsense or, at least, a minimum consensus on the social world.

But, as I suggested, the objects of the social world can be perceived and expressed in a variety of ways, since they always include a degree of indeterminacy and vagueness, and, thereby, a certain degree of semantic elasticity. Indeed, even the most constant combinations of properties are always based on statistical connections between interchangeable characteristics; furthermore, they are subject to variations in time so that their meaning, insofar as it depends on the future, is itself held in suspense and relatively indeterminate. This objective element of uncertainty—which is often reinforced by the effect of categorization, since the same word can cover different practices—provides a basis for the plurality of visions of the world which is itself linked to the plurality of points of view. At the same time, it provides a base for symbolic struggles over the power to produce and to impose the legitimate vision of the world. (It is in the intermediate positions of social space, especially in the United States, that the indeterminacy and objective uncertainty of relations between practices and positions is at a maximum, and also, consequently, the intensity of symbolic strategies. It is easy to understand why it is this universe which provides the favorite site of the interactionists and of Goffman in particular.)

Symbolic struggles over the perception of the social world may take two different forms. On the objective side, one may act by actions of representation, individual or collective, meant to display and to throw into relief certain realities: I am thinking for instance of demonstrations whose goal is to exhibit a group, its size, its strength, its cohesiveness, to make it exist visibly (Champagne 1984); and, on the individual level, of all the strategies of presentation of self, so well analyzed by Goffman (1959, 1967), that are designed to manipulate one's self-image and especially—something that Goffman overlooked—the image of one's position in social space. On the subjective side, one may act by trying to transform categories of perception and appreciation of the social world, the cognitive and evaluative structures through which it is constructed. The categories of perception, the schemata of classification, that is, essentially, the words, the names which construct social reality as much as they express it, are the stake par excellence of political struggle, which is a struggle to impose the legitimate principle of vision and division, i.e., a struggle over the legitimate exercise of what I call the "theory effect." I have shown elsewhere (Bourdieu 1980, 1986b), in the case of Kabylia, that groups—households, clans, or tribes—and the names that designate them are the instruments and stakes of innumerable strategies and that agents are endlessly occupied in the negotiation of their own identity. They may, for example, manipulate genealogy, just as we, for similar reasons, manipulate the texts of the "founding fathers" of our discipline. Likewise, on the level of the daily class struggle that social agents wage in an isolated and dispersed state, we have insults (which are a sort of magical attempt at categorization: *kathegorein*, from which our word "category" comes, originally means to accuse publicly), gossip, rumours, slander, innuendos, and so on. On the collective and more properly political level (Bourdieu 1981), we have all the strategies that aim at imposing a new construction of social reality by jettisoning the old political vocabulary, or at preserving the orthodox vision by keeping those words (which are often euphemisms, as in the expression "common folks" that I just evoked) designed to describe the social world. The most typical of these strategies of construction are those which aim at retrospectively reconstructing a past fitted to the needs of the present—as when General Flemming, disembarking in 1917, exclaimed: "La Fayette, here we are!"—or at constructing the future, by a creative prediction designed to limit the ever-open sense of the present.

These symbolic struggles, both the individual struggles of everyday life and the collective, organized struggles of political life, have a *specific logic* which endows them with a real autonomy from the structures in which they are rooted. Owing to the fact that symbolic capital is nothing other than economic or cultural capital when it is known and recognized, when it is known through the categories of perception that it imposes, symbolic relations of power tend to reproduce and to reinforce the power relations that constitute the structure of social space. More concretely, legitimation of the social world is not, as some believe, the product of a deliberate and purposive action of propaganda or symbolic imposition; it results, rather, from the fact that agents apply to the objective structures of the social world structures of perception and appreciation which are issued out of these very structures and which tend to picture the world as evident.

Objective relations of power tend to reproduce themselves in relations of symbolic power. In the symbolic struggle for the production of common sense or, more precisely, for the monopoly over legitimate naming, agents put into action the symbolic capital that they have acquired in previous struggles and which may be juridically guaranteed. Thus titles of nobility, like educational credentials, represent true titles of symbolic property which give one a right to share in the profits of recognition. Here again, we must break away from marginalist subjectivism: symbolic order is not formed in the manner of a market price, out of the mere mechanical addition of individual orders. On the other hand, in the determination of the objective classification and of the hierarchy of values granted to individuals and groups, not all judgments have the same weight, and holders of large amounts of symbolic capital, the *nobiles* (etymologically, those who are well-known and recognized), are in a position to impose the scale of values most favorable to their products—notably because, in our societies, they hold a practical *de facto* monopoly over institutions which, like the school system, officially determine and guarantee rank. On the other hand, symbolic capital may be officially sanctioned and guaranteed, and juridically instituted by the effect of official nomination (Bourdieu 1982). Official nomination, that is, the act whereby someone is granted a title, a socially recognized qualification, is one of the most typical expressions of that monopoly over legitimate symbolic violence which belongs to the state or to its representatives. A credential such as a school diploma is a piece of universally recognized and guaranteed symbolic capital, good on all markets. As an official definition of an official identity, it frees its holder from the symbolic struggle of all against all by imposing the universally approved perspective.

The state, which produces the official classification, is in one sense the supreme tribunal to which Kafka (1968) refers in *The Trial* when Block says to the attorney who claims to be one of the "great attorneys": "Of course, anybody can say he is 'great,' if he likes to, but in these matters the question is decided by the practices of the court." Science need not choose between relativism and absolutism: the truth of the social world is at stake in the struggles between agents who are unequally equipped to reach an absolute, i.e., self-fulfilling vision. The legal consecration of symbolic capital confers upon a perspective an absolute, universal value, thus snatching it from a relativity that is by definition inherent in every point of view, as a view taken from a particular point in social space.

There is an official point of view, which is the point of view of officials and which is expressed in official discourse. This discourse, as Aaron Cicourel has shown, fulfils three functions. First, it performs a diagnostic, that is, an act of knowledge or cognition which begets recognition and which, quite often, tends to assert what a person or a thing is and what it is universally, for every possible person, thus objectively. It is, as Kafka clearly saw, an almost divine discourse which assigns everyone an identity. In the second place, administrative discourse says, through directives, orders, prescriptions, etc., what people have to do, given what they are. Thirdly, it says what people have actually done, as in authorized accounts such as police records. In each case, official discourse imposes a point of view, that of the institution, especially via questionnaires, official forms, and so on. This point of view is instituted as a legitimate point of view, that is, a point of view that everyone has to recognize at least within the boundaries of a definite society. The representative of the state is the repository of common sense: official nominations and academic credentials tend to have a universal value on all markets. The most typical effect of the *raison d'Etat* is the effect of codification which is at work in such mundane operations as the granting of a certificate: an expert, physician or jurist, is someone who is appointed to produce a point of view which is recognized as transcendent over particular points of view—in the form of sickness notes, certificates of competence or incompetence—a point of view which confers universally recognized rights on the holder of the certificate. The state thus appears as the central bank which guarantees all certificates. One may say of the state, in the terms Leibniz used about God, that it is the "geometral locus of all perspectives." This is why one may generalize Weber's well-known formula and see in the state the holder of the monopoly of legitimate symbolic violence. Or, more precisely, the state is a referee, albeit a powerful one, in struggles over this monopoly.

But in the struggle for the production and imposition of the legitimate vision of the social world, the holders of bureaucratic authority never establish an absolute monopoly, even when they add the authority of science to their bureaucratic authority, as government economists do. In fact, *there are always, in any society, conflicts between symbolic powers that aim at imposing the vision of legitimate divisions,* that is, at constructing groups. Symbolic power, in this sense, is a power of "world-making." "World-making" consists, according to Nelson Goodman (1978), "in separating and reuniting, often in the same operation," in carrying out a decomposition, an analysis, and a composition, a synthesis, often by the use of labels. Social classifications, as is the case in archaic societies where they often work through dualist oppositions (masculine/feminine, high/low, strong/weak, etc.), organize the perception of the social world and, under certain conditions, can really organize the world itself.

III

So we can now examine under what conditions a symbolic power can become a *power of constitution,* by taking the term, with Dewey, both in its philosophical sense and in its political sense: that is, a power to preserve or to transform objective principles of union and separation, of marriage and divorce, of association and dissociation, which are at work in the social world; the power to conserve or to transform current classifications in matters of gender, nation, region, age, and social status, and this through the words used to designate or to describe individuals, groups or institutions.

To change the world, one has to change the ways of world-making, that is, the vision of the world and the practical operations by which groups are produced and reproduced. Symbolic power, whose form par excellence is the power to make groups (groups that are already established and have to be consecrated or groups that have yet to be constituted such as the Marxian proletariat), rests on two conditions. Firstly, as any form of performative discourse, symbolic power has to be based on the possession of symbolic capital. The power to impose upon other minds a vision, old or new, of social divisions depends on the social authority acquired in previous struggles. Symbolic capital is a credit; it is the power granted to those who have obtained sufficient recognition to be in a position to impose recognition. In this way, the power of constitution, a power to make a new group, through mobilization, or to make it exist by proxy, by speaking on its behalf as an authorized spokesperson, can be obtained only as the outcome of a long process of institutionalization, at the end of which a representative is instituted, who receives from the group the power to make the group.

Secondly, symbolic efficacy depends on the degree to which the vision proposed is founded in reality. Obviously, the construction of groups cannot be a construction *ex nihilo*. It has all the more chance of succeeding the more it is founded in reality, that is, as I indicated, in the objective affinities between the agents who have to be brought together. The "theory effect" is all the more powerful the more adequate the theory is. Symbolic power is the power to make things with words. It is only if it is true, that is, adequate to things, that description makes things. In this sense, *symbolic power is a power of consecration or revelation*, the power to consecrate or to reveal things that are already there. Does this mean that it does nothing? In fact, as a constellation which, according to Nelson Goodman (1978), begins to exist only when it is selected and designated as such, a group, a class, a gender, a region, or a nation begins to exist as such, for those who belong to it as well as for the others, only when it is distinguished, according to one principle or another, from other groups, that is, through knowledge and recognition (*connaissance et reconnaissance*).

We can thus, I hope, better understand what is at stake in the struggle over the existence or non-existence of classes. The struggle over classifications is a fundamental dimension of class struggle. The power to impose and to inculcate a vision of divisions, that is, the power to make visible and explicit social divisions that are implicit, is political power par excellence. It is the power to make groups, to manipulate the objective structure of society. As with constellations, the performative power of designation, of naming, brings into existence in an instituted, constituted form (i.e., as a "corporate body," a *corporatio*, as the medieval canonists studied by Kantorowicz [1981] said), what existed until then only as a *collectio personarium plurium*, a collection of varied persons, a purely additive series of merely juxtaposed individuals.

Here, if we bear in mind the main problem that I have tried to solve today, that of knowing how one can make things (i.e., groups) with words, we are confronted with one last question, the question of the *mysterium* of the *ministerium*, as the canonists liked to put it (Bourdieu 1984b): how does the spokesperson come to be invested with the full power to act and to speak in the name of the group which he or she produces by the magic of the slogan, the watchword, or the command, and by his mere existence as an incarnation of the collective? As the king in archaic societies, *Rex*, who, according to Benveniste (1969), is entrusted with the task of *regere fines* and *regere sacra*, of tracing out and stating the boundaries between groups and, thereby, of bringing them into existence as such, the leader of a trade union or of a political party, the civil servant or the expert invested with state authority, all are so many personifications of a social fiction to which they give life, in and through their very being, and from which they receive in return their power. The spokesperson is the substitute of the group which fully exists only through this delegation and which acts and speaks through him. He is the group made man, personified. As the canonists said: *status*, the position, is *magistratus*, the magistrate who holds it; or, as Louis XIV proclaimed, *"L'Etat, c'est moi"*; or again, in Robespierre's words, "I am the People." The class (or the people, the nation, or any other otherwise elusive social collective) exists if and when there exist agents who can say that they are the class, by the mere fact of speaking publicly, officially, in its place, and of being recognized as entitled to do so by the people who thereby recognize themselves as members of the class, people or nation, or of any other social reality that a realist construction of the world can invent and impose.

I hope that I was able, despite my limited linguistic capabilities, to convince you that complexity lies within social reality and not in a somewhat decadent desire to say complicated things. "The simple, wrote Bachelard (1985), is never but the simplified." And he demonstrated that science has never progressed except by questioning simple ideas. It seems to me that such questioning is particularly needed in the social sciences since, for all the reasons I have said, we tend too easily to satisfy ourselves with the commonplaces supplied us by our commonsense experience or by our familiarity with a scholarly tradition.

REFERENCES

BACHELARD, GASTON. [1934] 1985. *The New Scientific Spirit*. TRANS. Arthur Goldhammer. Boston: Beacon Press.

BENDIX, REINHARD, AND BENNETT BERGER. 1959. "Images of Society and Problems of Concept Formation in Sociology." Pp. 92–118 in *Symposium on Sociological Theory*. Edited by Llewelyn Gross. New York: Harper and Row.

BENVENISTE EMILE. 1969. *Le vocabulaire des institutions indo-européennes*. Vol. II: *Pouvoir, droit, religion*. Paris: Editions de Minuit.

BOURDIEU, PIERRE. 1968. "Structuralism and Theory of Sociological Knowledge." *Social Research* 35 (Winter): 681–706.

_____. [1972] 1977. *Outline of a Theory of Practice*. Cambridge: Cambridge University Press.

_____. 1980. *Les sens pratique*. Paris: Editions de Minuit.

_____. 1981. "La représentation politique. Eléments pour une théorie du champ politique." *Actes de la recherche en sciences sociales* 37 (February–March): 3–24.

_____. 1982. "Les rites d'institution." *Actes de la recherche en sciences sociales* 43 (June): 58–63.

_____. [1979] 1984a. *Distinction: A Social Critique of the Judgment of Taste*. Trans. Richard Nice. Cambridge: Harvard University Press.

_____. 1984b. "Delegation and Political Fetishism." *Thesis Eleven* 10/11 (November): 56–70.

_____. [1984] 1985. "Social Space and the Genesis of Groups." *Theory and Society* 14 (November): 723–744.

_____. [1983] 1986a. "The Forms of Capital." Pp. 241–258 in *Handbook of Theory and Research for the Sociology of Education*. Edited by John G. Richardson. New York: Greenwood Press.

_____. 1986b. "From Rules to Strategies." *Cultural Anthropology* 1–1 (February): 110–120.

CASSIRER, ERNST. [1910] 1923. *Substance and Function. Einstein's Theory of Relativity*. Trans. William Curtis Swabey and Marie Collins Swabey. Chicago: Open Court Publishing.

CHAMPAGNE, PATRICK. 1984. "La manifestation. La production de l'évènement politique." *Actes de la recherche en sciences sociales* 52/53: 18–41.

DURKHEIM, EMILE. [1897] 1970. La conception matérialiste de l'historie." Pp. 245–252 in *La science sociale et l'action*. Edited by Jean-Francois Filloux. Paris: Presses Universitaires de France.

GOFFMAN, ERVING. 1959. *The Presentation of Self in Everyday Life*. Harmondsworth: Pelican.

_____. 1967. *Interaction Ritual*. New York: Pantheon.

GOODMAN, NELSON. 1978. *Ways of Worldmaking*. Indianapolis: Hackett Publishing.

HUSSERL, EDMUND. [1913] 1983. *Ideas Pertaining to a Pure Phenomenology and to a Phenomenological Philosophy. First Book; General Introduction to a Pure Phenomenology*. The Hague: Martinus Nijhoff.

KAFKA, FRANZ. 1968. *The Trial*. New York: Schoken Books.

KANTOROWICZ, ERNST H. 1981. *The King's Two Bodies: A Study in Medieval Political Theology*. Princeton: Princeton University Press.

SCHUTZ, ALFRED. 1962. *Collected Papers*, Vol. I: *The Problem of Social Reality*. The Hague: Martinus Nijhoff.

THOMPSON, E.P. 1963. *The Making of the English Working Class*. Harmondsworth: Penguin.

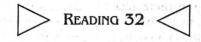

READING 32

AGENCY, INSTITUTION, AND TIME–SPACE ANALYSIS*

ANTHONY GIDDENS

1 THE GAP BETWEEN ACTION THEORY AND INSTITUTIONAL ANALYSIS

It is not difficult, I think, to see that the differentiation between so-called micro- and macro-sociological analysis has tended to coincide with a strongly embedded dualism in social theory and philosophy. This dualism has gone under various names and has taken various guises. In sociology, it has taken the form of an opposition between theories which emphasize human agency or "action" on the one side, and theories which emphasize "institutional analysis" or "structural analysis" on the other. In philosophy, it has normally taken the form of a contrast between those conceptions which emphasize the primacy of the "subject" (the knower or the locus of sense-experience) and those which take their point of departure from the

*From K. Knorr-Cetina and A.V. Cicourel, eds., *Advances in Social Theory and Methodology: Toward an Integration of Micro- and Macro-Sociologies* (London: Routledge and Kegan Paul, 1981), pp. 161–74. Reprinted with permission of Routledge.

"object" (the social or natural world that shapes the experience of the human being).

When we look at the development of the major traditions of social theory, we can set up a theorem which, broadly speaking, summarizes the division I have in mind. The theorem is: "strong on action theory, weak on institutional analysis." The reverse also holds: "strong on institutional analysis, weak on action theory." That is to say, those traditions of thought which have attributed some importance to human action—to the everyday phenomenon that we have reasons for what we do, and that those reasons in some way enter into the very nature of what we do—have on the whole not provided sophisticated treatments of the overall institutional structuring of societies. On the other hand, most traditions which have placed their main emphasis upon institutional or structural analysis have not made adequate recognition of the significance of human agency. Rather than attempting to provide a general classification of social theories in respect of this dualism, let me mention two particular examples of eminent sociological authors whose writings can serve to illustrate what I have in mind: Erving Goffman, on the one hand, and R. K. Merton, on the other. Goffman's writings, I would say, do give centrality to the notion of action: not as an abstract concept, but as exemplified by his style of sociological work. Those of Merton—and I am thinking here primarily of Merton's by now classical essays on functionalism in sociology—fall into the opposing category I have mentioned above.

First of all it is important to define "action" and "institution." The notion of human action has been much debated by philosophers, and has given rise to some considerable controversy. I shall understand "action" here, however, to refer to two components or aspects of human conduct, which I shall refer to as "*capability*" and "*knowledgeability*." By the former of these I mean that, whenever we speak of human action, we imply the possibility that the agent "could have acted otherwise." The sense of this well-worn phrase is not easy to elucidate philosophically, and I do not propose to attempt to spell it out in any detail here. Its importance to social analysis is nevertheless very substantial indeed. By the second term, "knowledgeability," I refer to the fact that the members of a society know a great deal about the workings of that society, and must do so if that society is recognizably a "human society." "Capability" must not be identified with the ability of human beings to make "decisions" or "choices"—as is posited in "utilitarian" social theory and also in most forms of game theory. "Decision-making" is a sub-category of capability in general, if it refers to circumstances where individuals consciously confront a range of potential alternatives of conduct, and make some choice among those alternatives. The vast bulk of day-to-day social activity is predicated upon capability, the possibility of "doing otherwise," but this is exercised as a routine feature of everyday behaviour. Much the same applies

to knowledgeability: it is a basic mistake to equate the knowledgeability of human agents with what is known "consciously," or "held in mind" in a conscious way. The knowledgeable character of human conduct is displayed above all in the vast variety of tacit modes of awareness and competence that I call "practical consciousness" as differentiated from "discursive consciousness"—but which actors chronically employ in the course of daily life.

Goffman's writings display a strong awareness of each of these features of human action. In this sense, in my opinion, they are superior to those of many philosophers who have analysed problems of action theory in a more abstract way, but who have conceptualized action in a "voluntaristic" manner, in terms of decision-making. Goffman treats human beings as capable and knowledgeable agents, who employ such capability and knowledgeability routinely in the production and reproduction of social encounters. The subjects Goffman portrays for the most part know what they are doing and why they are doing it: but much of this knowledge does not operate at an immediately "conscious" level. Goffman's writings have an appeal for those unacquainted with the literature of sociology which many other sociological writers do not. The reader of Goffman also often experiences a feeling of illumination of his or her conduct that appears relatively rarely in other types of sociological writing. Why this is so is not simply the result of Goffman's own writing skill, however significant this may be. It is, I think, because Goffman shows us many of the things we "know" about social conventions, and other aspects of society, but which we "know" in a tacit rather than an explicit sense. They become clear to us only when he points them out, but nevertheless we do already know them: and very dazzling and complex these forms of tacit knowledge turn out to be, however much we ordinarily take them for granted as members of any given society. Consider what is involved in knowing a language. To "know English" is to know a vast variety of syntactical and semantic rules and the contexts of their application. But linguists have to work very hard to elucidate what it is we already know, for if an ordinary English speaker is asked to actually spell out the rules and the pragmatics that he or she knows in order to speak the language, he or she is very unlikely to be able to identify more than a few of them. Goffman, in my view, is interested in laying bare the *tacit rules* and *resources* which competent social actors employ in the course of day-to-day life in much the same (although not exactly the same) sense as a linguist might be interested in specifying "what we already know" when we speak a particular language, or language in general in so far as all tongues share common characteristics. Of course, this is not to say that Goffman is only concerned with tacit knowledge or practical consciousness; rather, he shows how the tacit and the explicit are interwoven in the texture of everyday social activity.

The theorem "strong on action, weak on institutions" seems to me to apply with some force to Goffman's writings. Let me specify at this point how I want to use the term "institution." By institutions I mean structured social practices that have a broad spatial and temporal extension: that are structured in what the historian Braudel calls the *longue durée* of time, and which are followed or acknowledged by the majority of the members of a society. It is a banal enough criticism of Goffman's work to say that he does not explain, or seek to explain, the long-term development of the institutional frameworks within which his actors carry out the routines of their lives; but it seems to me one which is essentially correct. Just as, on a more philosophical plane, the forms of life within which Wittgenstein attempts to elucidate human action are taken

by him as "givens," so are the institutional backdrops which Goffman presumes. He has not elucidated an institutional theory of everyday life: rather, the institutional properties of the social systems within which his actors find themselves form an "environment" of their action. This judgment, I consider, is not affected by Goffman's more recent work on the "framing" of social interaction, since what is at issue is the absence of an attempt to explain how it is that "frames" originate in the overall institutional context of societal development.

Goffman's predominant concern is with how social interaction is organized in and through the capable and knowledgeable conduct of human actors (and the strains and tensions in which such actors are involved). I want now to try to show that the reverse theorem, "strong on institutions, weak on action" applies to Merton's codification of functionalism in what surely remains the most cogent presentation of functionalist theory to be found in the sociological literature. In his discussion of functionalism, Merton is certainly occupied mainly with what I have earlier identified as institutional analysis: with how the sociologist explains overall features of the organization and development of societies. Rather than concentrating his attention upon "action," he is primarily concerned with how social forces operate "behind the backs" of members of society so as to effect specific outcomes either stabilizing society or leading to social change.

Merton's now famous distinction between "manifest" and "latent functions," I shall try to show, fudges over some major characteristics of human action: in fact, precisely the two elements I have talked about above. I shall later want to say that the concept of function *en gros* is a redundant one in sociology—while accepting that functionalist authors have diverted attention to some fundamental exigencies of social analysis. But at the present juncture what is relevant are the deficiencies of the notion of "manifest function": an aspect of Merton's analysis that has been much less discussed in the sociological literature than other of his concepts and arguments. Perusal of what Merson says indicates: (a) that "manifest function" is ambiguous in respect of to whom it is manifest and in what way; and (b) that it is not at all clear what relation it bears to the capable and knowledgeable features I have held to be intrinsic to human action. These points can perhaps be most effectively demonstrated by reference to an example Merton himself uses. At one point in his articles he refers to the Hopi rain ceremonial as an illustration of the distinction between manifest and latent functions. The manifest function of the ceremonial, he says, is to produce rain. We know that it does not produce this result, and hence as sociologists we may enquire what accounts for its long-term persistence. Why does the institution of the rain ceremonial persist if it does not achieve its "manifest function," that of bringing about rain? Merton's answer is to appeal to the "latent functions" of the ceremonial in fostering group cohesion.

There are quite a number of critical points that can be made about this analysis, but I shall only concentrate upon those relevant to the present context. The "manifest function" of the ceremonial is to produce rain. But what relation does this "manifest function" bear to the reasons the participant actors have for enacting, and continuing to enact, the ceremonial? Is "manifest function" equivalent to "reason" (or perhaps "purpose")? If it is, it is certainly a deficient idea, for it is evident that the reasons people have for engaging in a particular activity are not necessarily equivalent to the "official charter" of that activity, and that reasons for participation may vary between individuals. Merton provides no analy-

sis at all as to how the Hopi perceive the nature of the ceremonial: they are, as it were, "written off" as capable and knowledgeable actors by the sociologist. Notice how different Merton's solution to the question of why the Hopi rain ceremonial persists is from that offered by Evans-Pritchard to a very similar problem. One of the issues Evans-Pritchard posed in his *Witchcraft, Oracles, and Magic among the Azande* was the following. Why do the Azande go on believing in and practising sorcery (when we, as Western observers, know that it does not produce the results that the members of that society think it does)? Evans-Pritchard's answer, however, is quite different from Merton's, and does not disregard the capable, knowledgeable character of the conduct of his Zande subjects. What might initially appear to the outside observer as an "irrational" cluster of beliefs and practices turns out to be a mode of behaviour which, if one is a member of Zande society, there are good reasons for continuing to accept. If one is "inside" the system of belief upon which Zande sorcery is based, there is no difficulty in explaining events which seem to the Western observer to contravene the ideas to which the Azande adhere; moreover there are sceptics in Zande society as elsewhere.

Evans-Pritchard's portrayal of Zande witchcraft has figured prominently in debates about the universality or otherwise of "rational belief," but is it not my intention to pursue the implications of these debates here. I wish only to point to the contrast between Merton's discussion of the Hopi ceremonial and Evans-Pritchard's view. My point is that what Merton talks of (ambiguously) as the "manifest function" of the practices in question, Evans-Pritchard shows to be comprehensible in the light of treating the Azande as capable agents who know (tacitly and explicitly) a good deal about what they are doing. In saying this, I do not however want to suggest that the sort of analysis Merton pursues is without value, or that that we should simply grasp the capable/knowledgeable character of human action and leave it at that. To do so would be equivalent to endorsing some sort of action theory without taking up the problem of how action analysis connects to institutional analysis. I want to propose that there are valid elements in the types of approach adopted by both authors, and that—appropriately explicated—they are not inconsistent but (in principle) complementary.

At this juncture what I have argued so far can be connected to the relation between so-called micro- and macro-sociological analysis. I repeat "so-called" because I want to place the distinction in question, at least as it is ordinarily understood. One might perhaps suppose that the dualism between acton and institutional analyses—which I have attempted to exemplify by particular examples but which I claim to be deeply embedded in sociology generally—is simply an expression of two perspectives in social analysis: the micro- and macro-sociological perspectives. Indeed, I think this is a view either explicitly adopted by many authors, or implicitly assumed to be the case. The origins of such a view can be traced in some part to specific developments within American sociology since the Second World War. One major theoretical tradition within American sociology, symbolic interactionism (to which one might claim Goffman's writings have a fairly strong affiliation), has generically embodied notions of human agency such as I have formulated it in this paper. The territory that symbolic interactionism has staked out has been mainly that of "social encounters" in Goffman's sense: face-to-face interaction between individuals. A second, vying tradition, functionalism, has claimed the domain of institutional analysis, in the sense in which I have employed that term above. The two traditions of thought, of

course, have been in some competition with one another; by and large, however, each seems to have respected the domain of the other. The result has been a sort of mutual accommodation, organized around a division of labour between micro-and macro-sociological analysis.

2 STRUCTURES AS RULES AND RESOURCES

I do not think that the dualism I have described between action theory and institutional analysis can be resolved merely by declaring that there can be a sort of sharing-out of the tasks of sociology. The problems involved lie at a much deeper level than that. Micro-sociological analysis cannot be identified *ipso facto* with action theory, or macro-sociological analysis with the theory of institutions. I want to suggest here the outlines of a theoretical scheme which I have developed in more detail elsewhere.[1] It involves providing a conceptualization of the notions of "action," "institution" and "structure," and indicating that there is a relation between these notions of rather profound importance for social analysis. I have already described in this paper, at least in a general way, how I wish to understand the concepts of action and institution. But I have not so far discussed the idea of "structure," which has generally loomed large in those traditions, including functionalism ("structural functionalism") which I have associated with a predominant emphasis upon institutional analysis. In the English-speaking sociological world at least, I think it would be true to say that the concept of structure has operated largely as a received one, and one which has not been subject to detailed examination. We have only to think, for example, of the controversies surrounding functionalism to see that this is so. While the notion of function has been debated almost *ad nauseam,* the concept of structure, which is used at least as often in a great deal of sociological literature, has received far less attention. It seems to me that when most sociologists speak of "structure," or "social structure," they have in mind a "patterning" of social relationships: they have in mind something like the girders of a building or the anatomy of a body. Moreover, they also tend to identify "structure" with "constraint." The *locus classicus* of this second aspect of the idea of structure is of course Durkheim, even if he himself rarely used the term itself. I do not want to discard the conception that it is useful and indeed necessary to think of social relationships between individuals or collectivities as "patterned"—which in my view means reproduced across time and space. But I do not propose to use the term "structure" to refer to such patterning, nor do I wish to link structure only with constraint. The equation of structure with constraint, in fact, is one of the major elements creating the dualism between action and institutional theories. If structure is conceived of as merely "external" to human action, it becomes regarded as a sort of autonomous form, independent of such action: or worse, as determining such action wholly through "social causes."

To consider how the concept of structure might usefully be reconceptualized in social analysis it is necessary to refer briefly to yet another popular sociological notion, that of "system." Most functionalist authors, and many others besides, employ both terms in their writings, and take the view that social systems *are* structures. The conception I want to propose, by contrast, is rather that social systems have *structural properties,* but are not as such structures—in the sense which I wish to attribute to that latter term. Most functionalist authors who have used the concepts of structure and system have thought of them as being distinguished from one another in the

following way, whether or not they have employed direct organic analogies. The structure of a society is like the anatomy of a body, so the reasoning runs: it is the morphology, or "patterning of parts." If we inject the "functioning"—if, in other words, we think of a living body—we have a system. A system is a "functioning structure." But however valid this may be in the case of a biological organism, it is inapplicable to a society. While one might (perhaps) accept that the anatomy of a body can be examined independently of its "functioning"—as in the case of dissecting a corpse, which has stopped "functioning"— such a separation has no sense when applied to a society. A society which ceases to "function"—to be reproduced across time and space—ceases to be. Hence it is not surprising that the distinction between structure and system tends to collapse, so that the two become used more or less synonymously.

I want to propose that what most sociologists have thought of as "structure," the "patterning" of relationships between individuals or collectivities, can be best dealt with by the notion of system. Social systems (and overall societies, as encompassing types of social system) consist of reproduced relationships between individuals and (or) collectivities. As such, social systems have always to be treated as situated in time–space. If we understand "system" in this way, we can free the concept of structure to perform other conceptual tasks. English-speaking sociologists can learn a good deal here from a general tradition of thought which has until now remained largely alien: the French tradition of "structuralism" (which, of course, like "functionalism" is internally diverse). Although I think there are several important contributions which structuralist thought can render to Anglo-Saxon sociology, I shall confine my attention here to the concept of structure itself. The best place to locate a discussion of this is at origin, in the work of Saussure, by general agreement the founder of "structuralist linguistics." Somewhat confusingly, Saussure used the term "system" rather than that of "structure," but this is not relevant to my argument at this point. The notion of structure in structuralist linguistics has reference to a part/whole relation of a different kind to that expressed by the "patterning" of social systems as described above. When I speak a sentence, the sentence is generated by, and understood by the listener in terms of, an "absent totality": that "absent totality" is the rest of the language, which has to be known for the sentence to be either spoken or understood. The relation between the speech act and the rest of the language is a moment/totality relation between "presences" (the spoken words) and "absences" (the unspoken, taken for granted knowledge of the rules and resources that constitutes "knowing a language"). This is a structural relation, where "structure" refers to the "structured properties" of a language. One should notice that in this sense structure does not exist anywhere in time–space—as speech acts do—except in the form of memory-traces in the human brain, and except in so far as it is instantiated in speech acts, writing, etc.

I suggest that the concept of structure can be applied in sociology in a sense which is formally parallel to, and substantively in some part includes (since language-use is intertwined with social practices), the Saussurean conception of the structural properties of language. "Structure" then refers to rules and resources instantiated in social systems, but having only a "virtual existence." The "rules" involved here are social conventions, and knowledge of them includes knowledge of the contexts of their application. By resources I mean "capabilities of making things happen," of bringing about particular states of affairs. There is a great deal more that can be said about the significance of resources than I shall be able to discuss in this paper, since the

notion of resources can be applied to connect the structural study of domination with the analysis of the *power relations* involved in social systems. To conceptualize structure as rules and resources (or structures as rule/resource sets) is to acknowledge that structure is both enabling and constraining. The one, so to speak, is the price of the other. This can again be illustrated by reference to the example of language. Every language involves relatively "fixed" categorizations that constrain thought at the same time as they make possible a whole variety of conceptual operations that without language would be impossible.

3 OVERCOMING THE DUALISM BETWEEN ACTION AND INSTITUTION: THE DUALITY OF STRUCTURE

This discussion of structure and system can now be connected to what I have remarked earlier about human agency. The structured properties of society, the study of which is basic to explaining the long-term development of institutions only exist (a) in their instantiation in social systems, made possible (b) by the memory-traces (reinforced or altered in the continuity of daily social life) that constitute the knowledgeability of social actors. This brings me to an essential part of my analysis, which consists in the thesis that the properties of society are fundamentally *recursive*. The recursive nature of the structural properties of social systems has to be understood as presuming what I call the *duality of structure*. The scheme I am putting forward here involves the claim that the traditional dualism of action theories and institutional theories can be avoided by the emphasis that action and structure—as I have formulated the notions—form a duality. That is to say, action and structure stand in a relation of logical entailment: the concept of action presumes that of structure and vice versa. I use the phrase "duality of structure" to mean that structure is both the medium and outcome of the social practices it recursively organizes. The sense of this can be illustrated by Saussurean linguistics, so long as one keeps in mind the proviso noted above. In using examples drawn from linguistics I do not mean to imply that society is a language, or can be studied as a language—the characteristic error of structuralism, in fact. So this example should be treated cautiously, but none the less helps indicate clearly what I mean by the "duality of structure." When I utter a grammatical sentence, I draw upon various syntactical rules of the English language in order to do so. But the very drawing upon of those rules helps reproduce them as structural properties of English as recursively involved with the linguistic practices of the community of English language speakers. The moment (not in a temporal sense) of the production of the speech act at the same time contributes to the reproduction of the structural qualities that generated it. It is very important to see that "reproduction" here does not imply homology: the potential for change is built into every moment of social reproduction (as a contingent phenomenon).

I can represent formally what I have been arguing as below:

Structure   Recursively organized rules and resources, having a virtual existence outside of time–space.

System   Reproduced relations between actors or collectivities, situated in time–space.

Structuration   Conditions governing system reproduction.

The introduction of the term "structuration" returns us to the problems I raised in the beginning part of this paper. For, as I emphasized there, we have to recognize that the issues theorized by functionalist authors—especially the fact that there are social influences which work "behind our backs," and which are centrally implicated in the long-term formation/transformation of social institutions—are of integral significance to social theory. To talk of "structuration," in the context of my discussion here at any rate, is to say: (a) that social systems are structured only in and through their continual and contingent reproduction in day-to-day social life; and (b) that the capability/knowledgeability of social actors is always *bounded* (although in historically mutable ways). The boundaries of the capability/knowledgeability that social agents apply in and through the duality of structure concern just those influences about which functionalist theories have maintained a prime interest: the *unintended consequences* of action. Such phenomena chronically enter into system constitution and hence have to be analysed as fundamental features *conditioning* social reproduction. But I do not think they should be regarded as "functions," latent or otherwise. The concept of function, as I have tried to show elsewhere, only has some plausibility as part of the technical vocabulary of sociology if we attribute "needs" to social systems.[2] But social systems have no needs, and to suppose that they do is to apply an illegitimate teleology to them. According to the ideas I have tried to formulate above, "social reproduction" is not an explanatory term: it always has itself to be explained in terms of the structurally bounded and contingently applied knowledgeability of social actors. It is worth emphasizing this, not merely in respect of criticizing orthodox functionalism, but also in regard of the not infrequent tendency of Marxist authors to suppose that "social reproduction" has magical explanatory properties—as if merely to invoke the term is to explain something.

Let me return again to the differentiation between micro- and macro-sociological analysis. It follows from the arguments I have advanced above that there can be no theoretical defence for supposing that the personal encounters of day-to-day life can be conceptually separated from the long-term institutional development of society. The most trivial exchange of words implicates the speakers in the long-term history of the language via which those words are formed, and at the same time in the continuing reproduction of that language. There is more than a fortuitous similarity between the *longue durée* of historical time of which Braudel writes and the *durée* of daily social life to which Schultz, following Bergson, draws our attention. Where the distinction between micro- and macro-sociological analysis, or something like it, is important is in respect of the time–space constitution of social systems as involving presences or absences. That is to say, the distinction can be treated as focusing upon the differences between social interaction where others are *present*, and social interaction with others who are *absent*. The conventional term "face-to-face interaction" perhaps will do to refer to the former, but we have no established term to refer to the latter. It should be clear, however, that the differences between these can only be adequately expressed in terms of time–space analysis. "Presence"—the presence of others in an immediate milieu of interaction—does not simply refer to the fact that there are people physically together in a room, shop or street where one happens to be. Or at least presence in this sense is sociologically uninteresting. What matters for purposes of sociological analysis is what might be termed *presence-availability*. Most face-to-face interaction, as ethnomethodological studies of "turn-taking" have helped to point out, is serial. At a cocktail party, there is a large amount of face-to-face interaction, but everybody does not talk to everybody else at once. What matters is that the interaction is characterized by what, for want of a less cumbersome phrase, I should call "high presence-availability." Others are "there" in the sense that they are available, they *can* be talked to directly. There probably are cocktail parties where everybody is expected, and does, at some point talk to everybody else.

NOTES

1. A. Giddens, *Central Problems in Social Theory* (University of California Press, 1979).
2. A. Giddens, "Functionalism: après la lutte," in A. Giddens, *Studies in Social and Political Theory* (London: Hutchinson, 1977).

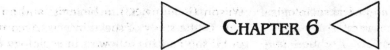

CHAPTER 6

NEW PERSPECTIVES
AND APPROACHES

Sociology, as a formal academic discipline, has been around for little over a century. As we have argued, the theoretical roots of sociology extend back much further, to the cosmological speculations of Plato, Ibn Khaldun, and the eighteenth-century Enlightenment. Sociological theory emerged, in its classical mode, in the work of the great nineteenth-century theorists: Spencer, Marx, Weber, Durkheim, Simmel. In the United States, the origins of a body of authentically American sociological theory date a bit later, in the writings of George Herbert Mead and the Chicago School. After a period of narrow empiricism and relative neglect of theory, the 1937 publication of Talcott Parsons' masterwork *The Structure of Social Action* ushered in a new era of theorizing in American sociology.

The following decade saw a revival of sociological theory due to the work of Parsons and several of his graduate students who themselves went on to become notable sociological theorists—Robert Merton, Kingsley Davis, and Wilbert Moore among them. From the late 1940s through the middle 1960s, Parson-

ian functionalism was the dominant theoretical approach in American sociology. At the end of this period, Kingsley David (1959) could truthfully remark, "We *are* all functionalists."

The criticisms of structural functionalism raised by Horton, Dahrendorf, Lockwood, Coser, and numerous others during the late 1950s and 1960s gave birth to several theoretical schools that have been covered in this book. Parsonian "Grand Theory" proved as untestable and vulnerable to criticism as its many dissenters had contended it would be. The retreat from the functionalist consensus in the 1960s was rapid. Many of the theoretical alternatives, however, left their supporters caught in either a methodological trap or an intellectual dead end. The conflict model's conceptualization of power and status, for example, was not easily amenable to testing: How does one get into the White House to observe the process of decision making? Symbolic interactionism, as developed by Mead and his followers at Chicago, especially Herbert Blumer, similarly was attacked for its seeming irrelevance to empirical sociological research, precipitating several splits in the symbolic interactionist school. And both symbolic interactionism and George Homans' exchange theory were criticized for their lack of attention to macro-level phenomena by more structurally-minded sociologists.

None of these theoretical statements gained the all-pervasive status of structural functionalism. Indeed, in the 1960s and 1970s, several more new theoretical schools developed in sociology—Marxism, ethnomethodology, sociobiology, structuralism, feminism. These were followed in the 1980s by another round of new theoretical approaches—neo-functionalism, neo-Marxism, rational choice theory, postmodernism. Today in the 1990s, as we have attempted to show, a number of theoretical perspectives and approaches exist side by side in sociology. We have already reviewed some of the most important of them in the preceding chapters. In this chapter, we will survey several of these new and challenging theoretical perspectives. (For general surveys of new theoretical approaches in sociology, see McNall, 1979; Ritzer, 1990.)

Prominent among these new approaches are *sociobiology* and *environmental sociology*. Although they are quite different in their particulars, both of these perspectives start from the premise that human societies cannot be understood in isolation from the larger evolutionary and environmental context in which human beings and their societies have developed. Both of these perspectives have been influenced by recent developments in biology—sociobiology by developments in population genetics and population ecology, and environmental sociology by the rise of terrestrial ecology and the larger environmental movement.

The origins of sociobiology, in fact, lie outside sociology, in the seminal work *Sociobiology: The New Synthesis* (1975) by Edward O. Wilson (Reading 33), a biologist and an expert in the study of social insects. According to Wilson and his followers in sociology (see Greene et. al. 1979), much of human behavior is, like the behavior of other species, genetically determined. While granting the importance of environment and culture in determining much that is characteristic of humans' social behavior. Wilson still maintains that in principle the same conventions that underly the study of animal societies are applicable to the study of human beings (see Wilson 1978). The reception of Wilson's ideas in sociology has, so far, been quite mixed. Some sociologists (Lopreato 1981, van den Berghe 1974, Wozniak 1984) have argued that the sociobiological model has great benefits to offer to sociology, and they have attempted to incorporate the sociobiological perspective into sociological theory. But that approach has come under considerable attack from other sociologists who reject the idea that human behavior can be explained in terms of genetic predispositions, "instinct," or the like (see Caplan 1978).

Environmental sociology has drawn on a different aspect of biology for its central insight. It has largely been developed at Washington State University in the work of the sociologists William Catton and Riley Dunlap (Reading 34; Catton and Dunlap 1980, Dunlap and Catton 1979). Dunlap and Catton criticize sociologists for holding to the notion that human societies can be understood apart from the larger natural ecologies in which they are embedded. In fact, it is the interaction between the biological environment and society that gives rise to much in the way of social structure and behavior that is distinctive of modern societies. Environmental sociologists argue that if we are to avoid the ecological disasters of soil erosion, depletion of energy reserves and raw materials, and drastic climatic change, we must become more sensitive to the impacts our chosen forms of social organization and lifestyle have on the delicate balance of our natural ecology. This same point has been made in a somewhat different way by socialist and radical environmentalists, who have focused their attention on what they view as the environmentally destructive nature of capitalism (see Bahro 1984, Bookchin 1990, Gorz 1980). All environmental sociologists claim that it is only by bringing our societies into harmony with nature and protecting our natural environment that we can ensure a successful future for human societies in an age of increasing scarcity and increasing environmental demands.

Of all the new theoretical paradigms to emerge since the 1970s, none has been more important or more radical in terms of its potential for transforming the discipline than feminist theory. In 1975, a landmark collection of feminist articles appeared that invited sociologists to observe that the sociological Emperor had no clothes (Millman and Kanter 1975, vii). And, indeed, for all its pretensions to be the "science of society," few could deny that sociology had from the very beginning been a male-centered discourse that had largely ignored the life and experience of women in society. A product of the feminist movement in the larger society, feminist sociology has been one of the fastest-growing approaches in the discipline over the last decade. Feminist criticisms have been raised concerning almost every theoretical school in traditional and contemporary sociology (see, for example, Readings 17 and 24). And feminist theorists have gone beyond criticism to develop an extensive body of feminist theory in sociology dealing with issues of gender stratification, everyday life, the family, housework, childhood socialization, politics, and social change (see Reading 35; also Chafetz 1988, MacKinnon 1989, Pateman and Gross 1986, Sargent 1981, Smith 1987, Wallace 1989). Judith Stacey and Barrie Thorne (Reading 35) argue that this feminist revolution, although an impressive accomplishment, has in fact not achieved its central goal of transforming the sociological discipline as a whole. They offer a perceptive assessment of the gains made by feminists in sociology and the obstacles that stand in the way of further transformation of the discipline.

As Arlie Hochschild observed (1975, 280), the failure of traditional sociology to look at the social world with a feminine eye meant that many topics of sociological importance simply went uninvestigated by the male-dominated discipline. One of the consequences of this historical blind spot, Hochschild argued, has been the relative lack of attention paid by sociologists to the sociology of feeling and emotion. The emergence of the sociology of emotion as a new theoretical area within sociology is clearly one of the consequences of the feminist revolution in sociological theory (see Hochschild 1975, 1983; Kember 1979, Shott 1979). Influenced by phenomenological and ethnomethodological currents in social theory, theorists working in this new area have focused on the ways in which emotion and feeling are socially constructed and the ways in which we learn to "feel" the appropriate emotions in different contexts. As Joanne Finkelstein (Reading 36) argues, the management of emotions within the public sphere should be seen as an important link between the taken-for-granted structures of the social world and the private experience of the individual.

One of the more intellectually challenging subfields within sociological theory has always been the area of historical sociology. The works of the great classical theorists Marx, Weber, and Durkheim were grand historical syntheses that sought to discern sociological patterns in the sweep of centuries-long historical processes. During the 1950s and 1960s, however, historical sociology entered into a decline, although even during this period important work continued to be done (see

Moore 1966). The prevailing functionalist theoretical model encouraged sociologists to study societies *synchronically*, as contemporary integrated systems, rather than *diachronically*, as evolving historical entities, and many sociologists argued that the age of grand historical schemes was past.

The 1970s and 1980s, however, have seen a great revival in the field of historical sociology (see Skocpol 1984). Sociologists have studied and reinterpreted the transition from feudalism to capitalism and the rise of the capitalist world order, the causes and consequences of social revolutions, and the emergence of the state and social stratification in several recent important works (Abu-Lughod 1989; Anderson 1974a, 1974b; Mann 1986; Skocpol 1979; Tilly 1978, 1990; Wallerstein 1974–1989). In Reading 37, noted historical sociologist Charles Tilly explains why this area remains a vital field of study within contemporary sociology and discusses the future of historical work in sociology.

If the reader is feeling at this point that modern sociological theory is fragmented into myriad competing paradigms with no particular reason for choosing one over the other, he or she may be pleased to know that there is in fact one sociological theory that embraces this confusion and declares it to be an inevitable and indeed a positive aspect of life in the fast lane of our modern (or perhaps we should say postmodern) age. *Postmodernism* is the name of this perspective, and it has emerged in sociology in only the last few years. Postmodernism as a form of theorizing about contemporary societies and their cultures was originally developed by theorists working in the areas of art and architecture during the 1970s, but it rapidly spread to the general area of cultural studies and has entered sociology through the sociology of culture (see Featherstone 1988, Nelson and Grossberg 1988).

To a large extent, postmodernism repre-sents a mood of cynicism and resignation concerning the perceived failure of the various radical projects that emerged in social theory during the 1960s and 1970s with the goal of transforming society—Marxism, feminism, environmentalism, socialism. For more politically conservative postmodernists, these transformative discourses were themselves "totalitarian," with their insistence on a self-aggrandizing "master narrative" (see Lyotard 1984). Thus, many postmodernists have retreated to a position "beyond" politics. They reject the very idea of political activism, viewing it as being meaningless and absurd (see Poster 1988).

This does not mean, however, that all postmodernists have retreated from the 1960s attitude of radical skepticism toward official society and culture. Some theorists have argued for a more radical or critical use of postmodernism, responding to Fredric Jameson's interpretation of postmodernism as the cultural logic of late capitalism (see Best and Kellner 1991, Jameson 1984, Kellner 1989). Postmodernists, then, are centrally concerned with the analysis of culture, in some ways not unlike the theorists of the Frankfurt School, which we discussed in Chapter 3. Many postmodern theorists generally share the Frankfurt School theorists' mood of cultural pessimism (see Marcuse, Reading 12). But postmodernists reject what they see as the insupportable and philosophically dangerous conceptions of knowledge and truth held by the earlier generation of radical theorists (see Lyotard 1984).

Although still only in formation, postmodernism represents a new and innovative way of conceptualizing life in contemporary society. Already, postmodernist approaches have had a striking impact on contemporary sociological theory, and this influence seems certain to grow in the coming years (see Lash 1990, Rosenau 1992, Seidman and Wagner 1992). In Reading 38, Norman Denzin discusses the challenge that postmodernism presents to the sociological theories we have surveyed in this volume. He argues that the postmodernist critique demands that those theories be rethought and revised. To this end, Denzin surveys the work of several important postmodern theorists and recent debates over the meaning of postmodernism which he believes are of special importance to sociological theory. For Denzin, the postmodern critique necessitates the abandonment of the positivist "foundationalist" discourse that has characterized traditional sociological theory, with its emphasis on the development of universalistic "true" descriptions and explanations of social reality. The postmodern critique has demonstrated the futility of such a project of "grand systems"; according to Denzin, we should refocus our efforts as theorists of society onto the development of more relativistic and situationally conditioned accounts of social experience.

This theme is taken up in the final essay in this volume (Reading 39), by Steven Seidman, a leading sociological proponent of postmodernism. Echoing Denzin's call for a new, more relativistic approach in sociological theory, Seidman emphasizes the intrinsically moral character of social theory. Seidman argues that the significance of classical social theory lay in its conscious involvement in the conflicts and public debates of the time. This sense of social significance has been lost over time as a consequence of the transformation of social theory from a moral and political discourse into an increasingly technical and positivistic mold. Like Denzin, Seidman calls for the end of scientific sociological theory and the revival of social theory—social narrative with a moral intent—advanced from the standpoint of postmodernism.

Many sociologists have responded negatively to this postmodern challenge, which sharply questions the legitimacy of the sociological enterprise and traditional theory (see D'Amico 1992; see also Bernstein 1985; Dews, 1987; Nicholson, 1990). But fundamental criticism and challenges to the prevailing theoretical paradigms have been, after all, at the heart of sociological theory since its origins in the eighteenth-century Enlightenment. And beginning with the premise of the rejection of traditional theory, postmodernism is itself very much a part of the sociological tradition it criticizes, a constantly evolving heterogenous body of theory that has ever renewed itself through criticism, conflict, and radical departures from the old. Undoubtedly this tradition will continue.

REFERENCES

ABU-LUGHOD, JANET. 1989. *Before European Hegemony: The World System A.D. 1250–1350.* New York: Oxford University Press.

ANDERSON, PERRY. 1974a. *Passages from Antiquity to Feudalism.* London: New Left Books.

_____. 1974b. *Lineages of the Absolute State.* London: New Left Books.

BAHRO, RUDOLF. 1984. *From Red to Green.* London: Verso.

BERNSTEIN, RICHARD, ed. 1985. *Habermas and Modernity.* Cambridge: MIT Press.

BEST, STEVEN, AND DOUGLAS KELLNER. 1991. *Postmodern Theory: Critical Interrogations.* New York: Guilford Press.

BOOKCHIN, MURRAY. 1990. *Remaking Society: Pathways to a Green Future.* Boston: South End Press.

CAPLAN, ARTHUR, ed. 1978. *The Sociobiology Debate.* New York: Harper and Row.

CATTON, WILLIAM, JR., AND RILEY DUNLAP. 1980. "A New Paradigm for Post-Exuberant Sociology." *American Behavioral Scientist* 24 (September–October):15–47.

CHAFETZ, JANET. 1988. *Feminist Sociology: An Overview of Contemporary Theories.* Itasca: Peacock.

D'AMICO, ROBERT. 1992. "Defending Social Science against the Postmodern Doubt." Pp. 137–55 in *Postmodernism and Social Theory,* ed. Steven Seidman and David Wagner. London: Basil Blackwell.

DAVIS, KINGSLEY. 1959. "The Myth of Functional Analysis as a Special Method in Sociology and

Anthropology." *American Sociological Review* 24 (December):757–72.

DEWS, PETER. 1987. *Logics of Disintegration,* London: Verso.

DUNLAP, RILEY, AND WILLIAM CATTON, JR., 1979. "Environmental Sociology." Pp. 243–73 in *Annual Review of Sociology,* vol. 5, ed. Alex Inkeles et al. Palo Alto: Annual Reviews.

FEATHERSTONE, MIKE, ed. 1988. *Postmodernism.* Beverly Hills: Sage Publishers.

GORZ, ANDRE, 1980. *Ecology as Politics.* Boston: South End Press.

GREENE, PENELOPE, CHARLES MORGAN, AND DAVID BARASH. 1979. "Sociobiology." Pp. 414–30 in *Theoretical Perspectives in Sociology,* ed. Scott McNall. New York: St. Martins Press.

HOCHSCHILD, ARLIE. 1975. "The Sociology of Feeling and Emotion: Selected Possibilities," Pp. 280–307 in *Another Voice: Feminist Perspectives on Social Life and Social Science,* ed. Marcia Millman and Rosabeth Kanter. New York: Anchor Books.

_____. 1983. *The Managed Heart: Commercialization of Human Feeling.* Berkeley: University of California Press.

JAMESON, FREDRIC. 1984. "Postmodernism, or the Cultural Logic of Late Capitalism." *New Left Review* 146 (July–August):53–92.

KELLNER, DOUGLAS, ed. 1989. *Postmodernism/ Jameson/Critique.* Washington, D.C.: Maissonueve Press.

KEMPER, THEODORE, 1979. "A Sociology of Emotions: Some Problems and Some Solutions." Pp. 431–49 in *Theoretical Perspectives in Sociology,* ed. Scott McNall. New York: St. Martins Press.

LASH, SCOTT. 1990. *Sociology of Postmodernism.* New York: Routledge.

LOPREATO, JOSEPH. 1981. "The Battle of BB Guns against Sociobiology." *Social Science Quarterly* 62 (June):234–42.

LYOTARD, JEAN. 1984. *The Postmodern Condition: A Report on Knowledge.* Minneapolis: University of Minnesota Press.

MACKINNON, CATHERINE. 1989. *Toward a Feminist Theory of the State.* Cambridge: Harvard University Press.

MCNALL, SCOTT, ed. 1979. *Theoretical Perspectives in Sociology.* New York: St. Martins Press.

MANN, MICHAEL, 1986. *The Sources of Social Power, Vol. 1: A History of Power from the Beginning to A.D. 1760.* Cambridge: Cambridge University Press.

MILLMAN, MARCIA, AND ROSABETH KANTER, eds. 1975. *Another Voice: Feminist Perspectives on Social Life and Social Science.* New York: Anchor Books.

MOORE, BARRINGTON. 1966. *Social Origins of Dictatorship and Democracy: Lord and Peasant in the Making of the Modern World.* Boston: Beacon Press.

NELSON, CARY, AND LAWRENCE GROSSBERG. 1988. *Marxism and the Interpretation of Culture.* Urbana: University of Illinois Press.

NICHOLSON, LINDA, ed. 1990. *Feminism/Postmodernism.* New York: Routledge.

PATEMAN, CAROLE, AND ELIZABETH GROSS, eds. 1986. *Feminist Challenges: Social and Political Theory.* Boston: Northeastern University Press.

POSTER, MARK. 1988. *Jean Baudrillard: Selected Writings.* Stanford: Stanford University Press.

RITZER, GEORGE, ed. 1990. *Frontiers of Social Theory.* New York: Columbia University Press.

ROSENAU, PAULINE MARIE. 1992. *Post-Modernism and the Social Sciences.* Princeton: Princeton University Press.

SARGENT, LYDIA, ed. 1981. *Women and Revolution.* Boston: South End Press.

SEIDMAN, STEVEN, AND DAVID WAGNER, eds. 1992. *Postmodernism and Social Theory.* London: Basil Blackwell.

SHOTT, SUSAN, 1979. "The Sociology of Emotion: Some Starting Points." Pp. 450–62 in *Theoretical Perspectives in Sociology,* ed. Scott McNall. New York: St. Martins Press.

SKOCPOL, THEDA, 1979. *States and Social Revolutions.* Cambridge: Cambridge University Press.

_____. ed. 1984. *Vision and Method in Historical Sociology.* Cambridge: Cambridge University Press.

SMITH, DOROTHY. 1987. *The Everyday World as Problematic: A Feminist Sociology.* Boston: Northeast University Press.

TILLY, CHARLES. 1978. *From Mobilization to Revolution.* Reading: Addison-Wesley.

_____. 1990. *Coercion, Capital and European States, AD 990–1990.* Cambridge: Basil Blackwell.

VAN DEN BERGHE, PIERRE. 1974. "Bringing Beasts Back In: Toward a Biosocial Theory of Aggression." *American Sociological Review* 39:777–88.

WALLACE, RUTH, ed. 1989. *Feminism and Sociological Theory.* Newbury Park: Sage Publications.

WALLERSTEIN, IMMANUEL. 1974–1989. *The Modern World-System,* 3 vols. Cambridge: Cambridge University Press.

WILSON, EDWARD. 1975. *Sociobiology: The New Synthesis.* Cambridge: Harvard University Press.

_____. 1978. *On Human Nature.* Cambridge: Harvard University Press.

WOZNIAK, PAUL. 1984. "Making Sociobiological Sense Out of Sociology." *Sociological Quarterly* 25 (Spring):191–204.

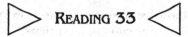
WHAT IS SOCIOBIOLOGY?*

EDWARD O. WILSON

I was surprised—even astonished—by the initial reaction to *Sociobiology: The New Synthesis* (1975). When the book was published in 1975, I expected a favorable reaction from other biologists. After all, my colleagues and I had merely been extending neo-Darwinism into the study of social behavior and animal societies, and the underlying biological principles we employed were largely conventional. The response was in fact overwhelmingly favorable. From the social scientists, I expected not much reaction. I took it for granted that the human species is subject to sociobiological analysis no less than to genetic or endocrinological analysis; the final chapter of my book simply completed the catalogue of social species by adding *Homo sapiens*. I hoped to make a contribution to the social sciences and humanities by laying out, in immediately accessible form, the most relevant methods

and principles of population biology, evolutionary theory, and sociobiology. I expected that many social scientists, already convinced of the necessity of a biological foundation for their subject, would be tempted to pick up the tools and try them out. This has occurred to a limited extent, but there has also been stiff resistance. I now understand that I entirely underestimated the Durkheim-Boas tradition of autonomy of the social sciences, as well as the strength and power of the antigenetic bias that has prevailed as virtual dogma since the fall of Social Darwinism.

I did not even think about the Marxists. When the attacks on sociobiology came from Science for the People, the leading radical left group within American science, I was unprepared for a largely ideological argument. It is now clear to me that I was tampering with something fundamental: mythology. Evolutionary theory applied to social systems is an extension of the great Western traditions of scientific materialism. As such, it threatens to transform into testable hypotheses the assumptions about human nature made by some Marxist philosophers. Its first line of ev-

*From Michael S. Gregory, Anita Silvers, and Diane Sutch, eds., *Sociobiology and Human Nature* (San Francisco: Jossey-Bass, 1978), pp. 1–12. Reprinted with permission of Jossey-Bass, Inc.

idence is not favorable to those assumptions, insofar as most traditional Marxists cling to a vision of human nature as a relatively unstructured phenomenon swept along by economic forces extraneous to human biology. Marxism and other secular ideologies previously rested secure as unchallenged satrapies of scientific materialism; now they were in danger of being displaced by other, less manageable biological explanations. The remarkably harsh response of Science for the People is an example of what Hans Küng (1976) has called the fury of the theologians.

But much of the confusion has come from a simple misunderstanding of the content of sociobiology. Sociobiology is defined as the systematic study of the biological basis of all forms of social behavior, including sexual and parental behavior, in all kinds of organisms, including humans. As such, it is a discipline— an inevitable discipline, since there must be a systematic study of social behavior. Sociobiology consists mostly of zoology. About 90 percent of its current material concerns animals, even though over 90 percent of the attention given to sociobiology by nonscientists, and especially journalists, is due to its possible applications to the study of human social behavior. There is nothing unusual about deriving principles and methods, and even terminology, from intensive examinations of lower organisms and applying them to the study of human beings. Most of the fundamental principles of genetics and biochemistry applied to human biology are based on colon bacteria, fruit flies, and white rats. To say that the same science can be applied to human beings is not to reduce humanity to the status of these simpler creatures.

Nor is there anything new or surprising about having such a discipline within the family of the biological sciences. The term *sociobiology* was used independently by John P. Scott in 1946 and by Charles F. Hockett in 1948, but the word was not picked up immediately by others. In 1950, Scott, who had been serving as secretary of the small but influential Committee for the Study of Animal Behavior, suggested *sociobiology* more formally as a term for the "interdisciplinary science which lies between the fields of biology (particularly ecology and physiology) and psychology and sociology" (p. 1004). From 1956 to 1964, Scott and others constituted the Section on Animal Behavior and Sociobiology of the Ecological Society of America. This Section became the present Animal Behavior Society. During 1950–1970, *sociobiology* was employed intermittently in technical articles, a usage evidently inspired by its already quasi-official status. But other expressions, such as *biosociology* and *animal sociology*, were also employed. When I wrote the final chapter of *The Insect Societies* (1971), which was entitled "The Prospect for a Unified Sociobiology" and when I wrote *Sociobiology: The New Synthesis* (1975), where I suggested that a discrete discipline should now be built on a foundation of genetics and population biology, I selected the term *sociobiology* rather than some other, novel expression because I believed it would already be familiar to most students of animal behavior and hence more likely to be accepted.

Pure sociobiological theory, being independent of human biology, does not imply by itself that human social behavior is determined by genes. It allows for any one of three possibilities. One is that the human brain has evolved to the point that it has become an equipotential learning machine entirely determined by culture. The mind, in other words, has been freed from the genes. A second possibility is that human social behavior is under genetic constraint but that all of the genetic variability within the human species has been exhausted. Hence our behavior is to some extent influenced by genes, but we all have exactly the same potential. A third possibility, close to the second, is that the human species is prescribed to some extent but also displays some genetic differences among individuals. As a consequence, human populations retain the capacity to evolve still further in their biological capacity for social behavior.

I consider it virtually certain that the third alternative is the correct one. Because the evidence has been well reviewed in other recent works, most notably Chagnon and Irons (1979), De Vore (1979), and Freedman (1979), I will not undertake to exemplify it or review it in detail. Instead, let me outline its content.

1. *Specificity of human social behavior*. Although the variation of cultures appears enormous to the anthropocentric observer, all human behavior together comprises only a tiny subset of the realized social systems of the thousands of social species on earth. Corals and other colonial invertebrates, the social insects, fish, birds, and nonhuman mammals display among themselves an array of arrangements that it is difficult for human beings even to understand, much less imitate. Even if we were to attempt to duplicate some of these social behaviors by conscious design, it would be a charade likely to create emotional breakdown and a rapid reversal of the effort.

2. *Phylogenetic relationships*. Our social arrangements most closely resemble those of the Old World monkeys and apes, which on anatomical and biochemical grounds are our closest living relatives. This is the result expected if we share a common ancestry with these primates, which appears to be an established fact, and if human social behavior is still constrained to some extent by genetic predispositions in behavioral development.

3. *Conformity to sociobiological theory*. In the case of the hypothesis of genetic constraints on human social behavior, it should be possible to select some of the best principles of population genetics and ecology, which form the foundations of sociobiology, and to apply

them in detail to the explanations of human social organization. The hypothesis should then not only account for many of the known facts in a more convincing manner than do previous attempts but should also identify the need for new kinds of information not conceptualized by the unaided social sciences. The behavior thus explained should be the most general and least rational of the human repertory, the furthest removed from the influence of year-by-year shifts in fashion and convention. There are in fact a substantial number of anthropological studies completed or underway that meet these exacting criteria of postulational-deductive science. Among them can be cited the work of Joseph Shepher (1971) on the incest taboo and sexual roles, Mildred Dickeman (1979) on hypergamy and sex-biased infanticide, William Irons (1979) on the relation between inclusive genetic fitness and the local set of evaluational criteria of social success in a herding society, Napoleon Chagnon (1976) on aggression and reproductive competition in the Yanomamö, William Durham (1976) on the relation between inclusive fitness and warfare in the Mundurucú and other primitive societies, Robin Fox (personal communication) on the relation of fitness to kinship rules, Melvin Konner (1972) and Daniel G. Freedman (1974, 1979) on the adaptive significance of infant development, and James Weinrich (1977) on the relationship of genetic fitness and the details of sexual practice, including homosexuality.

4. *Genetic variation within the species*. By 1977, more than 1,200 loci had been located on human chromosomes through the fine analysis of biochemical and other mutations (McKusick and Ruddle, 1977). Many of these point mutations, as well as a growing list of chromosomal aberrations, affect behavior. Most simply diminish mental capacity and motor ability, but at least two, the Lesch-Nyhan syndrome, based on a single gene, and Turner's

syndrome, caused by the deletion of a sex chromosome, alter behavior in narrow ways that can be related to specific neuromuscular mechanisms. The adrenogenital syndrome, which is induced by a single recessive gene, appears to masculinize girls through an early induction of adrenocortical substances that mimic the male hormone.

More complex forms of human behavior are almost certainly under the control of polygenes (genes scattered on many chromosome loci), which in turn create their effects through alternating a wide array of mediating devices, from elementary neuronal wiring to muscular coordination and "mental set" induced by hormone levels. In most instances, the role of behavioral polygenes can be evaluated—but only qualitatively—by the careful application of twin and adoption studies. The most frequently used method is to compare the similarity between identical twins, who are known to be genetically identical, with the similarity between fraternal twins, who are no closer genetically than ordinary siblings. When the similarity between identical twins proves greater, this distinction between the two kinds of twins is ascribed to heredity. Using this and related techniques, geneticists have found evidence of a substantial amount of hereditary influence on the development of a variety of traits that affect social behavior, including number ability, word fluency, memory, the timing of language acquisition, sentence construction, perceptual skill, psychomotor skill, extroversion and introversion, homosexuality, the timing of first heterosexual activity, and certain forms of neurosis and psychosis, including the manic-depressive syndrome and schizophrenia.

In most instances, there is a flaw in the results that renders most of them less than definitive: Identical twins are commonly treated more alike by their parents than are fraternal twins. They are instructed in a more nearly parallel manner, dressed more alike, and so

forth. In the absence of better controls, it is possible that the greater similarity of identical twins could, after all, be due to environmental influences and not their genetic identity. However, new and more sophisticated studies have begun to take account of this additional factor. Loehlin and Nichols (1976), for example, analyzed many aspects of the environments and performances of 850 sets of twins who took the National Merit Scholarship test in 1962. The early histories of the subjects, as well as the attitudes and rearing practices of the parents, were taken into account. The results showed that the generally more similar treatment of the identical twins cannot account for their greater similarity in general abilities and personality traits or even in ideals, goals, and vocational interests. It is evident that either the similarities are based in substantial part on genetic identity or else environmental agents were at work that remained hidden to Loehlin and Nichols.

My overall conclusions from the existing information is that *Homo sapiens* is a typical animal species with reference to the quality and magnitude of the genetic diversity affecting its behavior. I also believe that it will soon be within our ability to locate and characterize specific genes that alter the more complex forms of social behavior. Obviously, the alleles discovered will not prescribe different dialects or modes of dress. They are more likely to work measurable changes through their effects on learning modes and timing, cognitive and neuromuscular ability, and the personality traits most sensitive to hormonal mediation. If social scientists and sociobiologists somehow choose to ignore this line of investigation, they will soon find human geneticists coming up on their blind side. The intense interest in medical genetics, fueled now by new methods such as the electrophoretic separation of proteins and rapid sequencing of amino acids, has resulted in an acceleration of discoveries in human heredity that is certain to have profound consequences for the study of genetics of social behavior.

I wish now to take up the concerns expressed about human sociobiology. . . .

The first area of conflict that can be resolved is the relation of genes to culture. Many social scientists see no value in sociobiology because they are persuaded that variation among cultures has no genetic basis. Their premise is right, their conclusion wrong. We can do well to remember Rousseau's dictum that those who wish to study humans should stand close, while those who wish to study humanity should look from afar. The social scientist is interested in the often microscopic, but important, variations in behavior that almost everyone agrees are due to culture and the environment. The sociobiologist is interested in the more general features of human nature and the limitations that exist in the environmentally induced variation. He or she is especially interested in the fact that, although all cultures taken together constitute a very great amount of variation, their total content is far less than that displayed by the remaining species of social animals. By comparing the diagnostic features of human organization with those of other primate species, the sociobiologist aims to reconstruct the earliest evolutionary history of social organization and to discern its genetic residues in contemporary societies. The approach is entirely complementary to that of the social sciences and in no way diminishes their importance—quite the contrary.

Those immersed in the rich lore of the social sciences sometimes reject human sociobiology because it is reductionistic. But almost all of the great advances of science have been made by reduction, in the form of conjectures that are often bold and momentarily premature. Theoretical physics transformed chemistry, chemistry transformed cell biology and genetics, natural selection theory trans-

formed ecology—all by stark reduction, which at first seemed inadequate to the task. Reduction is a method by which new mechanisms and relational processes are discovered. In the most successful case histories of postulational-deductive science, propositions are expressed in forms that can be elaborated into precise, testable models. The other side of reduction, the antithesis of the thesis, is synthesis. As the new principles and equations are validated by repeated testing, they are used in an attempt to reconstitute the full array of the subject's phenomena. Karl Popper (1974) has correctly suggested that philosophical reductionism is wrong but that methodological reductionism is necessary for the advancement of science. Here is how I tried to summarize the role of sociobiological reduction in an earlier review (Wilson, 1977, p. 138):

The urge to be reductionistic is an understandable human trait. Ernst Mach [1974] captured it in the following definition: "Science may be regarded as a minimal problem consisting of the completest presentment of facts with the least possible expenditure of thought." This is a sentiment of a member of the antidiscipline, impatient to set aside complexity and get on with the search for more fundamental ideas. The laws of his subject are necessary to the discipline above, they challenge and force a mentally more efficient restructuring, but they are not sufficient for its purposes. Biology is the key to human nature, and social scientists cannot afford to ignore its emerging principles. But the social sciences are potentially far richer in content. Eventually they will absorb the relevant ideas of biology and go on to beggar them by comparison.

The strongest redoubt of counterbiology appears to be mentalism. It is difficult—for some it is impossible—to envision the existence of the mind and the creation of symbolic thought by biological processes. "The human mind," this argument often goes, "is an emergent property of the brain that is no longer tied to genetic controls. All that the genes can prescribe is the construction of the liberated brain." But the relation between genes, the brain, and the mind is only a practical difficulty, not a theoretical one. Models have already been produced in neurobiology and cognitive psychology that allow at least the possibility of mind as an epiphenomenon of complex but essentially conventional neuronal circuitry. Consciousness might well consist of large numbers of coded abstractions, some fed stepwise through a hierarchy of integrating centers whose lowest array consists of the primary sense cells, others originating internally to simulate these hierarchies. The brain—in Charles Sherrington's (1940) metaphor, the "enchanted loom where millions of flashing shuttles weave a dissolving pattern"— not only experiences scenarios fed to it by the sensory channels but also creates them by recall and fantasy. In sustaining this activity, the brain depends substantially on the triggering effect of verbal symbols. There is also a reliance on what have been called *plans* or *schemata*—configurations within the brain, either innate or experiential in origin, against which the input of the nerve cells is compared. The matching of the real or expected patterns can have one or more of several effects. It can contribute to mental "set," the favoring of certain kinds of sensory information over others. It can generate the remarkable phenomena of *gestalt* perception, in which the mind supplies missing details from the actual sensory information in order to complete a pattern and make a classification. And it can serve as the physical basis of will: The mind can be guided in its actions by feedback loops that lead from the sense organs to the brain schemata to the neuromuscular machinery and sense organs and back again until the schemata "satisfy" themselves that the correct action has been taken. The mind could be a republic of alternative schemata, programmed to compete for control of the decision centers, individually waxing and waning in power according to the relative urgency of the needs of the body being signaled through other nervous pathways passing upward

through the lower brain centers. The mind might or might not work approximately in such a manner. My point is that it is entirely possible for all known components of the mind, including will, to have a neurophysiological basis subject to genetic evolution by natural selection. There is no a priori reason why any portion of the foundation of human social behavior must be excluded from the domain of sociobiological analysis.

Some critics have objected to the drawing of analogies between animal and human behavior, especially as it entails the same terminology to describe phenomena across species. This reservation has always struck me as insubstantial. The definitions and limitations of the concepts of analogy and homology have been well worked out by evolutionary biologists, and it is difficult to imagine why the same reasoning cannot be extended with proper care to the human species. We already speak of the octopus eye and the human eye, insect copulation and human copulation, and earthworm learning and human learning, even though in each of these cases the two species are in different superphyla, and the traits listed were independently evolved. The questions of interest are in fact the degrees of convergence and the processes of natural selection that made the convergence so close. When biologists compare altruism in the honeybee worker with human altruism, no one seriously believes that they are based on homologous genes or that they are identical in detail. Slavery practiced by *Polyergus* and *Strongylognathus* ants resembles human slavery in some broad features and differs from it in others, as well as in most details of its execution. By using the same term for such comparisons, the biologist calls attention to the fact that some degree of convergence has occurred and invites an analysis of all the causes of similarity and difference. There is a Greek-derived term for insect slavery—*dulosis*—but its usage outside entomology would not only complicate language but would also slow the very comparative analysis that is of greatest interest.

I am most puzzled by the occasional demurral that sociobiology distracts our attention from the real needs of the world. The questions are raised, "How can we worry about the origins of human nature when the nuclear sword hangs over us? When people are starving in the Sahel and in Bangladesh and political prisoners are rotting in Argentinian jails?" In response, one can answer, "Do we want to know, in depth and with any degree of confidence, why we care? And, after these problems have been solved, what then?" The highest goals professed by governments everywhere are human fulfillment above the animal level and the realization of individual potential. But what is fulfillment, and to what ends can potential be expanded? I suggest that only a deeper understanding of human nature, which must be developed from neurobiological investigations of the brain and the phylogenetic reconstruction of the species-specific properties of human behavior, can provide humanity with the perspective it requires to formulate its highest social goals.

The excitement of sociobiology comes from the promise of the role it will play in this new humanistic investigation. Its potential importance beyond zoology lies in its logical position as the bridging discipline between the natural sciences on the one side and social sciences and humanities on the other. For years, the chief spokespersons of the natural sciences to Western high culture have been physicists, astronomers, geneticists, and molecular biologists—articulate and persuasive scholars whose understanding of the evolution of the brain and of social behavior was unfortunately minimal. Their perception of values and the human condition was almost entirely intuitive and hence scarcely better than that of other intelligent laypersons. Biology has been employed as a science that accounts for the human body; it concerns itself with technological manifestations such as the conquest of disease, the green revolution, energy flow in ecosystems and the cost-benefit analysis of gene splicing. Natural scientists have by and large conceded social behavior to be biologically unstructured and hence the undisputed domain of the social sciences. For their part, most social scientists have granted that human nature has a biological foundation, but they have regarded it as of marginal interest to the resplendent variations in culture that hold their professional attention.

In order for the fabled gap between the two cultures to be truly bridged, social theory must incorporate the natural sciences into its foundations, and for that to occur biology must deal systematically with social behavior. This competence is now being approached through the two-pronged advance of neurobiology, which boldly hopes to explain the physical basis of mind, and sociobiology, which aims to reconstruct the evolutionary history of human nature. Sociobiology in particular is still a rudimentary science. Its relevance to human social systems is still largely unexplored. But in the gathering assembly of disciplines it holds the greatest promise of speaking the common language.

REFERENCES

CHAGNON, N.A. 1976. "Fission in an Amazonian Tribe." *The Sciences* (New York Academy of Science) 16, 14–18.

CHAGNON, N.A., AND W. IRONS, eds. 1979. *Evolutionary Biology and Human Social Behavior*. Scituate, Mass.: Duxbury Press.

DE VORE, I., ed. 1979. *Sociobiology and the Human Sciences*. Chicago: Aldine.

DICKEMAN, M. 1979. "Female Infanticide and the Reproductive Strategies of Stratified Human Societies: A Preliminary Model." In N.A. Chagnon and W.G. Irons, eds. *Evolutionary Biology and Human Social Behavior*. Scituate, Mass.: Duxbury Press.

DURHAM, W.H. 1976. "Resource Competition and

Human Aggression." Part I: "A Review of Primitive War." *Quarterly Review and Biology*, 51, 385–415.

FREEDMAN, D.G., 1974. *Human Infancy: An Evolutionary Perspective*. Hillsdale, N.J.: L. Erlbaum.

———. 1979. *Human Sociobiology*. New York: Free Press.

IRONS, W. 1979. "Emic and Reproductive Success." In N.A. Chagnon and W. Irons, *Evolutionary Biology and Human Social Behavior*. Scituate, Mass.: Duxbury Press.

KONNER, M.J. 1972. "Aspects of the Developmental Ethology of a Foraging People." In N. Blurton-Jones, ed. *Ethological Studies of Child Behavior*. Cambridge: Cambridge University Press.

KUNG, H. 1976. *On Being a Christian*. New York: Doubleday.

LOEHLIN, J.D., AND R.C. NICHOLS. 1976. *Heredity, Environment, and Personality*. Austin: University of Texas Press.

MACH, E. 1974. *The Science of Mechanics*. (T.J. McCormack, Trans.) Lasalle, Ill.: Open Court.

MCKUSICK, V.A., AND F.H. RUDDLE. 1977. "The Status of the Gene Map of the Human Chromosome." *Science*, 196, 390–405.

POPPER, D.R. 1974. "Scientific Reduction and the Essential Incompleteness of All Science." In F.J. Ayala and T. Dobzhansky, eds. *Studies in the Philosophy of Biology*. Berkeley: University of California Press.

SCOTT, J.P. 1950. Forward to "Methodology and Techniques for the Study of Animal Societies." *Annals of the New York Academy of Sciences*, 51, 1003–1005.

SHEPHER, J. 1971. "Mate Selection among Second-Generation Kibbutz Adolescents and Adults," *Archives of Sexual Behavior*. 1(4), 293–307.

SHERRINGTON, C. 1940. *Man on His Nature*. Cambridge: Cambridge University Press.

WEINRICH, J.D. 1977. "Human Reproductive Strategy." Unpublished doctoral dissertation, Harvard University.

WILSON, E.O. 1971. *The Insect Societies*. Cambridge: Belknap Press.

———. 1975. *Sociobiology: The New Synthesis*. Cambridge: Harvard University Press.

———. 1977. "Biology and the Social Sciences." *Daedalus*. 106(4), 127–40.

ENVIRONMENTAL SOCIOLOGY:
A NEW PARADIGM*

WILLIAM R. CATTON, JR., AND RILEY E. DUNLAP

Sociology appears to have reached an impasse. Efforts of sociologists to assimilate into their favorite theories some of the astounding events that have shaped human societies within the last generation have sometimes contributed more to the fragmentation of the sociological community than to the convincing explanation of social facts. But as Thomas Kuhn (1962:76) has shown, such an impasse often signifies "that an occasion for retooling has arrived."

The rise of environmental problems, and especially apprehensions about "limits to growth," signalled sharp departures from the exuberant expectations most sociologists had shared with the general public. Environmental problems and constraints contributed to the general uneasiness in American society

*From William R. Catton, Jr., and Riley E. Dunlap, "Environmental Sociology: A New Paradigm," *The American Sociologist* 13:1 (February 1978), 11–19. For an expanded discussion of the issues treated in this article, see Catton and Dunlap, *American Behavioral Scientist* 24:1 (September-October 1980), 15–47. Reprinted with permission of the American Sociological Association and the authors.

brought about by events in the sixties. Sociologists, no less than other thinking people, are still grappling with the dramatic shift from the calmer fifties, when the American dreams of social progress, upward mobility, and societal stability seemed secure.

In 1976 the American Sociological Association, following precedents set a few years earlier in the Rural Sociological Society and in the Society for the Study of Social Problems, established a new "Section on Environmental Sociology." In this paper we shall try to account for the development of environmental sociology by showing how it represents an attempt to understand recent societal changes that are difficult to comprehend from traditional sociological perspectives. We contend that, rather than simply representing the rise of another speciality within the discipline, the emergence of environmental sociology reflects the development of a new paradigm, and that this paradigm may help to extricate us from the impasse referred to above.

The "New Environmental Paradigm" (NEP) implicit in environmental sociology is, of course, only one among several current candidates to replace or amend the increasingly obsolescent set of "domain assumptions" which have defined the nature of social reality for most sociologists. Environmental sociologists, no less than the advocates of the very different alternatives Gouldner (1970) has described, are attempting to come to grips with a changed "sense of what is real." Further, we believe the NEP may contribute to a better understanding of contemporary and future social conditions than is possible with previous sociological perspectives. To illustrate the power of this paradigm to shed new light on important sociological issues, we shall briefly describe some recent NEP-based examinations of problems in stratification. But first we must contrast the old and new sets of assumptions.

THE "HUMAN EXCEPTIONALISM PARADIGM"

The numerous competing theoretical perspectives in contemporary sociology—e.g., functionalism, symbolic interactionism, ethnomethodology, conflict theory, Marxism, and so forth—are prone to exaggerate their differences from each other. They purport to be paradigms in their own right, and are often taken as such (see e.g., Denisoff, et al., 1974, and Ritzer, 1975). But they have also been construed simply as competing "preparadigmatic" perspectives (Friedrichs, 1972). We maintain that their apparent diversity is not as important as the fundamental anthropocentrism underlying *all* of them.

This mutual anthropocentrism is part of a basic sociological worldview (Klausner, 1971:10–11). We call *that* worldview the "Human Exceptionalism Paradigm" (HEP). We contend that acceptance of the assumptions of the HEP has made it difficult for most sociologists, regardless of their preferred orientation, to deal meaningfully with the social implications of ecological problems and constraints. Thus, the HEP has become increasingly obstructive of sociological efforts to comprehend contemporary and future social experience.

The HEP comprises several assumptions that have either been challenged by recent additions to knowledge, or have had their optimistic implications contradicted by events of the seventies. Accepted explicitly or implicitly by all existing theoretical persuasions, they include:

1. Humans are unique among the earth's creatures, for they have culture.
2. Culture can vary almost infinitely and can change much more rapidly than biological traits.
3. Thus, many human differences are socially induced rather than inborn, they can be socially altered, and inconvenient differences can be eliminated.
4. Thus, also, cultural accumulation means that progress can continue without limit, making all social problems ultimately soluble.

Sociological acceptance of such an optimistic worldview was no doubt fostered by prevalence of the doctrine of progress in Western culture, where academic sociology was spawned and nurtured. It was under the American branch of Western culture that sociology flourished most fully, and it has been clear to foreign analysts of American life, from Tocqueville to Laski, that most Americans (until recently) ardently believed that the present was better than the past and the future would improve upon the present. Sociologists could easily share that conviction when natural resources were still so plentiful that limits to progress remained unseen. The historian, David Potter (1954:141), tried to alert his colleagues to some of the unstated and unexamined assumptions shaping their studies; his words have equal relevance for sociologists: "The factor of abundance, which we first discovered as an environmental condition and which we then converted by technological change into a cultural as well as a physical force, has ... influenced all aspects of American life in a fundamental way."

Not only have sociologists been too unmindful of the fact that our society derived special qualities from past abundance; the heritage of abundance has made it difficult for most sociologists to perceive the possibility of an era of uncontrived scarcity. For example, ecological concepts such as "carrying capacity" are alien to the vocabularies of most sociologists (Catton, 1976a; 1976b), yet disregard for this concept has been tantamount to assuming an environment's carrying capacity is always enlargeable as needed—thus denying the possibility of scarcity.

Neglect of the ecosystem-dependence of human society has been evident in sociological literature on economic development (e.g., Horowitz, 1972), which has simply not recognized biogeochemical limits to material progress. And renewed sociological attention to a theory of societal evolution (e.g., Parsons, 1977) has seldom paid much attention to the resource base that is subjected to "more efficient" exploitation as societies become more differentiated internally and are thereby "adaptively upgraded." In such literature, the word "environment" refers almost entirely to a society's "symbolic environment" (cultural systems) or "social environment" (environing social systems).

It is the habit of neglecting laws of other sciences (such as the Principle of Entropy and the Law of Conservation of Energy)—as if human actions were unaffected by them—that enables so distinguished a sociologist as Daniel Bell (1973:465) to assert that the question before humanity is "not subsistence but standard of living, not biology, but sociology,"

to insist that basic needs "are satiable, and the possibility of abundance is real," to impute "apocalyptic hysteria" to "the ecology movement," and to regard it as trite rather than questionable to expect "compound interest" growth to continue for another hundred years. Likewise, this neglect permits Amos Hawley (1975:8–9) to write that "there are no known limits to the improvement of technology" and the population pressure on nonagricultural resources is neither "currently being felt or likely to be felt in the early future." Such views reflect a staunch commitment to the HEP.

ENVIRONMENTAL SOCIOLOGY AND THE "NEW ENVIRONMENTAL PARADIGM"

When public apprehension began to be aroused concerning newly visible environmental problems, the scientists who functioned as opinion leaders were not sociologists. They included such individuals as Rachel Carson, Barry Commoner, Paul Ehrlich and Garrett Hardin—biologists. Leadership in highlighting the precariousness of the human condition was mostly forfeited by sociologists, because until recently, most of us had been socialized into a worldview that makes it difficult to recognize the reality and full significance of the environmental problems and constraints we now confront. Due to our acceptance of the HEP, our discipline has focused on humans to the neglect of habitat; consideration of our *social* environment has crowded out consideration of our physical circumstances (Michelson, 1976:17). Further, we have had unreserved faith that equilibrium between population and resources could and would be reached in noncatastrophic ways, since technology and organization would mediate the relations between a growing population and its earthly habitat (see, e.g., Hawley, 1975).

But, stimulated by troubling events, some sociologists began to read such works as Carson (1962), Commoner (1971), Ehrlich and Ehrlich (1970), and Hardin (1968), and began to shed the blinders of the HEP. As long-held assumptions began to lose their power over our perceptions, we began to recognize that the reality of ecological constraints posed serious problems for human societies *and* for the discipline of sociology (see, e.g., Burch, 1971). It began to appear that, in order to make sense of the world, it was necessary to rethink the traditional Durkheimian norm of sociological purity—i.e., that social facts can be explained *only* by linking them to other *social* facts. The gradual result of such rethinking has been the development of environmental sociology.

Environmental sociology is clearly still in its formative years. At the turn of the decade rising concern with "environment" as a social problem led to numerous studies of public attitudes toward environmental issues and of the "Environmental Movement" (see Albrecht and Mauss, 1975). A coalition gradually developed between sociologists with such interests and sociologists with a range of other concerns—including rather established interests such as the "built" environment, natural hazards, resource management and outdoor recreation, as well as newer interests such as "social impact assessment" (mandated by the National Environmental Policy Act of 1969). After the energy crisis of 1973, numerous sociologists (including many with prior interests in one or more of the above areas) began to investigate the effects of energy shortages in particular, and resource constraints in general, on society: the stratification system, the political order, the family, and so on. (For an indication of the range of interests held by en-

vironmental sociologists see Dunlap, 1975, and Manderscheid, 1977; for reviews of the literature see Dunlap and Catton, 1979 and Humphrey and Buttel, 1976.)

These diverse interests are linked into an increasingly distinguishable specialty known as environmental sociology by the acceptance of "environmental" variables as meaningful for sociological investigation. Conceptions of "environment" range from the "manmade" (or "built") environment to the "natural" environment, with an array of "human-altered" environments—e.g., air, water, noise and visual pollution—in between. In fact, *the study of interaction between the environment and society is the core of environmental sociology,* as advocated several years ago by Schnaiberg (1972). This involves studying the effects of the environment on society (e.g., resource abundance or scarcity on stratification) and the effects of society on the environment (e.g., the contributions of differing economic systems to environmental degradation).

The study of such interaction rests on the recognition that sociologists can no longer afford to ignore the environment in their investigations, and this in turn appears to depend on at least tacit acceptance of a set of assumptions quite different from those of the HEP. From the writings of several environmental sociologists (e.g., Anderson, 1976; Burch, 1971, 1976; Buttel, 1976; Catton, 1976a, 1976b; Morrison, 1976; Schnaiberg, 1972, 1975) it is possible to extract a set of assumptions about the nature of social reality which stand in stark contrast to the HEP. We call this set of assumptions the "New Environmental Paradigm" or NEP (see Dunlap and Van Liere, 1977 for a broader usage of the term, referring to emerging public beliefs):

1. Human beings are but one species among the many that are interdependently involved in the biotic communities that shape our social life.

2. Intricate linkages of cause and effect and feedback in the web of nature produce many unintended consequences from purposive human action.
3. The world is finite, so there are potent physical and biological limits constraining economic growth, social progress, and other societal phenomena.

ENVIRONMENTAL FACTS AND SOCIAL FACTS

Sociologists who adhere to the NEP readily accept as factual the opening sentences of the lead article (by a perceptive economist) in a recent issue of *Social Science Quarterly* devoted to "Society and Scarcity": "We have inherited, occupy, and will bequeath a world of scarcity: resources are not adequate to provide all of everything we want. It is a world, therefore, of limitations, constraints, and conflict, requiring the bearing of costs and calling for communal coordination" (Allen, 1976:263). Persistent adherents of the HEP, on the other hand, accustomed to relying on endless and generally benign technological and organizational breakthroughs, could be expected to discount such a statement as a mere manifestation of the naive presumption that the "state of the arts" is fixed (see, e.g., Hawley, 1975:6–7).

Likewise, sociologists who have been converted to the assumptions of the NEP have no difficulty appreciating the sociological relevance of the following fact: the $36 billion it now costs annually to import oil to supplement depleted American supplies is partially defrayed by exporting $23 billion worth of agricultural products—grown at the cost of enormous soil erosion (van Bavel, 1977). Environmental sociologists expect momentous social change if soil or oil, or both are depleted. But sociologists still bound by the HEP would probably ignore such topics, holding that oil and soil are irrelevant variables for sociologists. However, we believe that only by taking into account such factors as declining energy resources can sociologists continue to understand and explain "social facts." We will attempt to demonstrate this by examining some work by NEP-oriented sociologists in one of the areas they have begun to examine—social stratification.

USEFULNESS OF THE NEP: RECENT WORK IN SOCIAL STRATIFICATION

The bulk of existing work in stratification appears to rest on the Human Exceptionalism Paradigm, as it " . . . does not adequately consider the context of resource constraints or lack thereof in which the stratification system operates . . ." (Morrison, 1973:83). We will therefore describe recent work in the area by environmental sociologists, in an effort to illustrate the insights into stratification processes provided by the NEP. We will limit the discussion to three topics: the current decline in living conditions experienced by many Americans; contemporary and likely future cleavages in our stratification system; and the problematic prospects for ending self-perpetuating poverty.

Recent decline in standard of living: A majority of Americans are concerned about their economic situation (Strumpel, 1976:23), and in *Food, Shelter and the American Dream,* Aronowitz (1974) exemplifies the growing awareness that *something* is not going according to expectation—that old ideals of societal progress, increasing prosperity and material comfort, and individual and intergenerational mobility for *all* segments of society are *not* being realized (also see Anderson, 1976:1–3). Yet, even a "critical sociologist" such as Aronowitz seems impeded by the HEP in attempting to understand these changes. He views recent shortages in food, gasoline, heating oil, and so on, entirely as the result of "manipulations" by large national and supranational corporations, and is skeptical of the idea that resource scarcities may be real. Thus, his solution to the decline in the American standard of living would apparently be solely political—reduce the power of large corporations.

Although many environmental sociologists would not deny that oil companies have benefited from energy shortages, their acceptance of the NEP leads to a different explanation of recent economic trends. Schnaiberg, (1975: 6–8), for instance, has explicated a very useful "societal-environmental dialectic." Given the *thesis* that "economic expansion is a social desideratum" and the *antithesis* that "ecological disruption is a necessary consequence of economic expansion," a dialectic emerges with the acceptance of the proposition that "ecological disruption is harmful to human society." Schnaiberg notes three alternative *syntheses* of the dialectic: (1) an *economic synthesis* which ignores ecological disruptions and attempts to maximize growth; (2) a *managed scarcity synthesis* which deals with the most obvious and pernicious consequences of resource-utilization by imposing controls over selected industries and resources; and (3) an *ecological synthesis* in which "substantial control over both production and effective demand for goods" is used to minimize ecological disruptions and maintain a "sustained yield" of resources. Schnaiberg (1975:9–10) argues that the synthesis adopted will be influenced by the basic economic structure of a society, with "regressive" (inequality-magnifying) societies most likely to maintain the "economic" synthesis and "progressive" (equality-fostering) societies least resistive to the "ecological" synthesis. Not surprisingly, therefore, the U.S., with its "non-redistributive" economy, has increasingly opted for "managed scarcity" as the solution to environmental and resource problems.

Managed scarcity involves, for example, combating ecological disruptions by forcing industries to abate pollution, with resultant costs passed along to consumers via higher prices, and combating resource shortage via higher taxes (and thus higher consumer prices) on the scarce resources. There is growing recognition of the highly regressive impacts of both mechanisms (Morrison, 1977; Schnaiberg, 1975), and thus governmental reliance on "managed scarcity" to cope with pollution and resource shortages at least partly accounts for the worsening economic plight of the middle-, working, and especially lower-classes—a plight in which adequate food and shelter are often difficult to obtain. Unfortunately, these economic woes cannot simply be corrected by returning to the economic synthesis. The serious health threats posed by pollutants, the potentially devastating changes in the ecosystem wrought by unbridled economic and technological growth (e.g., destruction of the protective ozone layer, alteration of atmospheric temperature), and the undeniable reality of impending shortages in crucial resources such as oil, all make reversion to the traditional economic synthesis impossible in the long run (see, e.g., Anderson, 1976; Miller, 1972). Of course, as Morrison (1976) has noted, the pressures to return to this synthesis are great, and understanding them provides insights into contemporary and future economic cleavages.

Cleavages within the stratification system: Schnaiberg's ecological synthesis amounts to what others have termed a "stationary" or "steady-state" society, and it is widely agreed that such a society would need to be far more egalitarian than the contemporary U.S. (Anderson, 1976:58–61; Daly, 1973:168–170). Achieving the necessary redistribution would be very difficult, and opposition to it would be likely to result in serious, but unstable cleavages within the stratification system. In the long run, as environmental constraints become more obvious, ecologically aware "haves" are likely to opt for increased emphasis on managed scarcity to cope with them.

The results would be disastrous for the "have nots," as slowed growth and higher prices would reverse the traditional trend in the U.S. in which *all* segments of society have improved their material condition—not because they obtained a larger slice of the "pie," but because the pie kept growing (Anderson, 1976:28–33; Morrison, 1976). Slowed growth *without* increased redistribution will result in real (as well as relative) deprivation among the "have nots," making class conflict more likely than ever before. As Morrison (1976:299) notes, "Class antagonisms that are soothed by general economic growth tend to emerge as more genuine class conflicts when growth slows or ceases." Thus, in the long run the NEP suggests that Marx's predictions about class conflict may become more accurate, although for reasons Marx could not have foreseen.

In the short run, however, a very different possibility seems likely. The societal pressures resulting from managed scarcity are such that large portions of *both* "haves" and "have nots" will push for a reversion to the economic (growth) synthesis. In fact, Morrison (1973) has predicted the emergence of a Dahrendorfian (i.e., non-Marxian) cleavage: "growthists vs. nongrowthists," with *all* those highly dependent upon industrial growth (workers and owners) coalescing to oppose environmentalists (who typically hold positions—in the professions, government, education, for example—less directly dependent on growth). The staunch labor union support for growth, and the successful efforts of industry to win the support of labor and the poor in battles against environmentalists, both suggest the emergence of this coalition. Somewhat ironically, therefore, support for continued economic growth has united capitalists and the "left" (used broadly to include most labor unions, advocates for the poor, and academic Marxists). Not only does this support reveal the extent to which most of the left has abandoned hopes for real *redistribution* in favor of getting a "fair share" of a growing pie, but it also reveals a misunderstanding of the distribution of costs and benefits of traditional economic growth.

The "Culture of Poverty" solidified: Sociologists guided by the NEP have not only questioned the supposed universal benefits of growth, but they consistently point to the generally neglected "costs" of growth—costs which tend to be very regressive (Anderson, 1976:30–31; Schnaiberg, 1975:19). Thus, it is increasingly recognized that the workplace and inner city often constitute serious health hazards, and that there is generally a strong inverse relationship between SES and exposure to environmental pollution (Schnaiberg, 1975:19). Further, in his study of the SES-air pollution relationship, Burch (1976:311) has gone so far as to suggest that, "Each of these pollutants when ingested at certain modest levels over continuing periods, is likely to be an important influence upon one's ability to persist in the struggle for improvement of social position. . . . These exposures, like nutritional deficiencies, seem one mechanism by which class inequalities are reinforced." This leads him to suggest that efforts to eradicate poverty which do not take into account the debilitating impact of environmental insults are likely to fail.

CONCLUSION

We have attempted to illustrate the utility of the NEP by focusing on issues concerning stratification, for we believe this is one of many aspects of society that will be significantly affected by ecological constraints. As noted above, in the short run we expect tremendous pressure for reverting to the economic growth synthesis, for such a strategy seeks to alleviate societal tensions at the expense of the environment. Of course, the

NEP implies that such a strategy cannot continue indefinitely (and the evidence seems to support this—see, e.g., Miller, 1972). Thus we are faced with the necessity of choosing between managed scarcity and an ecological synthesis. The deleterious effects of the former are already becoming obvious; they help account for the trends described by Aronowitz and others. However, the achievement of a truly ecological synthesis will require achieving a steady-state society, a very difficult goal. As students of social organization, sociologists should play a vital role in delineating the characteristics of such a society, feasible procedures for attaining it, and their probable social costs. (See Anderson, 1976 for a preliminary effort.) Until sociology extricates itself from the Human Exceptionalism Paradigm, however, such a task will be impossible.

REFERENCES

ALBRECHT, STAN T., AND ARMAND I. MAUSS. 1975. "The environment as a social problem," Pp. 556–605 in A. I. Mauss. Social Problems as Social Movements. Philadelphia: Lippincott.

ALLEN, WILLIAM R. 1976. "Scarcity and order: The Hobbesian problem and the Humean resolution." Social Science Quarterly 57:263–275.

ANDERSON, CHARLES H. 1976. The Sociology of Survival: Social Problems of Growth. Homewood, Ill.: Dorsey.

ARONOWITZ, STANLEY. 1974. Food, Shelter and the American Dream. New York: Seabury Press.

BELL, DANIEL, 1973. The Coming of Post-Industrial Society. New York: Basic Books.

BURCH, WILLIAM R., JR. 1971. Daydreams and Nightmares: A Sociological Essay on the American Environment. New York: Harper and Row.

_____. 1976. "The peregrine falcon and the urban poor: Some sociological interrelations." Pp. 308–316 in P.J. Richerson and J. McEvoy III (eds.), Human Ecology: An Environmental Approach. North Scituate, Mass.: Duxbury.

BUTTEL, FREDERICK H. 1976. "Social science and the environment: Competing theories." Social Science Quarterly 57:307–323.

CARSON, RACHEL. 1962. Silent Spring. Boston: Houghton-Mifflin.

CATTON, WILLIAM, JR., 1976a. "Toward prevention of obsolescence in sociology." Sociological Focus 9:89–98.

_____. 1976b. "Why the future isn't what it used to be (and how it could be made worse than it has to be)." Social Science Quarterly 57:276–291.

COMMONER, BARRY. 1971. The Closing Circle. New York: Knopf.

DALY, HERMAN E. 1973. "The steady-state economy: Toward a political economy of biophysical equilibrium and moral growth." Pp. 149–174 in H.E. Daly (ed.), Toward a Steady-State Economy. San Francisco: W.H. Freeman.

DENISOFF, R. SERGE, OREL CALLAHAN, and MARK H. LEVINE (eds.). 1974. Theories and Paradigms in Contemporary Sociology. Itasca, Ill.: Peacock.

DUNLAP, RILEY E. (ed.). 1975. Directory of Environmental Sociologists. Pullman: Washington State University, College of Agriculture Research Center, Circular No. 586.

DUNLAP, RILEY E., AND WILLIAM R. CATTON, JR. 1979. "Environmental sociology." Pp. 243–273 in Annual Review of Sociology: Vol. 5. Palo Alto, Calif.: Annual Reviews, Inc.

DUNLAP, RILEY E., AND KENT D. VAN LIERE. 1977. "The new environmental paradigm: A proposed measuring instrument and preliminary results." Paper presented at the Annual Meeting of the American Sociological Association, Chicago.

EHRLICH, PAUL R., AND ANNE H. EHRLICH. 1970. Population, Resources, Environment. San Francisco: W.H. Freeman.

FRIEDRICHS, ROBERT W. 1972. A Sociology of Sociology. New York: Free Press.

GOULDNER, ALVIN W. 1970. The Coming Crisis of Western Sociology. New York: Basic Books.

HARDIN, GARRETT. 1968. "The tragedy of the commons." Science 162:1243–1248.

HAWLEY, AMOS H. (ed.). 1975. Man and Environment. New York: New York Times Company.

HOROWITZ, IRVING L. 1972. Three Worlds of Development: The Theory and Practice of International Stratification. 2nd ed. New York: Oxford University Press.

HUMPHREY, CRAIG R., AND FREDERICK H. BUTTEL. 1976. "New directions in environmental sociology." Paper presented at the Annual Meeting of the Society for the Study of Social Problems, New York.

KLAUSNER, SAMUEL Z. 1971. On Man in His Environment. San Francisco: Jossey-Bass.

KUHN, THOMAS S. 1962. The Structure of Scientific Revolutions. Chicago: University of Chicago Press.

MANDERSCHEID, RONALD W. (ed.). 1977. Annotated Directory of Members: Ad Hoc Committee on Housing and Physical Environment. Adelphi, Maryland: Mental Health Study Center, NIMH.

MICHELSON, WILLIAM H. 1976. Man and His Urban Environment. 2nd ed. Reading, Mass.: Addison-Wesley.

MILLER, G. TYLER, JR. 1972. Replenish the Earth: A Primer in Human Ecology. Belmont, Calif.: Wadsworth.

MORRISON, DENTON E. 1973. "The environmental movement: Conflict dynamics." Journal of Voluntary Action Research 2:74–85.

———. 1976. "Growth, environment, equity and scarcity." Social Science Quarterly 57:292–306.

———. 1977. "Equity impacts of some major energy alternatives." Paper presented at the Annual Meeting of the American Sociological Association, Chicago.

PARSONS, TALCOTT. 1977. The Evolution of Societies (ed. by Jackson Toby). Englewood Cliffs, N.J.: Prentice Hall.

POTTER, DAVID M. 1954. People of Plenty. Chicago: University of Chicago Press.

RITZER, GEORGE. 1975. Sociology: A Multiple Paradigm Science. Boston: Allyn and Bacon.

SCHNAIBERG, ALLAN. 1972. "Environmental sociology and the division of labor." Department of Sociology, Northwestern University, mimeograph.

———. 1975. "Social syntheses of the societal-environmental dialectic: The role of distributional impacts." Social Science Quarterly 56:5–20.

STRUMPEL, BURKHARD (ed.). 1976. Economic Means for Human Needs. Ann Arbor: Institute for Social Research, University of Michigan.

VAN BAVEL, CORNELIUS H.M. 1977. "Soil and oil." Science 197:213.

THE MISSING FEMINIST REVOLUTION
IN SOCIOLOGY*

JUDITH STACEY AND BARRIE THORNE

A decade ago feminist sociologists shared with our counterparts in other disciplines an optimistic vision about the intellectual revolution a feminist perspective promised to bring to all our fields. As Arlene Daniels (1975:349) proclaimed in her contribution to *Another Voice:*

> ... the women's movement contributes far more to sociology than a passing interest would. The development of a feminist perspective in sociology offers an important contribution to the sociology of knowledge. And through this contribution, we are forced to rethink the structure and organization of sociological theory in all the traditional fields of theory and empirical research.

By now there has been an extraordinary amount of sociological work on gender. It is likely that more gender-sensitive research has been "mainstreamed" in sociological periodicals and conferences than in those of most

other disciplines. Feminists can point with pride to important, even cutting-edge contributions such work has made to our understanding of society. Feminist perspectives have helped correct androcentric biases in established lines of work and have inspired much better research in the study, for example, of organizations, occupations (e.g., Epstein, 1981; Glenn, 1986; Kahn-Hut et al., 1982), criminology (Leonard, 1982; Smart, 1977), deviance (Millman, 1975; Piven and Cloward, 1979), health (Scully, 1980), and stratification (Acker, 1980; Blumberg, 1978). Feminist sociologists have helped revitalize the study of mothering (e.g., Bernard, 1974; Chodorow, 1978), housework (Berk, 1980; Glazer-Malbin, 1976), rape (Holmstrom and Burgess, 1978; Russell, 1982), contraception (Luker, 1975), marriage (Bernard, 1982), divorce (Weitzman, 1981), widowhood (Lopata, 1973), and the life-cycle (Giele, 1980; Rossi, 1980)—topics which previously had been devalued or studied in distorted ways. And by attending to women's experiences, feminists

* © 1985 by the Society for the Study of Social Problems. Abridged and reprinted from *Social Problems,* Vol. 32, No. 4, April 1985, pp. 301–302, 306–16. Reprinted with permission of the University of California Press and the authors.

have opened new topics for research, such as sexual harassment (McKinnon, 1979), wife battering (Breines and Gordon, 1983; Dobash and Dobash, 1979), compulsory heterosexuality (March, 1982; Rich, 1980), lesbian communities (Krieger, 1982), the feminization of poverty (Pearce, 1979), and the sociology of childbirth (Rothman, 1982). Feminists have also provided new insight into relationships between family and work institutions (Voydenoff, 1983), and women's and men's different experiences of being fat (Millman, 1980), of conversation (West and Zimmerman, 1983), of intimacy (Rubin, 1983), and of emotions like anger and love (Hochschild, 1983).

These are impressive achievements. And yet, we find that the impact of feminist thought on sociology, and the current relationship between feminism and the discipline as a whole, seem to fall short when measured against the optimistic vision of a decade ago. Peggy McIntosh (1983; also see Tetreault, 1985) has identified several stages in feminist transformations of knowledge. The initial period is one of filling in gaps—correcting sexist biases and creating new topics out of women's experiences. Over time, however, feminists discover that many gaps were there for a reason, i.e., that existing paradigms systematically ignore or erase the significance of women's experiences and the organization of gender. This discovery, McIntosh suggests, leads feminists to rethink the basic conceptual and theoretical frameworks of their respective fields. . . .

THE CONTAINMENT OF FEMINISM WITHIN SOCIOLOGY

Within sociology the feminist strategy of putting women at the center of knowledge has yielded valuable new insights and redirections of inquiry, as we detailed in the intro-duction. But we believe the results have been more contradictory and less successful, on the whole, than in anthropology, history, or literature. Specific subfields have been challenged, and many new topics added, but there has been less rethinking of basic conceptual frameworks. This may be due, in part, to the traditional subject matter of sociology, which was neither as gender-sensitive as in anthropology nor as dramatically male-centered as in history or literature.

In contrast with history and literature, the discipline of sociology was not organized around formal canons or narrowing definitions (e.g., history defined in terms of the politically powerful) which clearly excluded entire groups. Margaret Anderson (1983) and Helen Roberts (1981) have each noted that the "bedrock" assumptions of the field commit sociologists, at least *in theory,* to understanding all institutions and the experiences of their members, which in turn produces beneficial potential for including women in their analyses. *In practice,* however, the standpoints of the privileged (western, white, upper-middle class, heterosexual men) infuse traditional sociological knowledge.

In traditional sociology, sexual divisions of labor and gender-related issues were considered primarily in the subfields of family, demography, and community studies, where the presence of women could not be ignored. However, sociologists of occupations, politics, law, religion, formal organizations, and even social stratification and social movements virtually ignored women; they tacitly or explicitly assumed male experience without including gender as a category of analysis. The fact that gender was explicitly present in a few subfields—albeit present in distorted, androcentric ways—probably contributed to the containment of feminism within sociology; and note that the presence of *women,* not men, made gender a visible issue. Because the subject matter of traditional sociology was neither totally male-centered nor basically gender-sensitive, it fell into a co-optable middle ground.

Over a decade ago feminist sociologists began to raise fresh questions about gender and social life, but our queries have been co-opted in several basic ways. We are glossing enormous complexity by sketching these patterns of co-optation, and even by speaking of sociology as a discipline. Sociology is large and fragmented; since the 1960s, when functionalism was undermined as the dominant paradigm, sociology has been a field without a center (Becker, 1979). This fragmentation suggests that a unitary "feminist revolution" is unlikely; the conceptual transformations we might hope for would have to be multiple and diverse. Feminist transformations of the paradigms of sociology have been contained in three major ways: by the limiting assumptions of functionalist conceptualizations of gender, by the inclusion of gender as a variable rather than as a central theoretical concept, and by the ghettoization of feminist insights, especially within Marxist sociology.

Functionalist Co-optation

In the United States the sociological study of gender originated in functionalist family sociology and has been deeply shaped by the concepts developed by Talcott Parsons. Parsons (Parsons and Bales, 1955) translated gender divisions into the (female) "expressive role" and the (male) "instrumental role" within the traditional nuclear family. His analysis of the family (and hence, of gender) emphasized the function of "socialization," understood as integral to maintaining a smoothly functioning social order. This way of casting the subject matter has left a lasting imprint on the sociology of gender, shaping basic concepts (e.g., the language of "sex roles") and assumptions (for example, that gender is more central to the family than to other institutions, and that gender arrangements function primarily to insure social maintenance and reproduction).

Early on, contemporary feminists recognized the influence and limitations of functionalism as a framework for understanding gender. Several of the founding works of the contemporary women's movement criticized Parsons for what Betty Friedan (1963) called "the functionalist freeze," which tacitly legitimized women's subordination and their encapsulation within the family. Feminist sociologists have cleared away many of Parsons' blind spots by attending to gender in work and politics, as well as in families, and by emphasizing gender hierarchies. Yet functionalism has continued to exert a significant and, we believe, inhibiting effect on the development of feminist sociology.

Much of feminist sociology is cast in the language of roles ("sex roles," "the male role," "the female role") and emphasizes the process of "sex role socialization." This approach to the analysis of gender retains its functionalist roots, emphasizing consensus, stability, and continuity (Thorne, 1978). The notion of "role" focuses attention more on individuals than on social structure, and implies that "the female role" and "the male role" are complementary (i.e., separate or different but equal). The terms are depoliticizing; they strip experience from its historical and political context and neglect questions of power and conflict. It is significant that sociologists do not speak of "class roles" or "race roles." Functionalist assumptions linger more deeply in sociological conceptualizations of gender than of other forms of inequality. These functionalist assumptions have posed significant obstacles to feminist rethinking of basic orienting assumptions within sociology.

Gender as a Variable

Within the last decade an increasing number of empirical sociological studies have included attention to gender. For those working in more quantitative research traditions where problems are conceptualized in terms of variables, gender, understood as the division between women and men, has been relatively easy to include. Whether one is a man or a woman, after all, is highly visible; as it is socially constructed, the division encompasses the entire population and sorts neatly into a dichotomy.

A growing number of surveys (e.g., research on status attainment) now include gender (as well as factors like race, education, and income) as a variable, as do experimental studies (e.g., of processes of attribution). Here, as in other research traditions, sensitivity to gender has resulted in important revisionist work. For example, in status attainment research, measures of occupational prestige and socioeconomic position have been found to account more adequately for data about men—from whom the measures were derived—than for data about women (see review in Acker, 1980). Feminist sociologists working in this tradition have pursued fresh topics and developed new measures (e.g., to assess the occupational status of housewives [Bose, 1980]) suggested by attention to women's lives. The use of quantitative methods has provided information crucial to documenting problems such as gender segmentation of the labor force and the feminization of poverty (see literature reviewed in Ferber, 1982).

Much of this literature, however, is unreflective about the nature of gender as a social category. Gender is assumed to be a property of individuals and is conceptualized in terms of sex difference, rather than as a principle of social organization. Reducing social life to a series of measurable variables diminishes the sense of the whole that is crucial to theoretical understanding of social, including gender, relationships. The use of gender as a variable, rather than as a basic theoretical category, is a prime example of the co-optation of feminist perspectives.

The Containment of Feminism within Marxist Sociology

The development of feminist sociology has been contained not only by inadequate conceptualizations of gender, but also by ghettoization within dominant sociological traditions. Ghettoization is especially dramatic, and perhaps surprising, within Marxist sociology, where feminist theorizing has flourished, but apart from and with little influence on the "mainstream."

The relationship between feminism and Marxism is more complex and contradictory than the relationship of feminism to other sociological paradigms. On the one hand, feminist theory maintains its traditional status within Marxism as a continuation of the "Woman Question." On the other hand, feminists have generated a body of "Marxist-Feminist" theory that operates primarily outside "mainstream" Marxist discourse in the social sciences.

It can be argued that Marxist sociology has been even less affected by feminist thought than have more mainstream bodies of sociological theory. Analysis of sex and gender is not easily absorbed within a Marxist conceptual framework. The central Marxist categories which focus on production, labor, and class—as defined through men's relationship to production and labor—are more obviously androcentric than categories like "roles" or "social system."

It is possible, of course, to study women in traditional Marxist terms as is evident in the literature and debate about "domestic labor" and in the significant renaissance of interest in women's labor force participation (see literature reviewed in J. Smith, 1982; Sokoloff, 1980; and see Vogel, 1984). But such analyses, at their best, provide only partial understanding of women or of our relationships to men. And they do little to challenge or revise the epistemological or even conceptual foundations of Marxist thought.

On the positive side, Marxism has been subjected to full-scale critical scrutiny by feminists who have made a self-conscious, sustained attempt to develop a Marxist-Feminist theoretical paradigm that augments the theoretical effectiveness of both perspectives without subordinating one to the other (e.g., Eisenstein, 1979; Hartmann, 1981; Kuhn and Wolpe, 1978). In part this has happened because Marxism, a critical paradigm, tends to incite critical reflection on its own conceptual system. Thus feminists who work within a Marxist tradition begin with a critical stance as well as with a strong commitment to theoretical knowledge. More importantly, Marxist-Feminist work emerged in a political context that encouraged theoretical effort. Socialist-feminists who participated in the development of an autonomous women's movement sought to develop a relatively autonomous body of theory as a guide to political practice.

Somewhat ironically, however, this has allowed the ghettoization of the "Woman Question" tradition to continue, now in the form of "hyphen" literature. Marxist-Feminists have succeeded in developing entirely autonomous and almost exclusively female institutions, conferences and publications. Resistance of many Marxists to engage with this increasingly sophisticated body of literature has left the rest of contemporary Marxist thought remarkably untransformed. For example, Immanuel Wallerstein's (1979) influential book, *The Capitalist World Economy*, ignores sexual divisions of labor and is uninformed even by feminist critiques of sexist language. Using Marxist definitions of so-cial class, Erik Wright and his colleagues (Wright, Costello, Hachen, and Sprague, 1982) recently reported an empirical finding that "a sizable majority of the U.S. working class is composed of women and minorities." Yet they pursue none of the implications this suggests for rethinking Marxist theories of class to take more specific account of race and gender.

INTERPRETIVE VS. POSITIVIST KNOWLEDGE

Having briefly discussed the containment of feminist thinking within sociology, we return to the comparative question: What are the obstacles to feminist transformation within different disciplines? In addition to its traditional subject matter and conceptual frameworks, the basic epistemology of a discipline may affect its congeniality or resistance to feminist rethinking. We have observed that feminist thinking has made the most headway in fields (anthropology, literature, and history) with strong traditions of interpretive understanding. In contrast, fields more deeply anchored in positivist epistemologies—sociology, psychology, political science (excepting political theory), and economics—have posed more obstacles to feminist transformation.

Why has feminist thinking been more successful in revamping interpretive rather than positivist traditions? For one thing, interpretive approaches are more reflexive about the circumstances in which knowledge is developed. They are thus more open to the question: What are the effects of the social and political circumstances in which knowledge is created and received? Feminists modify this question to ask: What are the effects of the gender of the researcher, the audience, or those studied or written about? Positivist knowledge, in contrast, is phrased in abstract, universal terms. It claims to be "objective" and "unrelated to a particular position or a particular sex as its source and standpoint" (Smith, 1978:283).

Values and interests *do,* of course, infuse positivist knowledge, as critics of positivism long have argued. Max Weber initiated a line of analysis, continued by critical theorists like Jürgen Habermas, which connects positivist science to processes of rationalization and control in industrial society. Specifically, Habermas (1971) argues that the attitude of technical and instrumental rationality, which is at the core of positivist social science, serves dominant groups' interests in mastery and control.

Feminists have built upon this critique to argue that positivist knowledge serves the interests not only of dominant social classes (the focus of critical theorists), but also the interests of men, the dominant gender. Evelyn Fox Keller (1982; 1983), Dorothy Smith (1978; 1979), and Nancy Hartsock (1983) have each developed theories connecting masculine standpoints and interests to the structure of knowledge. They argue that the sexual division of labor and male dominance produce fundamental differences in the lives and experiences of women and men, with important consequences for knowledge. Using feminist revisions of psychoanalytic theories of development, Keller (1982; 1983) and Hartsock (1983) suggest that rationality divorced from feelings, and sharp separation between the knower and the known—an objectifying stance basic to positivist social science—may be founded in the organization of gender. This stance is characteristic of a rigidly autonomous personality that, for reasons of social organization and family structure, is more often found among men than women. "To what extent," Keller (1983:18) asks, "does the disjunction of subject and object carry an intrinsic implication of control and power?"

Feminist theorists, among others, are reconsidering the relationship between knower and known to develop a method of inquiry that will preserve the presence of the subject as an actor and experiencer. This approach, as Dorothy Smith (1979) has theorized it, embodies "the standpoint of women," a standpoint rooted in the production and maintenance activities of everyday life. Nancy Hartsock (1983) proposes the development of "a feminist standpoint," an achieved and critical perspective on those activities. By preserving the agency of female subjects, feminist epistemological theory promises significant contributions to the hermeneutic and neo-Marxist critiques of positivist social science. This critique may help to clarify the barriers to feminist transformation of knowledge posed by the positivist tradition.

THE STATE OF FEMINIST THEORY

Not all of the barriers to feminist reconstruction stand within the disciplines. Feminist theory is a fledgling endeavor; perhaps greater maturation is necessary before sociology can reap the full intellectual harvest it promises. It is unsurprising, but somewhat ironic, that thus far the major achievements of feminist theory have been grounded in analyses of family, kinship, and "domestic" relationships. Feminist theorists make the legitimate claim that analyses of the far-from "private" sphere have important theoretical implications for all other arenas of social life, but we have only begun to reconceptualize conventionally-defined political or economic relationships such as the nature of the state, revolutions, social class, or power. That is, we have only recently begun the work of developing knowledge that is "gendered" rather than androcentric or largely limited to the institutions associated with women.

We believe that this underdevelopment of feminist theory has more serious repercussions in sociology than it does in the fields where feminist thought has made more radical progress. This is due to the paradoxical status of theory in sociology. On the one hand, much mainstream sociological work is atheoretical. The aversion to developing theory, which is present among many sociologists, is certainly part of the problem. Although gender may be readily incorporated as a variable, or as a source of research topics, this does little to advance theoretical reconstruction. On the other hand, the subject manner of most sociological inquiry may make the adequacy of one's theoretical perspective especially important. Complex contemporary societies cannot be grasped, or even studied, whole. At the same time, the potential sources of accessible data are overwhelming. Yet a holistic view gives greater analytical significance to description.

Perhaps that is another reason why anthropology—where the favored subjects of inquiry are small societies which allow one to retain a sense of the whole (e.g., to conceptualize and later reconsider a public-domestic dichotomy)—has been such a fruitful site for feminist scholarship. Because anthropologists have a more holistic (and gendered) view of society, they have been in a better position than sociologists to question overall assumptions, such as the division between public and private (Rosaldo, 1980; Tsing and Yanagisako, 1983). Sociologists have yet to fully problematize the "public/domestic" division, which separates the study of the family from the study of occupations, the labor force, and politics.

In history as in anthropology, empirical depth can be a profound theoretical statement. As E.P. Thompson (1979) notes, close historical attention to the complex process and details of social change can generate analytical concepts sufficiently elastic to capture the irregularities and particularities of patterns of human experience. Thompson contrasts empirical depth with empiricism, which fetishizes facts as the only valid objects of knowledge.

However, in most sociological work, "thick description" will not suffice. This might have been less true had more feminist sociologists worked within the tradition of ethnography and community studies, but, for reasons unclear to us, few feminists are doing such work, and those few are mostly anthropologists (e.g., Stack, 1976; Whitehead, 1976). More conscious and developed theory may be necessary to produce equally compelling treatments of the complex, contemporary social world. Generally sociologists study only a part, and often a small part, of that world. We need theory to help us situate the part in the whole.

CONCLUSION

We wrote this paper in a spirit of invitation, rather than final statement. Our starting point, and immediate concern, is the state of feminist thinking within sociology. But this concern has taken us to a larger set of questions that deserve fuller discussion. With over a decade of work behind us, what is the relative impact of feminist theory on the construction of knowledge in different disciplines? And how have different disciplines contributed to feminist theory? We hope this essay will provide further discussion of these questions.

Questions like these rightfully take us across disciplines; feminist scholarship has always had a healthy disrespect for boundaries, and interdisciplinary work has provided critical perspectives on more narrowly defined fields of inquiry. This is an important corrective for the way we have cast our argument. By focusing on sociology as if it were a bounded endeavor, we have given the false impression that feminist sociologists, historians, or anthropologists mine in separate disciplinary tunnels. Comparison of feminist work in different disciplines must be sensitive to effects of disciplinary training, but it also should more fully probe our shared terrain.

Our analysis has emphasized the organization of knowledge and methods of inquiry of different disciplines. Perhaps ironically, we have neglected the sociological dimensions of this question. Feminist transformations of knowledge are surely affected by factors such as the demographic composition of a given discipline, its internal organization and structure of opportunities, the availability and forms of research funding, and the relation of the discipline to the making of public policy.

We want to emphasize another, crucial corrective. A feminist critique of knowledge is not the only missing revolution in sociology, nor could it, by itself, produce an adequate epistemology. Scholars (e.g., Ladner, 1973; Rich, 1980; Wolf, 1982) have also begun to analyze the effects on the discipline of the traditional erasure and distortion of the experiences of other subordinated groups—Blacks, Chicana/os, Native Americans, Asian-Americans, homosexuals, working-class people, the peoples of the Third World—half of whom are women. Our focus on gender was necessary to analyze the limitations of feminist efforts to transform sociology, but it may have given the impression that gender is *the* central category of analysis. Feminist theory has itself been charged, justifiably we believe, with falsely universalizing the category of "woman." Too often the experience of white, middle-class, heterosexual, Euro-American women has served as the basis for analyses that seek to generalize about the experience of WOMAN. The inclusive knowledge we seek would as equally attend to race, class, and sexuality as to gender. The paradigm shifts we hope for are much broader, and more complex, than we have implied.

Feminists have begun to seek a more complicated understanding of both unity and diversity among women, and among men. We have also begun to recognize some of the dilemmas that attend our analytic stance. Central to feminist scholarship is belief in the deep importance of gender, not only for understanding areas specific to the experiences of women, such as mothering or rape, but also for understanding class structure, the state, social revolutions, or militarism—phenomena which are also shaped by the organization of gender, although this point has been obscured by prior conceptualizations. Yet in our efforts to restore agency to women and to develop knowledge sensitive to gender, sexuality, race, and class, feminists often have employed frameworks that essentialize differences rather than understanding that differences are socially constructed and historically changing. Thus much feminist work has unintentionally reinforced the dichotomizing ideologies of contemporary Western culture. The challenge to feminist theory has been succinctly described by feminist scientist and theorist, Evelyn Fox Keller (1982:593–94):

. . . the task of a feminist theoretic in science is twofold: to distinguish that which is parochial from that which is universal in the scientific impulse, reclaiming for women what has historically been denied to them; and to legitimate those elements of scientific culture that have been denied precisely because they are defined as female.

Thus far, feminist tools have worked better to criticize than to reconstruct most bodies of theoretical knowledge. It is time, we believe, to follow the lead of our colleagues in anthropology who have begun to reconstruct the core theoretical frameworks and conceptual systems in their field. Feminist sociologists have a crucial role to play in this project, because sociological theory has significance far beyond our disciplinary borders. Many "applied" fields like speech communication, criminology, education, and social work rely upon sociological frameworks. And feminist scholars in literature, history, philosophy, and other fields turn frequently to sociology and anthropology either to organize and interpret their data or to situate abstract ideas. If we can effect a feminist revolution in sociology, the results will be far-reaching indeed.

REFERENCES

ACKER, JOAN. 1980. "Women and stratification: a review of recent literature." Contemporary Sociology 9:25–29.

ANDERSON, MARGARET L. 1983. "Thinking about women and rethinking sociology." Working Paper Series, Wellesley College Center for Research on Women.

BECKER, HOWARD, S. 1979. "What's happening to sociology?" Society 15,5:19–24.

BERK, SARAH FENSTERMAKER (ed.). 1980. Women and Household Labor. Beverly Hills: Sage.

BERNARD, JESSIE. 1974. The Future of Motherhood. New Haven: Yale University Press.

_____. 1982. The Future of Marriage. 2nd edition. New Haven: Yale University Press.

BLUMBERG, RAE LESSER. 1978. Stratification: Socioeconomic and Sex Equality. Dubuque, IA: Wm. C. Brown.

BOSE, CHRISTINE E. 1980. "Social status of the homemaker," Pp. 69–87 in Sarah Fenstermaker Berk (ed.), Women and Household Labor. Beverly Hills: Sage.

BREINES, WINNI, AND LINDA GORDON. 1983. "Review essay: the new scholarship on family violence." Signs 8:490–531.

CHODOROW, NANCY. 1978. The Reproduction of Mothering. Berkeley: University of California Press.

DANIELS, ARLENE KAPLAN. 1975. "Feminist perspectives in sociological research." Pp. 340–70 in Marcia Millman and Rosabeth Moss Kanter (eds.), Another Voice: Feminist Perspectives on Social Life and Social Science. Garden City, NY: Anchor.

DOBASH, R. EMERSON, AND RUSSELL DOBASH. 1979. Violence against Wives. New York: Free Press.

EISENSTEIN, ZILLAH (ed.). 1979. Capitalist Patriarchy and the Case for Socialist Feminism. New York: Monthly Review Press.

EPSTEIN, CYNTHIA FUCHS. 1981. Women in Law. New York: Basic Books.

FERBER, MARIANNE A. 1982. "Women and work: issues of the 1980's." Signs 8:273–95.

FRIEDAN, BETTY. 1963. The Feminine Mystique. New York: Norton.

GIELE, JANET. 1982. Women in the Middle Years. New York: John Wiley.

GLAZER-MALBIN, NONA. 1976. "Review essay: housework." Signs 1:905–22.

GLENN, EVELYN NAKANO. 1986. Issei, Nisei, War Bride: Three Generations of Japanese American Women in Domestic Service. Philadelphia: Temple University Press.

HABERMAS, JÜRGEN. 1971. Knowledge and Human Interests: Boston: Beacon Press.

HARTMANN, HEIDI. 1981. "The unhappy marriage of Marxism and feminism: toward a more progressive union." Pp. 1–42 in Lydia Sargent (ed.), Women and Revolution. Boston: South End Press.

HARTSOCK, NANCY. 1983. "The feminist standpoint: developing the ground for a specifically feminist historical materialism." Pp. 283–310 in Sandra Harding and Merrill B. Hintikka (eds.), Discovering Reality. Amsterdam: D. Reidel Publishing Co.

HOCHSCHILD, ARLIE RUSSELL. 1983. The Managed Heart. Berkeley: University of California Press.

HOLSTROM, LYNDA L., AND ANN W. BURGESS. 1978. The Victim of Rape: Institutional Reactions. New York: John Wiley and Sons.

KAHN-HUT, RACHEL, ARLENE K. DANIELS, AND RICHARD COLVARD (eds.). 1982. Women and Work. New York: Oxford.

KELLER, EVELYN FOX. 1982. "Feminism and science." Signs 7:589–602.

_____. 1983. "Feminism as an analytic tool for the study of science." Academe 69,5:15–21.

KRIEGER, SUSAN. 1982. "Review essay: lesbian identity and community: recent social science literature." Signs 8:91–108.

KUHN, ANNETTE, AND ANN MARIE WOLPE (eds.). 1978. Feminism and Materialism. London: Routledge and Kegan Paul.

LADNER, JOYCE. 1973. The Death of White Sociology: New York: Random House.

LEONARD, EILEEN B. 1982. Women, Crime and Society: A Critique of Theoretical Criminology. New York: Longman.

LOPATA, HELENA Z. 1973. Widowhood in an American City. Cambridge, MA: Schenckman.

LUKER, KRISTEN. 1975. Taking Chances—Abortion and the Decision Not to Contracept. Berkeley: University of California Press.

MARCH, ARTEMIS. 1982. The Changing Structure of

Control of Female Sexuality. Unpublished Ph.D. dissertation, University of California, Santa Cruz.

MCINTOSH, PEGGY. 1983. "Interactive phases of curricular re-vision: a feminist perspective." Working Paper Series, Wellesley College Center for Research on Women.

MCKINNON, CATHARINE 1979. Sexual Harassment of Working Women. New Haven: Yale University Press.

MILLMAN, MARCIA. 1975. "She did it all for love: a feminist view of the sociology of deviance." Pp. 251–79 in Marcia Millman and Rosabeth Kanter (eds.), Another Voice. Garden City, NY: Anchor.

_____. 1980. Such a Pretty Face: Being Fat in America. New York: Norton.

PARSONS, TALCOTT, AND ROBERT F. BALES. 1955. Family, Socialization and Interaction Process. New York: Free Press.

PEARCE, DIANA. 1979. "Women, work and welfare: the feminization of poverty." Pp. 103–24 in Karen Feldstein (ed.), Working Women and Families. Beverly Hills: Sage.

PIVEN, FRANCES FOX, AND RICHARD A. CLOWARD. 1979. "Hidden protest: the channeling of female innovation and resistance." Signs 4:651–70.

RICH, ADRIENNE. 1980. "Compulsory heterosexuality and lesbian existence." Signs 5:631–60.

ROBERTS, HELEN (ed.) 1981. "Some of the boys won't play any more: the impact of feminism on sociology." Pp. 73–82 in Dale Spender (ed.), Men's Studies Modified. New York: Pergamon Press.

ROSALDO, MICHELLE Z. 1980. "Use and abuse of anthropology: reflections on feminism and cross-cultural understanding." Signs 5: 389–417.

ROSSI, ALICE. 1980. "Life-span theories and women's lives." Signs 6:4–32.

ROTHMAN, BARBARA KATZ. 1982. In Labor: Women and Power in the Birthplace. New York: Norton.

RUBIN, LILLIAN. 1983. Intimate Strangers. New York: Harper and Row.

RUSSELL, DIANA E.H. 1982. Rape in Marriage. New York: Macmillan.

SCULLY, DIANA. 1980. Men Who Control Women's Health. Boston: Houghton Mifflin.

SMART, CAROL. 1977. Women, Crime and Criminology: A Feminist Critique. London: Routledge and Kegan Paul.

SMITH, DOROTHY E. 1978. "A peculiar eclipsing: women's exclusion from man's culture." Women's Studies International Quarterly 1:281–95.

_____. 1979. "A sociology for women." Pp. 135–87 in Julia A. Sherman and Evelyn T. Beck (eds.), The Prism of Sex; Essays in the Sociology of Knowledge. Madison: University of Wisconsin Press.

SMITH, JOAN. 1982. "The way we were: women and work." Feminist Studies 8:437–56.

SOKOLOFF, NATALIE J. 1980. Between Money and Love: The Dialectic of Women's Home and Market Work. New York: Praeger.

STACK, CAROL. 1976. All Our Kin: Strategies for Survival in a Black Community. New York: Harper and Row.

TETREAULT, MARY KAY. 1985. "Feminist phase theory: An experience derived evaluation model." The Journal of Higher Education 56: 363–84.

THOMPSON E.P. 1979. The Poverty of Theory and Other Essays. New York: Monthly Review Press.

THORNE, BARRIE. 1978. "Gender . . . how is it best conceptualized?" Unpublished paper given at annual meetings of the American Sociological Association.

TSING, ANNA LOWENHAUPT, AND SYLVIA JUNKO YANAGISAKO. 1983. "Feminism and kinship theory." Current Anthropology 24:511–16.

VOGEL, LISE. 1984. Marxism and the Oppression of Women. New Brunswick, NJ: Rutgers University Press.

VOYDENOFF, PATRICIA (ed.). 1983. Work and Family. Palo Alto, CA: Mayfield.

WALLERSTEIN, IMMANUEL. 1979. The Capitalist World Economy. New York: Cambridge University Press.

WEITZMAN, LENORE J. 1981. The Marriage Contract. New York: Free Press.

WEST, CANDACE, AND DON ZIMMERMAN. 1983. "Small insults: a study of interruptions in cross-sex conversations between unacquainted persons." Pp. 103–18 in Barrie Thorne, Cheris Kramarae, and Nancy Henley (eds.), Language, Gender and Society. Rowley, MA: Newbury House Publishers.

WHITEHEAD, ANN. 1976. "Sexual antagonism in Herefordshire." Pp. 169–203 in Diana L. Barker and Sheila Allen (eds.), Dependence and Exploitation in Work and Marriage. London: Longman.

WOLF, ERIC. 1982. Europe and the People without History. Berkeley: University of California Press.

WRIGHT, ERIK OLIN, CYNTHIA COSTELLO, DAVID HACHEN, AND JOEY SPRAGUE. 1982. "The American class structure." American Sociological Review 47:709–26.

CONSIDERATIONS FOR A SOCIOLOGY
OF THE EMOTIONS*

JOANNE FINKELSTEIN

Discussion of the emotions has been dominated by a desire for their definition, as if, by such a statement, the apparent spontaneity and equivocation of emotions would be made explicable. The pursuit of a definition has channelled understanding of emotions into a reductionist vision in which they are commonly regarded as physiological in character, reflexive in expression and instinctive in origin. For example, one of the early and esteemed studies of the emotions within the "scientific" community defined them as such:

Affect is any subjective experience, that, when examined introspectively, is considered to originate in or belong to the subject's individual organism. It may be felt to be either mental or physical, to be stimulated by sense perception, by a thought, or to be causeless. But in no case is it thought to be a quality of the stimulus, except in relation to the subject.... Emotional expressions are objective phenomena which may qualify instinctive behavior or betray an attitude. They consist of gestures, postures, movements of parts of the face, vocal expressions, modulations of the voice and many visceral changes. (MacCurdy 1925:44)

*From Norman K. Denzin, ed., *Studies in Symbolic Interaction*, vol. 3 (Greenwich, CT: JAI Press, 1980), pp. 111–21. Reprinted with permission of JAI Press, Inc.

James (1894) considered emotions as sensations devoid of rationality; Darwin (1896) saw them as essentially physiological responses; Freud (1894) regarded them as mechanical processes expressing the instincts and, even as early as Descartes (1596–1650), the emotions were defined as individuated experiences arising from the inherent nature of the person. Contemporary analyses of the emotions have moved away from this primacy-based view, suggesting instead that emotions can be cognitive estimations and moral judgments of the individual's place in the world (Sartre 1939), and integral parts of the social fabric which measure levels of civilization as well as patterns of thought and sensibility within individuals (Elias 1939). Mainstream sociology has generally omitted them from study leaving, psychology, and in particular, its cognitive sub-field, to define their nature. In this paper, emotions are placed at the heart of social discourse thereby suggesting that a sociology of emotions is a foundational question which has been overlooked. Part 1 of the paper discusses how emotions have been typically regarded in the reductionist view as descriptions of the individual's interior existence.

From this perspective, the contribution of emotions to the social construction of reality can be seen as much under-rated. To counterbalance this view, Part 2 of the paper argues from a phenomenological basis that emotions are significations of human consciousness and negotiated features of the social arena. The contention is that emotions should no longer be considered solitary, individuated, internal (private) experiences (as earlier theories suggest) but should be seen as emblematic of human consciousness and intrinsic to public decorum. For this latter point, Part 3 of the paper considers the connections between public life and private experience. By taking note of the styles in interaction, manners, etiquette and public demeanor as they have been shaped through the marketplace and the rise of the middle classes, the social management of emotions presents itself as an important part of the dialectic through which social structures and human sensibility are intertwined in the manufacture of reality.

PART 1

For Descartes, the passions were private mental events of an infallible nature. Feelings such as joy, emotions such as love, attitudes such as admiration, virtues such as courage, and traits of character such as shyness, were all passions of the soul, and as such, were aspects of human consciousness and intuition. Their purpose was to preserve the body. Nature instructed the soul to identify what was injurious or beneficial to the body via the sensations of pain and pleasure. These sensations produced passions which, in turn, directed the body toward appropriate action (1952:56, 120, 137, 144). In this way, the passions took on the characteristic of infallibility: they could not be deceived. As Descartes stated:

They are so close and so interior to our soul that it is impossible that they should be felt without their being in reality just as they felt . . . Even if a man is

asleep and dreaming, it is impossible that he should feel sad, or feel moved by any other passion, without it being strictly true that such a passion is in the soul. (1952:15–26)

Descartes saw the passions entering the soul in much the same way as did sensory perceptions (1952:28) and, in a similar way, they were, also, beyond the individual's will or control. While it was possible to shape the outward expression of the emotion by the exertion of will, it was not possible, in a similar fashion, to prevent the arousal of the emotion. Thus, for Descartes the emotions were mental events characterized by their interiority, privacy and infallibility.

Following theorists agreed with Descartes that the emotions were private, involuntary and infallible but, their reasons for doing so were different. Darwin, for instance, saw the emotions as largely the result of physiological and reflexive processes:

. . . only a few expressive movements . . . are learned by each individual. The far greater number of the movements of expression, and all the important ones, are, as we have seen, innate or inherited; and such cannot be said to depend on the will of the individual. (1896)

In accord with Darwin, James viewed the emotions as the products and expressions of altered body-states:

Bodily changes follow directly the perception of the exciting fact, and that our feeling of the same changes as they occur is the emotion. (1898:100)

The sequence that James suggested was, firstly, a perception, secondly, an action, and finally, an emotion. While this sequence differed from that offered by Descartes, these theorists, nonetheless, concurred on the point that emotions are experiences devoid of voluntary, cognitive process; as James stated:

Without the bodily states following on the perception, the latter would be purely cognitive in form, pale, colorless, destitute of emotional warmth. We might then see the bear, and judge it best to run, receive the insult and deem it right to strike, but we could not actually *feel* afraid or angry. (1894:188–205)

James separated the cognitive from the emotions by suggesting that the perception caused the action without the intervention of any "intellectual mind-stuff." The emotion resulted from the physical stimulus: "Every perception *must* lead to some nervous result." James acknowledged the limitations of this schema: it could not explain the more complex ("subtle") emotions derived from aesthetics, morality and intelligence. Nonetheless, he saw its applicability for the more common ("coarse") emotions of grief, fear, rage and love. Thus, James reinforced Descartes' basic ideas that the emotions were private and infallible because of their origins internal to the individual.

Again with Freud, the idea of the emotions being private, interior and infallible states, is further supported. Freud argued that emotion was an immeasurable attribute which increased, decreased, excited and activated the cardio-vascular and motoric body-processes. Emotion was a release of tensions and stimulations generated by the instincts. As such, the expression of emotion evidenced an unconscious or interior urge which could not be appreciably modified. An emotion followed its own law, and in this sense, was infallible. Freud saw that the expression and meaning of the emotion was a matter of symbolic consciousness separate from the emotion itself. In this way, he saw emotions as a common feature of personality development and social expectation. Nonetheless, because emotions stemmed from internal mechanisms which were beyond the control of human will they remained, by their nature, infallible. In following their own laws, emotions make anticipation and foreknowledge of them improbable: they were regarded, then, with some trepidation because they could intrude into consciousness and social activity without prior warning. Through Freud, then, emotions were further emphasized as commodities independent of human consciousness and true only to themselves.

PART 2

Whether they arise from the soul (Descartes) or from physiological mechanisms (Darwin, James, Freud), the emotions appear as independent of human intention or will and beyond conscious or cognitive control. In contrast to this perspective, Sartre (1939) views the emotions as social in origin. However, he nonetheless arrives at a conclusion similar to previous theories, insofar as he claims the emotions are final and infallible in their form and appearance, if not in their substance or nature.

While agreeing with Descartes that all is consciousness, Sartre disavowed the psychophysiological perspective which questioned the existence and nature of the emotions and asked, instead, for their significance. Sartre shares with Descartes an understanding of emotions as final and infallible in character, but, reaches the conclusion from a different argument. He sees that: "an emotion signifies *in its own manner* the whole of the consciousness ... the human reality." (1962:27) Emotion, then, is a final, eschatological understanding of social reality:

(Emotion) has its own essence, its peculiar structures, its law of appearance, its meaning. It cannot possibly come from *outside* the human reality. It is man, on the contrary, who *assumes* his emotion, and emotion is therefore an organized form of human existence. (1962:28)

To study emotions, then, is to examine the social construction of reality because emotions are emblematic of the individual's total consciousness:

an emotion is a specific manner of apprehending the world. (1962:57)

The emotion is a belief and a form of consciousness. Even though the body registers the excitation of the emotion and behaves in accord with it, the meaning of the activity and its differentiation into an emotion is signified by consciousness. Thus, the individual is not forced into actions by interior directives but only precipitated into *apprehending* the world anew.

Emotion is not an accident, it is a mode of our conscious existence, one of the ways in which consciousness understands (in Heidegger's sense of *Verstehen*) its Being-in-the-world. (1962:91)

Sartre reinforces the idea of the finality and infallibility of the emotions when he claims that they are beyond conscious intervention: "One cannot get out of it as one pleases; it fades away of itself, but one cannot put a stop to it." (1962:76) However, he makes that claim on the basis that it is human consciousness which differentiates the world and not the unreflected psycho-physiological impulses suggested by previous theories. Sartre argues that the meaning of the emotion is not inherent in the psychological or physiological excitation of the individual but rather, is realized through the processes of human consciousness—that is, through the individual's apprehension of the world. In this way, Sartre has established the individual's negotiated discourse of the public arena as an integral feature in the study of emotions. Emotions as human consciousness are not always fully articulated or deliberately shaped, but like other thoughts and ideas, they flow in the phenomenological stream of consciousness and emerge in the public realm with an appearance of finality.

As Sartre re-conceptualizes the emotions as displays of evaluated social participation through which the social world is apprehended, he unequivocally separates them from any physiological sources. In this separation from internal origins (in either the soul or the senses) Sartre recognizes the signifi-cance of everyday life as embedded within the emotions. Thus, from Sartre, a study of emotions is turned toward a consideration of their public management. By seeing emotions as apprehensions of the world, Sartre is outlining the process of reality construction. In so doing, attention is focused upon the process through which individuals order the world, and one of the obvious parts of this process is the practice of public decorum. How emotions are expressed and the meaning attributed to them in the social arena is clearly an important part of their study. Indeed, Sartre invokes the necessity for detailed analyses of particular emotions as they occur in the everyday as the means for understanding them (1962:73).

PART 3

The management of emotions within the public sphere is a bridge between the taken-for-granted structures of the social world and the lived-in world of the individual. The interpenetration of social structures and individual experience "is the structure of a man's personality," as Mead suggested:

A person is a personality because he belongs to a community, because he takes over the institutions of that community into his own conduct ... The structure, then, on which the self is built is this response which is common to all, for one has to be a member of a community to be a self. Such responses are abstract attitudes, but they constitute just what we term a man's character. (1934:136–44)

In viewing the emotions as integral parts of the social arena, attention is focused upon how they have been conventionalized and routinized, and thus, incorporated within the taken-for-granted world. Styles of interaction and the manners of public life express shared meanings as well as the individual's apprehensions. Thus, there is a connection between manners or public discourse and individual consciousness or emotions. As Mead describes the intermeshing of self and community, so public decorum and individual emotion are intertwined, thus suggesting that a sociology of emotions can be found embedded within the character of human discourse. So, in this section of the paper, a brief review is undertaken of the development of manners and public behavior as a way of showing how interconnected are the social world and the individual's sensibility, and thus, showing where a sociology of emotions can begin.

When Erasmus of Rotterdam produced *On Civility in Children* (1530), he established a concern for public demeanor that continued to be influential for the next three centuries. His treatise concerned "outward bodily propriety," that is, the conduct of the individual in the public domain. In this treatise, Erasmus was expressing an idea that was gathering force at the time, namely, that the inner worth of the individual is reflected in outward appearance. As the feudal order decayed and new social classes, such as the burgher-bourgeoisie, and the humanists-intellectuals were beginning to coalesce, the public domain was also changing. The old social ties were loosening, thereby allowing individuals from different social origins to encounter one another. The public domain thus came to hold increasingly differentiated perspectives towards honor, piety, civility and social order. It became necessary, then, for individuals to be more sensitive to the differences between themselves and, in turn, this encouraged a heightening of human observation. That is, styles of interaction, outward propriety, physical appearance and manners became points of focus and the means for evaluating others. In this way, the practices of social interaction became beacons to the evaluation of individuals as well as of the social order; as Elias (1939) suggests:

The "civilization" which we are accustomed to regard as a possession that comes to us apparently ready-made, without our asking how we actually came to possess it, is a process or part of a process in which we are ourselves involved. Every particular characteristic that we attribute to it . . . bears witness to a particular structure of human relations, to a particular social structure, and to the corresponding forms of behavior. (Elias 1978:59)

The construction of the social order, then, involved not only structural reorganizations, but, also, interpersonal changes. Where the feudal order had clear divisions in rank and privilege, the new social order increased mobility and obscured class-based rights. Where previously the courts of the aristocracy had been the scene for dispensing privilege and power, the marketplace now became the cornerstone of social location. In the public domain, the new currency was civility and manners, so, with a brilliant appearance and elegant manners, the individual could define a social position irrespective of origins and birthright (Sennett 1974):

People, forced to live with one another in a new way, become more sensitive to the impulses of others. Not abruptly but very gradually the code of behavior becomes stricter and the degree of consideration expected of others becomes greater. The sense of what to do and what not to do in order not to offend or shock others becomes subtler, and in conjunction with the new power relationships the social imperative not to offend others becomes more binding. (Elias 1978:80)

With emphasis being placed upon physical appearance and public behavior as the measure of the individual's value and rights to privilege, it soon followed that doubts arose over the sincerity of expressive, social behavior.

As Diderot (1778:14) argued, spontaneity in behavior resulted in confusion whereas more conventionalized and routinized practices established shared understandings. However, this stylized behavior, which was so important in defining the individual's social status, could be questioned as being a ploy for self-advancement. Thus, manners could become substitutes for sincere feelings and the exhibition of courtesy a facade that concealed the individual's virtues (or lack thereof). As the eighteenth century compendium of social manners states:

Courtesy undoubtedly gets its name from the court and court life. The courts of great lords are a theater where everyone wants to make his fortune. This can only be done by winning the favor of the prince and the most important people of his court. One therefore takes all conceivable pains to make oneself agreeable to them. Nothing does this better than making the other believe that we are ready to serve him to the utmost of our capacity under all conditions. Nevertheless, we are not always in a position to do this, and may not want to, often for good reasons. Courtesy serves as a substitute for all this ... To be sure, it should really be ability and virtue which earn us people's esteem. But how few are the correct judges of these two! And how many fewer hold them worthy of honor! People, all too concerned with externals, are far more moved by what reaches their senses externally, especially when the accompanying circumstances are such as particularly affect their will. (Zedler 1736)

Courtesy, good manners and civility, then, became integral to the evaluation of the individual: they became signposts to the individual's spiritual and internal condition (Callières 1963:97–101). Yet, at the same time, such artiface was seriously doubted, and many came to regard public demeanor as antithetical to understanding both the human condition and the social order (or level of civilization):

I marvel to see how our learned views, false on all points, are wrong on what we take to be civilization. If they were asked what civilization is, most people would answer: softening of manners, urbanity, politeness, and a dissemination of knowledge such that propriety is established in place of laws: all that only presents me with the mask of virtue and not its face, and civilization does nothing for society if it does not give it both the form and the substance of virtue. (Mirabeau:1760)

As the society becomes more complex, not only in its structural, economic-political features but, also, through its interpersonal practices, then the expression of emotions becomes correspondingly complex. With increasing nuances in the general stock of ideas and behaviors, emotions become equivocal and variegated. For instance, complex emotions develop such as anxiety, anomie, boredom and desire, where previously (in the feudal order) there had been piety/wickedness and virtue/evil. The thresholds of emotions are raised and differentiated at the same time that the frontiers of sensibility, reserve and good manners also change (Elias 1978:70). A relationship can be seen, then, between private experience and public demeanor. For example, the appearance of the Dandy in the figure of George Bryan (Beau) Brummell (1778–1840) illustrates this relationship. The achievement of the Dandy was the pedastalization of the self, where the self is tight, controlled and stylish as opposed to "instinctual reactions, passions and enthusiasms." (Moers 1960:18) The outward appearance and brilliance of wit are essential to the Dandy in that they proclaim a superiority of sensibility which in turn, defines the nature of the total individual consciousness: "Opinion pronounced him cold, freezingly cold, and so self-committed as to avoid personal entanglements of any kind." (Moers 1960:36)

There is, then, a mutuality between private experience and public display, and it is this crucial point which directs a sociological study of the emotions to the social sphere. Social structures and the construction of reality are intertwined with individual sensibility (Elias 1978:249). Manners, fashions and styles in behavior are a compendium of everyday life and speak to the character of social actors. Thus, fashion is not simply the "embroidery of history" but "a code, a symbolic vocabulary that offers a subrational but instant and very brilliant illumination of the characters of individuals and even entire periods, especially periods of great turmoil." (Wolfe 1976:197). This is a realization shared by the currently emerging field of semiology (see Barthes

1972:41–50 for a discussion of clothing and fashions through a semiotic perspective).

In a study of emotions, it is important to focus upon their public management because, not only does this reflect how emotions are differentially experienced between peoples, cultures and societies, but it also highlights the significance of particular emotions within the individual's lived-in world. For example, alienation in the modern society takes on a particular character at both the structural and individual levels. The variety of responses reflects how public displays and private experiences are intertwined. For instance, the pursuit of identity mirrored in such experimental situations as new religious cults, studies in extra-sensory and extra-terrestrial communications, the occult and astrology, the proliferation of utopian communities, and new trends in drug use, food preparation and physical exercise (Morgenthau and Person 1978:331) are contemporary responses to an age-old phenomenon. The individual's feelings of distress, anxiety, boredom, alienation, love, sympathy and so on, are manifestations of the personal and private apprehensions the individual has made of the world. As such, emotions are emblematic of the individual's understanding of self, others and the social milieu. Emotions are a lived-in perspective, which in their outward direction, express the moral platforms of individual consciousness: "In everyday life the mood that one establishes can be as basic to the organization of one's joint actions as are one's claims to power, status and social influence." (Denzin 1978)

In a discussion on culture and sensibility, Sontag notes the connection between private experience, public display and socio-cultural forms when she asks the question: "What other response than anguish, followed by anaesthesia and then by wit and the elevating of intelligence over sentiment, is possible as a response to the social disorder and the mass atrocities of our time . . . ?" (1965:301)

It is in this intertwining of individual emotion and social order that an understanding emerges. As Sontag elsewhere argues that sensibilities, ideas, emotions, and tastes are moral responses and intelligent (rational) assessments of the external world, the point of this paper becomes clear:

Most people think of sensibility or taste as the realm of purely subjective preferences, those mysterious attractions, mainly sensual, that have not been brought under the sovereignty of reason. They *allow* that considerations of taste play a part in their reactions to people and to works of art. But this attitude is naive. And even worse. To patronize the faculty of taste is to patronize oneself. For taste governs every free—as opposed to rote—human response. Nothing is more decisive. There is taste in people, visual taste, taste in emotion—and there is taste in acts, taste in morality. Intelligence, as well, is really a kind of taste: taste in ideas. (1964:278)

Emotions, then, penetrate into the heart of the dialectic through which reality is constructed. They are not predominantly psychophysiological mechanisms, nor are they "moments" in a ritual game but, rather, are stances towards the world, emblematic of the individual's apprehension of it and moral position within it: how the individual feels becomes how the individual sees. So, emotions are not accidental disturbances of the individual's psychic life but are, rather, a mode of consciousness which defines the individual's being-in-the-world: they do not emerge from a primordial source but are manufactured aspects of social reality.

REFERENCES

BARTHES, R. 1972. Critical Essays. Evanston: Northwestern University Press.
CALLIÈRES, FRANCOIS DE, 1963. On the Manner of Negotiating with Princes. Trans. A.F. Whyte. 1716. Reprint, South Bend: Notre Dame University Press.

DARWIN, C. [1896] 1965. The Expression of Emotion in Man and Animals. Chicago: University of Chicago Press.

DENZIN, N. 1978. "Moods, Selves and Social Interaction." Paper presented at the 9th World Congress of Sociology, Uppsala, Sweden.

DESCARTES, R. [1630] 1952. Les Passions de l'Ame in Philosophical Writings. Translated and edited by E. Anscombe and P. Geach. London: Routledge and Kegan Paul.

DIDEROT, D. [1778] 1957. The Paradox of Acting. Translated by W.H. Pollack. New York: Hill and Wang.

ELIAS, N. [1939] 1978. The Civilizing Process. Translated by E. Jephcott. New York: Urizen Press.

ERASMUS, D. [1530]. On Civility in Children. Quoted in and translated by N. Elias 1978.

FREUD, S. [1894] 1959. Collected Papers. Edited by J. Riviere. New York: Basic Books.

JAMES, W. 1894. "The physical basis of emotion." The Psychological Review 1:516–529.

_____. 1898. Psychology: The Briefer Course. New York: Charles Scribner's and Sons.

MACCURDY, J.T. 1925. The Psychology of Emotion. New York: Harcourt, Brace and Co.

MEAD, G.H. 1934. Mind, Self and Society. Chicago: University of Chicago Press.

MIRABEAU, V. 1760. Théorie de l'impôt. Trans. G. Weulersse 1910. Paris: P. Geuthner.

MOERS, E. 1960. The Dandy. Lincoln, Neb.: University of Nebraska Press.

MORGENTHAU, H., AND E. PERSON. 1978. "The Roots of Narcissism." Partisan Review 3:337–347.

SARTRE, J.P. [1939] 1962. Sketch towards a Theory of the Emotions. Translated by P. Mairet. London: Methuen.

SENNETT, R. 1974. The Fall of Public Man. New York: Alfred Knopf.

SOLOMON, R.C. 1976. The Passions. New York: Anchor Books.

SONTAG, S. 1965. "One culture and the new sensibility," in Against Interpretation. New York: Dell Publishing, 1969.

_____. 1964. "Notes on camp," in Against Interpretation. New York: Dell Publishing, 1969.

WOLFE, T. 1976. Mauve Gloves and Madmen, Clutter and Vine. New York: Farrar, Straus and Giroux.

ZEDLER, J.H. 1736. Grosses vollstandiges Universal-Lexikon aller Wissenschaften und Kunste. Leipzig and Halle. Translated by Philip Shorr 1932. London: P.S. King and Son Ltd.

FUTURE HISTORY*

CHARLES TILLY

PAST SOCIOLOGY

Sociology began its separate existence as historical speculation. Auguste Comte, coiner of the name for the enterprise that finally stuck, had no mean plans for his cherished sociology. He considered its future construction as the crowning achievement of scientific enlightenment. Just as astronomy displaced astrology and chemistry displaced alchemy, sociology would displace theological speculation about human affairs. Comte spoke of:

the invariant hierarchy, at once historical, dogmatic, scientific, and logical, of the six fundamental sciences, mathematics, astronomy, physics, chemistry, biology, and sociology, of which the first constitutes the sole point of departure and the last the sole essential goal of all positive philosophy.[1]

Dealing with the most complex subject matter and building on all the other sciences, according to Comte, sociology would take its place at the head of the scientific hierarchy, immediately above biology. Thus sociology had two equally gratifying roles to play, as analyst of the process by which humanity progressed from Theological to Metaphysical to Positive forms of thought, and as the very culmination of that process.

Comte's speculation about the stages of human understanding counts as metahistory, the effort to discern a temporal pattern in all human experience. We can usefully distinguish metahistory from history, which examines variation in human action as a function of time and place, and which normally deals with much less than the totality of human action. As history approaches universality, indeed, it becomes metahistory. On the whole professional historians shun metahistory, or treat it as a taste one ought to indulge outside of regular working hours. Metahistory enjoys some of the same disrepute among historians that the search for a single prototype of all human languages receives among linguists. In both cases, workaday practitioners do not so much doubt the possibility of such a discovery

*From Charles Tilly, "Future History," *Theory and Society* 17:5 (September 1988), 703–12. Reprinted by permission of Kluwer Academic Publishers.

in principle as sense its vulnerability to quackery, self-deception, and wasted effort in practice.

If few of Comte's successors publicly proclaimed sociology to be queen of the sciences, many of them continued to practice it chiefly as historical speculation of one variety or another. Herbert Spencer, Oswald Spengler, Pitirim Sorokin, and many lesser souls erected metahistories as the frames for their sociologies.[2] Another brand of historical inquiry, furthermore, appeared at the edge of sociology, among the followers of Karl Marx and Max Weber; both schools pursued ambitious inquiries into the actual unfolding of social processes in time and space, making arguments and achieving results that professional historians would recognize, however grudgingly, as impinging on their own enterprise.

Nevertheless, from the time of Durkheim onward, the main body of professional sociologists turned away from grand historical schemes, and from history itself. Sociology—especially American sociology—became the systematic study of the present. Sociologists became specialists in structures and processes, rather than times and places, on the presumption that currently observable uniformities in structures and processes transcend the limits of time and place.

Less so than economists but more so than political scientists, anthropologists, or geographers, sociologists built a discipline in which time and place served merely as convenient markers, not as systematic objects of analysis or ever-present bases of variation. By the time of a semi-official American review of the field in 1959, the editors could describe historical sociology as an "important subject," but omit it from their survey "because of limitations of space."[3] They reached their decision despite the fact that one of the editors, Robert Merton, was making distinguished contributions to the historical study of science. The authors of articles on sociological subjects that afore-

said limitations of space did allow into the volume, furthermore, rarely mentioned historical problems and material, doing so for the most part when sketching the intellectual background to the present-day, presumably more scientific, enterprise. From the 1959 publication, one could reasonably have concluded that, with the exception of an occasional oddity such as Merton's work, sociology and history had almost nothing to do with each other.

The history and sociology of that time did, in fact, dally now and then. In the 1950s, not only Merton, but also such scholars as Reinhard Bendix, George Homans and Barrington Moore, Jr., were pursuing historical research.[4] Within his metahistorical frame, Pitirim Sorokin was continuing his more specific historical inquiries into altruism.[5] Scholars who maintained self-conscious contact with European social thought commonly wrote in a historical idiom. Nevertheless, these historically oriented sociologists constituted a small remnant in a largely present-oriented discipline.

What is more, twentieth-century sociologists commonly adopted a dismissive definition of their relationship to historians. As Charles Ellwood described the division of labor in a widely read text first published in 1910:

History is a concrete, descriptive science of society which attempts to construct a picture of the social past. Sociology, however, is an abstract, theoretical science of society concerned with the laws and principles which govern social organization and social change. In one sense, sociology is narrower than history inasmuch as it is an abstract science, and in another sense it is wider than history because it concerns itself not only with the social past but also with the social present. The facts of contemporary social life are indeed even more important to the sociologist than the facts of history, although it is impossible to construct a theory of social evolution without taking into full account all the facts available in human history, and for this reason we must consider history one of the very important methods of sociology. Upon its evolutionary or dynamic side sociology may be considered a sort of philosophy of history; at least it attempts to give a scientific theory which will explain the social changes which history describes concretely.[6]

Answering in 1964 the question "What is Sociology?", Alex Inkeles offered a similar contrast: "The historian prides himself on the explicitness, the concreteness of detail which characterizes his discipline. The sociologist is more likely to abstract from concrete reality, to categorize and generalize, to be interested in what is true not only of a particular people's history but of the histories of many different peoples."[7] For some reason sociologists did not recognize the condescension in that distinction between those who gather the facts and those who explain them, those who describe and those who analyze, those who grub and those who pluck, those who scrub and those who polish.

HISTORY REDIVIVUS

In any case, the years since Inkeles's summary have seen a great revival of historical thinking and historical research in sociology. Perhaps "revival" is the wrong word, for two reasons: First, the sort of historical work sociologists have undertaken over the past quarter-century has few precedents in the speculative schemata of the nineteenth century. Second, the properly historical writing of founding fathers Marx and Weber had few repercussions inside academic sociology, especially its American variant, until the 1960s. Within standard sociology, there was little history to revive. To a large degree, the expansion of historical work among sociologists marked a new departure.

Why did the new growth occur? I have no intention of tracing the intellectual history of a strongly historical sociology, or even of proposing an explanation of its expansion. As an active participant in that expansion, I hope

someone else will do both. Here, in any case, is the most salient fact: Out of a sustained critique of the ideas of "development" and "modernization" that dominated sociological analyses of large-scale change for two decades after World War II grew an effort to historicize such analyses—to extend backward the period over which one analyzed great transformations, to seek past analogs of present changes, to try out general ideas concerning the consequences of sweeping processes on well-documented historical experiences of similar processes. At the same time a minority of historians, likewise critical of the models of large-scale change that prevailed in their own discipline, were turning to the social sciences, including sociology, for alternative ways of analyzing the past.[8]

The turn to history could have proceeded at any of four levels, metahistorical, world-systemic, macrohistorical, or microhistorical:

metahistorical: attempting to identify temporal patterns in all human experience
world-systemic: tracing the succession of world-systems, the largest connected sets of human interaction
macrohistorical: examining large-scale structures and processes within world-systems
microhistorical: studying the experiences of individuals and well-defined groups within the limits set by large-scale structures and processes

Some of sociology's historical revival has taken place at each of the levels. Anthony Giddens and Michael Mann have, for example, started to fashion new metahistories of power and social change.[9] Although most of their analyses have focused on change and variation within what they conceive of as the contemporary capitalist world-system, Immanuel Wallerstein and his collaborators have at least occasionally tried to chart the movement from one world-system to another. Numerous students of family structure, communities, inequality, and population processes have pursued microhistory. Yet the bulk of sociology's new historical effort has gone into macrohistory, the examination of large-scale structures and processes within world-systems. Thus we have sustained sociological treatments of farmers' movements in the United States, of the European fertility decline, of the emergence of different forms of the welfare state.

Comparisons among populations identified by national states have occupied a large (to my mind, disproportionate) share of sociologists' historical energy; analyses of the so-called transition from feudalism to capitalism have, for example, repeatedly compared entities labeled France, England, Prussia, and so on. National states have had a large weight in western history; they occupy an important place in my own historical work. But exclusive concentration on national states fosters a series of illusions: that behind the state stands a coherent society; that a single unit such as Prussia had an integrity making it possible to assign the unit a continuous history over many centuries, using schemes involving origins, stages, or developmental paths; that the important states, and therefore the ones worthy of sustained sociological analysis, were those that survived into the twentieth century; that comparison of the experiences of the survivor states will yield or test comprehensive explanations of the capitalism's development. As soon as historical analysts start taking economic regions, cities, mercantile networks, churches, linguistic blocs, and other crucial social groupings into serious account, the illusions begin to fade, and the possibility of relating the histories of national states to these other histories begins to open up.

Whether conducted at the national scale or not, most of this work partakes of historicism, asserting that how things happen depends strongly on when and where they happen. Historicism permits analysts to claim that late industrializers followed different paths than early industrializers, that the presence of great landlords in a region at one point in time affected the subsequent possibility of democratic politics in that region, that the state of the economy during a given birth cohort's childhood shapes its members' orientation toward childbearing, and so on. Historicism counters the old sociological faith in the generality of relationships inferred from the proper systematic analysis of contemporary social life. The various intellectual enterprises that observers group together as "historical sociology" lean implicitly toward historicism.

Not that they have great intellectual unity. The trouble with "historical sociology" as the name of a specialty is that it groups inquiries by their methods and materials rather than by the ideas and phenomena with which they deal. The term parallels such labels as "survey sociology" and "qualitative sociology"—perhaps realities as coalitions vis à vis the rest of the field, but treacherous bases for common intellectual endeavors. Historical sociology, as actually practiced, includes a variety of investigations at different edges of sociology: investigations of political processes, family structure, community organization, inequality, ideological orientations, scientific activity, economic transformation, and much more. On the whole, the ideas guiding such investigations bind the investigators to others who are studying similar phenomena much more strongly than to fellow sociologists who likewise work chiefly on the past rather than the present. Nevertheless, the disparate enterprises called historical sociology have greatly gained in popularity over the last two decades, especially in the United States.

In 1959, cutting through a great deal of criticism and counter-criticism, Kingsley Davis declared that all sociologists were really functionalists of one sort or another; "In a way it is appropriate to speak of functional analysis as something *within* anthropology," he wrote, "because there are branches of that field that have totally different subject-matters. A similar statement with respect to *social* anthropology or sociology, however, is tautological, for the reason that structural-functional analysis *is* sociological analysis."[10]

What should a thirtieth-anniversary version of Davis's presidential address say? Are we all now really historicists? Do we all now claim that where and when social changes occur strongly influence how they occur? No: In fact, plenty of sociology is still unclear about its time and place references, and unprepared to take time and place seriously. Although I have no survey to prove it, I would say that most sociologists in the United States and elsewhere still cling to the pursuit of generalities that transcend time and space, even large blocks of time and space such as world-systems. Historical sociology still represents a minority mood among sociologists.

FEARS AND HOPES

What future has historical work in sociology? Let me distinguish between my fearful predictions and my cherished hopes. Fearfully, I predict the institutionalization of historical sociology: fixing of a labeled specialty in sections of learned societies, journals, courses, a share of the job market. I fear these likely outcomes for two reasons: first, because the "field" lacks intellectual unity and, by its very nature, will forever lack it; second, because institutionalization may well impede the spread of historical thinking to other parts of sociology. The other parts need that thinking badly.

My cherished hopes run in a different direction. In the short run, I would be delighted if more historical sociologists would broaden their scope from national comparisons to (1) other macrohistorical investigations, taking regions, markets, modes of production, connections among capitalists, and other large structures as their units of analysis, (2) world-systemic analyses, including new attempts to examine the actual historical circumstances under which European capitalism came to dominate most of the world's economics, and (3) microhistorical studies of structures and processes that sociologists now examine chiefly in the contemporary world.

In the long run, I hope for a miracle elixir, one that will dissolve the specialty of historical sociology, and let its premises—especially its historicism—permeate all of sociology. Thus not only students of capitalism and of family change, but also demographers and survey analysts, would find themselves examining how the relation among their favored variables altered as a function of region and historical era. The result would be a historically grounded sociology of far greater intellectual power than its current incarnation.

A greatly broadened historical sociology can make two major contributions to the discipline. First, it can historicize sociological analyses: anchor them in time and place. If we now have established any important nontautological generalizations that hold across all historical eras, they have not come to my attention. I do not deny in principle that any such generalizations can exist, but insist that we are better off for the time being trying to ground all generalizations historically: specifying their time and place limits, and attaching them to other empirical generalizations that reliably characterize social life within those time and place limits.

Second, a greatly broadened historical sociology can also draw in important problems that are prominent in historical analysis and in lived history, but somehow remain neglected in sociology. Most notably, it can force sociologists to examine how the residues of action at a given time constrain subsequent action. Arthur Stinchcombe provided an important example of that sort of historicizing analysis in his discussion of the way that craft organizations persisted in some industries into the era of mass production.[11] Allan Pred, a sociologically inclined geographer, has similarly shown how the existing connections among cities in eighteenth-century North America constrained the subsequent growth of the North American urban system.[12] In a phrase faintly echoing Karl Marx, Pred has recently preached that "People do not produce history and places under conditions of their own choosing, but in the context of already existing, directly encountered social and spatial structures."[13]

The linking idea is simple and powerful: past social relations and their residues—material, ideological, and otherwise—constrain present social relations, and consequently their residues as well. Once an employer has established ties with a particular source of labor, those ties affect his subsequent recruitment of labor, and may well reproduce themselves. Once developers have laid down a certain urban structure, that structure defines the opportunities for further development. Once people adopt a certain national language, that language circumscribes the other people with whom they can easily communicate. Such processes produce connectedness within time and space that goes beyond simple temporal and spatial autocorrelation; every existing structure stands in the place of many theoretically possible alternative structures, and its very existence affects the probabilities that the alternatives will ever come into being. In short, social processes are path-dependent. That is why history matters.

Consider some examples. The social organization of migration affects the subsequent welfare of migrants and their descendants, among other reasons because some forms of migration build means of capital accumulation within families and ethnic groups, while others individualize whatever accumulation occurs. The proletarianization of one genera-

tion of workers strongly affects the opportunities of the next generation of workers to become capitalists, artisans, or peasants. The efforts of great powers to build up the military capacities of friendly Third World states shape the likelihoods that the national armed forces will take over those states. The creation of collective-action repertoires through struggles between powerholders and their challengers limits the possibilities of action for all parties in the next round of struggle. Intergroup conflicts over jobs, land, or political power create new social actors, whose presence then alters the character and outcome of conflict. In all these processes, time and place matter fundamentally; when and where they occur affects how they occur. They therefore fall into the domain of history.

Of course, some sociologists are addressing these topics, and others like them; the historical revival has made a healthy difference. But we need more, more, more—enough more to refashion sociology as a whole so that it automatically takes time and place seriously, and seriously engages the challenge of placing its regularities firmly within historical eras. If these things happen, sociology will have realized its potential as history of the present.

At that point, as Philip Abrams long since prescribed, the distinction between history and sociology will have disappeared. "Historical sociology is not," wrote Abrams,

a matter of imposing grand schemes of evolutionary development on the relationship of the past to the present. Nor is it merely a matter of recognising the historical background to the present. It is the attempt to understand the relationship of personal activity and experience on the one hand and social organisation on the other as something that is continuously constructed in time.[14]

Abrams barred the road to Comte, and opened it to Marx and Weber. Ultimately, however, the road back to anywhere concerned him less than the road forward: Where should the historical enterprise within sociology go? It should go on to become the foundation of all sociology.

NOTES

1. Auguste Comte, *Discours sur l'esprit positif* (Paris: Union Générale d'Editions, 1963), 133.

2. Herbert Spencer, *The Principles of Sociology* (London: Appleton, 1897; 2 vols.); Oswald Spengler, *The Decline of the West* (New York: Knopf, 1926–28; 2 vols.); Pitirim A. Sorokin, *Social and Cultural Dynamics* (New York: Bedminster, 1962; 4 vols.)

3. Robert K. Merton, Leonard Broom, and Leonard S. Cottrell, Jr., editors, *Sociology Today: Problems and Prospects* (New York: Basic, 1959), vi.

4. Reinhard Bendix, *Work and Authority in Industry* (New York: Wiley, 1956); George C. Homans, *Sentiments and Activities* (New York: Free Press, 1962); Barrington Moore, Jr., *Social Origins of Dictatorship and Democracy* (Boston: Beacon, 1966).

5. Pitirim A. Sorokin, *Altruistic Love: A Study of American "Good Neighbors" and Christian Saints"* (Boston: Beacon, 1950).

6. Charles A. Ellwood, *Social Problems and Sociology* (New York: American Book Company, 1935), 18.

7. Alex Inkeles, *What is Sociology?* (Englewood Cliffs: Prentice Hall, 1964), 21.

8. Olivier Zunz, editor, *Reliving the Past* (Chapel Hill: University of North Carolina Press, 1985).

9. Anthony Giddens, *The Nation-State and Violence* (Berkeley: University of California Press, 1985); Michael Mann, *The Sources of Social Power I. A History of Power from the Beginning to A.D. 1760* (Cambridge: Cambridge University Press, 1986).

10. Kingsley Davis, "The Myth of Functional Analysis in Sociology and Anthropology," *American Sociological Review* 24 (1959), 771.

11. Arthur L. Stinchcombe, "Social Structure and Organizations," in James G. March, editor, *Handbook of Organizations* (Chicago: Rand McNally, 1965).

12. Allan Pred, *Urban Growth and the Circulation of Information: The United States System of Cities, 1790–1840* (Cambridge: Harvard University Press, 1973).

13. Allan Pred, "Interpenetrating Processes: Human Agency and the Becoming of Regional Spatial and Social Structures," *Papers of the Regional Science Association* 57 (1985), 7–17. (Pred 1985:8).

14. Philip Abrams, *Historical Sociology* (Ithaca: Cornell University Press, 1982).

POSTMODERN SOCIAL THEORY*

NORMAN K. DENZIN

My intentions are to review the major themes and problematics that have emerged over the last decade in postmodern social theory (see Foster 1983a; Bernstein 1985; Jameson 1983, 1984a; Huyssen 1984; Jencks 1985; Newman 1985). I will examine the works of two leading French postmodern theorists, Lyotard (1971, 1974, 1984) and Baudrillard (1968, 1970, 1972, 1975, 1981, 1983a, 1983b, 1983c) against the backdrop of the poststructuralist and Critical Theory formulations of Barthes, Lacan, Althusser, Levi-Strauss, Derrida and Habermas. I hope to relate American social theory more closely to postmodern formulations. At the same time it is my desire to make social theory more alive to the current crises that grip the present world economic and cultural structures (Denzin 1986). Because Lyotard and Baudrillard offer explicit and implicit critiques of the Frankfurt School and Habermas, it will be necessary to briefly speak to Habermas's theory of communicative ac-

*From Norman K. Denzin, "Postmodern Social Theory," *Sociological Theory* 4:2 (Fall 1986), 194–204. Reprinted with permission of the American Sociological Association and the author.

tion (1975, 1983) as it applies to the legitimation crisis in post-capitalist societies.

I will take up in order the following topics: (1) the current state of American social theory; (2) a brief discussion of the defining characteristics of postmodern theory; (3) an analysis of the major themes in Baudrillard and Lyotard's works; (4) a discussion of the Habermas critique of postmodernism and postmodern theory; (5) a set of proposals concerning the future directions social theory and empirical research might take, in light of the postmodern critique.

THE CURRENT STATE OF AMERICAN SOCIAL THEORY

Recent dialogue and debate within American social theory have centered mainly on the works of Collins, Alexander, Giddens and Habermas. If there has been a dialogue in contemporary theory it has been among varying proponents of conflict theory (Collins, Dahrendorf, Coser), microstructuralism (Blau, Giddens), exchange theory (Homans, Blau, Emerson), interactionism

(Blumer, Turner, Stryker, McCall and Simmons), ethnomethodology (Garfinkel, Cicourel), functionalism and neo- or post-functionalism (Parsons, Merton, Alexander, Luhmann, Münch; see Turner, 1986). In the background have been powerful Marx-Weber (Antonio and Glassman 1985; Wiley 1986b) debates as well as world-systems (Wallerstein 1980), historical-comparative (Skocpol 1978) and feminist (Benjamin 1981; Chodorow 1978; Clough 1987; Dinnerstein 1976) currents of theorizing (see also Hall 1980).

Some claim that a new age of theorizing is beginning (Hayes 1985). Others argue that sociology is tired and some contend that American sociology is in an interregnum (Wiley 1985) and has been in one since the late 1960's. New efforts at grand, or synthetic theorizing (Alexander, Habermas, Giddens) have not been met with universal acclaim (see Hayes 1985; Livesay 1985; Lukes 1985).

It is clear that large portions of the new theory work in American sociology share the following commitments: (1) a desire to conceptualize societies as totalities; (2) an attempt to wed the micro and the macro levels of experience; (3) an effort to form sociology into a science of society; (4) a desire to speak to the conflict and crisis that appear in post-or-late-capitalist societies. At the same time there is an undertheorizing of language, the human subject, the mass media, commodity relations in the consumer society, and the legitimation crisis surrounding science, knowledge and power in the modern world. These topics are the major problematics in postmodern social theory.

DEFINING POSTMODERN

I define postmodernism as both a form of theorizing about societies and a period in social thought. Postmodern social theory is characterized by (1) a departure from theorizing in terms of grand systems which conceptualize the social as a totality; (2) an intense preoccupation with the crises of legitimation and experience that characterize the modern computerized, media dominated world cultural system; (3) a move in theorizing that goes beyond the phenomenological, structural, poststructural and critical theory formulations of Barthes, Derrida, Levi-Strauss, Sartre, Merleau-Ponty, Foucault, Adorno, Horkheimer, Marcuse, Lukács, and Weber; (4) a radical conceptualization of language, linguistic philosophy and pragmatism (Peirce); (5) a critique of scientific knowledge and realism in the late-capitalism era; (6) a critique of the subject in social theory; (7) a return to the commodity as a central theoretical problematic; (8) a concern for the collapse of meta-narratives (science, religion, art) in everyday life; (9) a call for new images of the social, society, language and the human subject; (10) a profound distrust of reason and science as forces which will produce a utopian society based on consensus, rational communicative action, and human freedom (see Lyotard 1984, pp. 64–67, 79–82; Baudrillard 1983c, p. 133).

Postmodern theory has emerged within the last decade. The term has been primarily used to describe changes and developments in the fields of architecture and art. It was first used in the United States to describe changes in modernist dance and architecture in 1949, and again in 1974, and more recently in 1985 (Jencks 1985). In the 1970's postmodernism was seen as migrating to Europe in the works of Kristeva, Lyotard, Baudrillard, Habermas, Foucault and poststructuralism more generally (Huyssen 1984). The time period for the beginning of postmodernism in social theory would be the late 1960's and the early to middle 1970's, although C. Wright Mills used the term in 1959 (Mills 1959, p. 166).

Post modernist theorists suggest that culture can be conceptualized as a set of myths produced within a communication system.

The texts of culture can no longer be read as "realist" extensions of actual lived experiences. Rather culture is a semiotic, linguistic production. The meanings of culture must be deconstructed, taken apart and traced back to the productional activities of readers, audiences, and authors. This position produces a crisis, often termed "the death of the subject" (Foster 1983b, pp. x–xi). It signals the loss of master narratives in Western culture (i.e., the belief in a human subject immune to the structural forces of a larger society). At the same time it turns interest in the direction of the modern consumer society in which the commodity has become the focal object of experience (Baudrillard 1970, 1975).

Since Foucault, correspondence theories of truth have been seriously challenged. Simplistic causal models which argue for structural dominations that flow from the cultural, social, historical, political, or symbolic realms are now questioned. That is, domination and reflection theories (i.e. the economic determines the cultural, or the cultural reflects the social) have been displaced in favor of articulation, archaeological and genealogical studies of contemporary and historical structures of power (see Grossberg 1985, p. 146).

BAUDRILLARD

Baudrillard's texts embody, in varying degrees, each of the features of postmodern theory as sketched above. Four key terms, or processes organize his analysis: (1) the simulacrum; (2) the mass media, (3) the sign, and (4) communication. I will take these up in order.

Simulacrum

A basic thesis structures Baudrillard's interpretation of the postmodern situation. It is contained in the term *simulacrum* which means an image, the semblance of an image, make-believe, or that which "conceals" the truth or the real (Baudrillard 1981, pp. 32–33). He opens his book (*Simulations* 1983a, p. 1) with the following elliptical statement: "The simulacrum is never that which conceals the truth—it is the truth which conceals that there is none. The simulacrum is true." With Barthes and Deleuze, Baudrillard asserts that the modern situation was defined by the power of the simulacrum; that is by the power of images and signs which have come to stand for the objects (commodities) that make up the everyday lifeworld of late-capitalism.

He elaborates this position as follows. Four historical orders of appearance have characterized Western culture: (1) the realistic order of Feudalism, in which symbols correspond to external reality, (2) the "Counterfeit" period, from the Renaissance to the industrial revolution, (3) the order of "Production," which was the dominant scheme of the industrial era, and (4) the order of "Simulation," which is the reigning scheme in the current phase (Baudrillard 1983a, p. 83). These four historical orders of appearance correspond to successive phases of the image of the real: (1) the image is a reflection of basic reality, as when a map depicts a geo-political territory; (2) the image perverts a basic reality, e.g. a religious icon subverts or trivializes religious dogma; (3) the image masks the *absence* of a basic reality as in magic or sorcery; (4) the image bears no relation to any reality, e.g. Disneyland (Baudrillard 1983a, p. 11).

As indicated, Baudrillard asserts the centrality of four historical moments: (1) pre-Renaissance, i.e., the feudal order where there was little social mobility. In this order there is a total clarity of signs, for each sign refers to an assigned social position or status; (2) the Renaissance in which signs are no longer obligated to refer to a fixed social stratification system. In this moment the arbitrary sign appears. It no longer links two person in an unchanging relationship. "The signifier starts referring back to the disenchanted universe of the signified, common denominator of the real world toward which no one has any obligation" (Baudrillard 1983a, p. 85).

At the same time Baudrillard argues there is a movement into a democratic political ideology in which there is a transference of values and signs of prestige from one class to another. This makes it possible for one class to imitate, or simulate the value and prestige of another class. There is thus a proliferation of signs of value and prestige (fashion). Signs and images become *counterfeit;* that is they now extend to materials, and social statuses which are no longer clearly bounded by a fixed stratification system. The modern sign is thus born in the Renaissance. It simulates the real world, and produces a nostalgia for the past. The sign no longer has a fixed, referential relationship to a fixed, stable social world of social objects and persons.

If the Renaissance creates the false (i.e. baroque theatrical machinery, stucco interiors) (3) the industrial revolution ushers in a period where signs no longer have to be counterfeited. Now they can be mass produced with machines. The problem of their origin, uniqueness, or authenticity is no longer relevant. Following Walter Benjamin (1968), Baudrillard argues that the work of art (and the sign) in the age of technical reproduction is one in which there is no longer any problem concerning the relationship between a sign and its object. The Counterfeit period is over. We are in the age of mass production. Objects become undifferentiated simulacra (imitations, reproductions) of one another. At the same time the men and women who produce these objects also become simulacra. This is the essence of the modern division of labor according to Baudrillard (see 1983a, p. 97; 1975, p. 30).

The industrial age produces the mirror of production, in which men are induced to believe that their labor (use value) defines their worth (exchange value). The assumption that use value (concrete value behind exchange value) structures economic production emerges in the early capitalist period. This moment is organized in terms of an ideology which links man as a producer to man as moral being. The myth or mirror of production thus underlies Marxism's analysis of capitalism (Baudrillard 1975, p. 31) for it convinces men that they are alienated because they sell their labor power. Marxism thus becomes ideological at the very moment when it should provide a radical critique of the political economy it has set out to analyze.

Marxism, like capitalism, appeals to a model of simulation which controls the industrial period; that is it codes human experience in terms of use and exchange value without realizing that these terms have come to rule the entire capitalist system in a symbolic fashion (see below). What Marxism misses is that capitalism, in the industrial age, has shifted from a model of the real sign to an age in which the image masks the absence of a basic reality. (4) In the age of reproduction we are in the third post-feudal order of simulacra where the entire order of production is governed by operational simulation. This is the postmodern age. There is no longer a basic reality to which objects and their signs refer. This is the age of the *hyperreal.* Disneyland is a perfect model of how each of the proceeding orders of the image and appearance are entangled. There are pirates, the frontier, a future world, a world of castles, a world controlled by robots, a make-believe world in which all values are exalted, simulated and presented to the viewer (Baudrillard 1983a, pp. 25–26).

The third-order of the simulacrum contains the postmodern experience. It constitutes a form of social organization in which the polity, the economy, culture and the mass media endlessly reproduce one another in a proliferation of signs and codes. The industrial order is replaced by a computerized, cybernetic model. A logic of deterrence operates in this historical moment, as does a discourse of crisis. The only weapon of power has become the attempt to inject realness and referentiality into the world of the mass media. Everywhere there are attempts to convince us that the social is real; the economy is in a grave situation, and solid political leadership will take us out of this crisis. Hyperreality and simulation thus become deterrents in the system; that is "the very definition of the real becomes: *that of which it is possible to give an equivalent reproduction*" (Baudrillard 1983a, p. 146, italics in original). We live, Baudrillard argues, in a time in which the political, social, historical and economic have incorporated the "simulatory dimension of hyperrealism" (Baudrillard 1983a, p. 147).

The Mass Media

The media is the hyperreal agency personified. It stages and reproduces the deterrence drama. It brings alive the contradictions and oppositions between peace and war, terror and security, inflation and economic stability, employment and unemployment, hold-ups, hijacks and bombings (Chang 1986; Baudrillard 1983a, p. 41). The media provides the public with the illusion of reality and actuality. The media overproduces information. It fabricates communication, when non-communication is its goal (Baudrillard, 1981, p. 169). The media has created information consumers. Information has become the central commodity of the current age. The media short circuits events which occur in the realm of the political and the economic by broadcasting them and creating the illusion of an abstract, universal public opinion. The media actualizes the simulation models of the third-order of the simulacra (Baudrillard 1981, p. 179). It creates and circulates a form of universalized opinion that excludes communication between interlocutors. What is communicated is a univocal voice which socially controls public opinion.

The Sign

The internal structure of the sign operates in terms of a political economy. The signifier and signified (as the two sides of the sign), correspond to the two sides of a commodity (exchange value and use value). Just as exchange value corresponds to use value, or the commodity form and the object form, the systems of signifier and signified designate two codes: sign value and symbolic exchange.

Ideology no longer stands outside everyday life as an infrastructural relation between productions of signs (culture) and contradictions in the base. *Ideology has invaded the very sign that signifies the commodity objects that capitalism produces.* Ideology is "actually *that very form* that traverses both the production of signs and material production—or rather, it is the logical bifurcation of this form into two terms . . ." (1981, p. 144). Exchange value (EV) and use value (UV) thus lie on opposite sides of the signifier (Sr) and the signified (Sd). "*The logic of the commodity is the internal logic of the sign.*" ([Baudrillard, 1981: 144, italics in original].

Several important conclusions flow from this analysis of the sign. First, the structure of the sign is the structure of the commodity. Hence the two have become inseparable— sign and commodity, T.V. and the television set, etc. Second, the commodity that dominates in the postmodern world is information. Third, what is consumed is not objects, or commodities per se, but signs of these objects. The commodity is produced as a sign of itself, as sign value. Signs are produced as commodities (Baudrillard 1975, p. 147). The world that the sign invokes is nothing but a shadow, or hyperreal simulation of the real, which has now been mass produced. Fourth, a social logic now governs the production and consumption of objects. This logic turns on four conceptions of value: (a) use value, (b) exchange value, (c) sign value, (d) symbolic exchange. Objects no longer have an empirical status in the world, except as they are captured within a sign. The pure object is a myth (Baudrillard 1981, p. 63).

Objects now circulate through a political economy of signs in which symbolic exchange value (the prestige of an object as signaled by its sign value) replaces use value (which has become an alibi for the commodity), while pure exchange is now governed by the rules of decorum, status and prestige. The logic of prestige and status thus controls the commodities which are consumed. All everyday objects must now submit to the duality of a code which simultaneously confers prestige and effort (symbolic exchange and use value). What is critical is that the symbolic has invaded the commodity and its signs and this has occurred through the realm of the ideological which has now taken control over the political economy of signs. The object in the new political economy of postmodernism is indissoluably both commodity and sign (Baudrillard 1981, p. 148). In this analysis Baudrillard radicalizes the traditional Marxist critique of the political economy and drives the semiotics of experience directly into the sign structures which surround the commodities that are produced and consumed in the public and private spheres of everyday life.

Communication

Communicative understanding is now transformed into a fascination with the "spectacle"; with the latest ecological, geo-political, monetary, or personal crisis that is presented to the silent majority on the television screen (Baudrillard 1983b). The hyperreal of the media neutralizes the social, leaving the meaning of events to be determined by media experts who interpret the hyperreal as real for the public.

The media thus creates the illusion of audience or viewer participation in the events of the day. A fantasy of communication is created (Chang 1986, p. 175). The audience participates in an anti-drama which is created for them by the media. The hyperreal that is created is thus given a structure of meaning that makes it more real than the real that it has replaced. Reality is erased, as in Disneyland and elsewhere.

The mass emerges out of the mass media as an undifferentiated entity whose representation is no longer possible (Baudrillard 1983b, p. 22). The mass is that which is surveyed and tested by sociologists. Yet it remains mute and silent, its attitudes and feelings to be represented back to it through public opinion polls. The masses lack a historical mission. They engulf mass culture, swallow up its fashions, and contribute to a system of social stratification which bases itself on the prestige and status symbolism of the commodities the economy makes available.

All of this is structured by a collapse of the division between the public and private in everyday life. A new historic scene has emerged in which the interiority of private space (the home) has been invaded by the media. The domestic universe has become a public space in which the news of the world plays out its drama on the television set. Individuals are no longer actors in their homes, but controllers of information terminals which connect them to the entire world system. They have become receivers of information. The home has become the setting for the simulation of the real. Here work, leisure, sexuality, family, education, banking, consumption and social relations are all played out. Here we project ourselves into fantasy worlds (Baudrillard 1983c).

This situation produces an obscenity of experience wherein the most private of events become fodder for the media. There are no longer any secrets concerning the personal, sacred realms of daily existence. Information on the person is now contained with information banks, held by hospitals, the Social Security System, the workplace, the Internal Revenue System, the bank, and the loan agencies. The media exploits ruptures in the realm of the private through its endless circulation of information and news. The old divisions between public and private have disappeared.

Interpretations

As Chang (1986, p. 161) and others have observed, Baudrillard's work is a reaction to the inadequacy of the Marxist and semiotic analysis of the political economy of the present postcapitalist situation. His work shows how "revolutionary ideologies can end by reaffirming what they intend to subvert" (Chang 1986, p. 161). Marxism remains within the political economy of production and exchange. Semiotics has revealed a hesitance to locate the signifier and the signified in the logic of the political economy of signs that merges with the postmodern economic situation. Baudrillard's insight has been to merge these two concerns, as evidenced in his critique of the political economy of the sign. It is clear that it will no longer be possible to perform a sociological and Marxist or Weberian analysis of the economy without a model which merges the economic with the linguistic.

Baudrillard's work can be read as an elaboration of the early Frankfurt School's argument that the cultural has produced a one-dimensionality of experience. But his interpretation thickens this position and brings it up to date in the modern computerized age. At the same time his work challenges the latest efforts of Habermas to build an utopian theory of rational, communicative action. Baudrillard's work suggests that we have transcended that historical moment in which the real, the rational and the symbolic can unproblematically connect. His work, grounded

as it is in a descriptive analysis of the postmodern experience (Chang 1986), suggests that the ecstasy of communication, far from being competent and rational, has produced its own circular emptiness, which is solitary and narcissistic (Baudrillard 1983c, p. 132). Intersubjectively shared meanings, grounded in rationality and reason, have slipped away as a dominant motif of the postmodern period. We are in an age where there is a forced exteriority of interiority (Baudrillard 1983c, p. 132). We are trapped in a historical moment where the instantaniety of things gives rise to feelings of no defense and no retreat. We are at the end of intimacy and private interiority. We have been overexposed to the world at large. The image Baudrillard (1983c, p. 133) leaves us with is the following. The postmodern individual

can no longer produce the limits of his own being, can no longer play nor stage himself, can no longer produce himself as a mirror. He is now only a pure screen, a switching center for all the networks of influence.

LYOTARD

Lyotard's most recent work (1984) may be read as a polemic against Habermas's (1971a, 1971b, 1975, 1981) and Luhmann's (1969) conception of the legitimation crisis in postindustrial societies and the nature of scientific knowledge in those societies. The vision of a noise-free, fully communicative social order, based on rationality and consensus is rejected by Lyotard. If Habermas and Luhmann locate the legitimation crisis in the technical realm of the political economy, which then displaces itself in the sphere of the cultural and the everyday, Lyotard locates the crisis in the production and distribution of scientific knowledge in the modern computerized society. Hence Lyotard's critique centers on knowledge and its production, while Habermas's is focused on the state and its need for legitimation. Lyotard attempts to expose a flaw in the post modern system which, if correct, cuts to the core of the legitimation crisis Habermas attempts to repair through his concept of rational communicative action. Hence, while concurring with Habermas on the presence of a crisis in contemporary social life, Lyotard contends that the crisis is one of representation, science and knowledge and not communication.

The following problematics structure Lyotard's argument: (1) Knowledge, paralogy and legitimation in postmodern societies; (2) language games and postmodern science; (3) the nature of the social bond under postmodernism; (4) a critique of Habermas and (5) a consideration of what postmodernism is.

Knowledge and Legitimation in Postmodern Societies

Postmodernism is a different moment in the socioeconomic organization of society. Capitalism has moved to a third stage, consumerism, having surpassed prior stages where market and monopoly capitalism dominated. This third stage has produced a media society, a society of the spectacle, a bureaucratic society controlled by consumption and the computerization of knowledge. This has created a crisis in the legitimation of science, technology and society. The grand narrative legitimating structures of the past turned on two myths: the belief that science could liberate humanity (the French Revolution), and the belief that there is a unity to all knowledge, producing cumulative rational understandings of man, nature and society (German idealism). Incorporated in this latter myth was a systems theory of society, i.e., as a unified totality. Lyotard contends that these myths have collapsed, leaving postmodern science in a situation where its task is no longer one of producing an adequate model of reality, but rather one of producing more knowledge, more work, and more information. The realist epistemology, which underwrote the old version of science (positivism), argued that science could reproduce reality objectively. It was a mirror of reality, and its categories were adequacy, accuracy and truth.

Postmodern science, which Lyotard sees as emerging over the last 40 years, has displayed a preoccupation with language and theories of representation. It has moved from epistemological realism to a concern for theories of nonrepresentational, simulated practices. The leading sciences over the past forty years have had to do with language:

phonology and theories of linguistics, problems of communication and cybernetics, modern theories of algebra and informatics, computers and their languages, problems of translation and the search for areas of compatibility among computer languages, problems of information storage and data banks, telematics and the perfection of intelligent terminals, paradoxology. The facts speak for themselves (and this list is not exhaustive) (Lyotard 1984, pp. 3–4).

Postmodern science no longer rests on the search for stabilities. Since Goedel's theorem, Kuhn's theory of revolutions in knowledge structures, and Thom's catastrophe theory, instabilities, discoveries of unpredictabilities, innovations, and discontinuities have become the scientific norm. Science now legitimates itself through *paralogy*, or the production of knowledge which undermines previous understandings, and seeks legitimation through new narratives which are pragmatic; that is, the new knowledge works for a limited period of time, only to be overturned by a new de-stabilizing discovery. Thus paralogy represents the hallmark of postmodern science. It involves the attempt, not to reach agreement within a framework, but to undermine, from within the framework, prior assumptions held under the assumptions of "normal science" (Jameson 1984b, p. xix).

Examples from many fields can be cited to

support this claim by Lyotard: game theory, artificial intelligence, utility theory, behaviorism, debates within structural-functionalism, competing research paradigms in the sociology of science, conflicts between literary theorists concerning constructionist and deconstructionist readings of texts, etc. In each of these examples a theorist, scientist, or critic poses a countertheoretical interpretation of a class of phenomenon. He or she justifies this question in terms of its ability to generate new knowledge and new arguments regarding the subject matter at hand.

Language Games and Postmodern Science

Two new performative criteria for science have thus emerged. The first highlights efficiency, production and performance. This is the criteria of information technocrats and bureaucrats, both governmental and corporate. The second criterion is the one that questions the very legitimacy of the scientist's theory. This is the criterion of paralogy, i.e. a permanent tendency toward scientific revolution. These two criteria clash. Hence, while an anti-model opposing scientific stability underlies postmodern science, this model has been required to fit itself to the bureaucratic model of performance efficiency demanded by the larger system.

By conceptualizing postmodern science in this manner Lyotard is able to incorporate recent philosophies of language and pragmatics into his model. Drawing upon Wittgenstein, Austin and Searle, he argues that language games have become the model for postmodern science. The pragmatics of language use, the study of language in speaking situations, and the understanding that language is always an unstable interactive exchange of messages between sender and receiver, leads him to offer a conflictual, "agonistic" version of science and the social bond (Lyotard 1984, p. 10).

Lyotard distinguishes two types of knowledge, narrative and scientific. He also distinguishes two types of language games, narrative (which rely upon rules of competency that are not purely objective and denotative but promissory, performative, prescriptive) and scientific (which rely upon denotative rules). Narrative knowledge, which does not equal scientific knowledge, corresponds to the taken-for-granted knowledge structures everyday individuals in a society employ and have access to, i.e. ordinary language. Narrative knowledge includes myth, folklore and ideology. It is the raw material for the social bond. It is played out in language games which are agnostically structured. Narrative knowledge carries its own authority. It absorbs the past into the present.

Scientific knowledge requires the language game of denotation to the exclusion of all others. It has, until recently, been set aside from the language games that form the social bond. Yet it has influenced the social bond through institutions of education and higher learning. Science games and scientific knowledge judge narrative knowledge to be inferior, while narrative knowledge tolerates scientific knowledge.

Lyotard argues that knowledge in the postmodern period displays a fundamental tension between narrative and scientific forms. Science now appeals to narrative when it attempts to legitimate itself in the public's eye. Pragmatically, postmodern science invokes the new authorities of the state and the university, transforms the "people" into heroes, and promotes the narrative myth that science is in the service of the people.

Postmodern science has been invaded by the language games of narrative knowledge. It has invested itself in a search for metanarratives which would legitimate it. The contemporary incredulity toward metanarratives, however, (Lyotard 1984, p. xxiv) reflects a crisis in philosophy, science and the university.

In the past these structures could appeal to the metanarrative myths of the grand tradition: science equals reason. Today this is not possible; and to the extent that such appeals are made they are done in the name of a new metanarrative structure which masks the decline of the old orders of reason, tradition and consensus.

The Social Bond

As indicated above Lyotard postulates a conflictual, agonistic model of the social order. Conflict, not consensus, structures society. This view derives from his theory of language games. Scholars such as Parsons, Habermas and Luhmann value a systemic, consensual, conformist, system-legitimating model of science and society. Lyotard rejects this view and the partitioning of knowledge into positivist, technological, and critical-reflexive categories that it presupposes (Habermas). Such a division, he argues, reproduces the problems of computerized knowledge in postmodern societies. It is out of step with postmodern knowledge which has fallen into the domain controlled by administrators, machines, data banks, archives and libraries. *Such a division fails to raise the central problematic of the postmodern period; that is who owns the data bank?*

A composite layer of corporate classes now sits astride computerized society. These classes and their members (high level administrators, heads of major corporations, heads of professional, labor, political and religious organizations) are replacing the old power structure which moved between the nation-state, the middle and working classes, institutions of higher learning, and the traditions embodied in the grand narratives of the past. This breaking up the grand narratives produces for Lyotard, not the dissolution of the social bond, as it does for Baudrillard (Lyotard 1984, p. 15) but a new form of social organization in which the conflictual language game predominates. In this era the self comes to exist in a "fabric of relations that is now more complex and mobile than ever before" (Lyotard 1984, p. 15).

Each individual is located at the center of specific and multiple communication circuits or points. Multiple language games (political, economic, sexual, interactional, ideological) now play across the biographies of individuals. At the same time more and more information about each person is being generated, collated and located within ever larger data banks. The reserve of knowledge about each person is inexhaustible. The computerization of society, coupled with the pragmatics of science which now legitimates itself in terms of paralogy, has produced a heterogeneity of language games which defies consensus. (Lyotard 1984, pp. 65–66)

Habermas

Heterogeneity and the search for dissent (the hallmarks of postmodern science) destroy the very assumptions of Habermas's theory. In particular they contradict

a belief that still underlies Habermas's research, namely that humanity as a collective (universal) subject seeks its common emancipation through the regularization of "moves" permitted in all language games and that the legitimacy of any statement resides in its contributing to that emancipation (Lyotard 1984, p. 66).

For Lyotard consensus has become an outmoded value, as has discourse toward consensus. The model of society that Habermas idealizes would produce, for Lyotard, a new communicative community, terrorized by conformity and enforced consensus. The older models of society and science must be rejected because they have in fact been rejected by society. Here Lyotard lays to rest Parsonian systems theory, functionalism and outdated Marxist theories which see society as a dialectic of two classes struggling with one another.

The rights of the social and society have low priority in the postmodern period. Alleviations of social problems are of concern only if such attention can improve the system's performance. The needs of the underprivileged are no longer a concern of the system. The system has become a vanguard machine dragging humanity along with it (Lyotard 1984, p. 63). It dehumanizes humanity "in order to rehumanize it at a new level of normative and performative capacity." Lyotard states:

The technocrats declare that they cannot trust what society designates as its needs; they "know" that society cannot know its own needs since they are not variables independent of the new technologies. Such is the arrogance of the decision makers—and their blindness (Lyotard 1984, p. 63).

It can now be seen why Lyotard cannot follow Habermas. Habermas's emphasis on rules which are valid for all language games, where dialogue can produce consensus, is meaningless for Lyotard. Consensus can never be an end; it is a state in discussion. Its end is paralogy. The heterogeneity of rules in language games and the search for dissent question Habermas's model. Discourse can never be a weapon against a stable system, as Habermas argues in his criticism of Luhmann, or so Lyotard contends (1984, p. 66).

What Is Postmodernism?
Lyotard and Habermas

Lyotard (1984, pp. 71–82) analyzes the multiple meanings of postmodernism. He addresses Habermas's (1981, 1983) critique of the postmodern project and its reaction to the modernist agenda of the Enlightenment. I will first take up Habermas's critique and then Lyotard's response.

In "Modernity—An Incomplete Project" Habermas argues that postmodernism pre-sents itself as being antimodern; that is as being against the modernist impulse. The relation of the modern to the classical has thus been lost.

Certain neoconservatives, such as Daniel Bell, have linked cultural modernity with nihilism, hedonistic values and a general weakening of the rational in everyday life. These critics welcome societal modernization but not cultural postmodernism. They fail to see, however, that a crisis in the communicative infrastructures of everyday life arises from the clash that has occurred between administrative and communicative rationalities in the present period. Nor do they grasp Weber's point that cultural modernity involved a separation of substantive reason in religion and metaphysics into three areas: science, morality and art. With this separation rose the great claims of the Enlightenment for truth, normative rightness, authenticity and beauty. Each domain of the cultural could be seen as becoming institutionalized, professionalized and subject to specific forms of rationality, including the cognitive-rational, and the moral.

The 18th century project of modernity proposed a rational organization of everyday life. Art and science would reflect and control nature, producing understanding, moral progress and human emancipation. The 20th century has shattered this premise.

Habermas sees the various versions of modernity and postmodernism as contributing to this demise of the Enlightenment belief structure. Modern art failed to give a rational structure to everyday life. Rather it shattered any belief in a consensual, normative order. The antimodernism and postmodernism of such critics as Foucault, Derrida, and Batille have further undercut the modernist project. They have celebrated de-centered subjectivity, located self-expression in a far away land, justified the postmodern in the name of the new and juxtaposed the will to power and instrumental reason. Habermas, accordingly, rejects the postmodern project.

Lyotard responds in kind. He rejects Habermas's claim that the modernist project never had a chance and should not be abandoned. Lyotard turns Benjamin's arguments concerning art in the age of reproduction against Habermas, suggesting that capitalism has always reproduced the familiar and the artistic, while subjecting such productions to the technical criteria of the best possible performance. Habermas's model is thus one based on nostalgia and a longing for a return to an age of realism.

Where Habermas would have artists return to an age of realism, Lyotard endorses an art that questions and challenges the canons and traditions of the past. Realism avoids the basic question of "What is Reality?" This is the question postmodernism asks over and over again and it is the question Habermas wants to avoid; or so Lyotard argues.

Redefining the Postmodern

For Lyotard postmodernism (1984, pp. 79–82) has the following characteristics: (1) it is part of the present, modern period; (2) it is a reflective reaction to the present; (3) it is a withdrawal from, and a critique of the real. It questions the power of representation to present the sublime; (4) it emphasizes the jubilation of being and the invention of new rules of the game; (5) it rejects a nostalgia for the past; (6) it attempts to present the unpresentable; (7) time, not the subject becomes the hero; (8) the signifier is given primacy; (9) the grammar and vocabularies of language are no longer just accepted. Postmodernism plays with language in an attempt to present the unpresentable.

Modernism, in contrast, presents the real and the sublime in an aesthetic that is acceptable, and produces solace and pleasure. The "real" sublime, however, produces pain and discomfort and this is the underlying goal of postmodernism; to produce, that is, a massive and painful reflection on the present. Postmodernism works with rules that are constructed as the game is played. It rejects tradition and the old rules of the game, whether this be in art, literary criticism, political theory, social theory, or philosophy.

The postmodern task becomes one that (1) does not simplify reality, but (2) invents new allusions to the conceivable that cannot be presented under old terms; (3) will not produce a theory that reconciles the chasm of a totality which is missing; (4) pays the price for the terror that is produced by dis-order; feeling that for too long we have paid for nostalgia and a desire to reconcile the real with the conceivable. Postmodernism thus urges a war on totalities, while it bears witness to the unpresentable and activates the differences that exist in the social, cultural and historical realms of the everyday.

Interpretations

Lyotard's study offers a penetrating analysis of the knowledge structures of postmodern life. Postmodern science now legitimates itself in terms of the rules of two language games: science and everyday narratives. By analyzing the discourse structures that now legitimate postmodern science he shows how a new mode and form of power has come into play in everyday life. His archeological and genealogical interpretation of the transformations that have occurred in the communications and language sciences suggests that we are in a neo-representational age. The image of reality and computerized information about that reality has, for all practical purposes, replaced any direct contact with the world of the real. We live the real through the mediated knowledge structures postmodern informational systems give us. These knowledge structures no longer carry their own proof of verification, for their rules of legitimation have become absorbed into the very language games they presuppose for their existence. The implosion of meaning and information that Baudrillard identified is thus given new meaning by Lyotard. We are in an age where the terror of over-information surrounds us.

Lyotard's and Baudrillard's interpretations call for serious study and research. We do not know how this new information age is lived on a daily basis by ordinary people. We do not know how the meaning structures which are arising in the postmodern age find verification in ordinary lives. Schutz's man on the street has been transformed into an expert on the happenings within the global village that constitutes the world system. How this information then enters and circulates within the realm of the taken-for-granted is not understood.

More deeply Lyotard and Baudrillard's works can be read as massive critiques in the sociology of science and knowledge. Each questions how what passes for knowledge in the postmodern age becomes constituted as knowledge. Each questions the relationship between power, truth and knowledge and each offers an analysis of the state as an agent which structures science and truth. At the same time their works can be read as critical phenomenological studies in the everyday life worlds of the postmodern period.

REFLECTIONS

It is now necessary to reflect on the directions social theory and empirical research might take in the near future. First, it is clear that, with the exception of feminist theory, current American social theory evidences an attempt to salvage from the great early modern social theorists (Marx, Weber, Durkheim) and the modern theorists (Parsons, Merton, Homans, Garfinkel, Goffman) a model of the social and the interactional that still sees societies as totalities. This impulse to theorize about the totality is a modernist, not a post-modernist theme. These theories and the rereadings of the classic texts that they rest upon still valorize the subject, while locating sociology's subject matter in a present world that reacts against the changes and transformation that have occurred in the last 40 years. That is, American social theory has not theorized language, the problematic of the subject, nor has it critically reflected upon the grand narratives of the past that gave rise to sociology in the first place.

Second, recent theory work remains within, while its very actions deny, the positivistic paradigm. Attempts to formulate causal interpretations of the social reveal this commitment. Yet the very theory work of Collins, Giddens and Alexander evidences a move into the language games of the postmodern that Lyotard so convincingly analyzes. These new readings of classic texts are justified, not because they yield better readings, or more truth, *but because they are new.* Thus if current social theory is to critically reflect back upon itself it must learn how to analyze the language games it plays as new theory and new textual readings are produced.

Third, sociological theories and studies of the postmodern situation must be undertaken—if not within the frameworks of Baudrillard and Lyotard, then at least within frameworks that challenge the old sociological modernist theories, i.e., conflict theory, neo-functionalism, interactionism, ethnomethodology, world-systems theory, etc. Theory and research must be fitted to the empirical situations of the postmodern period. Old social stratification paradigms, old theories of the family, of small groups, religion, education, science, urbanization, media, communications, demography, social organization, criminology and deviance must be rethought. These theories presumed structural causation models which could be fitted to theories of societies as totalities, which were functionally integrated at micro and macro levels. Such models overlook the massive implications of the Foucault project which requires careful empirical study of specific discourse sites where power and knowledge structures interact so as to reproduce particular images of subjects and subjective experience.

Lyotard and Baudrillard offer a challenge to American theorists. With Foucault they ask that we re-theorize the social so that our theories and understandings may be better suited to the postmodern period. Sociology no longer serves society. It has become swallowed up by the social. The challenge is to learn how to reflect on this condition so that we may better understand the current situation that engulfs all of us. To not confront this challenge, to continue to rework classical and modernist theories in the name of the new is to risk final annihilation by the social. This is my reading of Baudrillard's and Lyotard's message to American sociology.

REFERENCES

ANTONIO, ROBERT J., and Ronald M. GLASSMAN (eds.). 1985. *A Weber-Marx Dialogue.* Lawrence, KA: University of Kansas Press.

BAUDRILLARD, JEAN. 1968. *Le Système des Objects.* Paris: Gallimard.

_____. 1970. *La Société de Consummation: Ses Mythes, Ses Structures.* Paris: Gallimard.

_____. 1972. *Pour une Critique de L'Economie Politique du Signe.* Paris: Gallimard.

_____. 1975. *The Mirror of Production.* St. Louis: Telos Press, Ltd.

_____. 1981. *For a Critique of the Political Economy of the Sign.* St. Louis: Telos Press, Ltd.

_____. 1983a. *Simulations.* New York: Semiotext(e), Foreign Agent Press.

_____. 1983b. *In the Shadow of the Silent Majorities.* New York: Semiotext(e), Foreign Agent Press.

_____. 1983c. "Ecstacy of Communication." Pp. 126–134 in *The Anti-Aesthetic: Essays on Postmodern Culture,* edited by Hal Foster. Port Townsend, WA: Bay Press.

BENJAMIN, JESSICA. 1981. "The Oedipal Riddle: Authority, Autonomy, and the New Narcissism." Pp. 195–224 in *The Problem of Authority in America,* edited by J.P. Diggins and M.E. Kann. Philadelphia: Temple University Press.

BENJAMIN, WALTER. 1968. "The Work of Art in the Age of Mechanical Reproduction." Pp. 219–254 in W. Benjamin, *Illuminations.* New York: Harcourt, Brace and World, Inc.

BERNSTEIN, RICHARD J. (ed.) 1985. *Habermas and Modernity.* Cambridge, MA: MIT Press.

CHANG, BRIANKLE. 1986. "Mass, Media, Mass Media-tion: Jean Baudrillard's Implosive Critique of Modern Mass-Mediated Culture." *Current Perspectives in Social Theory* 7:157–181.

CHODOROW, NANCY. 1978. *The Reproduction of Mothering.* Berkeley: University of California Press.

CLOUGH, PATRICIA T. 1987. "Feminist Theory: The Subject and the Critique of Social Psychology." *Studies in Symbolic Interactionism,* vol. 8, edited by N.K. Denzin. Greenwich, CN: JAI Press.

DENZIN, NORMAN K. 1986. "On a Semiotic Approach to Mass Culture." *American Journal of Sociology* 92:678–683.

DINNERSTEIN, DOROTHY. 1976. *The Mermaid and the Minotaur: Sexual Arrangements and Human Malaise.* New York: Harper and Row.

FOSTER, HAL (ed.). 1983a. *The Anti-Aesthetic: Essays on Postmodern Culture.* Port Townsend, WA: Bay Press.

_____. 1983b. "Postmodernism: A Preface." Pp. ix–xvi in *The Anti-Aesthetic: Essays on Postmodern Culture,* edited by Hal Foster. Port Townsend: WA: Bay Press.

GROSSBERG, LAWRENCE. 1985. "Michel Foucault." Pp. 143–146 in *Biographical Dictionary of Neo-Marxism,* edited by Robert A. Gorman, Westport, CN: Greenwood Press.

HABERMAS, JURGEN. (1960) 1971a. *Knowledge and Human Interests.* Boston: Beacon.

_____. (1963) 1971b. *Theory and Practice.* Boston: Beacon.

_____. (1973) 1975. *Legitimation Crisis.* Boston: Beacon.

_____. (1980) 1981. "Modernity versus Postmodernity." *New German Critique* 22:3–11.

_____. 1983. "Modernity—an Incomplete Project." Pp. 3–15 in *The Anti-Aesthetic: Essays on Postmodern Culture,* edited by Hal Foster. Port Townsend, WA: Bay Press.

HALL, STUART. 1980. "Cultural Studies and the Center: Some Problematics and Problems." Pp.

15–47 in *Culture, Media, Language: Working Papers in Cultural Studies, 1972–1979,* edited by Stuart Hall. London: Hutchinson.

HAYES, ADRIAN C. 1985. "Causal and Interpretive Analysis in Sociology." *Sociological Theory* 3:1–10.

HUYSSEN, ANDREAS. 1984. "Mapping the Postmodern." *New German Critique* 33:5–51.

JAMESON, FREDRIC. 1983. "Postmodernism and Consumer Society." Pp. 111–125 in *The Anti-Aesthetic: Essays on Postmodern Culture,* edited by Hal Foster. Port Townsend, WA: Bay Press.

———. 1984a. "Postmodernism or the Cultural Logic of Late Capitalism." *New Left Review* 146:30–72.

———. 1984b. "Foreword" to Jean-Francois Lyotard. Pp. vii–xxi in *The Postmodern Condition: A Report on Knowledge.* Minneapolis: University of Minnesota Press.

JENCKS, CHARLES. 1985. *The Language of Postmodern Architecture.* New York: Basic Books.

LIVESAY, JEFF. 1985. "Normative Ground and Praxis: Habermas, Giddens: and a Contradiction with Critical Theory." *Sociological Theory* 3:66–76.

LUHMANN, NIKLAS. 1969. *Legitimation durch Verfahren.* Neuweid: Luchterhand.

LUKES, STEVEN. 1985. Review of Anthony Giddens, *The Constitution of Society: Outline of the Theory of Structuration. Times Literary Supplement* 18 October: 1163.

LYOTARD, JEAN FRANCOIS. 1971. *Discours, figure.* Paris: Klincksieck.

———. 1974. *Economie libidinal.* Paris: Editions de Minuit.

———. (1979) 1984. *The Postmodern Condition: A Report on Knowledge.* Minneapolis: University of Minnesota Press.

MILLS, C. WRIGHT. 1959. *The Sociological Imagination.* New York: Oxford University Press.

NEWMAN, CHARLES. 1985. *The Postmodern Aura.* Evanston, IL: Northwestern University Press.

SKOCPOL, THEDA. 1978. *States and Social Revolutions.* New York: Cambridge University Press.

TURNER, JONATHAN H. 1986. *The Structure of Sociological Theory.* 4th ed. Chicago: Dorsey Press.

WALLERSTEIN, IMMANUEL. 1980. *The Modern World-System* II. New York: Academic Press.

WILEY, NORBERT. 1977. "Review Essay of D. Bell, *The Cultural Contradictions of Capitalism,* J. Habermas, *Legitimation Crisis,* and J. O'Connor, *The Fiscal Crisis of State." Contemporary Sociology* 6:416–424.

———. 1985. "The Current Interregnum in American Sociology." *Social Research* 52:179–207.

———. 1986a. Introduction in *The Marx-Weber Debate,* edited by Norbert Wiley. Beverly Hills, CA: Sage Publications.

——— (ed). 1986b. *The Marx-Weber Debate.* Beverly Hills, CA: Sage Publications.

THE END OF SOCIOLOGICAL THEORY:
THE POSTMODERN HOPE*

STEVEN SEIDMAN

Sociological theory has gone astray. It has lost most of its social and intellectual importance; it is disengaged from the conflicts and public debates that have nourished it in the past; it has turned inward and is largely self-referential. Sociological theory today is produced and consumed almost exclusively by sociological theorists. Its social and intellectual insularity accounts for the almost permanent sense of crisis and malaise that surrounds contemporary sociological theory. This distressing condition originates, in part, from its central project: the quest for foundations and for a totalizing theory of society.

To revitalize sociological theory requires that we renounce scientism—that is, the increasingly absurd claim to speak the Truth, to be an epistemically privileged discourse. We must relinquish our quest for foundations or the search for the one correct or grounded set of premises, conceptual strategy, and explanation. Sociological theory will be revitalized if and when it becomes "social theory." My critique of sociological theory and advocacy of social theory as a social narrative with a moral intent will be advanced from the standpoint of postmodernism.

Anticipating the end of sociological theory entails renouncing the millennial social hopes that have been at the center of modernist theory. Postmodernism carries no promise of liberation—of a society free of domination. Postmodernism gives up the modernist idol of human emancipation in favor of deconstructing false closure, prying open present and future social possibilities, detecting fluidity and porousness in forms of life where hegemonic discourses posit closure and a frozen order. The hope of a great transformation is replaced by the more modest aspiration of a relentless defense of immediate, local pleasures and struggles for justice. Postmodernism offers the possibility of a social analysis that takes seriously the history of cruelty and constraint in Western modernity

*From Steven Seidman, "The End of Sociological Theory: The Postmodern Hope," *Sociological Theory* 9:2 Fall 1991), 131–33, 136–46. Reprinted with permission of the American Sociological Association and the author.

without surrendering to the retreat from criticalness that characterizes much current conservative and liberal social thought.

SOCIOLOGICAL THEORY/SOCIAL THEORY: A DIFFERENCE THAT MATTERS

I'd like to posit a distinction between social theory and sociological theory. Social theories typically take the form of broad social narratives. They relate stories of origin and development, tales of crisis, decline, or progress. Social theories are typically closely connected to contemporary social conflicts and public debates. These narratives aim not only to clarify an event or a social configuration but also to shape its outcome—perhaps by legitimating one outcome or imbuing certain actors, actions, and institutions with historical importance while attributing to other social forces malicious, demonic qualities. Social theory relates moral tales that have a practical significance; they embody the will to shape history. Marx wrote *The Communist Manifesto* and the successive drafts of his critique of political economy in response to current social conflicts, as a practical intervention for the purpose of effecting change—to wit, contributing to the transformation of wage labor into the proletariat (i.e., into self-identified members of the working class antagonistic to capitalism). Weber wrote the *The Protestant Ethic and the Spirit of Capitalism* in part to stimulate the building of a politicized German middle class willing to seize power. Durkheim wrote *The Division of Labor in Society* in order to legitimate and shape the Third Republic against attacks from the right and the left. Social theories might be written to represent the truth of social matters, but they arise out of ongoing contemporary conflicts and aim to affect them. Their moral intent is never far from the surface. They are typically evaluated in terms of their moral, social, and political significance.

Sociological theory, by contrast, intends to uncover a logic of society; it aims to discover the one true vocabulary that mirrors the social universe. Sociological theorists typically claim that their ideas arise out of humanity's self-reflection as social beings. They position theory in relation to a legacy of social discourse, as if theorizing were simply humanity's continuous dialogue on "the social." Sociological theorists aim to abstract from current social conflicts to reflect on the conditions of society everywhere, to articulate the language of social action, conflict, and change in general. They seek to find a universal language, a conceptual casuistry that can assess the truth of all social languages. Sociological theory aims to denude itself of its contextual embeddedness; to articulate humanity's universal condition. Insofar as sociological theory speaks the language of particularity, it is said to have failed. It must elevate itself to the universal, to the level of theoretical logics or central problems or to the study of social laws or the structure of social action. The intent of sociological theorists is to add to the stock of human knowledge in the hope that this will bring enlightenment and social progress.

The story I wish to tell is not that of a movement from social theory to sociological theory. Social theory and sociological theory, at least since the eighteenth century, have lived side by side and frequently have been intertwined. Marx wrote social theory but also sociological theory; Weber may have penned the *Protestant Ethic*, but he also wrote methodological essays that attempted to offer ultimate grounds for his conceptual strategies. Durkheim wrote the *Division of Labor in Society* but also the *Rules of Sociological Method*, which set out a logic of sociology; Parsons wrote the *Structure of Social Action* but also *The American University*. Although sociological and social theory intermingle in the history of social thought, I want to suggest that within the discipline of sociology, especially since the post–World War II period, the emphasis has been on sociological theory. Indeed, social theory is often devalued; it is described as ideological. Sociological theorists are encouraged to do sociological theory, not social theory. In the discipline of sociology, sociological theorists stake their claim to prestige and privilege on their ability to produce new analytic approaches to supposedly universal problems. I want to claim further that the hegemony of sociological theory within sociology has contributed to rendering sociological theorists insular and making their products—theories—socially and intellectually obscure and irrelevant to virtually everyone except other theorists. As sociological theorists have moved away from social theory, they have contributed to the enfeeblement of public moral and political debate. . . .

THE POSTMODERN HOPE: SOCIAL NARRATIVE WITH A MORAL INTENT

Foundational theorizing is by no means a product of the social scientific disciplines. The attempt to resolve conceptual disputes or to authorize a particular conceptual strategy by appealing to some presumably universal or objective justification has accompanied modern social thought. Yet the institutionalization of social science and the phenomenal growth of the disciplines in the twentieth century has contributed greatly to the rise of theory specialists whose expertise revolves around metatheoretical or foundational concerns. Although foundational discourses may play a beneficial role at certain sociohistorical junctures (e.g., during periods of epochal transition, such as the 18th century), my view is that today they contribute to the social and intellectual insularity and irrelevance of much sociological theory. Moreover, I have voiced an epistemological doubt about the likely success of the foundational project. This suspicion has been a systematic feature of modern Western social consciousness at least since Marx's time. Postmodernism evokes this suspicion as current.

From a postmodern perspective, justifications of conceptual strategies appear to be unable to avoid a local, ethnocentric character. This is not an argument denying the possibility of foundations; I offer no proof of the impossibility of achieving a grounded social discourse. My epistemic doubt is local, it you will. It stems from my reflection on the historical failure of foundational efforts; it reflects a sympathy for the relentless epistemic doubt generated by modernist social science itself. If a genius comes along tomorrow and proves to the satisfaction of the social scientific community that he or she has succeeded in providing foundations, I will relinquish my standpoint. Until then, however, I propose that we renounce the quest for foundations in favor of local rationales for our conceptual strategies. Instead of appealing to absolutist justifications, instead of constructing theoretical logics and epistemic casuistries to justify a conceptual strategy, to lift them out of contextual embeddedness and elevate them to the realm of universal truths, I propose that we be satisfied with local, pragmatic rationales for our conceptual approaches. Instead of asking what is the nature of reality or knowledge in the face of conflicting conceptual strategies—and therefore going metatheoretical—I suggest we evaluate conflicting perspectives by asking what are their intellectual, social, moral, and political consequences. Does a conceptual strategy promote precision or conceptual economy? Does it enhance empirical predictability? What social values or forms of life does it promote? Does it lead to relevant policy-related information? Postmodern justifications shift the debate from that of Truth and abstract rationality to that of social and intellectual consequences.

does not like

The quest for foundations has been connected intimately to the project of creating a general theory (Seidman and Wagner 1991). Many modern social theorists have sought to elaborate an overarching totalizing conceptual framework that would be true for all times and all places. The search for the one right vocabulary or language that would mirror the social world, that would uncover the essential structures and dynamics or laws of society, has been integral to sociological theory. In *The German Ideology*, Marx and Engels believed that they had uncovered a universally valid language of history and society. In their view, the categories of labor, mode of production, class, and class conflict crystallized what they considered to be a general theory that captured the essential structure and dynamics of history. Durkheim proposed in *The Division of Labor in Society* and in *The Rules of the Sociological Method* the dual categories of collective representations and social morphology as the conceptual basis for a universal theory of society; Parsons wrote *The Structure of Social Action* and *The Social System* to reveal a universal set of premises and concepts that would unify and guide all social inquiry. This quest to discover the one true language of the social world, to uncover its laws, general structure, and universal logic, has been an abiding aim of sociological theory.

The quest for a totalizing general theory, in my view, is misguided. My reasoning parallels my reservations about foundationalism. General theories have not succeeded; their basic premises, concepts, and explanatory models, along with their metatheoretical rationales, consistently have been shown to be local, ethnocentric projects (Turner and Wardell 1986). The project of general theory has pushed theorists into the realm of metatheory as theorists attempt to specify an epistemic rationale to resolve conceptual or paradigm disputes; it has isolated theorists from vital ongoing research programs and empirical analyses; the quest for foundations and for a totalizing theory has marginalized theorists in regard to the major social events and public debates of the times. Moreover, when concepts are stretched to cover all times and places or to be socially inclusive, they become so contentless as to lose whatever explanatory value they have. These flat, contentless general categories seem inevitably to ignore or repress social differences (Nicholson 1991). For example, the categories of labor, mode of production, or class conflict may be useful in explaining nineteenth-century England, but are much less so, I think, in explaining nineteenth-century France or Germany or the United States and are virtually irrelevant for societies that are more kinship-centered or politically centered (e.g., Balbus 1982; Baudrillard 1975; Habermas 1977, 1984, 1987; Nicholson 1986; Rubin 1975).

If social theorists renounce the project of foundationalism and the quest for general theories, as I am recommending, what's left for us? Undoubtedly some theorists will want to argue that a more modest version of the project of general theory is still feasible, such as Merton's middle range theories or some variant, say, in the mold of Skocpol's *States and Social Revolutions*. I won't dispute here the value of these alternatives, although I believe that they remain tied too closely to scientism and the modernist ideology of enlightenment and progress that have been suspect for decades. Instead I wish to propose that when theorists abandon the foundationalist project in the broad sense—elaborating general theories and principles of justification—what they have left is social theory as social narrative. When we strip away the foundationalist aspects of Marx's texts, what remain are stories of social development and crisis; when we purge Durkheim's *Division of Labor in Society* of its foundationalist claims, we have a tale of the development of Western modernity. The same applies to Parsons, Luhmann, Munch, or Habermas. I am not recommending that we simply return to the grand stories of social evolution from Condorcet to Habermas. If social theory is to return to its function as social narrative, I believe it must be a narrative of a different sort than those of the great modernists. In the remainder of this section, I will outline briefly one version of a postmodern social narrative.

The postmodern social narrative I advocate is event-based and therefore careful about its temporal and spatial boundaries. By event-based, I mean that the primary reference points of postmodern narratives are major social conflicts or developments. As event-based narratives, postmodern social analyses also would be densely contextual. Social events always occur in a particular time and place, related to both contemporary and past developments in a specific social space.

The grand narratives of the great modernist social theorists responded to the major events of the day but typically disregarded their temporal and spatial settings. Instead of locating events in their specific sociohistorical setting, these grand narratives framed events as world historical and evolved stories of the course of Western, if not human, history. Instead of telling the story of capitalism or secularization in, say, England or Italy, they analyzed these events as part of a sketch of "Western" or human development. Thus, instead of analyzing the unique industrial development of England or Germany, which had "capitalistic" aspects, by being attentive to their dramatic differences and singular histories, Marx proposed a theory of capitalism that purported to uncover essential, uniform processes in all "capitalist" social formations. His "theory of capitalism" outlined a history of Western and ultimately human development that disregarded the specificity of particular

"Western" and non-Western societies. To be sure, Marx counseled that the uniform operation of capitalism would vary in different societies even if the essential dynamics and direction of history were set by the "laws of capitalism." Marx assumed that the fact that different societies have divergent national traditions, geopolitical positions, and political, cultural, familial-kinship, gender, racial, and ethnic structures would not seriously challenge the utility of his model of capitalism as setting out the essential dynamics and direction of human history.

In my view, this was a serious mistake. Even if one takes Marx's model of capitalism to be of some utility for analyzing nineteenth-century dynamics of socioeconomic change, I believe that the immense sociohistorical differences among European and Anglo-American societies and between them and non-Western societies would affect seriously the form and functioning of industrializing dynamics. Individual societies evolve their own unique configurations and historical trajectories, which are best analyzed historically, not from the heights of general theory.

The Eurocentrism of these grand narratives has been exposed thoroughly (e.g., Baudrillard 1975). Human history in these modernist tales really meant Western history. Non-Western societies were relegated to a marginal position in past, present, and future history; their fate was presumed to be tied to that of Europe and the United States. The West, in these stories, was the principal agent of history; it showed the future to all of humanity. Behind this conceit was the arrogance of the western theorists, with their claim that the western breakthrough to "modernity" carried world historical significance. The great modernists claimed not only that Western modernity unleashed processes which would have world impact, but also that modernization contained universally valid forms of life (e.g., science, bureaucracy, socialism, organic solidarity, secularism). Not much effort is required to see that behind the aggrandizing intellectualism of the modernists were the expansionist politics of the age of colonialism.

These grand narratives seem to bear the mark of their own national origin. They contain an element of national chauvinism. Modernists projected their own nations' unique development and conflicts onto the globe as if their particular pattern were of world historical importance. These totalizing conceptual strategies that attempted to sketch a world historical story seem today extremely naive and misguided. The grand narratives of industrialization, modernization, secularization, democratization, these sweeping stories that presume to uncover a uniform social process in a multitude of different societies, these stories with their simplistic binary schemes (e.g., Tonnies's *Gemeinschaft* to *Gesellschaft*, Durkheim's mechanical to organic solidarity) which purport to relate a story of change over hundreds of years, should be abandoned. They repress important differences between societies; they perpetuate Western-world hegemonic aspirations and national chauvinistic wishes; they are, in short, little more than myths that aim to authorize certain social patterns.

Although I believe we should abandon the great modernist narratives, general stories are still needed. This is so because in all societies there occur certain events and developments that prompt highly charged social, moral, and political conflicts. The various parties to these conflicts frequently place them in broad conceptual or narrative frameworks. In order to imbue an event with national moral and political significance or to legitimate a specific social agenda, advocates elaborate social narratives that link the event to the larger history and fate of their society or humanity. This process is clear, for example, in the case of the

AIDS epidemic: the spread of HIV in the United States occasioned social discourses that relate a fairly broad story of the failure of the "sexual revolution" or, indeed, the failure of a liberal, permissive society (Seidman 1988; Sontag 1988; Watney 1987). The construction of broad social narratives by theorists still has an important role.

These narratives offer alternative images of the past, present, and future; they can present critical alternatives to current dominant images; they can provide symbolic cultural resources on which groups can draw in order to redefine themselves, their social situation, and their possible future. I consider paradigmatic, for example, texts such as Linda Gordon's (1977) *Woman's Body, Woman's Right,* which offered a novel feminist interpretation of the conflict over birth control; Jeffrey Weeks's (1977) *Coming Out: Homosexual Politics in Britain,* which proposed a new social and historical reading of homosexuality; Barbara Ehrenreich's and Deirdre English's *For Her Own Good* (1979) or Robert Bellah's *The Broken Covenant* (1975). These texts offer redescriptions of the present that open up new ways of defining the present and the future (Seidman 1991). Broad social narratives that cover large chunks of time and space are still important, provided that they remain deeply contextual and event and nation-based.

Postmodern social narratives will depart from those of the great modernists in an additional way: such narratives abandon the centrality of the ideas of progress or decadence that have served as the unifying themes of modernist social thought. From *philosophes* like Condorcet or Turgot to Comte, Marx, Durkheim, and Parsons, these stories of social development are little more than variations on the motif of human advancement. They amount to millennial, salvationist tales. In reaction to the stories of the enlighteners, there appeared the great tales of lament or decadence by Rousseau, Bonald, Schiller, Weber, Simmel, Spengler, Adorno, and Horkheimer. Both the great modernist narratives of progress and the counterenlightenment motif of decadence are decidedly Eurocentric. In all cases the site of the fateful struggles of humanity is the West. Indeed, national histories are important in these grand narratives only insofar as they exhibit a pattern of progress or decadence. These stories typically disregard the enormous social complexities and heterogeneous struggles and strains within a specific society at a specific time. They have one story to tell, which they rehearse relentlessly on a national and world historical scale. They utterly fail to grasp the multisided, heterogeneous, morally ambiguous social currents and strains that make up the life of any society. In the end they amount to little more than rhetorics of national and Eurocentric chauvinism or rhetorics of world rejection.

The great modernist stories of progress or decadence almost always operate with one-dimensional, virtually mythic notions of domination and liberation. Ignoring actual complex conflicts and power dynamics with their ambiguous calculus of gains and losses, benefits and costs, pleasure and pain, these grand narratives frame history and social conflicts in grossly simplifying millennial or apocalyptic images. For these modernists, the dynamics of domination are merely a matter of freedom lost or gained; whole strata, indeed whole epochs, are described as unfree, alienated, or repressed; large chunks of time are regarded as periods of darkness or light, freedom or tyranny. History is thought to play out a unidimensional human drama revolving around the human quest for liberation against the forces of domination.

These images of liberation and domination are often tied to essentialist concepts of the human subject. The modernists presuppose a notion of humanity as having a fixed, un-

changing identity and dynamic regardless of historical variation and social considerations such as gender, race, ethnicity, class, or sexual orientation. This unified human subject is thought to be in a constant struggle for freedom. The forces of oppression, in this tale, aim to deny humanity's quest for liberation. Human freedom is identified with the realization of human nature. Most modernist social narratives are underpinned by these notions of progress, liberation, domination, the human subject who is oppressed and striving for emancipation. As an obvious example, in the *1844 Manuscripts* Marx relates a story of the struggle of humanity to actualize its full nature by overcoming an alienated human condition. Although this tale of humanity's struggle for self-realization is later transfigured into the struggle of the working class to overcome capitalist oppression, there is no change in the focus on a grand world historical drama in which "humanity"—now in the guise of the working class—resists oppression to achieve a state of freedom. The same symbolic configuration reappears in the more contemporary social discourses of the black liberationist, women's, and gay movements. In all these movements, a world historical drama is depicted, involving humanity's struggle to overcome a state of domination to achieve liberation.

The problem with this discursive strategy relates not only to the shortcomings of the categories of progress, to the flattened-out concepts of domination and liberation, as I've stated already, but also to the concept of the human subject that is built into these discourses. Although Marxists, feminists, or gay liberationists may have abandoned the essentialist strategy of speaking of humanity as if "humanity" referred to a fixed, unchanging essence across all times and places, they continue to appeal to the agency of women, blacks, homosexuals, or the working class. Yet these categories are no more fixed or uniform in their meaning than the concept of humanity. Without rehearsing an argument that is now being played out with a vengeance among people of color, feminists, and gay and lesbian intellectuals, I believe that the language of agency, whether that of womanhood or of the working class, is viewed by many parties to these debates as normative (e.g., Spelman 1988).

For example, postmodern feminists have criticized the essentialist discourse of gender—both androcentric and gynocentric—that posits a bipolar gender order composed of a fixed, universal "man" and "woman." According to these postmodernists, such agentic concepts are understood as social constructions in which the discourse of gender, including the feminist discourse, is itself a part of the will to shape a gendered human order. The discourse of gender is tied to ongoing struggles to assign gender identities and social roles to human bodies. Womanhood and manhood are seen as neither a natural fact—nor a settled social fact but as part of a ceaseless, contested struggle among various groups to establish a gender ordering of human affairs. Therefore those who appeal to the agency of women or homosexuals or African-Americans intend to become part of the clamor of voices and interests struggling to shape a system of identity, normative order, and power. Discourses that use categories such as woman, man, gay, black American, and white American need to be seen as social forces embodying the will to shape a gender, racial, and sexual order; they seek to inscribe in our bodies specific desires, needs, expectations, and social identities.

My point is not that such categories of agency should not be used but that we need, first of all, to recognize their socially efficacious character. Although they are attached to a discourse of truth, they are inextricably entangled in the very constitution of identities, normative orders, and power relations. Second, we must be sharply aware that just as there is no "humanity" which acts as an agent (because humans exist always as particular national or tribal, gendered or aged, religious or ethnic beings), the same is true with respect to "women" or "blacks" or "homosexuals." These categories do not have a uniform meaning and social import across different societies or even within any given society. For example, same-sex intimacies do not carry an essentially fixed and common meaning across different histories. As many historians have argued compellingly, the concept of homosexuality and the homosexual exhibit historically and culturally specific meanings that cannot be applied to all experiences of same-sex intimacies (e.g., Katz 1983; Seidman 1991; Weeks 1977; Williams 1986). Moreover, even within a given society at a specific historical juncture, these categories of identity and agency (woman, man, homosexual, black American) not only acquire diverse meanings but do so, in part, because categories of identity are always multiple and intersect in highly idiosyncratic and diverse ways. Just as individuals are not simply instances of the abstraction "humanity," we are not embodiments of the abstractions of woman or man. Even within the contemporary United States, "woman" does not have a uniform meaning. It varies by ethnic, racial, religious, or class status as well as by factors relating to sexual orientation, age, or geographical/regional characteristics. There is no reason to believe that a middle-class southern heterosexual Methodist woman will share a common experience or even common gender interests with a northern working-class Jewish lesbian. It is equally naive to assume that whatever gender commonalities they do share will override their divergent interests and values.

This argument suggests, of course, that the experience of oppression and liberation is not flat or unidimensional. Individuals are not simply oppressed or liberated. Just as an individual's identity mix is varied in innumerable ways, his or her experience of self as empowered or disempowered will be similarly varied and multidimensional. We need to shift from an essentialist language of self and agency to conceiving of the self as having multiple and contradictory identities, community affiliations, and social interests. Our social narratives should be attentive to this concept of multiple identities; our stories should replace the flat, unidimensional language of domination and liberation with the multivocal notion of multiple, local heterogeneous struggles and a many-sided experience of empowerment and disempowerment.

Insofar as postmodern social discourses are seen simply as narratives with all the rhetorical, aesthetic, moral, ideological, and philosophical aspects characteristic of all storytelling, their social role would have to be acknowledged explicitly. Postmodern social analyses amount to stories about society that carry moral, social, ideological, and perhaps directly political significance.

Postmodern social narratives would do more than acknowledge their moral and social character; they would take this moral dimension as a site for a more elaborated analysis. I believe that there are fruitful possibilities here for sociological theorists to shift their reflexive analytical focus from metatheoretical foundational concerns to practical-moral ones (cf. Bellah et al. 1985; Rosaldo 1989). In other words, I am urging that the effort which theorists have invested in foundational, general theorizing, an effort that has yielded so little and has cost us so dearly, be shifted in part to moral analysis.

Needless to say, I am not counseling a shift to foundational moral theory or to the search for universal values or standards of justification. I wish to endorse a pragmatic, socially informed moral analysis (e.g., Seidman 1992). From a postmodern pragmatic standpoint, it would not be sufficient simply to invoke general values (e.g., freedom, democracy, solidarity, order, material comfort, pleasure) or moral imperatives (e.g., that individuals should be treated with respect or dignity or should be treated as ends) either to justify or to criticize current social arrangements or to recommend changes. Social criticism must go beyond pointing to the deficiencies of current social realities from some general moral standpoint. It would be compelled to argue out its standpoint through an analysis that is socially informed and pragmatic. The social critic has a responsibility, it seems to me, not only to say what is wrong with current realities in some broad, abstract way but also to make his or her critique as specific as possible so as to make it socially relevant. Similarly, the critic should be compelled at least to outline in some detail the social changes desired and the consequences that would follow for the individual and society. Again, this process forces social criticism to be potentially socially useful to (say) policy makers, activists, and legislators. It also makes theorists more accountable for their criticisms.

Finally, insofar as the social critic cannot appeal to transcendent or universal moral standards to justify his or her moral standpoint, the critique must be justified by an appeal to local values or traditions. Lacking a transcendental move, the postmodern critic must be satisfied with local justifications of those social forms of life which he or she advocates. The justification perhaps will take the form of endorsing a specific social arrangement because it promotes particular social values that are held by specific communities. This kind of pragmatic moral argumentation must be informed by a sociological understanding that allows one to analyze the impact of proposed changes on individuals and society. For example, a postmodern feminist critique of gender arrangements should do more than document and criticize general inequalities and discrimination against women from a moral standpoint that values freedom and equality. It also should show what a gender order of equality in specific social domains would be like and what social impact such changes towards gender equality would have. In addition, feminist critique in a postmodern mode would appeal to local traditions, practices, and values to justify these changes.

Recognizing that all social narratives have a socially effective character, we would not try to purge them of this character but would try to acknowledge it and, indeed, to seize it as a fruitful source of an elaborated social reason. How so? Not, as I've said, by simply offering a general criticism or defense of social forms from the high ground of some abstract moral values or standpoint. And certainly not by trying to ground one's moral standpoint in an appeal to some objective universal element (e.g., nature, God, natural law). Rather, I have recommended a pragmatic, socially informed moral analysis in which the critic is compelled to defend social arrangements by analyzing their individual and social consequences in light of local traditions, values, and practices. The values of the community of which the critic is a part stands as the "ultimate" realm of moral appeal.

Theorists would become advocates. We would be advocates, however, of a slightly different sort from (say) public officials or social activists. Unlike the advocacy of these partisans, which typically might take the form of rhetorical, moral, or national appeals, the presentation of documents or data, or appeals to particular social interests, the advocacy of theorists would take the form of elaborated social and moral argumentation about consequences and social values. Like other partisans, we would be advocates for a way of life, but unlike them, we would be compelled to produce elaborated social and moral discourses. As theorists we would be in a role of encouraging moral public discussion; we would be catalysts for public moral and social debate. We would be advocates, but not narrow partisans or politicos. Our value would be both in providing socially informed analyses that would be useful to partisans and in promoting an uncoerced public moral discussion in the face of various partisans who repeatedly act to restrict such elaborated discourse. We would become defenders of an elaborated reason against the partisans of closure and orthodoxy, and of all those who try to circumvent open public moral debate by partisan or foundational appeals.

CONCLUSION

Sociological theory, in my view, has become insular and irrelevant to all but theory specialists. At least in part, this insularity is connected to a foundationalist project that has been at the center of modernist social thought. Ironically, the institutional successes of sociology have been accompanied by the growing obtuseness of sociological theory. Today, sociological theorists are largely entangled in metatheoretical disputes revolving around the search for a general, universal grounded science of society.

I have suggested some reasons why there is little likelihood of escaping this morass. Moreover, although the foundationist project may have had beneficial practical significance from the eighteenth century through the latter part of the nineteenth century in Europe and the United States, which was linked to legitimating "modernity" against its critics, it has lost most of its social benefits, at least in the contemporary United States and perhaps in many western European nations. The argument that the foundational project is important for the defense of certain desirable social arrangements can hardly be entertained seriously in view of the social and intellectual insularity of disciplinary theory. I don't doubt that the foundational, totalizing theoretical project might still be valuable for promoting a reflexive, critical reason. Yet the same intellectual and social values can be cultivated just as easily in the postmodern project.

Under the banner of postmodernism, I have pressed for a major reorientation of sociological theory. To be revitalized, theory must be reconnected in integral ways to ongoing national public moral and political debates and social conflicts. This vital tie between theorizing and public life accounts for the continuing attractiveness of classical social theory, but that connection has been broken. To reestablish that tie I have urged that sociological theory reaffirm a core concept of itself as a broad, synthetic narrative, I have proposed, however, that a postmodern social narrative should depart in certain important ways from those of the great modernists. I recommend an event-based, nation/society-based narrative. Postmodernist narratives would be well advised to discard the configuration of core modernist concepts such as progress, domination, liberation, and humanity. The basic postmodern concepts will revolve around the notion of a self with multiple identities and group affiliations, which is entangled in heterogeneous struggles with multiple possibilities for empowerment.

Finally, postmodern narratives would acknowledge their practical-moral significance. Moral analysis would become a part of an elaborated social reason. Theorists would become advocates, abandoning the increasingly cynical, unbelievable guise of objective, value-neutral scientists. We would become advocates but not narrow partisans or activists. Our broader social significance would lie in encouraging unencumbered open public moral and social debate and in deepening the notion of public discourse. We would be a catalyst for the public to think seriously about moral and social concerns.

REFERENCES

BALBUS, ISAAC. 1982. *Marxism and Domination.* Princeton: Princeton University Press.

BAUDRILLARD, JEAN. 1975. *The Mirror of Production.* St. Louis: Telos.

BELLAH, ROBERT. 1975. *The Broken Covenant.* New York: Seabury.

BELLAH, ROBERT, RICHARD MADSEN, WILLIAM SULLIVAN, ANN SWIDLER, STEVEN TIPTON. 1985. *Habits of the Heart.* Berkeley: University of California Press.

EHRENREICH, BARBARA, and DEIDRE ENGLISH. 1979. *For Her Own Good.* New York: Doubleday.

GORDON, LINDA. 1977. *Woman's Body, Woman's Right.* New York: Penguin.

HABERMAS, JÜRGEN. 1977. *Communication and the Evolution of Society.* Boston: Beacon.

_____. 1984. *The Theory of Communicative Action,* Vol. 1. Boston: Beacon.

_____. 1987. *The Theory of Communicative Action,* Vol. 2. Boston: Beacon.

KATZ, JONATHAN. 1983. *Gay/Lesbian Almanac.* New York: Harper and Row.

NICHOLSON, LINDA. 1986. *Gender and History.* New York: Columbia University Press.

_____. 1991. "On the Postmodern Barricades: Feminism, Politics and Theory." Pp. 82–100 in *Postmodernism and Social Theory,* edited by Steven Seidman and David Wagner. Cambridge: Blackwell.

ROSALDO, RENATO. 1989. *Culture and Truth.* Boston: Beacon.

RUBIN, GAYLE. 1975. "The Traffic in Women." Pp. 157–210 in *Towards an Anthropology of Women,* edited by Rayna Reiter. New York: Monthly Review.

SEIDMAN, STEVEN. 1988. "Transfiguring Sexual Identity: AIDS and the Contemporary Construction of Homosexuality." *Social Text* 19/20 (Fall): 187–205.

_____. 1991. *Romantic Longings: Love in America, 1830–1980.* New York: Routledge.

_____. 1992. *Embattled Eros: Sexual Politics and Ethics in Contemporary America.* New York: Routledge.

SEIDMAN, STEVEN, and DAVID WAGNER (eds.). 1991. *Postmodernism and Social Theory*. New York: Blackwell.

SONTAG, SUSAN. 1988. *AIDS and Its Metaphors*. New York: Farrar, Strauss, and Giroux.

SPELMAN, ELIZABETH. 1988. *Inessential Woman*. Boston: Beacon.

TURNER, STEPHEN, and MARK WARDELL (eds.). 1986. *The Transition in Sociological Theory*. Boston: Allen and Unwin.

WATNEY, SIMON. 1987. *Policing Desire*. Minneapolis: University of Minnesota Press.

WEEKS, JEFFREY. 1977. *Coming Out: Homosexual Politics in Britain, From the Nineteenth Century to the Present*. London: Quartet.

WILLIAMS, WALTER. 1986. *The Spirit and the Flesh*. Boston: Beacon.